WOMEN IN SEVENTEENTH-CENTURY FRANCE

Women in Seventeenth-Century France

WENDY GIBSON

Lecturer in French Studies
University of Reading

St. Martin's Press   New York

First published in the United States of America in 1989

Printed in the People's Republic of China

ISBN 0–312–02347–2

Library of Congress Cataloging-in-Publication Data
Gibson, Wendy, *1944–*
Women in seventeenth-century France.
Bibliography: p.
Includes index.
1. Women – France – History – 17th century.   I. Title.
HQ1613.G53   1989   305.4'0944   88–18176
ISBN 0–312–02347–2

Contents

Contents

v

To the Reader

Un auteur à genoux, dans une humble préface,
Au lecteur qu'il ennuie a beau demander grâce;
Il ne gagnera rien sur ce juge irrité,
Qui lui fait son procès de pleine autorité.

(Satire IX, v. 187–90)

With Boileau's warning in mind, suffice it to say that in this book I have attempted to give an outline of the role of women in France from 1600 to 1700, dates which have been stretched occasionally to allow for full coverage of some exemplary personage whose career began just prior to, or extended just beyond, them.

The names of those to whom I am obliged for my material will be evident from the text and the notes. There is a debt which is not acknowledged therein, the most important, which I wish to mention here: that is the one owed to my two favourite matriarchs, my mother and grandmother, for the support and devotion of a lifetime. May this book not seem to them unworthy of all the sacrifices which they have made on my behalf.

1
Birth and Childhood

'C'est une fille!' The midwife's pronouncement was calculated to bring little joy to the exhausted mother or her expectant relatives in seventeenth-century France. Queen Marie de Médicis 'pleura fort et ferme' in 1602 on learning that she had supplied France with a princess, Elisabeth, instead of a second heir to the throne and 'ne s'en pouvait contenter'.[1] In 1662 Louis XIV's first sister-in-law Henriette d'Angleterre (Madame), having impatiently ascertained the female sex of the child that she was in the actual process of bearing, 'dit qu'il la fallait jeter à la rivière, et en témoigna son chagrin à tout le monde'.[2] Outside the royal circle the sense of anti-climax was equally keen. Memorialists recording the birth of a girl into an aristocratic family speak of the 'great regret' and 'ordeal' of the father, and of the mother's 'misfortune'.[3] Gazette-writers and other well-wishing versifiers stress that couples will rapidly work to correct their mistake:

> Mais, n'étant qu'un Amour femelle,
> Les époux, redoublant leur zèle,
> Vont travailler sur nouveaux frais
> A faire un Amour mâle après.[4]

Grandmothers for their part seek to guard against a second 'accident' by stern injunctions to daughters not to let their unborn offspring 'devenir fille'.[5]

The general disappointment could take on more palpable forms. When a royal prince was born the occasion was marked by prolonged rejoicings: cannon salvoes, bonfires, pyrotechnic displays, processions and services of thanksgiving, free distributions of wine in the streets, and the release of prisoners.[6] But when, after the birth of his third daughter Henriette in 1609, Henri IV summoned the Paris Parlement to make 'signés de réjouissance en la manière accoutumée', the First President replied 'que l'on n'a point accoutumé de faire aucunes cérémonies pour les filles, hormis pour la première, et qu'il ne s'en trouvera aucune registrée au Greffe, en l'Eglise de Paris, ni en l'Hôtel de Ville'.[7]

1

That women should accept and join in the chorus of disparaging remarks which greeted the arrival of a member of their own sex caused some amazement to contemporaries like the Comte de Bussy-Rabutin, who maliciously interpreted it as a tacit admission of male superiority.[8] But there were other, more practical, reasons for the prevailing attitude. In a country such as France, where women were excluded from the right of succession to the throne and from effectively holding public office, and where titles and property were normally passed on from generation to generation through the eldest male, the absence of an heir could constitute a real disaster. 'Les mâles,' as Gui Patin wrote, 'dans une grande famille, sont fulcra et columnae diuturnitatis.'[9] Lack of them might necessitate the abandonment of rank and possessions laboriously acquired over the centuries to rival dynasties and households interested in making posterity forget to whom they owed their elevation and lustre.[10] Expressions of chagrin over births of girls are accordingly always most pronounced amongst royalty and the aristocracy, who had most to lose by them. Lower down in the social hierarchy the bourgeoisie note the event with a non-committal wish for the infant's future virtue:

Dieu lui fasse la grâce d'avoir sa crainte et amour en recommandation et la remplisse de ses grâces.[11]

Dieu lui fasse la grâce d'être blanche de nom et de fait devant Dieu et devant les hommes.[12]

Dieu fasse la grâce à cette enfant de vivre et mourir dans sa sainte crainte et son saint amour![13]

The reactions of the peasantry, in the absence of direct written records of their sentiments, remain still more inscrutable. But any pleasure experienced at the thought of an extra worker in the family was bound to be tempered by the awareness of an extra mouth to feed, an extra 'establishment' to provide in later life.

For the birth of a daughter meant that sooner or later a dowry would have to be handed over to a husband or to a convent, a consideration which affected every class of society. Whatever the size of the dowry it represented the cession to outsiders of cash and property which, if invested in a son's marriage or career, would either have remained within the bosom of the family or yielded appreciable returns in the form of wages, perquisites and social distinction. The unhappy father had, moreover, the invidious task of safeguarding his daughter's virginity against the stratagems of designing gallants, on pain of sullying the family name and honour.

Born into a society disposed to regard her as more of an encumbrance than a blessing, the little girl began at once a struggle for survival against the host of physical perils and superstitions that beset the seventeenth-century infant. Birth, like the other two major events of human existence, marriage and death, was surrounded by its own age-old set of rituals. Some – the custom of blowing wine into the newborn child's mouth to prevent future inebriation and epilepsy, rubbing the baby's lips with a piece of gold to ensure their redness, inducing fashionable dimples by placing peas under the cheekbones – were comparatively innocuous. Others risked causing irreparable damage. Infant heads were kneaded to give them a good shape, or tightly bound with narrow bands, producing an elongation by which Parisian children were instantly recognisable. Noses were bound, pulled and pinched to correct real or fancied deformities. A cruel operation was performed on the infant girl's breast in the belief that this would facilitate the suckling of children in later life.[14]

Cleansed without by a mixture of water and wine, and within by means of soap suppositories, the infant had then to submit to the straitjacket[15] of swathing bands in which it would spend the first eight or nine months of life, sometimes longer in the case of girls. The main purpose of swaddling, apart from that of providing warmth and protection, was to render the body upright and the limbs straight and to accustom the child to stand instead of crawling in an unseemly and unhealthy fashion over floors that were cold, damp and littered with human and animal droppings. In practice the reverse effect was often achieved. In their anxiety to develop a plump, well-rounded breast in their nurslings, misguided wet-nurses subjected infant thoraxes to such compression that permanent humpbacks, projecting shoulders and curvatures of the spine resulted. Constriction of the hips, impeding their proper broadening, caused serious problems when the age of child-bearing was reached. Legs emerged from their wrappings bent, twisted and chafed.[16]

To the discomfort of cramped and sore limbs was added that of a diet calculated to extinguish rather than to sustain life. Instances of children in the upper strata of society being suckled by their natural mothers were already sufficiently rare in the sixteenth century to make Marguerite de Valois, future wife of Henri IV, start at the sight of an aristocratic hostess tranquilly calling for her baby to breast-feed before guests at a feast.[17] A powerful coalition of ignorance, vanity and selfishness militated against the performance of what indignant preachers and moralists represented as a fundamental maternal duty.[18] Human milk was popularly supposed to be formed of blood which flowed from the womb to the breasts, where it was mysteriously whitened.[19] Suckling, therefore, could only have a debilitating effect upon the constitution of the mother, draining her of precious life-blood. Worse still, her youthful silhouette was threatened by this messy chore, and just at a time when it was important to have the wherewithal to cajole and mollify a husband impatient for the resumption of normal conjugal services. In consequence, the infant scarcely had time to rejoice in the maternal smiles and caresses over which pedagogues waxed lyrical before being despatched to the arms of a local village wet-nurse whose own frequently scanty milk[20] was quickly supplemented with the notorious *bouillie*.[21] This glutinous concoction of flour and cow's milk worked wonders in silencing cries of hunger, sometimes permanently.[22]

Minute prescriptions for the choice of an ideal *nourrice* were listed in every gynaecological treatise of the day.[23] The sum total of opinions was that she should be a brunette of twenty-five to thirty years and of healthy stock, with good teeth, ample but not excessive proportions, a pleasant and virtuous disposition, and clear pronunciation, the last two qualities in order that her nursling would not contract any undesirable habits or modes of speech. Sexual continence during breast-feeding, with a view to maintaining high quality milk, was a further requirement, but one which was likely to be half-heartedly obeyed and to precipitate the introduction of weaning well before the recommended stage of the appearance of teeth.[24]

The paragon of integrity described by the specialists appears in real life to have eluded even the most earnest parental seekers of her services. For private and public journals testify to a negligence of duty on the part of the *nourrice* that caused, at best, disfigurement or crippling, at worst, death. The philosopher John Locke, conversing with a physician at Orléans in 1678, learned that the lameness of the local children was due 'more to the negligence of nurses than anything else, carrying them always wrapped up and on one side, and he thinks this to be the cause, because this lameness lights more on girls that are tenderer, than boys who are stronger and sooner out of their swaddling clothes'.[25] At the opposite end of the century Pierre de l'Estoile made a grim entry in his Journal for 1608 to the effect that 'force petits enfants' had been 'étouffés par leurs nourrices',[26] though he failed to specify whether the stifling was done deliberately or came about through the habitual accident of the wet-nurse rolling on the baby in bed.[27] The very person, then, entrusted with the rearing and physical well-being of infants presented yet another threat to their continued existence.

Maladies of different kinds, some arising from congenital malformations and clumsy post-natal care, others contracted in insanitary homes filled to capacity with humans[28] and livestock,[29] and all aggravated by the bleedings and purgings which doctors ordered with gay abandon,[30] accounted for further deaths. All sections of society had a high rate of infant mortality. The Protestant leader Henri, Duc de Rohan, managed to rear to adulthood only one of his nine children, and Henri IV's minister, Sully, only four of his own ten offspring.[31] *Livres de Raison*, diaries kept by the heads of households, depress by their long casualty lists. Simon Le Marchand, a bourgeois of Caen, recorded between 1612 and 1635 the birth of twelve offspring, ten of whom were overtaken by death within a maximum of two years, and mostly within a matter of days or months.[32] Usually the fatal occurrence is just starkly noted, an eloquent testimony to its commonplace nature. Sometimes a pious ejaculation, touching in its resignation, accompanies the entry:

Dieu lui fasse paix.[33]

Dieu par sa grâce lui vueille avoir fait miséricorde, n'imputant point en elle le péché de ses père et mère, et encore grandement entâchée.[34]

Deus dedit, Deus abstulit, sit nomen Domini benedictum. L'âme est au ciel et le corps en notre sépulcre, proche celui de sa bonne mère. Plaise à la divine majesté que les âmes soient ensemble dans le ciel.[35]

Only occasionally does the note of serene acceptance waver a little, betraying a proud parent whose hopes for the future have been

cruelly shattered: 'Etait bien apprise et promettait beaucoup
... Avait un grand esprit, savait lire dès l'âge de cinq ans et
avait toutes les bonnes inclinations et passions de sa défunte
mère.'[36]

The extreme precariousness of infant existence helps to account
for the emphasis that was placed on rapid baptism. Such was the
concern to avert the tragedy of a Catholic baby's soul being
condemned to wander in limbo[37] and the body confided to a
specially demarcated portion of the cemetery because death had
intervened before the accomplishment of this vital ceremony that
provision was made for the administration of a preliminary form of
baptism known as the *ondoiement* to any new-born child whose life
was considered to be in imminent danger of extinction. Anyone,
male or female, lay or ecclesiastic, Catholic or non-Catholic, could
perform the *ondoiement*,[38] provided that they used natural water
and pronounced in whatever language they knew the formula: 'I
baptise you in the name of the Father, and of the Son, and of the
Holy Ghost'.[39] It sufficed for only a part of the child to protrude
from the mother's body for the emergency baptism to be legitimate, and syringes were invented for use within the womb in cases
of obstructed birth.[40]

Formal presentation of the infant at the parochial church font
was generally carried out with speed, whether an *ondoiement* had
already been performed or not. At eight in the evening on 8
August 1677 Ferdinand Jacque, a Parlement advocate of Dôle,
hastened to church the daughter who had arrived just before two
o'clock that same day.[41] Boys and girls born into the Froissard-
Broissia family, also of Franche-Comté, were rushed to the font
within as little as one or two hours after birth, a practice which
proved remarkably effective in weeding out the weaker scions.[42]
Usually, however, parents managed to curb their zeal sufficiently
to give the newly-born twenty-four hours to gather strength before
being exposed to the elements.

Fairly frequent exceptions to the rule for speedy baptism were
royal and aristocratic children whose official admission to Catholicism was delayed for reasons of state or convenience. Louis XIII
and his sister Elisabeth, born respectively in September 1601 and
November 1602, were not baptised until 14 September 1606, along
with their sister Christine, who had joined the family in the
February of that year.[43] The Duchesse de Montpensier, Louis's
niece, received her baptism in July 1636, at the age of nine.[44] Mlle

de Béthune, a grand-daughter of Chancellor Séguier, was obliged to wait fourteen years before being christened.[45]

In the choice of godparents, a considerable amount of latitude was allowed. Children of a very young age are themselves often found acting in this capacity.[46] The grand-daughter of the illustrious Marquise de Rambouillet was allowed to be a godmother at four years because she could answer the necessary questions when interrogated by the local priest.[47] In 1688 Racine's daughter Madeleine had as godparents her elder brother and sister, despite the fact that the latter, aged seven, was unable to sign the baptismal register.[48] Having brothers and sisters serve as godparents, a popular custom, was a useful means of reinforcing with spiritual bonds the ties of blood already existing. Respectable introductions between youngsters of the opposite sex could also be made at the baptism ceremony, forming the basis of future marriages.[49] Just as age was taken very little into account in the selection of godparents, so was social status. The attachment and gratitude of domestics was strengthened by holding their offspring at the font[50] and by permitting them to do likewise with the infants of their employers.[51] The supreme gesture of piety and humility consisted in handing children for baptism to a couple of paupers,[52] and in performing a reciprocal service for the offspring of the poor. Thus Marguerite de Valois acted as impromptu godmother to the son of an Irish beggar-woman delivered one day in her path.[53] Not only individuals but collective bodies also could stand as godfather or godmother. Evidence of this phenomenon is more common in connection with boys, baptised under the aegis of municipal authorities or the Provincial Assemblies (*Etats Provinciaux*). But Tallemant mentions a lady-love of the Duc de Guise who had the town of Marseille as godparent,[54] while the abbess of Sainte Croix at Poitiers, Flandrine de Nassau, Princess of Orange, owed her unusual forename to the fact of being the godchild of the *Etats* of Flanders.[55]

Custom decreed that the infant be given as a first name that of the godmother or godfather, as appropriate. For the Catholic girl the name would normally be that of a saint whose virtues she might imitate and whose protection she might implore;[56] for the Protestant girl the name of an Old Testament heroine such as Rachel or Sarah would be first choice. The addition of second and third names was regarded by the Church as superfluous. There were, however, few blue-blooded girls without at least a double-barrelled forename, an abuse described towards the end of the century as spreading to the *Tiers Etat*, who considered that the possession of several names conferred on their infants an air of nobility.[57] The Church also disliked the abbreviation of baptismal saints' names to familiar diminutives;[58] but judging from the Manons, Catauts, and Margots sprinkled in letters and *Livres de Raison*, the rebuke fell on deaf ears.

It was not at all unusual for several children in a family to bear the same forename. When an elder child died prematurely what seems in retrospect like a pathetic attempt at resuscitation would sometimes be made by passing on the same name to the next brother or sister that came along. But a succession of living children might equally be christened alike, for religious or family reasons. The pious Ducs de Beauvillier and de Noailles bestowed the name of Marie, the former on all of his nine daughters, the latter on seven out of eleven daughters.[59] In the Savelli household to which Mme de Rambouillet belonged the name of Lucine, a saint of the family, was added to that of all daughters on baptism.[60] The usage was not without causing a certain amount of confusion, and was one of the reasons which prompted the authorities to insist on the regular keeping of parish baptismal records.[61]

Baptism being essentially a solemn sacrament, the Church saw little reason for it to be accompanied by merry-making and jollification. The faithful, however, begged to differ, seeing in the occasion a glorious excuse for lavish expenditure, gastronomic indulgence and letting off steam generally.[62] Plenty of noise was obligatory. Music from violins, fifes and tabors (or salvoes from guns in the case of the nobility) would accompany the infant to church. Guests would while away the time that it took the priest to perform the familiar ritual – exorcisms,[63] introduction of salt into the child's mouth (a symbol of wisdom and preservation from vice), aspersion with holy water, anointment with oil, imposition of the christening bonnet (*chrémeau*), reading from Saint John's Gospel and exhortation to the godparents – by laughing, joking, promenading and exchanging kisses. Peals of bells would signal the termination of the ceremony.[64] At that point the new Christian was apt to be whisked away to the nearest tavern and released only when the parents gave the merry kidnappers the means to wet the baby's head.[65] Parents of substance would seek to render the event more memorable by keeping open house over a number of days and by giving presents to the populace. Consecration of the family name and largesses in the pages of the *Mercure Galant* was secured in October 1697 by the Marquis de Cruzy, who celebrated the baptism of his fifteen-year-old daughter by free distributions of liquor and sweetmeats, and by having two tables served throughout a week of festivities.

Swift to censure what they saw as reprehensible vestiges of paganism, the clergy were so dilatory in fulfilling their more important obligation to record baptisms that they had to be reminded by periodic edicts issued throughout the late sixteenth and early seventeenth centuries.[66] Registration of baptism was essential at a time when precise records of the actual birth were not universally or officially kept, and when recourse was consequently had to the fallible memory of relatives and friends to determine age. Mme Guyon, the mystic, begins her autobiography with the telling phrase: 'Je naquis, à ce que disent quelques-uns, la veille de Pâques, le 13 avril (quoique mon baptême ne fut que le 24 de mai) de l'année 1648.'[67] Marie-Jeanne d'Aumale, biographer of Mme de Maintenon, admits that the date of birth which she gives for the latter is only a surmise based on the luckily preserved extract from a baptismal register.[68] Not that contemporaries seem to have been unduly disturbed by this state of affairs. Indeed writers jested about it, or used it as a pretext to pay compliments to ladies delighted to find themselves suddenly rejuvenated by the discovery of a baptism certificate.[69]

Delicate infants, perhaps born before time, or those whose mothers had made special vows in return for a safe delivery, sometimes received, in addition to baptism, an extra form of spiritual protection. This consisted in dedicating them to God, the Virgin Mary, or one of the saints, in honour of whom they would adopt a religious type of raiment for a number of years stipulated by their parents. Madeleine de Sourdis, a future abbess whose precarious health had caused her to be offered at six weeks of age to the Virgin, 'afin qu'il lui plût d'être sa Protectrice, et de trouver bon qu'elle portât l'habit blanc en son honneur, jusqua'à l'âge de sept ans', lived to be an octogenarian.[70] Less fortunate was the prematurely-born daughter of Louis XIV, who died in December 1664, a fortnight after being taken to the Récollettes in the Faubourg Saint Germain and committed to assuming the habit and scapulary of the order for the first three years of her life.[71] White or blue were the usual colours of the garments worn by girls consecrated in this way, and a service in church commemorated the moment when they were formally exchanged for ordinary, worldly clothes.[72]

Children were clothed, as paintings and engravings of the period show, in scarcely modified versions of the heavy dress of their elders. Aristocratic girls bowed beneath the weight of jewels and elaborate coiffures. 'Elle succombe sous l'or et les pierreries', wrote Mme de Maintenon of the tiny young Duchesse du Maine, 'et sa coiffure pèse plus que toute sa personne. On l'empêchera de croître et d'avoir de la santé.'[73] To induce them to preserve an upright carriage beneath the load they had stiffening material inserted into the corsage of their dresses[74] and wore a type of bodice similarly strengthened with bone or metal.[75] Hunchbacks like the three daughters of the Maréchale de la Mothe were condemned from childhood onwards to life in an iron corset.[76]

Young and not so young shared games and pastimes too. The meanest little towns boasted of a tennis court in which children outshone mothers and fathers by their precocious dexterity with a racket.[77] Strollers in the gardens of the Tuileries were charmed by the spectacle of groups of girls playing at bowls and skittles, and engaging in jumping competitions terminated by the solemn crowning of the winner with flowers or laurel. Over in the enclosure of the Palais de Justice impoverished girls who assisted the numerous merchants selling their wares there were in the habit of tossing to and fro a ball or shuttlecock while digesting their lunch.[78] Gentlewomen did not disdain shuttlecock, since it was permitted during recreation hours at Mme de Maintenon's aristocratic boarding-school at Saint-Cyr, along with games such as spillikins, chess, draughts and *trou-madame* (played by rolling balls into holes) which the foundress of the establishment regarded as exercising the brain or the memory.[79] Juvenile play-acting, included under the same utilitarian rubric, became as popular at Saint-Cyr as it was in the rest of upper-class society;[80] but it underwent an enforced eclipse after sumptuous performances of Racine's *Esther* before the court in 1689 had stirred dangerous emotions in the bosom of actresses and spectators. Mme de Maintenon continued, however, to let her girls entertain small, select audiences in conditions of strict privacy and sobriety, and did not oppose the theatrical bent of her most important charge, the Duchesse de Bourgogne, whom she schooled after the ten-year-old princess's arrival at court in 1696.[81] She even

condescended to the occasional game of blind man's buff which all
the high-ranking ladies of the court had to play in order to amuse
the king's effervescent grand-daughter-in-law. [82]

Early participation by children in the social, and especially in the
religious, life of the community was encouraged. It was the
youngest members of the family who pronounced the benediction
at mealtimes[83] and handed round portions of the bean cake
traditionally baked on New Year's Eve. [84] Under a watchful
maternal eye they distributed alms to the poor[85] and solicited
offerings from the congregation in church. [86] Theirs were the hands
trusted to select winning tickets in public lotteries. [87] Attired in
angelic or other symbolic raiment they marched in pious processions, saluted dignitaries on the occasion of a ceremonial entry into
town or installation in office, and paraded at times of national
rejoicing. Though contemporary recorders of such events habitually fail to specify the sex and age of the children involved, it is
obvious from scattered references that young girls played their part
in public ceremonies of welcome, thanksgiving and supplication.
They came into their own when it was a question of greeting
high-born ladies who had come to take up temporary or permanent residence in the locality. As Louis XIII processed through
Angers with Marie de Médicis in 1614 they were confronted at the
entrance to the Rue St-Michel-du-Tertre by a theatre with two
rustic grottoes, out of the first of which emerged a young boy to
recite verses to the king, while out the second appeared a young
girl, representing an oread, to do likewise to the queen mother. [88]
During the course of the triumphal entry of the Duchesse de
Richelieu into the seat of the duchy in 1685 she was complimented
by a deputation of boarders from a local convent, the smallest of
whom captivated onlookers by her graceful manner of presenting
crowns of flowers to the visitor. [89] Boarders were again on hand at
the abbey of Vernon in Normandy to declaim praises in honour of
Mme de Berthemet on the February day in 1687 when she was
consecrated as the new abbess. [90] As members of the so-called
'devout sex', [91] girls were naturally associated with corporate
demonstrations of piety. It was they who led a procession to
implore the Divinity for rain to fall on their drought-stricken town
of Châlons in the summer of 1624. [92] Young daughters of upper-
class families of Marseille learned an object lesson in humility
when, arrayed in virginal robes, they each escorted a female from
the poor-house in a procession of 1688 which ended with some of

their mothers waiting upon the impoverished women at table.[93] But certain restrictions seem to have been in operation. The *Mercure Galant*, reporting in 1681 on the annual Trinity Sunday procession from Flavigny to Alise-Sainte-Reine (Burgundy), in which girls played a leading part, describes as unusual the fact that they were allowed to carry sacred relics.[94]

It goes without saying that community life was not all play and pageantry. The sober reality of work intervened at an age which struck travellers in France by reason of its earliness: 'les plus petits enfants sont élevés au travail', remarked Elie Brackenhoffer of Strasbourg after a trip to Grenoble.[95] Albert Jouvin of Rochefort made an identical observation at the arsenal of Toulon: 'On y voit ... travailler ... jusqu'aux plus petits enfants.'[96] The poverty of parents who needed every hand available, every *sou* earned, in order to maintain the family bread supply was the major factor in turning children out into the fields or the forerunners of the factories as soon as they had sufficient intelligence and strength to be able to mind livestock and perform simple mechanical operations. Seven or eight was the age at which the exercise of reason was thought to commence.[97] But grown-ups were impatient: children in the vicinity of Alençon were employed to manufacture pins at the ripe old age of six.[98] Any qualms over child labour were easily stifled by the reflection that children were not worked to the point of exhaustion. Even in a poor-house like the famous La Charité at Lyons, where indigent and orphaned girls and boys were constrained from the age of seven to rise at five in the morning and busy themselves with silk-making till dark in winter and six in the evening in summer, John Locke felt that 'counting their mass and breakfast in the morning, collation in the evening and time of dinner, their work is not hard'.[99] The idea was firmly ingrained, moreover, that the young needed to be trained and to be preserved from the evils of slothfulness. Parents who suffered no economic duress still believed in delegating household chores to their daughters at the first opportunity and in making sure that every minute of the day was fruitfully filled.[100] 'I observed here one thing as I walked along the streets', wrote Francis Mortoft on a visit to Nantes in 1658, 'that none of the women were idle, but the gentlewomen and little girls, as they sat at their doors or walked about the streets, had their spinning work in their hands.'[101] No devil was going to find mischief for idle young hands to do if mothers like these could help it.

Inevitably children so rapidly established in the adult roles of wage-earners and, if they were well-to-do, of marriage partners, [102] were judged by adult criteria. Judgements were harsh. The great classical writers in general show themselves to be impervious to the charms of childhood, viewing it with some horror as an age of physical and mental weakness, essentially lacking in dignity. 'L'enfance est la vie d'une bête', was the terse verdict of Bossuet when he considered the impotence of the child's will and reason to combat the force of passions. [103] 'Les enfants ... sont déjà des hommes', that is to say, possessed of all vices, according to La Bruyère. [104] The genial La Fontaine underlines their stupidity, harshness and cruelty. [105] Boileau and Bayle would banish them from the epic as undermining the requisite lofty tone. [106] Dramatists and novelists use them sparingly and seek to give them a wisdom in advance of their years. [107]

Manifestations of affection towards these miniature adults appear decidedly inhibited by modern standards. The few brief insights into the sentiments of the peasantry left by seventeenth-century observers attest to a certain detachment between parents and offspring, of the kind which characterises the expressions and stances of the group depicted in the painting *Famille de Paysans*, attributed to Louis Le Nain, where each figure seems physically withdrawn from the others and immersed in his or her own private world. The ex-soldier turned moralist, Fortin de la Hoguette, cites peasant fathers and children as an example of the purely pragmatic relationship, what he calls 'un sentiment d'amitié fort obscur du père au fils, du fils au père ... qui ne subsiste qu'en tant que le requiert la communauté de leur travail', that develops when parents tend their progeny like their livestock, nurturing the body at the expense of the soul. [108] At best the generalisation would avowedly apply only to fathers and sons, leaving unsettled the question of whether peasant fathers were equally unfeeling towards daughters, and vice versa. In addition it was penned by an 'outsider' from a higher social bracket who shared with a good many of his equals the propensity for interpreting peasant behaviour in the light of that of animals. [109] The attitude taken by some sections of fashionable society towards demonstrating love for children hardly justified feelings of superiority. Coulanges, Mme de Sévigné's cousin, in a lengthy *Chanson* entitled 'Avis aux Pères de Famille', pleads for fathers to observe public silence about their offspring and to make sure that the latter eat apart from civilised company:

> Sachez, encor, mes bonnes gens,
> Que rien n'est plus insupportable,
> Que de voir vos petits enfants
> En rang d'oignons à la grand'table,
> Des morveux qui, le menton gras,
> Mettent les doigts dans tous les plats.[110]

The sight of a learned man stooping to play with his own child brought a pitying smile to the lips of Vigneul-Marville:

> Les savants ont aussi leur ridicule. Qui aurait pu s'empêcher de rire, en voyant Melancthon, le plus grave et le plus savant théologien d'entre les Luthériens, tenir d'une main un livre dans lequel il lisait, et de l'autre bercer son enfant pour l'endormir? Je vis un jour dans une posture peu différente de celle-là feu M. Esprit. Il lisait Platon, et de temps en temps quittant sa lecture, il faisait sonner le hochet de son enfant, et badinait avec ce marmot.[111]

However, as this passage reveals, there *were* fathers[112] willing to brave public ridicule and the prejudices of what were for the most part childless scholars in order to show affection for, and interest in, their young children.

Letters provide a precious testimony in this respect since, out of the public gaze, in the intimacy of a page designed only for the perusal of a loved one or a friend, a father could abandon himself unashamedly to the promptings of paternal affection. Henri IV confides to his mistress Mme de Verneuil his pleasure in the wit, or naivety, of their four-year-old Gabrielle: 'notre fille a entretenu ce soir trois heures ma femme et moi et toute la compagnie, qu'elle nous a cuydé faire mourir de rire'.[113] The Maréchal de La Force preoccupies himself with keeping his daughter's complexion free from sunburn in his absence, and threatens her with the ultimate sanction of no Christmas presents if she persists in talking through her nose and failing to study diligently.[114] In the later part of the century Racine's letters are full of homely chatter about little Nanette's difficulty in cutting her teeth, the wit and intelligence of young Madelon, and his delight at receiving a bouquet for his *fête* from his youngest daughters while he is busy working.[115] But perhaps the most touching memorial to the bond between a father and his small daughter is that enshrined within the memoirs of

Henri de Campion, a nobly-born military man who died in 1663. Louise-Anne entered his life on 2 May 1649, 'si belle et si agréable que dès le moment de sa naissance je l'aimai avec une tendresse que je ne puis exprimer'. Scarcely had Campion time to savour the joys of paternity before death robbed him of the child on 10 May 1653:

> Lorsque je pensais que j'étais séparé pour toute ma vie de ce qui m'était le plus cher, je ne pouvais aimer le monde, hors duquel était ma félicité. Je sais que beaucoup me taxeront de faiblesse, et d'avoir manqué de constance dans un accident qu'ils ne tiendront pas des plus fâcheux; mais à cela je réponds, que les choses ne font effet sur nous, que selon les sentiments que nous en avons, et qu'ainsi il n'en faut pas juger généralement comme si nous avions tous la même pensée. Il faut savoir le prix que nous estimons les choses, avant que de louer notre patience quand nous les perdons ... J'avoue que je jouerais le personnage d'une femme si j'importunais le monde de mes plaintes; mais chérir toujours ce que j'ai le plus aimé, y penser continuellement en éprouvant le désir de m'y rejoindre, je crois que c'est le sentiment d'un homme qui sait aimer, et qui, ayant une ferme croyance de l'immortalité de l'âme, pense que l'éloignement de sa chère fille est une absence pour un temps, et non une séparation éternelle.[116]

Even the fondest of fathers, it seems, was uncomfortably aware of indulging a culpable weakness in loving and grieving for his own child.

It was not, therefore, a very welcoming face that seventeenth-century society presented to the infant girl. From a physical point of view life was fraught with dangers to which her tender constitution often succumbed. From a moral point of view she suffered doubly. As a child she was an object of mistrust to theologians, moralists and certain men of letters who saw in her essentially the product of Original Sin, a wilful animal needing, they urged with some success, to be kept at a distance even from her own parents until the process of reason began to operate. As a female she was a disappointment because she was 'fragile' in all respects and inapt to maintain her family's material status. This initial burden of prejudice was to accompany her continually, and not least throughout the second major phase of existence, her education.

2
Education

From amongst the insipid pieces continually inspired by the interminable *Querelle des Femmes*, the debate over equality of the sexes, a new theme emerged in the seventeenth century. The same hackneyed arguments were still advanced for or against the superiority of woman[1] but an increasing amount of space came to be devoted to the hitherto neglected subject of her education. That the issue was vital was recognised and stressed by pamphleteers early on in the century. The gossips who gather round the bed of the newly delivered mother in an anonymous opuscule of 1622 entitled *Les Caquets de l'Accouchée* decide that if only a fraction of the care lavished upon the education of men was devoted to that of the opposite sex, 'on verrait des merveilles'.[2] In a publication of the same year, *L'Egalité des Hommes et des Femmes*, Marie de Gournay marvelled that the paltry education given to women did not prevent them altogether, let alone in most cases, from rising to the heights attained by men, and she asked the pertinent question: 'Et pourquoi leur institution ou nourriture aux affaires et lettres à l'égal des hommes, ne remplirait-elle ce vide qui paraît ordinairement entre les têtes des mêmes hommes et les leurs?'[3] To demolish obscurantist bastions, however, a more solid assault was needed than the passing protest of a satirist or the laborious pamphlets of a *savante* whose personal eccentricities were a dubious advertisement for her claims. The assault was launched by various churchmen and moralists who sought to prove that it was in the interest of both men and women that the latter should not be left in ignorance.

The gist of their arguments was as follows. The difference between the sexes is more apparent than real and in no way extends to the functioning of the brain; possessing all the necessary organs, women are capable of exactly the same mental processes as men.[4] Delicacy of body is only calculated to predispose them to subtlety of mind, and their renowned *légèreté* to quicker thinking.[5] Women also have at their disposal considerably more leisure time and privacy than men, and what better way for them to avoid the proverbial vices engendered by idleness than to occupy themselves with study?[6] Several advantages will result. The first and most important is that a woman will be able to discern where her duty lies and to do it, despite all the besetting passions and impulses to which she is notoriously subject.[7] Feminine morals are more safely guarded by knowledge than by ignorance.[8] Secondly, the educated woman makes a much more agreeable companion than the one whose ignorance renders her mute or limits her conversation to the latest fashions.[9] Thirdly, a woman will have the means of contenting herself in solitude, even if there exists no public outlet for the knowledge she has acquired.[10]

While ostensibly championing woman's right to education these writers were in fact making a number of substantial concessions to the opposing party, who aligned themselves behind an ancient Breton duke in proclaiming a woman sufficiently learned if she could distinguish between her husband's doublet and his shirt.[11] Prevailing views about the weaknesses of the female constitution and temperament are accepted, as is shown by the clumsy attempt to explain them away as assets for study purposes or as susceptible of correction by the pursuit of learning. The suggestion is put forward that men will profit from the enlightenment of women in that the latter will become more virtuous and entertaining companions. Admission is made that there is no use for a woman's knowledge beyond her own self-perfection and satisfaction, thereby anticipating La Bruyère's caustic analogy between the blue-stocking and the finely polished weapon, 'pièce de cabinet, que l'on montre aux curieux, qui n'est pas d'usage'.[12]

Moreover when it came to the problem of outlining a concrete educational programme for women hitherto progressive theorists were wont to become suddenly reactionary. If the Franciscan Du Bosc is willing to allow the learning of music, history and philosophy, he quickly makes it clear that he regards the study of morality to take precedence.[13] The Jesuit Caussin, in his anxiety not to form 'des Sibylles et des Muses', settles for 'une honnête science des choses qui servent à la direction des mœurs'.[14] His colleague Le Moyne promptly follows a generous declaration that women are capable of studying speculative philosophy with a qualification that virtually nullifies the original concession:

Quoi que j'ai dit néanmoins, mon intention n'est pas d'appeler les femmes au collège. Je n'en veux pas faire des licenciées, ni changer en des astrolabes et en des sphères, leurs aiguilles et leurs laines. Je respecte trop les bornes qui nous séparent: et ma question est seulement de ce qu'elles peuvent, et non pas de ce qu'elles doivent, en l'état où les choses ont été mises, soit par l'ordre de la nature, soit par une coutume immémoriale, et aussi vieille que la nature.[15]

In stating that he is concerned merely with what women can do, not with what they should do, the Jesuit underlines a basic flaw in the argumentation of contemporary educational treatises, one which limits the value of an ultra-revolutionary work like Poulain de la Barre's *De l'Egalité des Deux Sexes*, where the assertion that women are capable of taking up all the offices and careers at present closed to them is not accompanied by the corollary that the existing status quo should be altered to allow them to do so.[16]

Another factor restricting the import of seventeenth-century educational theory was the obligation placed upon the educated woman to conceal her knowledge. Connotations of shame and sin were introduced to discourage potential rebels. 'Il y a des dames de qualité fort savantes dans les belles-lettres, qui s'en cachent comme d'une chose un peu honteuse et elles ont raison', argues the Jansenist moralist Pierre Nicole, 'car il est toujours un peu honteux de s'être chargé d'une science inutile.'[17] Archbishop Fénelon, whose proposed curriculum of the three Rs, scripture, elementary law, literature, history, Latin, music and painting places him amongst the most liberal advocates of feminine instruction, nevertheless issues to instructors a forceful prescription for avoiding the kind of arrogance commonly associated with the brainy female: 'Retenez leur esprit le plus que vous pourrez dans les bornes communes et apprenez-leur qu'il doit y avoir pour leur sexe une pudeur sur la science, presque aussi délicate que celle qui inspire l'horreur du vice.'[18] The equation between learning and vice, made with all the authority of a respected man of the Church, can scarcely have helped the cause to which Fénelon purported to give his backing.

The scope of educational treatises was further narrowed by a third qualification basically inspired, like the previous two, by the desire to ensure that woman did not stray far from her traditional role of housekeeper and child-bearer and give herself airs unsuited to her station. It concerned the class of women for whom the treatises legislated. To give a literary education to the plebeian girl was considered superfluous. The young *bourgeoise*, according to Mme de Maintenon, needed only a sound training in her domestic duties, the rudiments of reading and writing, and enough arithmetic to be able to keep accounts and memoranda, if she were to retain a salutary awareness of her divinely ordained place in society.[19] Pursued to its logical conclusion the argument tended to debar girls at the bottom of the social scale from the right to even the fundamentals of education. Louise de Marillac, helper of Vincent de Paul, writing to the future saint on 22 August 1647 about schooling arrangements for children installed in the poorhouse at Bicêtre, gave her opinion that it was not expedient 'que les filles apprennent à écrire'.[20] Neglecting the vast bulk of the female population, educationalists concentrated on adorning the minds of the aristocracy, the upper aristocracy for preference.[21] Examples of imitable conduct were almost invariably drawn from the same elevated social class as that of the intended reader. In Caussin's *Cour Sainte* the necessary precepts are placed on the lips of an empress. The sheer range of De Grenaille's course of studies – religion, logic, physics, astronomy, philosophy (ethics), politics, metaphysics, eloquence, poetry and cosmography – indicates that he cannot be addressing himself to the multitude, and in effect he speaks 'pour des reines devant que de travailler pour des suivantes'.[22]

The procedure of De Grenaille typifies that of all those writers who contributed to the discussion. Much ink was expended on gallant proofs of woman's ability to study, none on the practical use to which the fruits of her intellectual labours might be put for the benefit of persons other than the men in her life. Programmes of study, sometimes elaborate, were devised, but always there was some qualification to restrict the efficacy of their application. Behind the liberal façade a fundamental conservatism persisted.

A consideration of the actual means of education at the disposal of women, and the results achieved from using them, will show the practical repercussions of this attitude. The education available may be divided for the sake of clarity into three main types: domestic, formal and informal.

It had long been a tradition that a girl's education should be confided to her mother in the home, a responsibility which somewhat bemused fathers were only too glad to hand over to their partner.[23] In some cases the responsibility was conscientiously assumed. Mme de la Guette, who came of the minor provincial nobility, remembered with affection how her 'bonne mère' began to occupy her as a child with little tasks around the house, 'et me faisait toujours rendre compte de ce qu'elle m'avait commandé'.[24] The second wife of Louis XIV's brother, Charlotte de Bavière, prided herself on the moral training which enabled her daughter to remain virtuous in the midst of a corrupt court: 'On m'a demandé comment je m'y étais prise pour l'élever aussi bien: j'ai répondu que c'était en lui parlant toujours raison, en lui montrant pourquoi telle ou telle chose était mal ou bien, en ne lui passant aucun caprice, en cherchant autant que possible à ce qu'elle ne vît aucun mauvais exemple, en ne la rebutant point par des accès de mauvaise humeur, en louant la vertu et en lui inspirant l'horreur du vice en général.'[25] As these two examples demonstrate, the type of instruction demanded of the mother was not particularly exacting, consisting of housewifery and morals. But rare were those mothers in a position to provide more solid intellectual fare and to emulate a Mme de Sévigné or a Mme d'Aubigné in introducing their daughters to the study of a foreign language or of Greek literature.[26] Often poorly educated themselves, and preoccupied with their *toilette* and the social round, many failed to take their natural role of instructress seriously or far enough. Some fashionable ladies contented themselves with a passing injunction about posture or etiquette in the manner of the Duchesse de Montpensier's stepmother, who addressed nothing but a peremptory 'Tenez-vous droites; levez la tête' to her daughters when she granted them a quarter of an hour's audience morning and evening.[27] Others considered their maternal duty fulfilled if they showed an extreme severity. Javotte, the heroine of Furetière's *Roman Bourgeois*, who spends her life silently sewing in her room under her mother's eye,[28] seems merely the exaggerated product of a satirist's colourful imagination. Yet Mme de Maintenon has real-life 'horror stories' to tell of housebound girls released only for a Sunday airing or forced to stand every day mutely watching aristocratic mothers gamble.[29]

More often than not the task of keeping a daughter under surveillance was passed on to a female domestic, a chambermaid or a so-called *gouvernante* who would in all probability be merely a chambermaid with a grander title.[30] The functions of the *gouvernantes* were essentially those of a nursemaid. They kept the person and room of their young charges clean, saw them in and out of bed, gave them their meals and made sure that they came to no harm. They were also expected to be able to teach children how to pray and make the sign of the cross,[31] and to inculcate some notions of social etiquette. If the instructional duties required of them extended no further this was for the very good reason that the majority were extremely ignorant. Mme de Maintenon, whose educational vocation had first manifested itself in the teaching of her own *gouvernante* to read and write, paints for the pupils of Saint-Cyr a colourful picture of the fate that overtakes their equals outside its portals:

> ... votre mère aurait au plus deux femmes de chambre, dont l'une serait votre gouvernante. Quelle éducation pensez-vous qu'une telle fille vous donnerait? Ce sont ordinairement des paysannes, ou tout au plus de petites bourgeoises qui ne savent que faire tenir droite, bien tirer la busquière, et montrer à bien faire la révérence... La plus habile est celle qui sait quatre petits vers bien sots, quelques quatrains de Pibrac[32] qu'elle fait dire en toute occasion, et qu'on récite comme un petit perroquet.[33]

What education the *gouvernante* might conceivably provide in the way of setting a good example was also not to be relied upon. The *gouvernante* to the daughters of the future Regent, Philippe d'Orléans, ruined herself through gambling.[34] The one assigned to the daughter of the financier Montauron spawned illegitimate offspring.[35] Several are recorded as having connived at the dishonour of girls in their care.[36] It is not surprising therefore that popular literature of the day delighted in mocking the vices and insufficiencies of the *gouvernante*,[37] holding her up as an importunate figure of ridicule to girls already disposed to regard her as little more than a social inferior set to spy on them. Attempts to assert authority were futile and met with resistance that occasionally took the form of physical violence. Mme de Fiesque was locked in her room and tormented for seeking to discipline the headstrong Duchesse de Montpensier.[38] Mlle de Quaat, on taking a whip to correct Charlotte de Bavière, suffered 'tant de coups dans son vieux ventre qu'elle tomba tout de son long... et faillit se tuer'.[39]

In view of the unwillingness or inability of the mother to dispense instruction, and the notorious inadequacies of the *gouvernante*, it was necessary to call in assistance in the form of private tutors if the girl remaining at home was to acquire at least one or two accomplishments with which to attract a prospective husband. But recourse to outside instructors created rather more problems than it solved. Not without cause were parents urged to select God-fearing applicants for the post and to keep them under close surveillance.[40] Tutors, like contemporary school-teachers in general, often sprang from the lowest strata of society,[41] a factor which tended to be reflected in their mores. Within their ranks it was not unknown to find men who improvised as instructors merely to obtain easier access to the object of their affections. The Chevalier de Méré, relating to the Duchesse de Lesdiguières the story of an amorous friend who masqueraded thus in order to see a country noblewoman, gives an interesting glimpse of these nomadic and libertine 'tutors': 'ce sont des vagabonds qui ne vont deça, delà que pour apporter du scandale et séduire quelque innocente, et quand on les pense tenir ils ne manquent jamais de faire un trou à la nuit'.[42] Supposing, however, that the tutor's morals were above reproach, he was still a man and as such susceptible to the charms of an attractive pupil. As the poet Tristan L'Hermite put it in some verses addressed 'A son Ecolière':

> O sujet vraiment plus qu'humain,
> Amour qui ne nous quitte guère
> Me fait conduire votre main
> Pour former de beaux caractères:
> Mais voyant vos yeux m'enflammer
> Le traître tout bas me vient dire
> Que je profite à vous instruire,
> Et que j'apprends à bien aimer
> En vous montrant à bien écrire.[43]

The quiet and privacy required for teaching, the hours spent tête-à-tête, all favoured embarkation on the kind of idyll that immortalised Eloisa and Abelard. Méré confesses to having lost his heart while working to endow the young Mme de Maintenon with those social graces that later won for her the hand of a king.[44] Gilles Ménage's relations with Mme de Sévigné, who signed herself 'toute ma vie la plus véritable amie que vous ayez', were sufficiently intimate for her to confide to him subsequently her husband's infidelities,[45] while his devotion to his 'dulcissima Laverna', Mme de Lafayette (née Marie-Madeleine de la Vergne), lasted a lifetime.[46] Where the pupil was in a position to reciprocate the affection of the master the relationship might ripen into marriage[47] – or degenerate into debauchery.[48]

In fairness to the tutor, his flammable passions were not the only obstacle to effective schooling: he had also to reckon with the demands of his employers and with the dispositions of his pupil. In some ways the services required of him resembled those provided by the 'finishing school' of more modern times. He would often be engaged to instruct not a young child, but a young adolescent on the verge of marriage and needing to acquire the smattering of general knowledge and the indispensable talents that would enable her to hold her own at social gatherings. When tutors are mentioned in connection with girls it is nearly always in their capacity as instructors in the arts of leisure – music, singing, dancing – or those that pandered to snobbery, such as modern languages, rather than as teachers of more basic subjects. Appointed at a time when many valuable years of potential training had already been lost, they would find themselves obliged to supply a kind of instant knowledge in a matter of weeks or months.[49] And how could any tutor hope to fix on his lessons the attention of a pupil dreaming about her wedding or the exciting life that awaited beyond the confines of the parental home?[50]

Domestic education then, when dispensed by mothers, *gouvernantes* or tutors, appears for various reasons to have been either superficial or completely negative. Only one group of girls escaped its potentially stultifying effects, namely those who were lucky enough to have in the background some enlightened male relative to discern, and supervise the cultivation of, their nascent talents. Madeleine de Scudéry, an orphan confided at the age of six to the care of a learned uncle who facilitated her acquisition of an encyclopedic culture, is a classic example.[51] So is Anne Dacier, who was permitted to learn Greek, Latin and Italian from her erudite father Tanneguy le Fèvre after a timely intervention in her brother's lessons.[52] And Elisabeth-Sophie Chéron, who excelled in poetry and music, translated psalms and canticles from Hebrew and followed in her painter father's footsteps to become an affiliated member of the Royal Academy of Painting and Sculpture.[53] Did the irony escape contemporaries, one wonders, that the summits of female academic achievement in the seventeenth century were reached precisely by those who, for lack of a sufficiently noble pedigree, had been explicitly and implicitly condemned by educationalists never to raise their eyes above their prayer-books, ledgers and embroidery?

Should parents decide to send their girls outside the family home for instruction, their choice of educational establishments was limited. Higher education was out of the question since the University resolutely closed its doors to women,[54] and there existed no female equivalent of the colleges at which the Jesuits gave secondary education to boys. Public education for girls was essentially of the primary type, designed to inculcate the rudiments but not to broaden knowledge already acquired. It was obtainable from three[55] principal sources: from charity schools, generally founded and maintained by pious individuals or religious bodies;[56] from the 'little schools' (*petites écoles*), so called to distinguish them from the large grammar schools which prepared boys for university entrance;[57] and from the convents.

The *petites écoles* laboured under numerous difficulties. In many areas they were simply non-existent, and provinces made fruitless appeals for their establishment[58] to a central government that showed little interest in educational matters until the Revocation of the Edict of Nantes in 1685 made the diffusion of Catholic instruction imperative. The absence of sustained direction and subsidies from the state had unavoidable repercussions on school accommodation, on personnel and, in turn, upon the level of instruction that could be offered. The most that a girl could hope to learn from frequenting a makeshift schoolroom in the living quarters of the master, whose wife would probably be co-opted to teach her, was a notion of the three Rs and of handiwork. Even that meagre allowance was in constant danger of being reduced. Legislation concerning the *petites écoles* is characterised by an obsession on the part of the clergy with keeping boys and girls segregated both from each other and from teachers of the opposite sex. After listing official decrees to that effect issued by his ecclesiastical superiors, Claude Joly, Precentor of the Church of Paris, comments: 'Il n'est pas nécessaire qu'une fille sache l'écriture dans sa perfection: mais il est nécessaire qu'elle soit en lieu sûr et non suspect.'[59] Better an ignorant girl than one exposed to the perils of consorting with men.

Such risks could be lessened by sending a girl to board at a convent school, the habitual choice of upper-class parents who were anxious, into the bargain, to avoid the physical and moral contagion that ensued from rubbing shoulders with the lower orders.[60] Innumerable orders of nuns in the seventeenth century devoted themselves wholly or in part to the instruction of their sex, the Ursulines, who took a special fourth vow to that effect, being perhaps the best known. Christian charity prescribed that poor girls should be educated free as day pupils, while paying boarders usefully supplemented convent revenues. But the sisters did not perform their self-appointed task without a certain amount of soul-searching. Time spent in attending to the physical, spiritual and educational needs of their pupils was so much time deducted from that which could have been occupied in the statutory conventual pursuit of self-perfection. Angélique Arnauld, abbess of Port-Royal, writing on 25 January 1658 to the Queen of Poland in connection with the persecution to which the Jansenist stronghold was becoming subjected, expresses the dilemma of her peers, with on the one hand the desire to save souls, and on the other the concern to avoid distractions from the religious life: 'Nous sommes bien aises de servir ces petites âmes pour essayer de leur aider à conserver leur innocence. Mais après tout, si Dieu permet qu'on nous les ôte, nous en serons plus en paix et moins distraites, leur service nous donnant beaucoup d'occupation.'[61] To console the nuns and allay their misgivings it was thought necessary to stress that rearing the young could in fact be a means of sanctification, a daily penance that God was sure to take into special account when passing final judgement.[62]

The regime to which these conscript instructresses submitted their pupils understandably resembled the conventual ideal as far as possible[63] and impresses by its almost unrelieved austerity.[64] Rising took place around half past five, and as early as four o'clock for the older boarders at Port-Royal. Every action was framed by prayers, and every day ended with an examination of conscience. Silence was observed as far as was practical outside recreation hours, the latter consisting of two periods morning and evening of no more than an hour's duration each. Pupils were kept under constant surveillance. Letters, and anything brought into the convent for the boarders, were censored by the mother superior or class mistresses. Visits to and from relatives were discouraged, as was the slightest familiarity with mistresses or with fellow pupils. Punishments, notably at Port-Royal, took conventual forms such as kissing the feet of an offended companion or wearing a paper describing the fault committed. On Sundays and during religious festivals the routine differed little from normal except by an increase in the number of pious exercises to be performed. As a treat Port-Royal gave its boarders one hour's instruction in arithmetic on holy days.

The curriculum was dominated by religious instruction. This was administered both directly in the form of explanations of the catechism, training in prayer, and preparation for confession, communion and confirmation; and indirectly through the pious observations that mistresses were encouraged to introduce discreetly into their remarks at every possible opportunity. Moral training formed an indispensable complement. Pupils had instilled into them not only the Christian love of virtue, hatred of vice and contempt for worldly goods, but also an admiration for the conventual way of life and a deep mistrust of the wicked ways of the opposite sex.[65] Initiation into reading, writing, spelling and arithmetic took second place. The first was commonly taught by having the mistress read out a page or two which the pupils would follow in their books and repeat together in an undertone, then aloud one after the other so that their mistakes could be corrected. The reading of Latin preceded that of French, the theory being that Latin is easier to grasp because the pronunciation of the words resembles their spelling more closely than is the case with French.[66] When writing, girls began by learning how to hold their pen 'de bonne grâce, avec trois doigts', then proceeded from the formation of single letters to groups of the same letter and finally to proper words, in both Roman and Gothic script.[67] Spelling was inculcated by means of dictation, after which pupils corrected their work with the help of their books and rewrote the passage in question until they ceased to make errors.[68] Additional educational benefit was sometimes derived from using as a basis for writing and spelling lessons legal and business documents which pupils were likely to encounter in later life, or, more frequently, maxims of piety.[69] For arithmetic lessons counters were employed in simple calculations and an ability to handle money was taught by making pupils pay for imaginary purchases in various kinds of coinage.[70] Instruction in needlework and tapestry,[71] in good manners and in correct posture[72] completed the average programme.

The defects of convent education spring to the eye. As regards teaching methods, undue emphasis was laid upon the simple retention of facts by memory.[73] Repetition was the means by which comprehension was ascertained. The kind of dialogue between mistress and pupil brought about by the asking and answering of questions is mentioned only in connection with religious instruction, and certain provisos are made: 'Tout ce qu'on doit leur permettre, c'est d'exposer simplement ce qu'elles n'entendent pas et d'en demander l'intelligence. . . gardez-vous d'en faire des discoureuses qui questionnent pour le plaisir de parler.'[74] Where the curriculum was concerned, the fact that considerations of moral and social utility took precedence over purely intellectual profit made for some important omissions. Mme de Maintenon frowned on the teaching of history because she regarded the example of the pagan sages, once extolled to the girls of Saint-Cyr, as being responsible for perniciously exalting their imagination and diverting them from 'la simplicité convenable à notre sexe'.[75] Foreign languages are classed among those subjects which 'prennent un temps qu'on pourrait employer plus utilement'.[76] The same was implied of geography at a time when 'Un fils de famille peut entreprendre un voyage, passer les mers, aller aux extrémités du monde; mais une fille ne doit pas même sortir de sa maison sans ordre'.[77] And prospects for a significant extension to the range of subjects, or the depth in which they were studied, did not seem very bright so long as the Church anathematised a spirit of enquiry and curiosity as being conducive to schisms and heresies.[78]

Whereas criticisms of convents and their inmates abound in the seventeenth century,[79] they appear only rarely to have been extended specifically to the education provided by these establishments. Molière indirectly jibed at the system in *L'Ecole des Femmes* by depicting the convent as the ideal prison for the mind as well as the body of Arnolphe's ward, but the point was not laboured.[80] Fénelon had some trenchant advice to give to the Comtesse de Montberon in 1700 about her grand-daughter's education: 'évitez, si vous le pouvez, un couvent. Le meilleur la gênera, l'ennuiera, la révoltera, la rendra fausse et passionnée pour le monde.'[81] But the archbishop's misgivings were expressed at the dawn of the eighteenth century, and later still were those of Mme de Staal, who in her memoirs attributed all the misfortunes of her life to the manner of her upbringing in various Normandy convents of the late 1690s.[82] The virtual absence of derogatory comment, particularly in the later part of the century, when the question of female education had stimulated much discussion and when writers and thinkers generally were beginning to attack the most sacred institutions, invites the conclusion that the majority of the population were content with the education received by their daughters in the convent. In what proportions this contentment signifies genuine satisfaction with the educational services rendered, ignorance of conventual procedures, or mere relief at having persons onto whom the onerous burden of a girl's training could be shifted, it is unfortunately impossible to establish.

The generally scanty intellectual fare provided by conventual education, as by the domestic kind, could be, and frequently was, supplemented in later life by a third kind of knowledge gained informally from day-to-day experience and conversation, from private reading and from the use of various educational facilities placed at the disposal of the public.

In the case of the peasant woman, whose schooling, if any, had probably been interrupted by periods of seasonal work on the land and in the home, the chances of extending her competence beyond the routine household and agricultural chores were remote. But further up the social ladder intellectual horizons progressively widened. Active involvement in a business, or in the running of a large middle-class or aristocratic household, a task traditionally delegated to the wife, necessitated the development of managerial and mathematical talents if accounts were to be properly balanced, transactions advantageously made, estates and domestic personnel efficiently overseen. The rudiments of legal procedure and terminology might equally have to be mastered in order to bring about the successful conclusion of the lawsuits in which countless seventeenth-century families were embroiled, to the extent of passing them on from one generation to another.[83] Proficiency in the organisation, at least, of domestic industries such as sericulture and the carding and spinning of wool would be expected of the country housewife.[84] It was the mother of the household, too, who instructed herself in elementary medicine so that she could concoct her own remedies for the family's ills.[85] These were practical skills which served chiefly to safeguard the material well-being of a household and advance its station. In conversation, on the other hand, the element of a woman's personal pleasure and profit was more pronounced.

Universally enjoyed by contemporaries, conversation was raised to the level of an art by the formulation of rules which laid emphasis, somewhat paradoxically, on naturalness and proscribed all pedantry. Discussion was to be 'plus souvent de choses ordinaires et galantes, que de grandes choses',[86] a precept admirably calculated to facilitate assimilation of the subject matter by an untrained female mind. But the content of the average salon conversation was perhaps less important than the opportunity which the occasion provided to match and sharpen minds one against the other, meet people of various professions, ask questions – exercises which were foreign to the girl secluded all day in her mother's room or behind convent walls. Social intercourse with the writers who figured prominently in the salons might also give rise to fruitful exchanges of letters in which an aristocratic correspondent would not hesitate to debate with her mentor the 'grandes choses' that etiquette and decorum outlawed in public discussion.[87]

Books presented at the outset less instant appeal than conversation as a means of improving the mind. Great ladies were noted either to get by without them, as did Louis XIII's queen who 'n'a[vait] point lu',[88] or to turn to them only when in need of a distraction from misfortune and solitude.[89] In the first place they were costly items,[90] particularly when bound and illustrated for the adornment of a library shelf. In the second place books in female hands smacked of pedantry. Huet, bishop of Avranches, tells a revealing anecdote about the shame of the future Marquise de Castries on being surprised reading Plato, and her plea to him to keep the matter secret.[91] The only permissible works to have on view were the devotional manuals that formed the staple part of the representative Frenchwoman's library.[92] Thirdly, 'solid' works were composed in Latin and presented in a Scholastic form that could attract only the despised bluestocking.

As the century progressed, however, a movement was begun to place specialist knowledge within reach of the layman and, more especially, the laywoman. Descartes may be said to have led the field with his doubly epoch-making decision in 1637 to entitle the prospectus of his philosophical system *'Discours' de la Méthode*, instead of the more ponderous *'Traité'* or *'Commentaire'*, and to write in the vernacular so that 'les femmes même pussent entendre quelque chose'.[93] In the second half of the century the movement accelerated to produce a spate of engagingly entitled *Dialogues* and *Entretiens* which claimed to have pre-digested even the most abstruse subjects.[94] Where the word *philosophie* was retained in the title, an amplification clarified the nature of the public for whom the work was intended: *Fine Philosophie Accommodée à l'Intelligence des Dames* (1660), *Philosophie des Gens de Cour* (1680).[95] These works recommended themselves by their overall brevity, by the variety derived from having several interlocutors presenting (opposing) ideas, and by the use of step-by-step definitions, short sections and homely images, of the kind which make Fontenelle's *Entretiens sur la Pluralité des Mondes* (1686) the epitome of the genre.

In the preface to the *Entretiens* Fontenelle had promised his female readers that the amount of application necessary to grasp the essentials of astronomy would not exceed that required for the comprehension of a popular novel. The remark testifies both to the favourite literature of the contemporary female public, and to the reputation of that literature for being unexacting on the intelligence. Yet novels too had their part to play in the instruction of women. Denounced by most moralists as dangerous stimuli of the passions and mocked by satirists for divorcing readers from the real world, novels were justified by their composers on the grounds that they performed a genuine educational service. By virtue of their setting in ancient times and faraway lands they could boast of initiating their readers into history, mythology and geography, subjects which girls barely touched upon in school.[96] They might also act as disguised philosophy manuals: in Abbé d'Aubignac's curious *Macarise* (1664) giants, monsters and phantoms, verses and billets-doux contrive to relieve an arid exposé of Stoicism. Above all novels schooled the uninitiated in the social graces, with what success may be judged from the example of Mlle Desmarets who, by five years of diligent application to novel reading, repaired that ignorance of 'l'esprit du monde' in which her mother had let her flounder for fourteen years, and went on to merit a place in Somaize's *Dictionnaire*[97] as one of the most accomplished *précieuses*.

Women's magazines, in the modern acceptation of the term, had still to be invented, but progress was made towards their creation. To keep abreast of developments literate ladies in the early seventeenth century had the choice of consulting news-sheets and pamphlets (mostly political or sensationalist in content), the *Mercure Français* or, from 1631 onwards, the government-controlled *Gazette*. Recourse was also possible to the simple, if slow and by no means sure, expedient of exchanging letters with acquaintances living or travelling in distant climes. In the salons the information thus conveyed would sometimes be rendered more piquant by putting it into verse and sending it collectively to the absent member of the group. This practice gave rise, around the middle of the century, to a number of rhymed gazettes, the most famous being the *Muse Historique* (1650–65) in which Jean Loret addressed to his patroness, Marie de Longueville, weekly reports on every kind of society event and scandal that came to his attention. The immense popularity of this venture, exploited and prolonged after Loret's death by various contemporary poetasters, inspired a monthly publication that partook of the newspaper, the recently founded *Journal des Savants*[98] and the women's magazine. This was the *Mercure Galant*.

Begun in 1672 by Jean Donneau de Visé, the *Mercure Galant* was placed, like the rhymed gazettes which preceded it, under the auspices of a woman, an imaginary Marquise confined to the provinces and desirous of not losing touch with the major events of the day. It interspersed reports of the latest happenings in the capital, the provinces and abroad with all manner of gallantries in verse and prose, romantic short stories, news of Paris fashions,[99] lengthy descriptions of high society weddings and similar items of ultra-feminine interest. The more substantial articles dealt with curiosities in the medical and scientific fields, as well as with literary, linguistic and moral topics, 'la variété des matières de mes lettres', as the editor rightly claimed in the June 1693 issue, 'étant cause qu'il n'y a personne, de quelque goût qu'il puisse être, qui n'y trouve quelque chose qui lui convienne'. The ladies were duly seduced. From being passive readers, many became active contributors. One month it was some female laureate whose prize-winning ode or sonnet appeared in the *Mercure's* columns; the next month it might be a short treatise from the pen of a learned spinster; the next, a letter from a provincial *savante* relating a local celebration. Periodic notices informed the public of when and where Madame such-and-such's latest book could be obtained, and lavished praise on those muses who had passed to a better life. Informative, entertaining, the *Mercure Galant* could thus offer its feminine readers, in addition, the useful service of establishing a nascent literary reputation or enhancing one already achieved.

Attendance at intellectual tournaments and lectures to hear experts discoursing on their specialist subjects helped those interested in completing the work begun through the medium of conversation, books and periodicals. The promotion of public conferences was yet another facet of the general movement to bring knowledge outside the confines of the Schools and Universities for the benefit of a broader section of the population. Impetus was given to the scheme by the enterprising editor of the *Gazette*, Théophraste Renaudot, who began in 1633 to invite the public to hitherto private weekly assemblies of men of culture at his Paris headquarters, the Bureau d'Adresse. Except for religion and politics, every conceivable topic, including a number of direct feminine concern,[100] was aired by panels of from two to six speakers expressly instructed to keep the use of Latin and learned citations to an absolute minimum. Renaudot's example encouraged other polymaths and scholars to throw open their cabinets and laboratories and give lectures and demonstrations. The erudite Dutchman Christiaan Huygens, visiting Paris in 1660 and attending public expositions of Cartesianism at the house of the physicist Jacques Rohault, encountered amongst the press of listeners Mmes de Guederville and de Bonneveau, who requested the pleasure of his company at the sessions of scientific experimentation and philosophical discussion which they held every Saturday.[101] Pierre-Sylvain Régis's open lectures on Descartes at Toulouse in 1665 won for him an appreciative following of female tutees, one of whom, 'fort habile cartésienne', successfully defended a thesis disputed in French.[102] 'Beaucoup de femmes', nuns as well as laywomen, are said to have looked for enlightenment to Louis Carré, mathematician and disciple of Malebranche, who liked their freedom from preconceived ideas and their attachment to what they had once learned.[103] The decision of professional philosophers, men of science and mathematicians to propagate the fruits of their research from the public rostrum was a momentous one for women. Philosophy, and mathematics beyond simple arithmetic, formed no part of their school timetable. Sciences were generally neglected even in boys' educational establishments in favour of a predominantly literary culture. These branches of knowledge therefore had the powerful attraction of novelty, which is one of the reasons why endeavours to diffuse them met with a singularly warm feminine response.

An element of snobbery, also, cannot be discounted in the rush to the laboratory and the lecture-hall. Sitting at the feet of great intellectuals of the day was the fashionable pursuit of the second half of the century,[104] the pastime that allowed for a little pleasurable boasting in the same way that a visit to court or attendance at a triumphant operatic *première* might do. The desire to be remarked undoubtedly accounted in large measure for the presence of women at academic functions which, unlike the public lectures, were not specially geared to their needs. It is true that college authorities, in an occasional fit of gallantry, would open their doors to the ladies and consent to lower the tone of their normal exercises. On 26 August 1683 the Jesuit college of Arles invited a throng of women to hear some theses contested, in French, on eloquence, history and drama, including one on whether a woman could be the subject of a tragedy.[105] The Jesuit college of Toulouse allowed mothers to listen to their young sons debating publicly in French, putting them 'hors d'œuvre derrière les ceintures de chaises des personnes invitées, de sorte que sans être beaucoup aperçues, elles voient et entendent le répondant'.[106] Usually, however, theses were disputed in Latin, a language of which the matron with schooldays well and truly behind her might retain just sufficient to be able to recite her Pater Noster and Ave Maria. If she figured as a spectator at academic ceremonies it was not so much to expand her knowledge as to support a disputant with whom she had connections or with whose relatives she wished to curry favour.[107]

In the final analysis the motives which drove women to the salons, the bookstalls and the conference rooms matter less than the fact that they made the effort to go there and that their minds were consequently exposed to forms of education elsewhere denied them.

It remains now to attempt to gauge the overall results of the three types of education – domestic, formal and informal – to which women were submitted, and to estimate the level of culture generally achieved. Regrettably such a study presents some insurmountable difficulties. Modern researchers have found themselves hampered not only by the magnitude of the enquiry but also by a frequent dearth of official documents before the eighteenth century, particularly those bearing upon the *petites écoles*. Information so far established about the education of the lower classes, girls and boys, has therefore been necessarily fragmentary and of a general nature.[108] What evidence there is suggests widespread female illiteracy,[109] which would accord with the poverty of educational facilities provided. Beyond that supposition it is at present impossible to proceed.

The only women about whose educational standards anything can be said with certainty are those members of the aristocracy and of the bourgeoisie whose 'quality' or connections assured for their accomplishments a paragraph in collections of *Femmes Illustres*, verbal portrait galleries, and the like. These documents, though subject to caution because of their primarily laudatory nature, nevertheless make repeated mention of proficiency in certain subjects and pass over others in silence, a circumstance which gives some indication of priorities and lacunae in female education of the time.

Prominent on the lists of talents are those connected with music: singing, dancing, or the playing of a stringed or keyboard instrument.[110] Virtuosity in more than one instrument was not unknown. The Duchesse de Ventadour 'touch[ait] du clavecin, de la basse viole et de divers autres instruments'.[111] Mme de Creil, wife of an *intendant* of Normandy, 'jou[ait] admirablement bien du lut, du théorbe, du clavecin, et de la guitare'.[112] Mlle Petit was credited by a portraitist with knowing how to play a phenomenal total of forty instruments.[113] Having no visible associations with book-learning and enabling women, as they did, to appear in a graceful and decorative role, musical skills reinforced the traditional image of femininity and could accordingly be cultivated with impunity.

The same observation applies to needlework. Whereas it was shameful to be caught book in hand, to be seen busy with embroidery or tapestry-work was 'feminine' and showed a laudable concern to shun idleness even in leisure moments. Thus the Duchesse de Sully 'se délassait dans ses heures perdues, à travailler en tapisserie et en broderie, avec ses filles et ses dames d'honneur',[114] while Mme de Maintenon would sit with head becomingly bent over her tapestry as Louis XIV and his ministers decided in her apartment the destiny of France.[115] Heroines of contemporary fiction, often mere transpositions of real life personages, can always ply their needle well, if only to provide some entranced cavalier with a hand-made favour.[116]

Skill in drawing and painting was another, somewhat less conventional, form of manual dexterity to which women dared to own. By personally drawing up the plans for the embellishment of one of their country houses, the Duchesse de Liancourt had enticed a libertine husband away from court and converted him to piety.[117] Mme de Rambouillet's expertise in drafting the plans of her immortal Hôtel was such that her pet poet Vincent Voiture flatteringly compared her to her compatriot Michelangelo.[118] Great ladies showed an interest in perfecting their technique by engaging reputed painters to guide their pencils and brushes: the Duchesse de Montpensier took lessons in her youth from Pierre Mignard,[119] and Charles Le Brun schooled the second wife of Nicolas Fouquet, disgraced superintendant of finances.[120] Tuition in the subject was also given to girls of humbler station,[121] a few of whom won admission to the Royal Academy of Painting and Sculpture.[122] The majority, however, concentrated on buying and commissioning works of art[123] rather than on developing the ability to produce them personally.

By contrast an impressive number of women strove to familiarise themselves with a foreign language. Of the two classical languages Greek was confined to a handful of nuns, who acquired it in order to peruse sacred texts at first hand,[124] and to a few *savantes* who needed it for studying or business purposes.[125] Latin, the language in which girls learned to read at school and in which they continued to recite church liturgies, was relatively more widely diffused, not only in convents[126] and amongst the erudite bourgeoisie[127] but in aristocratic circles also.[128] Of the modern languages Italian and Spanish enjoyed the most favour,[129] probably because their affinity with French made them easier to learn and because interest in the culture of Italy and Spain was stimulated by dynastic links between Medicis, Habsburgs and Bourbons. The latter consideration ought logically to have applied in the case of England and Germany also, given the marriage of Henriette-Marie to Charles I in 1625 and the number of English and German brides who entered the French royal family in Louis XIV's reign. But northern languages were viewed askance as being too guttural for delicate throats,[130] and mentions of any seventeenth-century Frenchwoman conversant with them are virtually non-existent.[131]

In the general enthusiasm to acquire a foreign tongue the study of French was sadly neglected. Women themselves affirm the ignorance of their sex on the subject. Mme de Sévigné declared in 1689 that the majority of Frenchwomen did not know their own language.[132] Mme de Maintenon told her confessor that in everything women wrote there were always 'mille fautes contre la grammaire'.[133] Women of the nobility were amongst the worst offenders. Saint-Evremond, in a letter to the Duchesse Mazarin, recalled the epistolary assistance that he once had to give her at a time when 'la construction ne vous manquait pas moins que l'orthographe'.[134] Mme de Choisy obliged the crowned heads with whom she corresponded to make a considerable effort of interpretation since 'il n'y avait point d'orthographe dans ses lettres'.[135] Not only was their spelling and grammar bizarre, but women also had difficulty in forming actual characters on paper. 'J'écris si mal qu'on a toutes les peines du monde à lire mon écriture', the Duchesse de Montpensier candidly admitted.[136] 'Le plus souvent la vivacité de mes pensées emporte ma plume et me fait griffonner avec une mauvaise orthographe', was Mme de Saintot's excuse.[137] Masculine recipients of illegible scripts could ill conceal their exasperation beneath polite acknowledgements.[138] But one would-be apologist was happy to find therein proof of his novel contention that the fair sex had never been suspected of forgery: 'Elles ont bien de la peine à former une vraie écriture, comment auraient-elles assez d'habileté pour en faire de fausse?'[139] If women seemed unconcerned about their reputation for faulty penmanship,[140] their complacency was given every encouragement. A certain orthographic negligence, they were assured, was becoming in persons of quality, strict accuracy being the hallmark of the professional author, not to say the pedant.[141] Besides, admirers and secretaries were always in plentiful supply to take dictation and to transform scribble into calligraphy. The absence, nevertheless, of such basic aptitudes as those of correct spelling and legible writing in a class which alone, according to the theorists, had the right to a literary education, and the best chance of implementing that right, opens a gloomy perspective on the level of female literacy lower down the social scale.

At this point, it will be recalled, and indeed often far short of this point, the theorists had ceased to issue their prescriptions and scholastic establishments had ended their attempts to put them into practice. An acquaintance with reading, writing and harmless drawing-room pursuits, the latter replaced by elementary arithmetic and handiwork in proportion as illustriousness of birth decreased, was all that the majority had sought for the nation's women. What would nowadays be regarded as essential subjects for study tended to become superfluous in the seventeenth century the moment some threat to the 'purity' of women or to their awareness of their 'proper' place in the home and in society was scented. For a variety of reasons women had, however, begun on their own initiative to cast off the educational blinkers by which they were confined and to enjoy the sensation of venturing into more arduous and, for them, unexplored fields of knowledge – philosophy, science and advanced mathematics – where they signalised their curiosity and enthusiasm, if not always their expertise.

The spectacle of women learning philosophy was, for contemporaries, a minor miracle. In the later part of the century serious thinkers could still be found expounding the view that the female brain was capable of apprehending data received through the senses, but incapable of the prolonged, abstract reasoning necessary to the search for more profound truths. 'Pour l'ordinaire elles sont incapables de pénétrer les vérités un peu difficiles à découvrir. Tout ce qui est abstrait leur est incompréhensible', as Malebranche put it.[142] Only moral philosophy, of the type summarised by the Ten Commandments, was considered to be within their grasp, and commended in proportion to the expectation that in cultivating it women would be incessantly reminded of their duties and obligations to men.

One abstract philosophy nevertheless had an undisputed female following, and that was Cartesianism. Mentor to two learned princesses, Elizabeth of Bohemia and Christina of Sweden, Descartes might be called the ladies' philosopher. His biographer Adrien Baillet emphasises the pleasure he took in philosophical conversations with women, finding them 'plus douces, plus patientes, plus dociles, en un mot, plus vides de préjugés et de fausses doctrines que beaucoup d'hommes'.[143] The admiration was mutual. Women appreciated the unpedantic air of this widely travelled ex-soldier who had thought to cast some of the results of his meditations in a deceptively accessible French form. Their imagination must have been fired by the boldness of a philosophy which purposed to sweep away all the errors of the past but which at the same time reassured their fundamental piety by ostentatiously placing the truths of revealed religion out of reach of methodical doubt. Perhaps also the fact that the teaching of Cartesianism was viewed askance by large sections of the orthodox intelligentsia lent to it the irresistibility of that forbidden fruit which moralists solemnly noted to have precipitated the downfall of the first female. All these attractions, heightened by the efforts of disciples to disseminate Cartesian theories in Paris and the provinces, produced what contemporaries represent as a veritable army of *cartésiennes* with, in the vanguard, such distinguished personages as the Comtesse de Grignan,[144] the Marquise de Sablé,[145] the future Baronne de Staal[146] and the Duchesse du Maine.[147] Enthusiasm waxed even stronger as soon as popularisers like Louis Carré had had time to do for Descartes's disciple Malebranche and his *De la Recherche de la Vérité* (1674–5) what the Rohaults had done for the master himself. In fact the fervour of lady *malebranchistes* reached such a pitch that some were heard professing to 'vivre et mourir' in pursuit of that same Truth which the metaphysician had brandished before them.[148]

Some prompt deflation of the female ego, dangerously swollen by all this sudden inrush of Knowledge, was obviously called for. Things were getting out of hand. Fashionable ladies were perceived to be hob-nobbing with mathematicians and becoming rather familiar with Euclid.[149] Algebra was preserving its hermetic reputation with difficulty, for interest in its mysteries was growing apace, 'même parmi les dames de la cour et de la ville'.[150] Botany was being forced to yield its secrets to determined lady herborists.[151] Laboratories were springing up in back rooms as frequenters of Nicolas Lémery's chemistry demonstrations busily distilled[152] and pored over Marie Meurdrac's *Chimie Charitable et Facile en faveur des Dames* (1666) in an effort to discover the elusive philosophers' stone.[153] Undesirable nudities were being exposed on dissecting-tables for the benefit of ladies whose passion for anatomy outweighed concerns of propriety.[154] Exasperated husbands were alleging the conjugal bed to be deserted while wives repaired to the attic to study stars and comets through their telescopes.[155] 'O tempora! O mores!' chorused the mockers, as they sharpened their quills to repel the threat. Chappuzeau,[156] Molière,[157] Abbé de la Roque,[158] Fatouville,[159] Boileau[160] discharged periodic broadsides against the new breed of petticoat philosophers and scientists, seeking, by way of a reaction, to recall them to the devotions and domestic arts which had traditionally constituted all the educational baggage of a woman. The very repetition of these sallies indicates the persistence in the second half of the century of the phenomenon against which they were directed. It also indicates lingering opposition to the whole idea of the learned woman, even when she laboured to acquire the wherewithal to make a solid claim to that title.

The seventeenth-century Frenchwoman received her education, in sum, despite society rather than with its assistance or approval. Few overtly contested her right to some instruction other than in

household management. However even the most ostensibly generous claims on her behalf were rendered hollow by two factors:
firstly by the restrictions and taboos with which they were
surrounded in an effort to preserve, ultimately, masculine superiority and peace of mind; secondly by the substitution of haphazard, privately directed modes of schooling in place of a regular,
centrally organised system.

If women were saved from crass ignorance it was largely due to
their own initiative: that of the charitable ladies who financed and
ran classes for young girls; that of the mothers and nuns who,
whatever their own intellectual or pedagogical shortcomings, bore
the brunt of the responsibility for educating their sex; and that of
the autodidacts who doggedly pursued specialised studies ordinarily refused them on the grounds of mental incapacity or
wastage of time. Then, if they made so bold as to manifest
enthusiasm for learning, the public responded with irony, ridicule
and the inevitable reminder that a woman's most fitting occupation
in life was to school herself to catch and retain a husband.

3

The Preliminaries to Marriage

Of all the virtues which pedagogues strove to inculcate into girls, few received more emphasis than obedience, 'le partage de notre sexe' in the words of Mme de Maintenon.[1] The reason is not far to seek. The physical, mental and emotional weaknesses of women, as consecrated by tradition and by contemporary legislation, bent them in an eternally submissive posture before the stronger sex from whom they derived all their well-being. They were the dependent sex. 'Qui dit femme, dit une chose dépendante', affirmed one moralist.[2] Women are like vines, declared another: 'elles ne sauraient se tenir debout, ni subsister par elles-mêmes; elles ont besoin d'un appui, encore plus pour leur esprit que pour leur corps'.[3] The notion of female independence was not easily comprehensible to a seventeenth-century mind. At every stage of their life steps were taken to place women under some form of tutelage, ideally masculine. For those unwilling to make a graceful exit into the cloister this normally meant passing straight from the hands of one guardian, the father, into those of another, the husband.

Despite the fact that marriage was the event towards which the average girl's life was exclusively orientated, contemporaries considered the institution with some disdain. Christianity taught that virginity was the most perfect state to which the individual could aspire, marriage being a last resort for those unable to contain their baser instincts ('Melius est nubere quam uri'). Inspired by this tradition, churchmen painted a black picture of conjugal life in the pious hope of swelling the number of recruits for the convents. Marriage was not synonymous with pleasure, they warned the naive; instead it brought in its wake all manner of pains and anxieties which by implication were never experienced in the tranquillity of the cloister. 'L'état du mariage est un état qui requiert plus de vertu et constance que nul autre; c'est un perpétuel exercice de mortification', wrote the future saint François

41

de Sales to a girl contemplating matrimony.[4] 'C'est un nom de joug et de souffrances, une communauté de maux et de peines, une société de soins et d'offices', agreed Le Moyne.[5] Secular moralists, with and without the benefit of personal experience, took up the refrain: 'point de mariages délicieux'; 'lourd fardeau sous lequel l'homme succombe'; 'l'état où l'on éprouve le plus de tribulations'.[6] Popular writers in turn reinforced the images of the yoke, the burden and the ordeal, by dwelling complacently on the theme of the incompatibility of love and marriage. Matrimony, as portrayed in light literature, did not signify the continuation and deepening of love, but rather its instant dilution or cessation. 'Il y a grande différence de l'amour au mariage', asserts the wise Léonide in Honoré d'Urfé's widely acclaimed novel *l'Astrée*, 'parce que l'amour ne dure qu'autant qu'il plaît, mais le mariage se rend d'autant plus long qu'il est plus ennuyeux: le premier, c'est le symbole de la liberté, parce que l'amour ne contraint personne que par la volonté; au contraire, le mariage, c'est le symbole de la servitude, parce qu'il n'y a que la mort qui en puisse dénouer les liens.'[7] On the stage a plaintive supporting chorus arises from heroines aghast at the thought that wedlock has metamorphosed the submissive gallant into the exacting master:

> Tant qu'ils ne sont qu'amants, nous sommes souveraines,
> Et jusqu'à la conquête ils nous traitent de reines;
> Mais après l'hyménée ils sont rois à leur tour,

and that sateity breeds contempt:

> Je te suis odieuse après m'être donnée![8]

Not that much pity was wasted on female victims of the institution. The martyrdom of husbands, described under expressive titles like *Le Purgatoire des Hommes Mariés*[9] and *Discours sur les poignantes traverses et incommodités du mariage, où les humeurs et complexions des femmes sont vivement représentées*,[10] engaged all the writers' sympathy.

The representation of marriage as a joyless and, above all, a loveless estate is amply justified by the way in which the affair was advanced and concluded in the seventeenth century. Paradoxically the two chief actors in the drama played virtually no part until it was time to pronounce the fateful *'Volo'* ('I will') in church. Their union was arranged for them, often in spite of them, and for considerations likely to benefit their progenitors and posterity.

Marriage was regarded essentially as a family concern, not that of two private individuals. The choice of husband or wife had repercussions on the social standing and material welfare of the family. A household would gain not only a whole new set of allies and social relations, but ultimately a series of heirs to perpetuate the family name. It stood to acquire the financial advantages that would ensure general prosperity and facilitate advancement in the social hierarchy – or a legacy of debts and mortgages that might drag it into the mire. Justice and prudence alike dictated that the family should select and vet any new member to be introduced within its ranks. The point was forcefully put in 1634 by Mathieu Molé, at the time *procureur général* of the Paris Parlement, during discussions over the validity of the clandestine marriage of Louis XIII's brother, Gaston d'Orléans, to Marguerite de Lorraine: 'les mariages s'exécutent, non pour la considération de la personne qui contracte, mais pour l'honneur et l'avantage des familles; ... l'on passe contrat non comme un accord particulier, mais commun à tous les parents, puisque l'on leur donne des héritiers et des alliés, ce qu'ils ne peuvent recevoir contre leur gré'.[11] Since the then heir presumptive was not dispensed from his obligations in this respect, still less could the ordinary citizen expect to be.

As a result of this view marriage negotiations were almost always conducted by the families of the parties concerned, sometimes by the actual parents but more often by a relative or friend acting as their representative, in order that they would not be directly involved in any unseemly haggling that might be necessary.[12] The dutiful daughter was urged, in the meantime, not to entertain love lest she be forced by those on whom her destiny depended to belie the promptings of her heart.[13] Not until and unless invited to do so by her parents did propriety allow her to manifest openly her feelings for any man. A negative response was permissible on such an occasion but not the expression of a preferred alternative.[14] Her right of choice was distinctly limited.

In selecting a prospective partner negotiators rarely allowed themselves to be swayed by considerations of sentiment, mindful that 'peu de mariages succèdent bien, qui sont commencés et acheminés par les beautés et désirs amoureux'.[15] More solid advantages – political, financial and social – were always sought first and foremost, love entering into the contract if and where it could.

Princely households had long taken it for granted that their female scions would be despatched as brides wherever they might be useful to the state, and that they would close their eyes to the fact of being united to a 'heretic'[16] or a Francophobe[17] in favour of the diplomatic alliance secured, the territorial dispute settled or the war averted. In ministerial circles female relatives were regularly farmed out as a means of procuring influential relations, quietening powerful and potentially seditious families or strengthening positions against the attacks of rivals. Cardinal Richelieu developed the procedure into a fine art. On 28 November 1634 he simultaneously gave three cousins in marriage: Mlle du Plessis-Chivray to the Comte de Guiche, the elder Mlle de Pontchâteau to the Duc de La Valette, and her younger sister to Puylaurens, Gaston d'Orléans's favourite.[18] The suitability of the respective grooms may be gauged from the facts that Guiche secured Richelieu's favour by noisily declaring for the Cardinal against Gaston in the midst of a drunken stupor;[19] that La Valette was commonly believed to have poisoned his first wife[20] and had subsequently to flee to England to avoid decapitation for treason; and that Puylaurens was allowed to savour less than three months of married life before being conducted to prison on the Cardinal's own orders and allowed to die there. A more successful calculation, from the political point of view, was the marriage in 1641 of a niece, Mlle de Maillé-Brézé, to the great general Condé, but from the human point of view the match was disastrous, involving a lifetime of misery for a wife scorned by her princely husband and their son, and eventually relegated to the grim fortress of Châteauroux to die.[21] Even Richelieu's best-loved niece, the Duchesse d'Aiguillon, was not spared. As Mlle de Vignerot she had been united to the Duc de Luynes's nephew Combalet, 'mal bâti et couperosé', to seal the new alliance between the two uncles after the rout at the Ponts-de-Cé in 1620.[22] Combalet's premature death at the siege of Montpellier in 1622 brought a welcome release from a husband 'qu'elle ne pouvait souffrir', and to avoid a similar ordeal in the future the widow hastily announced, and renewed at intervals, her vow to become a Carmelite.[23] In the event, however, it was only the unequivocal manifestation of aristocratic prejudice on the part of the Comte de Soissons that saved her from being sacrificed a second time to the *raison d'état* by her resolutely matchmaking uncle.[24] But Richelieu was posthumously avenged, for during the next reign the haughty Soissons were forced to accept Olympe

Mancini, one of the seven nieces whom Mazarin distributed amongst the French and Italian nobility in imitation of his predecessor's policy.

Viewed in the context of state security, the 'political' marriage at least had a certain air of elevation about it, and protests against the custom were limited to the complaints of potential *esclaves couronnées* in novels and plays. The marriage for money, on the other hand, had an aura of baseness that caused it to draw fire from a variety of writers[25] safe in the knowledge that to attack a suitably impersonal Mammon was not calculated to bring down on their head the wrath of the powerful and the influential. The preoccupation with material assets, 'nœud de presque toutes les alliances',[26] is not surprising. Amassing wealth and possessions seemed to all sections of the population to be a comforting insurance and a bulwark against the ups and downs of life in a highly unstable age. The bourgeoisie had always been noted, and mocked, for the thrift which drove fathers to enquire firstly of a prospective son-in-law 'exactement de la quantité de son bien, s'il n'était point embrouillé, et s'il n'avait point fait de ... dettes'.[27] But it was the aristocracy who were perhaps the most unashamedly tenacious in pursuit of the wealthy bride. A characteristic case was that of the Marquis de Gesvres in 1690. Having passed over the daughter of the *lieutenant civil* Le Camus with a dowry of 400 000 *francs* in cash and 100 000 *francs* 'en bons effets', the Marquis became alarmed when it appeared that Mlle de Boisfranc, a financier's daughter who was on the marriage market with a dowry of 700 000 *francs*, 20 000 *écus* in jewellery and 5000 *pistoles*[28] destined to pay his debts, was slipping from his grasp. He owed a considerable amount of money and his elevation to the peerage was in jeopardy because the family estates were on the point of being seized by creditors. To put an end to this cruel predicament the Marquis and his friends petitioned the king, whose intervention clinched the desired transaction.[29] Misalliances with rich commoners such as Mlle de Boisfranc, already sufficiently prevalent in the first half of the century to worry Sully and Richelieu,[30] grew to epidemic proportions in the late seventeenth and early eighteenth centuries as aristocratic finances dwindled and morals became increasingly lax.[31] To those who expressed horror at the mingling of patrician with plebeian blood the nobility could always quip that even the best lands needed manuring from time to time.[32]

In the race to secure a useful in-law or a coffer of money the personality of the particular individual through whom these prizes were obtainable was the last consideration. Ambitious men did not trouble to hide their cynical attitude. The Comte de Guiche, on being asked by Richelieu to marry Mlle du Plessis-Chivray instead of Mlle de Pontchâteau, replied that 'c'était son Eminence qu'il épousait, et non ses parentes, et qu'il prendrait celle qu'on lui donnerait'.[33] There were girls, too, for whom the name and social status of a likely husband outweighed all other considerations. The Duchesse de Montpensier, fated never to marry one of the successive princes to whom she aspired, admitted that she was less interested in their person than in their rank.[34] Mlle de Rambures, seeking Louis XIV's approval for her marriage to the Marquis de Polignac, was asked 'L'aimez-vous? – Non, Sire, lui répondit-elle, mais c'est un homme de grande qualité que j'aime mieux épouser qu'un autre'.[35] Those who could extend to a wife the coveted *tabouret* – the privilege whereby duchesses were allowed to be seated on a low stool in the presence of the queen – were besieged with offers of life companionship.[36]

The time taken to bargain for a marriage partner varied from a matter of years to one of minutes. The habit of many parents of staking their claim to a title, estate or fortune well in advance by betrothing their children in the cradle[37] allowed for substantial changes of circumstances, and therefore for second thoughts and fresh negotiations, before fiancés reached the official nubile age of twelve for girls and fourteen for boys. It was not uncommon for a girl who had been obliged to regard herself as the future wife of one man to be expected to suddenly transfer her affections to another to suit parental or royal convenience. Henry IV's dealings with his minister Sully are particularly enlightening in this respect. The king's sister, the Duchesse de Bar, had originally proposed the Duc de Rohan as a husband for Sully's daughter Marguerite, but the girl had also been sought in 1603 by the Comte de Laval. Henri had ordered Sully to prefer Laval's suit, and the marriage was about to be accomplished in 1605 when the king changed his mind and commanded the marriage with Rohan to be performed in three days' time.[38] The situation was virtually repeated several years later in the arrangements for the marriage of Sully's son, the Marquis de Rosny. Mlle de Créquy had been Henri's original choice as bride, but then he decided that one of his own bastard daughters would be a more suitable match. Another change of mind effectively delivered into Rosny's hands in 1609 Mlle de

Créquy, who was barely ten years old at the time.[39] No mention is made in either case of the slightest concern for the feelings of the girls involved, let alone of any semblance of consulting their wishes.

At the opposite extreme to that of protracted negotiations curious instances are recorded of marriages being settled, by parents and relatives, on the spur of the moment. The marriage of the Duc de Saint-Aignan's daughter was thus 'l'affaire d'un quart d'heure: en louant le fils de Sanguin à son père, celui-ci loua aussi Mlle de Saint-Aignan. Le duc lui dit: "Si nous les mariions tous deux ensemble?" Sanguin lui répondit: "Ce me serait trop d'honneur, monsieur, quand vous ne lui donneriez qu'une paire de gants." "Allons-en parler au roi" dit M. le duc de Saint-Aignan. Ils le firent, et voilà comment se fit ce mariage.'[40] Examples of what La Fontaine poetically termed 'impromptus d'amour'[41] could easily be multiplied.[42] So that moralists had some justification in lamenting that the rapidity with which marriages were concluded gave scant time to a couple to prepare themselves to fulfil their conjugal responsibilities properly.[43]

When parents deigned to consult their children about the partner selected – and they were by no means obliged to do so – it was all too often purely for form's sake. Mme de la Guette's father arranged for his unsuspecting daughter to meet her destined husband at a convent, and then sprang his decision upon her: 'Je vous recommande de le recevoir de bonne grâce, parce que j'en veux faire votre mari'.[44] Her spiritedness in dismissing the importunate stranger enabled her subsequently to make a love-match of her own choice, but others were not so lucky. Présidente Ferrand described in her autobiographical *Histoire des Amours de Cléante et de Bélise* the prelude to a marriage that inspired her 'haine insupportable' for her partner: 'Aussitôt qu'il [son père] eut trouvé un parti qui convenait autant à ma famille qu'il convenait peu à mes sentiments, il m'engagea, comme c'est la coutume, sans m'en parler, et m'apprit qu'il ne fallait plus, pour consommer cette terrible affaire, qu'un consentement qu'il ne croyait pas qu'il me dût demander.'[45] A similarly unhappy aftermath awaited the young girl who became Mme Guyon, bestowed upon a gentleman whose opulence recommended him to the parents: 'On le [mariage] fit, sans m'en parler ... et même l'on me fit signer les articles du mariage sans me dire ce que c'était ... Je ne vis point mon accordé jusqu'à deux ou trois jours avant le mariage.'[46] In the first of these three instances a daughter was precipitated into a clandestine marriage; in the second, into adultery; and in the third, into a vagabond existence that culminated in confinement to the Bastille. Yet parents persisted in their naive belief that the wedding night and the mere fact of cohabitation would be sufficient to overcome a bride's repugnance.[47]

Enlightened thinkers tried to open their compatriots' eyes to the folly of uniting two strangers for material gain.[48] A visit to Holland enabled Saint-Evremond to make a suggestive comparison between Dutch conventions, which allowed a girl to become well acquainted with her future husband, thereby encouraging marital fidelity later, and French conventions which, by stressing acquaintance with a dowry instead of a person, predisposed to adultery men rendered indifferent to their partner in advance:

> En France où l'on se marie quasi toujours par intérêt, les personnes sont peu examinées et souvent la sûreté des conventions précède la simple curiosité de se voir. La raison est qu'on cherche moins à posséder un cœur qu'à se donner du bien; qu'on songe plus à la commodité d'une maison et aux moyens de faire de la dépense qu'au rapport des humeurs et aux qualités de la femme qu'on doit épouser. Quelque belle qu'elle puisse être, nous sommes tous préparés à n'aimer pas longtemps ce qu'on ne saurait aimer toujours et prévenant le sentiment du plaisir de l'imagination du dégoût nous nous engageons indifféremment au mariage, dans un dessein tout formé de nous consoler ailleurs d'un domestique lassant et d'une société ennuyeuse. En Hollande, où l'on se livre de bonne foi et où la délicatesse de ces réserves est peu entendue, on croit ne pouvoir jamais assez connaître ce qu'on veut toujours aimer.[49]

Not only did French customs appear absurd, but they also exposed couples to positive moral dangers and threatened to undermine the whole institution of the family.

From the feminine point of view, curtailment or absence of courtship meant the shattering of the young girl's dream: to have a suitor attentive to her slightest need, downcast by a cold glance, uplifted by a gracious smile, melancholy at the approach of rivals, reassured by the bestowal of an innocent favour; in short, to savour the endless little pleasures of amatorial despotism before roles were reversed in marriage. Though mocked, the clamour of

Molière's *précieuses ridicules* for a full ceremonial wooing in the best novelistic tradition prior to matrimony 'et ce qui s'ensuit' (sc. 4) must have struck a sympathetic chord in more than one spectator's heart. To victims of hard-headed parents light literature offered an inflammatory portrait of pre-marital dalliance and a means of vicariously indulging frustrated youthful desires. Plots of novels and plays centred on a courtship, or series of courtships, with all their vicissitudes, material and emotional. Each crucial moment of falling in love – the first meeting, the first avowal, the first hand-clasp – was elaborately mapped out and unfolded. Eliciting a 'je vous aime' from the heroine, let alone a kiss, was a work of art which could involve the dauntless swain braving whims, tantrums and scruples for anything up to ten bulky volumes. The outcome of this leisurely promenade through the labyrinths of the heart was given short shrift. Dramatists and novelists subscribed to the notion that marriage was the legitimate aim of faithful love, but were wont to terminate their productions brusquely with the wedding ceremony.[50] At that point producers and consumers were unanimous in considering that the idyll ended.

As well as enabling women to play in imagination the flattering part of courted and capricious sweetheart, novels and dramas led a general protest movement against acts of tyranny in sentimental matters. Throughout the century they joined with moral treatises and satirical works[51] in denouncing the traffic in human liberty that passed for marriage, and in claiming the right to bestow love and select a partner without third-party interference.[52] Condemnation was both explicit in tirades and implicit in situations. Only in rare instances did heroines bow before parental oppression, employing all manner of ruses, elopements and suicide bids rather than be robbed of the hero of their choice. Here again plays and romances provided a useful safety-valve for feminine emotions, a figuration and crystallisation of instincts of revolt which many girls must have experienced, however ephemerally, on being forced into a loveless marriage, but which they could not bring themselves to voice openly. Hence one of the reasons for the tremendous popularity of both genres with seventeenth-century Frenchwomen, exposing as they did real and fundamental injustices in the female status quo at a time when feminist pamphlets remained largely preoccupied with trivial 'proofs' of women's superiority over men.

In the novelistic and stage worlds stubborn parents invariably saw the error of their ways in time for the ending and gave their blessing to the union hitherto opposed. In real life too mothers and fathers were persuaded to relent, but the lovers' victory was not always so neat, honourable or bloodless.

If a girl had attained her majority of twenty-five years she could, provided that she made an official summons to dissenting parents for permission to marry (*sommation respectueuse*), contract a valid marriage without their being able to disinherit her by way of reprisal.[53] If, however, she married under age and without parental consent she was deemed to have been suborned into marriage, the union was termed clandestine, and her partner became liable to the death penalty.[54] In practice the latter was rarely applied. Parents balked at the idea of resorting to a noose to dissolve an otherwise legally binding marriage and preferred to give their belated consent rather than expose their daughter and the family name to further dishonour.[55] Relying on this form of emotional blackmail, girls consented to being abducted by their suitors. Society was inclined to view the seizure of a bride with indulgence. When the future Duc de Châtillon carried off Mlle de Montmorency-Bouteville in 1644 his action met with a chorus of poetic approval.[56] Abductors had little difficulty in finding powerful protectors amongst the nobility,[57] even if kings and ministers did their best to stamp out a practice that rendered precarious the liberty of every rich, unattached heiress.[58]

Such despair did the prospect or accomplishment of a forced marriage cause on occasions that the ultimate expressions of protest were not shunned. Girls are found resorting to the cloister,[59] murdering the offending parent,[60] committing suicide. One incident of this kind seems to have momentarily shocked contemporaries out of their habitual complacency, judging from repeated references to it. In November 1651 the twenty-five-year-old daughter of an expert engraver, Varin, was 'sold' in marriage to the son of a wealthy fish-merchant. The groom had the distinction of being lame, hump-backed and scrofulous, and the spectacle of four men occupied in undressing him and unscrewing his iron leg horrified his bride on their wedding night. Just over a week later she sprinkled an egg with poison and swallowed it, 'dont elle mourut trois quarts d'heure après sans faire d'autre bruit, sinon qu'elle dit: "Il faut mourir, puisque l'avarice de mon père l'a voulu".'[61] The tragedy of Mlle Varin highlights, in an extreme form, the fate suspended over many of her sex and suggests that the Molières and the Furetières had less far to look for originals of their grotesque fiancés than might at first be supposed.

Open filial revolt was, however, the exception rather than the rule. Generally speaking girls were content, or resigned themselves, to accept the husband whom their parents chose for them, and this for a number of reasons. Dutifulness and fear undoubtedly played a large part in filial submission. Seventeenth-century offspring were reared to regard their parents, as authors of their being, in the same light as God and to hold them in the same respectful awe.[62] They were *Monsieur* and *Madame*, somewhat remote beings in whose presence children stood until instructed otherwise, and whose permission might have to be obtained for such a simple action as going into the garden.[63] When they descended from their Olympian heights it was, after the fashion of divinities, to punish misdemeanours with a devastating severity justified by the argument that the young were incapable of responding to mere appeals to reason.[64] Adult sons and daughters were not spared: news of the thrashings administered by Colbert to his wayward son, of the slaps and kick in the stomach dealt by the Maréchale de Châtillon (Anne de Polignac) to her straying daughter, echoed round society.[65] It was a brave, or a foolish, girl who defied these formidable personages and risked physical violence or incarceration in a convent by means of a *lettre de cachet*.[66] Besides, marriage was the one sure way of escaping parental domination since almost everywhere it legally emancipated a girl from paternal authority.[67] Though she exchanged one form of tutelage for another, that exercised by the husband was generally less rigid in practice than that of the father, and being a wife had many extra advantages in terms of social prestige. The alternative to resignation threatened to place a girl in a frightening no-man's-land outside the social and moral structures with which she was familiar. The heroines of books and plays, significantly, resisted parental oppression long enough to display becoming qualities of resourcefulness and devotion to the hero, but almost always some opportune event enabled the desired union to be consummated and order to be restored to the family unit after temporary chaos. Readers and spectators could safely enjoy, by proxy, all the thrills of revolt, but no one cared to contemplate the problematical situation of the girl whose rebellion definitively placed her outside the family, or the respectable social pale.

The choice of husband having been made to the satisfaction of parents and relatives, if not to that of the daughter, there remained a series of formalities to be fulfilled and rituals to be accomplished before a couple could begin married life together. The first priority was to make sure that there were no circumstances capable of preventing a legal union. Impediments to marriage existed in large number and were divided into two groups, *empêchements prohibitifs* and *empêchements dirimants*. The former group comprised certain obligations imposed by the Church (for example, the necessity to be absolved from a religious vow before marriage) which halted marriage proceedings only so long as they remained unfulfilled. The latter group, on the other hand, theoretically constituted irremovable obstacles to matrimony. They included conditions aimed to prevent unions where there was some physical incapacity; where persons were related by blood or through marriage up to the fourth degree inclusive,[68] or possessed some spiritual affinity such as that between godparent and godchild; and where the proper formalities had not been completed.[69] In practice the so-called *empêchements dirimants*, particularly those concerning relationships, were often waived by Church or royal authority to enable members of the aristocracy to keep estates and titles within the family by means of close intermarriage. Criticisms of papal liberality in the matter of dispensations were voiced, notably by the Jansenists,[70] but since the sect was not viewed as representing orthodox Church opinion their remonstrances were calculated to have little influence.

The next step involved publicising the marriage by means of the official betrothal or *fiançailles*, and the calling of the banns. Betrothal was originally designed by the Church to give prospective partners an opportunity to meditate on the gravity of the engagement they were about to undertake. Opinions about the desirability of the institution were revised, however, when impatient fiancés were observed to be treating it as a licence to cohabit prematurely. The custom arose for dispensing with *fiançailles* altogether or performing them only a few days before the nuptials.[71] In royal and aristocratic families betrothal and wedding ceremonies were habitually telescoped in this way.[72] But the evidence of *Livres de Raison* suggests that though certain of the more prosperous members of the middle classes imitated this custom,[73] bourgeois fiancés preferred to wait at least a month before definitively tying the marriage-knot.[74]

Betrothal was also meant to allow time for verification of a couple's legal right and capacity to enter into marriage, an intention that was reinforced by the publication of the banns. Importance attached to this formality as a means of combating the clandestine marriages that had multiplied during the early sixteenth century in consequence of the validity accorded to marriages effected by the simple exchange of promises before a notary, without priest, banns or witnesses. The 1579 *Ordonnance de Blois* sought to remedy the situation by stipulating that three banns had to be called prior to the wedding and that at least four witnesses must be present when the contracting parties were 'épousées publiquement' (Article 40). Sensing that the vagueness of these terms might lead to genuine or wilful misinterpretation, the government promulgated on 26 November 1639 a *Déclaration sur les Formalités du Mariage* in which all possible ambiguity was removed: 'ordonnons que la proclamation des bans sera faite par le curé de chacune des parties contractantes, avec le consentement des pères, mères, tuteurs ou curateurs, s'ils sont enfants de famille, ou en la puissance d'autrui. Et qu'à la célébration du mariage assisteront quatre témoins[75] dignes de foi, outre le curé qui recevra le consentement des parties, et les conjoindra en mariage suivant la forme pratiquée en l'église'.[76] Loopholes were still found in the law. During the civil wars of the Fronde a magistrate named Gaulmin conceived the idea of exchanging promises of marriage with his fiancée before a notary and then informing his *curé* of the existence of the contract, a procedure which rendered impossible any enquiry into the legal fitness for marriage of the persons concerned. The clergy repeatedly protested to the king, pointing out in 1680 that these purely civil unions were becoming 'très fréquentes dans les diocèses' on the part of those to whose marriage there was some impediment, on that of minors, and on that of Catholics wishing to engage in mixed marriages with Protestants.[77] The response was a *Déclaration sur l'Invalidité des mariages faits par d'autres prêtres que les curés des contractants* in 1697 which enjoined perpetrators of *mariages à la Gaulmine* to have their marriages rehabilitated by the local bishop or archbishop.[78] The government blunted the impact of its own salutary measures, however, by failing to rescind a clause in Article 40 of the *Ordonnance de Blois* permitting dispensations from the second and third banns,[79] and by tolerating marriages without banns on the part of minors who had the consent of parents or guardians.[80]

The signature of the articles of marriage and of the contract, the third major formality, occurred at varying stages in the proceedings, and where the contract was concerned this was sometimes before the betrothal,[81] sometimes between the betrothal and the wedding,[82] sometimes after the nuptials.[83] The effect of the articles of marriage, signed by the future partners and their relatives, was to oblige the former to proceed to the celebration of their union, on pain of payment by the dissenting partner of damages and expenses. A notary would then be summoned to draft the marriage contract proper. The contract was an elastic document into which any clauses could be inserted provided that they did not contravene the law or public morality.[84] The standard wording consisted of an opening declaration that two parties had mutually promised 'la foi de mariage' and were about to accomplish that promise, followed by details of the material and financial contributions that each was making to the conjugal community and the advantages that should accrue to the surviving party. A flourish of signatures terminated the list of dotal provisions, custom decreeing that as many notables as possible be invited to sign along with parents and relatives in order to enhance the social standing of the family.[85] Before adding their signatures, the well-bred young couple would bow in the direction of their parents to request permission.[86]

The figure fixed for the dowry was almost certain to be elevated in proportion to paternal resources: it was important to appear opulent for reasons of prestige, and the cost of dowries rose catastrophically during the course of the century. Humorists like Furetière produced tables showing a girl precisely what class of husband she could expect to buy for her money, ranging from a small merchant or minor legal official for 2000 to 6000 *livres* to a Parlement president, a superintendant of finances or a genuine aristocrat for 100 000 to 200 000 *écus*.[87] Unable to foot the bill, desperate fathers began to propel their daughters towards the convents, where a dowry was still required, but of a relatively less costly nature. The government, alarmed in turn at possible repercussions on the country's birth-rate, planned to examine means of regulating dowries, but did not get past the stage of good intentions.[88]

The paternal predicament was eased somewhat by the fact that payment of the monetary element of the dowry could be spread out and deferred in several ways. Part of the sum promised, sometimes all of it, might consist of expectations in the form of inheritances,[89] repayments by debtors[90] and parental undertakings to pay for the upkeep of one or both of the newly-weds for a given period.[91] Custom allowed, moreover, for a certain proportion only of the money stipulated in the contract to be handed over at the time of the actual wedding, the remainder being paid in instalments, with or without interest, over an agreed number of years.[92] Considerable good faith was necessary all round for such a practice to work well, and abuses were not unknown in the highest circles.[93] It was Spain's failure to pay Marie-Thérèse's dowry of 500 000 gold *écus* that gave Louis XIV a pretext to start the War of Devolution in 1667.

The dowry comprised other effects besides money. The upper-class bride usually brought to the conjugal community some of what were known as *biens immeubles*, that is to say estates, houses and other such properties which could not be transported from place to place, as opposed to *biens meubles* like sums of money, which were movable. She might also be able to offer a husband an army command, or a post as lieutenant of the king or governor in the provinces.[94] In addition every bride was provided, or provided herself, with a trousseau of jewels, clothes or household articles. These varied in magnificence from the pendants worth 10 000 *écus* that hung from the ears of the minister's new daughter-in-law[95] to the 'half-belt' (*demi-ceint*) of silver that girdled the waist of the betrothed maidservant;[96] from the 50 000 *francs* of gems and movables that sealed the aristocratic misalliance[97] to the bed-linen and kitchen utensils that set up the peasant household.[98]

In line with the requirements of the law, the observances of the Church and the financial expectations of her future in-laws and husband, the fiancée was now ready to perform the rituals that would carry her over the threshold of matrimony. She would have been warned in advance by the local matrons not to marry in May, nor on a Wednesday or Friday, for fear of bad luck.[99] The *curé* would issue a reminder that the Church frowned upon the celebration of nuptials on Sundays and holy days, and during the periods of Lent and Advent.[100] Otherwise the ceremony might legally take place from any hour of the early morning until late into the night. A nocturnal wedding merited serious consideration, since it was well-known that the casting of charms such as the dreaded *nouement d'aiguillette*, which prevented consummation, was rendered more difficult in darkness.[101]

From the rapid pictures of the bride's adornment painted by contemporaries, it appears to have differed greatly from region to region and from one social class to another. The common denominator was the expense and care lavished upon its purchase and arrangement, as befitted such an important occasion in life. A picturesque custom still survived in certain localities for the bride to proceed to church with her hair flowing loose around her shoulders, a symbol of the veil which in ancient times girls wore to show their submission to their future husband.[102] At Lyon brides affixed silken stars to their coiffure.[103] Protestant girls preferred orange-blossom or jasmine.[104] The peasant bride of Touraine favoured colour and sparkle with her scarlet robe and head-dress embroidered with imitation jewellery, while her relatives donned garments of blue drawn from coffers perfumed with lavender, rose petals and rosemary.[105] The fashion for a white bridal gown was not yet firmly established. Accounts of princely weddings show popular colours to have been crimson and purple, scattered with fleurs-de-lys,[106] or silver, cloth of which was worked with jewels and sometimes overspread with froths of silver lace to match.[107]

If the marriage was to take place in church, as opposed to the private chapel of an aristocratic *château* or royal palace, a long procession would wend its way thither on the appointed day. Plebeian fiancés of Lyon marched hand in hand behind their relatives, with the respective sets of parents bringing up the rear. Kitchen-boys followed alongside bearing the utensils of their trade, including a massive cauldron from which soup was later distributed to the poor. Accompanying musicians coaxed tunes from portable organs and psalteries to put everyone in an appropriately joyous mood.[108] Not that guests needed much encouragement to display their gaiety and exuberance, if ecclesiastical monitions are anything to go by.[109] Volleys of musket shots, both inside the church and out,[110] signalled to the world that yet another bride was in the process of receiving from her groom the ring and traditional pieces of money,[111] symbols of eternal fidelity and of the dower which assured her material welfare in the future.[112] Blows from well-wishers anxious to avert the effects of evil charms were directed at the heads and feet of the couple as they knelt for mass or to receive the nuptial blessing beneath the *poêle*, a piece of cloth or veiling extended over them in representation of the nuptial couch.[113] Once the ceremony was over, boisterousness increased in proportion as copious draughts of wine washed down gargantuan plates of victuals, in defiance of government regulations,[114] and bodies jigged and swayed to rustic orchestras, an exercise deemed by delighted doctors to be propitious to the reproduction of the species.[115] Entering into the spirit of the occasion the local overlord might come jovially to claim his wedding due, which was rumoured in darker ages to have involved deflowering the vassal brides on his estates but which had long since been commuted into a cash, or other symbolic, payment.[116]

The bourgeoisie and aristocracy were credited with a taste for quieter celebrations.[117] Where such was the case this was no doubt due partly to the desire to dissociate themselves from the bacchanalia of plebeians; partly also to the need to reduce heavy wedding bills[118] for which pride and decorum prevented them from seeking reimbursement after the fashion of their social inferiors, namely by obliging the guests to pay their own share in cash or in kind.[119] Nevertheless upper-class weddings were scarcely distinguished by their austerity. More sophisticated entertainments – firework displays, boat trips, balls, concerts, ballets, operas and especially performances of plays[120] – may have replaced revels in the village square; but princes surpassed commoners in their gastronomical feats,[121] worthy bourgeois abandoned their gravity to the enticements of the dance,[122] and provincial notables squandered immense sums to provide amusements and largesses that would immortalise their name in local memory.[123]

All classes were united in their somewhat indelicate insistence on the purpose for which marriage was instituted. That the newlyweds' life would revolve around the conjugal bed was underlined repeatedly, both during the ceremony in the use of the *poêle* and in the preacher's exhortation,[124] and throughout the subsequent festivities. Leaving aside the dubious jokes and pranks to which the couple might be subjected, a respectable usage ordained that the priest, who was not above participating with gusto in the rejoicings,[125] should bless the nuptial couch.[126] Eminent lords and ladies would hand a royal bride and groom their respective chemises, and solemnly close the bed-curtains for the benefit of privileged onlookers, though they might well be redrawn shortly afterwards and a couple too young to consummate their marriage be separated until such time as vigilant attendants pronounced them ripe for reproduction.[127] On the day after the wedding, custom obliged brides of all ranks to deck themselves out in their finery and recline on their bed to receive visits of congratulation.[128]

Intimate questions were commonly posed on this occasion by inquisitive relatives and friends about the husband's performance on the previous night,[129] and some candid replies given.[130]

The seventeenth-century marriage thus retained throughout a strictly functional aspect. Conceived as the union of titles, estates or fortunes, negotiated by third parties, presented as a *fait accompli* to virtual strangers, vetted and approved by the Church and the law, it reserved at the last merely a blunt reminder that its aim was procreation, the giving 'incessamment des présents à l'Eglise et à l'Etat'.[131] Individuals and personalities counted for little in the process, romance still less. Love had to develop, if it could, at that precise moment when its failure to materialise was susceptible of none but partial and doubtful remedies.

4

The Estate of Matrimony

The arbitrary and impersonal nature of the process by which young men and women were matched and mated in the seventeenth century meant that for the bond of mutual affection and understanding which modern generations have come to regard as a vital prerequisite of marriage was substituted at best an initial indifference, at worst an active resentment against the person to whom fidelity had to be vowed until death. The onus for closing this emotional breach rested largely, it was stressed, with the wife.[1] On her flexibility and deference, on her willingness to accept subordinate status, and on her power to resist pressures that threatened to divide her still further from her spouse, depended the degree of marital harmony that could be established.

In theory marriage was a partnership. Moralists of the day were fond of retelling the story of how Eve was drawn from Adam's side to demonstrate that woman was created to be the companion and helpmate of man, neither his slave nor his master.[2] In practice the relationship was that of subordinate to superior. The cosy anecdote of the Creation was invariably followed by a citation or paraphrase of Saint Paul's stern injunction to the wife to submit herself unto her husband as unto the Lord, 'se persuadant, quand elle parle à son mari, qu'elle parle à son maître, à son seigneur, à son Roi, et ce qui surpasse infiniment tout cela, qu'elle parle à Jésus Christ même, dont il soutient à son égard la personne et l'autorité'.[3] The corollary was that blind obedience should not be expected at all times, for this might conceivably lead to acts contrary to the laws of God and man; but in all reasonable matters, submission to a husband's wishes was obligatory.[4] The ideal wife would in any case have no wishes or desires separate from those of her husband. So carefully would she study to efface from her personality all traces of thoughts and feelings that did not accord with his or did not centre on him that she would become as 'le bon miroir qui représente fidèlement la face, n'ayant aucun dessein, amour, pensement particulier'.[5]

The wifely subordination which tradition recommended was

underlined by certain aspects of the complex legal system governing marriage. In place of one uniform legal code throughout the country, every French province, enclaves within particular provinces and many of the large towns had their own individual legal usages or *Coutumes* which in the south had retained a stronger imprint than elsewhere of ancient Roman legislation and were known collectively as the 'written law' (*droit écrit*). The general tendency of written law was to separate the interests of husband and wife in accordance with the premise underlying Roman law that women were weak, easily influenced beings who needed protection from the consequences of their foibles. It granted a woman absolute jurisdiction over all her personal possessions which were not expressly included in the dowry (*paraphernaux*) and the option of deciding whether or not to consent to the transference of that jurisdiction to her husband.[6] The dowry itself, the profits from which belonged to the husband,[7] had been safeguarded from alienation without the wife's consent by a Roman law, the *Lex Julia*, subsequently expanded by the Emperor Justinian I to forbid alienation even with her consent.[8] In the same spirit a decree of the Roman Senate, the *Senatus-Consultus* of Velleius, prevented married (and celibate) women from contracting any legal obligation on behalf of, or in the interests of, others, for example by acting as guarantor for the payment of debts. In the seventeenth century these laws were felt by the French government to constitute a hindrance to commerce. Taking advantage of a fashion for inserting into marriage contracts a clause renouncing the Velleian decree, Henri IV abolished it in 1606.[9] In 1664 his grandson repealed the *Lex Julia* in Lyon and surrounding districts, and authorised women to pledge their dotal possessions as well as their *paraphernaux*.[10] The concern to foster trade resulted in greater legal freedom for wives, but at the same time it exposed them to the kind of pressure from prodigal husbands that Roman legislation was designed to forestall.

Under customary law (*droit coutumier*) marriage was envisaged as a community of possessions (*communauté des biens*) to which the two partners brought goods on entering married life and to which they added others (*conquêts* and *acquêts*)[11] during the course of their union, the total revenues thereof being designed to support the household. The notion of a community was misleading in so far as the husband, as head of the association, administered and disposed of the property held in common virtually as he chose, a point made clear by the Paris *Coutume*: 'Le mari est seigneur des meubles et conquêts immeubles, par lui faits durant et constant le mariage de lui et sa femme. En telle manière qu'il les peut vendre, aliéner ou hypothéquer, et en faire et disposer par donation ou autre disposition faite entre vifs, à son plaisir et volonté, sans le consentement de sa dite femme, à personne capable et sans fraude.'[12] It is true that the husband was legally prevented from disposing of property to the prejudice of the dower to which the wife was entitled after his death,[13] and that he could not sell, exchange, mortgage and so on without her consent those patrimonial *immeubles* which had been bequeathed or donated to her;[14] but then neither could she so dispose of her own property without his authority.[15] As a general rule the husband's official permission had to accompany all the legal actions of the wife,[16] whether she wished to sign a contract,[17] appear before a court of law,[18] accept a donation or legacy,[19] or enter into a legal agreement on another's behalf, with the exception in the last instance of those wives engaged in a business completely distinct from that of their husband (*marchandes publiques*) and those judicially separated from their partner.[20] In some *Coutumes* the making of a will was subject to the same provision.[21] Where the husband refused permission the wife could resort to a legal tribunal, but authorisations thus granted were limited in their sphere of application.[22]

The authority which the husband possessed over his wife's property and legal actions was extended to her person. As her 'maître et bon seigneur' he was entitled to her 'honneur, révérence et respect'.[23] She was obliged to serve him and follow him wherever he might choose to lead her,[24] on pain under some *Coutumes* of losing her dower.[25] The husband's right to 'correct' his wife for her faults still subsisted intact from the medieval period when codification of the *Coutumes* first began. The seventeenth century theoretically condemned the use of any corporal punishment and the beaten wife was able to obtain a separation.[26] But the law was ill equipped to bridle hypersensitive temperaments disposed to outbursts of violence by the repeated experience of war and insurrection and, more important, by the absence of sophisticated methods of easing the tensions and frustrations of living precariously in a universe where countless unexplained phenomena awed and terrified. If they abandoned the use of *Martin bâton* recommended by their forebears, contemporary husbands from all walks of life were remarkably free with their slaps, punches and kicks.[27] Wives were fortified with the thought that ill-treatment was in the natural order of their subjection to men[28] and left to make novenas to Saint 'Raboni' for the amendment of the heavy-handed spouse.[29] When it was a question of punishing a wife's sexual aberrations husbands could, quite literally, get away with murder.

Adultery offered an obvious form of revenge and compensation to those who had been bundled into marriages for which they were not prepared from either the physical or the emotional point of view, or both. Men, as Saint-Evremond was seen in the previous chapter to confess, submitted to the loss of their bachelor freedom with the tacit intention of recovering it by means of illicit liaisons, and the early stages of upper-class wedlock[30] increased rather than diminished temptation to implement that intention. In some instances brides were too young to consummate the marriage, which meant that while they continued to play with their dolls[31] the husband betook himself to the wars or immersed himself in affairs and travels until such time as his partner was capable of assuming her full wifely role. The risk of permanent emotional estrangement and worse, ensuing from this suspension of normal conjugal relations, was high. Brides in their middle or late teens were commonly drawn straight from the convent,[32] where the mention of marriage was taboo, or from the confines of the maternal chamber, where males other than relatives were not freely admitted, and thrust without further ado into those *Terres Inconnues*[33] of which the few novels that they might have perused in secret spoke with a disconcerting vagueness. Sexual education, other than that gleaned from remarks overheard at weddings,[34] would probably be confined to the awareness of an imprecise obligation to 'coucher contre un homme vraiment nu', as the *précieuses* put it.[35] Respectable manuals on the subject such as Dr Nicolas Venette's *Tableau de l'Amour considéré dans l'état du mariage* (1687) appeared late in the century and there is no proof that this was studied by the young girls for whom the author avowedly thought his revelations to be profitable.[36] Great pains were taken, on the other hand, to ensure that the young groom was sufficiently knowledgeable to be able to perform his conjugal duties without hitches, to the extent of having him practise on women of loose morals before the wedding.[37] By the time that the necessary adjustments had been made between an ignorant bride and an experienced groom the latter might well have impatiently sought sentimental and sexual satisfaction elsewhere, inviting his for-saken spouse in her turn to follow his example.[38]

Society treated forbearingly those breaches of conjugal faith committed by the husband. Marriage, everyone knew, was a 'religieuse et dévote liaison'[39] instituted for the production of heirs, not for the gratification of sensual desires.[40] The healthy male, however, could hardly be expected to contain himself within such narrow limits, in which case it was better for him to take his pleasure with mistresses and prostitutes than to commit what Montaigne had called 'incest' by bringing to the marriage-bed 'les efforts et les extravagances de la licence amoureuse'.[41] Not only his physical fitness but his reputation also was at stake. It was a feather in the cap of any man to have, or at least to appear to have, more than one woman at his disposal,[42] and failure to do so signified a derisive lack of wit or opportunity.

The same tolerance was not accorded to the opposite sex. Women, it was agreed, had far greater sexual appetites than men.[43] But the religious and social taboos which sought to prevent voluptuous intercourse, to ban embraces in front of the children[44] and to outlaw all public demonstrations of affection meant that marriage afforded them 'peu de rafraîchissement'.[45] That women should assuage their frustrated desires with a lover was neverthe-less unthinkable. Pollution of the race would result, legitimate heirs would be deprived of their birthright by bastards, and once a woman lost her chastity, the prime female virtue, she was bound to lose simultaneously her aversion for all vices and crimes.[46] One and the same act when committed by a man was labelled gallantry, by a woman, infamy.

The injustice of this double standard of morality did not escape notice. Moral and religious treatises reminded husbands that preserving their own conjugal fidelity was the best way to safeguard that of a wife.[47] The theatre in particular, always quick to champion the cause of women, aired the problem in forceful terms throughout the century.[48] In act two, scene one of Hauter-oche's comedy *Crispin Médecin* (1673) the servant Dorine asks the married master who tries to cajole her what he would say if his wife elected to behave likewise:

> *Mirobolan*: Oh! ce n'est pas la même chose. La gloire d'un homme est de cajoler plusieurs femmes, mais la vertu d'une femme est de n'écouter que son mari.

Dorine: Je ne crois pas que là-dessus les hommes aient plus de privilège que les femmes, et qu'il leur soit permis de faire ce qu'elles n'oseraient entreprendre.
Mirobolan: La loi a voulu que cela fût ainsi.
Dorine: Il fallait que cela fût tout au contraire.

In asserting that the 'law' authorised male philandering the amorous master presumably meant the law of nature, but he might equally have invoked contemporary legislation, which connived at a husband's debauchery by refusing the wife the right to bring a charge of adultery against an unfaithful spouse.[49] If her husband strayed and broke his conjugal vows the wife had two courses open to her: she could signify her displeasure with open reproaches, or she could suffer in silence. The first tactic had the advantage of showing a husband that his affections were not a matter of indifference, but few advocated it apart from Richelieu, who cuts a curious figure as marriage guidance counsellor.[50] The second tactic was much more in keeping with the ideals of wifely submission and respect epitomised by Boccaccio's long-suffering Griselda. 'Quand il y a du péché, pleurons-le', advises Caussin's spokeswoman, 'tâchons à y remédier par prières, par discrétion, par patience ... nous nous trouverons fortes dans le silence, et l'espérance, et non pas dans les assiduelles crieries, qui ne font qu'égratigner les plaies, et renouveller les désastres.'[51] Tears, prayers and patience, these were the only weapons allowed to the betrayed wife.

The betrayed husband laboured under no such restrictions, legal or moral. In past ages he had been able to invoke degrading and savage penalties that included parading the adulterous wife naked round the town, under the lash of the executioner.[52] In the relatively civilised seventeenth century exposure to public mockery was still practised: in Poitou the guilty party was dragged by the hangman through the streets tied to the tail of a mule, then left bound with her hands behind her back to a stake set up in a well-frequented place for passers-by to insult.[53] But the standard legal punishment was confinement of the adulteress to a convent for two years, during which time the husband had the option of taking her back into the conjugal home. If there was no reconciliation by the end of that period the wife had her head shaved, was dressed in nun's garb, and was obliged to spend the rest of her life in the cloister.[54] Her dower and other such advantages stipulated in the marriage contract were forfeit to the husband in return for the pension he paid to keep her in the convent, and he could usually claim her dowry in addition if the marriage was childless.[55]

Recourse to justice to avenge dishonour was not, however, widely favoured, especially in conjugal matters where the complainant would lay himself open to scorn and ridicule.[56] Husbands much preferred to take the law into their own hands and to inflict bloody reprisals on wives and their accomplices. In 1602 the pregnant Comtesse de Cheverney was strangled in bed by her wronged spouse.[57] In 1619 Constant d'Aubigné, Mme de Maintenon's father, despatched his first wife and her gallant into the next world, 'après l'avoir fait prier Dieu'.[58] In 1627 a Parisian sadler's wife was stabbed to death by the irate husband who discovered her *in flagrante delicto* with a neighbouring barber.[59] In the provinces these summary vengeances were taken to extremes of brutality. Espinchal, one of a number of noblemen from the Auvergne whose favourite sport was terrorising the local inhabitants, forced his wife to take poison, then castrated and hung up to die the page whom he suspected of making him a cuckold.[60] The law adopted a lenient attitude towards this usurpation of its prerogatives and accorded virtual impunity to the murderer. The prevailing view was succinctly resumed during the trial of one Scipion, who in March 1602 had surprised his young wife in bed with her lover and killed them both.[61] On this occasion the lawyer for the crown was heard to declare: 'Il n'est pas permis au mari de tuer sa femme, quoiqu'il la surprenne en adultère, quelque part que ce soit; il est seulement permis au père, en sa maison propre, ou de son gendre. C'est chose qui répugne aux principes de la justice et de l'humanité, de donner licence à un particulier de se venger soi-même. Le mari n'est donc pas exempt de peine, quand il lui arrive de tuer sa femme surprise en adultère, mais les lois ont pitié de lui. On le punit, parce qu'il a transgressé la loi; mais on le punit doucement.'[62] So heinous was the crime of female adultery considered to be that the law could countenance murder of the offending wife by her father and could acquit an avenging husband, as in this case, on payment of a token fine, or on facile procurement of royal letters of remission.[63]

During Louis XIV's personal rule mentions of private executions disappear from the pages of the memorialists. Not that the incidence of adultery decreased, as these same pages testify. On the contrary. But a greater complacency towards conjugal misdemeanours seems to have infiltrated contemporary morals, assisted by the growing practice for couples to lead their lives independently of one another.

Since time immemorial the seasonal migration of husbands in search of work[64] or their departure for service in the army and at court had accustomed wives throughout society to long separations, during which they kept the home fires burning and bore children, after being impregnated during home-comings.[65] What appeared as a novelty was the artificial prolongation of such separations by the genteel, their transformation from a necessity into a fashion. To place some physical distance between oneself and one's partner, by means of separate beds, separate domiciles or separate life-styles, became indispensable to those who did not wish their mode of existence to be called old-fashioned and low-class. The arrangement increased chances of alleviating that sense of loss of personal liberty which in the popular view made matrimony so burdensome. It realised almost exactly the ideal of the *précieuses*, whose watchword was freedom, and who wanted to render conventional marriage, defined as 'l'abîme de la liberté', more elastic.[66] The various forms of trial marriage which they were credited with preaching[67] had necessarily to remain on the purely imaginary level. The 'half-marriage', however, allowed for a compromise between freedom and social convention: society's requirements were met by a legal union which engaged merely two indifferent names and bodies and provided a respectable façade behind which couples who had nothing, or were unable to develop anything, in common were free to pursue their individual interests and amours.

By the 1660s the phenomenon had reached such proportions as to attract the attention of moralists and satirists. Charles Sorel was one of the first to expose the new vogue: 'Il semble qu'ils [gens mariés] soient chacun condamnés à faire bande à part. De se gouverner d'autre sorte, c'est vivre comme les bonnes gens du temps passé, du moins en ce qui est de ceux qui suivent l'air du grand monde. C'est assez pour faire soulever le cœur aux personnes galantes, de voir seulement le mari et la femme dans un même carrosse. La mode veut qu'ils se fuyent l'un l'autre.'[68] Other observers report that husbands who thought to pass the time of day with their wife were regarded as jealous importunates[69] and condemned for their 'bourgeois' habits.[70] To risk a caress in public was 'tout à fait ridicule' according to the manuals of correct behaviour.[71] By 1690 just to be seen out together was a 'shameful' lapse.[72]

The degree of success achieved by the campaign to ban all outward manifestations of conjugal intimacy may be gauged from the extreme reserve with which allusions are made to marriage partners even in the most personal documents. It was taken as axiomatic that the husband should rarely speak about his wife.[73] In letters to friends he merely noted the state of her health or passed on her respects,[74] whilst reserving the right to dilate at length on his mistresses. The Comte de Bussy-Rabutin, so sparing with references to his two successive Comtesses, fills whole pages of his correspondence with the activities of the faithless Mme de Montglas. In personal memoirs one or two fleeting evocations of a wife's qualities usually sufficed. Tallemant des Réaux, who reveals a multitude of highly intimate details about his contemporaries, devotes a bare three or four lines to his wife's beauty and to her youthful inexperience as housekeeper.[75] Saint-Simon keeps for his last will and testament the expression of a profound conjugal tenderness visibly contained throughout his voluminous memoirs.[76] The recording or remembrance of a wedding day or, more especially, of a wife's death, are the only two occasions on which discreet effusions are judged permissible. 'C'était une très digne et très vertueuse personne avec laquelle j'avais doucement vécu pendant notre mariage' is the souvenir that a lawyer preserves of his 'chère épouse'.[77] 'Dieu me fasse la grâce de la voir dans le ciel', cries a doctor in his 'grandes afflictions' over the loss of a partner 'toute sa vie vertueuse, obligeante'.[78] 'A bien vécu et est bien morte . . . C'était la meilleure femme du monde' is the brisk funeral oration pronounced by a Parlement advocate.[79] 'Le samedi XX novembre [1683], à cinq heures et demie précises du matin, à ma montre et à l'horloge de la ville avec lequel elle convenait très bien, ma femme a rendu son âme à Dieu,' specifies a notary crisply; 'C'était une bonne âme; elle se confessait et communiait tous les samedis; aussi vit-elle sa dernière heure venir avec joie . . . Elle était âgée de 45 ans 10 mois 5 jours.'[80] The bourgeoisie, derided for their unfashionable displays of marital love, cannot have been entirely oblivious to the opinions of the smart set since they thought fit to curb their emotional expansiveness in papers which were destined only for the eyes of family and friends.

Wives for their part subscribed to the silence imposed upon husbands. Those who left their mark on the century were mostly *mal mariées* of one kind or another who had in any case no wish to evoke the memory of a husband from whom death or distance conveniently parted them. In well over a thousand extant letters Mme de Sévigné makes but two disparaging mentions of a husband killed prematurely in a brawl over a wanton.[81] Françoise Bertaut's memoirs refer for completeness to the authoress's marriage to Président de Motteville, but understandably do not expatiate on the nature of her relationship with a man more than four times her own age.[82] Mme Scarron, long before her union with Louis XIV forbade all reminiscences of her previous inglorious alliance, had definitively buried with an enigmatic '[sa mort] m'a donné assez de douleur, et assez d'affaire' the indebted cripple who saved her from becoming a nun.[83] Wives who do profess affection for their husband stress the outmoded or forbidden nature of the gesture. In the very first of her long series of *Lettres Historiques et Galantes* Mme Dunoyer tells an imaginary provincial correspondent: 'je suis d'assez bonne foi pour avouer que j'aime mon mari, quoique à Paris, on regarde cette faiblesse comme un des vices du temps de Jean de Verd,[84] que les mœurs de ce siècle ont corrigé'. The poetess Mme Deshoulières, despatching to an absent husband a rhymed news bulletin, wishes that she dared adopt a more loving tone:

> Si l'on osait aux époux,
> Ecrire d'un style doux,
> Je pousserais des Hélas;
> Mais aux chères précieuses,
> Le bon air ne le veut pas.[85]

Sentimental incontinence may have been a quality universally attributed to women, but the necessity for them to keep their feelings in check, even in a legitimate liaison, was quite clearly spelt out.

So it was that the note of estrangement on which couples were accustomed to enter into matrimony tended to be prolonged throughout their married life. Legal discrimination, religious taboos and social pressures, by undermining the status of women and debasing conjugal love, all contributed to put asunder those whom God had joined together. The seventeenth-century husband was conditioned to regard his nominal co-partner as an inferior whose physical and mental weakness justified his almost complete control over her property and person. She was the being from whom public opinion encouraged him to live remote, physically if possible, emotionally at least. Never must he show assiduity or passion for her, lest he excite derisive comment, such demonstrations of interest and affection being more properly reserved for the mistress who compensated him for marital abstinences. On only one occasion did conjugal intimacy receive unanimous approval and that was when, mindful of the Church's instructions, the husband united, staidly, with his wife for the purpose of propagating the human race.

5

Maternity

Mme de Turgis, who was wedded, Tallemant assures us, to 'la plus grosse bête' of all those that sat in the Paris Chambre des Comptes, jibbed at cohabitation with such a poor specimen of masculinity. However every twenty months, without fail, the family solemnly assembled to enforce a temporary restitution of conjugal rights whereupon, just as regularly, a child was conceived.[1] The memorialist's illuminating tale demonstrates at once the fecundity of the seventeenth-century Frenchwoman and the seriousness with which contemporaries took to heart the Divine precept 'Be fruitful and multiply'.

Within twelve months of marriage a healthy woman could expect to bear her first child. Subsequent births would gradually space themselves out until they reached intervals of two or more years. Such is the predominant pattern revealed by domestic registers of the century. The *Livre de Raison* of Pierre Boyer, a doctor in a small Lyonnais town, contains a typical record. On 4 February 1621 Pierre took to wife Jane [sic] Berthon, who gave him their first child, Blanche, on 7 January 1622. There followed André on 19 April 1623; Pierre on 10 April 1624; Marie-Flavie on 9 August 1626; Jean on 3 December 1627; Françoise on 13 December 1628; Guillaume on 13 June 1630; Jacques-François on 10 April 1632; and twins on 31 July 1633. Mme Boyer's child-bearing career was abruptly terminated on 19 August by a fever contracted shortly after the birth of the twins.[2] Representing a higher social bracket the *Livre de Raison* of Jacques de Fontainemarie, councillor at the Cour des Aides et Finances of Guyenne, gives a similarly eloquent picture of marital assiduity. The councillor's wife, Jeanne de Saint-Angel, produced a son on 15 November 1661, barely nine months after their marriage on 21 February of that year. A second child arrived on 9 October 1662, and a third on 4 December 1663, after which, on 25 July 1664, occurred a miscarriage in the second month of pregnancy. Further pregnancies were successfully accomplished on 28 May 1665, on 4 September 1666 and on 10 August 1667. Another miscarriage on 6 August 1669 preceded the seventh full-term pregnancy on 12 June 1670, the eighth on 3 July 1671, the ninth on 1 February 1673, the tenth on 7 April 1674 and the eleventh on 16 March 1676. After a series of miscarriages on 15 April 1677, 1 March 1678 and 22 October 1678 Jacques de Fontainemarie finally conceded defeat and there was no more issue of the marriage.[3] The results of this intense conjugal activity were veritable prodigies of fertility amongst mothers of the leisured and moneyed classes, whose rhythm of production was less vulnerable than that of their impoverished peasant and urban counterparts to interruption by famine, disease, premature senescence and death. Women like Mme Arnauld, mother of the militant Jansenist leader Antoine Arnauld, Mme de Chavigny, wife of the secretary of state, the Duchesses de Biron and de Noailles, had twenty and more deliveries to their credit.[4] The Présidente de Marbeuf of Rennes 'se portait assez bien' after giving birth to no fewer than thirty-one children.[5]

Though many offspring quickly renounced the struggle to stay alive, the fruitfulness of French mothers enabled them to be replaced with equal speed. At Clermont-Ferrand, where the bearing of ten sons was regarded as a mere trifle and several ladies boasted of eighteen offspring each, smallpox could strike down more than a thousand infants without leaving any visible gap in the population.[6] At Montpellier arrivals of twins and triplets swelled the birth-rate with a frequency such that 'un cahier entier' would not suffice to record them, according to a local observer.[7] One traveller through Dol, in Brittany, had the impression of stumbling across some vast nursery.[8] Seventeenth-century France was a land that seemed literally to swarm with children.

The creation of large families was encouraged not only by the Church, which placed married couples under a solemn obligation to reproduce, but also by that other omnipotent institution, the State, whose interests were served by a high birth-rate that provided manpower for the land, for industry and especially for the army. An edict of 1666 granted exemption from taxes and other impositions to all non-noble Catholic parents of ten or twelve living children who were not priests or conventuals, and annual pensions of 1000 or 2000 *livres* were awarded to aristocrats in the same position.[9] Unfortunately the projects for increasing the population had soon to be sacrificed to those of filling a permanently depleted Treasury. By the early 1670s Colbert was spreading the word that the government largesses were not to be paid,[10] and in

1683 the edict was officially repealed.[11] Prolific provincials nevertheless continued to evoke its clauses to secure exemptions at times when their tax burden became particularly onerous.[12]

Perhaps the most significant boost to the birth-rate was given by unreliable methods of birth control. In the seventeenth century there were only two practical alternatives: abortion, or abstention from full sexual relations. To combat recourse to the former an edict had been promulgated in 1556 obliging women to make an official declaration of their pregnancy and decreeing the death penalty for those whose infants died unbaptised after a concealed pregnancy or delivery.[13] The risk was scarcely worth taking even for the unmarried mother anxious to suppress the result of her weakness. Provided that her seducer could not prove any notorious debauchery on her part she could claim from him lying-in expenses and damages for the upkeep of the child.[14] If she later decided to marry the father, their offspring could be legitimised by the simple formality of extending the *poêle* over the child during the ceremony.[15] Bastards were in any case regarded with the same indulgence as the act that produced them. From a legal point of view most *Coutumes* permitted them to dispose freely of their goods in favour of their own legitimate children, and to accept donations and bequests from their parents on condition that the interests of legitimate heirs were not unduly harmed thereby.[16] From the social and moral points of view little visible discrimination operated apart from the obligation for the legitimised bastards of noblemen to have a bar painted across their coat-of-arms. Women of the time showed a motherly concern for the fortunes of children illicitly begotten by male relatives, superintending their upbringing and furthering their careers.[17] But then Henri IV and Louis XIV set a striking example to the nation of how to raise legitimate and illegitimate offspring in one big, ostensibly happy, family, the latter monarch bestowing so many rights and privileges on the children of La Vallière and la Montespan that an indignant Saint-Simon spoke of the 'Golden Age of bastards'.[18]

Conjugal abstinence was facilitated by the vogue for couples to sleep separately and generally to live their lives apart. But, since this mode of existence was viewed in the second half of the century as a convenience to enable husband and wife to consort with other partners, only the rate of legitimate births was likely to be affected. For faithful and loving partners it was a haphazard method of family planning indeed. All Mme de Sévigné's eloquence, her studiedly jocular rebukes and pleas to her son-in-law to grant his ardour some intervals of repose, failed to save her willingly fatigued daughter from a series of pregnancies that rapidly robbed her of a once famed beauty.[19]

The risk to health and physical charms caused by 'les contre-coups de l'amour permis'[20] was the argument advanced by the only articulate group of protestors against maternal servitude in the seventeenth century: the *précieuses*. A young wife's fertility, according to Eulalie in Michel de Pure's *Prétieuse*, exposed her 'tous les ans à un nouveau poids, à un péril visible, à une charge importune, à des douleurs indicibles, et à mille suites fâcheuses'. Aracie in the same novel would limit the duration of marriage to the birth of a couple's first child: 'Après ce premier ouvrage et cette marque de bénédiction des honnêtes feux dont ils auraient brûlé l'un pour l'autre, ils partageraient le butin; l'enfant demeurerait au père et la liberté à la femme que le père reconnaîtrait de quelque somme considérable, et qui répondrait au mérite de son ouvrage.'[21] The somewhat exaggerated rhetoric of the first quotation, and the fact that in the second the birth of a child is seen as a *bénédiction* bestowed on a legitimate union, undermine the apparent revolutionism and betray a masculine author not wholly sympathetic to the creeds of the *précieuses* which he undertook to transmit to posterity. Much the same procedure is used by the dramatists. Female characters who voice their horror at the prospect of a burdensome collection of brats are represented as the sycophants of disgruntled mothers or as oddities desirous of reserving their time for the more 'useful' pursuits of frequenting the theatre and watching for men in the moon.[22] Overt rejection of maternity, though rare, was considered a dangerous eccentricity to be curbed by the ready expedient of public mockery.

Once her pregnancy had been ascertained the prospective mother observed attentively the steady thickening of her body and the colour of her complexion. Rosy cheeks and marked swelling of the right side of her torso indicated that a boy was on the way, whereas pallour and swelling on the left, the 'sinister' side, betokened the arrival of a girl.[23] If these signs were inconclusive the sex could still be foretold from the moment when the infant first quivered in the womb. Boys began to stir around the third month; girls, slower to form, did not make their presence felt until approximately the fourth month.[24] The matter of predictions was simplified after the first birth, when close scrutiny of the formation of the placenta made it possible for the midwife to inform clients of the number and gender of the offspring that they were destined to mother.[25] The pre-natal regime to which the pregnant woman was subjected[26] resembled in many, though not all, respects that of the present day. Naturally she was advised to rest adequately, eat bland foods, avoid all emotion and refrain from exercise that involved jolting,[27] but bathing was also forbidden for fear of prematurely opening the womb. All attempts to maintain a shapely silhouette by constriction with whalebone-fortified dresses were denounced as conducive to foetal malformation and prolicide.[28] Loose and flowing *robes battantes* of the kind invented by Mme de Montespan to hide the results of her adultery[29] were a far preferable type of concealment. Great care had to be taken with regard to the objects presented to the mother's gaze during pregnancy, for it was believed that their image could be imprinted on the unborn child. This was all very well in the case of the Dauphin, whom Louis XIV considered to take after the figure of a Christ-child in the room of the pious Marie-Thérèse,[30] but disastrous in that of the Burgundian labourer's wife whom the *Mercure Galant* reported as giving birth to Siamese twins after contemplating a picture of two angels intertwined.[31]

Unlike the other rules, the question of when and whether to bleed a pregnant woman gave rise to a certain amount of controversy amongst medical men. Some were against phlebotomy.[32] Others thought that it could be usefully employed in moderation, depending on individual circumstances.[33] The majority favoured copious blood-letting, invoking the sacrosanct authority of Galen to prove that stifling of the foetus occurred otherwise.[34] The operation was carried out particularly during the last months of pregnancy, and even during labour itself in the belief that the child would be delivered more easily.[35] Patients were cheered by the thought that a doctor's pregnant wife had lived to tell the tale of forty-eight blood-lettings, while another robust mother had survived a total of ninety.[36] Doctors prudently kept silent the casualty figures resulting from this legalised vampirism.[37]

Keen interest was displayed in every stage of pregnancy, for the birth of a new baby could checkmate many a carefully planned political move and alter an entire order of succession to thrones and other coveted properties. From the moment that the high-born woman was elaborately bedded with her husband she was watched for tell-tale signs of morning sickness and interrupted carriage rides. The fluttering of royal and aristocratic foetuses in the womb was gravely registered in all court memoirs and letters.[38] Poets and poetasters eager to curry favour with influential patrons rhapsodised over the advent of a baby hero[39] – at the risk of having to hastily change their imagery when the infant was perverse enough to belie universal expectations that it would be a male. In 1638 court etiquette was relaxed to allow privileged courtiers to place a hand on the person of Anne d'Autriche to feel the first movements of the unborn Louis XIV.[40]

Privacy was a luxury denied to royalty even at the intimate moment of birth. Fears of a substitution of infants in child-bed obliged the royal mother to bear her child virtually in public. Princes as well as princesses of the blood had the right to be present whenever the queen was delivered. At the commencement of labour they were summoned for that purpose, along with other males concerned (the husband, father or father-in-law), medical and religious personnel, and ladies-in-waiting. Louise Bourgeoise, midwife to Marie de Médicis, specifies that when the queen gave birth to Louis XIII in 1601, seated in a special chair, 'les Princes étaient dessous le grand pavillon vis-à-vis d'elle'. Immediately after the birth Henri IV opened the door and let in the huddle of courtiers who had been waiting in the ante-rooms: 'Je crois qu'il y avait deux cents personnes, de sorte que l'on ne pouvait se remuer dans la chambre pour porter la Reine dans son lit.'[41] The stifling press of onlookers and the disorders to which they gave rise continued to be signalled in the second half of the century. On 6 August 1682 'les douleurs commencèrent à presser Mme la Dauphine après qu'elle eût été saignée; et le Roi, avec toute la famille royale, étant revenu dans sa chambre, toute la cour ne quitta plus son appartement'. The birth of the Duc de Bourgogne ten and a half hours later led to scenes of wild rejoicing during which the *canaille* broke all the window panes of the delivery room.[42]

To help them through the ordeal of labour seventeenth-century mothers relied on both divine and human assistance. During the birth of Louis XIV several bishops relayed one another at an altar in Anne d'Autriche's apartment to pray for the successful termination of twenty-two years of royal childlessness.[43] In less exceptional circumstances recourse was had to religious images, notably those in which the Virgin and Child figured. Relics and lives of saints were particularly esteemed as a means of easing pain and procuring a safe delivery. The belt or bones of Saint Margaret were regularly lent to mothers in childbirth, or her biography read to them;[44] though no one knew exactly which of the three saints who bore that name possessed the necessary therapeutic powers, and the invocation of the Virgin was advised as a useful supplement.[45] Special prayers were composed for pregnant women but their consolatory effect was dubious since they stressed the pain and suffering that justly ensued from the sinful act of conception.[46]

The proverbial wages of sin were paid in full. Not only were anaesthetics and analgesics unknown, but the unskilled 'help' rendered to mothers only prolonged and intensified, instead of abbreviating, the pangs of birth. In country areas the expectant mother would interrupt daily toils, which continued right up to the onset of labour,[47] to call in her female relatives and one or two neighbouring matrons whose several offspring presupposed at least some practical expertise in the matter of childbirth. Provided that there were no complications and nature was allowed to take its course, the peasant woman, inured to pain and hardship, probably suffered less than the more delicate townswoman and châtelaine who summoned so-called professional medical assistance. Though moves to train midwives were made in the seventeenth century,[48] many dispensed themselves from such formalities. Those who did observe them encountered prejudice from their own sex, who preferred male obstetricians (accoucheurs),[49] as well as strong opposition from doctors and surgeons resentful of all feminine interference in the medical field and openly contemptuous of professional inadequacies from which they were themselves by no means exempt. Obstetrical manuals relate in horrific detail the mutilations suffered by mothers and children at the hands of inexpert assistants:

D'une femme qui avait eu deux fâcheux accouchements, dans lesquels ses enfants avaient eu les bras et les jambes rompues, par la faute de la sage-femme et du chirurgien qui l'avaient accouchée

D'une femme qui mourut par l'ignorance d'un chirurgien qui lui avait violemment tiré la matrice, croyant que ce fût un corps étrange

D'une femme qui mourut dès le même jour qu'elle fut accouchée, sa sage-femme lui ayant fait trop de violence pour la délivrer de l'arrière-faix resté en sa matrice[50]

The ignorance and precipitation of these licensed torturers, abetted by lack of hygiene and antiseptics, were more than sufficient, as these same case histories indicate, to despatch hapless mothers into an early grave.

Women gave birth in a variety of postures: standing, kneeling, seated on specially pierced chairs such as those used at the main Paris hospital (Hôtel-Dieu), or lying on small beds appropriately known as 'lits de misère'.[51] They liked to have a candle lit nearby or a rose of Jericho placed in holy water, the burning of the former and the opening of the latter supposedly corresponding to the gradual dilation of the cervix.[52] Village women had faith in the efficacy of perching on a heated cauldron or putting their husband's hat on their nether regions to quicken the process.[53] Immediately after delivery the mother would have her stomach encased for a few hours in the skin of a freshly-killed sheep or hare and then bandaged, a practice designed to assist stretched organs to return to normal size.[54] Enemas to clean the entrails and fomentations to remove unwanted milk completed the post-natal programme.[55]

As soon as the mother had recovered some of her strength she set about preparing to entertain well-wishers who, in accordance with tradition, would come to offer felicitations and bring gifts. The fine linen and coverlets which had perhaps been used for the similar reception that followed the wedding night would once again drape the bed on which she was laid, resplendent in her best clothes, to acknowledge the greetings of callers. In bourgeois households female neighbours sat for long hours round the bed feasting, drinking and exchanging gossip, and often returned to repeat the process on several successive days. Husbands groaned over the expense, satirists condemned the display of luxury and doctors warned of the strain on the mother's constitution.[56] But the 'abuse' was a very ancient one, and therefore eminently respectable in the eyes of those who clung to it.

Frenchwomen were remarked for the rapidity with which they rose to their feet again and resumed their former pattern of existence after a confinement. Those with whom Sir John Lauder conversed on his travels through France in the mid-1660s were surprised to learn that his Scots countrywomen kept to their bed for a month when they themselves were used to rising after a week, or at most a fortnight if childbirth had left them very feeble.[57] Swifter recovery still was imposed upon the woman whose pregnancy could not be openly avowed. The mistresses of kings and courtiers, diplomatically declared 'unwell' when their flowing gowns no longer sufficed to hide their fault from prying eyes, would give birth in a morning and within three or four days – some said within the space of an afternoon – would show their wan face once more to the world.[58]

Though the Catholic woman, unlike her Jewish counterpart, was not officially held by her religion to be in a state of impurity after giving birth, public opinion required her to undergo a ceremony of purification before she began to circulate again in society. On the occasion of the *relevailles*, as the ceremony was called, she presented herself at the parish church to hear mass, accompanied by the attendant midwife to hand over for ritual burning on Ash Wednesday the bonnet used to cover the child's head after baptism. When mass ended, while the mother knelt before the altar with a lighted candle in her hand, the priest took up a large loaf of bread which she had donated, blessed it and broke it into several pieces, one of which she was given to eat, the rest being divided between the relatives at home and all those present in the congregation. The mother kissed the priest's stole, beneath which her head had been bowed during his reading of the Purification of Mary from the second chapter of Saint Luke's Gospel, and, absolved, cleansed, exhorted, went on her way rejoicing. So vital was churching to the contemporary way of thinking that if a woman died in childbirth the ceremony was performed over her coffin or over a female substitute so that she might not be denied the sight of God in the next world.[59]

The mother's most important obligation, to become acquainted with her newborn child, had frequently to be deferred because of her refusal to breast-feed and the necessity to employ a wet-nurse who found it convenient to carry out her appointed duties in her own domicile. Right from the start the elementary bond created by the mother's nourishing and holding of her child was severed, and the emotional ties that would normally develop from physical contact were correspondingly handicapped. By contrast the constant physical proximity of the *nourrice* and her charge, plus the fact of her social inferiority, removed inhibitions created by etiquette and favoured the establishment of lasting and intimate relations. Members of the bourgeoisie such as Descartes and Racine expressed their gratitude to former *nourrices* by the payment of life pensions.[60] Louis XIV's *nourrice* received the signal honour of permission to be amongst the first to enter the royal bed-chamber in the morning to plant a kiss on her erstwhile nursling.[61] *Nourrices* of princes and princesses prolonged their services to the point of accompanying the latter to foreign lands at the time of their marriage.[62] The *gouvernante*, who took over or supplemented the care provided by the *nourrice* once the weaning stage was past, inspired similar attachments and affectionate memories. Louis XIII, whose first maternal caress was withheld until six months after his birth, called his *gouvernante* Mme de Montglat by the significant name of 'Mamanga'.[63] Mme de Maintenon, who received but two maternal kisses in her lifetime, readily exerted herself to educate and perform menial tasks for her own *gouvernante* Mme Delisle.[64] The Duchesse de Montpensier and Charlotte de Bavière, for all their wilful intolerance of certain *gouvernantes*, came across others after their own heart to whose virtues and devotion they paid tribute.[65] Fiction faithfully reflected the closeness of these quasi-maternal relationships. Seventeenth-century literature represents girls and grown women as turning instinctively to their *nourrice* or *gouvernante* for comfort, advice and practical assistance in moments of stress, and receiving them all unstintingly. Mothers are cast for preference in the role of jealous rivals and general obstacles to filial happiness.[66]

The initial affection and ascendancy that the mother forfeited by opting out of her prime responsibility for her baby's physical welfare stood to be regained if she actively interested herself in the child's education. Few mothers were so heedless that they did not attempt to inculcate, however sporadically, into their children simple precepts tending to enable them to comport themselves with integrity and efficiency in the estate for which they were destined in adult life. Mothers of sons were noteworthy for their zeal in furnishing moral guidance, encouragement and such formal instruction as their own rudimentary education permitted. Jean Rou, a Protestant advocate in the Paris Parlement, recalls that he found his lessons so difficult when he was first sent as a day-pupil to college at the age of five 'que ma mère, qui avait pour moi des complaisances que j'admire encore, quand j'y songe, se donnait la peine, pour me donner courage, d'apprendre elle-même toutes mes leçons de compagnie avec moi, me promettant mille "bon-bons", comme on parle, en cas que je fusse le premier à venir à bout de notre innocente tâche'.[67] In a parallel Catholic household the fertile wife of Jacques de Fontainemarie is praised by one of her grateful sons for having laboured incessantly to educate her numerous offspring:

Dès que je fus en état de profiter des premières instructions qu'on donne aux enfants, ma mère prit elle-même le soin de m'apprendre à prier Dieu; ensuite elle m'enseigna le catéchisme, après quoi elle me montra à lire, et enfin ce fut elle qui m'apprit le commencement du rudiment. Jamais mère n'a eu plus d'attention qu'elle à l'éducation de sa famille et il y en a peu qui en ayent eu autant; elle n'a rien négligé ni rien épargné pour nous rendre tous honnêtes gens et elle a travaillé dans tous les temps avec une application singulière et une tendresse qui ne s'est jamais démentie à nous inspirer des sentiments de religion, d'honneur et de probité.[68]

But the efforts of model mothers like Mme de Fontainemarie were apt to be brusquely curtailed by the custom of removing boys from the care of women as soon as they were deemed physically capable of fending for themselves, lest they should grow up 'soft' and molly-coddled. At the age of approximately seven years[69] they were placed under the direction of male tutors or sent away as boarders to a college or military academy to acquire skills and sciences of which the average mother had little knowledge. Beyond the training-schools lay marriage, and the prospect for the mother of sharing her influence or seeing it effaced by that of another woman.

Girls seemed much better placed to enjoy maternal solicitude and attention in respect of their education. No stigma attached to their remaining in the parental home and being trained by their mother, regarded as their natural instructress. However examples quoted in Chapter 2 have shown mothers who could have made time to educate their daughters either abandoning that responsibility to outsiders, or treating them in a manner likely to engender the opposite of confidence and intimacy. It was not just that mothers resorted to outside help because of a modest awareness of their own intellectual limitations; or that they had been conditioned to pin their hopes for the family's social elevation on their male progeny, whose education and establishment in a career were given top priority. Daughters were an encumbrance to a mother with a busy social life, not least because their age betrayed hers and their youthful freshness distracted admiration from her mellower charms. In an epoch when a woman was considered past her prime at twenty and half way to her dotage at thirty, vain mothers went to ridiculous and extraordinary lengths to belie the involuntary testimony to their age constituted by adult offspring. Learning that her daugher had inadvertently confessed at court to being twenty-seven years old, the Duchesse de Vitry made herself a laughing-stock by promptly appearing there in an ostentatiously youthful *toilette*, 'toute couverte de rubans couleur de rose, la gorge ouverte, disant qu'elle n'avait que trente-deux ans, et que quand on avait de grands enfants à cet âge-là on ne laissait pas de porter des couleurs'.[70] Rather than wait till the situation was past remedying, far-sighted mothers were careful to send their daughters away from home to relatives and convents as soon as was decently possible.[71] The Comtesse de Murat's mother, 'trop jeune pour voir croître auprès d'elle une fille qui aurait si bien marqué son âge', despatched her to a grandmother for rearing and subsequently to a nunnery.[72] The convent became abused to such an extent as a repository for daughters whose presence embarrassed that dramatists inveighed against the practice in comedies satirising coquettish mothers.[73] Even when entry into a cloister was strictly for educational purposes and not a pretext for permanent imprisonment, the arrangement still meant parting more or less completely for a number of years, during which any rift between mother and daughter had ample opportunity to widen. At the end of that time the daughter would be ready to pass forever from under her parents' jurisdiction to that of a husband and to set up her own separate household.

In the absence of mutual understanding and sympathy, the growth of which so many circumstances contributed to impede, there remained always the legal rights and the authority which the mother possessed over her children. Her consent, as well as that of the father, was officially required for the marriage of a minor, and if she refused it a *sommation respectueuse* had to be made to her in the same way, on pain of disinheritance.[74] When her husband predeceased her she almost automatically received tutelage over any minor children of the marriage. Recommendations in his will or similar documents often tended towards the strengthening of her position as head of the family after his demise. The Comte de Souvigny stipulated that the dowry of 20 000 *livres* bequeathed to his daughter should be reduced by half if she married without her mother's consent, and that if either of his sons committed the same fault they should be deprived of their inheritance.[75] The ageing Fortin de la Hoguette addressed a touching exhortation in his *Testament* to the children whom he felt that his younger wife would shortly be left alone to bring up: 'Elle est si bonne et si avisée, que je ne fais point de doute qu'à mon défaut vous ne trouviez en elle seule une affection de père et de mère. Si cela arrive, comme ses bons offices se redoubleront envers vous, si vous désirez que la bénédiction de Dieu vous accompagne, vous réunirez alors aussi toutes les puissances de votre âme, pour lui rendre à elle seule tout l'honneur et tout le respect que vous nous devez à tous deux en commun.'[76] The mother's powers were, however, neither as extensive nor as firmly established as those of the father, and could normally be overruled or replaced by the latter. In 1601 the moralist Pierre Charron published the loaded statement that since the mother was in subjection to her husband she could not have personal control over her children.[77] In the 1660s government legislation concerning mixed marriages between Catholics and Protestants capitalised on this idea to decree that children born of Catholic fathers should automatically be baptised and raised in the Catholic faith, regardless of the wishes of the Protestant mother.[78] The legal guardianship of the mother over her children ceased as soon as she remarried, though the widower in an equivalent position maintained his tutelary rights.[79] Obviously it was just as easy, too, for a husband to limit his wife's authority by testamentary provisions as it was for him to reinforce it.[80] Even when he placed his offspring under his wife's control legal tribunals could quash his last wishes in this respect.[81] The legislators' preoccupation with ensuring male supremacy combined with the vagaries of a husband's dispositions to render maternal jurisdiction decidedly precarious.

The approach to child-bearing and -rearing in the seventeenth century can be seen to have encouraged between the mother and her children the same kind of distance, physical and emotional, as that prescribed between the mother and father. Pregnancy was not so much a private affair as a matter to be publicised in the minutest detail. Its frequent occurrence was calculated to diminish the mother's chances of being able to minister personally to the individual needs of each of her offspring, and to induce her to follow the lead given by women of fashion in handing babies over to social inferiors to be raised and nurtured. When the child succumbed as a result of an outsider's negligence, the mother was predisposed by the repetition of such events and the knowledge that a replacement would soon arrive not to upset herself unduly. When the child thrived on account of an outsider's devotion she, the real mother, risked becoming the outsider in her turn and having to re-establish her influence later in the face of strong competition from the teachers and marriage partners who monopolised her son's or daughter's attention in rapid succession. From the legal, in addition to the moral and emotional, points of view the mother was at a disadvantage in that her rights over her children – recourse to which would in any case be tantamount to confession of failure – were eclipsed by those of the father during his lifetime. After her partner's death, provided viduity was not abandoned, she obtained in this as in many other spheres a greater measure of freedom.

6
The Dissolution of Marriage

One of the greatest drawbacks of marriage, in the popular estimation, was the everlasting nature of the commitment. Whereas a lover could always be discarded for failing to please, a spouse had to be endured for the lifetime of torment that stretched between the two blissful days of the wedding and the funeral.[1] Needless to say the sceptics and the wags were guilty of exaggeration in suggesting that death alone released those unhappily locked in matrimony. In the first place their witticisms took no account of the marital discipline observed by the Protestant minority. Article 36 of the *Discipline Ecclésiastique* laid down by the first national synod in 1559 expressly recognised the right of a spouse whose partner was convicted of adultery to be set free from the alliance after reconciliation had proved impossible. Article 9 of the acts of the synod of 1562 went further, specifying that the injured party must obtain proof of a partner's guilt in the form of a magistrate's sentence and present it to the Consistory, which could then grant permission to remarry. The guilty party might also engage in matrimony a second time, but not before the innocent one had remarried or formally renounced remarriage, and not until public penance had been done.[2] In spite of the narrowness of the grounds on which divorce proceedings could be instigated and the number of conditions, time-consuming and sometimes humiliating, which had to be satisfied prior to embarkation on a second union, there was at least a clearly defined escape-hatch for both partners in a Protestant marriage broken by a fault common enough to give remedial measures a potentially broad sphere of application.

The position of the Catholic majority of the nation was more complex, and here the misogamists had a certain amount of justification for their grumbles. Adultery, with which the husband could formally charge the wife but not vice versa, did not liberate Catholic couples from their marriage vows, and divorce in the modern sense was not permitted before the Revolution. But legal substitutes existed to loosen or to break bonds which proved for some reason to be intolerable.

The first of these was the judicial separation. Separations were either of properties, or of properties and persons. The *séparation des biens*, which could operate from the start of marriage if a clause to that effect was inserted in the contract, protected a woman's fortune against a husband's indigence or prodigality. It gave her a free hand in the administration of her *meubles* and revenues from her *immeubles*, in respect of which she could appear before a legal tribunal and enter into engagements on behalf of third parties without her husband's consent.[3] The latter was, however, still needed if she wished to alienate her property.[4] An ordinance of 1673 required separations of goods to be made public in the case of bankers, merchants and businessmen so that creditors and other interested parties should not be defrauded.[5] Not that wives were inclined to make much secret of their plans to secure financial independence. Bussy-Rabutin was able to compile an impressive list of those who had taken the plunge or were poised to do so in 1686: 'Il y a bien des femmes qui se veulent séparer: mme de Fontenilles, mme de Saint-Géran, mme de Foix; mme de Poussé a déjà fait le saut; la marquise de Coislin et encore une douzaine d'autres; la plupart parce qu'elles font trop de dépenses. Les maris autrefois ne s'y opposaient pas, parce que les amants donnaient des jupes; présentement qu'ils veulent faire l'amour but à but, les maris grondent et n'ont pas d'ailleurs les talents qui font finir la dispute; ainsi les femmes aiment mieux se séparer.'[6] Bussy's conclusion that wives were driven to petition for a *séparation des biens* by an unwillingness to tolerate rebukes over their prodigality towards gallants who did not reciprocate seems an ironic reversal indeed of the reasons for which the procedure had originally been instituted. Separation in such cases was merely an outward manifestation of the deeper emotional rift between partners. Nevertheless it was an arrangement revocable by mutual consent and did not normally include any obligation to live apart, so that appearances could still be preserved.

The *séparation des corps* did not allow for similar ambiguities. It was obtainable chiefly in the event of physical or emotional cruelty on the husband's part or his installation of a mistress in the conjugal home. The effect of this separation was to free the wife from her obligation to cohabit with her husband, and it always implied a *séparation des biens*. The wife usually withdrew during the court hearing to a place of refuge – a convent or her parents' domicile – which might become her permanent residence thereafter.[7] Physical separation between husband and wife was regarded by the Church and by the law as an extremity arrived at only when all attempts to compose disputes had failed. In fashionable circles it rapidly became the vogue, as was seen in Chapter 4, and the successful petition for a *séparation des corps* must have had an air of rendering official that which had been practised unofficially for a number of years past. Aristocratic husbands treated the matter as a joke and even used it to pay their court to the king: 'M. de Ventadour a dit au roi qu'il était fort fâché que sa femme le trouvât plus laid que quand elle l'épousa, mais que ce n'était pas sa faute; que n'était pas beau qui voulait, et que si on pouvait se donner la figure qu'on voudrait, il serait fait tout comme sa Majesté.'[8] Their wives, however, were discouraged from following suit by loss of privileges. The Duchesse de Ventadour in question (Charlotte-Eléonore-Madeleine de La Mothe-Houdancourt) was put in a convent which she was forbidden to leave without an escort of four ladies nominated by the king. The breakaway spouse of the Marquis de Châtillon lost to the latter all but her wages as wardrobe mistress to Charlotte de Bavière and was obliged to forfeit to him their apartment in the Palais-Royal.[9] King and court asked of a wife only that she should maintain the semblance of a legal union for decorum's sake,[10] on which condition adulterous desires could be indulged at will.

Judicial separation ruled out the possibility of a second marriage until one of the partners died, since the original marriage was deemed still to subsist. For remarriage to take place during a partner's lifetime it was necessary to secure an annulment, which implied that no valid union had ever been contracted. Annulment was awarded on proven contravention of an impediment laid down by the Church or failure to fulfil a legal requirement. In trying to safeguard public morality by the erection of a substantial number of hurdles before matrimony, ecclesiastical and civil authorities in a sense defeated the purpose which these hurdles were intended to serve. It was relatively easy to unearth a certain formality that had supposedly gone unobserved at the time of the wedding, to 'remember' that an ecclesiastical dispensation had not been obtained for a prohibited degree of kinship, or to assert that a marriage had never been properly consummated, and so to rid oneself of a partner whose presence displeased. Doubtless the availability of annulment was vital to protect victims of coercion like Jeanne de Schomberg, a martyr to paternal ambition whose peremptory refusal in 1618 to consummate marriage with the stupid and ugly Comte de Brissac resulted in nullification on the grounds of the husband's impotence.[11] The very same case, however, illustrates the abuses to which the procedure laid itself open. Brissac's lack of virility was made a pretext for invalidating the marriage when it was common knowledge that his unwilling bride had not permitted him to perform his conjugal duties.

Early in the century the facility with which annulments were being obtained, particularly on the grounds of physical incapacity, had given cause for alarm. The surgeon Charles Guillemeau in his *Traité des abus qui se commettent sur les procédures de l'impuissance des hommes et des femmes* (1620) describes the charge as 'aujourd'hui . . . tant fréquente et commune, qu'il semble que nos palais [de justice] et plaidoyers ne retentissent d'autres plaintes',[12] and forcefully condemns those women who applied for the infamous *congrès* to substantiate their accusations. No one knew the precise origins of the *congrès*, but it was thought to date back to the late sixteenth century[13] when years of religious, political and social upheaval had left the moral fibre of France profoundly weakened. It involved nothing less than an inspection of the plaintiff's and the defendant's genitals by doctors and midwives, and a performance of the sexual act before the same audience. The semi-public nature of the ordeal was guaranteed to cause frigidity in the boldest and to produce results that made a mockery of justice. The Marquis de Langey, who dismally failed the test in 1658, belied the aspersions which his first wife had cast upon his manhood by fathering seven children with a second wife. His first wife also remarried and had three children.[14] The *congrès* inspired revulsion in a generation not easily shocked[15] and was abolished in 1677, though the Marquise de Gesvres tried to resurrect it in a famous lawsuit of the year 1712.[16]

The wife was not therefore completely disarmed in the event of an uncongenial marriage, having at her disposal means of artificially terminating her conjugal duties and obligations without waiting for the natural intervention of death. The fact remained that a husband's demise had the great advantages of removing in one fell swoop all ambiguities in the wife's position, maintaining her social prestige and granting her undisputed independence. If the deceased's household and business affairs had been properly managed she was also endowed with some solid financial assets, which she did her best to increase.[17]

There were a large number of widows in seventeenth-century France. The numerous wars with which the period was fraught cost the nation's men dear. During campaigns in Germany in 1644 the provinces of Burgundy, Bresse and Berry alone lost, apart from the unmentioned rank and file, nine hundred noblemen whose widows magnanimously rejected a decree permitting them to pass on their late husband's name and privileges to a second partner.[18] Civil strife in turn took a heavy toll of lives. The spectacle of 'beaucoup de pauvres veuves . . . chargées d'enfants' amongst the emaciated peasants who dragged themselves from the devastated countryside to the towns for sustenance was commonplace in the terrible years of the Fronde.[19] In peacetime the habit of settling personal quarrels and so-called affairs of honour in combats where seconds as well as the chief protagonists fought to kill plunged many a wife into premature viduity.[20] The practice of marrying girls to husbands many years their senior also helped to swell the ranks of widowed women. Marie de la Noue began at the age of thirteen to render her famous Protestant name even more so by getting through three successive husbands – a quinquagenarian, an octogenarian and a septuagenarian – within a couple of decades.[21]

Whatever the way in which her husband died, and whatever her private feelings on the subject, the widow was obliged to mourn in the grand style. For the first forty days after the tragedy she was supposed to remain in a room hung with black draperies where she received those who came to pay their respects and offer condolences.[22] During this *quarantaine* she did well to relieve herself of any inclination to shed floods of tears, tear hair or gnash teeth, for the seventeenth century unanimously condemned noisy public manifestations of vidual grief as sheer hypocrisy.[23] When she emerged from seclusion a black crêpe *bandeau* worn low down on the forehead after the manner of the nun's head-dress evoked her recent loss.[24] Black was the accepted symbol of mourning, though Richelieu's merrily widowed niece, the Duchesse d'Aiguillon, set the fashion for wearing all sorts of colours except green.[25] In 1674 the *Mercure Galant* reported that widows were adopting an all-white attire within the home 'pour ne point porter de bandeau'.[26] Mourning costume was paid for by the husband's heirs out of money derived from his personal property and included not only the widow's clothes but appropriate livery for her domestics and carriage draperies if the deceased was of high rank. Since no sum was set aside for such expenses in the case of widows 'du bas peuple' they were dispensed from wearing exterior marks of their affliction.[27] Under both customary and written law official mourning lasted for twelve months, known as the *an vidual* or *de grand deuil*, after which the widow hastened to cast off her weeds, if indeed she had persisted in wearing them for the full term demanded by propriety. Widows like Mme de Nogent and Mme de Navailles who preserved the *bandeau* until death were remarked as belonging to a species long since extinct.[28]

The widow could be forgiven for not prolonging her sorrow indefinitely since reflection on her new position revealed a somewhat enviable state of affairs. True, she had lost a partner, but at the same time she had lost a master, without forfeiting any of the prestige that attached to the status of the married, as opposed to the celibate, woman. Privileges which her late husband had enjoyed through his headship of the household, his employment or his rank would often be continued in her person. The tutelage of minor children was usually granted to her as of right and her authority within the family benefited from being no longer shared.[29] If her husband had possessed an office during his lifetime, for example in the financial sector, in one of the sovereign courts or a royal household, she profited from the various tax exemptions and honours attached thereto;[30] and if she sold the office she received half the sale price, the other half going to the husband's heirs.[31] Where the husband had been engaged in a trade she was normally permitted to carry on the business for the duration of her viduity.[32] The nobleman's widow, provided that she refrained from remarriage to a commoner, retained aristocratic privileges, while the noblewoman who had married beneath her station regained the privileges of her rank which were reputed to be dormant during her marriage.[33]

Steps were taken to safeguard the widow's material interests by her option, under customary law, to renounce the marital *communauté*, and by a number of gains which, under both customary and written law, accrued to her as the surviving partner. The decision to accept or to renounce the *communauté des biens* was a fairly reliable gauge of the care exercised by the husband in his administration of community property. Acceptance meant that the widow would be held responsible for payment of debts contracted by her partner prior to, as well as during, the marriage.[34] Renunciation enabled her to evade an obligation which his mismanagement or dissipations might have rendered extremely onerous. Three months were accorded to her in which to produce a 'bon et loyal' inventory of her husband's property, plus a standard period of forty days during which to opt for or against the *communauté*, the latter decision requiring legal registration.[35] To stop the widow from fraudulently withholding or concealing goods, *Coutumes* stipulated that renunciation entitled her to take only certain personal effects – a set of clothes, a bed, sometimes jewellery, furniture, crockery or a prayer book[36] – in addition to her dower.

The dower represented a reward for the care and attachment that the wife was presumed to have shown for her husband, as well as a kind of payment for her sexual surrender. Some of the older *Coutumes* specified with quaint forthrightness that 'la femme gagne son douaire au coucher'[37] or 'ayant mis le pied au lit',[38] but the later ones referred more modestly to the nuptial benediction as the moment at which the dower came into operation.[39] The amount of the dower could either be set forth in the marriage contract (*douaire conventionnel* or *préfix*) or prescribed by the relevant *Coutume* (*douaire coutumier*). The latter type of dower assigned to the widow usufruct of one half,[40] or sometimes one third,[41] of the husband's *immeubles*, on condition that she kept them in good repair and continued to pay any necessary dues to the overlord.[42] Provision for the widow to choose the *douaire coutumier* in preference to the *préfix* if she found it more profitable was generally made either in the contract or in the actual *Coutume*.[43] So vital was the dower considered to be that its payment took precedence over that of all other debts with which the *communauté* was encumbered.[44] The dower was forfeit, however, if a wife was convicted of debauchery during marriage or viduity, or if she had left her husband against his wishes and without just cause.[45]

Over and above benefits awarded by the law the widow received any advantages that the marriage contract stipulated should come to her despite renunciation, for example her dowry, legacies acquired during marriage, or what was known as the *préciput conventionnel*, consisting of either money or personal effects, or both.[46] She might also be entitled to come into possession of the *don mutuel*, a reciprocal and exactly equal donation of goods which partners made by a special contract, on the understanding that the surviving one should benefit.[47] But the *don mutuel* operated as a rule only when there were no children at the dissolution of the marriage[48] and was sometimes incompatible with tenure of the dower.[49]

Under the names of *gains nuptiaux* and *gains de survie* written law endowed the widow with benefits parallel to those obtained under customary law. The equivalent of the dower was the *augment de dot*, which consisted ordinarily of usufruct of the deceased husband's property in proportion to the nature and amount of the dowry brought to the marriage by the wife.[50] Assessed in the same way, the right of *bagues et joyaux* granted the widow of certain provinces such as Dauphiné and Lyonnais an additional payment, originally in kind, later in cash, on a par with the *préciput* of customary law.[51] Provided that she was legally emancipated her dowry was restored to her; otherwise her father had the use of it but was obliged to reconstitute it if she remarried. Whether she had brought a dowry or not, a certain sum of money was allocated for her upkeep during the vidual year.[52] Written law prohibited partners from making any donations to each other except in the form of bequests in a will. The surviving partner always inherited from the other as long as there were no heirs to claim the inheritance. If heirs subsisted and the surviving partner was impoverished then he or she obtained a quarter of the goods of the deceased. Finally the payment of all these gains received the same preferential treatment as under the *Coutumes*, and was liable to forfeiture in similar circumstances.[53]

Liberated thus from material worries, in theory at least, the widow was expected to lead henceforth a pious and withdrawn existence devoted to three principal tasks: the rearing of her husband's children, the cultivation of his memory and her own personal sanctification. It was scarcely conceivable that worldly pomps and vanities could hold any further attraction for one literally bereft of her better half and since gathered to the bosom of Christ, the celestial husband who would never abandon her.[54] The widow who hurled herself into a round of pleasures was reproved for being dead in soul if not in body. The 'true' widow was as the chaste turtle-dove, perpetually mourning for a lost mate. She imitated the modest March violet, shrinking from the glances and the contact of the crowd. Like the aromatic lamp burning more sweetly after the extinction of its flame, she signalled her presence only by the odour of her sanctity.[55]

The moralists' persuasive imagery appealed to women whose

heart was genuinely broken, as well as inspiring those who had reasons for wishing the world to believe it so. Many throughout the century were prompted to retire temporarily or permanently into a cloister after a husband's death. In some families the gesture was a pious tradition: several wives of the great Arnauld household joined their celibate relatives at Port-Royal as soon as viduity freed them from their marital commitments.[56] Elsewhere it permitted the realisation of a previously thwarted yearning for the religious life and fulfilled a profound desire to be of service to humanity: Mme de Chantal, saintly collaborator with François de Sales in the creation of the Visitandines, Mme de Belle-Isle, foundress of the Filles du Calvaire, and Mme de Lestonnac, instigator of the teaching order of Notre-Dame, were just three of the most illustrious widows who found their true vocation in this way.[57] In the case of the Duchesse de Montmorency a long and rigorous immurement proved the means of winning that universal acknowledgement and respect which a hitherto unremarkable existence and a husband decapitated for treason seemed likely to deny her.[58] Retreats were also dictated by sheer necessity. The installation of Mme de Sablé at Port-Royal in 1656 was motivated by acute financial difficulties resulting from lawsuits against her children over vidual dues.[59] The future Mme de Maintenon, credited with marrying Scarron precisely to avoid the convent, was obliged to enter one when he died in 1660 bequeathing her debts of 22 000 *francs*.[60] In 1694 the Maréchale d'Humières, rendered penniless by her husband's demise, was forced to tread the same path.[61] For women left destitute the convent had the double advantage of allowing urgent economies to be made while saving face in public.

Without visibly severing relations with the world by boarding in a convent or taking the veil, some widows lived quasi-eremitical lives in their own homes, forsaking all but indispensable public engagements and voluntarily limiting their horizons to domestic affairs, prayer and the performance of good works. It was a favourite compromise for women prevented by a sense of responsibility towards young children from pursuing their salvation full-time in a religious order. The decision took moral courage, for many were still sufficiently young and attractive to inspire proposals of remarriage. Henri de Campion's mother, widowed at thirty-three and 'fort aimable', refused 'plusieurs personnages considérables et riches' in order to dedicate herself to the education of her five children.[62] Mme de Sales, wife of a president in the Bordeaux Parlement, preserved her viduity for sixty-one years from the age of twenty-five, 'afin de pouvoir, disait-elle à ceux qui la sollicitaient à un second lit, élever ses enfants et les rendre accommodés par son soin et ménagement'.[63] A Breton *châtelaine*, Mme de Brézal, won renown throughout the province no less for her persistence in viduity from the age of twenty-two in favour of an only son than for her charitable attention to housing the elderly poor on her estates and educating young gentlewomen whom eager parents pressed upon her.[64] A comparable portrait of self-abnegation, energy and devoutness emerges from a memorialist's obituary of the Marquise de Lavardin, who was laid to a well-earned rest in 1694: 'étant demeurée veuve à l'âge de vingt-deux ans, et n'ayant qu'un fils, elle n'avait pas voulu se remarier pour l'amour de lui, l'avait fait élever avec grand soin, avait par son économie rétabli sa maison, qui était ruinée, et l'avait ensuite enrichie par la succession de son frère ... Elle avait couronné cette vie si louable selon le monde par beaucoup d'aumônes et de piété pendant les dernières années de sa vie.'[65] Lacking the glamour of the retreat within convent walls, such existences nevertheless demanded the same resolution, the same ability to combat temptation, the same spirit of sacrifice perpetually renewed.

Despite numerous and outstanding proofs of virtue and continence given by individual widows, collectively they were an object of suspicion to society. Their sexual experience and their freedom from the masculine yoke at an early, or comparatively early, age made them a butt for gossip and slander. The efforts of religious and lay moralists over the centuries to persuade them to lead sequestered lives already denotes a concession to current prejudices. Literature from ancient times onwards had pandered to public malice by representing widows as skittish, hypocritical, and utterly ruthless in pursuit of a replacement for their deceased spouse. The seventeenth century duly brought to the common fund its own variations on Petronius's evergreen tale of the Widow of Ephesus,[66] suitably modernised to become the *veuve à la mode*, prostrate with grief when the curtain rises but planning marriage with her late husband's heir by the time it falls.[67] Alerted by the moralists' admonitions and by the satirists' jibes, writers of letters and memoirs in turn scrutinised widowed neighbours and acquaintances and did not hesitate to corroborate the popular image of their conduct. Women confided to friends and to posterity their disbelief in the sincerity of vidual tears. Mme de Maintenon ironically insinuated that Mme de Lionne's laments and prolonged sojourn in a convent were due less to the recent demise of her husband, Louis XIV's minister, than to the fact that her family opposed her departure from the disguised prison to which her notorious debauchery had forced him to relegate her.[68] The Duchesse de Montpensier, at odds with Mme de Nogent, under-mined the latter's claim to be an inconsolable widow by asserting that husband and wife were on the point of separation before his fortuitous death in battle.[69] Masculine writers were more con-cerned with exposing the sexual licence of widows, which they themselves had often exploited in a mis-spent youth. The Maréchal de Bassompierre divulged that his legendary vigour had once deserted him after five consecutive days and six nights occupied in charitably relieving the frustration of a bereaved teenage bride.[70] Bussy-Rabutin confessed that his youthful innocence had suc-cumbed to the advances of a certain deprived widow of Guise.[71] Tallemant, who also had first-hand experience of the 'frailty' of widows, amused himself by repeating scabrous rumours about the Duchesse d'Aiguillon's ability to satisfy the lust of both her uncle and her perverted friend Mme du Vigean, and cited the Duchesse de Rohan's libertine viduity as being responsible for the contem-porary loss of respect for her sex.[72] Variously accused of affecta-tion, infidelity, coquetry and licentiousness, the widow paid in terms of reputation a substantial price for her envied freedom.

There was one obvious means by which she could both silence malicious speculation about her morals and abandon with honour an allegedly irksome chastity: remarriage. Yet this was the one course upon which everything conspired to prevent her from embarking.

Simultaneously with the loss of her husband a woman gained, in the eyes of the Church, a second virginity which, though not of such pure alloy as the first, was infinitely preferable to the 'state of sin' in which the payment of the conjugal debt had forced her to exist. Ideally she was required to remain in this superior state and to channel earthly affections towards the Divine Spouse with whom she could hope for reunion at life's end.[73] Bearing in mind, however, its own precept that to marry was better than to lust, the Church did not expressly forbid second marriages, being content to stress that continence represented the greater virtue.[74]

Where the Church merely issued a directive, the law saw fit to impose sanctions. The latter were designed to shield a husband's memory against the insult of his widow's hasty remarriage, to prevent misalliances and to protect existing offspring. Second nuptials within the vidual year were viewed with particular severity under written law, influenced by ancient Roman traditions: the Parlements of Toulouse and Grenoble deprived widows in such circumstances of all matrimonial gains such as the *augment de dot* and forbade them to inherit from children of the first marriage.[75] Unions with social inferiors were discouraged in some *Coutumes*, as was seen above, by loss of noble prerogatives, while the non-noble widow of a nobleman had sometimes to renounce aristocratic privileges on remarriage.[76] Article 454 of the Brittany *Coutume*, inspired by Article 182 of the Ordinance of Blois, obliged a widow remarrying with a domestic to forfeit her dower, and where there were any children of a previous marriage, rendered her legally incapable of disposing of her property.[77] Special precautions were taken to ensure the material and moral well-being of offspring of the first marriage. The amount of property transferable to a second husband was limited, in Article 279 of the Paris *Coutume* for example, to a part of the wife's goods not exceeding the smallest portion due to any one of his step-children. Certain *Coutumes* ruled that the widow had to leave ownership of all gains and advantages acquired during the first marriage to the issue of that marriage.[78] In rare instances where the *don mutuel* was permissible despite the existence of children it was revocable when a second marriage took place.[79] Remarriage also incurred immediate loss of tutelage over minors, for whom a replacement guardian had to be provided.[80] Confronted with such a barrage of penalties the widow could only draw the intended conclusion that in entering upon a second engagement she was wronging her late husband, his children and herself.

Society had its own method of giving the matrimonially-minded widow a guilty conscience. Her wedding night was a signal for the local scapegraces to band together, arm themselves with anything that would make a noise – drums, trumpets, cauldrons, pans, basins, guns – and proceed to create uproar outside the newly-weds' house until paid money to go away. The *charivari*, as it was called, sometimes lasted for several days[81] and gave rise to acts of violence. Homes were forcibly entered and strewn with horns, the symbol of cuckoldry; couples were insulted in the nuptial chamber;

shots were exchanged between the intruders and the victims' relatives, wounding uninvolved bystanders.[82] Such incidents, together with a growing habit of inflicting unwelcome serenades on all kinds of newly-weds deemed to merit public mockery (because of an age discrepancy, especially), prompted civil and religious authorities to react with bans and excommunications. The result was that *charivaris* continued unabated.[83]

In all the various situations in which a wife might find herself when the marriage bond was relaxed or broken the same trait is discernible: society's uneasiness over her acquisition of independence. The seventeenth century recognised the injustice of forcing a woman to continue to associate her property and her person with a husband who abused his rights over either or both, but refused to release her entirely from his authority if she obtained a separation, and waived her obligation of eternal fidelity only upon proof that no valid marriage had ever been contracted. When death rendered impossible any continuation of the husband's physical authority attempts were made to prolong at least his moral authority beyond the grave. Widows were urged to perform promptly the Christian equivalent of suttee, to chain themselves to the memory of the deceased and to bury themselves in seclusion and pious works. Rejection of an emotional death in favour of remarriage was punished with sanctions and humiliations. A new master might be acquired thereby, but this advantage was outweighed by uncertainty as to the potential ignominies which a wife might commit to the detriment of her husband's memory or his children in the euphoria of a second union.

In some way or other woman had to be kept on a lead, though jurists and moralists always spoke chivalrously in terms of protecting female weakness. But what of this famous weakness when it came to the necessity of earning her daily bread?

7

Women at Work I

That a woman should earn her keep by homemaking, as had countless generations of her sex, seemed as natural in the seventeenth century as that she should wear skirts and bear children. Expertise in housewifery, 'la plus utile et honorable science et occupation de la femme',[1] was the cornerstone of her education, and those with loftier aspirations were rapidly recalled to 'leurs aiguilles et leurs laines'.[2] However this Golden Age vision of the female, seated at the hearth tranquilly plying needle or distaff while her menfolk ventured into the outside world to procure the family's sustenance, glossed over certain harsh realities. Not every woman had a man to help support her. A substantial number of the population were widowed in their prime and urged by public opinion to remain so. Economic necessity, unwillingness to relinquish a husband's flourishing enterprise, concern to avoid an idleness propitious to the invasion of painful memories, might well induce a woman in this position to undertake some outside work or business. In the case of spinsters who had no private income starvation was the simple alternative to obtaining paid employment. Even married women, who seemed the best placed of the three groups, were often driven for reasons of finance or prestige to occupy themselves with other than strictly domestic chores, though these, when done conscientiously, were apt to provide more than sufficient occupation for both body and mind.

For the fashionable noblewoman the necessity to earn a living was a vulgar fact of life contemplated in the persons of her social inferiors rather than experienced at first hand. Court ladies had a reputation for being able to muster just enough energy to perform their elaborate toilet, after spending most of the day sleeping off the effects of the previous night's round of pleasures.[3] Nevertheless life in the shadow of the monarch was not entirely one of elegant inertia. The woman who wished to distinguish herself from the crowd, an ambition that became strongly advisable when Louis XIV intimated that he took as a personal insult lack of

97

assiduity around his person,[4] would endeavour to signal her zeal by securing a post in the household of the queen or some other female member of the royal family. If unmarried she hoped for nomination as a *fille d'honneur* or *dame d'atours*, the latter always styled 'Madame' whether single or not. If married or widowed she aimed to be chosen as principal *femme de chambre, dame du palais,*[5] *dame d'atours, gouvernante* of the maids of honour or the royal children, *dame du lit,*[6] *dame d'honneur* or *surintendante.*[7] These posts were the object of fierce competition.[8] They carried eye-catching wages and pensions, without which the luxurious mode of living at court was impossible, plus all manner of occasional gratifications in cash and in kind. In Henri IV's reign the Dauphin's *gouvernante* was entitled to keep his silver plate on retirement from her functions.[9] Her counterpart under Louis XIV, along with the *dames d'honneur* of the queen, Dauphine and Duchesse de Bourgogne, received every New Year's Day a purse full of silver.[10] The privileges attached to such offices were no less inviting. Apart from enjoying the tax immunities granted to members of royal households generally, the female retinue of queens and princesses rode in royal carriages, dined in royal company and, depending upon a particular individual's function, slept in the royal bedroom.[11] The queen's *surintendante*, or in her absence the *dame d'honneur*, exercised effective control over the selection and suspension of those who filled subordinate posts in the household, a control underlined by her solemn reception of oaths of allegiance from incomers.[12] Numerous occasions arose in this way to advance relatives and clients, or to thwart enemies, thereby strengthening the position of the attendant and her family at court. Privileges were jealously guarded, a phenomenon observable in all sections of contemporary French society, and appeals were regularly lodged with the king by disgruntled *surintendantes* or *dames d'honneur* anxious to prevent encroachments on their duties.[13]

The chief attraction of serving in a royal household was doubtless that of easier access to the powers in the land. The attendant's dutiful presence at the most intimate moments of her employers' physical existence often preluded an emotional expansiveness on the part of royal mistresses, not to mention masters, which made her a power in her own right. Of Marie de Médicis's entourage her *dame d'atours*, Léonora Galigaï, alone possessed the privilege of one or two hours' private confabulation before the royal bedtime, and used them to further the interests of her husband Concino Concini and their friends.[14] Marie-Thérèse's good graces were won at the price of abasement before her ugly and haughty *femme de chambre* Molina.[15] Louis XIV's daughter-in-law, the withdrawn Dauphine de Bavière, made no secret of the fact that she was approachable only though her *femme de chambre* Bessola, 'l'unique dépositaire de ses pensées, de ses réflexions et de sa conduite'.[16] Mme de Maintenon, who had herself risen spectacularly from the position of *gouvernante* of the royal bastards to that of uncrowned queen of France, confided in Nanon Balbien to the extent that a duchess thought it worthwhile to bribe the former maidservant to obtain a coveted court post.[17]

The service of the great had its risks and its snags. The notorious capriciousness of royal employers and their susceptibility to outside influence rendered existence in their neighbourhood extremely insecure. Those who lacked the necessary suppleness or subtlety were prone to rapid falls from grace. Marie de Hautefort, *dame d'atours* and long-standing favourite of Anne d'Autriche, who had once been entrusted with a delicate mission to save her mistress's honour, was disgraced in 1639, then virtually exiled from court in 1644 for her intransigent refusal to comply with the policies of Richelieu and Mazarin.[18] In 1664 a similar fate overtook Mme de Navailles, *gouvernante* of the maids of honour, when, after rejecting Louis XIV's proposals to 's'accommoder à ses volontés avec quelques honnêtes apparences', she barred the amorous monarch's access to her charges by means of iron grilles.[19] With lesser fry employers did not stop to parley. A chambermaid who ventured to speak to Anne d'Autriche in favour of rebel Paris at the outset of the Fronde was ejected from her post without delay.[20] Another chambermaid's imprudent confession that she had married for love earned her a summary dismissal from Louis XIV's bizarre cousin the Duchesse de Montpensier, who professed an aversion for that passion.[21]

To the uncertainties of preserving royal goodwill were added the physical discomforts and the disagreeable duties. Ordinary waiting-women were commonly allotted whatever lodgings happened to be available after their superiors had accommodated themselves, regardless of whether they were properly ventilated or heated.[22] Meals might be a makeshift affair consisting of the remnants of the mistress's supper, disputed with those who had served it.[23] Hours were long, since retirement for the night could not be contemplated before the lengthy ritual of the mistress's disrobing and bedding had been accomplished, and attendance at the reverse process early next morning had to be contrived despite the irresistible urge to sleep.[24] Etiquette demanded that subordinates should remain standing in the presence of their masters and mistresses.[25] On occasions when permission was granted to kneel[26] or to sit on the floor or a low seat to converse with a great lady, those favoured found the alternative postures less comfortable for their muscles and their pride than keeping on their feet.

The obligation to accompany a mistress everywhere might involve anything from exposure to the elements to confrontation with a dissected corpse. Ladies-in-waiting were expected to be able to participate, on horseback wherever possible, in the great hunts for which French monarchs showed an unwavering passion, and had to school themselves to paint expressions of pleasure and admiration on faces worn with tiredness and lashed by wind and rain.[27] From time to time affairs of state or the itinerant urge which had possessed his forebears would prompt the king to promenade his wife, the ladies of the court and their retinues around the various outposts of the realm, making them suffer all the usual inconveniences that beset the seventeenth-century traveller: roads that became mud-bogs in winter, dustbowls in summer; beds hurriedly composed of mattresses thrown on the ground or cushions in the back of a carriage; and victuals so tough that exasperated diners segmented them by means of a tug-of-war.[28] Fatigues of a different kind, albeit intermittent, awaited survivors of these exhausting cavalcades. Whenever a royal mistress gave birth her attendants were required to help in the delivery-room and, in the case of the appointed *gouvernante*, to receive and entertain the press of visitors and well-wishers.[29] When she sickened or died the most repugnant chores had still to be dispatched unflinchingly: assisting at the medication of contagious and foul-smelling maladies;[30] witnessing the opening of the corpse by the royal surgeons;[31] accompanying to their last resting-place containers of embalmed entrails which at least once exploded 'avec une puanteur subite et intolérable'.[32] Distinguished though their ancestry might be, members of a royal entourage were still 'domestics' in the eyes of their superiors, who assigned duties to them accordingly.

Despite the very real servitude of their mode of existence, few ladies valued their independence to the extent of renouncing court life for that of the provincial *châtelaine*. In the seventeenth century withdrawal to country estates was in nine cases out of ten enforced by a formal order (from king, husband or others) to leave the court, or by the necessity to save money. It was a course of action undertaken because of coercion or expediency rather than out of personal choice. For everyone knew the fate that awaited those unfortunates severed from the manifold distractions, cultural and amatorial, offered by the capital:

> D'abord chez le beau monde on vous fera venir;
> Vous irez visiter, pour votre bienvenue,
> Madame la baillive et Madame l'élue,
> Qui d'un siège pliant vous feront honorer.
> Là, dans le carnaval, vous pourrez espérer
> Le bal et la grande-bande, à savoir deux musettes,
> Et, parfois, Fagotin et les marionnettes.[33]

As a matter of fact a large proportion of French noblewomen did stand the risk of never hearing any orchestra more melodious than the village bagpipes or conversation more elevated than the gossip of the local functionaries' wives. Only a small fraction of the French aristocracy were permanently clustered around the court; the majority resided on ancestral domains in the countryside. Being of provincial stock or domiciled in the provinces in no way prevented the country nobleman from bringing himself to the attention of the sovereign by volunteering for military service or pursuing a sinecure at court. But someone had to stay at home to manage affairs in his absence and the obvious candidate for the job was his wife. She probably accepted the arrangement without undue distaste. The rough life of the army camp had charms for none but amazons and prostitutes, while only day-to-day frequentation of the court could enable a woman to avoid the minute blunders in dress, speech and etiquette which betrayed the provincial and rapidly drew the contemptuous smile and the polite sarcasm. Besides, the amount of work which devolved upon her left little time for regrets or repining. The diary of Madeleine-Ursule des Porcellets, Comtesse de Rochefort, has a vivid tale to tell in this connection.[34]

In May 1689, on the departure of her husband for a period of army service, the Comtesse began to keep a detailed record of her daily activities during the five months of his absence. Like many of his peers the Comte was heavily in debt and took with him all the money that remained, together with his financial overseer. The Comtesse was therefore left to cope on her own save for her domestics and her two small sons. Her rising often coincided with, and sometimes preceded, that of the sun.[35] An early start was vital, for almost every day she made a point of visiting some part of her estates on the confines of Provence and Languedoc. On arrival she would enquire about repairs to be made to her rural tenements and their appurtenances,[36] inspect woods and ditches,[37] tour harvest fields,[38] note ways of improving crop yields,[39] listen to advice about viticulture and flood prevention,[40] organise wool-spinning and sericulture.[41] On her return, or when bad weather kept her indoors, there were complaints from vassals to be heard[42] and accounts to be drawn up – endless accounts with tradesmen, tenants, domestics.[43] Trying to balance the books was a nightmare because the Comtesse was harassed on all sides by creditors and pensioners whom she alternately appeased by promises of payment at harvest time or threatened with the *lettres d'état* which she (wrongly) believed would give her immunity from prosecution for debt.[44] Book-keeping was followed by the composition of memoranda of things to be done or bought in the course of her travels,[45] and for the instruction of agents sent 'en plusieurs endroits pour aller chercher de l'argent'.[46] A vast correspondence, both business and personal, clamoured for attention in turn, the Comtesse now and then devoting to it as much as a whole day.[47]

In between there was the house proper to be run. Time was set aside for periodic inspections of furniture and hangings,[48] as a result of which arrangements were made for the appropriate refurbishments.[49] The servants had their names neatly inscribed in a fresh register, and some were lucky enough to receive new liveries,[50] for the Rocheforts would present no shabby exterior to the world even if they were within an ace of insolvency. The children were not neglected. The mother cut out their linen with her own hands and sacrificed her old skirts to make robes for '[son] fils le chevalier'.[51] Somehow she planned her overcrowded days so as to leave an hour spare here and there in which to keep abreast of the news via a subscription to the *Gazette*,[52] and to satisfy the demands of her fervent piety, which occasionally conflicted with those of her no less fervent rank-consciousness. When the local curate tried to dodge his obligation to present her with holy water in church, the scandalised Comtesse forthwith denounced his sin of omission to his superior.[53] However impoverished and indebted the provincial nobility might be, they never suffered the slightest breach of the privileges and respect to which the 'purity' of their blood entitled them.

The Comtesse de Rochefort's journal gives a sobering insight into the physical and mental stamina required by a wife left to shoulder the burden of a large seventeenth-century household. She herself reveals, in an isolated entry for 30 May 1690, how she almost succumbed beneath the weight but found the strength to resume the perpetual struggle to make ends meet:

> Depuis le dix de novembre jusqu'au premier de février, j'ai été si fort accablée de mélancolie, par le mauvais état où je voyais mes affaires, que je ne mangeais ni ne dormais; j'avais fort maigri, et j'étais assurément dans le cas de tout craindre ... Enfin, le bon Dieu nous a fait la grâce de remédier à l'état de nos affaires, dans le temps que j'y pensais le moins. J'espère, moyennant sa grâce, de les régler dans quelques années. Mais il faut pour cela que la maison soit bien réglée; il faut même épargner tout ce que l'on peut; car, autrement, on ne saurait lier les deux bouts dans les mauvaises années.[54]

With only her faith and her sense of *noblesse oblige* to sustain her, the provincial *châtelaine* must often have led a life of anxious toil that differed little from that of her vassals.

The financial burden of many a noblewoman, Parisian as well as provincial, stood a chance of being eased if she or her husband could repair their dilapidated fortunes by engaging in a commercial or private enterprise. That the project appealed to ladies of quality there is no doubt. Throughout the century, for example, their names are mingled with those of plebeian women in what proved to be a popular livelihood for the sex, the carriage and sedan-chair business.[55] Towards the end of the 1600s they were embarking upon some of the most progressive commercial ventures. The Maréchale de Créqui undertook the construction of ironworks on the river Aisne.[56] The Comtesse de Beuvron obtained permission to establish factories wherever she chose for the preparing of different kinds of skins and hides.[57] In all right-thinking quarters, however, the idea of the blue-blooded openly demeaning their rank and prostituting their talents for the sake of sordid gain was totally unacceptable. Trading or industrial activity neither sufficiently well concealed under the cover of estate management or an assumed name, nor authorised by a royal warrant, constituted the crime of *dérogeance* for which the penalty was deprivation of noble status and privileges.

The bourgeoisie were not hidebound by the same traditions and prejudices. While their betters subsisted precariously on pride and credit they busied themselves with amassing riches by various means that included all those – trade, industry, business, usury – deemed to be beneath aristocratic dignity. Wealth enabled them to buy land and to accumulate those venal offices in administration and the magistracy which, by virtue of the aristocratic prerogatives attached thereto, went far towards cleansing the holders of the original sin of plebeian birth. Possessing both opulence and influence this new aristocracy found it not unduly difficult to tempt the old, scornful but envious, into countenancing the practice if not the theory of intermarriage, which epitomised the fulfilment of every ambitious bourgeois's plan to erase the last vestiges of a 'base' provenance.

The enrichment and ascension of the bourgeoisie was hastened by the aspirations and enterprise of their womenfolk. Bourgeois women were credited with one great passion in life: aping the nobility.[58] Aristocratic fashions, modes of speech and pastimes, such as opening salons, were all copied faithfully. But superficial imitation was not enough for many, who wanted the substance as well as the shadow of an aristocratic life-style. Not all of them could hope to reach the same dizzy heights as some whose fabulous dowries had bought thoroughbred in-laws, powerful spur though the sight was to latent ambitions. It was possible, however, by a husband's judicious purchase of estates and fiefs or by his installation in an office carrying fiscal exemptions to save precious pin-money from flowing into the tax-collector's pocket and, more important, to replace by an imposing 'Madame de . . .' the humiliating 'Mademoiselle' by which the bourgeois wife was addressed.[59] Husbands were consequently badgered into bettering themselves. In a *Relation of the State of France* drafted in 1609 for James I, the English ambassador Sir George Carew expressed the opinion that French towns would be much more prosperous 'were it not that all offices being vendible in this kingdom, the merchants employ their money rather in buying offices than in exercising traffic, because officers' wives go before merchants' wives'.[60] That pressure upon husbands never eased is evident from the report of a provincial *intendant* in 1698: 'Les femmes, par gloire et vanité, engagent leurs maris d'acheter [sic] des charges qui ont quelque relief ou qui leur donnent quelque rang.'[61] But land and offices cost money, the price of the latter in particular rising steeply throughout the century. To satisfy the exigences of her vanity and to help earn the wherewithal to maintain a standard of living commensurate with her pretensions, the bourgeois wife was prepared to take on, in addition to her domestic tasks, almost every trade of which she was physically capable and from which she was not debarred by what the twentieth century has termed male chauvinism.

The easiest way for a woman to augment the family income was to assist her husband in his business, acting as saleswoman in his shop perhaps, keeping his accounts and handling customers' money. The indications are that she adjusted rapidly and ably to her role as vendor. In the smart *boutiques* that lined the streets of prosperous Lyon it was the men who acted as assistants and errand-boys while the women took charge of sales and cash: 'Les femmes y ont les principaux emplois, elles tiennent les écritures en partie double, elles vendent, elles invitent les pratiques à acheter, leur montrent poliment les marchandises, comptent l'argent, le serrent et le gardent... Bref, les maris et les pères servent de commis et de garçons de boutique.'[62] Tradesmen were only too happy to efface themselves, realising the extent to which sales were promoted by having an attractive woman behind the counter. Those located in the famous galleries of the Palais de Justice in Paris saw to it that their merchandise was displayed by 'les plus avenantes et les plus jolies' of their womenfolk, supplemented if need be by girls bought from impoverished families for an agreed period of time. At the end of this they would be either married off or well recompensed and returned to their parents.[63] Apart from their purely decorative value women could be relied upon to show the necessary perseverance when it came to the delicate operation of extracting debts from recalcitrant customers. Mme de Sévigné's aristocratic susceptibilities smarted at the news that a Parisian tradeswoman had travelled all the way to Provence to harass her prodigal daughter into settling some overdue accounts.[64] In 1693 the *marchandes'* tenacity received literary recognition when Dancourt introduced into his comedy *Les Bourgeoises à la Mode* (act one, scene seven) the personage of Mme Amelin, whose demands upset heroines bent on emulating the aristocracy down to the detail of unpaid bills. Whether exasperated or amused, contemporaries could scarcely deny the tradeswomen's business acumen and competence.

It was perfectly feasible for a woman, as well as working in conjunction with her husband, to branch out in business on her own account. The *Coutumes* encouraged female enterprise of this kind by permitting the wife whose business was entirely separate from any run by her husband to buy, sell and borrow without his authorisation where commercial dealings were concerned, and by making him liable for payment of debts where a *communauté des biens* existed between them.[65] The regulations of the various trade guilds were also to a certain extent favourable to the solitary businesswoman. The majority contained a set clause to the effect that a member's widow would be allowed to continue her husband's trade on four conditions: that she received assistance from an able journeyman or men (variously referred to as *compagnons, valets, garçons, serviteurs* and so on); that she took on no apprentices other than those already being trained by her late husband; that she paid the guild dues and abided by the regulations; and that she did not remarry with a man practising a different trade.[66] If she disregarded the last condition she had to close her shop or abandon her stall, and hand back to the guild any hallmark or seal which her first husband might have used to stamp his products.[67] Remarriage within the guild caused no problems. On the contrary, the widow of a master-guildsman who married a *compagnon* was often able to gain him dispensation from some, if not all, of the dues and practical tests which barred the way to the mastership (*maîtrise*).[68]

The precise role played by women in the guilds during the seventeenth century is difficult to determine. Whereas statutes of the medieval period mentioned *apprentisses* and *maîtresses*, and employed expressions such as 'Que nul ne nulle...', in later centuries the tendency was to formulate all prescriptions in the masculine gender and to refer specifically to women only in the clauses dealing with widows and daughters of master craftsmen (*maîtres*). The evolution in terminology is symptomatic of the contemporary desire for the masculine element to predominate in corporative life. There were certain types of work – building, metallurgy, large areas of medicine – from which women were automatically excluded on the grounds of the arduous or repellent nature of the labour involved, or their lack of technical skills. Where no obvious barrier existed men tried hard to create one. An outstanding example was that of the tailors of Paris in their dealings with the local women dressmakers. The tailors considered it their right to monopolise the fabrication of both men's and women's clothes, and relaxed their restrictions only so far as to permit the wives and daughters of their *maîtres* to make clothes for children under eight. The employment by a master tailor of any *couturière* was strictly prohibited, and senior guild officials were empowered to visit domiciles to make sure that garments were not being manufactured outside the pale of the guild.[69] Since the *couturières* worked on a private and individual basis they seemed doomed to be crushed by pressure from the determined and organised guild of their rivals. But they refused to be brow-beaten. Despite seizures of their products and interdictions procured by the tailors they continued business as usual, strong in the knowledge that their services were being increasingly demanded by customers of their own sex. In 1675 they decided to unite against the opposition by forming a guild for the protection of their interests. Article 3 of their statutes expressly forbade the tailors any right of inspection over their work; but with regard to the actual manufacturing of clothes concessions had to be made. The *couturières* were allowed to sew clothes for children of both sexes under eight and most women's clothes. The tailors, however, reserved the right to make dress-bodices and -bottoms and all garments for the members of their own sex.[70] The struggle of the Paris dressmakers was echoed in the provinces, with similar results: women were not prevented from working but their sphere of action was limited by specifications as to the amount of cloth they could use or the persons whom they could clothe.[71]

Masculine prejudice did not stop women from infiltrating into a large number of guilds, even if it was generally successful in excluding them from taking any official part in the management of corporative affairs. Women made their presence felt, not unnaturally, in those trades closest to their ordinary domestic occupations – in the clothing, food and allied industries. The Paris guilds were typical in this respect. Three were exclusively feminine: the linen-drapers (*lingères*), the oldest, largest and richest;[72] the *couturières*; and the flower-sellers (*bouquetières*), both smaller and poorer. A fourth guild, the linen and hemp workers (*linierschanvriers*), was almost exclusively feminine despite the retention of the masculine title.[73] In mixed guilds the position of women varied. The grain merchants (*grainiers*) and wig-makers (*perruquiers*)

quiers) admitted them to the *maîtrise* and elected them to the *jurande*, the governing body of the guild.[74] The fruiterers, on the other hand, formally denied them entry into the *jurande*.[75] Specific prohibitions of the latter kind are rare in the sixteenth and seventeenth centuries, but formal references to the election of *maîtres* as members of the *jurande* (*jurés*) in statutes which elsewhere reveal the presence of *maîtresses* in the guild invite the conclusion that women were not eligible for the post.[76] As widows continuing their husband's trade they might, however, be allowed to participate in the election of *jurés*.[77] Other guilds – the trimmers and buttoners, hatters and plume-makers, belt manufacturers, second-hand clothes dealers and minters amongst them – went a step further by stipulating that no girls should be taught the trade unless they were the daughters of *maîtres*.[78]

Membership of a guild, albeit voiceless membership, entailed adherence to a rigid code of professional conduct which regulated in minute detail the nature and quality of the articles to be manufactured, methods of fabrication, hours of labour, the mode of advancement in the corporative hierarchy and the penalties for transgressors of the rules. Every girl, with the occasional exception of those related to a *maître* or *maîtresse*, was obliged to begin by serving an apprenticeship. In return for the document authorising apprenticeship, the *brevet d'apprentissage*, she usually paid a fee (*droit d'apprentissage*) which ranged from the modest twenty *sous* disbursed by apprentice tailoresses at Abbeville in 1644[79] to the daunting twelve *livres* and five *sous* exacted from apprentice *lingères* at Rouen by 1700.[80] Apprenticeship lasted on average two to three years, though it might be prolonged for up to six years, as was the case with the Paris grain merchants.[81] Along with technical instruction the *apprentisse* received bed, board and clean linen from the master or mistress to whom she was attached, and undertook in return to learn the trade to the best of her ability and to serve out her full term.[82] Apprenticeship was traditionally followed by a further period of approximately two years' service as a *fille de boutique*, during which wages were paid. For many girls and women achievement of the status of paid ancillary worker in shop or workshop represented the limit of professional advancement. Henceforth they would merge with the anonymous masses classed in official documents as *ouvrières*, though individualised in their respective trades by quaint and expressive appellations: *esnoueuses*, *esplucheuses*,[83] *devideuses*, *molinières*,[84] *meneuses de table*,[85] *tres-*

seuses[86] and so forth. The rest, who had theoretical access to the *maîtrise*, faced barriers devised to prevent overcrowding at the top of the profession. Apart from supplying proof of Catholicism, respectability and completion of apprenticeship, candidates were required to demonstrate their technical competence by means of a practical test known as the *chef-d'œuvre*, performed in the presence of senior *maîtresses*. If kinship with a master or mistress could be claimed the *chef-d'œuvre* might be waived. So might the high reception fees that had to enter guild coffers before successful candidates became fully-fledged *maîtresses* with, in those guilds that allowed it, the prospect of rising to the honoured status of presiding officials.

The latter, comprising the *jurées* or *gardes*, plus those *anciennes* who had held all the guild offices, had several main duties: the administration of guild finances and property; the periodic inspection of merchandise produced by members, to ensure that it came up to standard; the examination of aspirants to the *maîtrise*; the summoning of fellow *maîtres* and *maîtresses* to corporative assemblies and to the prayers and processions that commemorated the death of one of their number.[87] In addition they might assume some responsibility in managing the affairs of their *confrérie*,[88] a religious association composed mainly (though not exclusively) of guild members, financed by apprenticeship and reception fees, and often maintaining in a local church a special chapel, dedicated to the guild's patron saint, for the celebration of corporative acts of worship and piety.

Another type of confraternity with which women were associated and which was related to, yet distinct from, the guild was the *compagnonnage*. The *compagnonnages* closely resembled the later freemasons' societies. They consisted of groups of young male *compagnons* who banded together in secrecy for purposes of mutual instruction, social and moral assistance, and protection against exploitation by the *maîtres*. Certain women known as *Mères* were chosen to preside over the material and moral welfare of the various sub-groups of *compagnons*, acting chiefly as hostesses to those engaged in the *tour de France*, the customary journey from town to town during which professional training was completed. They enjoyed undisputed authority and respect, and occupied a place of honour at a number of ceremonies.[89] Association with the *compagnonnages* was somewhat hazardous because the secrecy on which they prided themselves made them perpetually suspect to the authorities. In 1697 one Marguerite Guyot, wife of a Parisian *compagnon* and *Mère* to his blacksmith workmates, was fined fifteen *livres* for allowing them daily meetings at her house 'pour comploter et monopoler entre eux', and the assemblies were suppressed.[90] Women other than the *Mères*, who had no say in administration and organisation, were rigorously excluded from the *compagnonnages*. Female equivalents of the *compagnons* appear neither to have been permitted to join such associations nor to have formed their own.

By virtue of their trade monopolies, their strong internal organisation and, in the case of the larger ones, the wealth and influence of their leaders, the guilds were formidable bodies whose privileges outsiders disregarded at the risk of suffering interminable professional vexations. This is not to say that the corporative Juggernaut was never resisted. Quite the reverse. Two groups of workers, in both of which women were conspicuous, notably defied attempts to regularise their activities – and not unsuccessfully, judging from the vehemence with which the guilds denounced them.

The first group was that of the *revendeurs* and the *regrattiers*, hucksters who bought for resale many different kinds of merchandise, principally foodstuffs, fuel, clothes, furniture and jewellery. Sometimes the guilds tried to curb their enterprise by means of an official agreement. The 1661 statutes of the *merciers-ciriers-épiciers-droguistes* of Amiens allowed a prescribed number of ten *revendeurs* and *revenderesses* to sell their wares in the town market but not in their homes or shops.[91] More often a simple clause of prohibition was formulated:

Item, pour régler, le temps à venir, le nombre effréné de ceux qui se mêlent de vendre, regratter les dites denrées, défenses sont faites à toutes personnes dorénavant, soit hommes ou femmes, à peine de confiscation et d'amende arbitraire, de revendre aux places publiques ni autres endroits de la dite ville [Paris] aucunes sortes de fruits, œufs, beurres et fromages.[92]

Défenses à toutes revenderesses de hardes d'exposer ni porter par les rues ou maisons aucunes toiles, par pièces ou morceaux, œuvrées ou non œuvrées.[93]

The guilds were assisted in their campaign by municipal authorities disturbed by the threat which the huckstresses in particular constituted to public order. The least offensive of their habits was that of obstructing the highway with their wares and leaving malodorous heaps of rubbish in their wake.[94] 'Nation entreprenante et tumultueuse',[95] they would band together on the slightest pretext[96] into vociferating mobs quite capable of righting by their own rough methods the wrongs of which they complained. Their tongues and morals were notoriously unbridled. In Paris a special class of *revendeuses à la toilette* were known to present themselves at the morning toilet of female clients with offers to sell jewels, clothes and articles of haberdashery that were often stolen or contraband,[97] and to earn extra money from dubious sidelines: usury, fortune-telling, marriage-broking, procuring.[98] The authorities of Nancy forbade *revenderesses* 'd'injurier ni d'insulter aucun bourgeois lorsqu'il marchandera', and obliged them to wear a right sleeve in the colour of the town's liveries (green or yellow) as a distinguishing mark.[99] The mayor of Poitiers had suspended in the town square a swinging cage in which to imprison the delinquents and blasphemers in their ranks.[100] Corporative and municipal harassment was calculated not so much to bring about a cessation of the commerce on which the huckstresses depended for a livelihood as to drive them to adopt the kind of tactics practised by the second group of rebel workers, who came under the rubric of *chambrelans*.

The *chambrelans* subscribed neither nominally nor financially to the guild system. They operated on an individual basis in the privacy of their own or their customers' home, usually undertaking, in the case of women, some form of needlework. Prospective clients for sewing and lace-making were lured by means of advertisements which dwelt upon the charitableness and cheapness of the arrangement: 'Si quelques personnes charitablement veulent faire travailler au point de fil sur le patron à l'aiguille, nous savons une pauvre veuve qui s'en acquittera consciencieusement, et avec la satisfaction de ceux qui lui feront l'honneur de l'employer; pourvu qu'on lui fasse quelque petite redevance raisonnable, tant pour son fil, que pour lui avoir [sic] les choses nécessaires à la vie.'[101] The nature of their services and the locality where they were performed made it difficult to discern whether these 'underhand' workers were merely going about their ordinary domestic duties or acting in a professional capacity. The tailors' guilds, which were directly affected, tried to eliminate unauthorised competition by sending inspectors round to suspect homes on periodic witch-hunts in order to enforce payment of guild dues, especially where apprentices were being employed.[102]

The existence of huckstresses and 'clandestine' needleworkers is a significant pointer to the number of working women who preferred independence to the stifling protection of the guilds. Membership of a corporation did not, in effect, offer palpable advantages to the majority at a time when advancement depended less on technical skill than on money and blood relatives within the ruling oligarchy of *maîtres* and *maîtresses*, and when women had a minimal say in the direction of guild affairs. There were those who chose to evolve their own internal discipline and usages to take the place of statutes and official incorporation. The one thousand or more *crieuses de vieux chapeaux*, wives and daughters of poverty-stricken Parisian craftsmen and soldiers who dealt in old clothes and furniture, had their own distinct hierarchy and apprenticeship scheme whereby a novice paid an experienced *crieuse* to teach her the business.[103] Even when the decision was taken to form a guild, the process was often a slow one. The Paris *couturières* did not organise themselves until 1675, nor did the *bouquetières* until 1677. Moreover Paris was a city in which guilds had flourished since the Middle Ages, but other large towns like Dijon and Lyon opposed their imposition.[104] In provinces such as Poitou they were the exception not the rule.[105] The peasants, who constituted the bulk of the population, were scarcely touched by corporative institutions.

But where the guilds were non-existent, or relaxed their vigilance, other authorities intensified their own. Whenever the working woman overstepped the bounds of her traditional tasks in life she could expect to encounter suspicion, prejudice, hostility and sanctions.[106]

8
Women at Work II

The bourgeoisie was a perpetually shifting and, for that reason, ill-defined social class in the seventeenth century. Its wealthy members gravitated towards the old aristocracy, with whom they had in common the possession of land, titles, privileges and cultural tastes, if not that of a lengthy warrior lineage. Its lower ranks merged with the underprivileged masses, sharing their illiteracy and the stigma of poverty. There was no question at the latter end of the scale of work being merely a distraction or a means of providing luxuries, as it was for the tradesman's wife, or as she carefully pretended it was. Contemporary wages scarcely kept the manual worker, particularly the woman worker in receipt of half a man's pay, at subsistence level. There was little question either of being fastidious in the choice of work undertaken. Women of the lower classes turned their hand to virtually every trade. Indeed necessity often forced them to practise several concurrently, however taxing they might be physically or however repulsive morally.

One occupation which attracted a large number of refugees from economic distress was that of domestic service. Via personal recommendation or that of a *Bureau de Recommandaresses*[1] peasant girls would seek to enter bourgeois households in the capacity of servants and chambermaids, as a means of escaping from miserable home backgrounds and of assembling a modest dowry that they hoped would lead to an advantageous marriage.[2] Even bourgeois women in straitened circumstances were compelled to swallow their pride and take employment, preferably as companions and *gouvernantes*, with the aristocracy or the richer members of their own class.[3] The social come-down was disguised, though none the less resented, when an impoverished girl earned a living in the service of well-to-do relatives. The phenomenon was sufficiently widespread in the early 1630s for Pierre Corneille to devote a cautionary comedy of manners, *La Suivante*, to a lively portrayal of the rancour harboured by *déclassées* obliged

113

to suffer all manner of subtle humiliations as a daily penance for their impecuniosity.

The snubs and slights which a temperamental mistress had leisure to think out and inflict were just one of the drawbacks of domestic service. Concerned moralists undeniably took pains to make employers aware of their obligation to treat servants with humanity and affection, assist them in all their physical and spiritual needs, pay them fairly, reprove them tactfully and praise them for jobs well done.[4] But the very fact that employers needed reminding that their domestics were human beings, in subjection merely because of the vagaries of fortune, betrays an outlook at variance with the ideal of Christian charity. Fénelon was not exaggerating when he wrote of mistresses who handled servants 'à peu près comme des chevaux'.[5] Women of all ranks were in the habit of striking their domestic staff. Dramatists depict irascible *bourgeoises* raising their hand to cuff unfortunate maids.[6] Medical men instance miscarriages brought about by the beating and kicking of lackeys.[7] Authors of memoirs, letters and gazettes cite thrashings administered by great ladies. The Marquise de Vervins, wife of the chief royal butler, crowned a long career of servant-beating by flogging a maid and having her thrown out of the window.[8] Mme d'Aymet, allied by marriage to the egregious La Force family, dealt her child a near fatal blow aimed at its *nourrice* and 'battit sa demoiselle à outrance'.[9] Louis XIII's nieces were all disposed to hit their domestics,[10] a mania shared by the Princesse d'Harcourt until a lusty chambermaid decided to return the outrage.[11]

To add insult to injury, mistresses were fond of working their domestics hard and then refusing to remunerate them properly. The possession of servants was a status symbol, but a potentially costly one. A favourite way round the difficulty consisted in employing the smallest possible number and making them serve in several different capacities simultaneously.[12] When company arrived all that was necessary to save appearances was to instantly decorate the *servante* with the grander title of *demoiselle* or *femme de chambre*.[13] A 'Hé quelqu'un!' when service was required preserved the fiction of an army of domestics waiting to hand;[14] just so long, that is, as the solitary representative of that army did not involuntarily reveal by her bewilderment the falseness of her mistress's pretences.[15]

Once the guests had departed the maid resumed her accustomed role as provision-buyer, cook, bottle-washer, bed-maker, cleaner and child-minder.[16] In return for her sundry labours wages payable both in cash and in kind were agreed. The servant was promised a fixed sum per annum, plus a pair of shoes, a chemise or a length of material.[17] In the interim she might benefit from gifts of her mistress's discarded clothes.[18] Agreements were not, however, always honoured with the requisite punctuality. The practice of yearly, as opposed to weekly or monthly, settlements of wages allowed the unscrupulous employer to conveniently forget the date on which they were due and to postpone payment indefinitely, relying on the likelihood of the domestic remaining with the household in the hope of eventually coming into possession of what she had been promised. In the event of over-insistent demands a pretext could always be found for dismissal without any recompense whatsoever. Even honourable employers seem to have considered their domestics' wages as the least important debt to be liquidated. Marguerite Mercier, Protestant wife of a royal butler, paid her chambermaid Esther, but months and years in arrears. 'J'ai payé à Esther toute l'année 1651. Quand nous serons à la fin de l'année 1654 je lui devrai trois années' reads a casual entry in her *Livre de Raison*.[19] Not only was Esther irregularly paid but she was obliged to make substantial loans to her mistress![20]

Failure to pay wages encouraged servants to compensate themselves by illicit means. An accusation repeatedly made against them was their propensity to 'ferrer la mule':[21] to cheat employers over the price of commodities, appropriate their property, guzzle and tipple at their expense, and generally make what illegal profits they could for subsequent squandering on lotteries[22] and fine clothes.[23] Penalties for theft were draconian. The 1628 version of the Bouillon *Coutume* prescribed whipping for the first offence; whipping, branding and banishment for the second; hanging for the third.[24] And penalties did not merely exist on paper. Magistrates felt duty-bound to mete out exemplary punishment to those who in their way were ridiculing and rebelling against the principle of authority, represented as much by the magistrates themselves as by ill-served employers. The judges who condemned one Louise Bellanger to the gallows at Angers in 1617 for having introduced her husband and son into her master's house to commit robbery were trying to obliterate all traces of social upheaval as well as warn her peers when they ordered the corpse to be taken down and burned.[25] Severity became more marked at times when the central authority of the realm, the monarchy, was struggling to assert or reassert itself. Hence the number of light-fingered maidservants sentenced to hang on the eve of the Fronde.[26] But since well-to-do employers on the whole disdained close surveillance of household affairs as beneath them, the risk of being caught and disciplined was minimised.

Disorders of a different type were caused by the reluctance of masters and mistresses to engage other than single domestics.[27] Married domestics were considered to have a greater incentive to steal from employers and to render inferior service because part of their attention was constantly diverted elsewhere.[28] This prejudice commonly led to concubinage, either with the menservants of the household, tolerated until pregnancy rendered dismissal necessary to avert scandal;[29] or with the master,[30] prolonged until or unless a misalliance regularised the liaison.[31] Promiscuity in turn resulted in the spread of venereal diseases[32] and in a high incidence of cases of abortion and infanticide amongst maidservants.[33]

First-hand witnesses, or accomplices, of all the shortcomings of their equals and their superiors, domestics felt under no obligation to keep their observations to themselves. Outsiders desirous of ascertaining what went on behind respectably closed shutters had only to prompt the maid to discover all that they wanted to know, and more:

> ... lorsqu'on les envoie acheter quelque chose, la plupart des gens leur demandent, Aha, ma fille, vous êtes donc à présent chez Monsieur ou Madame une telle? Oui, Madame, répond la servante. Y a-t-il longtemps que vous y êtes, répond l'autre? Non, Madame, répond encore la servante. Vraiment, continue l'autre, ils en changent souvent. Quelles gens sont-ce donc, que font-ils? Comment vivent-ils? Ils sont donc bien difficiles, puisqu'ils changent si souvent. Alors la servante entre tout à fait en matière, et dit de son maître et de sa maîtresse tout ce qu'elle sait, et ce qu'elle ne sait pas.[34]

Information was that much more readily volunteered and embroidered when the servant thought that she had been unfairly dismissed, and many a mistress's reputation suffered from vengeful calumny.[35] Abuse of the confidential nature of their position was, in the eyes of contemporaries, the really mortal sin of domestics, by comparison with which their pilfering and lubricity were but venial. For this they were regarded as dangerous enemies – 'les plus dangereux de nos ennemis', specified the Comtesse de Murat[36] – and charged with censuring every action they witnessed 'selon la bassesse de leur génie et par l'infamie de leurs débauches'.[37] Amidst the imprecations the fact that employers bore partial responsibility for this state of affairs was overlooked.

The wantonness of the servant population placed them on familiar terms with a second important body of working women, the midwives. They shared the same kind of social backgrounds, being drawn from impoverished bourgeois families[38] or from the peasantry. They also had in common an unedifying public image. The highly intimate nature of the services rendered by midwives, not only in childbirth but also in the verification of allegations of impotence,[39] automatically cast suspicion on their personal morals. Rumours were not silenced by scandals resulting from assistance given to women of easy virtue.[40] But according to their critics the biggest scandal of all was the midwives' ignorance, incompetence and stubbornness, which had frightening repercussions on patients:

> Les unes timides ou déconcertées n'osent déclarer l'état des choses et demander du secours. D'autres attachées à leur intérêt s'efforcent de s'en passer. La plupart, entêtées de leur prétendue habileté, n'en veulent absolument point . . . Je dis par nécessité ce que je n'ai vu qu'à regret, des cordons rompus, des enfants contus, meurtris, disloqués ou morts; des délivres en pièce; des matrices relâchées, tombées et perverties; des femmes jetées mal à propos dans les pertes de sang, sources des symptômes les plus fâcheux qui puissent accompagner les travaux.[41]

Loudest in their denunciations, as here, were the male members of the medical profession. For conservative doctors and surgeons the existence of midwives constituted an impudent and unwarranted intrusion into jealously guarded masculine preserves. To halt the invasion they sought both to discredit their female competitors in the eyes of the public and to prevent them from gaining access to means of improving their knowledge and techniques. In the first half of the century women were forbidden to assist at the relevant dissections in the medical schools,[42] despite appeals and offers to pay for the privilege,[43] and despite the precedent set by other European countries like Spain.[44]

However the risk to human life from untrained hands was too great to be ignored, and steps were eventually taken to attack the basic problem of insufficient professional instruction. In the large towns prospective midwives were called upon to serve an apprenticeship in the main hospital of the locality, or alternatively with a qualified midwife or surgeon specialising in obstetrics, before presenting themselves for examination by doctors and surgeons. In Paris letters patent of 1664 created the offices of two *sages-femmes jurées* who were to present examinees before a panel consisting of the chief royal barber, his deputy and the four directors of the surgeons' guild, with the dean of the Medical Faculty presiding.[45] At Rouen candidates who had completed one year's apprenticeship with a master surgeon or at the Hôtel-Dieu, or two years with an expert midwife, were to undergo a four-hour examination carried out by surgeons, for which an entrance fee of sixty *livres* was paid.[46] Those who passed the test took a solemn oath[47] at municipal headquarters before being officially received into the profession. The control exercised by doctors and surgeons over the admission of midwives went some way towards soothing masculine susceptibilities, but not far enough for the liking of certain practitioners, who saw to it that they were prevented from giving any medicines to mothers and infants.[48]

The idea of formal training courses for midwives was slow to materialise and made no substantial advances before the eighteenth century.[49] In the meantime, rudimentary and haphazard though they might be, municipal training schemes were a considerable advance on the procedure adopted in country areas. An excerpt from the diary of Michel Lalande, rector of the parish of Siran in Languedoc, describes a characteristic method of selecting and swearing-in the country midwife:

L'an 1697 et le 21ᵉ mars, l'ancienne femme-sage[50] qui était en exercice d'aider les femmes dans leurs couches et d'élever les enfants, étant devenue hors de pouvoir de le faire davantage par maladie et vieillesse ... il était nécessaire d'y pourvoir d'une autre, ce que nous recteur aurions fait en examinant les approbations que les femmes donnaient pour cela à Marianne Sonière, femme de Jean Cros de la présente paroisse, par la confiance avec laquelle elles l'envoyaient quérir et par le témoignage qu'elles nous en ont rendu, nous certifiant qu'elles la jugent fort capable de cela, à quoi nous avons d'autant plus connivé que nous voyons qu'elle est mère d'un nombre considérable d'enfants, d'autant plus qu'elle nous a paru par sa conduite de bon exemple dans la paroisse. C'est pourquoi étant d'ailleurs assuré de sa foi dans l'église et de sa suffisance dans la doctrine, l'ayant instruite particulièrement de la manière de conférer le baptême dans le cas de nécessité, nous aurions reçu son serment qu'elle a fait en mettant la main sur les saints évangiles, qu'elle s'en acquittera avec soin, diligence et fidélité pour le salut des enfants et des mères, et nous l'avons ainsi reçue pour femme-sage en présence de plusieurs autres femmes qui se sont trouvées à l'église en convoi à la sortie des couches de Thérèse Falquière, femme de Jean Cathala.[51]

The rural midwife's competence was therefore measured by the satisfaction of her clients and the number of her own progeny. Her examiner, the local priest, was a man who, if he minded his calling, was as remote from childbirth as it was possible to be. He looked primarily not for professional skill but for good morals, Catholicism[52] and the ability to administer the *ondoiement* to moribund infants. That a baby might die through making an imperfectly assisted entry into the world aroused rather less concern than that it should die in the orthodox religious manner.

The tenure of an official licence to practise midwifery did not spell professional security. Midwifery was a science in which every woman who had borne a child considered herself something of an expert and capable of passing on the benefit of her experience to relatives and neighbours in *travail*. The presence of these im-promptu midwives, more comforting to the patient than that of a stranger, not only hindered the qualified midwife in her work but also represented a potential source of business rivalry. More serious competition stemmed from male *accoucheurs*, who had at their disposition the best training facilities and who enjoyed the confidence of royalty.[53] Salaries, too, were not high. By way of compensation midwives were sometimes accorded tax exemp-tions. Midwives at Nancy, for instance, known as *basles*, were dispensed from paying ordinary and extraordinary customs duties (*aides*).[54] But when this was insufficient to balance the budget more remunerative sidelines had to be undertaken simultaneously.[55]

Midwifery was the only official access for women to the medical profession. All hopes of becoming doctors and surgeons were rudely dashed. 'C'est un sot animal qu'une femme qui se mêle de notre métier', stormed Dr Gui Patin; 'cela n'appartient qu'à ceux qui ont un haut-de-chausses et la tête bien faite.'[56] Insults did not deter women from practising medicine in a number of private capacities. Convents that wished to limit their contact with the outside world of men and to devote themselves to healing the sick and the poor trained nuns as nurses and apothecaries.[57] In the home women treated common family ailments with potions and powders which they had made themselves from flowers, herbs and roots.[58] Whenever they imagined that superfluity of blood was responsible for an indisposition they opened one of their veins.[59] If an internal spring-clean became necessary the maidservant mixed and administered the appropriate douche or clyster.[60] Outside the home women were hired to nurse invalids and newly delivered mothers.[61] During plagues and epidemics they exposed their lives to help ease the indescribable sufferings of the victims. The municipal registers of Troyes in Champagne record the quiet heroism of a certain Babeau, 'femme expérimentée et de longue main versée en telles affaires', who in 1606 shut herself away with the plague-stricken 'pour [les] panser et médicamenter selon les avis qui lui en seraient donnés de la part des médecin et chirurgien de la santé'.[62]

In the reign of Louis XIV women took to advertising and setting down on paper the medical skills which they had acquired through observation and experiment. The *Mercure Galant* in September 1685 broadcasts the successes of a young bone-setter from the Bourbonnais, Mlle de Remirand, and in July 1700 recommends Mme de Vaux's cure for hernia, approved by the royal doctor. Memorialists exalt the poultices of Mme Fouquet,[63] mother of the disgraced superintendant of finances, whose collected remedies were printed for the benefit of the public in 1675. Two years later Marguerite Du Tertre, a qualified midwife at the Hôtel-Dieu in Paris, obtained the approval of the Faculty of Medicine for the publication of her *Instruction Familière et Utile aux Sages-Femmes* which the administrators of the hospital had commissioned.[64] The king himself was an excellent publicity agent for female healers since he willingly allowed their balms and ointments to be applied to sore spots on the royal anatomy.[65]

Professional practitioners viewed with ill-concealed fury the activities of amateurs, or *empiriques* as they were branded, who had never mumbled Latin in the medical schools and who relied solely on practical experience. When the English doctor Martin Lister travelled to Paris in 1698 his French colleagues grumbled to him about the disrepute into which medicine had fallen because of the 'boundless confidence and intruding of quacks, women, and monks'.[66] By the end of the century women had become a force to be reckoned with in the medical profession, even if they had been obliged to sneak in through the back door.

Active in the relief of physical ills, women were also alert to the intellectual needs of their sex. In the teaching as in the healing sphere the religious orders had led the way and it was they who commanded the best-trained female personnel. In the seventeenth century they possessed a virtual monopoly of girls' education, but their efforts were supplemented, particularly in the instruction of the lower classes, by those of laywomen.

It often came about that individuals or small groups of friends, moved by piety and compassion, dedicated their lives to saving young girls from the perils of ignorance, taking them into their homes to instruct them in the rudiments that would enable them to make an honest living. Sometimes small groups of devout laywomen formed the nucleus of a future teaching order[67] or merged with an existing one,[68] in which case they proceeded to adopt the traditional conventual methods of education described in Chapter 2. But there were in addition a number of laywomen, distinct from any religious body, who aspired simply to earn their keep by teaching. The precise origins of these women, their educational standards and methods, their way of life, are all shrouded in obscurity. Memoirs, letters, travellers' accounts, fiction, pass over them in almost complete silence, as indeed they do the school-master. Government briefs and despatches recall their existence in the last decades of the century when the monarch's eyes were opened to the key role that teachers had to play in his campaign to wipe out the Protestant 'heresy'.

From the sparse information available it appears firstly that emphasis was placed upon subordinating the schoolmistress, like the contemporary midwife, to ecclesiastical authority. In the capital the Church precentor had jurisdiction over the reception and dismissal of masters and mistresses. The latter were authorised by *lettres de provision* to teach for one year, at the end of which the *lettres* had to be renewed at a cost of ten *sous*.[69] This arrangement, it was thought, kept teachers on their toes. The precentor himself examined new recruits into the profession. He required proof of Catholicism and good repute,[70] and was careful to inspect the intending schoolmistress's handwriting: 'Que si aucunes n'ont pas ce talent, il leur permet de faire venir dans leurs écoles à leurs dépens d'autres femmes expertes, ou des maîtres d'école, et même des écrivains jurés, qui enseignent leurs filles en leur présence.'[71] The standard of education demanded from the schoolmistress was obviously not very high. It sufficed that she was in a position to give elementary religious and moral instruction to her pupils, the rest being of secondary importance.[72] The examination terminated, the accepted candidate would be sent forth to impart what knowledge she possessed with a reminder that she had to be at work every day except Sundays and holy days from eight till eleven in the morning and from two till five in the afternoon, and must keep prominently displayed in her schoolroom a crucifix or image of the Virgin before which prayers could be said at the commencement of lessons.[73] Under no circumstances was she to instruct boys, but she could accept Protestant girls as pupils.[74] Since the precentor had the right not only to fix the number of pupils but also to prescribe what should be taught to them[75] there was little room for innovation. Evidence from elsewhere in France proves that mistresses were content to use the time-honoured methods of instruction. Thomas Du Fossé penned the following rare portrait of some schoolmistresses whose work he paused to watch when travelling through Pithiviers (Loiret) in 1691:

> Nous vîmes avec grande édification dans Pluviers [sic] deux damoiselles très sages, qui tenaient l'école des filles et s'en acquittaient avec tout le soin et toute l'habileté possible. C'était une chose curieuse que d'entendre ces jeunes filles réciter toutes ensemble, et toutes séparément, les articles différents qu'on leur demandait du catéchisme ou d'autres choses. Car, en même temps que la maîtresse avait achevé la demande, la première du banc commençait la réponse; la seconde continuait; la troisième reprenait; et ainsi des autres, chacune à son tour...[76]

Rote-learning and the cultivation of the memory were both fundamental to the techniques employed by nuns.

After the Revocation of the Edict of Nantes the availability of pedagogues for indoctrination purposes became a matter of urgency. Formal legislation obliging all parishes still devoid of schoolmasters and mistresses to institute them at the rate of 150 *livres* per annum for men and 100 *livres* for women was tardily promulgated in December 1698.[77] Prior to that date, however, provincial *intendants* had been asked to report on the possibility of installing them in the different localities and to indicate means of remunerating them. Replies were optimistic. Foucault, *intendant* at Poitiers, proposed to Louis XIV in 1687 the establishment of thirteen schoolmistresses in the diocese of Poitiers, eight in that of Luçon and six in that of La Rochelle. They were to be drawn from the *Nouvelles Catholiques* of Poitiers, that is to say from amongst the newly converted Protestants, and paid forty *écus* per annum. Louis naturally hesitated to confide the instruction of youth to recent 'heretics', but while waiting for time to test the sincerity of their abjurations he made no objection to the wages suggested since they could be paid from the proceeds of confiscated Protestant property.[78] Not every area had within reach such a facile source of money. It was usual in the seventeenth century, when a collectivity required extra finances for a particular project, to raise the money by increasing, or freshly imposing, taxes. The *intendant* of Moulins, Le Vayer, wrote to his superiors on behalf of the parishioners of Aubusson on 26 April 1699 requesting permission for them to levy thirty *sous* on every barrel of wine sold, 'pour fournir à l'entretien de trois ou quatre régents et de deux ou trois maîtresses'. By 25 November he was reporting that the levy had been dropped to ten *sous* per barrel, deemed sufficient to provide 450 *livres* for the upkeep of a reduced number of two masters and two mistresses.[79] Increased taxation has never been welcomed in any age, but in the seventeenth century, when tax-payers laboured under a crushing burden of direct and indirect levies, it rapidly became intolerable. Parents summoned to defray the cost not only of the schoolmistress's wages but also of fees for their children to attend classes were likely to view her installation as more of a liability than an asset. Teachers' wages quickly fell into arrears[80] and, with a major incentive to enter the profession removed, posts became impossible to fill.[81]

At no stage therefore were lay mistresses able to present a serious challenge to their cloistered counterparts. Their level of education left much to be desired, their continuation in office was not automatic, they could rely upon no permanent schoolroom of the type that could easily be made available in a convent and, above all, they lacked the venerable aura which surrounded the religious orders. Nevertheless their services were such as to command respect and consideration. Into their hands were confided the moral and intellectual formation of a community's womanhood. Their very ability to read and write, if fully developed, made them potentially as valuable outside school hours as within. Help given in composing or deciphering letters and documents afforded access to the intimacies of family life and contact, perhaps, with parish leaders. Any social or church work[82] that they might be invited to undertake as a result could only enhance their status. Though sprung from humble origins and living and working amongst those of similar provenance, their calling and their tincture of learning served to elevate them above the amorphous masses to which no one cared to be assigned: 'le bas peuple' or 'la lie du peuple'.

Yet grouped under these vague and derogatory headings lay a very considerable part of the population, in terms of both numbers and usefulness to the community. Marshal Vauban reminded readers of his *Dîme Royale*, composed in 1698, that these social Untouchables constituted the very arteries of the nation because they not only paid the most taxes but in addition executed 'tous les gros ouvrages des villes et de la campagne, sans quoi ni eux, ni les autres ne pourraient vivre'.[83] The 'gros ouvrages' in question – the backbreaking, dangerous and dirty jobs shunned by the rest of society – were carried out no less by the so-called weaker sex than by the strong one. In a social stratum where work was often temporary and seasonal in nature a woman's ability to contribute to the family exchequer even during the full employment, but especially during the unemployment, of her menfolk meant the difference between starvation and subsistence. Of all the ways of earning open to her the most popular was to increase the output from her domestic spinning, lace-making or stocking-knitting until she had a surplus to sell to passing traders and merchants. Alternatively, or rather simultaneously, she reared a few livestock – a couple of hens if the family was very poor, a pig, goat or cow whenever the budget stretched that far – the produce from which was used for home consumption or sold or bartered for other commodities. If the household was fortunate enough to own a strip of land, without which Vauban saw little chance of its survival, she grew vegetables, herbs, perhaps a few cereals, for the table or the market.[84]

Her labour, in common with that of her menfolk, had always to be at the disposal of outsiders. No doubt she preferred those jobs which were an extension of familiar household occupations or those where she could deploy her charms and eloquence – suckling the babies of the rich, taking in laundry, [85] selling every conceivable commodity from water to tourist souvenirs[86] – but she had to be prepared to turn her hand to sterner tasks. In the countryside women tilled the soil, cut the corn and cultivated the vine alongside the men, adopting in some areas the same dress for greater ease of movement.[87] Subject to the feudal due of the *corvée*, they paid it by assisting in the construction of canals and fortifications.[88] In the towns, likewise, they were employed in moving earth and stones for masons,[89] but had more opportunity to demonstrate their versatility. In Paris they pushed behind two-wheeled carriages known as *vinaigrettes*, while a man pulled in front.[90] At Lyon they plied little boats on the river and pestered passers-by for their custom.[91] On occasion they deputised for the public executioner.[92]

Returns for their exertions were poor. Women at Montpellier in the winter of 1676 received five *sous* a day for shifting earth in baskets, as opposed to the twelve *sous* a day earned by the men. At harvest time they could expect seven *sous*; the men, eighteen.[93] Around the same time Colbert rebuked his overseer of fortifications for giving men engaged on the *corvée* ten *sous* a day and women six *sous*, and ordered payment to be reduced to munition bread only, as had been the custom in the past.[94] Women's wages were as a rule slightly more or less than half those of men, and totally disproportionate to the physical effort and time expended. In the silk mills at Tours girls walked an estimated seven leagues every day in the process of turning a machine that twisted and wound yarn from more than 120 spools simultaneously. Their work began at five in the morning and lasted until night-time, with only two one-hour breaks. Their recompense was five *sous* a day.[95] Yet they were the lucky ones. A peasant woman from the vicinity of Bordeaux told John Locke in 1678 that her husband earned seven *sous* a day, out of which their two selves and three children had to be maintained and house-rent and taxes paid. 'She indeed got 3 or 3½ s. [*sous*] per diem when she could get work, which was but seldom. Other times she span hemp, which was for their clothes and yielded no money.' Handicapped by their inability to offer special skills and by their domestic responsibilities, many women hunted for work in vain. Inevitably they sank into abject poverty. Locke's interlocutress dwelt in a 'poor one room and one storey open to the tiles, without window', on a diet of rye bread and water varied by an occasional dish of offal. The tax-collector had not long ago seized all her cooking utensils, 'money not being ready'.[96]

Locke's observations were made well before the French provinces felt the full impact of the ruinous wars into which Louis XIV plunged his people. By 1698 Vauban calculated that nearly one tenth of the 'peuple' were reduced to mendicity and over half the remainder to approximately the same state.[97] For daring to shatter the myth of a happy and thriving population he died in disgrace.[98] Kings and courtiers judged the condition of the rabble on the strength of the prettified village girls who danced at their *châteaux*[99] and the prosperous *marchandes* glimpsed at trade fairs during sporadic visits to Paris.[100] The bourgeoisie, composed of absentee landlords for the most part, was blissfully ignorant of things rural[101] and took care to preserve a healthy distance between itself and the urban riff-raff. Out of touch with the true plight of the masses, the social élite were that much more disposed to accept as reality the idyllic fictions imagined by men of letters sprung from their own ranks, and to believe that shepherdess Marion actually did while away the hours with shepherd Robin at nothing more strenuous than amorous dalliance. The process of disillusionment was long and slow, and belongs to the history of the following century, when the unlovely face of want and toil was quite literally thrust before disbelieving aristocratic eyes.[102]

Survival, for the lower-class woman, depended on her adaptability. Limitation to one trade meant liability to starvation every time the national or local economy traversed one of the crises to which they were fatally prone. The only hope of counteracting the effects of inflation, unemployment and redundancy lay in a woman's ability to switch from one occupation to another according to season and demand. In this respect disreputable trades offered much better prospects than the reputable kind. The work involved might still be subject to fluctuations in demand, but less so than in most conventional jobs because it tended towards the satisfaction of perennial desires and weaknesses in human nature. Profits were high in return for little effort compared with that needed to plough a field or drudge in a mill all day. Success spelt not only freedom from material worries, but also fame, influential patrons, distinguished protectors. In the face of such powerful arguments scruples were apt to fade and penalties to seem easily payable.

9
Women at Work III

The need to find avenues of escape from the rigours of existence was as keenly felt in the seventeenth century as at any epoch in mankind's chequered history. Discounting suicide, forbidden to every Christian, the simplest solution to the problem consisted in beating a hasty retreat from the immediate source of pain or anxiety, were it the insatiable creditor, the marauding soldier, the killer disease or the storm-wrecked home. But even supposing that the cause of distress could be easily located, physical flight was not always practicable or adequate. Psychological withdrawal into realms of illusion and fantasy was a tempting substitute which cost seekers-after-release either as little as a flight of the imagination or as much as they cared to pay for aids to bolster fallacious hopes and induce artificial sensations of well-being. Taking the sting out of living was a prosperous business on which sizeable groups of women flourished. In respectable circles their reputation was unenviable. Yet at the same time they attracted a large and select clientele and achieved in some cases a fame that won for them a place in factual and fictional documents denied to more orthodox luminaries of their sex.

Amongst the purveyors of dreams actresses occupied a privileged position. The exercise of their profession kept them constantly in the public eye, surrounded by all the accessories proper to the transformation of the humdrum into the exotic and the sublime. That they used their advantages to the full may be deduced from expressions of concern over the permanence of illusions contracted in the theatre. Women themselves were considered exceptionally vulnerable to this form of make-believe. In his *Traité de la Comédie* Nicole maintained that those who witnessed the adventures and adoration of their sex on the stage absorbed the romantic vision of existence to the extent that real life soon became intolerable:

> ... les femmes principalement, prenant plaisir aux adorations qu'on y rend à celles de leur sexe ... s'impriment tellement dans

la fantaisie cette sorte de vie, que les petites affaires de leur ménage leur deviennent insupportables. Et quand elles reviennent dans leurs maisons avec cet esprit évaporé, elles y trouvent tout désagréable, et surtout leurs maris, qui étant occupés de leurs affaires, ne sont pas toujours en humeur de leur rendre ces complaisances ridicules, qu'on rend aux femmes dans les comédies.[1]

To the argument that drama divorced the spectator from reality supporters of the theatre retorted that it did indeed have a diverting action, but that this tended in the salutary direction of discouraging vice and promoting virtue.[2]

The prolonged dispute over the merits and demerits of the theatre had the effect, invaluable for the historian, of casting the spotlight onto the life and customs of those who worked there, as brochures, novels and plays in abundance vied to introduce the public backstage so that they could judge for themselves. Actresses, sometimes playing their real selves as in Molière's *Impromptu de Versailles*, were shown in the hustle and bustle of preparing for performances, rehearsing lines with their co-stars, arguing with the director, complaining loudly about the importunities of stage-door admirers and about their public image.[3] The theatre was a province wherein the nascent feminism of the century could observe the uncontested achievement of some of its more sane ideals. By tacit agreement women in the acting profession had always been regarded as the equals of their male associates. Once they had completed a period of apprenticeship in minor utility parts and, as fully trained performers, had signed a contract with a company for one or more years,[4] their approval had to be sought before any change affecting the company was made: 'L'autorité de l'état [théâtral] est partagée entre les deux sexes, les femmes lui étant utiles autant ou plus que les hommes, et elles ont voix délibérative en toutes les affaires qui regardent l'intérêt commun.'[5] They had the right to be present when new plays were being considered for acceptance, though out of modesty they preferred to leave this chore to their masculine colleagues.[6] When takings were shared out at the end of the day they queued alongside the actors to receive their stipulated portion.[7]

The usefulness of women to the troupe explains the deference with which they were treated. The beauty of the actresses was a box-office attraction on a level with, and sometimes surpassing, that of the play itself. High prices were paid for seats on the actual stage from which the actresses' charms, tantalisingly displayed in low-cut dresses,[8] could be ogled at closer quarters.[9] For those who could only afford to stand in the pit there was still the opportunity, once the concluding farce was over, to crowd into the actresses' dressing-room and attempt familiarities seemingly authorised by the licence of the stage role just abandoned.[10] Playwrights, bewitched in turn, took to composing roles specially for their favourites,[11] and paid public tribute to the way in which actresses ensured the success of productions. An aspiring actor in Gougenot's *Comédie des Comédiens* (1633) is made to declare that 'quelque peine que puisse prendre le meilleur acteur du monde, on donne toujours l'avantage aux femmes', to which his companion replies, 'Il est vrai. J'étais l'autre jour à l'Hôtel de Bourgogne, où j'entendais mille voix, dont les unes disaient: Ha! que voilà une femme qui joue bien! et les autres: Celle-là fait encore mieux.'[12] Actors obviously found it difficult to hold their own, though a spirit of competition improved the quality of performances.[13]

Professional recognition and success brought both social and material gains. Though not as base-born as some insinuated,[14] actresses were on the whole of modest origins,[15] a circumstance which outside the profession would have forever closed to them all the doors that mattered. But as the popularity of the theatre, and their own, increased, they began to contract solid bourgeois alliances[16] and to frequent, both in a business and in a private capacity, persons of quality and the court. Playing to a full house or before a select company developed a confidence and fluency which stood them in good stead when called upon to mingle with their social superiors, while a veneer of culture, acquired in the last resort from the dramas they performed, enabled them to acquit themselves honourably in polite conversation.[17]

They profited from their distinguished contacts to strengthen their material position. Wealthy patrons were persuaded to commission plays to set off their talents,[18] to hire their company at times of family rejoicing,[19] to provide cash subsidies,[20] theatrical props[21] and, above all, new costumes. Performers were frequently required, when signing contracts, to undertake to supply the costumes necessary for the representation of all their various roles.[22] The obligation was hard on the purse. Costumes not only had to be sufficiently eye-catching to satisfy the audiences' perpetual craving for spectacle and novelty, but needed to change according to prevailing fashions[23] since scant attention was paid to reproducing authentic historical dress. In the early days, when funds were low, troupes fell back upon second-hand clothes merchants,[24] but the increasing practice by which patrons donated used finery helped actors and actresses to cut their costs while presenting a smart appearance to the auditorium.[25]

All the plaudits, social satisfactions and material gratifications that came their way could not alter the fact that actresses pursued a calling which all God-fearing citizens understood that it was their duty to deplore and to shun. The metropolitan Church, bearing in mind the spectacles which the first Christians had been condemned to provide in the Roman arenas, ranked those who perpetuated kindred amusements with adulterers, usurers, sorcerers and blasphemers as persons unworthy to receive the sacraments unless they renounced their impious activity. Even the champions of the dramatic art hesitated to give its interpreters an absolutely clean bill of morality. Scudéry recalled in his apologetic *Comédie des Comédiens* (1635) that the theatrical mode of living was commonly pictured as 'un libertinage, une licence au vice, à l'impureté, à l'oisiveté et au dérèglement' (I.ii) and that virtuous actresses were hailed as prodigies (III.i),[26] before he went on to give one such prodigy a chance to refute the critics. Scarron depicted the actress heroines of his *Roman Comique* (1651–7) as models of impeccable virtue, but slyly insinuated that they had few imitators: 'Ce n'est pas à dire qu'il n'y en [de femmes] ait de la profession qui n'en [de vertu] manquent point, mais dans l'opinion du monde, qui se trompe peut-être, elles en sont moins chargées que de vieille broderie et de fard.'[27]

In defence of actresses it was pointed out that their morals were judged on the strength of the uninhibited manners characteristic of the works which they were asked to represent in the early decades of the century.[28] This excuse was removed when Louis XIII, officially approving a recent purge of stage morals, passed an edict in 1641 to the effect that, provided the purity of the drama was maintained, actors and actresses were no longer to suffer because of any social stigma hitherto attached to their profession.[29] The monarch's expectations regarding the drama were by and large fulfilled, but the same could not be said of the morals of the acting personnel, which if anything deteriorated. Actresses in Louis XIV's France, as in Charles II's England, were the acknowledged mistresses of the highest in the land, trailing the king's own son

and nephew amongst their retinue of gallants.[30] Far from concealing their debauchery they complacently paraded the rewards that
it brought, a sight which roused the ire of the *curé* of Versailles: 'On
les voyait avec horreur être vêtues comme des princesses, avoir des
meubles très magnifiques, des trains superbes, de belles maisons à
la ville et à la campagne que leurs galants leur achetaient, amasser
du bien, se faire des revenus, en un mot profiter autant qu'elles le
pouvaient de leurs crimes et entasser chez elles les dépouilles des
plus grandes maisons du royaume'.[31] Not surprisingly the clergy
refused to soften its rigorous attitude towards members of the
profession. In 1694 Bossuet was still arguing that a tomb was
preferable to an actress's life,[32] and on the threshold of the
so-called Age of Enlightenment Voltaire was still protesting against
the denial of Christian burial to Adrienne Lecouvreur,[33]

> Celle qui dans la Grèce aurait eu des autels.

Adulated but despised, the actress was financed, applauded and
fêted by that same public who subscribed to her spiritual ostracism
from the community.[34]

Though the theatre was a form of escapism patronised by high-
and low-born alike, theatrical productions of any substance were
aimed primarily at a socially and intellectually refined minority –
the *honnêtes gens* to whose enlightened judgement playwrights
were so fond of appealing. But there were other diversions which
required no cultural preparation whatsoever for their morale-
boosting effects to be fully appreciated. One of the most popular,
in every sense of the word, was alcohol.

The ordinary dispenser of this valued commodity, the tavern
landlady (*hôtesse*), was quite a 'character' and seems to have
completely overshadowed her counterpart, the landlord, in the
memories of her clients. Contemporaries depict her as a woman of
generous dimensions, the result of Low Country origins or too
frequent sampling of her own merchandise.[35] The sharpness and
quickness of her tongue were legendary. Bishop Huet relates how
as a youth he and a travelling companion decided to amuse
themselves by addressing everyone they met in impromptu verse,
and how a landlady whom they greeted in the agreed manner
replied instantly in the same strain with a volubility that made
them ashamed of their slowness.[36] Two vices were attributed to
those of her trade. The first was rapacity, particularly where

unsuspecting foreigners were concerned.[37] The trait was excusable in view of the number of customers, princes and clerics[38] among them, who tried to dodge payment for refreshments and accommodation. But cheating *hôtesses* was inadvisable; in 1600 one of them conspired to poison Henri IV for failing to settle an old debt.[39]

The second vice, laxity of morals, was encouraged by the overcrowding, familiarity and promiscuity that were part and parcel of tavern life in seventeenth-century Europe generally.[40] Patrons remarked upon the hostess's eagerness to present herself for the kiss with which every new female acquaintance was customarily saluted in France,[41] and gossiped about her engagement in prostitution and procuring.[42] In the novel and on the stage her stock role was that of a woman of flammable passions who spent an undue amount of time in pert dalliance with handsome clients.[43] Her lapses, however, did not diminish the *hôtesse's* clientele nor prevent her from winning general esteem. Tallemant, ordinarily no respecter of females, has warm praise for Mme Du Ryer, owner of a famous hostelry at Saint-Cloud, whose charitable actions effaced a wanton youth and convinced initially scrupulous ladies that their reputation would not suffer from wining and dining in her establishment.[44]

Fine ladies needed no persuasion to frequent the *devineresse* or fortune-teller, whose assurances of secrecy and discretion augured well for the preservation of a decorous façade. Clandestinity played an important part in creating an air of mystery fit to impress the gullible and deceive the credulous. It was also vital for the *devineresse's* protection, since in the popular imagination she differed little from the sorceress whose fancied ability to cast spells on man and beast caused panic terrors leading in backward country districts to massacres[45] and in towns to the scaffold and the stake.[46]

The French nation was profoundly superstitious. Ignorant or imperfectly informed about the causes of natural phenomena, men and women readily attributed them to the workings of occult powers. These powers might stem from God and manifest themselves in the protective and curative actions of guardian angels, saints and the king, whose touch was thought to heal the scrofulous; or they might issue from Satan and take the form of Lucifer himself or that of malevolent demons and evil spirits. Angels and demons were propitiated and conjured with equal fervour by means of prayers, exorcisms, charms, incantations and sacrifices. Belief in the occult transcended all barriers of class and culture. A man of the social and intellectual distinction of Cardinal Richelieu upheld the power of talismans to ward off disease.[47] Blaise Pascal's devout and learned family was convinced that he owed his survival to the removal of a curse put upon him in infancy.[48] Contemporaries liked to think, however, that magic and superstition enthralled the female half of the population, whose minds were too weak to resist and whose imaginations were easily inflamed.[49] They pointed to the pious Mme de Maintenon's relations with a reputed sorceress, Mme Arnoul,[50] and her bosom friendship with Mme d'Heurdicourt, an astrology enthusiast.[51] They cited the vogue of the Italian occultist and graphologist Primi Visconti, who numbered among his consultants Louis XIV's cousin, the Duchesse de Montpensier, and Cardinal Mazarin's niece, the Comtesse de Soissons.[52] Above all they quoted the series of resounding trials in Paris which between 1679 and 1682 had suddenly exposed the dangerous excesses of which the fortune-tellers and their clients were capable.

The trials were set in motion by the arrest early in the year 1679 of three *devineresses*: Marie Bosse, widow of a horse-dealer; Marie Vigoureux, a tailor's wife; and Catherine Deshayes, better known as La Voisin, wife of a ruined haberdasher. The confessions of these women were such as to precipitate further arrests of their associates and dupes and the establishment of a special tribunal, the Chambre Ardente, to judge all those taken into custody. Interrogations revealed that La Voisin and her emulators had used fortune-telling as a cover for their real specialities: procuring abortions,[53] mixing potions to win indifferent lovers, supplying poisons to dispose of unwanted husbands, and arranging for perverted priests to say black masses at which infants were sacrificed.[54] Reeling from disclosures even more horrifying than those which had emerged during the trial of the mass poisoner Marie de Brinvilliers, decapitated three years earlier,[55] Parisians were astounded to learn that the fortune-tellers' clientele was drawn from the élite of the court and the city. La Voisin had kept a list of her clients' names, along with the reasons for their visits. The naive had approached her with harmless enough requests for beauty aids. The Duchesse de Foix wanted a preparation to fill out her bust, and Mme de Vassé something to develop her hips and height.[56] But the lovelorn queued behind Louis XIV's mistress

Mme de Montespan to collect philtres and to book the unholy masses, performed over their own naked bodies, from which they departed clutching phials of fresh human blood.[57] Women tormented by ambition, revenge and adulterous passion asked boldly for help in eliminating obstacles to their desires. The Comtesse de Soissons, another of Louis's favourites, the Comtesse du Roure and the Vicomtesse de Polignac were indicted for planning to do away with Mlle de La Vallière, who had preceded Mme de Montespan in the good graces of the king.[58] Mme de Vivonne was accused of similar designs on the life of Colbert and of attempting to further them by participating in black masses and having her unborn child consecrated to the devil.[59] Présidente Le Féron was charged with procuring her viduity by means of one of La Voisin's poisons, and Mme de Dreux, sister of the royal presenter of ambassadors, and the Duchesse de Bouillon, sister of the Comtesse de Soissons, were arraigned for taking steps to imitate her.[60] The Princesse de Tingry was cited to appear before the tribunal on the allegation of having murdered the fruits of intercourse with her own brother-in-law, the Maréchal de Luxembourg.[61]

As the list of turpitudes grew progressively longer, high society trembled for its reputation and its liberty.[62] A movement of revulsion swept through the public. 'Cela fait horreur à toute l'Europe', wrote Mme de Sévigné on 29 January 1680, 'et ceux qui nous liront dans cent ans plaindront ceux qui auront été témoins de ces accusations.'[63] But the reaction was short-lived. The incriminated classes, of whom Mme de Sévigné was a typical spokeswoman, rapidly convinced themselves that there was more suspicion than substance in the charges made, and that 'ces sorcières . . . font horreur à toute l'Europe d'une bagatelle'.[64] Louis XIV, besmirched by the involvement of Mme de Montespan with the *devineresses*, and his ministers, concerned over the defamation of France's name abroad, connived at this face-saving interpretation of events. The high-born female defendants in the case paid lightly for what was presented as a mere scatterbrained impulse on their part. The Comtesse de Soissons was openly allowed time to escape across the French frontier, taking with her another suspected poisoner, the Marquise d'Alluye, so that they should avoid trial.[65] The Princesse de Tingry and the Duchesse de Bouillon, summoned to appear before the tribunal, were escorted thither in triumphal procession by their noble relatives.[66] The Duchesse, according to Mme de Sévigné, 'entra comme une petite reine' and proceeded to mock the presiding magistrate La Reynie, with a verve slightly coloured by the reporter's prejudices.[67] Her punishment, like that of her equals, consisted of a mild banishment from the capital.[68]

The weight of royal 'justice' fell much more heavily on the low-born *devineresses* in that an example had to be made to deter others and their compromising revelations had to be smothered at all costs. The means employed to achieve those ends highlighted the barbarity of seventeenth-century criminal procedure. Detainees whose lives were spared were dispersed amongst outlying strongholds of the kingdom, and officials responsible for their close confinement received instructions to use terrorism to keep them quiet: 'empêcher que l'on n'entende les sottises qu'ils pourront crier tout haut, leur étant souvent arrivé d'en dire touchant Mme de Montespan, qui sont sans aucun fondement, les menaçant de les faire corriger si cruellement au moindre bruit qu'ils feront, qu'il n'y en ait pas un qui ose souffler'.[69] The remainder had their tongues permanently stilled. Section 19, Articles 1 and 3 of the *Code Criminel*, promulgated in 1670, allowed those suspected of crimes carrying the death penalty to be tortured to obtain definite proof of guilt, and further provided for a condemned person to undergo torture before execution in order that the names of accomplices might be divulged. Their sex in no way saved the principal actresses in this lugubrious drama from the application of the letter of the law. Mme de Sévigné, an avid collector of details about the death agonies of the fortune-tellers, told of one who, on the point of being tortured and hanged, was refused her life in return for promising a full confession and so made a vow, which she kept, that pain would not unseal her lips: 'On lui donna la question ordinaire, extraordinaire, et si extraordinairement extraordinaire, qu'elle pensa y mourir'. The Marquise went on to mention, 'en passant', 'une autre qui expira, le médecin lui tenant le pouls', a probable reference to the inaptly named Marie Vigoureux, who died at the hands of her tormentors in May 1679.[70] La Voisin's death sentence also comprised preliminary torture. As with several of the *devineresses* considered too delicate or too fat to withstand it, the authorities humanely spared her the torture which consisted of inserting a funnel into the victim's mouth and pouring in water until a confession, or suffocation, ensued. Instead they used the *brodequins* which gradually crushed the sufferer's legs.[71] The *devineresse* recovered with the help of bottles of liquor, and when she was taken to execution the ruddiness of her complexion matched that of the flames in which she was burned alive.[72] Mme de Sévigné, who had personally witnessed the march to the stake, was edified to learn afterwards that 'certains petits adoucissements' were practised when burning women: logs were thrown on top of them and the executioner's assistants tore off their heads with iron hooks.[73]

With the scattering of the *devineresses'* ashes to the winds France breathed again, but uneasily. The trials spread such fear and mistrust that a simple attack of indigestion was apt to lead to accusations of poison and to mass arrests of cooks and domestics. They brought to public attention, too, the utility of poison in hastening the conclusion of marriages and the receipt of legacies.[74] To help calm apprehensions and to forestall any possible recrudescence of poisonings, recourse was had to ridicule. In 1679 what was undoubtedly a government-approved if not government-inspired play, *La Devineresse* by Thomas Corneille and Jean Donneau de Visé, belittled fortune-tellers in the personage of Mme Jobin and mocked the credulity of their clientele. Mme Jobin is represented as being able to satisfy the women from all classes of society who troop to consult her about their looks or their love-life, not because she possesses any special powers of magic or clairvoyance, but because they unwittingly reveal their own affairs to her. The details she fills in with the help of spies and domestics who assist her in performing supposed enchantments. She is made to explain carefully for the benefit of the audience that what clients take to be manifestations of the supernatural are merely the adroitly staged inventions of a fertile imagination and deceive only because of the onlookers' terror. Abruptly divested of their supernatural aura, the *devineresses* appeared in the reassuringly human light of clever charlatans.

To reinforce the message of *La Devineresse* an edict appeared in August 1682, a month after the final session of the Chambre Ardente, banishing all magicians and fortune-tellers from France and subjecting the manufacture and sale of poisons to stringent controls.[75] A definitive gesture of purgation had, it seemed, been made. But literary sallies against fortune-tellers and their dupes continued to revive memories down to the end of the century[76] and old terrors needed little incitement to break out afresh. On 13 June 1701 the royal attorney of the Châtelet tribunal in Paris informed his superiors of recent rumours that children were being abducted, their throats cut and their blood used for the bath of a person of quality. 'Ces visions et ces mouvements de la fureur du peuple ne sont pas nouveaux,' he continued; 'j'en ai vu arriver ... qui se portèrent à un tel excès, qu'en divers quartiers de Paris il y eut des femmes presque assommées de coups et prêtes à être jetées dans la rivière et dans des égouts, parce qu'on les accusait d'être des preneuses d'enfants.'[77] Government reassurances were manifestly impotent to erase the impressions made by three long years of suspicion, accusation, arrest, exposure, torture and execution.[78]

Like the fortune-teller's trade, that of the prostitute was practised in a twilight world rarely illuminated save by the fulminations of the law and the lampoons of the satirists. Both were as old as time itself and in many instances overlapped. Prostitutes acquired, or availed themselves of, the *devineresses'* skill in making charms and potions to heighten sex appeal,[79] and of their expertise in abortion and infanticide. The *devineresses* were for their part notoriously promiscuous in morals and participated in rites and black masses where the sexual element was pronounced. Relations between the two groups could only be cemented by the fact that both had to operate on a clandestine or semi-clandestine basis since both were liable to persecution. Though prostitutes never became embroiled in the kind of national scandal that sent the leading *devineresses* to the stake, they plied their trade forever in the shadow of the police, the penitentiary and the public executioner. From time to time authorities would be seized with the urge to spring-clean the streets, both literally and metaphorically. Police ordinances would be issued enjoining all debauched women to leave town within a brief span, on pain of diverse sanctions.[80] Those too slow in going underground were rounded up and taken either to a correctional prison or to a convent that served in its stead. Paris possessed a number of such institutions, of which the most famous were La Refuge and La Salpétrière, offshoots of the Hôpital Général, and the convent of the Madelonnettes[91] which gave hospitality for a while to the impenitent Ninon de Lenclos. The grimness of life within prison walls is revealed by a set of regulations drafted in 1684 for the treatment of offenders incarcerated in La Salpétrière. In between morning and evening prayers they were constrained to work 'le plus longtemps, et aux ouvrages les plus rudes que leurs forces et les lieux où [elles] seront le pourront permettre'. They were dressed in coarse cloth and sabots and fed on soup, bread and water, unless the fruits of their labour procured them the wherewithal to buy supplementary victuals. Laziness and other faults were punished by withdrawal of the soup ration, increased work, stricter confinement and the pillory.[82] Harsh though these conditions appeared, the alternatives were more so. When detention centres were full, prostitutes were speeded out of town by public whipping, branding or mutilation.[83] An ordinance of 1684, confirmed in 1687, condemned camp-followers in the Versailles area to have their nose and ears slit (*coupés*).[84] As an ultimate deterrent the government suspended over the prostitute's head the threat of deportation to the colonies, first put into effect long before tears were shed over the tragic fate of Manon Lescaut.[85]

The reiteration and the savagery of penalties against prostitutes smack of desperate remedies tried by authorities conscious of fighting a losing battle. Skilled in the arts of pleasing and cajoling, a pretty debauchee would have little difficulty in circumventing police officials[86] or in contacting admirers to help her break her way out to freedom. In 1640 the 'bonnes dames' of Le Puy were just congratulating themselves on having secured the incarceration of the local whores when they learned that a band of gallants had demolished the prison wall to set the captives free.[87] Ninon owed the brevity of her stay with the Madelonnettes to the necessity for the watch to patrol nightly round the convent for fear of its invasion by the young rakes of the court.[88]

The popularity of harlots stemmed from talents other than the obvious ones. Like workers in orthodox trades they had their own professional hierarchy, ranging from the street-walker to the courtesan, who was in a class apart. The courtesan continued the traditions of the *hetaira* of ancient Greece and the *cortegiana* of Renaissance Italy, whose company had been sought as much for their breeding and culture as for their fabled physical charms. The two outstanding courtesans of seventeenth-century France, Marion de Lorme and Ninon de Lenclos, both sprang from the minor provincial nobility. Both could sing and play musical instruments, and Ninon was well versed in modern languages and philosophy.[89] Men of eminence and learning were their intimates, as well as ladies whose morals had to be above suspicion. Marion succeeded in tickling the fancy of Richelieu, his aristocratic victim Cinq-Mars, the future Maréchal d'Albret and a string of Parlement presidents.[90] Ninon was firm friends, amongst a host of others, with Boisrobert[91] and Saint-Evremond,[92] and consulted by Molière on the subject of his plays.[93] She maintained cordial relations with her old acquaintance Mme de Maintenon[94] and was cited by Queen Christina of Sweden as the only ornament lacking for the perfection of the French court.[95] Contemporaries marvelled at the deference and esteem accorded to the courtesan. 'On t'offre le tapis même à la Comédie,' testified Antoine Mareschal in an early comedy of manners, Le Railleur (1636):

> On y marque ta loge, et le vaillant portier
> A te la conserver signale son métier;
> Ton carrosse est suivi de laquais et de pages;
> Tes sœurs les craignent tant, tu les as à tes gages;
> Le nombre des seigneurs qui passent par tes bras
> Hausse á deux mille écus la rente de tes draps. (II.1)

Wonderment increased as the careers of Marion and Ninon unfolded and drew to their close. 'Une autre, en faisant ce qu'elle faisait, aurait déshonoré sa famille; cependant comme on vivait avec elle avec respect!' exclaimed Tallemant of Marion. 'La considération, chose étrange, qu'elle s'était acquise, le nombre et la distinction de ses amis et de ses connaissances [continuèrent] quand les charmes cessèrent de lui attirer du monde', echoed Saint-Simon of Ninon.[96] Honoured by their superiors, respected by their inferiors, surrounded by wealth and luxury, the courtesans reigned supreme within their own domains.

To add to the general paradox of their existence they were moral and virtuous after a fashion. Certainly they were lascivious and stooped to the iniquities common amongst the basest members of their profession. But they lived according to creeds which had a persuasive air of rationality, and they knew the meaning of charity, generosity and piety. Ninon, equally frank in signifying her pleasure to any man who attracted her and her dismissal of him immediately the attraction faded, remained technically faithful to the chosen lover during his period of favour. She had no scruples about using certain of her admirers, les payeurs, purely as suppliers of finances, but took little or nothing from those who temporarily won her inconstant heart.[97] Her art of retaining ex-lovers on terms of friendship was renowned.[98] Her purse and her influence remained always at the disposal of her friends, who willingly confided to her safe-keeping deposits of money and important secrets.[99] Reunions at her house were normally conducted with an outward decency invited by the naturally serious and respectable mien of the hostess.[100] Though in youth her libertinism had extended to her views on religion, she 'donna à Dieu' the last years that preceded her death in 1705.[101] The death of Marion de Lorme, the brusque result of an overdose of the drugs with which she habitually terminated unwanted pregnancies, left little time for formal repentance. She nevertheless insisted on making repeated confessions of her manifold sins and died 'fort chrétiennement' in an odour of purity: 'Elle a été mise en lit de parade, parée et vue de tout le monde le lendemain, comme si c'eût été une princesse. Elle avait une couronne de fleurs d'oranger sur la tête.'[102] It was subsequently learned that the fine clothes, jewels and silver plate which she always exacted from her lovers in lieu of cash had not only satisified her own passion for magnificence and prodigality, but also contributed to the upkeep of a large number of financially embarrassed relatives.[103]

The suspect businesses and morals of actresses, landladies, fortune-tellers and prostitutes simultaneously repelled and fascinated a society morally bound to dispense with their acquaintance, but physically and emotionally unable to steer clear of it. Well patronised, they reaped ample compensation for the invectives of their critics. Hounded, they bided their time, safe in the knowledge that the commodities which they sold would become superfluous only when the human condition coincided exactly with each man's dreams and aspirations.

10
Women in Political and Civic Life

The makers of France's constitution, mindful of female infirmities, had shown themselves reluctant to give women a fair share and a say in the running of the country. The misapplication of a disposition of Frankish Salic law prevented any woman from sitting on the French throne and holding sway as did Elizabeth I of England until her death in 1603 or Christina of Sweden prior to her abdication in 1654. Government offices were closed to practically all members of the sex except queens and a few of their intimates,[1] whose powers were more nominal than real. Courts of justice were tranquilly possessed male provinces. Voting in elections was largely a masculine prerogative too.

That women had the theoretical right to govern and administer, and even the necessary expertise, was not altogether denied. A gallant platitude of the day affirmed that women governors were likely to be better served and honoured than their male counterparts because of the deference and attachment inspired by their charms.[2] A more convincing argument advanced in their favour was that the successful administration of a country in no way depended upon the possession of a beard or austere countenance, but on that of mental and moral qualities which were as readily encountered in the one sex as in the other. 'Si les femmes sont autant capables que nous de se bien conduire elles-mêmes', asserted Poulain de la Barre, 'elles le sont aussi de conduire les autres, et d'avoir part aux emplois et aux dignités de la société civile.'[3] Saint-Evremond professed astonishment at the exclusion of women from affairs, 'car j'en trouvais de plus éclairées et de plus capables que les hommes'.[4] The trouble was that everything hinged on the insidious word 'capable'. As in the educational sphere, men were prepared to declare women *capable* of anything so long as they were not obliged to abdicate any of their own power and dominion to provide concrete outlets for feminine capacities. Fulsome flattery all too often masked the belief that

141

woman was fundamentally *incapable* of holding authority. Saint-Evremond eased many masculine consciences when he immediately followed his tribute to the administrative intelligence of the sex with the pronouncement that women are unfortunately not ruled by the head but by the heart, 'faible, incertain, trop assujetti à la fragilité de leur nature. Telle qui gouvernerait sagement un royaume aujourd'hui, se fera demain un maître, à qui on ne donnerait douze poules à gouverner, pour me servir des termes de M. le Cardinal Mazarin.' In a society where pretensions to power-sharing were deftly brushed aside with bouquets of compliments women in the normal course of events had little hope of exercising direct political or civic influence. But there was still room for indirect intervention – through a masculine relative or lover – and the scarcity of 'normal' circumstances, especially in the turbulent years that preceded the personal rule of Louis XIV, sometimes gave women the opportunity to play roles of which the most fervent modern feminist could approve.

Twice during the century France was prematurely bereft of her king, and twice a queen consort – Marie de Médicis in 1610, Anne d'Autriche in 1643 – was called upon to hold the reins of government until her eldest male child came of age. As wife of the reigning monarch the queen of France naturally enjoyed extensive privileges, being paid the same honours and generally associated in all the more imposing manifestations of royal authority such as the consecration ceremony (*sacre*)[5] and official visits to Parlement (*lits de justice*). But, as with any ordinary wife, it was during the absence or incapacity of her husband that she really came into her own, for it was then that the powers of regent could legally be conferred upon her.

The regency[6] belonged by right to the nearest prince of the blood royal, but fear lest an ambitious man might make himself powerful at the expense of an infant heir to the throne had favoured the policy of handing over power to the queen. As a woman she was prevented by the Salic law from usurping the throne. As a mother she had a prior claim to the tutelage of her minor son by the law of nature. The memory of competent regents in the past, such as Blanche de Castille, also contributed to sway public opinion in support of a female interregnum. Regency powers could devolve upon a queen during her consort's lifetime if he had some sickness of body or mind that made it impossible for him to rule, if he was imprisoned or if he made a journey outside the realm,[7] as well as in the event of his death. By the seventeenth century these rights were uncontested. Marie de Médicis was unanimously recognised as regent on the very day of Henri IV's assassination and her status was solemnly confirmed in Parlement on the following day. Anne d'Autriche was proclaimed regent shortly before Louis XIII's death, though since he mistrusted both her loyalty to France and her capabilities, the king tried to ensure that her authority would be subordinate to that of a regency council in which all major state issues would be decided on a majority vote. Four days after Louis's death Anne successfully appealed to Parlement to have the terms of the declaration altered to enable her to select the members of the council herself and to evade any obligation to follow a majority decision.[8]

Neither of the two regencies under discussion impressed upon contemporaries the benefits of female rule. Both queens were of undistinguished intelligence and had little experience of, or interest in, the mechanism of government prior to their assumption of power.[9] As a result both were forced to lean on advisers, Marie de Médicis on the Concinis[10] and Anne d'Autriche on Mazarin.[11] In each case these advisers were Italians, detested for the element of foreign interference which they represented and for the avidity with which they accumulated wealth and posts of eminence. On each occasion some of the resentment felt by the French populace towards the favourites was extended to the queen. Accusations against Marie de Médicis ranged from that of acting as Concino Concini's paramour[12] to that of keeping the young Louis XIII in ignorance of politics in order not to have to relinquish control of affairs.[13] Anne d'Autriche's manifest piety reduced the charge of fornication to that of a secret marriage with her particular confidant,[14] but she too was credited, unjustly, with clinging to power at the expense of a deliberately subjugated and uneducated son.[15] The growing unpopularity of the two regents and their associates afforded the many dissident factions in the state a golden opportunity to raise the standard of revolt. The period of Marie de Médicis's domination, effectively prolonged by her son's tardiness in asserting himself, was clouded by a succession of aristocratic and Protestant uprisings in the midst of which Concini was assassinated and mutilated and his wife decapitated and burned on a trumped-up charge of sorcery. The queen mother herself subsequently appeared at the head of the very rebels whom she had sought to bribe into quiescence. Several decades later, when *frondeur* nobles and Parlementarians vied for self-advancement on the hackneyed pretext of liberating France from foreign tyranny, Anne d'Autriche suffered the same humiliations of a thinly disguised captivity and a fugitive existence as had her mother-in-law, and allowed her twice-exiled minister to have a price put on his head. The French could be forgiven for thinking that misery, anarchy and carnage were the price that had to be paid for putting the helm of state in a woman's hands.

But even when an adult male sat on the throne there could be no certainty that he would not fall under some baneful female influence. Wives, with whom relations were never close, and mothers – long dead in the case of Henri IV, unloved and exiled in that of Louis XIII, respectful of filial power in that of Louis XIV – were less feared in this connection than the mistresses and favourites who jockeyed incessantly for pre-eminence at the French court. The position of royal mistress was prized on a par with, if not more highly than, official court posts, for it promised rapid fame, fortune and the confidence of the king, and carried no particular stigma of shame. It was appreciated that the king, in common with all his male subjects, might need to compensate himself elsewhere for a loveless marriage contracted with a view to breeding heirs; and any bastards he might sire were, after all, so many proofs of his fitness to produce legitimate successors to the throne. The habit of French monarchs for selecting concubines from amongst their own nobility countered objections from true and false patriots, while the beauty or wit of the women concerned testified to royal discernment as well as going far to silence all masculine opposition. In her own fashion the favourite was performing a valuable service for her king, supplying him with relaxation and entertainment that lightened the burden of government and providing an attractive focus for the endless court fêtes concocted to impress subjects and foreigners alike. But what if the favourite refused to content herself with a purely sexual or decorative function?

In the seventeenth century the problem scarcely arose. Two of Henri IV's mistresses, Gabrielle d'Estrées and Henriette de Balzac d'Entragues, had made a serious bid for the throne, the second armed with Henri's promise of marriage in return for her surrender. But Gabrielle died a sudden, opportune, death in 1599 and Henriette was coerced into relinquishing her promise of marriage in 1604.[16] In Louis XIII's reign any hopes that were raised by the king's well-known coldness towards his wife and by the precariousness of her position during twenty-two years of barren marriage were dashed by his unusual chastity and by the vigilance of Richelieu, who despatched the only two platonic loves of Louis's life, Louise de Lafayette and Marie de Hautefort, into a convent and exile respectively the moment he considered their influence to be outweighing his own.[17] Louis XIV, realising his inability to imitate paternal continence but determined to avoid grandpaternal aberrations, invited his ministers in 1663 to warn him if they ever saw any woman gaining a hold over him, whereupon he promised to jettison her within twenty-four hours.[18] He kept his first two declared mistresses, Louise de La Vallière and Athénaïs de Rochechouart de Mortemart, Marquise de Montespan, in a state of semi-imprisonment, forbidding them visitors for fear that these might persuade them to intercede with him and that it might be said that the women governed him.[19] In actual fact neither showed any inclination to meddle in state affairs. Mlle de La Vallière was universally celebrated for her disinterestedness,[20] though this did not prevent her from accepting, amongst other trifles, the duchy of Vaujours and the sumptuously furnished Palais Brion for herself, the abbey of Chelles for her sister, a rich heiress for her brother and the elevation of her surviving bastard daughter to the rank of Princesse de Conti.[21] Mme de Montespan restricted the 'ambition sans bornes' with which she was credited[22] to manoeuvring, likewise, numerous relatives and protégés into advantageous positions,[23] to soliciting occasionally on behalf of religious establishments,[24] and to procuring material goods for herself.[25] It was Mme de Maintenon who posed the only real challenge to Louis's cherished independence of decision and action.

Françoise d'Aubigné, Marquise de Maintenon, possessed a combination of personal qualities which Louis had not previously had occasion to appreciate in any one woman: beauty, intelligence, modesty of manner, discretion, reasonableness and devotion to his interests. While she was still acting as *gouvernante* to Mme de Montespan's illegitimate infants Louis had been impressed by the charm and sensibleness of her conversation and had acquired the habit of confiding in her.[26] Whatever may have been the initial nature of their relations, she became his wife by a secret marriage after death removed Marie-Thérèse in 1683. Marks of deference[27] and trust were heaped upon her. Early on Louis took to working with one or two of his ministers in her apartment[28] while she sat decorously reading or sewing. Also in her apartment returning ambassadors and generals saluted the king,[29] war councils were held[30] and a full council of state took place in 1710.[31] That she was not expected to close her ears to the discussions taking place in her presence is shown by the fact that Louis often interrupted them to ask for her opinion.[32] In the crucial debates of 1700 as to whether Louis should accept for his grandson, the Duc d'Anjou, the legacy of the Spanish throne, she cast her vote, in the affirmative, immediately after that of the Dauphin.[33]

Saint-Simon, the memorialist who furnishes the most detailed account of Mme de Maintenon's political activities, alleges that as a result of these private sessions she was able to control the distribution of well over three-quarters of available posts and gratifications. But he feels constrained to add that her participation in state affairs proper was 'beaucoup moins ordinaire' and achieved only by roundabout methods: 'cette femme habile faisait presque tout ce qu'elle voulait mais non pas tout, ni quand et comme elle voulait'.[34] Coming from a witness whose hostility towards the favourite made him keen to ferret out all her machinations, such a testimony is valuable. In effect Mme de Maintenon did not always have her own way and could scarcely hope to do so. She had, firstly, many highly placed enemies: rank-conscious members of the royal family,[35] resentful at having access to Louis only through the widow of a grotesque poet;[36] the powerful War Minister Louvois[37] and the king's Jesuit confessor La Chaise,[38] both of whom staunchly opposed the public declaration of her marriage; and behind all these personages a swarm of envious courtiers like the Duc de Saint-Simon, anxious for her disgrace[39] and intriguing to usurp her position for themselves or their protégés. Secondly, and more important, Mme de Maintenon had the formidable barrier of the king himself standing in the way of any inordinate ambitions that she may have cherished. Louis XIV never lost his youthful horror of the slightest appearance of being governed, though with advancing years his grip on affairs automatically slackened somewhat and methods of circumventing him became proportionately easier to employ. Mme de Maintenon, according to Saint-Simon, would work out in advance with the appropriate minister the course of action which best suited her interests, leave it to him to present a biased list of options to the king, feign a becoming ignorance when a perplexed Louis appealed for her advice, then ultimately support the minister's view.[40] With the connivance of the ministers, whose authority she skilfully balanced by extending her protection to each in turn,[41] she was able to ensure that news was carefully filtered before reaching the king.[42] She herself wrote to the Archbishop of Paris, Noailles, in 1696 that she was obliged to 'cacher beaucoup de choses' from Louis, because of the difficulty of effacing first impressions from his mind.[43] Sudden assertions of authority on the king's part nevertheless remained a threat to the best-laid plans, and Mme de Maintenon's ill-concealed tears continued to remind the court from time to time of who was master.[44]

During critical moments of the reign, when the activity of this elusive woman emerges fairly clearly, her role was less than glorious. Her marked enthusiasm for the conversion of Protestants[45] lent colour to the charge that she had instigated the persecutions that hastened the Revocation of the Edict of Nantes, though the Protestant ambassador of Brandenburg, Spanheim, equitably suggested that she could only hold her position by a show of zeal for the king's policies and was powerless to prevent excessive violence against her former co-religionists.[46] In the 1690s she again appeared as persecutress, this time of Fénelon and his quietist supporters, whose downfall she was all the more ardently pledged to secure in that she had figured as the dupe of their religious orthodoxy and had risked compromising herself irrevocably with the intolerant Louis.[47] A diplomatic animosity towards the Jansenists led her to work to foment Louis's undisguised dislike of the sect; but she in turn was 'used' by her spiritual directors to further complex intrigues aimed at discrediting her former protégé Noailles[48] and obtaining papal condemnation of the Jansenist doctrines with which he sympathised.[49] Her only memorable excursion into foreign affairs – her entry into an ultimately abortive pact with the ambitious Princesse des Ursins, chief attendant of the Savoyard queen of Spain, for the purpose of ruling that country through the queen's influence over her docile French husband Philip V – similarly illustrated her tendency to be swayed by those who paid their court adroitly.[50] Rather than being a directing force at court Mme de Maintenon seems frequently to have let herself be directed, either by the king's aversions or by individual intriguers.

On the whole, therefore, Louis XIV succeeded in his aim of resisting domination by his immediate female entourage. His favourites mostly channelled any propensity for intrigue into acquiring property, cash, titles and posts for themselves and their clients. His queen was effaced, devout and totally submissive. Nor did the king encounter any overtly subversive political activity on the part of the ladies of his court.[51] His reign was regarded as one in which women had ceased to meddle in politics and were discouraged from even discussing them. Père Rapin asserted that 'depuis que le roi prenait soin de ses affaires, les dames ne se mêlaient plus de rien et l'on ne les écoutait que peu'.[52] Charlotte de Bavière made an identical observation about her late brother-in-law's day: 'De son temps, on avait appris aux dames à ne pas parler des affaires d'Etat; ce n'était pas l'usage.'[53] As the Jesuit and the princess indicated, the ladies had not always appeared so quiescent.

The civil wars of the late sixteenth century had sharpened the political awareness of women and increased their participation in national affairs on a hitherto unprecedented scale. Long accustomed to intriguing at the Valois courts,[54] they had found themselves additionally obliged, during the absences of warring husbands, to enter the actual battle arena to defend threatened homes and possessions. They had risen magnificently to emergencies, fortifying strongholds and arming towns against invaders of opposing factions, exhorting and animating discouraged troops.[55] They developed a taste for combat which was manifested throughout the seventeenth century by the number of budding amazons who learned to handle weapons,[56] engaged in duels,[57] joined or formed armies[58] and fought alongside their menfolk during sieges.[59] Every other heroic novel and tragi-comedy sported its warrior maid,[60] and the most talked-about epic of the day, Jean Chapelain's *Pucelle* (1656), magnified Jeanne d'Arc, the finest home-produced specimen of the breed.[61]

Playing a man's role in time of war seemed to give women the right, which they claimed energetically, to prolong that role in time of peace. They began to turn up at peace conferences, not merely to keep their men company but as influential negotiators in their own right. At the conferences of Loudun (1616), which brought about a lull in the protracted power struggle between the crown and the aristocracy, the presence of the Comtesse de Soissons (Anne de Montafié), the Duchesse de Longueville (Catherine de Gonzague) and the Princesse de Condé (Charlotte de la Tremoille) was considered indispensable to a successful settlement. 'Beaucoup de gens n'approuvèrent pas que des femmes fussent assises, et eussent voix dans une assemblée telle que celle-là,' wrote a contemporary, 'mais il fallut bien le souffrir, pour les obliger à vouloir la paix, et y contribuer autant qu'elles avaient fait pour la guerre.'[62] Masculine resentment notwithstanding, female intervention was to become a permanent feature of the political scene during the next few decades.

By the late 1620s many of the old generation of amazons and activists born in the previous century had died, women like the Duchesse de Nevers (Catherine de Lorraine, d. 1618), leader of a resistance movement when the city of Nevers was besieged by royalist troops in 1617,[63] and the Princess de Condé (d. 1629), would-be instigator of street riots in Paris when the peace of Loudun was rapidly shattered.[64] But they were swiftly replaced by a new, more famous generation of *intriguantes* who, if they relied on winsomeness rather than on feats of arms to overcome the opposition, were none the less gifted in the noble art of causing political havoc.

The ministry of Richelieu served as a good test of the aristocratic conspiratresses' mettle, for the Cardinal was committed to reducing that power which mutinous elements in the royal family and the nobility tried to arrogate at the king's expense. Throughout his term of office his person and his policies were a target for females intent on destroying both. In 1626 his most persistent enemy, the Duchesse de Chevreuse, came close to having him assassinated by one of her numerous lovers, Chalais, as part of a conspiracy to prevent Louis XIII's brother, Gaston d'Orléans, from marrying the woman of the Cardinal's choice.[65] In 1631 the exile of his former protrectress Marie de Médicis and her confidants, the Princesse de Conti (Louise-Marguerite de Lorraine, d. 1631) and the Duchesse d'Elbœuf, signalled an almost successful attempt to dislodge him from Louis XIII's favour.[66] In 1632 the Duchesse de Montmorency, a distant relative of Marie de Médicis, was a party to the engagement of her husband, the governor of Languedoc, in a fruitless plot to rouse the province in support of Gaston's seditious partisans.[67] In 1633 the Duchesse de Chevreuse, back from exile at the court of the enamoured Duc de Lorraine whom she had worked to unite with England against France, began passing to him state secrets charmed out of the infatuated Keeper of the Royal Seals, Châteauneuf, a crime that earned her another exile, in Touraine.[68] In 1637 Anne d'Autriche, whose name had been linked with several previous conspiracies against a prime minister whom she detested, was caught imparting vital information to her native Spain, France's declared enemy at that juncture, and to her confidant the Duchesse de Chevreuse, who this time fled across the Spanish frontier.[69] Harassed on all sides the Cardinal more than once confided to his papers his dread of female intrigues:

> Il se trouve souvent, dans les intrigues des cabinets des rois, des écueils beaucoup plus dangereux que dans les affaires d'Etat les plus difficiles; et, en effet, il y a plus de péril à se mêler de celles où les femmes ont part ... que des plus grands desseins que les princes puissent faire en autre nature d'affaires[70]

> ... il n'y a rien qui soit si capable de perdre un Etat que de mauvais esprits, couverts de la faiblesse de leur sexe.[71]

His antagonists were either too high-ranking, or too slippery, or sometimes too attractive to the Cardinal[72] to suffer the decapitation and imprisonment that commonly befell their male accomplices. Exile, as the case of the Duchesse de Chevreuse plainly illustrated, was an ineffectual deterrent. Richelieu's answer to the problem was to employ women loyal to his cause to exercise a covert surveillance over suspect persons. Mmes de Brassac and de Lansac were thus set to watch over Anne d'Autriche from the vantage-points of *dame d'honneur* and *gouvernante* of the Dauphin respectively.[73] Mlle de Lacroix was appointed *dame d'honneur* to Richelieu's niece, wife of the Prince de Condé, so that she could keep an eye on a nest of traitors.[74] A lady-in-waiting, Mlle de Chemerault, was instructed to insinuate herself into the confidence of Mme de Hautefort, who was privy to the secrets of both the king and queen.[75] The Marquise de Rambouillet was approached with a proposition to spy on the intrigues of the Prince de Condé's mother (Charlotte de Montmorency) and the Cardinal de la Valette, members of her salon.[76] Any woman who could furnish information in this way, from cook to countess, was pressed into service.[77] The benefits of Richelieu's policy of using women as intrigue-detectors were not to be lost upon his disciple and successor Mazarin.[78]

The death of Richelieu in December 1642, followed by that of Louis XIII five months later, was a godsend for impatient *intriguantes*. Every circumstance favoured their enterprises. Anne d'Autriche – 'si bonne!'[79] – began her regency by granting an amnesty to a host of political exiles, including the Duchesse de Chevreuse, whose return the moribund king had expressly forbidden. Anne's prime minister, Mazarin, was a very different opponent from Richelieu, a man who, to maintain authority, preferred to resort not to the scaffold but to the negotiations, secret deals and counter-plots in which women delighted. Finally the outbreak in 1648 of a five-year civil war, the Fronde, created, as had the upheavals of the late sixteenth and early seventeenth centuries, a state of turmoil extremely favourable to the satisfaction of female fantasies. Government and reforms replaced fashions and hairstyles as the chief topics of conversation.[80] Sex was postponed until after husbands and lovers had reported on the latest political developments.[81] And infant noblewomen were heard to gravely request their elders: 'parlons d'affaires d'état, à cette heure que j'ai cinq ans'.[82]

A variety of motives underlay the decision taken by the ornaments of the *beau monde* to join forces with rebel factions. Some were blatantly intent on making money. The Duchesse de Montbazon fixed the price of her submission at 100 000 *écus*.[83] For three times that amount the Princesse Palatine and Mme de Choisy offered to put the Duchesse de Montpensier on the throne.[84] The hope of extorting social distinctions was another incitement to revolt. On a long list of demands presented to the regency government in 1649 the mention of a *tabouret* for the wife of such-and-such a *frondeur* general figured repeatedly.[85] The excitement of running round to nocturnal assignations in disguise, plotting with whoever was willing to plot, appealed to women like the Duchesse de Chevreuse, for whom 'les négociations, les rendez-vous nocturnes, les déguisements, avaient . . . un charme infini',[86] and Mme de Rhodes, who 'avait pris un si grand goût aux intrigues qu'elle s'y jetait à corps perdu, sans se mettre en peine de quoi il était question'.[87] Not infrequently there lurked somewhere in the background a masculine influence, a relative who needed the feminine touch to help him win supporters, or a lover to be served or secured. The inoffensive Princesse de Condé (née Maillé-Brézé), hurled into the *mêlée* by her arrogant husband, faithfully campaigned, harangued and suffered the privations of siege and exile on his behalf.[88] The Duchesse de Montpensier thought, by turning the Bastille cannons on his troops, to persuade Louis XIV personally to save her from an embarrassingly prolonged spinsterhood.[89] The Duchesse de Longueville (Anne-

Geneviève de Bourbon) joined the Fronde to keep company with her lover La Rochefoucauld and dissuaded her brother Condé from accepting the court's peace overtures so that she would not be forced to return to an unloved husband.[90] Tipping the scales most heavily in favour of rebellion, perhaps, was the consideration that it was an unrivalled opportunity for conspiratresses to impress upon the public at large the magnetism of their personality, the nimbleness of their wits and the extent of their power. The Duchesse de Longueville's burning desire, fanned by La Rochefoucauld, was to enjoy the reputation for cleverness that would ensue from visibly directing affairs.[91] The Duchesse de Châtillon (née Montmorency-Bouteville), by persuading one lover, Nemours, to offer his services to another, Condé, and then assuming the role of peacemaker between Condé and the court, aimed to demonstrate the superiority of her beauty and intellect over those of the Duchesse de Longueville, her rival for domination of the two princes.[92] The Princesse Palatine, negotiating with the government on behalf of Condé and his princely relatives, revelled in the heady sensation of being everyone's confidant and holding the destinies of others in her hands.[93]

The fact that there were almost as many different motives as there were *frondeuses* underlines the highly individualistic nature of their participation in the revolt and the basic selfishness of their designs. The Princesse Palatine's memoirs sum up the situation in a nutshell: 'Les projets n'avaient rien de fixe; des qualités brillantes, le courage, l'esprit, éclataient dans quelques personnes. Mais l'intérêt personnel dirigeait seul tous ceux qui attisaient le feu de la faction; ils n'étaient dominés par aucun système.'[94] There was scarcely any question of concerted action, political or otherwise. As the Longueville-Châtillon feud showed, the civil war served not to patch up old quarrels but to settle old scores. Lady conspiratresses, like gentleman conspirators, had no discernible political objective beyond the agreeable diversion of toppling Mazarin. Several of the most intelligent amongst them, the Duchesse de Chevreuse and the Princesse Palatine especially, manifested the lukewarmness of their political convictions by changing sides during the course of the rebellion, plotting now against the minister, now on his behalf. To these women the Fronde was a means of escape from the tedium of the daily routine into the kind of world which they had read about in novels, where capricious princesses led great warriors by the nose and set whole

continents aflame. Their menfolk, catching the novelistic contagion, pandered to their foibles. The custom of wearing a loved
one's colours in battle was revived.[95] Beribboned troops gave
military reviews for the ladies' benefit and entertained them to
collations in their tents.[96] During the brief siege of the Bastille in
January 1649 chairs were taken to the Arsenal gardens so that
ladies could sit and watch the show in comfort.[97]

Despite their frivolity and mutability *frondeur* noblewomen
spread enough chaos and consternation to inspire that respect for
their capabilities after which they hankered. Mazarin, looking back
over events in later years, described the Duchesses de Chevreuse
and de Longueville and the Princesse Palatine as being 'capables
de renverser dix états'.[98] The contemporary historian Benjamin
Priolo attributed to four unspecified women, probably the three
named by Mazarin plus the Duchesse de Châtillon, sole responsibility for plunging France into the civil war.[99] The *frondeuses'* image
of power was projected onto their sex as a whole. Testimonies to
the indispensability of female intercession to secure advancement
at court, or indeed in any walk of life, were penned in increasing
numbers, even by such independent males as Colbert and Saint-
Simon.[100] Foreign nations took their cue accordingly, making sure
that ambassadors presented themselves to the ladies with rich gifts
and, if possible, a handsome mien proper to elicit the state secrets
which they were thought to have in their possession.[101] The
knowledge that they had cost the 'gredin de Sicile'[102] more than
one sleepless night, that their prowess was consecrated in the
annals of history and their omnipotence blazoned abroad, in some
measure compensated for the necessity to stop playing chivalric
games under the forbidding eyes of Louis XIV and Colbert.

The concentration of government in the hands of the king and a
few hand-picked ministers narrowed the scope of high-born
intriguantes and removed from politics the spectacular and exciting elements that had seduced them into the Fronde. They did not
on that account abstain from scheming, as certain short-sighted
contemporaries naively imagined. In 1670 the Savoy ambassador
Saint-Maurice, despatched to France amongst other things to
recommend his sovereign's interests to Colbert via the Duchesse
de Chevreuse, confided to a progress report his wonderment at the
undiminished vigour with which the septuagenarian conspiratress
was busy plotting, in collusion with Mazarin's nieces and Mlle de
La Vallière, the overthrow of Mme de Montespan: 'ainsi, vieille et

décrépite comme elle est, sans bouger de son cabinet, elle gouverne la cour'.[103] Restless females had merely bent their energies in directions less likely to bring them into head-on collision with the guardians of law and order. Outmanoeuvring rivals for the affections of the king had regained all its former popularity.[104] Fresh impetus was given also to dabbling in affairs susceptible of yielding monetary rewards. Impecuniosity had become the nightmare of an aristocracy whose finances, already drained by long years of anti-Establishment activity and by inflation, were being finally depleted by the cost of the luxurious trappings upon which Louis XIV insisted for his courtiers, and by the heavy gambling to which the latter resorted to fill both their coffers and the emptiness of their lives at court. As during the Fronde, *intriguantes* hovered round those who wielded the most power, but it was financial rather than political power which attracted them now. Noblewomen wormed their way into the houses of superintendants of finances and wealthy tax-farmers and made friends with their flattered wives. Once installed in favour they proposed to their hosts ideas for the imposition of new taxes or the creation of new saleable offices, in return for the promise of a lump sum or a pension if the affair succeeded. By way of a lucrative sideline they sold their protection to men whose merits or length of service were inadequate to secure advancement through the regular channels, obtaining the desired promotion either directly through their financier cronies or indirectly through the cultivation of faithful agents in government bureaux.[105]

It was, therefore, only the fashion in conspiracies that varied, never the passion for plotting. Intrigue represented, for those noblewomen epitomised by the Duchesse de Chevreuse, a whole way of life, indeed the very breath of life, and as such could only be renounced with existence itself.

While aristocratic ladies hatched their plots at court and rode round the land in search of thrills and lovers, plebeian women did not sit idly by. They, the mothers, wives and daughters of peasants and petty craftsmen, had their own grievances to air and did not scruple to profit from the government's moments of vulnerability, from the insurrections of their overlords and from the rancour of their menfolk to make their dissatisfaction known. The end result of their agitation – perpetual disruption of governmental machinery – resembled that achieved by their aristocratic equivalents, but the two groups differed in their aims and methods of accomplishing them.

For the peasant woman or the urban *ouvrière* intrigues and rebellion were not a way of life nor lightly undertaken to procure satisfactions of vanity. Ordinarily they were too absorbed in the daily struggle for survival to have the desire or leisure to weave plots and to participate in demonstrations subject to severe repression by the authorities. Only when the struggle for survival was rendered practically impossible were they moved to take action. This state of affairs arose chiefly as a result of fiscal pressure from the government, unemployment crises and food shortages. At such times deprivation had to be endured by all, but its effects were calculated to strike most forcibly and cruelly those women obliged to stop at home and watch the progressive starvation of their children. In sheer desperation the women of the people lashed out, verbally and physically, at what they saw to be the immediate cause of their misfortunes.

The king was rarely blamed. Seventeenth-century insurgents, of whatever social rank, studiously avoided attributing to the monarch any responsibility for the miseries of his people. He was envisaged as a mere tool in the hands of his guardians, ministers or bureaucrats, who hid from him their oppression of his subjects. Thus prior to, and during, the Fronde Anne d'Autriche and Mazarin had borne the brunt of popular discontent over fiscal exactions, the former in particular being singled out for attack by the members of her sex. As early as 1645 groups of women took to waylaying the queen on her weekly visits to Notre-Dame, clamouring for justice, accusing her of squandering the king's money, and threatening to abandon their children to her to feed 'puisqu'on leur ôtait leur pain'.[106] Women were instrumental in printing and hawking the pamphlets (*Mazarinades*) denouncing her regency and the nature of her relations with her prime minister.[107] Respect for her sank so low that she was referred to only as 'madame Anne', a name she shared with a fishwife from the Halles who was eventually incarcerated in the lunatic asylum for having broadcast seditious opinions about the regent.[108] But then, during these exceptionally turbulent years, no person of standing was safe from affronts and maltreatment by female mobs. The Prince de Condé was publicly insulted for the famine and misery that he had caused while blockading Paris from January to March 1649.[109] The Maréchal de la Meilleraye, guilty of repressive conduct during the street barricades in August 1648, had to flee from a horde intent on stabbing him to death.[110] Members of Parlement lived in terror of their lives as women milled around in the courtyard of the Palais de Justice, pistols and daggers in hand, pursuing any who chanced to provoke their ire and periodically invading the debating chambers to remind the assembly 'qu'ils s'amusaient à travailler et gagner de l'argent pendant qu'elles mouraient de faim'.[111]

In provincial areas remote from the court, where the heads of government were inaccessible, feminine fury was wreaked upon minor bureaucrats sent round to ensure the execution of unpopular measures decided in the capital, upon representatives of authority and generally upon anybody suspected of profiteering at the public's expense. It was women who appeared as the most jealous guardians of the community's privileges and well-being, raising the alarm the moment that either seemed threatened[112] and taking to the streets with their female companions in martial array if the threat persisted.[113] Official *communiqués* mention time and again not just the simple participation of women in riots, but their active instigation of disturbances. In 1645 an uproar over the imposition on Montpellier craftsmen of a tax designed to pay a due levied on the occasion of the king's accession to the throne was said by the local lieutenant-general to have been 'commencé par les femmes et suivi avec beaucoup de chaleur par leurs maris'.[114] The *intendant* of Languedoc apprised the government in 1691 of 'une espèce d'émeute' at Toulouse 'excitée par quelques femmes, qui ont battu un des commis du traitant des offices de jurés crieurs publics'.[115] In 1699 the *intendant* of Lyon began a report on the jostling and beating of the city's magistrates during an insurrection caused by grain shortages, with the words: 'il s'attroupa dans la place des Terreaux, au pied du perron de l'hôtel de ville, environ cinq ou six cents femmes, et, de moment à autre, le nombre grossissait; il s'y mêla quelques hommes'.[116] Having once started a commotion and drawn their menfolk into the fray,[117] women had little hesitation in employing physical force against the objects of their execration. If the latter had fled, their property suffered in their stead. A whole series of tax-collectors' domiciles at Montpellier were pillaged and burned in a veritable female orgy of destruction.[118] Those unlucky enough to be caught by the mobs were beaten, murdered, mutilated. Normandy women used their spindles to put out the eyes of a *gabeleur* accused of trying to establish the detested salt-tax in their locality.[119] In the course of savage uprisings 'pour le fait de la gabelle' at Agen in 1635 one man was castrated and another had the eyes torn from his battered corpse.[120] Right to the end women had a star part, for their names appeared on the list of offenders condemned to the whippings, brandings, hangings and banishments that invariably terminated these sanguinary tragedies.[121]

For all the tumult and bloodshed to which their outbursts gave rise, there is no real evidence that the women of the people were politically motivated, any more than their sister rebels higher up the social ladder. Their resentment was directed against individuals rather than against bodies or institutions, individuals whose exactions were blamed for causing pain and hardship and who exercised powers to silence protesters. The violence that characterised reprisals against tax-collectors and the like was spontaneously born of a sense of despair and outrage, and intensified by the heat of the moment. The inescapable fate that would await rebellious towns and villages when royal troops swooped upon them to restore order was temporarily forgotten in the desire to return, with interest, suffering previously and currently experienced. Passionate in their affections as well as in their enmities, the women of the people idolised those who made specious promises of ending their oppression, and those who could overcome feelings of repugnance sufficiently to descend often into their midst. The women of the Paris Halles, the most insubordinate and outspoken of the *frondeuses*,[122] illustrated well the political myopia of their kind by selecting as their hero the Duc de Beaufort, a man despised even by his fellow conspirators for his fatuity, but possessed of the common touch and a most alluring mane of golden curls.[123]

Though women wielded greater power at times of national crisis, when men were otherwise engaged, their role in peaceful political and civic contexts was not negligible. Here the chance to make their mark depended upon social status, women of pedigree and property having access to dignities of state and political assemblies from which the rank and file of their sex were excluded.

The highest dignity, after royalty, to which a woman could accede in her own right was the peerage. Possession of the proud title 'Pair de France'[124] came about in the seventeenth century mostly through inheritance of a fief elevated into a peerage[125] by the Crown and made transmittable to the female heirs of the original beneficiary in default of the male.[126] Several new peerages were, however, created in favour of women who had merited well of their king. The letters patent by which the honour was bestowed upon the Marquise de Senecé in 1663 for her 'services extraordinaires' in the double capacity of *dame d'honneur* to Anne d'Autriche and *gouvernante* to the young Louis XIV enunciated the monarch's feminist policy in this respect:

> Considérant qu'il est de la prudence et de la justice des rois, autant que de leur grandeur et munificence, non seulement de soutenir les principales maisons de leurs états, par des titres et prérogatives d'honneur, mais aussi de les augmenter, et d'élever ceux qui en sont issus, et qui par leurs vertus et signalés services se sont rendus recommandables, et se sont distingués des autres, les honorant des premières dignités, qui leur fassent garder un rang proportionné à leurs mérites, et donnent à connaître à la postérité en quelles considérations ont été leurs personnes; ce que nous estimons devoir aussi bien être pratiqué en faveur des femmes, que des hommes, quand elles sont parvenues à un haut point de vertu, et qu'elles ont toutes les rares qualités et ont rendu tous les services dont leur sexe est capable.[127]

According to this and similar preambles, the peerage was a reward for the virtues of the recipient and for the services rendered both by herself and members of the noble lineage to which she belonged. The conferment of the distinction on Louise de La Vallière in 1667[128] and on Louise de Kéroualle, mistress of Charles II of England, in 1684[129] showed the king's extremely elastic interpretation of the virtues and services in question. Peeresses were empowered by royal provisions to pass on their peerages to female relatives[130] or to husbands.[131] They enjoyed the much prized *honneurs du Louvre*: the right to drive a carriage within the precincts of the royal palace, to be seated before the queen and to have a cushion on which to kneel in church in the presence of the sovereigns.[132] One right, crucial from the political point of view, which they no longer shared with male peers was that of being formally received into Parlement and participating in sessions and debates.[133]

Allowing women to take an active part in Parlement business would have been something of an anomaly. The Paris Parlement, which had a dozen counterparts in the chief provincial capitals, was a body with the power to remonstrate against acts of royal legislation judged not to be in the public interest and to exercise a veto by refusing to register them. But the Parlements were first and foremost sovereign courts of law, and women could not sit as public magistrates, nor any longer officially preside as judges and arbitresses on their own estates once seigneurial justice was replaced by that of the king.[134] Entry into Parlement was not absolutely forbidden. Queens and princesses, flanked by ladies-in-waiting, were customarily present during the solemnity known as the *lit de justice* when the king went in person to Parlement to signify his wishes.[135] A substantial attendance of female relatives was a familiar sight at the investiture of an eminent Parlementarian in office.[136] At times other than ceremonial occasions women were at liberty to sit in the *lanternes* or public galleries overlooking the debating chamber. They could in this way listen in on whatever interested them – lawsuits, religious or political discussions[137] – and gain a valuable insight into the internal affairs of the realm. The facts that the women mentioned in these connections are invariably aristocratic and upper middle class and that the appearances of women of the people in the Paris Parlement during the Fronde are described in terms of illegal intrusions imply, however, that Parlements did not admit female spectators at random. They were vetted beforehand and had to be of a certain social standing.

Most of the periodic assemblies which complemented the permanently established Parlements in the exercise of governmental and juridical functions – the *Etats Généraux*, the *Etats Provinciaux* and the *Grands Jours*[138] – likewise banned women from their personnel but not entirely from participation in their affairs.

The *Etats Généraux* met only once during the century, in 1614, with no woman in the ranks of the deputies. The extent to which the woman in the street was able even to influence the choice of deputies[139] was to all appearances nil. In rural districts preliminary election work was done at the assemblies of inhabitants which the local judge or comparable functionary convoked whenever decisions had to be made affecting the life of a particular community as a whole.[140] No formal legislation denied women the right to be present at these assemblies. La Poix de Freminville in his *Traité Général des Biens et Affaires des Communautés d'Habitants* (1760) specified that, when issues of permanent import to the community were at stake, 'il faut que tous les habitants soient assemblés sans exception'. He added, however, that when it was merely a matter of nominating temporary community officials ten inhabitants were regarded as constituting a quorum.[141] This latter trend is the one most marked in seventeenth-century election proceedings. In the typical parish a number of males only, representing 'la plus grande et meilleure [or "saine"] partie des habitants', would be convened for the purpose of drafting a list of the community's grievances (*cahier de doléances*) which would be taken by one or two elected participants to a superior functionary, usually the bailiff (*bailli*), who in turn conveyed it to a further electoral meeting at the principal town of the administrative circumscription. Here the bailiff, henceforth acting as spokesman for the effaced villagers, met urban representatives of the Third Estate, municipal officials deputed chiefly by their male peers,[142] and delegates of the two higher orders in the state, the Clergy and the Nobility. All these persons combined their grievances into a final *Cahier* and elected deputies to represent them at the Estates General proper. Members of the nobility, male and female, and sometimes the clergy[143] enjoyed the distinction of being personally summoned by minor bureaucrats to the meeting for the definitive election of deputies. The detailed publication of the *Cahiers de Doléances* of Troyes shows, for example, that four summonses to noblewomen were issued in that area,[144] one of which stipulates that the recipient, a widow, shall present herself 'en personne et non par procuration'.[145] But even supposing that these women, and others in the same position, discharged their civic duties as requested, the amount of influence that their minute number could have brought to bear on an assembly dominated by men is questionable.

Coming after an interval of over twenty years since the last meeting in 1593, and at a time when pressure groups were in a state of ferment, the Estates of 1614 roused considerable interest, not least among the ladies. On the opening day, 27 October, the vast hall of the Hôtel Bourbon in Paris where the debates were to take place was so packed that the deputies could hardly enter in the confusion: 'tout était plein de dames et damoiselles, de gentilshommes et autres peuples, comme si l'on se fut transporté là pour avoir le divertissement de quelque comédie'.[146] This tart comment from a crushed deputy, Florimon de Rapine, unveils what was probably the prime motive behind the ladies' ostensible political fervour. The Estates were a novelty and distraction for them, a chance to see and be seen, exactly on a par with the latest theatre production.

The general procedure of the *Etats Provinciaux* – assemblies of the three orders which met annually or biennially in a number of provinces, chiefly to attend to financial matters and to vote a subsidy (*don gratuit*) to the king – was to admit representatives on the basis of ownership of land within the province. Since under most *Coutumes* women were permitted to inherit and to possess estates there was no theoretical barrier to their indiscriminate admission along with men. Though in the Middle Ages women had exercised their rights, during the century at issue they seem rarely, if ever, to have done so. The seventeenth-century historian of Provence, Honoré Bouche, records the presence amongst the deputies at the Estates of Aix in 1390 of 'La Magnifique Dame de Baux, Phanete de Baux, femme de Berenguier de Pontivez, Chevalier Seigneur de Lambesc, Dame de la Barben', but for the contemporary period only the mention of 'seigneurs et gentilshommes' is encountered.[147] No woman's name is found on the lists of deputies to the Norman or Burgundian Estates.[148] The Estates of Brittany formally debarred women from their sessions, though non-Breton nobles who had taken a wife within the province had the right of entry.[149] The Estates of Languedoc were more subtle. In the early seventeenth century noblewomen in possession of domains to which the right of entry was attached were not allowed, apparently, to attend in person but could send one, or sometimes two, male representatives.[150] In 1655 the regulations were tightened: possession of the aforementioned domains still gave right of entry to the Estates, but it was stipulated that those acquiring them should be of the military profession. Since any representatives that they wished to send in their place had, by a ruling of 1612, to be 'gentilshommes d'ancienne race, de nom et d'armes', all participation by women was neatly excluded.[151] It is legitimate to suppose that women here and elsewhere did not view their exclusion as too great a deprivation. The seventeenth-century provincial nobility in general often showed an apathetic attitude towards their Estates, taking no interest in the election of representatives and failing to appear at meetings.[152]

Yet the Provincial Estates were not all business and tedious discussion of governmental minutiae. Mme de Sévigné, a spectator at the Breton Estates for the first time in 1671, retained a very different impression:

C'était une grande joie de me voir aux états, où je ne fus de ma vie; je n'ai pas voulu en voir l'ouverture, c'était trop matin. Les états ne doivent pas être longs; il n'y a qu'à demander ce que veut le Roi; on ne dit pas un mot: voilà qui est fait. Pour le gouverneur, il y trouve, je ne sais comment, plus de quarante mille écus qui lui reviennent. Une infinité d'autres présents, des pensions, des réparations des chemins et des villes, quinze ou vingt grandes tables, un jeu continuel, des bals éternels, des comédies trois fois la semaine, une grande braverie, voilà les états.[153]

For the wives and lady-friends of governors, *lieutenants du roi*, *intendants* and other representatives of royal authority in the provinces, the holding of the Estates was always a break in the daily round and, if they were used to life in the capital, a chance to see fresh scenery and faces, to observe new customs, to hear unfamiliar dialects. Relieved of all the administrative worries that beset their menfolk, they could surrender to the pleasure of being fêted by provincials concerned to belie their reputation for being boorish and outmoded gallants and to curry favour with Monseigneur through assiduity towards his females.[154] From the very moment of their entry into town they would be cornered by a municipal deputation, lengthily harangued,[155] presented with symbolic gifts of food and drink, paraded beneath triumphal arches, complimented by local schoolchildren and deafened by cannon salvoes and trumpet blasts.[156] In the days that followed wine flowed freely, tables groaned beneath piles of delicacies, legs ached from dancing and eyes from a kaleidoscope of pageantry and entertainments. But a little graciousness paid handsome dividends. In gratitude for compelling them to vote an enormous *don gratuit* the Estates would obligingly award the governor and his aides a substantial cash present each and include their wives in the liberalities. In 1614 the Duchesse de Montmorency, wife of the ill-fated governor of Languedoc, received 3000 *livres* and similar sums were given to her mother-in-law and to her husband's sister, the latter being married to the lieutenant-general of the province.[157] The apparent ease with which money was forthcoming from the Estates led greedy women to view the provinces as a gold-mine for their own personal exploitation. In 1680 the Maréchal de Créqui demanded on behalf of his wife one hundred gold *pistoles*, on the pretext that this gift was an annual perquisite of governors' wives in the duchies of Lorraine and Bar, and overruled protests by means of threats.[158] The Marquise de la Baume, 'femme très avide d'argent et aussi prodigue qu'avide', pounced on the province of Dauphiné when her son was installed as royal lieutenant there in 1678 as on 'une proie certaine' in the words of a local historian; but she was constrained to return to Paris empty-handed, 'ce qui blessa fortement son esprit'.[159] Mme de Castries, widow of a governor of Montpellier, not content with the income of bribes from dishonest traders, sold the mud from the town's ditches.[160]

Sessions of the *Grands Jours*, royal assizes which circulated from time to time in the provinces to hear cases considered difficult or dangerous for local tribunals to handle, were immune from feminine interference insofar as the presiding judges were specially commissioned Parisian magistrates. But they despatched business, much as did deputies at the Provincial Estates, in between entertaining a bevy of female relatives, brought along to see to their creature comforts, and provincial matrons, come to brush up on the latest fashions, manners and gossip from the capital. There was always a chance that from amongst the wide-eyed retinue a woman of vigour and initiative would emerge and start to play havoc with red tape. Mme Talon's ostensible reason for attending the famous *Grands Jours* of Auvergne in 1665, immortalised by Fléchier, was to superintend the domestic affairs of her son Denis, who was acting on the tribunal as royal attorney. But as soon as she arrived at Clermont she manifested a reforming zeal that shook the town to its foundations. Civil and criminal affairs were all grist to her mill. Her first efforts were directed towards properly policing the town and introducing taxes on commodities to prevent avaricious merchants from taking advantage of the presence of the assizes to make illicit profits. On discovering, from a personal examination of their weights and measures, that Clermont tradesmen were cheating customers of the full amounts, she loudly campaigned for a corresponding reduction in prices. Local gentlewomen, inclined to associate piety with old age and ugliness, found themselves mobilised at her instigation into charity groups. Nuns of teaching and nursing orders who attracted her attention by their lax ways were persuaded of the necessity to mend them. Nothing escaped Mme Talon's vigilance, not even the upkeep of prisoners or the hangman's wages. A quietly amused Fléchier wondered that she had not received her warrant to sit on the judges' bench since she was doing their job so energetically.[161]

Humouring ladies with influential connections was, however, the limit beyond which no right-thinking deputies and magistrates were prepared to go. Women might be tolerated within their sanctums, but never as colleagues in the debating chamber, only as onlookers from the gallery. In dealings with foreign nations active feminine participation was in some measure more acceptable because more remote. Having women serving as ambassadresses and agents for France outside the confines of the country cushioned the blow to masculine pride. So did the small percentage of high-ranking women involved, and the fact that the missions confided to them were of the kind most decorously and most unobtrusively performed by members of their sex.

It had always been tacitly understood that French princesses married to foreign potentates should try to use their influence over their husband to promote home interests abroad. Indeed a niece of Louis XIV acquitted herself of the task so well after her marriage to Charles II of Spain in 1679 that her sudden death in 1689 was attributed to her poisoning by the anti-French faction at the Spanish court.[162] Foreign princesses marrying into the French royal family were also enrolled as diplomats. They were expected to renounce completely their country of origin, even in such details as use of their native language,[163] and to further wholeheartedly the policies of their adoptive country, whatever mental suffering this might cause.[164] Acclimatised brides like Henriette d'Angleterre, employed on a successful mission to England in 1670 to win support for her brother-in-law Louis XIV from her brother Charles II, admirably fulfilled expectations. But then Henriette could feel little allegiance towards compatriots who had decapitated her father and forced her mother and herself into a long, impoverished exile across the Channel.[165]

Princesses passing to and fro across the frontiers needed escorts, not just troops and bodyguards but women to tend to their personal needs, to prevent violations of propriety and etiquette, and generally to iron out problems arising during the transition from one homeland to another. Incoming wives of French princes were met by the leading ladies of their future households usually at the relevant border, though penetration into foreign lands to fetch the bride was also sometimes required. The Princesse Palatine, who had negotiated the second marriage of Louis XIV's brother with her husband's niece, was thus deemed the most appropriate person to officially collect the new Madame from her native Germany in 1671.[166] Outgoing French princesses were accompanied to foreign climes by an aristocratic *ambassadrice* of mature years to act as chaperone and to see her charge safely delivered to her new master before returning to France. The Maréchale de Guébriant was created 'Surintendante du Voyage et Ambassadrice Extraordinaire' for the purpose of escorting the newly married Marie de Gonzague to her husband the king of Poland early in 1646, and she was honoured accordingly at the Polish court. She received there the blessing of the bishop of Poznania, a privilege reserved for sovereigns, and processed triumphally back to France via Hungary, Austria and Italy, saluted all along her route with the pomp and pageantry accorded to personages of distinction.[167] The dignity bestowed upon the Maréchale was not repeated for the benefit of any of her peers,[168] despite the occasional protest from a rank-conscious escort who wanted a grander title than that of plain *ambassadrice* to figure in the letters patent of her appointment.[169] The designation was, in effect, ambiguous since it applied equally to those women who acquired it simply by virtue of their marriage to an ambassador.

The ambassador's wife accompanied her husband on missions abroad primarily to minister to his domestic needs. But though in his shadow she still, whether she wished it or not, had a representational role. She was a yardstick by which foreigners would judge her compatriots and her conduct was therefore not unimportant. At European courts she could scarcely with decorum remain confined to her home. She had to pay her respects to the ruling family and participate in court ceremonial. If she wanted to avoid fatal blunders she had to acquaint herself with key personages and current affairs, taking care that her enquiries were not misconstrued as intrigues. Circulating at court and gathering information could even provide a rudimentary diplomatic training from which at least one wife profited to assume her husband's functions in an emergency.[170]

The trials of being an ambassador's wife in the seventeenth century are entertainingly narrated in a series of letters written to her friend Mme de Coulanges in Paris by Marie de Villars, wife of the ambassador to Spain. Mme de Villars preceded her husband on his second embassy to Madrid late in 1679, just prior to the arrival of Charles II's new French queen. Her first impulse was to bury herself in solitude, for she was painfully aware of her ignorance of the customs of the court and the country: 'Je n'ai pas encore voulu recevoir de visites. J'attends le retour de M. de Villars. Il y a tant de manières et tant de cérémonies à observer, qu'il faut qu'il m'instruise de tout... Rien ne ressemble ici à ce qui se pratique en France.'[171] As the king and queen approached the capital, a feeling of panic set in: 'Que j'appréhende de m'habiller, et de commencer à sortir! Je ne suis point du tout née pour représenter.'[172] But an effort had to be made to emerge from comforting seclusion and plunge into the fatiguing ritual of court audiences and complimentary visits: 'Je ne vous dirai point les pas comptés que l'on fait pour aller recevoir les dames, les unes à la première estrade, les autres à la seconde, ou à la troisième: car, par parenthèse, j'ai un très grand appartement. Tirez de là, en soupirant pour moi, la conséquence de ce qu'il m'en coûte à le meubler. Il faut, en entrant et en sortant, passer devant toutes ces dames. Celle qui me conduisait avait assez d'affaires à me redresser. Car j'oubliais souvent le cérémonial. Ces visites durent tout le jour.'[173] Spain and its people had few charms for the ambassadress, whose power of communication was limited by her imperfect grasp of the language. She was bored by the claustrophobic atmosphere at court, nauseated by recreations like the *auto-da-fé*, exhausted by the intense heat and plagued by the flies. Remaining solvent was a constant anxiety: her salary of 12 000 *écus*, she complained,[174] was worth just under half that sum at Madrid owing to devaluation, and 9000 *francs* were consumed in rent alone. She could not even be sure that her husband would keep his vulnerable post. Incidents in 1680 during which attempts were made to rouse the populace against Villars because of dissatisfaction over the treatment of his Spanish counterpart in France drove home the fact that ambassadors were sitting targets for manifestations of resentment against the policies of their government, who nevertheless blamed them for disorders: 'Quand ces désordres-là arrivent, les plaintes ne manquent pas d'être portées en France, et un pauvre ambassadeur est condamné, sans avoir pu dire ses raisons.'[175] The lament was prophetic since in the following year Mme de Villars was accused together with her husband of plotting at the Spanish court, despite the studied assurances of political indifference that filled her letters from the start,[176] and the embassy terminated under a cloud.[177]

Transplantation to foreign soil involved hazards and fatigues such that women were rarely called upon to sojourn abroad for long periods in any official capacity. The privileged few who were engaged in rendering diplomatic services gave a mixed account of themselves, in some cases working loyally and competently to further French interests, but showing in others that propensity for intrigue that seemed to be the fatal inheritance of the seventeenth-century noblewoman.

In political and civic life seventeenth-century Frenchwomen did not appear, or were not allowed to appear, to their best advantage. An infinitesimal fraction alone of the female population were invited to play any part in the internal administration or external affairs of the country. This same minority were eligible for admission to official assemblies, but with the idea that they should watch and admire, never take the floor. Men clung tightly to the reins of effective power, and it was in the name of men and through men that women from the queen regent downwards swayed events if they were so minded. Hence the gravitation of the ambitious towards the men of the moment – ministers, financiers, bureaucrats – who could be intimidated or cajoled into furthering the projects of themselves and their clients.

It was the petty aspects of politics that attracted contemporary women most: the chance to intrigue, above all, to satisfy personal vengeances and grievances, and to parade in the public eye. A solid political inspiration or plan of reform was discernible neither in the frenzied plotting and farcical capers of aristocratic conspiratresses, nor yet in the destructive fury of plebeian insurgents. Ironically their escapades worked to their detriment. The government was distracted from applying itself to those very reforms for which the women of the people clamoured as a matter of life and death, and to which heedless noblewomen paid lip-service. And provoked statesmen, whom more rational procedures might ultimately have persuaded otherwise, were merely fortified in the opinion that Richelieu once feelingly expressed: 'Le gouvernement des femmes est d'ordinaire le malheur des états.'[178]

11
Women in the Cultural Sphere

Taking a positive part in the intellectual life of the nation was a challenge which women were ostensibly as ill-equipped to meet as they had been to secure recognition of their potential for significant political and civic action. Placed at a serious disadvantage by their exclusion from institutions dispensing secondary and higher education, they were additionally handicapped by the risk of being mocked whenever they showed an impulse to improve their mind or to commit themselves in print. Official reunions of the French intelligentsia were in the main sympathetic to the policy adopted by the Académie Française on its foundation in 1635 of limiting its forty Immortals to members of the male sex. Nothing daunted by bans and prejudices, women used their ingenuity, as always, to find means of getting round them. They opened up relations with the art world by employing all kinds of masters to create at their bidding. They took pains to make of their homes inviting rendez-vous where men of learning were glad to forgather with colleagues and social superiors, away from the regimented atmosphere of the academies. They capitalised on their reputation for possessing greater refinement than the opposite sex to set themselves up as judges of literary works which authors hastened to submit to them out of deference and gratitude. They also ventured to publish on their own behalf, using stratagems to ensure that the dictates of modesty were not violated.

Of all the ways in which women intervened in cultural affairs the least resented and the most appreciated was undoubtedly that of patronage. The system had obvious advantages for both sides. The artist benefited from full employment, from the prestige acquired in serving eminent persons and receiving tangible marks of their satisfaction,[1] and from the stimulation of his genius. The patroness beautified her existence, enhanced her social standing and, with luck, immortalised her name after death. And both made fruitful contact with an environment different from their own.

Architects, landscape gardeners, painters and sculptors were in ceaseless demand, perhaps because the nature of their works seemed to offer the most imposing and durable guarantee against oblivion. Thanks to their assistance the great ladies of the seventeenth century were able to indulge a marked predilection for the construction, reconstruction and ornamentation of retreats which were forever changing the face of Paris and its environs. Marie de Médicis, true to her ancestral heritage, disbursed ruinous sums to enable her architect Salomon de Brosse to renovate Catherine de Médicis's old *château* of Montceaux, and later to build the Luxembourg palace, both envisaged as refuges from the constraints and formalities of the Louvre.[2] With a similar idea in mind Mme de Rambouillet personally replanned her famous Hôtel to accommodate more comfortably her chosen circle of friends.[3] Royal favourites, whose need for privacy was especially pressing, liked to have domains laid out where they could entertain the king and relax away from the curious eyes of the courtiers. Mme de Montespan was able to commandeer the services of Jules Hardouin-Mansart to erect a luxury *château* at Clagny, to the east of Versailles, while André Le Nôtre superintended work on the gardens.[4] Two years later, in 1676, Le Nôtre was busy designing the gardens of Maintenon, a somewhat dilapidated estate which the proprietress took a keen interest in restoring and running[5] until the time when her marriage to Louis XIV obliged her to reside almost permanently at court.

To make the interior of their palaces and residences match in splendour the façades and approaches, ladies called in the great painters of the day. Eustache Le Sueur was one of the many whose brush was scarcely ever idle as he painted now stately Junos on the walls of Anne d'Autriche's Appartement des Bains at the Louvre; now episodes from the lives of Solomon and Moses on the ceilings and chimney of the Comtesse de Tonnay-Charente's Paris abode; now an allegorical representation of her services as royal *gouvernante* on the ceiling of Mme de Senecé's house at Conflans; now an oratory for the Prince de Condé's mother.[6] Amongst the infinite variety of ornaments which fashion and individual caprice dictated, one which rarely failed to grace the walls of town house or country mansion was a painting of the mistress of the household.[7] When expense was no object renowned artists from abroad might be summoned to do the portrait. On the instances of Marie de Médicis Rubens spent three years (1622–5) adorning one of the galleries of the Luxembourg with a series of twenty-one portraits highlighting the important moments in his patroness's life.[8] But France possessed artistic talent of her own and certain painters made their name by specialising in female portraiture. The Beaubrun cousins, Henri and Charles, were overwhelmed by requests from potential sitters who appreciated their knack of improving upon less than perfect features without completely altering the resemblance.[9] To heighten the majesty of their mien ladies were fond of being represented as mythological deities or saints. Marie de Médicis commanded Simon François to depict her portly person in the guise of the Virgin holding a Christ child featuring the infant Louis XIII.[10] The wives of Louis XIV and his brother were transformed into Juno and Spring respectively, Anne d'Autriche into Cybele, the Duchesse de Montpensier into Diana and her three half-sisters into Graces, in a vast allegorical portrait of the royal family by Jean Nocret.[11] Ironies, unconscious or otherwise, resulted from this practice. The wanton Duchesses de Chevreuse and de Montbazon had themselves painted, the former as the chaste goddess of hunting, the latter as the mother of Christ.[12]

Not all wished merely to gaze upon reproductions of their own faces. Those with well-filled purses snapped up any paintings of renown that came within reach and sometimes formed impressive private collections. The Duchesse d'Aiguillon, an art enthusiast like her distinguished uncle, commissioned a *Rape of the Sabines* from Nicolas Poussin to place alongside his *Capture of Jerusalem* in a boudoir filled with rare and costly ornaments.[13] The Comtesse de Brassac paid her court in an original way by maintaining a private art gallery consisting of almost a hundred portraits of the French royal family.[14] Middle-class women of means also took steps to surround themselves with valuable canvases,[15] either because of a genuine interest in art or because of a perennial desire to imitate the aristocracy.

The feminine passion for collecting kept a whole host of craftsmen, apart from painters, hard at work, for it extended over a wide range of precious objects: jewels, porcelains,[16] silver plate,[17] medallions,[18] tapestries[19] and antiques of every description. Wealthy aesthetes began to earn a reputation for amassing treasures and curios that was reflected in the appearance of their addresses in guide-books and the eagerness of tourists to view their bulging galleries and cabinets.[20]

Commerce between women and artists was boosted by the

frequent recourse which the former had to the latter to help them manifest their piety in concrete ways. When a nobleman died it was still fashionable for his widow to perpetuate his memory by means of a sumptuous tomb in which she herself might eventually be laid to rest. One of the most outstanding funereal monuments of the period, the mausoleum of the decapitated Duc de Montmorency at Moulins, came to be sculpted thus under the direction of François Anguier on the initiative of the grieving Duchesse.[21] Joys as well as sorrows were commemorated. A humble Parisian cook-shop proprietress named Anne asked the Belgian-born artist Philippe Buyster to model a statue of her patron saint teaching the Virgin to read, as a thank-offering for the profits made by herself and her late husband in the sale of poultry.[22] At the opposite end of the social hierarchy her namesake, Anne d'Autriche, exhilarated at having produced a Dauphin in 1638, ordered the sculptor Jacques Sarrasin to model a silver angel holding a golden child, and then dedicated the statuette to Our Lady of Loreto to fulfil a vow made during pregnancy.[23] The queen's decision to reconstruct the Benedictine convent of Val-de-Grâce, whither she periodically withdrew throughout her reign for shelter and meditation, was inspired by the same motive of thanksgiving for an event which had given her a claim to the nation's esteem.[24] Large convents like this royal sanctuary were storehouses of artistic treasures, for artists lavished their talents on designing and decorating chapels and high altars, fabricating votive offerings and painting pious pictures, at the request of nuns and their devout benefactresses.[25]

As patronesses and promoters of music women were equally to the fore. The early acquaintance of girls with the means of making their own music[26] often ripened into an abiding love of the art, for which would-be suitors were earnestly advised by Molière to cater: 'La plupart des femmes aujourd'hui se laissent prendre par les oreilles; elles sont cause que tout le monde se mêle de musique, et l'on ne réussit auprès d'elles que par les petites chansons et les petits vers qu'on leur fait entendre.'[27] Princesses and favourites fostered the development of music by keeping their own retinue of musicians, paying pensions, accepting dedications from composers and persuading their intimates to lend an ear to the virtuosi summoned to perform in their apartments. Marguerite de Valois continued until her death in 1615 to support 'bon nombre d'excellents musiciens et joueurs d'instruments qu'elle employait à faire le divin service et à sa récréation ordinaire'.[28] From the 1650s onwards the Duchesse de Montpensier, Mlle de Guise, last survivor of the powerful Guise branch of Lorraine princes, and Madame appeared amongst the leading Maecenases of the musical profession. Mlle de Montpensier's entourage comprised a troupe of violinists whom her enemies accused of playing in the Place Royale during an illness of Louis XIV.[29] The songwriter and singer Michel Lambert, doted upon by salon hostesses,[30] found favour in her circle.[31] His sister-in-law Hilaire Dupuy, one of the most sought-after female singers of the day, was her pensioner.[32] For a while Jean-Baptiste Lully was also in her employ.[33] A subsequent adversary of the acquisitive Florentine, the composer Marc Antoine Charpentier, was similarly launched on his career through being taken under the wing of Mlle de Guise, and repaid a lengthy sojourn at the Hôtel de Guise by means of pieces specially arranged for his benefactress.[34] Henriette d'Angleterre seems to have found in music some of the charms necessary to soothe away the frustrations of marriage to an effeminate homosexual. The gazettes record a succession of vocal and instrumental concerts given in her apartment to an appreciative audience of 'maintes belles'.[35] In 1661 her name appropriately adorned the dedication of Lambert's *Nouveau Livre d'Airs*. Towards the close of Louis XIV's reign the avowedly unmusical Mme de Maintenon bestirred herself to organise concerts of chamber music to divert the king from his partiality for the opera, which was thought to be endangering his immortal soul.[36]

Women took a special delight in music when combined with other arts such as mime and dancing. They made a vital contribution to the triumph of the opera, though mainly in their role of professional entertainers (in the broadest sense),[37] a role which basically differed little from that of the ordinary actress.[38] By comparison the ballet was less of a closed shop. Already a standard form of diversion by the end of the sixteenth century, the ballet achieved its most magnificent expression at the court, where members of the royal family and the aristocracy took the principal parts, assisted when necessary by professional dancers and singers. At first men seemed to dominate the proceedings. King or princes instigated ballets which they danced with the gallants of their entourage, the use of a mask enabling them to perform female roles without undue absurdity.[39] But women quickly edged their way on to the scene, both as composers[40] and as dancers. Marie de Médicis, whose enthusiasm for ballets was such that in 1612 she commanded the lords of her court to provide her with one every Sunday,[41] realised the political advantages to be derived from allegorical spectacles on a large scale. She started organising her own lavish representations, notably on the occasion of her eldest daughter Elisabeth's marriage to the future Philip IV of Spain in 1615.[42] Prior to her viduity she was not averse to joining in the dancing herself,[43] and encouraged her daughters to do likewise from infancy.[44] Her example was imitated by Anne d'Autriche[45] and Marie-Thérèse[46] in the early years of their respective reigns when youth and absence of pregnancies permitted the exercise. Queens were seconded and overshadowed by talented princesses,[47] by ladies-in-waiting, and ultimately by professional ballerinas.[48] Songstresses, absent from ballets in the reigns of Henri IV[49] and Louis XIII, warbled many a harmonious solo at the court of the Sun King.[50] Ballets were not limited to court precincts but staged in the private residences of the aristocracy[51] and the rich bourgeoisie.[52] Even the convents did not remain impervious to their attractions. Six emancipated nuns from Poissy are on record as paying with exile for their impulse to tread a measure at Saint-Germain before the eyes of Louis XIII.[53]

Producing a successful opera or ballet required a prodigious feat of collaboration between musicians, singers, dancers, stage designers and, last but not least, men of letters. Poets and dramatists were responsible for the composition of opera libretti and the booklets of verses which were distributed to onlookers before the commencement of ballets and understood to be recited by the different performers while dancing. To lend pungency to their verses they tried to render them appropriate at the same time to the performer and to the personage represented, evoking traits and circumstances common to both. The acknowledged master of the art was Isaac de Benserade. The lines which he wrote for the wife of the obese superintendant of galleys, the Comtesse de Vivonne, who figured as a nereid paying homage to Venus (Henriette d'Angleterre) in the *Ballet Royal de la Naissance de Vénus* (1665), show his talent at its best:

> Il est vrai que je sors de mon antre profond
> Pour rendre à la Déesse un hommage fidèle;
> Et ce que par plaisir toutes les autres font,
> Je le fais pour l'honneur de danser avec elle:
> Mais je danserai mieux, et bien plus à propos,

Au retour d'un Epoux si fameux sur les flots;
De quels transports de joie aurai-je l'âme pleine!
A toute heure je crois qu'il s'en va revenir,
    Et jusqu'à la moindre Baleine,
    Tout m'en fait ressouvenir.[54]

Apposite versifying of this kind necessitated on the part of the composer a reasonably close acquaintance with his subject's character and private life, to avoid indiscretions and forestall hidings, and implies relations of a certain intimacy.

Contact between fashionable ladies and men of letters was facilitated by the writers' custom of attaching themselves to the top people – sometimes on a formal basis as tutor, secretary, librarian, almoner, steward or business manager – in the hope of obtaining the upkeep and protection necessary for the undisturbed incubation of their promised masterpieces. In return for shelter and support they worked to embellish the public image of the household and helped their patrons to shine in the social circles in which the latter moved. Gazette-writers were eminently suited to discharge these functions and willingly allowed themselves to be commandeered by the ladies. Jean Loret placed his *Muse Historique* under the aegis of Marie de Longueville right from the outset, and kept the public minutely informed of her health, qualities, activities, travels and payment of his pension. The Schomberg family, old acquaintances, were offered their share of tributes through their most beautiful and virtuous member the Maréchale de Schomberg (née Marie de Hautefort), renowned amongst literary men for her munificence.[55] The lucky rhymster also attracted the attention of the opulent Duchesse de Montpensier, for whom he discreetly propagandised during her disgrace after the Fronde, and that of Anne d'Autriche, who stimulated his zeal for her son's cause by periodic donations.[56] The continuators of Loret pursued his fruitful policy of seeking female patronage. La Gravette de Mayolas took over for a while as official reporter to Marie de Longueville. Robinet elected to dedicate his rhymed news-bulletins to Madame, whose generosity was solicited by flattering vignettes recalling the pleasures she derived from the arts, music and dancing. More fickle in their allegiances, Boursault and Subligny aimed to multiply patronesses and gratifications by addressing themselves to different ladies in turn or to two simultaneously.[57]

In addition to serving as publicity agents, patronised writers could expect to be tapped for entertainment, erudition and, generally, any commodity for which their patroness felt the need. They had to devise, to order, compositions in prose and verse on any subject that happened to catch her fancy, regardless of their own natural bent and preferences.[58] It fell to their lot to trace the gallant epistles and stanzas with which she liked to surprise friends or express gratitude for paeans, gifts and favours received.[59] If she personally was moved to compose, they assisted with the mechanics of literary creation, eliminating errors and polishing style.[60] They racked their brains to invent and arrange diversions for the amusement of her guests,[61] afterwards recording them in literary form for the benefit of absentees or of posterity.[62] They also came in handy to shed lustre, by their learned reputation if not their eccentricities,[63] on her salon.

The most illustrious of the salons, or *ruelles*[64] to use contemporary parlance, were formed and flourishing prior to the personal reign of Louis XIV. In some respects they were a typical manifestation of the spirit of individualism and resistance to centralisation which permeated French society in the first half of the century and which successive heads of government tried to curb in the interests of rendering monarchical power more absolute. Each salon revolved around a woman who for a variety of reasons – poor health, unorthodox political or religious convictions, undistinguished lineage or nonconformist temperament – was unable to figure advantageously at the royal court yet unwilling to forfeit the pleasures and company to be found there, and who created her own private little court instead. The impetus for the foundation of salons had come from a politically restless class, the aristocracy, faithfully imitated by the bourgeoisie. Certain salons engaged, or were suspected of engaging, in subversive activities, and were objects of government surveillance: the Hôtel de Rambouillet, for instance, patronised by the Condés and their clients;[65] the circle of Mme des Loges, a Protestant *bourgeoise* intimate with Gaston d'Orléans;[66] the Hôtel de Nevers, directed by Mme du Plessis-Guénégaud, a Jansenist opponent of Mazarin.[67] The declared purpose of their existence, however, was to enable *honnêtes gens* to meet decorously together in pleasant surroundings for conversation and mutual entertainment. Qualification for the title of *honnête homme* or *honnête femme* meant little more than being of acceptable provenance and possessing a modicum of culture and social polish. Where the morals of their guests were concerned salon-holders showed themselves to be singularly undemanding. It is true that some could hardly insist upon an unblemished record without being guilty of flagrant hypocrisy. But even a woman of irreproachable virtue like Mme de Rambouillet over-looked patent disreputableness[68] in favour of high birth or talents proper to enhance the status of her salon and secure useful protection.

Assiduity at one particular salon did not preclude attendance at others. The *habitués* of aristocratic salons liked to prolong their pleasures in those of the bourgeoisie,[69] and the bourgeoisie asked for nothing better than to be able to reciprocate the compliment. Men of letters in their endless quest for patrons found it profitable to circulate widely among the different *ruelles*. Ladies learned how to run a successful salon by frequenting as many recognised mistresses of the art as possible and absorbing their techniques. Intercommunication was helped by the fact that salons, instead of being limited to a set venue, were held now at one, now at another of the various domiciles owned by the hostess and her friends.[70]

The basic occupations of the salons changed little from place to place and from decade to decade. The mock-chivalric 'Ordre des Egyptiens' created *circa* 1635 by Mlle du Pré, self-styled Queen Epicharis, for the gallants of Metz[71] found an echo in the 'Ordre de la Mouche à Miel' at the *château* of Sceaux, to which the familiars of the Duchesse du Maine vied for admission at the dawn of the eighteenth century.[72] But hostesses were well aware of the necessity to satisfy diverse tastes, the crude as well as the refined, if they were not to see their salons deserted. They therefore strove within the conventional framework to vary their programme of entertainments as much as ingenuity and finances permitted.

Three topics provided focal points for conversation and pastimes: love, literature and philosophy. The last of these was the speciality of coteries presided over by women who had received an exceptionally solid education and whose intellectual emancipation sometimes spread to their morals, such as Mme Deshoulières,[73] Mme de la Sablière,[74] Ninon de Lenclos.[75] Less exclusive salons ventured excursions into arduous philosophical realms, but members felt happier confining themselves to a particular branch of the discipline, namely moral philosophy, about which it was possible to talk without possessing specialist knowledge. The thinly dis-guised account of her Saturday receptions which Mlle de Scudéry published in the form of the ten-volume novel *Clélie* (1654–60) alludes to conversations on metempsychosis and reason in animals.[76] But the bulk of the serious discussion centres on vices and virtues and on death,[77] subjects with which everyone would be sufficiently well acquainted to be able to proffer an opinion.

While the 'pedants' fired theories at one another in a corner, the younger and more frivolous members of the company amused themselves with an assortment of games and recreations designed for the most part to pay homage to the ladies present. Love, in the form of studied gallantry, was a major preoccupation of worldly *ruelles*. Rechristened with poetic pseudonyms[78] that helped transport them in imagination back to some Arcadia, ladies and gentlemen assembled as in the fabled 'Courts of Love' of medieval times to pose ticklish 'love-questions': 'Savoir si la présence de ce que l'on aime cause plus de joie que les marques de son indifférence ne donnent de peine; S'il est plus doux d'aimer une personne dont le cœur est préoccupé qu'une autre dont le cœur est insensible; Si le mérite d'être aimé doit récompenser le chagrin de ne l'être pas'.[79] The solution of amatorial problems led naturally to the analysis of sentimental phenomena and the drafting of guides to correct wooing. With a typical seventeenth-century relish for dissecting and fixing in palpable formulas even the most fleeting manifestations of emotional activity, the *habitués* of the salons pinpointed nine different kinds of 'amitié', as many again of 'estime', twelve varieties of sighs, sixteen shades of 'complaisance'.[80] Love-play they codified in curious maps,[81] and interminable lists of *Maximes d'Amour* and *Lois de la Galanterie* which prescribed, by straightforward injunction or by ironical antiphrasis, the elaborate ritual whereby a lady's favour was won.[82] When the last sentimental conundrum had been unravelled to everyone's satisfaction guests turned to parlour games that allowed them to reveal personal inclinations instead of merely expatiating on love in the abstract. Rules were remarkably accommodating. In a collection of pastimes expressly destined for 'des personnes de bonne condition, nourries dans la civilité et la galanterie', Charles Sorel gives instructions for a number of games 'où l'on baise', including one in which a woman would be asked to imagine herself in bed between two men of the company and to kiss the one whom she declared that she would choose to face for preference![83] Gallantries of a more decorous and conventional nature generally concluded the evening's entertainment: plays,[84] concerts, promenades, collations or quiet conversation, '[le] plus souvent de choses ordinaires et galantes'.[85]

Gallantry was inseparable from literature in the minds of those who flitted from *ruelle* to *ruelle*. They needed little prompting to air their views on the latest trends in literary composition,[86] especially that of novels, which served them well as huge compendiums of ideas for gallant conversations and distractions. They were also fond of elaborating works themselves. One of the most popular parlour games of the century was the 'Jeu du Roman', in which participants took turns to add to a story from the point where the previous person chose to break off the narrative, or wove a tale from a series of disconnected words.[87] The exercise was a useful initiation into the solo composition of not only full-length novels, but also shorter pieces of prose such as portraits and maxims, more easily completed during the limited period of a salon session.

The salons' output of prose was secondary, however, to that of poetry. They poured forth veritable streams of verse, forgotten now save for the sixty-two-piece poetic garland offered by the familiars of Mme de Rambouillet to her eldest daughter Julie d'Angennes as a birthday present in May 1641.[88] Inspirations were compressed into whatever form happened to be fashionable at the time of writing: *rondeaux*, odes, enigmas, *métamorphoses*, sonnets, madrigals, gazettes. Subjects were never lacking because the most trivial and even vulgar happenings in the everyday life of the salon and its members furnished a pretext for rhyming: an exchange of gifts,[89] the death of a pet,[90] a malady or its cure.[91]

The most important function of the salons from the literary point of view was that of a testing-ground where men of letters essayed their works prior to publication. In deference to a firmly established ritual, authors about to deposit a manuscript with a publisher first consulted the women of their acquaintance on the finer points which, as creatures of greater subtlety and delicacy than men,[92] they were considered better qualified to appreciate. The practice cast writers into a somewhat abject posture. Edme Boursault, unable to read at an agreed hour one of his compositions to Mme Tallemant, a financier's daughter who protected minor dramatists like himself,[93] placated the deity with sedulous flattery: 'je ne pourrai avoir le bien d'aller demain soumettre ma pièce à votre correction, dont je profite plus que de tout ce que je puis apprendre dans les livres. Vous êtes si accoutumée à dire toute chose de bon sens, que votre suffrage seul règle le destin de tous les ouvrages qu'on vous montre.'[94] Georges de Scudéry gloried in his religious submission to the whims of Julie d'Angennes, to whom he had made a vow 'de tenir pour maximes indubitables toutes [ses] opinions, et pour arrêts souverains tous les sentiments de ces excellentes personnes, qui firent un miracle en [lui] donnant l'être'.[95] Servility was perhaps to be expected from financially dependent poetasters, but even the most eminent authors acknowledged the authority of feminine censors. Corneille,[96] Pascal,[97] Racine,[98] Boileau,[99] La Fontaine,[100] Bossuet[101] repeatedly looked to women for approval of their widely divergent productions. The haughty La Rochefoucauld despatched to Mme de Sablé for correction maxim after maxim accompanied by flowery compliments: 'vous savez ... que les sentences ne sont sentences qu'après que vous les avez approuvées... Je vous envoie ce que j'ai pris chez vous en partie. Je vous supplie très humblement de me mander si je ne l'ai point gâté, et si vous trouvez le reste à votre gré.'[102] Ducal pen-pushers and the commoner sort all recited their litanies at the same shrine.

Truly knowledgeable women greeted appeals to act as arbitresses of literary works with modest protestations of their unsuitability to undertake the task.[103] There were plenty of less enlightened females, however, who jumped at the chance to pose as legislators of Parnassus. These were the ones who aimed to run their salons along the lines of an official academy in which women merely sat in judgement on literary offerings presented by men, without making any attempt at genuine converse and exchange of ideas. The Vicomtesse d'Auchy's Tuesday assembly was the epitome of the type. Chapelain, an academician, was dogged by a reputation for pedantry yet recoiled in disgust from the 'nouveauté ridicule' of an academy of ageing 'fées' where 'les femmes n[e] font que recevoir, et les hommes... donnent toujours'.[104] The phenomenon which Chapelain qualified as a 'novelty' in the 1630s proliferated to the point where it sparked off a reaction against the tyranny of female coteries. Donneau de Visé poured scorn on the author who consented to mutilate his work in order to obtain from a gaggle of capricious females letters of recommendation to the cliques of their featherbrained friends.[105] Michel de Pure,[106] Antoine Furetière[107] and Molière[108] exposed the mania of petty *bourgeoises* and *précieuses* for destructive criticism and the dangerous power complex they derived from the persuasion that no work could succeed without first passing muster in their circles. To show their contempt rebellious authors deliberately tested their works on women who offended the susceptibilities of the orthodox *bourgeoise* and the authentic *précieuse*. Molière gave preliminary readings of his comedies to his servant, Mlle Forest,[109] and to a courtesan, Ninon de Lenclos.[110] But so long as writers continued to seek approbation from members of the female sex, however dubious their social or moral status, what some regarded as the stranglehold of women over literary creation could not be said to be broken.

The interference of the *ruelles* in a closely allied sphere, that of language, stirred up fresh ripples of opposition. Here again women exploited their position as patronesses and their reputation for refinement and good taste to elect themselves as judges of perfection. Before the century was very old Mlle de Gournay, a learned authoress and salon holder,[111] began levelling ponderous philippics against the 'paidagoguesses poupines' and their 'mig-nardes Ruelles' whose every linguistic caprice was a law unto writers anxious to 'attrape[r] les bons dîners'.[112] It was easy to ridicule or to ignore the rambling protests of an eccentric spinster openly committed to preserving the philological and stylistic heritage of the Ronsardian era. The grammarian Vaugelas continued unperturbed his consultation of salon hostesses and court ladies,[113] convinced, as he stated authoritatively in the resultant *Remarques sur la Langue Française* (1647), that women of breeding could be relied upon to produce instinctively the correct forms of polite speech. As a reward for his discernment his *Remarques* found a place of honour on the bookshelf of every dazzled *précieuse*[114] engaged in linguistic revision.

The emendation of the language was a foreseeable extension of the efforts of the *précieuses* to purify and dignify relations between the sexes, which drew scarcely fewer sneers than their liberal views on marriage and female education. Objection was taken to their invention of a 'jargon' in which far-fetched and hyperbolical expressions replaced terms condemned as provincial, pedantic or vulgar.[115] Satirical lists appeared, purporting to contain the euphemisms substituted for breasts ('coussinets d'amour'), chamber pot ('l'urinal virginal'), commode ('la soucoupe inférieure'), lavatory ('la lucarne des antipodes')[116] and similar locutions '[d']une rudesse capable d'égorger en passant un pauvre gosier'.[117] Comedies and farces diverted the public with the spectacle of the *précieuse* half-swooning at the slightest solecism and recovering only to lecture in doctoral tones to the offending and uncomprehending interlocutor.[118] A spate of pamphlets and engravings representing a caricatural blacksmith named Lustucru (*L'eusses-tu cru?*) vainly endeavouring to hammer women's heads into shape underlined the fact that the *précieuses'* folly was irremediable.[119]

Unfairly detractors turned a blind eye to the idealistic and potentially beneficial aspects of the *précieuses'* linguistic innovations. Their yearning to transcend the banality and crudity, linguistic and otherwise, of everyday life for a grander, nobler plane of existence was construed as an arrogant desire to set themselves apart from the common herd. The purge and vocabulary transfusion which they sought to administer to language was dismissed as a ridiculous affectation or interpreted as an attempt to create a hermetic mode of communication proper to further separatist tendencies. Criticism of the *précieuses'* linguistic fastidiousness was sharpened by opposition to their more radical social ideas and by exasperation over their claim to issue certificates of literary excellence, but it was also an expression of impatience at the restraints that attendance at the salons sometimes imposed. In the pages of his *Historiettes* Tallemant relieved himself with satisfaction of the word 'cul', which he dared not pronounce in the presence of Mme de Rambouillet, 'un peu trop délicate', or her daughter Angélique, who 's'évanouissait quand elle entendait un méchant mot'.[120] The confession, if it seems to justify the epithet of *ridicules* that still sticks to the *précieuses*, suggests that their call for linguistic reform was not entirely superfluous.

Fraternising with writers in the salons, discussing their works and techniques, improvising the occasional maxim, poem or short story in the course of a parlour game, aroused a spirit of emulation in enterprising women and orientated their thoughts towards publication. The step was a daring one to take. Having works formally printed conjured up visions of burning the midnight oil, poring over learned tomes, labouring for mercenary ends, visions with which self-respecting gentlemen, let alone ladies, were reluctant to be associated. To save face, recourse was had to subterfuges: anonymity, pseudonyms, dedications and prefaces which spoke of papers 'stolen' by friends and submission to pressure from patrons. The procedure of the Comtesse de Lafayette exemplifies the sentiments of her contemporaries on this issue. Of her four short stories two – the *Princesse de Montpensier* (1662) and the *Princesse de Clèves* (1678) – were published anonymously, while *Zaïde* (1669–71) appeared under the name of a literary collaborator, Segrais, and the *Comtesse de Tende* (1724) came out over a quarter of a century after her death.[121] Her letters communicate something of the frustration of wanting to be acknowledged as the composer of works which sold out rapidly, yet at the same time fearing to be labelled as a professional writer. To Ménage, who was superintending the publication of the *Princesse de Montpensier*, she discloses her impatience to see her book in print, but urges him, 'si vous en entendez parler, de faire bien comme si vous ne l'aviez jamais vue et de nier qu'elle vienne de moi si par hasard on le disait'.[122] Huet is taken to task for passing on to his sister a copy of the story that Mme de Lafayette had given him for that very purpose, 'mais je ne vous l'avais pas remise pour la lui donner comme une de mes œuvres. Elle croira que je suis un vrai auteur de profession, de donner comme cela de mes livres.'[123] A month after the publication of the *Princesse de Clèves* she disavows point-blank to another correspondent having had any part in its composition, but treats herself to a compensatory review of the good points of the story.[124] Such was the persistence of old prejudices, even at this late stage in the century, that a woman of integrity preferred to tell, and connive at the propagation of, untruths rather than publicly own to being . . . an authoress.

In spite of the tyranny of public opinion women were some of the most fertile writers of the period, from the quantitative, if not always from the qualitative, point of view. There were few literary forms in which they failed to publish. But they turned for preference to genres that allowed for the inclusion of a large personal element, or those which the salons favoured. In each case they could, if need be, then escape the stigma of the professional authoress by claiming that their productions were composed solely for their own private amusement or that of friends.

Letter-writing was one of the genres in which they were considered to best exercise their pens. The women of the seventeenth century had a passion for letters. Each time that the acclaimed expert in the field, Guez de Balzac, brought out a new edition of his epistles, there was a press to purchase them: 'C'était le présent le plus agréable que les galants pussent faire à leurs maîtresses.'[125] Happily they rarely thought to copy Balzac's magniloquence any more than they did the stereotyped phrases offered as models of epistolary elegance in Guides for Correspondents. [126] Instead they seemed to abandon themselves to the inspiration of the moment, to be concerned more with an exact rendition of their feelings than with the construction of symmetrical periods or the achievement of technical perfection. Everyone agreed that women were for the most part completely ignorant of the niceties of spelling, grammar and punctuation, but that once their correspondence had been deciphered it was discovered to possess an indescribable charm. 'Elles sont heureuses dans le choix des termes, qu'elles placent si juste, que tout connus qu'ils sont, ils ont le charme de la nouveauté,' enthused La Bruyère in one of his rare tributes to women; 'il n'appartient qu'à elles de faire lire dans un seul mot tout un sentiment, et de rendre délicatement une pensée qui est délicate ... Si les femmes étaient toujours correctes, j'oserais dire que les lettres de quelques-unes d'entre elles seraient peut-être ce que nous avons dans notre langue de mieux écrit.' [127]

La Bruyère's panegyric is noteworthy in that at the time when he published it, in 1689, scarcely any collected editions of women's letters had appeared in print. The Comtesse de Brégy had issued in 1666 a selection of her efforts that did less to enhance her literary glory than to heighten her social prestige as the correspondent of queens and princesses. [128] But those letter-writers whom contemporaries lauded and those, not always the same persons, whom modern generations have admired published nothing in their lifetime. They had no need to. Their rank or their position as salon hostesses guaranteed them all the publicity they could desire. Though ostensibly private communications, letters were frequently passed around in the original or copied versions, whether to inform, impress or simply please friends. Fully aware of this practice, women took care, beneath an appearance of complete naturalness, to display their wit to best advantage and to win the esteem and sympathy of potential recipients. The letters of Mme des Loges found their way into an enviably large number of august hands owing to the writer's familiarity with princes and dukes and the accolade of 'tenth Muse' which the peerless Balzac bestowed upon her[129] – unjustifiably it was thought in some quarters. Malherbe acknowledged receipt of a batch from the Marquis de Racan, though his interest was such that he mislaid them. [130] Tallemant credited Mme des Loges with being 'la première personne de son sexe qui ait écrit des lettres raisonnables', but subsequently judged those that came into his possession 'pas trop merveilleuses' and endorsed the decision to prevent their publication by Conrart.[131] Soon even Balzac's allegiance wavered when Chapelain triumphantly heralded the appearance of a brighter star on the epistolary horizon in the form of Mme de Sablé:

> ... j'ai eu une extrême consolation de voir que mes sentiments sont conformes touchant la façon d'écrire de Mme la marquise de Sablé. Et certes il ne se peut plus délicatement ni plus flatteusement exprimer ses pensées qu'elle a fait dans cette lettre que je vous ai envoyée d'elle, et si toutes celles qu'elle écrit sont de ce style, comme je le crois, je n'ai garde de douter si je la dois préférer à votre amie à qui l'on ne saurait ôter qu'elle n'ait beaucoup d'esprit et qu'elle ne parle bien, mais qui aussi écrit si ambitieusement et se pique tellement de quintaine [sic] de lettres polies, que c'est tout ce que je puis faire que de la souffrir ...[132]

The custom of circulating letters and the seventeenth-century prescription for successful correspondence, that is to say delicate flattery and contrived negligence, were both therefore taken for granted well before Mme de Sévigné began to let her 'unbridled' pen[133] trace piquant gazettes[134] of court life into which she knew that persons other than her daughter looked to find their own embellished reflection.[135]

With their wealth of detail about events and personalities in the news, as well as about the writer's own actions and reactions, letters such as those of Mme de Sévigné, Mme de Maintenon and Charlotte de Bavière were distinguishable only in form from another branch of literature to which women were attracted, that of memoir writing. Composers of memoirs fell, broadly speaking, into one of two categories. The first category consisted of women who, out of a sense of gratitude to an employer or benefactress, undertook to write her life history, with which their own had been inextricably mingled. The observations of female memorialists differ from, and complement, those of their male counterparts in that they centre less on public conduct in wars and politics than on private life, which, as Mme de Motteville shrewdly said, is a surer guide to the true character.[136] The nature of the relationship between the memorialist and her chief subject made impartiality difficult. The familiars of Mme de Maintenon – Mlle d'Aumale, Mme de Caylus and the Dames de Saint-Cyr – are universally laudatory in their appraisal of her actions. Mme de Lafayette sees of Henriette d'Angleterre primarily '[les] grâces et les charmes... répandus en toute sa personne'.[137] And for all the air of strict neutrality with which she quotes official declarations and documents, Mme de Motteville can always find extenuating circumstances for Anne d'Autriche's shortcomings.[138] Criticisms, albeit veiled, are willingly reserved for members of the heroine's entourage or family. If Henriette d'Angleterre flirted this was because her manifold charms were wasted on a husband whose homosexuality Mme de Lafayette exposes with a delicately barbed phrase: 'le miracle d'enflammer le cœur de ce prince n'était réservé à aucune femme du monde'.[139] Yet partiality, from which few historians and biographers have been immune, does not so blind the memorialists as to render their testimonies completely at variance with those from unfriendly sources, and in a way their attitude does credit to their loyalty. Their heroine's conduct had at times been the object of speculation and controversy, and they were anxious to vindicate her in the eyes of present and future generations.

The apologetic intention predominates in the works of the second category of memorialists, but this time it is a question of a personal justification for activities that had incurred some form of social disgrace and punishment. The promoter of the quietist heresy, Mme Guyon, tries to enlist sympathy by narrating the long calvary of her life at the mercy of a hostile family and government.[140] The Duchesse de Montpensier profited from exile in Normandy to explain at the request of 'quelques personnes que j'aime' why a 'demoiselle qui n'aimait pas à se contraindre' like herself had the right to turn traitor on her king and cousin during the Fronde.[141] A vehicle for the apologetics of religious and political dissidents, memoirs were also the recourse of women who had amatory sins to be pardoned. Wives with records of imprisonment in convents, entanglement in lawsuits and bohemian existences in foreign climes explained how their original innocence had been exploited by insensitive parents who yoked them to husbands inclined to jealousy, debauchery, insanity and murder; and how their partner's brutality had driven them to follies which they now confessed in the earnest hope that others might learn to 'éviter les malheurs qui tiennent lieu de crimes, et à s'éloigner des occasions qui peuvent donner atteinte à la réputation des femmes'.[142] Some accounts were the work of professional writers of fiction. Others bore fictional titles: *Aventures ou Mémoires de la Vie de Henriette-Sylvie de Molière; Histoire de Cléante et de Bélise.*[143] Without forfeiting all claims to veracity, since the seventeenth century was one in which it could truthfully be said of certain individuals that they lived what others only dreamed, these memoirs blur the dividing line between fact and fantasy.[144] The extremist characters, the colourful escapades, the moralising pretensions, all make the subject matter interchangeable with that of any popular novel.

The novelistic domain proper was one where, having ventured tardily, women soon outstripped their masculine rivals. Prior to the 1650s gentlemen novelists – D'Urfé, Gomberville, La Calprenède – monopolised the composition of best-sellers. Then, in 1649, Madeleine de Scudéry's *Grand Cyrus* started to roll from the printing press, marking the beginning of an era of female literary triumphs that led a discerning judge, Pierre Bayle, to remark in 1697: 'Nos meilleurs romans français, depuis longtemps, se font par des filles ou par des femmes.'[145] Abandoning with distaste the so-called realist novel to male bourgeois colleagues like Paul Scarron and Charles Sorel, who could write unblushingly of pot bellies and excretion, women concentrated on multi-volume romances, subsequently reduced to shorter, romantic *nouvelles,*[146] in which allusions to natural functions and to the world of nature were kept to a stereotyped minimum. Their stories were set against backgrounds outwardly remote in time or space from seventeenth-century France, though the distance gradually narrowed from the ancient world favoured by Mlle de Scudéry to the medieval and Renaissance periods popularised by Mme de Lafayette. Historical authenticity became something of a fetish: fashionable novels styled themselves *Annales* and *Mémoires* and were accompanied by bibliographies of factual sources.[147] But history rarely furnished more than the framework of a few striking names and occurrences. It was precisely those intrigues of love and ambition that the history books were said to have passed over in silence that authoresses pretended to reveal to their readers. Frequently the intrigues concerned were based more or less loosely upon events of the day, in which case the historical trappings became at once a shield against accusations of libel and a means of stimulating the reader's curiosity.

The chief protagonists, themselves often lightly camouflaged portraits of persons known to the authoress, were drawn from the social élite and superlative in every respect. Their beauty was stunning, their sentiments extraordinary, their actions unprecedented. Who but the incomparable Mandane could have survived, honour intact, a stupendous succession of abductions;[148] and who but the inimitable Princesse de Clèves would have taken the amazing step of confessing to a husband in a million her passion for a rival masterpiece of masculinity?[149] When these paragons erred, strictly for the purpose of keeping the story moving, their lapse was generally attributable to the overwhelming force of love, and good was shown to come out of evil. The offended party would give further proofs of heroism and constancy; the offender would have an edifying fit of remorse on pain of dying a nasty death at the end. Presenting the story as an illustration of a moral truth or truths was a preoccupation that remained constant throughout changes in the form and style of the novel and shifts of emphasis in the content. Authoresses contrived to make their moral message not only implicit in the actions and situations of the characters, but also explicit by means of interruptions in the narrative or statements in prefaces, dedications and the like. Mlle de Scudéry wrote of adding to the ancient Greek romances and D'Urfé's *Astrée*, whence she freely admitted culling much of her material, 'un peu plus de morale afin de les éloigner de ces romans ennemis des bonnes mœurs, qui ne peuvent que faire perdre le temps'.[150] Later novelists, whilst portraying man and his passions in a more satirical and cynical light[151] inspired by changes in contemporary mores and by their own personal experiences, endorsed Mlle de Scudéry's view. Mme de Villedieu, whose existence testified to the deleterious effects of passion[152] that she relished describing under sensationalist titles – *Portraits des Faiblesses Humaines, Désordres de l'Amour* – reassured her readers that there was method in her licence:

> Du reste, j'ai tâché de renfermer un sens moral dans les choses qui paraissent les plus déréglées ... si je pousse la débauche de quelques femmes jusqu'à l'effronterie, c'est pour donner des couleurs plus fortes à l'impudicité. Il est quelquefois dangereux de ne faire qu'une faible ébauche du vice: telle personne se laisse emporter à la tentation, qui l'aurait, peut-être, surmontée, si elle en avait connu toutes les suites: et pour enchâsser des préceptes utiles dans les exemples que je propose, j'observe exactement la maxime de punir le vice, et de récompenser la vertu.[153]

Mindful of the low moral rating given to the genre by connoisseurs,[154] women of Mme de Villedieu's stamp repeated their didactic refrain with a view to earning an attestation of public respectability that might be extended from novel to novelist.

The crusade against humanity's baser impulses was pursued in other literary media where the aims of authoresses stood forth less ambiguously than in the romantic novel or *nouvelle*. Mmes de Sablé and de Maintenon imitated La Rochefoucauld in condensing their respective moral reflections into ever-popular maxims.[155] Mlle Durand supplied proverbs, written to be enacted as charades.[156] Verbal portraits of the *Coquette*, the *Bigote*, the *Joueuse* and others stigmatised aberrations to which La Bruyère's *Caractères* had opened the eyes of Mme de Pringy.[157] The Moral Conversations which Mlle de Scudéry lifted from her novels and elaborated for separate publication were so highly esteemed that the girls of Saint-Cyr used them as textbooks.[158] The morality expounded in these opuscules offered nothing new, but it derived a semblance of novelty from the form of the exposition. The systematic homily and the 'traité des passions' were passed over in favour of less erudite formats with attractive titles: *Avis ou Présents*,[159] *Différents Caractères des Femmes du Siècle*.[160] Sensitive to changes in literary as in other fashions, women complied with the new trend for making instructional works palatable[161] and dispensed morality in readily assimilable doses. To this end poetry, recitable and therefore easily retained, was employed alongside prose. The female literary camp could boast of no La Fontaine, but the fabulist's example was not lost on Mlle l'Héritier de Villandon, who accentuated the moral of her prose *nouvelles* by versifying it and risked the occasional apologue entirely couched in verse.[162] Mme Deshoulières rhymed platitudinous *Réflexions Diverses* in the style of Pibrac's *Quatrains*, and embroidered idyll upon idyll on the theme of man's wretchedness in comparison with the rest of nature.[163] Poetesses were not wont, however, to linger unduly over the thankless task of enlightening and correcting their neighbour. Ethics and religion most noticeably kindled poetic fervour at times when the onset of illness and old age had given the composer a salutary reminder of her mortality.[164] In days of youth and health the tone was lighter and more gallant.

Professional poetesses, those whose verses from about 1660 onwards padded the current 'Anthology of the Finest Contemporary Verse' or later swelled the columns of the *Mercure Galant*, celebrated the age-old occupations of man:

... je chante sur ma lyre
Ou le Dieu des Guerriers, ou le Dieu des Amants.[165]

They liked to clothe love in bucolic garb to render it more idyllic, and to imagine it as unhappy and unrequited to lend it greater piquancy. Now and again, to be sure, Damon or Tirsis would discard his indifference, to the accompaniment of what contemporaries, nurtured on the idea that a woman should not give utterance to her passion, must have regarded as torrid exclamations of triumph from the beneficiary:

Aujourd'hui dans tes bras j'ai demeuré pâmée,
Aujourd'hui, cher Tirsis, ton amoureuse ardeur
Triomphe impunément de toute ma pudeur,
Et je cède aux transports dont mon âme est charmée.[166]

But accents of genuine emotion were rare. Propriety forbade the experienced from making their eclogues and elegies too openly confessional, while the spinsters who contributed to the *Mercure* were honour bound at least to feign that their sentiments had never passed beyond the stage of what their *doyenne*, Mlle de Scudéry, demurely called *'Tendre-sur-Inclination'*. Fortunately that other major literary theme and pastime of the century, war, provided an extra source of inspiration that was perennially renewed by Louis XIV's victories in the field and round the conference table. Every town captured, every peace concluded, gave rise to a shoal of odes and sonnets praising the rout of Bellona by the modern Alexander.[167] The poetesses were ardent monarchists. When the king rested on his laurels they magnified his home policies,[168] worried about his health,[169] wrote prayers for his conservation[170] and composed encomiums to those princes of his blood who deputised for him at the battle front.[171] They vowed that their zeal was disinterested:

Non, depuis que des Dieux je parle le langage,
Je n'ai point (on le sait) prodigué mon encens

wrote Mme Deshoulières proudly to Mme de Maintenon.[172] But when Louis proved dilatory in granting anticipated favours, he and his controller-general of finances were harried with covert verse appeals from the chagrined muse.[173] The conquests which they extolled perhaps seemed a trifle less glorious to poetesses who found themselves the victims of economies necessary to finance them.

In view of the acclaim which greeted their elegies and idylls and the number of prizes won by their entries in poetry contests, [174] it is surprising that poetesses were not inclined to embark upon longer and more ambitious works of verse. Scarcely any woman tackled an epic. [175] Few ventured to enlarge the repertoire of dramatic poetry. Paris could supply the names of only three female dramatists, Mme de Villedieu, Mlle Bernard and Mme Deshoulières. The first two were credited with receiving substantial assistance from their writer friends D'Aubignac and Fontenelle respectively, [176] while Mme Deshoulières created less of a stir with her tragedy *Genséric* than by her alliance with the enemies of Racine's *Phèdre*. [177] To these three names the provinces added those of the Lorraine amazon Mme de Saint-Balmont, who composed a martyr tragedy in between duels; Marthe de Cosnac, a protégée of her Norman compatriot Pierre Corneille; and Françoise Pascal from Lyon, whose inspiration ran to the composition of six plays. [178] Further experiments were conceivably discouraged by the fact that women felt less free to express themselves in the dramatic medium, to which, especially in the case of tragedy, a number of stringent rules were recognised to apply, than in other much more loosely defined genres like the novel.

The inability to let fancy wander may also in part have deterred the sex from becoming involved in professional translation. A majority were automatically excluded from the field by their lack of fluency in a foreign language, and indeed in their own mother tongue. But those who possessed the necessary qualifications were partial to imitations or paraphrases [179] which allowed more latitude for the play of the imagination – and for any errors of interpretation that might be made. In these circumstances the career of Mme Dacier, who devoted a lifetime to making the ancients intelligible to her fellow countrymen, was highly unusual. [180] But then so was everything about her: her delayed, then intensive, education; her fruitful marriage to an intellectual equal; her employment as official translator of Greek and Latin classics for the obtuse Dauphin. [181] Her translations were criticised, [182] and her literary idol Homer disfigured by the irreverent Houdar de la Motte; whereupon, possessed of that battling spirit so often evidenced by seventeenth-century females, she riposted energetically: 'le moyen de voir dans un si pitoyable état ce qu'on aime, et de ne pas courir à son secours!' [183] Yet she was remembered as a modest, unassuming woman who never allowed her erudite activities to interfere with spinning and baking for her family, and who spoke in commonplaces instead of oracles.[184] In Mme Dacier the declining seventeenth century was able at last to admire its ideal of a *savante* and an authoress who redeemed the highest intellectual pursuits by the studious attention she gave to husband, to chores and to concealment of knowledge.

Such was the impact made by the diverse opuscules which flowed from the pens of prolific authoresses that the question was mooted as to whether some might not be worthy of admission into that masculine holy of holies, the academy. Men of the seventeenth century liked to take no important step without first finding a precedent which they could cite to justify their action. In this instance they did not have too far to seek. The Palace Academy of Henri III, an offshoot or continuation of the Academy of Poetry and Music founded in 1570 under Charles IX, had admitted a few select auditresses and suffered them to participate in disputations.[185] In more recent years the academy of the Ricoverati at Padua had become accustomed to granting nine 'Muses' at a time the status of associate members. Mme de Rambouillet (d. 1665) had been honoured in this way. Mlle de Scudéry, Mme Dacier and the leading women novelists and poetesses of France followed in her footsteps.[186] Not to be outdone in gallantry, French provincial academies began to unbar their doors. Mme Deshoulières was made an *associée* of the academy of Arles.[187] The Lanternistes of Toulouse violated previous custom to introduce the poetess Mlle l'Héritier de Villandon into their midst.[188] But the process was a slow and grudging one. Membership of the academies was either purely honorary, as in the case of the Ricoverati, who could be reasonably certain that women would not shuttle between France and Italy for the pleasure of attending their sessions;[189] or of an associate nature which implied a degree of inferiority and a limitation of the rights pertaining to full membership. With the exceptions of the Academies of Painting and Music,[190] the official academies in Paris, those enjoying royal patronage, refused to follow the lead given by the provinces.[191] The Académie Française showed the only type of concession that it envisaged on the occasion of the reception of Fontenelle in 1691, when an epistle of Mme Deshoulières on the subject of Louis XIV's conquests was read out to the assembly.[192]

There remained the possibility of women exercising an influence in the academies by securing the election of masculine friends and protégés as vacancies occurred. But canvassing on their part appears to have been so discreet as to be barely discernible.[193] Understandably so. For it was the protectors of the academies who effectively controlled the election of candidates[194] and in the seventeenth century these were powerful, if not forbidding, men – Richelieu, Chancellor Séguier, Colbert, Louis XIV – who brooked no outside interference with their policies. The situation was to change rapidly in the eighteenth century, when a Marquise de Lambert could boast that half of the Académie Française owed their seats to her solicitations.[195]

Social taboos and lack of education did not stop seventeenth-century Frenchwomen from taking more than just a dilettante interest in cultural affairs. They provided commissions that kept the artist or writer solvent, protection that gave him a sense of security and venues where he could meet his colleagues, exchange ideas, display his talents and win further contracts and patrons. Their efforts to reform language, their judgements and criticisms of works of art, even when misguided, as certain susceptible males protested was the case, were calculated to encourage reappraisals and revisions of the kind that maintained the high standard of artistic perfection for which the century is renowned. Not content with creating, as it were, through the intermediary of the opposite sex, they dared to create for themselves, choosing literature, into whose mysteries salon games and discussions had initiated them, as their favourite mode of expression. The volumes with which they bombarded editors and booksellers took the public by storm. Louis XIV's generation was alternately stirred by strains of sensuality and romantic melancholy, and edified by transports of moral and patriotic fervour. Tributes and honours showered down, while here and there an academy door half-opened to a happy few. Success, plus the modesty with which the chief laureates affected to conceal their literary enterprises, excused the bold gesture of exposure on the book market. Provided always that the authoress and *savante* was effaced behind the solicitous wife and mother or the gracious salon hostess, contemporaries were disposed to suspend their censure and their ridicule and to allow themselves to be pleasurably bewitched by that indefinable literary charm that woman seemed to add to all her others.

12

Women, Manners and Morals

'Les femmes sont d'une substance plus délicate que les hommes.'[1]
On the basis of what appeared to be a self-evident physiological
truth, deducible from women's muscular inferiority and their
traditionally sheltered life, the seventeenth century concluded that
the sex was endowed with a correspondingly greater delicacy of
mind and taste. Certain spectacles, actions and words unlikely to
disturb the average man would, it was imagined, give instant
offence to his companion, wounding her keen sense of fitness and
propriety. The sensitivity attributed to them resulted in the
elevation of women to the position of arbitresses of elegance. 'C'est
aux femmes à décider des modes, à juger de la langue, à discerner
le bon air et les belles manières', pronounced Malebranche; 'Elles
ont plus de science, d'habileté et de finesse que les hommes sur ces
choses. Tout ce qui dépend du goût est de leur ressort.'[2] Not
everyone shared the philosopher's persuasion that women should
be allowed to dictate in matters of fashion, still less in those of
language. But none objected to the idea of comely mentors having
a shot at polishing manners.

The frequentation of women constituted for a man a vital second
education. The first, often painfully acquired in gloomy surroundings under the surveillance of masters who did not spare the rod
and university professors who could see no further than the end of
their Aristotle, was thought proper only to turn out unsociable
dolts and pedants. To rid himself of the boorishness that made
harmonious social intercourse impossible a young man was
advised to attach himself to the circle of an accomplished woman
of the world who could train him in the social arts and graces
which lay outside the competence of the pedagogues. In her
company he would learn to abandon the trenchant remark and
gesture for a more gracious and deferential attitude. His manners
would lose their stiffness without sacrificing their politeness. His

193

conversation would end up sparkling with that quintessence of wit guaranteed to spellbind every interlocutor.[3]

The choice of possible 'finishing schools' was embarrassingly vast, but by far the largest concourse of pupils pressed round the door of ladies whose multiple gallantries designated them as excellent instructresses in the art of pleasing. Prior to lapsing into hypochondria and devoutness Mme de Sablé busied herself with transmitting the fruits of her experience to a rapt audience: 'tous les jeunes gens avaient accoutumé de [lui] rendre de grands devoirs, parce qu'après les avoir un peu façonnés, ce leur était un titre pour entrer dans le monde'.[4] It was Ninon de Lenclos, however, who succeeded in eclipsing all her rivals by her willingness to reward aptitude with supplementary lessons in lovemaking: 'Quand quelqu'un de la cour avait un fils qui n'était pas dégourdi, on l'envoyait à son école. Son éducation était si excellente, qu'on faisait bien la différence d'un jeune homme dressé des mains de [Ninon], d'avec un autre. Elle leur apprenait à faire l'amour, la délicatesse de l'expression, la manière jolie; si peu de peine qu'elle se donnât, pourvu qu'elle trouva un naturel docile, en peu de temps elle le rendait honnête homme.'[5] The terms *honnête homme* and *galant homme*, recurrently used to denote the end product of feminine tuition, underscore its limitations. Converse with women along the lines indicated produced a man who knew how to be supple, insinuating and entertaining, particularly where the opposite sex was concerned. But rarely did the polish penetrate from the exterior to the interior, from manners to morals. If his tutoress had pretensions to being virtuous her charge was liable, once her back was turned, to compensate himself liberally for any restraint exercised in her presence. If she were a wanton, moral improvement would come low down on the curriculum.

Ample testimony to the superficiality of the civilising influence which women of the seventeenth century were able to exert over their menfolk is furnished by the attitude and conduct of the latter towards the former, often disrespectful when not frankly cynical and brutal.

The female person, to begin with, was gleefully stripped and explored in all its intimate parts. The importunate neckerchief concealing snowy 'twin monticules' was cursed by poets:

> Sa gorge, où le désir s'égare,
> En deux petits monts se sépare,

L'un de l'autre assez éloignés,
Un importun voile les cache,
Qu'ils repoussent fort indignés
Et semble que cela les fâche.[6]

Dramatists went one better and had it constantly uplifted, physically as well as verbally, by stage lovers for the delectation of their audiences.[7] Posteriors and genitals, glimpsed in the course of accidents and bathes, were invariably bared a second time in the prose and verse of peeping Toms.[8] The functioning of the female anatomy, especially the digestive and reproductive systems, was a perpetual source of curiosity and speculation. When a fashionable lady took a purge some nosy parker was almost sure to broadcast the event.[9] The contents of her chamber-pot were scrutinised by gallants in search of an original theme for complimentary epistles.[10] No queen could suffer from intestinal or menstrual irregularities without the public being apprised of the disorders of the monarchy.[11] And the consummation of an aristocratic marriage might inspire anything from the earthy epithalamium –

Riez, sautez, dansez, Comtesse fortunée.
Que du ventre, d'où sort l'eau chaude que pissez,
Puisse bientôt sortir une heureuse lignée.[12]

– to the amused account of the bride's shock at losing her virginity.[13]

Far from being simply a literary phenomenon, the unceremonious treatment of women was a common feature of everyday life. Manuals of correct behaviour published during the century show how little accustomed or disposed men were to shed army-camp manners at polite social gatherings. Antoine de Courtin in his *Nouveau Traité de la Civilité* (1671) amplifies the standard admonitions against nail cleaning, nose picking, spitting, gobbling, belching and scratching in company with instructions to masculine readers to refrain from handling the persons and possessions of the women present: 'Il n'est pas d'un homme de qualité, s'il se trouve en compagnie de Dames . . . de baiser par surprise, d'ôter la coiffe, le mouchoir, quelque bracelet, de prendre quelque ruban, de s'en faire une faveur, de se l'attacher pour faire le galant, le passionné; d'emporter des lettres d'une Dame, ou de ses livres; de regarder dans ses tablettes, etc.' It is equally indecent, warns

Courtin, for a guest or host to start removing his coat, doublet and wig, adjusting his garter or changing into a dressing-gown and slippers. Never must the gentleman present himself in public, either, with clothes improperly fastened and 'quelque chose d'entr'ouvert, qui doit être clos par honnêteté'.[14] Just as the ladies' eyes were not to be shocked by the sight of any unwarranted masculine nudity, so their ears were not to be scorched by the use of any equivocal or dishonourable speech.[15] Courtin's prescription was both timely and necessary. The habit of swearing in front of women was on the increase,[16] and men who moved in the highest social circles proffered 'ordures horribles' to their interlocutresses.[17]

Love for a woman, a sentiment fondly imagined by novelists to be an indispensable spur to acquiring social refinement,[18] appears in reality to have had the opposite effect. The woman who surrendered to her lover could count on having details of her physique and performance discussed with all his other friends. If she withheld her favours she was liable to be credited with having granted them just the same, so pronounced was the masculine inclination to boast of amatory successes, real and imaginary.[19] When the lover was in good humour his sweetheart was subjected to boisterous demonstrations of affection. One of Mme de Gondran's many admirers 'crut faire une belle galanterie' by slapping her across the cheek with a piece of roast meat at dinner.[20] The Comte de Braisne expressed his passion for Mlle de Saint-Nectaire by surprising her in bed, ripping her chemise from top to bottom when she made to flee, and taking 'tout plein d'avantages sur elle'.[21] When the lover was in a bad temper the beloved suffered on her person the marks of his displeasure. Retz, who ended his days as a cardinal, seized Mme de Guémené by the throat during a quarrel over his infidelities.[22] Malherbe, beside himself with jealousy, caught hold of the Vicomtesse d'Auchy and struck her till she screamed for help.[23] After an *affaire* ended men were careful to retrieve any jewels and presents bought in the first flush of romance.[24] Those who bore a grudge took revenge by distributing their former mistress's letters in public and spreading scandalous gossip about her morals.[25]

What is striking about these indiscretions and brutalities is their prevalence amongst the upper crust of French society. In their insolence towards women aristocrats and churchmen rivalled that notoriously displayed by the lackeys whom they despised.[26] Even royalty indulged in regrettable horseplay. Louis XIV's adolescent brother had to be deterred by the threat of flogging from trying to raise the skirts of every lady-in-waiting he met and addressing them in 'termes étranges et lascifs'.[27] The monarch himself, by way of a youthful diversion, had once been observed to go round overturning from behind the armchairs in which court ladies were sitting.[28] On the strength of such incidents His Majesty's subjects could perhaps be excused for imagining that respect for women was something that went out with the likes of Galahad.

The ladies did not allow discourtesy to go unchallenged. Mme Deshoulières voiced a feeling protest in the name of her sex against the aspiration of modern lovers to omit tiresome preliminaries to a rapid sexual victory about which they could brag:

> Si des amants soumis, constants, discrets,
> Il est encore, la troupe en est petite.
> Amour d'un mois est amour décrépite.
> Amants brutaux sont les plus applaudis.
> Soupirs et pleurs feraient passer pour gruë
> Faveur est dite aussitôt qu'obtenue.
> On n'aime plus comme on aimait jadis.[29]

But the nostalgic poetess recognised, in common with other observers, that women, by their laxity, had helped to foster masculine nonchalance and impertinence.

For as long as everyone could remember Frenchwomen had enjoyed a large measure of freedom in their relations with the opposite sex. French diplomats and travellers in other European countries were always taken aback by the difficulty of access to women there in comparison to the ease with which their own female compatriots could be approached. The French ambassador Fontenay-Mareuil described the day-long imprisonment of Italian girls in their rooms, 'sans les faire pratiquer parmi le monde, comme on fait en France', and the type of purdah in which their Spanish counterparts were kept: 'On n'y visite pas les femmes aussi librement qu'on fait en France, et elles ne sortent guère que pour aller aux églises, et autres lieux de devoir.'[30] Foreign visitors to France were for their part surprised, agreeably or disagreeably, to find women who stared them boldly in the eye,[31] walked arm in arm with men along the street[32] and presented lips or cheek to complete strangers for the customary kiss of salutation.[33] At first this policy of non-restraint seemed to work well. Without by any means being uniform models of virtue and chastity, women during Louis XIII's reign and the early years of the subsequent regency at least made some effort to veil their lapses. But as time went on the ladies showed less inclination to keep themselves in check. That they had abused the freedom granted to them was an explanation that automatically occurred to uncharitable eye-witnesses like Tallemant, who wrote that France probably harboured the most scarlet women because 'presque partout ailleurs elles sont comme enfermées, et ne peuvent pas faire galanterie, puisqu'elles ne voient point d'hommes'.[34] There were those, on the other hand, who considered that women had become bolder precisely because they no longer felt as free as before to mingle with men in public. According to the memorialist La Fare, the severity towards passion and women that Louis XIV affected even with regard to, and despite, his seraglio of fertile mistresses discouraged polite social intercourse and prompted women to manifest with an unaccustomed directness natural desires which refused to be suppressed. The situation had been vastly different, La Fare alleged, during the lifetime of Anne d'Autriche, whose combination of impeccable morals and gallant manners had provided a shining example of how to maintain respect and courtesy without prudery or hypocrisy:

> Fière et polie en même temps, elle savait ce qui s'appelle tenir une cour mieux que personne du monde, et quoique vertueuse souffrait même avec plaisir cet air de galanterie qui doit y être pour la rendre agréable et y maintenir la politesse dont en ce temps-là tout le monde faisait cas, mais qui depuis est devenue inutile, et peut-être même ridicule. On peut dire que les mœurs des hommes et des femmes sont changées entièrement... par exemple, il est certain que, comme les femmes paraissaient se respecter plus qu'à présent, on les respectait aussi davantage.[35]

Whilst disagreeing over the root cause of the trouble – too much or too little freedom – contemporaries were united in their opinion that a steady decline in the standards set by women was taking place and that this decline was having repercussions on the conduct of their men. Mlle de Scudéry in the tenth volume of her weighty *Grand Cyrus* (1653) pointed out that men took the cue for their behaviour from the women with whom they associated:

'C'est aux femmes à qui il se faut prendre de la mauvaise galanterie des hommes: car si elles savaient bien se servir de tous les privilèges de leur sexe, elles leur apprendraient à être véritablement galants, et elles n'endureraient pas qu'ils perdissent jamais devant elles le respect qu'ils leur doivent.'[36] When women failed to command the necessary deference, the manners, and ultimately the morals, of both sexes were bound to suffer. The public was alerted to the gradual evolution in female behaviour by the number of scandals to which women, individually and collectively, gave rise, and by a bulk of literature denouncing them.

As if in answer to the prayers of inquisitive poets and gallants, ever preoccupied with divining the forms that lay hidden beneath whalebones and flounces, women were remarked to grow more negligent in their concern to hide their intimate charms from view. Dresses which left shoulders and much of the breast and back exposed had long ceased to be confined to prostitutes, actresses and women of loose conduct; but pious souls were horrified to see them being worn regularly for attending confession and communion and for taking the collection in church.[37] Insistence on keeping the breast covered in public led to whispers of malady and malformation which were silenced only by an unveiling ceremony.[38] While cleavages plunged, hemlines were being raised to reveal further instruments of masculine damnation. Guides to etiquette issued stern reminders that no lady worthy of the name ever uncovered an ankle in a thoroughfare. Still less did she hitch up her clothes to warm herself before the fire, another 'immodestie très grande' of which titled persons were guilty.[39]

Immodesty of dress was accompanied by greater licence of speech. Here again the phenomenon was not totally unprecedented. Women of common birth had never been at a loss for colourful expletives to bandy about in public places. But there were unmistakable signs that coarseness and indecency of language were spreading beyond the tradeswomen in the markets. Already in the early 1660s a tour of France had left the Englishman Philip Skippon with the overall impression that 'swearing and cursing, with the addition of obscene words, are customary in both sexes'.[40] Had he penetrated the corridors of Louis XIV's court Skippon might have overheard the Duchesse Mazarin boasting of her sexual equipment,[41] or the Princesse de Monaco belittling that of the king with the assertion 'que, quoique sa puissance fût grande ... son sceptre était très petit'.[42] By 1682 women had become so open in making and inviting vulgar and ambiguous remarks that even their habitual champion the *Mercure Galant* protested. Working on the familiar assumption that without women 'point d'honnêteté, de politesse, et de galanterie, qui sont les trois sources des belles et des grandes conversations', the Extraordinary issue of October concluded that a grave misuse of feminine authority had occurred: 'mais il faut avouer que les femmes ont rendu depuis quelque temps la conversation un peu trop licencieuse, et qu'elles l'ont déréglée sous prétexte d'une plus grande liberté, et d'un plus grand enjouement... Les femmes se sont accoutumées aux mots libres, et à double sens; et la licence qu'elles ont permise aux cavaliers de leur en dire, fait qu'elles ont aujourd'hui mauvaise grâce de s'en offenser.' The insertion of the statement in a periodical frequently used to publicise government policies implied official recognition of linguistic excesses and the desire to eradicate them without recourse to the almost certainly inefficacious expedient of legislation.

Shocking though they were to respectable eyes and ears, vestimentary and linguistic improprieties paled beside the depravity of which women showed themselves capable in pursuit of their pleasures. Too many were ready to adopt as their motto the 'Je n'aime pas les plaisirs innocents' that had slipped from the lips of the Duchesse de Longueville,[43] angel-faced fomenter of the Fronde. Instead of curbing this propensity to indulge in harmful pleasures the progressively staid and sombre rule of Louis XIV[44] exacerbated it. Obliged to renounce all the old thrills of cardinal-baiting and to feign conventual habits as their formerly libertine king was pressed into piety, women with time on their hands recouped themselves for their complaisance by means of diversions aimed at stimulating their blunted senses and giving them at least an illusion of the risks and exhilaration needed to brighten the intolerable drabness of existence. The fact that some diversions offered the prospect of making money as well as of experiencing strong sensations was an added incentive to banish any lingering remorse over participation.

It was precisely this promise of suspense and excitement and the mirage of quick, easy profits that lured women into gambling. In the first half of the century female gamblers were sensible enough to draw little attention to their activities. The liking of maidservants for a flutter on the *blanque*[45] and the assiduity of provincial housewives at the card tables[46] occasioned one or two sharp comments, but that was all. In the second half, by contrast, the *Joueuse* was pilloried by every other satirist and moralist who put quill to paper.[47] The reason for this unwelcome publicity was that gambling mania had gripped the female population. Ladies grew pale and haggard as they sat into the early hours of the morning wagering exorbitant amounts in a bid to scoop the jackpot that would restore them to temporary solvency and pay for further pleasures.[48] Good luck, or sleight of hand, enabled the occasional punter to live on her winnings.[49] But all that the majority had to show for their nightly vigils were losses estimated to run into as many as seven figures,[50] and the inevitable mounting debts. During a single night at the basset table in 1679 Mme de Montespan frittered away 400 000 *pistoles*. Having made good her losses by eight o'clock the next morning, she insisted on continuing until she won an additional 100 000 *pistoles* with which to settle debts to fellow players who had no other monetary resources. Thirty thousand *pistoles* still owing were extracted from Louis XIV,[51] who was summoned with monotonous regularity to salvage in this way the honour of his favourite, his bastard daughters[52] and his consort.[53] Only a favoured few, however, could rely upon their menfolk to extricate them from the appalling financial entanglements into which heedlessness, greed and desperation plunged them. The rest turned to unavowable expedients in order to obtain not so much a respite from their creditors, as the wherewithal to continue gambling.[54] They invented new ways of squeezing tax-payers in return for pensions from opulent financiers and tax-gatherers, accepted bribes to use their influence with persons in authority,[55] pawned jewels,[56] cheated,[57] prostituted themselves.[58] Husbands were in a state of cruel uncertainty as to whether to attribute to successful betting or generous lovers the sums of money which appeared in their spouses' hands.[59] Gambling wives had little time for husbands, or for children, who were either left to their own dangerous devices[60] or taken along to the card tables by their mothers[61] and exposed to the contagion of gambling fever in turn. The financial and moral detriment to households was incalculable.

In an attempt to halt the epidemic the authorities multiplied acts of legislation banning specific games along with gambling assemblies. The game of *hoca* alone was the object of six Parlement prohibitions from 1658 to 1661.[62] Also in 1661 a separate Parlement decree struck at the feminine craze for lotteries[63] by forbidding private individuals to organise them, though the decree had to be supplemented by royal and police ordinances in 1670, 1681, 1687 and 1700.[64] So-called academies of gambling, often established and run by women, were officially suppressed in 1678.[65] These measures, repeated almost annually, spoke eloquently of the government's concern to eradicate the problem, but underlined their lack of success. Ordinary citizens had little incentive to renounce inveterate habits when they witnessed their king draining the Treasury to pay the debts of his flippant females and tolerating in his entourage heavy gambling 'qui ne sentait pas la misère où la meilleure partie du royaume était réduite en ce temps-là'.[66] The characters in Dancourt's *Désolation des Joueuses* (1687), a drama inspired by a recent ban on *lansquenet*, epitomised the prevailing view when they expressed their determination in the twelfth scene to continue playing the game regardless, if need be in the attic, the cellar or any clandestine hovel. Gambling was never extirpated, merely driven underground in cases where addicts did not feel themselves powerful enough to defy the law openly.

Rather than flouting the law another class of females took advantage of its weaknesses to pursue an amusement that had potentially dire consequences for social justice and stability. These were the 'professional' *plaideuses*. Like the *joueuses*, the *plaideuses* aspired to mingle profit-making with pleasure. They were women who, having at some stage become involved in litigation, had developed a perverse taste for legal chicanery, to the point of exclaiming with Racine's Comtesse de Pimbesche: 'vivre sans plaider, est-ce contentement?'[67] Mme de Pringy, analysing their curious mentality in her *Différents Caractères des Femmes du Siècle*, concluded that they were motivated by an innate love of discord and by the satisfaction gained from a public display of their endowments. *Plaideuses* were said to savour the effect of their beauty on the vulnerable judges whom they harangued and solicited, and to relish the challenge of a battle of wits with men. Legal wrangling was also in the nature of a pleasurable emotional exercise: 'Elles nourrissent, elles réveillent, elles contentent toutes leurs passions par ce moyen.'[68] But while they were busy gratifying turbid passions *plaideuses* brought about the ruin of others. Collantine, a rapacious apparitor's daughter caricatured by Furetière, is made to boast of the ravages that she has caused throughout society by her practice of buying lawsuits from those ignorant of affairs and then tying her newly acquired opponents in such legal knots that they are forced to purchase the lucrative settlements on which she subsists: 'J'ai déjà ruiné sept gros paysans et quatre familles bourgeoises, et il y a trois gentilshommes que je tiens au cul et aux chausses. Si Dieu me fait la grâce de vivre, je les veux faire aller à l'hôpital.'[69] The devious enterprises of real-life Collantines were favoured by the extreme complexity, slowness and costliness of judicial procedure and by rivalries between the many different legal tribunals. By lodging objections against judges, impugning evidence, obtaining stays of proceedings, requesting evocations and similar tricks, litigants could prolong lawsuits indefinitely, relying upon financial exhaustion to bring opposing parties to heel. Some idea of the chaos that one resolute *plaideuse* could spread is given in a letter of 1645 addressed to Chancellor Séguier by his *intendant* in Normandy, a province reputedly skilled in pettifogging. It concerns a certain Mlle de Tourlaville of Cotentin, described as a cancer 'qui ayant consommé les chairs proches de soi se prend aux plus éloignées'. Having been arrested by order of the Customs and Excise court (Cour des Aides) for consummating the ruin of seven or eight parishes in her home area, Mlle de Tourlaville broke out of prison and appealed to another tribunal, Parlement, against her captors. When the latter denounced her crimes she changed her tactics to baffling her adversaries by embroiling the multiple lawsuits in which she was engaged:

... encore qu'au procès criminel qu'on lui fait au Parlement elle n'ait qu'une partie, elle y brouille des procès qu'elle a contre ses frères, d'autres contre des particuliers, et d'autres qu'elle suppose être parties qui ne le sont point et ainsi consomme ses parties en frais qui sont contraintes d'abandonner. Il a [sic] plus de quatre-vingts témoins d'examiner contre elle et sans faire informer avec M. le Procureur général, elle prétend évoquer et comme ses parties ne sont pas assez fortes pour supporter ces grands frais elle échappera et sera une peste qui ruinera le pays.[70]

This strongly worded report from an agent likely, if anything, to minimise the extent of the disorder in the hope of impressing superiors with his ability to cope is evidence of the authorities' awareness of, and alarmed reaction to, the depredations of the *plaideuses*. At the same time it demonstrates the ease with which, in the absence of any fundamental reform of the whole juridical system, these women could escape detection until considerable damage had been done and then evade retribution by means of the very machinery that should have brought them to justice.

The remaining indulgences – gastronomical, nicotian and sexual – which brought noteworthy opprobrium on the female sex had a predominantly sensual appeal. The appreciation of women in France for the pleasures of the table and the amount of edibles that they managed to ingest had provoked comment since the beginning of the century. The English voyager Robert Dallington informed his compatriots in *The View of France* (1604) that the diet of the French was to observe none, 'for they feed at all times, there being among them very few, which besides their ordinary of dinner and supper, do not "*goûter*", as they call it, and make collations, three or four times a day, a thing as usual with the women as men, whom you shall see in open streets before their doors, eat and drink together'.[71] At court ladies habitually consumed such quantities of victuals as to surprise even their own fellow-countrymen. A leading French magistrate, attending a royal ballet in 1667 and perceiving that the dancers did nothing but eat, was told that 'les dames de la cour ne sentaient plus que la soupe et le ragoût et avaient bu à neuf heures du matin cinq ou six sortes de vins'.[72] Both Anne d'Autriche and Marie-Thérèse were remarked for their large appetites,[73] a disposition encouraged by the food-loving Louis XIV, who never promenaded ladies in his carriage without forcing them to partake of an endless supply of refreshments.[74]

Comment turned to condemnation when women began to reject ordinary food and drink as too insipid for their taste. A fashion set in amongst those who could afford it for tickling their jaded palates with only the most pungent fare: heavily spiced meats and sausages, spirits and strong liqueurs.[75] The results of the new regimen were painfully apparent in the exhibitions of incontinence to which the public were treated. Ladies of quality presented themselves at social gatherings in a visible state of inebriation and had to be carried, comatose, from supper parties.[76] The contents of their overloaded stomachs and bowels they discharged on the spot, regardless of surroundings and persons present. The Princesse d'Harcourt was literally unapproachable because of her habit of overeating and promptly relieving herself where she stood.[77] Mmes de Saulx and de la Trimouille, constrained one day to use their box at the theatre as a lavatory, 'hygienically' threw their excreta down onto the spectators in the pit.[78] Even in her moments of greatest abandon the Duchesse de Longueville, summoned to reprimand the two offenders, had never so degraded her sex.

Bouts of gorging and carousing were interrupted to savour the properties of tobacco. The plant had first been introduced into France in the sixteenth century. Judging from the startled reaction of contemporaries[79] it was not until the 1690s, however, that a sizeable number of women took to sampling tobacco in public. Smoking remained something of a rarity. Whereas across the Channel Englishwomen were never seen to stir without their pipe,[80] Frenchwomen appear loth to have included one amongst their accessories. When the Duchesses de Bourbon and de Chartres, bastards of Louis XIV, wanted a quiet smoke they borrowed pipes belonging to their father's Swiss guardsmen.[81] Inhaling tobacco in the form of snuff was considered the more elegant mannerism, despite the halitosis and stained nostrils to which it gave rise.[82] Ladies who hesitated to carry around a pipe rushed to acquire a snuff-box. The finest specimens cost princely sums, and lengthened queues outside the pawnbroker's door.[83] In keeping with the spirit of the era painters adorned the inside of snuff-boxes with suggestive images,[84] a reminder of sexual pleasures experienced and anticipated.

Sex,[85] like every other diversion, had moved with the times. The traditional roles of the male as the hunter and the female as the prey were showing signs of being reversed. Now it was women who, existing husbands notwithstanding, started and stalked a quarry.[86] The king was clearly a prime target for feminine assiduities. 'Il n'est pas une dame de qualité dont l'ambition ne soit de devenir la maîtresse du roi', claimed the memorialist Visconti; 'Nombre de femmes, mariées ou non, m'ont déclaré que ce n'était offenser ni son mari, ni son père, ni Dieu même que d'arriver à être aimée de son prince.'[87] To achieve the distinction of fornicating with God's lieutenant on earth women strove to insinuate themselves either with the queen[88] or with some former favourite ready to turn procuress to maintain an influence that her own attractions had lost.[89] Becoming ladies-in-waiting also placed designing females in an excellent position to catch Louis XIV's roving eye. The frequency with which the conduct of the so-called ladies and maids of honour belied their majestic title was a subject of perennial amusement.[90] Louis XIV did nothing to dispel the ribald laughter by surrendering his virginity at the instance of his mother's one-eyed attendant Mme de Beauvais,[91] and by proceeding to use the entourages of the queen and princesses as a kind of private nursery of concubines.[92]

Hope of capturing the king's affections was open to any woman since he democratically slept with the very humblest, as well as the more exalted, of his subjects.[93] The majority, however, perforce lowered their sights to more readily available males. To lend lustre to their charms they might well offer to relieve a lover of all financial worries by paying his upkeep and his debts.[94] To the growing number of impecunious 'gentlemen' who could not or would not subsist by honourable means, the largesses of women represented a useful supplement to the proceeds obtained from more or less honest gambling.[95] Besotted females parted with fabulous sums in return for a few distracted caresses accorded between sessions at the gaming tables. The dissolute wife of Louis XIV's Foreign Minister, De Lionne, who lavished money on young courtiers 'comme le ferait un amant avec des maîtresses', spent a prodigious 50 000 *écus* on the Comte de Saulx alone – but then her daughter did use his services simultaneously.[96] The moment that coffers were emptied and expedients for refilling them exhausted, beaux departed in haste, leaving belles to repent at leisure.[97]

Liaisons with rakes whose noble birth, or invented titles, risked giving a specious appearance of grandeur to vice proved too tame still, too commonplace. So ladies cheated boredom by abandoning themselves to men whom social prejudices taught them to regard as outcasts and inferiors: entertainers, for example, and domestics. Actors were surrounded by females wishing to sample the titillating embraces of men grown rich through heady stage triumphs for which they braved pulpit threats of damnation.[98] Valets, whose regulation duties in the seventeenth century included assisting their mistress to dress and disrobe,[99] were good sport and had the advantage of being there to command whenever a partner in debauchery was required. The law maintained the polite fiction that menservants were responsible for any scandals that ensued by decreeing that those convicted of intercourse with their mistress should suffer the death penalty, commutable to banishment or to the galley if the woman was of age or admitted acting as temptress.[100] But the hint of danger only whetted appetites and persuaded liveried gigolos to set upon their labours of love a price that might be fixed in terms of millions[101] or of marriage.[102]

In order to pursue their amours unhindered and to preserve a hold over the unconcerned objects of their affection, women stooped to the extremes of crime and depravation – black masses, abortions, infanticides, poisonings – that rocked the Paris boat in the 1670s and 1680s. The lurid Poison Trials emphasised as never before the extent of the rot that had set into female mores from top to bottom of the social hierarchy, and the powerlessness of the authorities to halt its fatal growth. The government had unquestionably reacted with tough measures. But the severity of the torture and execution meted out to the lower-born villainesses was offset by the clemency extended to the high-born, and by the attempts of Louis XIV and his ministers to play down the gravity of the situation in the public eye. Invited to regard criminal acts and intentions as bagatelles and punishment as an unlikely possibility, women allowed the fuss to die down a little and then resumed old habits. In 1699 Louis and his government were confronted with a recrudescence of actual and attempted murders by wives of their wedded lords.[103] One Mme Tiquet, wife of a councillor in the Paris Parlement, was tortured and decapitated to encourage conservation of the threatened species, despite the facts that her assassination bid had been unsuccessful and that the intended victim had pleaded for her life. But once again cabinet calculations were upset. Mme Tiquet bore with such fortitude the multiple blows needed to sever her head that the hordes of fickle spectators at the execution changed their animosity into admiration for her courage.[104]

A would-be murderess executed in a blaze of glory is a fitting symbol of the sorry distinction in vice and crime achieved by women in the sunset years of Louis XIV's reign. Forsaking traditional roles as polishers of manners and propagators of refinement, at which they had worked with a show of enthusiasm in the preceding reign, women seemed to connive at the impudence with which their unruly menfolk were only too disposed to treat them, and to lose all self-respect. The disorders and vices into which they plunged were certainly not without precedent, either in terms of recent French history or that of the human race. But they arrested attention and provoked censure because women abandoned all concern for sacrosanct appearances, to the point of blatantly parading their turpitudes in public.

The culprits whose names were on the tip of every censor's pen belonged to the royal family and to the Parisian aristocracy. Boredom and inoccupation were the root causes of their misconduct, aggravated by the prudery which Louis XIV sought to impose upon them in expiation for his own youthful debaucheries. Dissoluteness was not, however, the prerogative of Parisian court ladies. The latter, in order to procure their pleasures and perpetrate their crimes, drew upon assistance from a veritable female underworld suddenly brought to light by the Poison Affair. The Poison Trials, and that of Mme Tiquet, also showed that the bourgeoisie, which in many respects formed the moral backbone of the nation, had become infected by loose behaviour and criminal tendencies. Bourgeois satirists, the most vigorous in denouncing female vices, abundantly confirmed the degeneration of their womenfolk. Noblewomen and *bourgeoises*, fanning out into the provinces on holiday or business, or as exiles, found the ground well prepared for the transplantation of fashionable vices from the capital. Here, where the morose eye of the king could not see and where his judicial arm operated for the most part spasmodically and inefficiently, women could indulge themselves all the more easily in that they enjoyed a greater amount of social freedom than their Parisian counterparts.[105] The acknowledged extremism of passions in the French provinces[106] and the custom of swift recourse to force to obtain satisfaction acted as further inducements to moral laxity and crime. The provinces did not witness any mass trials comparable to those of La Voisin and her clients; but individual cases involving the slaughter of children[107] and husbands,[108] witchcraft[109] and demoniacal possession[110] kept local magistrates and visiting metropolitan judges amply occupied. The convents, too, were tainted with violence and debauchery.[111]

Corruption was widespread, but not universal. Virtue had its heroines as well as vice, though their names rarely made headline news. Even those whose lives testified to the notorious 'fragility' of the female sex often mingled a strangely fervent piety with their licentiousness and redeemed their sins by charitable works and exemplary conversions. The vision of women as the spiritual leaven in society was not wholly chimerical since they could, and did, work as industriously for good as for evil.

13
Women, Religion and Charity

The special hopes which the Church pinned on feminine assistance in the furtherance of its cause and work were recalled in the seventeenth century by a multitude of references to its bestowal upon women of the engaging title of 'the devout sex'.[1] Hopes were not disappointed, though their realisation caused a certain amount of embarrassment to the establishment that cherished them. Convents bulged with new recruits, but disturbing incidents within sacred precincts gave rise to questions about the soundness of vocations. Houses of God ushered into their portals gratifying numbers of female communicants, penitents and pilgrims, but observers discerned and castigated impure motives behind the outward regularity. Charitable institutions mushroomed, but the morals of the ladies who cultivated them were sometimes such as to spell danger for the physically and spiritually destitute. The zeal with which women propagated, suffered and even died for their religion was on everyone's lips, but the religion concerned had often been pronounced heretical. The devout sex showed a touching desire to merit its accolade, only it did not always proceed along the strictly orthodox lines that pious ecclesiastics envisaged.

Opportunities were open to women to proclaim their piety in one of three ways: formally, by becoming nuns; semi-formally, by joining special kinds of sisterhoods; informally, by abstaining from veil and vows but scrupulously and actively practising the Christian faith, especially through the performance of charitable works.

Any number of reasons might determine entry into a convent. The obvious one – a genuine desire for the cenobitic life – was most in evidence while Henri IV, religious turncoat and incorrigible profligate, sat on his hard-won throne. During these years of comparative peace the movement by the Catholic body of the nation to rebuild the spiritual ruins left by over thirty years of internecine war against the Huguenots, and to rid Catholicism of abuses which had served as a pretext for the Reformation, surged victoriously forward. The repercussions of this Counter-Reformation upon conventual life were portentous. A vigorous reform of the old, existing orders was undertaken by abbesses who preached humility and mortification by their own example of drinking from skulls, licking pus from cancers and tracing crosses in the dirt with their tongue.[2] A host of new orders, many imported from Spain and Italy, were installed by dedicated laywomen of the calibre of Barbe Avrillot (Mme Acarie), who introduced the Carmelites into France (1604), and Jeanne de Chantal, co-foundress of the Visitandines (1610), both of whom enrolled amongst the members of their respective communities. Uplifted by the spectacular actions of the great saints and mystics in which their generation was prolific, girls throughout the land swarmed into the convents, choosing for preference those where regulations were most austere.[3] Wives persuaded husbands to release them from conjugal vows[4] and mothers forsook children[5] in order to be able to devote themselves wholeheartedly to God. Even during this first burst of enthusiasm, however, witnesses were struck by the number of religious professions due to motives less pure than simple devoutness, and the impression was fortified as the rush to the cloister lost its original impetuosity.

Religious vocations were often quite suddenly discovered, the result of some deep personal disillusionment or pressure from outsiders. Bereavement, particularly in straitened or humiliating circumstances, induced widows to bury their sorrow or shame in a nunnery.[6] Girls cheated of prospective husbands for whom they yearned, or threatened with those whom they execrated, committed emotional suicide as a complex gesture of despair, revenge and determination to keep faith with loved ones.[7] Mistresses who no longer captivated fickle princes recovered their dignity and self-respect through long years of seclusion and penance.[8]

'Romantic' motives, however, accounted for only a small portion of convent admissions in comparison with the efforts of designing relatives. Within aristocratic and bourgeois families, the chief suppliers of novices, it was, to quote the celebrated preacher Bourdaloue, 'une espèce de loi' for parents to decide on a religious career for a child before or soon after the actual birth.[9] Many eminent Benedictine abbesses of Henri IV's and Louis XIII's reigns had been deposited with nuns as babes in arms or infants little past the toddling stage and given the religious habit before they had any proper awareness of what was happening to them.[10] Girls of an age to exercise their reason were insinuated into convents under the pretence of receiving their education. Their impulses to taste of life outside were cleverly stifled by sermons and brief object lessons on the tribulations of worldly existence,[11] and they were left to languish behind the walls of their disguised prison until the impressiveness of the surroundings and the blandishments of the sisters had produced the desired effect.[12] Often these unfortunates were paying the price of an ugly face or a deformed body which shamed their relatives and rendered them improper to catch a husband.[13] Often, too, they were the younger members of a family, sequestered in the interests of establishing elder brothers in a career or elder sisters in an advantageous marriage.[14] Sometimes they were atoning for the sins of a parent who had conceived them out of wedlock.[15] A number had fallen foul of rapacious brothers-in-law who stuck at nothing to seize an extra dowry or legacy.[16] Small wonder that Bourdaloue could find no more appropriate metaphor to describe the disposition in which nuns were making their profession than that of the bound victim immolated on pagan altars.[17]

Before the sacrifice of unwanted daughters could be definitively consummated, certain formalities had to be satisfied. Age was of little consequence. The Ordinance of Blois (1579) officially forbade the pronouncement of vows by those under sixteen,[18] but in view of the tender years at which girls were introduced into convents training might begin early and regulations be waived accordingly. Social standing was of more importance. All the smart convents were the preserve of the aristocracy and the wealthy bourgeoisie. Persons of high birth, explained bishop Bossuet, kept up the spiritual tone of a convent by virtue of the natural elevation of their sentiments and their superior education, apart from the fact that their spiritual needs were greater than those of the common people.[19] In order not to violate too flagrantly the Christian principle of equality in the eyes of the Lord, girls of humble parentage were taken in, but on the footing of *sœurs converses*. This meant in effect that they acted as servants to the nuns proper, doing the cooking and all the menial tasks.[20] In the late sixteenth and early seventeenth centuries women of quite modest extraction had been known to instigate the foundation of religious communities.[21] The establishment of the Ursuline convent at Bordeaux was due to the initiative of a maidservant who, having solemnly vowed to educate her sex, obtained the local archbishop's permission to cloister herself and her helpers, despite criticism of her base birth and 'la familiarité que plusieurs femmes et filles d'entre le peuple avaient eu avec elle pendant sa première condition'. By 1607 the convent was the richest and most esteemed in town but, for those very reasons, proper to attract only women of higher rank than that of the foundress.[22]

The prime consideration was money. Seventeenth-century convents, with few exceptions,[23] sold dearly the privilege of becoming a bride of Christ. Applicants were required to pay a dowry, a pension for their upkeep, and all expenses incurred during the festivities and ceremonies surrounding the taking of the novice's habit and, later, that of the final vows. In addition items such as bedding and religious books might have to be supplied, a gift made to the convent church and the important office-holders of the community rendered favourably disposed towards the new recruit by means of suitable presents.[24] Tariffs varied depending on the standing of a convent, the locality and the epoch concerned. In 1646 a mayor of Bourges managed to put two of his daughters in the local nunnery of Saint Laurent at the relatively moderate cost of providing their vestments and accoutrements, a dowry of 1800 *livres* each and 100 *livres* for board. In 1658 the dowry exacted for veiling a third daughter was 2500 *livres*, plus 100 *livres* for the church.[25] Fashionable convents asked for much higher sums. Eusèbe Renaudot, *régent en médecine*, disbursed nearly 8000 *livres* in 1667–8 to assure his daughter of a place in the Benedictine abbey of Gif in the region of Paris.[26] Around the same time the convent of Saint Pierre at Lyon, which admitted only titled ladies, was demanding of prospective entrants an initial payment of 30 000 *francs*, in cash.[27] Mother superiors had no scruples about haggling over dowries down to the last *livre*,[28] nor about taking drastic action over tardiness in paying the stipulated price. The doctor of a town in the Lyonnais area relates how in 1626 his cousin was expelled after three years with the local Ursulines and sent back to her father, 'alléguant les dites religieuses ... que son père ne lui avait voulu donner les sommes d'argent qu'elles désiraient, ce qui fut trouvé fort étrange en des personnes religieuses qui ont quitté le monde'.[29] Indignation and alarm at conventual mercenariness was expressed by all articulate sections of society: by members of the clergy, appalled at the rejection of novices who lacked sufficient wealth to take a vow of poverty;[30] by the aristocracy, financially incapable of meeting the convents' demands;[31] and by the bourgeoisie, unwilling to dig ever deeper into carefully hoarded savings to buy their daughters a passport to sanctity.[32] In response to the continual outcry the Paris Parlement decreed the abolition of pensions and dowries in 1667. The ban had little effect and was lifted in 1693 to allow communities established since 1600 to accept life pensions of a maximum 500 *livres* per annum for each nun or a dowry not exceeding the value of 8000 *livres*.[33] The change in policy was attributed to the solicitations of highly placed protectresses of the convents,[34] an indication both of the tenacity with which the latter defended their pecuniary privileges and of the pressure which they could bring to bear in the world outside the cloister.

Peopled for the most part by educated women from influential backgrounds, handsomely dowered and pensioned, convents were in a strong position which was further fortified by a competent system of internal organisation. Each was a microcosm of the state, with a clearly defined hierarchy of officers catering for the needs of a community obliged by its very nature to be self-supporting to the fullest possible extent.

At the top of the hierarchy reigned the abbess, prioress or mother superior, appointed by the king or by a majority vote of the sisters. The nomination system was ripe for abuse. Mere children – nine-year-old Louise Rouxel at Almenesches and ten-year-old Angélique Arnauld at Port-Royal, both in 1602 – had thrust upon them the headship of abbeys.[35] Key posts were monopolised by aristocratic families whose daughters, attached as *coadjutrices* to related abbesses, promptly replaced the latter in the event of retirement or death.[36] Impatient of any outside intervention in their affairs, nuns manifested, with violence where legal wrangling failed, their opposition to royal nominees[37] and their preference for the relatively more democratic procedure of electing a superior[38] whose average three-year period of office could be curtailed or prolonged according to her capabilities. Mother superiors still possessed many of the extensive rights and powers granted to their medieval predecessors. At Fontevrault, a vast abbey in the diocese of Poitiers which grouped communities of both monks and nuns, and on which depended an estimated 150 outlying priories, supreme authority had been vested in an abbess ever since the time of foundation in the eleventh century.[39] Her counterpart at Montivilliers in Normandy had within her jurisdiction fifteen parishes overseen by a *grand vicaire* of her choosing through whom she controlled the local *curés* and the Capuchin monks of Harfleur.[40] The abbess of Ronceray exercised juridical rights over several localities in and near Angers of which she was *dame*, nominated candidates for 'un grand nombre de bénéfices, cures, prébendes, et chapelles', and received substantial pensions from eight of her nuns in charge of rich priories.[41] Even in large and old-established convents, however, abbesses were prevented by their sex from exercising the routine functions of a priest.[42]

The slightest move that savoured of an attempt to curb the privileges and authority of which an abbess or her equivalent considered herself to be in possession met with stout resistance. Henriette de Lorraine contested for two whole years Bossuet's right of jurisdiction over her abbey of Jouarre, bombarding the Vatican and the Paris Parlement with appeals, and compelling the bishop to resort to the minions of the law to be able to carry out his regulation visits of inspection.[43] A similar dispute over episcopal versus abbatial prerogatives at the abbey of Saint Andoche at Autun led to a literal breaking of the deadlock by soldiers called in to force the refractory abbess's barricaded doors.[44]

In between battles for supremacy with her brothers in Christ, the mother superior was summoned to attend to her chief duty of procuring the spiritual and physical welfare of the souls in her charge. To assist her in the onerous task she disposed of an *Assistante* or a *Prieure*[45] sufficiently experienced in the management of the convent to be able to take complete charge in her absence. Other senior nuns, variously known as *discrètes, conseillères* and *anciennes*, acted as a supreme council to give advice as needed. When important issues arose – projects for constructing and repairing buildings, borrowing and spending large sums, engaging in lawsuits, admitting or dismissing novices – a general assembly (*chapitre*) was called at which all professed nuns qualified to vote (*vocales*) gave their opinion in order of rank before casting their vote to reach a final decision. The *secrétaire* took the minutes of the meeting and ensured that major decisions were consigned to the annals of the convent.

Temporal affairs were the province of the *dépositaire* (or *économe*). Her job was to keep up-to-date records of the lands and properties, if any, owned by the convent, the revenues which they and other sources (such as private bequests and donations, reception fees) provided, and all expenditures made. Balancing accounts and preserving the community from the heavy debts in which many became enmeshed[46] depended upon close collaboration with nuns directed to buy provisions and victuals (*procureuses* or *dépensières*) and with those who distributed them to the sisters: the *lingère* in the vestry, the *cellerière* in the refectory.

The spiritual advancement of the community was work towards which everyone, from the abbess down to the lowliest *sœur converse*, was expected to contribute, but certain nuns were additionally responsible for seeing to the practicalities involved. The novice-mistress was the prime figure in this domain since the lessons that she could instil into raw recruits in the one to two years at her disposal gave a crucial impetus to the spiritual harmony and perfection which the ideal convent endeavoured to radiate. Her colleague the *sacristine* promoted the faith in a more tangible way by taking charge of the upkeep of the nuns' church and the arrangement of the services continually performed therein. To help ensure that religious rituals were properly observed and that the requisite standards were maintained in the chanting and recitation of the liturgy, a *maîtresse du chœur* kept a vigilant eye and ear open.

The ostensibly few recreational facilities that convents possessed each had assigned to them a special custodian. Most establishments had at least a modest collection of books for teaching and reference purposes, and consequently a *bibliothéquaire* to keep check on them. In Ursuline convents the librarian did double duty as a *zélatrice*, a charitable informer on any signs of discontent within the community. Physical relaxation was traditionally taken in the form of a stroll round the gardens, which hired labourers or pious masculine associates of the convent tended under the supervision of the *jardinière*. Her function was important because the gardens had to be not simply decorative but productive of crops for the *cuisinière* and of herbs which the *pharmacienne* dispensed for use by the *infirmière* on invalid nuns and on the sick poor who came begging for remedies. Contact with the outside world was officially assured by two or three doorkeepers (*portières*) and by an equal number of *tourières*. The latter received incoming visitors, relayed messages and purchased all necessities for the convent. Regulations emphasised that they should be of middle age and of a virtue capable of withstanding continual exposure to worldly temptations.

The diversity of the offices that made up the fabric of convent life meant that the tastes of almost any kind of entrant could be catered for. Women with a good head for organisation and business had a chance to show their mettle in one of the senior administrative or bursarial posts. The learned put their knowledge to use as secretaries, archivists and teachers. The artistic displayed their gifts in painting and embroidering for the adornment of their church and in writing for the glorification of their Saviour. The practically-minded could apply their talents in the kitchen, garden or infirmary. Those who understood the notion of helping their neighbour to extend beyond propitiatory orisons to the Divinity had a never-ending opportunity to perform the invaluable social service of delivering the needy from sickness, poverty and ignorance. Moreover nuns enjoyed a freedom to pursue unconventionally feminine occupations that was rarely granted to the woman in the street. Convents were not liberated entirely from masculine supervision, but the formal exclusion from the cloister of all men save ecclesiastical inspectors and spiritual directors limited surveillance chiefly to the religious sphere. Outside that sphere nuns indulged with impunity their inclination to become administrators, treasurers, doctors and the like. At the head of large monastic complexes they acquired an eminence and a power to direct men that made them truly queens of all they surveyed. In communities permitted to elect a mother superior every ambitious novice might hope to rise up through the ranks and obtain a lease of command easily renewable if she proved popular and capable. Should Providence not favour her climb to the heights she still possessed the theoretical right to choose, by her vote, those who would govern her and the policies they would adopt, a right for which her secular counterparts were to wait for nearly two and a half centuries.

The discovery that the convent was not devoid of ways to achieve fulfilment came as a pleasant surprise to some victims of parental coercion and transformed a life of potential misery into one of passable contentment. Girls like Mme de Montespan's sister Marie-Madeleine-Gabrielle, abbess of Fontevrault, made a virtue out of necessity and settled down to become model superiors admired for their learning and piety.[47] At the opposite extreme fretted the inevitable misfits who never succeeded in making the necessary adjustments and in resigning themselves to curbs on their freedom. In the course of his observation of the procedure of the *Grands Jours* in Auvergne, Fléchier marvelled at the succession of nuns who appealed to the tribunal for permission to shed a monastic habit unwillingly assumed. One pathetic case cited by the prelate summed up their plight, that of a novice who, when asked at the ceremony of her profession the ritual question as to what she sought from the company, demanded the keys of the convent so that she could leave.[48] Whilst obtaining release from vows pronounced under duress was feasible,[49] finding a means of subsistence afterwards was sufficiently problematical to discourage the taking of such drastic action. Parents callous enough to immure their daughter in the first place were unlikely to welcome a 'renegade' back into the bosom of the family, unless, that is, the premature death of brothers and sisters had rendered her sole heiress.[50] Prospective husbands, too, were apt to experience misgivings at the thought of taking a bride once destined for Christ. There was no place for the apostate nun in society, no honourable place at least. Faced with this harsh fact the restless concluded that their best course was to remain, sheltered and pensioned, in the cloister, while flouting more or less discreetly any vows and rules that irked.

Conventual traditions and obligations favoured the slackening of discipline. Nunneries were far from being the hermetically sealed units that their policy of female segregation suggested. Irruptions of the outside world into their precincts were frequent, causing suspensions of regulations from which mischief-minded inmates were quick to profit. In the first place convents had to receive a procession of callers who came on business or simply as tourists. The rank or reputation of the nuns meant that their visitors were often people of importance unaccustomed to travelling around without an escort of male and female retainers who had to be fed, watered, taken on tours of inspection and generally entertained in accordance with elementary laws of hospitality.[51] The performance might well have to be repeated when secular boarders were the object of visits. For convents acted, in the second place, as reception centres for laywomen of all ages who went thither to charge and recharge their spiritual batteries, or to find refuge. Young girls receiving education shared the ministrations of the nuns with older women making spiritual retreats. Periodic retirement into a cloister for meditation was common in devout circles, especially around important Church festivals. Withdrawal on the occasion of bereavement, social and political disgrace, or any difficulty at home which rendered alternative accommodation necessary was customary whatever the degree of a refugee's religious conviction. Pupils, penitents and asylum-seekers were welcome insofar as the pensions that they paid swelled revenues, but their presence could be a source of grave disorder. Gallants parted from women for whom they pined slipped into convent parlours to pursue their suit in the guise of brothers and cousins, and violated sacred enclosures to carry girls off by main force.[52] Women estranged from husbands and lovers alleviated boredom and chagrin by inculcating the fruits of their amatory experience into the naive, who 'faisaient un noviciat de coquetterie, en même temps qu'on croyait leur en faire faire un de religion'.[53] The danger of moral contamination was intensified when convents were required to supplement state prisons and workhouses as places of confinement for female lawbreakers. Mother superiors already worried over the effect upon their nuns of serving as wardresses to debauchees saw the former exposed to different spiritual hazards from contact with the religious dissidents incarcerated by order of Louis XIV. Protests to the government having achieved nothing, superiors responded by openly abetting the escape of burdensome and embarrassing charges.[54]

Secular intrusions into the cloister generated a perpetual current of unrest which completed the process of unsettling those whose vocations were forced and whose backgrounds had in no way prepared them for a life of self-restraint and self-denial. Of the monastic estate indifferent and recalcitrant nuns preserved little beyond the recital of the divine office, plus the habit, trimmed and gathered in closest possible conformity with the latest fashion.[55] Enclosure, greatly relaxed as a result of wars which forced communities to disperse in the path of predatory soldiers, was a memory that proved difficult to revive.[56] Conscientious abbesses of the early 1600s laboured in the face of bitter opposition to confine nuns accustomed to wandering down to fairs and markets to buy and sell produce like ordinary housewives, or to joining the locals for dances and entertainments in nearby villages.[57] But just as many superiors could not be bothered to enforce the regulation of strict enclosure because they were too busy absenting themselves for months at a time on the allegedly urgent business of visiting other convents of their order,[58] attending the consecration of their equals,[59] instructing lawyers in the capital[60] or curing maladies at fashionable spas.[61] Token sojourns at the base-convent were occupied by flighty superiors and their flocks in living lives of ease and self-indulgence. The fundamental obligation to subsist as a community with all property held in common was tacitly relinquished in favour of inhabiting separate apartments and owning individual possessions.[62] Equally offensive to aristocratic sensibility, the vow of poverty was dispensed with in the larger abbeys so that nuns could inherit goods on a par with secular persons.[63] Elsewhere it was honoured with most punctiliousness when national crises, or extravagance and mismanagement, plunged convents into debt. In times of prosperity nuns showed a concern for money-grubbing and a taste for luxury displeasing to those who subsidised their foibles. The channels into which flowed dowries and donations pressed from parents were all too apparent on ceremonial occasions when the convent church emerged resplendent with silken tapestries, Persian carpets, gold embroidery, silver chalices, priceless chandeliers and croziers,[64] and the community sat down alongside their guests to feast lavishly[65] from tables spread with the mother superior's collection of silver plate.[66] Appetites, of all kinds, seemed to be sharpened rather than dulled by official prohibitions. The reason for scandalous infractions of the vow of chastity, according to contemporaries, was because the walls and grilles that surrounded conventuals, the flowing robes which enveloped their person and their undertaking to remain continent were so many tantalising obstacles that begged to be surmounted.[67] It could not be denied that frisky nuns endeavoured to satisfy their needs discreetly by consorting with monks and priests.[68] Yet the occasional abbess would persist in letting the side down by giving birth in the middle of the court,[69] or swearing oaths by the fourteen bastards she had borne.[70] Reactions to moves aimed at preventing gross infringements of cloistral regulations expressed the contempt of nuns for their vow of obedience. Laurence de Budos, abbess of the Trinité at Caen, provoked a twelve-month uproar by urging her subordinates to renounce their white habit of delicate serge and their elegantly pleated surplices for something plainer.[71] Sisters of the Sainte Trinité at Poitiers broke out into nine years of open revolt when their superior Jeanne Guichard presumed to impose enclosure upon them.[72] Inmates of the abbey of Montmartre, resentful of a presence that hindered their assignations with neighbouring monks, made repeated attempts to murder their abbess Marie de Beauvilliers by poison and by the sword.[73]

Imbued from childhood with an awareness of their rank, the necessity to maintain it by outward and visible signs, and the privileges to which it entitled them, high-born nuns were markedly unwilling to abandon at the convent door their arrogance, their love of pomp and pleasure, and to acknowledge any authority other than their own caprices.

The glaring abuses of one sort and another that came to light overshadowed the successes of the movement for conventual reform and increased growing doubts about the utility of monastic life. Doubts were voiced not merely by epicureans allergic to austerities[74] and bourgeois scornful of aristocratic idlers,[75] but by the country's leaders, who had solid reasons for believing that the proliferation of religious establishments was harmful to the national interest. To the industrious Colbert nuns, like monks, were 'des gens inutiles dans ce monde',[76] an unproductive section of society who dodged work that could contribute to the public good. By committing themselves to celibacy, the minister observed, they robbed the country of children who could serve in useful capacities.[77] Furthermore in many areas religious communities commandeered the biggest share of land and revenues, to the detriment of the lay population.[78] These arguments, presented to Louis XIV in a series of memoranda during the years 1664 and 1665, appealed both to the monarch's passion for aggrandisement and to his youthful dislike of moral rigorism.[79] A campaign to slash the convents' recruitment figures was accordingly begun. In December 1666 the establishment of religious (and secular) communities without royal authorisation was banned.[80] Almost simultaneously tax exemptions were granted to those who married before they were twenty, and fathers of priests and conventuals were prevented from collecting newly instituted benefits for large families.[81] In the following year, as was seen above, the acceptance of dowries and pensions from nuns was prohibited. But the campaign was a hollow gesture. So long as a loophole remained for the creation of new communities, until financial backing was available for the proper implementation of the pension and tax relief schemes, and while dowry restrictions could be circumvented with impunity, the flood of willing and unwilling novices into the cloister was scarcely likely to dwindle to the respectable trickle that the government desired.

The great variety of religious orders and communities in seventeenth-century France allowed for those who so wished to live within a framework of devout ceremonies and practices but without committing themselves to all the regulation vows or to the obligation of enclosure. The arrangement was designed to meet the needs of women free from family responsibilities who chose, for the sake of convenience, propriety or spiritual salvation, to lead a conventual way of life, but who did not contemplate renouncing the world definitively. There were two main institutions that received these 'semi-conventuals': the Third Orders and the chapters of canonesses.

Most of the leading religious orders had their own affiliated *Tiers Ordres*, fraternities and sororities that grouped laymen and laywomen under less rigorous rules than those to which their cloistered counterparts were subjected.[82] The regulations of the *Tiers Ordre de Notre-Dame du Mont-Carmel et de Sainte Thérèse*, which will serve as an example of how the institution functioned, are prefaced by the statement that *Tiers Ordres* are established for the benefit of 'les gens du monde, afin de les rendre participants des mérites de tant de bonnes œuvres qui se font dans les religions, en portant seulement un petit habit de l'ordre, et en observant dans leurs maisons les points de la règle, qui sont compatibles avec leur état'.[83] This particular Carmelite affiliation admitted widows and spinsters of good family and independent means who would not have to miss assemblies to earn a living. Members took vows of obedience and chastity after an eleven-month novitiate and an examination of morals and dispositions.[84] They were entitled to reside at home and to dress in ordinary, sober, clothes according to their estate, though they were advised to wear underneath a wool tunic with a black belt and a scapulary and, for special ceremonies, a long white wool cloak and black veil.[85] Apart from fulfilling all the usual duties of the practising Christian, they recited the appointed conventual offices daily and observed silence at prescribed times.[86] No mother superior was elected. Instead a male 'director' selected officers to supervise the administration of the community's frequent assemblies, property, charity to the sick and poor, and the chapel.[87]

The Third Orders studied to copy closely the organisation and religious formalities of the parent orders. The chapters of canonesses diverged much more noticeably from the conventual norm. Secular canonesses, as they were named to distinguish them from 'regular' canonesses who lived in obedience to the rule of Saint Augustine,[88] flourished on the northern and eastern borders of

France and in Germany. Ultra-aristocratic in composition, their chapters were open only to women who could prove the long-standing nobility of both maternal and paternal ancestors. Entrants pronounced no vows and performed no religious duties, save that of reciting the office of the Virgin.[89] They were at liberty to withdraw and to marry whenever they wished.[90] Obliged simply to respect the statutes of the establishment into which they were taken, canonesses could give themselves up to all kinds of worldliness without compunction. At the ancient abbey of Remiremont in Lorraine, which housed the most celebrated chapter, the abbess backed her title of Princess of the Holy Empire by the possession of extensive fiefs, benefices and juridical prerogatives in the locality. Wherever she processed a major domo walked in front to bear her crozier and a lady-in-waiting followed behind to carry her train.[91] The canonesses of Mons, which fell to Louis XIV in 1691, were besieged by tourists eager to view the ermine, lace and ruffles with which their comely persons were adorned,[92] and to compliment them in amorous letters and poems that did not go unanswered.[93] When it was a question of overcoming temptation, canonesses inclined with cloistered nuns to believe that the best solution was to yield to it, and involved themselves in some distasteful scandals.[94]

'Semi-devotional' sisterhoods performed the useful function of giving shape to the lives of women who for various reasons hovered between the world and the cloister. At the same time they shared with the regular orders a distinctly aristocratic bias and an organisation designed primarily for the benefit of unattached Catholics, which meant that large numbers of the devout sex could not be accommodated within their ranks. This did not prevent well-meaning laywomen from groping for salvation in their own individual ways, sometimes applauded, often condemned, rarely deterred.

Simultaneously with their drive to purge the convents of impurities accumulated over the ages, promoters of the Counter-Reformation worked diligently to raise the level of spirituality amongst the general public. Women, with their reputed inclination towards piety and ability to influence the opposite sex, were ready targets for campaigners. It was to an imaginary 'amoureuse de

Dieu', Philothée, that François de Sales addressed his *Introduction à la Vie Dévote* (1608) in which piety was represented as a virtue that could be practised in any worldly estate, without undue hindrance to the everyday routine. A morning prayer and evening orison, a passing meditation here, a brief search of conscience there, a godly word, a charitable action, did not interfere with worldly pleasures, nor, feminine readers were delighted to learn, involve any sacrifice of the polite manners that attracted *honnêtes gens*. The old image of Christian perfection as a process of self-torture leading to melancholia and solitude was well and truly buried.[95]

Piety thus adorned made a tremendous impact on the devout sex. The *Introduction*, re-edited five times before the author's death in 1622, rapidly attained the status of a spiritual classic which, in the enlightened opinion of Mme de Maintenon, ranked with the New Testament and the *Imitation de Jésus-Christ* as an adequate guide for the whole of life.[96] More significant perhaps were the practical results which the handbook, and others like it, achieved. Budding Philothées besought the future saint for individual sets of rules for devout living and consulted him incessantly on all manner of scruples that newly troubled them: whether or not to veil daughters, embark on pilgrimages, take frequent communion, abide by specific fashions, indulge in popular amusements.[97] Consciences were reawakened to the needs of others also. Devoted women gave unstintingly of their time, energy and money to relieve physical and spiritual indigence wherever they came across it, amongst their domestics and vassals, in schools, hospitals, workhouses and prisons. The task of directing this immense fund of goodwill into fruitful channels fell to (Saint) Vincent de Paul, who emerged as the leading successor to François de Sales at the head of the female devotional movement.

Vincent de Paul's speciality was to harness the strength and powers of endurance of women owning to the same popular origins as himself, while soliciting the benevolence and co-operation of great ladies whose organisational ability and financial support were indispensable to the smooth running of his enterprises. He had begun in a small way in 1617 by setting up, first at Chatillon in Bresse,[98] then in other rural communities around the capital, associations of local women to care for the sick poor. These *Charités*, as they were called,[99] were sometimes joined to analogous confraternities of men who looked after the able-bodied poor, though women kept control of their own administration and finances to avoid disputes with their male colleagues.[100] The success of the country *Charités* attracted the attention of devout ladies in Paris, who appealed for the establishment of similar associations in their parishes. Vincent complied with their wishes, but soon discovered that the ardour of his high-born helpers cooled when they were required to serve meals, make beds, administer remedies and generally perform 'les plus basses et viles fonctions'. He overcame the difficulty by recruiting and training some of his 'bonnes filles des champs' in 1631–2 to do the dirty work repellent to their betters. In 1646 they were organised into an official *Confrérie* of Filles de la Charité separate from the higher-born Dames de Charité. They adopted a conventual mode of life without, however, taking nuns' vows or forsaking their peasant dress. The Filles were employed in almost all of the numerous charitable schemes launched by their founder. They helped to form new *Charités* in and around Paris, served impoverished patients under the supervision of Vincent's company of Dames de l'Hôtel-Dieu,[101] reared foundlings,[102] ministered to galley slaves, visited prisoners, taught poor girls and cared for the aged and insane.[103] Large-scale execution of these ambitious projects would not have been possible without the collaboration of upper-class women. Responsibility for instructing the Filles in piety and medicine before deploying them in town and countryside lay with the gaunt Louise de Marillac, widow of a secretary of Marie de Médicis, who was to Vincent de Paul what Jeanne de Chantal had been to his saintly predecessor, a spiritual protégée, a friend, a confidant, a right hand.[104] Subsidies for the different missions lightened the purses of opulent widows, amongst whom the Duchesse d'Aiguillon, Richelieu's much maligned niece, signalised her liberality.[105] With great ladies as his allies Vincent could be sure of having protectresses and liaison officers in all the right places, including the royal circle, where a *Charité* was implanted amidst great demonstrations of enthusiasm.[106] Despite an ill-disguised aversion for soiling their hands, ladies of quality performed some very real and worthwhile services for the cause.

The outbreak of civil war in 1648 caused a meteoric rise in the numbers of the sick and starving whose misery the Filles and Dames de Charité had taken it upon themselves to ease. Charitable zeal, far from being diminished by the immensity of the task in hand, was redoubled. Women of the upper bourgeoisie, less absorbed in intrigues than their aristocratic counterparts, now came to the fore[107] in organising relief for famished human beings reported by Vincent's missionary priests to have turned cannibal in their desperate search for something to eat.[108] The full extent of their beneficence, crowded into the corner of gazettes and memoirs by more exciting details of princely plots, was rarely known to the public at large. But those who profited from it did not forget. When the corpse of Marie de Lamoignon, wife of a Parlement president, was lain in the Paris church of Saint Leu Saint Gilles in 1651, ready for transportation to a conventual tomb, the poor, 'se souvenant des grandes aumônes qu'ils avaient receues de sa libéralité pendant sa vie', touchingly expressed their desire to retain their benefactress in their midst by digging a grave and burying her on the spot while the family mourners were at dinner.[109]

The passing of the Fronde appeared, on the surface, to be the signal for yet another spiritual revival on the part of women. The death of Vincent de Paul in 1660 left a void which no prelate of comparable stature filled. But before departing this life he had been able to witness with satisfaction the increase of *Charités* in the towns,[110] and the foundation by women of independent relief institutions which continued to flourish, amalgamate and branch out from Paris to the provinces or vice versa.[111] Prospects for fund-raising, one of Vincent's abiding worries, looked bright as devout princesses sold their jewels to feed the poor.[112] Displays of repugnance at close contact with human wretchedness became a thing of the past. Exalted personages like Marie-Thérèse publicly washed the feet of the poor,[113] and Mme de Maintenon suffered patiently the lice which she caught from her beggarly little catechists.[114] The willingness with which ladies breathed the infected air exhaled by the dying in the hospitals, and tarried in hovels to comfort the sick, was praised in prose and verse.[115]

From the point of view of general religious awareness all the outward signs pointed in the same edifying direction. New orders for women were still springing up,[116] albeit at a slower pace than before. Female exactitude in the observance of church rituals was to all intents and purposes as pronounced as it had ever been, indeed more so in certain quarters. Interest in doctrine, kindled by skilful controversialists who predigested arid dogmas for the benefit of the public, led animated ladies to engage in religious polemics and to champion 'new' creeds. The century even produced its crop of female martyrs, so staunch in their faith that they viewed abjuration with more horror than the stifling of their life by incarceration or the hangman's noose. But there were shadows on this rosy picture of good works and pious transports. The Catholic devotional movement in the era after the Fronde lost something of its original freshness and spontaneity. The *dévotes* upon whom public attention was focused now were not the ardent idealists who had thronged into the cloisters in François de Sales's day, nor the unsophisticated peasant maids who had trooped under the banner of Vincent de Paul. Instead they were mature and calculating women driven to piety as a means of expiating the sins of the past or concealing the failings of the present. Prominent converts were former *frondeuses* and *intriguantes* who sought in religion consolation for desertion by lovers and relatives, a distraction from inoccupation, and the chance to cut a figure once more in society. The Duchesse de Longueville transferred her twin passions for domination and for her disloyal paramour La Rochefoucauld to the directors and defenders of Port-Royal, whom she protected and guided in their polemical contact with the outside world.[117] Ensconced within the precincts of the Jansenist citadel, the 'fragile' Marquise de Sablé found not only the germ-free seclusion that she craved but fresh openings for intrigue and a consideration denied her by an intractable family.[118] Port-Royal had a special attraction for this group[119] because of a distinguished reputation that set its neophytes in a class apart and because its militant stand against enemies and detractors recalled happy days of plotting and rebellion. Ex-conspiratresses were imitated in their gestures of contrition by ambitious beauties who saw in devotion a stepping-stone to royal favour. Mme de Maintenon, whose own career yet resembled that of the persons whom she mocked,[120] informed her brother of the piety sported by wantons at court as soon as the death of Marie-Thérèse left a vacant place beside the converted Louis XIV: 'Je crois que la reine a demandé à Dieu la conversion de toute la cour: celle du roi est admirable, et les dames qui en paraissaient les plus éloignées ne partent plus des églises. Mme de Montchevreuil, Mmes de Chevreuse, et de Beauvilliers, la Princesse d'Harcourt, et, en un mot toutes nos dévotes, n'y sont pas plus souvent que Mmes de Montespan, de Thianges, la Comtesse de Grammont, la Duchesse du Lude et Mme de Soubise; les simples dimanches sont, comme autrefois, les jours de Pâques.'[121] Unfortunately for their designs Louis was alerted to the reality behind the mask when a practical joker from the royal bodyguard tricked the large congregation of ladies dutifully assembled in the chapel at Versailles into believing that the king was not coming, and then jubilantly watched all but one or two hasten away before his surprised master arrived to worship in unaccustomed isolation.[122] Worldlings whose looks had lost their power of enticement also threw in their lot with the devout. By sacrificing rouge and patches and affecting censorious manners, middle-aged coquettes hoped to retain the attention and esteem which had nurtured their vanity of old. In the event they merely succeeded in making themselves noticed by writers searching for traits with which to blacken portraits of the *fausse dévote*.[123]

Constrained by ostentatious avowals of repentance to go through the motions of piety, self-styled Magdalenes were pleased to find how easily certain ritual practices of the Catholic faith lent themselves to the pursuit of old habits. They reckoned to begin by selecting an ecclesiastic or layman other than their confessor to assume the direction of their conscience and conduct. Spiritual directors collectively had an obnoxious reputation in the seventeenth century.[124] Heated protests were formulated against their readiness to absolve sins in order to insinuate themselves with persuasible penitents, meddle in their temporal affairs, fleece them and sometimes perpetrate with them those vices which both parties were under a moral obligation to shun. But women who needed at least a spiritual substitute for the lovers they had lost,[125] or a scapegoat for any faults into which they lapsed, tranquilly persisted in consulting a director about their every move and thought.[126]

Leave to perform devotions in a public place of worship was something which few directors refused, save a minority of Jansenist rigorists who objected to communion being taken too frequently, with insufficient spiritual preparation.[127] Yet the house of God was acknowledged to be a favourite spot for Satan to lay his snares. Worldly women clad in daringly low-cut dresses[128] would sweep into church, after the service had begun for maximum effect, and while sinking in a graceful froth of lace upon their *carreau*[129] would rapidly survey the assembled congregation to see where their pulchritude had made the greatest impression. Loud chatter and horseplay with acquaintances, a dispute with neighbours or officiants forgetful of ceremonial dues,[130] would serve to fix an interested male's attentions and eye-play from behind a prayer-book to reassure him that they were not disdained. A promenade up the aisle to take the collection or retrieve a straying lap-dog, a whispered exchange, and a satisfied worshipper would resume her place with a beatific smile mistakenly attributed to a sudden pious inspiration.[131]

Facilities not only for assignations but also for surreptitious holidays with lovers were involuntarily provided by the Church. When a restive wife wanted an honourable pretext to keep company with her paramour for a week or so away from home she would announce the desire to go on a pilgrimage. Journeys to holy cities abroad had to be made subject to conditions laid down by the government in an effort to stop the exodus of Protestant fugitives. An ordinance of 1665, reiterated in progressively stronger terms in 1671 and 1686, decreed that all pilgrims intending to travel outside the realm must obtain certificates from local civil and religious authorities.[132] But ordinances did not apply to France itself, which offered a wide choice of sacred places[133] where hastily invented vows could be fulfilled and cures sought for feigned maladies. Credulous husbands, tied to their work yet fearful of the dangers on the roads, made no difficulty over allowing their spouse to travel with a joyous band of neighbours and escorts, to which the favourite of the moment unobtrusively attached himself.[134]

Tepid converts and impenitent hypocrites who used religion as a cover for worldly failures and gallant diversions were an unsightly excrescence which the body of the Church had nevertheless borne for centuries without visible hindrance to its development. Their outward zeal, when all was said and done, edified the naive and provoked raillery rather than reprehension from more perspicacious onlookers. In the general view the women really responsible for sapping the vitality of the Church were, paradoxically, those of sincerer convictions who believed that they were working for the clarification and purification of the faith.

Catholic Frenchwomen were reared on the idea that the mysteries of religion were beyond their comprehension and that it was sufficient to subscribe to them without examining the evidence for belief. Directors and confessors scrupled to place the Bible even in the hands of nuns,[135] preferring that their charges should absorb the principles of Christianity at second hand through spiritual guides composed by saints, mystics and churchmen. Laywomen who had grown to maturity in Louis XIII's reign gloried in their unquestioning acceptance of orthodox dogma, emphasising that theological matters were not a fitting subject for discussion by the members of their sex.[136] There was an element of reaction in this obscurantist attitude, reaction against those who were forgetting the modest ignorance imposed by their femaleness and embroiling themselves in the thorniest religious controversies.

The case most often quoted was that of the Jansenist sympathisers. Jansenism exercised a powerful fascination over women. The focal point of the movement consisted of two Cistercian nunneries, Port-Royal des Champs near Paris and its offshoot in the heart of the capital. Both housed dedicated followers of the Dutch bishop Jansen's extremist Augustinian doctrines, posthumously published in 1640, and diffused and defended in France by the fertile Arnauld family and its associates, whose daughters were the life and soul of the convents in question. Despite repeated condemnation of their tenets by popes, hostile bishops and the Jesuits – perhaps in part because of it – the Port-Royalists won a not inconsiderable following amongst the female laity too. Their terrorist images of fallen humanity's wretchedness in the sight of an awesome, hidden God made their brand of religion the last word in breath-taking drama, and the sustained asceticism of their conduct revived obscure yearnings for a purity and virtue long abandoned. On a more mundane level the presence in the Jansenist camp of the Duchesse de Longueville, a princess of the blood royal, and that of other titled ladies gave it the appearance of a select club, membership of which distinguished the fashionable penitent from the flock. Always eager to increase the number of their protectors and adherents, the controversialists of Port-Royal made a point of airing doctrinal quarrels with their foes in public by means of witty opuscules, elegantly phrased and attractively printed and bound, that passed from hand to hand in the salons and infiltrated the humblest strata of society. Soon there was no more popular topic of conversation in female circles than grace and predestination or the discomfiture of the Jesuits. It mattered little that doctrines were imperfectly grasped. To be able to cite a passage of Saint Augustine or the name of a Jesuit casuist was sufficient testimony to a flattering acquaintance with a sect which quickly became renowned for its intellectual, as well as moral, superiority.[137]

Certain vital protectresses, however, resisted Port-Royal's manifold seductions. Anne d'Autriche, who was opposed to all religious innovations generally, had been fortified in her aversion for Jansenism during her regency by the Marquise de Senecé, her *dame d'honneur*, and Mme de Hautefort, her *dame d'atours*.[138] Mme de Maintenon, guided by directors hostile to Jansenism, showed persistent animosity towards members of the sect.[139] The influence of these two women completed the alienation of Louis XIV from a party which harboured refugees of *frondeur* persuasion and exemplified the moral rectitude of which 'Le Roi Très-Chrétien' had set such a poor example. The slightest connection with Jansenism came to be punished with unambiguous marks of royal disfavour. A spiritual retreat to Port-Royal des Champs where she had been educated cost the Comtesse de Gramont a suspension of the highly valued privilege of relaxing with the monarch in the pavilions of Marly.[140] Loss of the post of *dame d'honneur* to one of Louis's bastards and of access to the queen's carriage warned the Marquise de Vibraye that her Jansenist sympathies had not gone unnoticed.[141] Exile in Normandy put a stop to the process of Jansenist indoctrination which Mme de Mondonville, supervisor of the Filles de l'Enfance de Jésus for the education of girls at Toulouse, was accused of carrying out in her community.[142] But it was the nuns of Port-Royal who bore the brunt of the king's displeasure. In 1661 a long campaign of intermittent persecution was begun during which they were deprived step by step of their boarders, novices and spiritual directors, dispersed to other convents, forbidden the sacraments, and subjected to interrogations and menaces designed to harass them into signing without reservations a Formulary condemning the teachings of Jansen. The majority refused or retracted until persuaded, in 1669, by their hitherto intransigent directors of the necessity to buy with their signatures a precarious Paix de l'Eglise, which ended abruptly on the death of their protectress Mme de Longueville ten years later. The ultimate outcome of events was typical of the strong-arm tactics which Louis XIV employed to crush opposition from religious dissidents. In 1709 the by now ageing remnants of the band of indocile nuns, who had been rounded up at Port-Royal des Champs to keep them separate from the more tractable sisters left at Port-Royal de Paris, were evicted by a police squad. Their convent and church were demolished and, as a supreme gesture of contempt, their graveyard was allowed to be desecrated.[143]

Towards the end of the century Jansenism was rivalled in its capacity to inflame and incense by another unorthodox spiritual movement in which women were prominently involved: Quietism. The essence of Quietism, which preached total abandonment to the will of God and indifference to conventional aids to salvation like prayers and acts of penitence and charity, was defined by the seventeenth-century Spanish theologian Miguel de Molinos. But the propagation of Molinosist ideas in France was due to one extraordinary woman, Jeanne-Marie Bouvier de la Motte, better known as Mme Guyon. Liberated in 1676 by the death of her Parlement councillor husband, this pock-marked widow set out from her native Montargis with her spiritual director (some said her lover), the Barnabite father La Combe, to shed upon the public the torrents of mystic inspiration later to be poured into her manuals of Quietism. After a number of years' highly successful proselytising in Gex, Piedmont and Grenoble Mme Guyon, whose doctrines had disturbed Church leaders encountered on her travels, was cornered in Paris and imprisoned by *lettre de cachet* in a Visitandine convent in 1688. At this stage her reputation was sufficiently sound and widely established for Mme de Maintenon to intervene to procure her release and for an illustrious charity worker, Mme de Miramion, to offer her shelter. With the backing of Fénelon, spiritual director of Mme de Maintenon, and the help of Mme de la Maisonfort, a relative and one of the teaching nuns at Saint-Cyr, Mme Guyon proceeded to consolidate the esteem of her protectress and to broaden her sphere of influence. Colbert's daughters, the Duchesses de Beauvillier, de Chevreuse and de Mortemart, intimate friends of Mme de Maintenon, and the Duchesse de Charost, Fouquet's daughter, fell under her spell. Fénelon, charmed by the quietist vision of the creature's childlike dependence upon its Creator, showered her with assurances of his docility to her instructions. The nuns of Saint-Cyr began to succumb to her persuasive tongue. Eventually Mme de Maintenon's eyes were opened to the spiritual disquiet and laxity that her protégée's ideas were causing at Saint-Cyr. To justify herself Mme Guyon offered in 1694 to submit her writings to a panel of ecclesiastical judges led by Bossuet, who, in consideration of her expressed willingness to subscribe to the condemnation of any errors detected, issued a certificate of her fitness to take the sacraments. The respite was only temporary. Ecclesiastical censure of certain of Mme Guyon's mystical treatises was followed, in December 1695, by her incarceration at Vincennes. In June 1698 she exchanged that prison for the Bastille, where she spent almost five years before being relegated to Blois. Mme de la Maisonfort and other tainted nuns were expelled from Saint-Cyr. Fénelon, who lacked Mme de Maintenon's ability to repudiate spiritual allies grown too compromising for comfort, paid for his loyalty with disgrace and disguised exile. As in the Jansenist affair Louis XIV showed that he considered no punishment too severe to silence heretics and deter their disciples.[144]

By dealing harshly, and at times brutally, with religious dissenters the king succeeded in making martyrs of them, stiffening the resolution of their followers and publicising the very doctrines that he sought to suppress. Nowhere was this more strikingly illustrated than in the example of the Huguenot minority.

Women were the pillars of Protestant resistance in seventeenth-century France. The persecution to which their sect had been subjected at intervals ever since its birth in the previous century had bred in them a toughness and a resilience that impressed co-religionists and Catholic opponents alike. In the early years of Louis XIII's reign, when animosity persistently smouldered and flared up between the two religious camps, Protestant women had steeled themselves to run a gauntlet of abuse and mud-slinging as they made their way to worship in their temples.[145] At times of armed insurrection the aristocrats in their midst had animated opposition to royalist forces and set an example of courage and endurance to the besieged, whose privations they loyally shared.[146] Women of the people had meanwhile stood repeatedly at the side of their men in the breaches of battered strongholds, repulsing Catholic assailants with stones and swords, and cheerfully accepting the loss of limbs and lives for their cause.[147]

The tolerant peace treaty of Alais in 1629 gave Protestant amazons a breathing-space that lasted until Louis XIV, his hands freed by the defeat of the *frondeurs* and his conscience pricked by Catholic zealots, renewed the hue and cry against the '*Prétendus Réformés*'. The edicts which rained down upon the Protestants with mounting frequency and severity during the monarch's personal reign affected not only freedom of worship but all kinds of individual liberties by which women set great store. Richelieu and Louis XIII had contented themselves with breaking the political and military power of the Huguenots. Louis XIV, fired by the triple desire to make an impression on the pope, outshine the Emperor's anti-Turkish crusade and atone sensationally for the double adultery with la Montespan, determined to extirpate the religion from the very hearts and minds of his subjects. He accordingly struck with particular violence at the family unit, a literal as well as

metaphorical breeding-ground of 'heresy'. Mixed marriages between members of the two rival faiths were banned in 1680.[148]
Marriages performed by Protestant pastors, the only ministers that
devout Huguenot fiancés could contemplate choosing to unite
them, became illegal when the Revocation outlawed the pastors in
1685.[149] The loophole of marriages abroad was closed.[150] To
safeguard babies against infection from heresy Protestant midwives were prevented from exercising their profession and Catholic midwives authorised to baptise the infants of Protestant
mothers.[151] Children could be declared converted and transferred
to the care of orthodox relatives at an age which was progressively
lowered to five years in January 1686.[152] Parents who refused to
abjure lost the right to disinherit unconverted children or to
oppose their marriage by withholding consent.[153] Protestant
schools, gradually limited in preceding years to specified areas and
to the teaching of the three Rs only, were abolished in 1685,[154] and
parents fined if they neglected to send their offspring to be
brainwashed in Catholic schools. Wives and widows who refused
to follow their husband's example of abjuration were deprived of
the right to dispose of their property and to profit from any kind
of *gains nuptiaux*, the latter being handed over to their Catholic
offspring or, if the marriage was childless, to the nearby
hôpitaux.[155] With an attention to details that was typical of the man,
Louis even decreed that Huguenot households should employ
only Catholic domestics.[156] Families not already thrown into a
confusion propitious to recantation were tempted by the insidious
system of rewards (pensions, tax relief, cession of confiscated
property and so on) offered to converts, or intimidated by the
covert form of terrorism which consisted in billeting dragoons on
Protestant homes and allowing them to make life quietly insufferable for the occupants.

It took a sturdy faith and a stout heart to withstand the combined
onslaught of cajoleries and brutalities. Predictably there were
defections from the party. Upper-class ladies disguised their
capitulation by means of strategic spiritual retreats[157] and the
organisation of private religious conferences between Catholic and
Protestant ministers from which they emerged 'enlightened'.[158]
Plebeian women saved face amidst the mass conversions of
townships and provinces that resulted from the missionary zeal of
the dragoons.[159] But an elated Catholic government and clergy

soon realised that they had little cause for self-congratulation. Wherever the freshly converted could find a pretext to gather together – a charitable enterprise, a visit to a friend, a duty call on a Protestant ambassador from abroad – they turned the assembly into an impromptu prayer meeting.[160] They politely ignored instructions to send their children to Catholic schools, or else re-indoctrinated them with Protestantism out of school hours.[161] On their deathbed they often publicly regretted their conversion and refused Catholic priests and rites, a crime punished by dragging the corpse round the streets on a hurdle before tossing it into an unconsecrated grave.[162]

There remained a hard core of Protestant women, of both distinguished and undistinguished lineage, for whom abjuration, even with the lips alone, was anathema. Intransigents with the means and opportunity went into exile abroad, travelling clandestinely along the escape routes which members of their sex were helping to organise[163] when their standing with the king did not permit them to take the broad highway.[164] Irreconcilables left behind suffered the grief and humiliation of seeing children shut up in convents and workhouses,[165] husbands bribed into submission[166] and the intimacy of conjugal life violated.[167] The most stubborn were interned, shaven-headed, in forbidding fortresses and conversion-convents and there abandoned to a living death.[168] Torture and execution overtook feminine prayer-leaders caught arranging secret assemblies[169] whither co-religionists stole away to chant their beloved psalms[170] and listen to young peasant 'prophetesses' foretelling amidst trances and convulsions the triumph of the steadfast over their enemies.[171] But the prospect of martyrdom for their faith seemed to invigorate and inspire these diehards, and to rekindle all their old battling instincts. When the guerrilla war of the Camisards, the last significant Protestant insurrection under the *Ancien Régime*, broke out amongst the Cévenols of Languedoc in 1702, women of the party soon showed that they had lost nothing of their great-grandmothers' expertise at routing royal troops with stones and sabres.[172]

The religious controversies which women, albeit well-intentioned, helped to fuel, and which Louis XIV prolonged and aggravated by spectacular acts of intolerance, had repercussions on the Christian faith which both sides imagined themselves to be championing. The persecution of the Huguenots not only multiplied the number of perjurers and estranged hesitators who might have been won by gentler methods of persuasion, but it made Catholics uneasy about their religion. In June 1700 the central government received from one of its agents in Rouen a significant communication relating the scandal occasioned by the flight of a local Protestant lawyer after his wife had been threatened with internment: 'Le remède à tant de maux, c'est laisser les religionnaires en repos, et un seul ne sortira [du royaume]', the agent wrote with unexpected bluntness; 'mais que l'on prenne leurs enfants avec force, comme l'on fait, et enfermer les pères et maltraiter les mères, comme l'on fait d'une dame ... que l'on dit être la plus vertueuse femme de France, cause bien du murmure parmi les catholiques et les fait douter de la religion: ce qui cause un grand scandale parmi nous. L'on m'a assuré qu'il y a une paroisse ici où plusieurs personnes n'ont pas voulu communier à Pâques.'[173] Professing a religion which employed physical violence against the defenceless and the virtuous evidently troubled consciences, all the more so when the victims were former co-religionists.

Another source of disquiet was the uncertainty in which adherents of the warring Christian sects were being kept. Arguments over the doctrinal solidity of various shades of Christianity dragged on interminably, leaving the faithful unsure as to what to believe and whether an episcopal or papal pronouncement might not render them heretics overnight. 'Epaississez-moi un peu la religion, qui s'évapore toute à force d'être subtilisée', cried Mme de Sévigné, exasperated by all the theological bickering.[174] Mme Guyon, anxious that her disciples should not have to live in an intolerable spiritual vacuum, pressed Bossuet to hasten his judgement of her teachings.[175] The situation was indeed grave. In a letter addressed to the Comtesse de Maure during the early stages of the Jansenist controversy Mme de Choisy, wife of Gaston d'Orléans's chancellor, had questioned the right of the party's champion, Antoine Arnauld, to meddle with religious reform and plunge minds into a disarray proper to 'faire des libertins ou des impies'. 'J'en parle comme savante', she continued, 'voyant combien les courtisans et les mondains sont détraqués depuis ces propositions de la grâce, disant à tous moments: Hé! qu'importe-t-il comme l'on fait, puisque si nous avons la grâce, nous serons sauvés, et si nous ne l'avons pas, nous serons perdus. Et puis ils concluent par dire: Tout cela sont fariboles.'[176] Minds in a state of suspension were open to doubt, and from doubt to incredulity the transition was disturbingly easy.[177]

According to Pierre Bayle, whose works became the breviary of anti-Christian thinkers in the eighteenth century, women were too preoccupied with futilities and too poorly equipped mentally to proceed as far as rejecting religion altogether.[178] The sex had nevertheless been associated throughout the century with groups of *'esprits forts'* and *'libertins'*, as contemporaries called freethinkers. An anonymous brochure of 1622, *Le Génie des Malfortunés*, deplored the admission of 'plusieurs dames et damoiselles' into a confraternity of shameless court voluptuaries whose prime rule was to be 'peu ou point religieux'.[179] The presence of females in the same or a related band of nonconformist courtiers affecting, with a 'grimace impie et ridicule', to 'ne suivre jamais la créance commune', was subsequently denounced in Jean Claveret's comedy of manners *L'Esprit Fort*, written *circa* 1630.[180] The interlude of the Fronde, when respect for all forms of established authority deteriorated, encouraged certain women to indulge in acts of irreverence only slightly less colourful than those committed by their menfolk.[181] The Comtesse d'Olonne caused an outcry by appearing at a court masquerade with her friends attired in the robes of a Capuchin monk.[182] Ninon de Lenclos was reporting for having, in the course of a Lenten orgy, thrown a meat-bone out of her window onto a passing priest.[183] In the company of the Prince of Condé the Princesse Palatine experimented with burning a sacred relic.[184] The pall of devoutness which gradually descended upon the court after the death of Marie-Thérèse sent repressed noblewomen scurrying for a breath of emancipation to fringe societies of unorthodox aristocrats and writers, the most notorious of which was presided over by the two crapulous Vendôme brothers at the Temple[185] and frequented, in between exiles, by their aunt the Duchesse de Bouillon.[186] As the century, and then the reign of Louis XIV, expired, well-born authoresses became bolder in communicating to the public the results of their contact with anti-Catholic mentors, in satirical poems, novels and letters.[187]

A few melodramatic gestures of derision did not, however, signify a general lapse into unbelief. Women of the people are rarely on record as committing acts of sacrilege[188] and their faith, judging from eye-witness accounts of its manifestations,[189] seems to have remained firm and wholesome, if crude and uninformed due to lack of education and of preachers conversant with regional dialects.[190] During that same Fronde which provoked exhibitions of aristocratic aggressiveness towards religion, women of the bourgeoisie were busy giving magnificent proofs of Christianity in action. Whilst some pens traced impious formulas, others combated godlessness.[191] Demonstrations, not so much of atheism as of anti-Catholicism and anti-clericalism, were almost always confined to three groups: noblewomen, courtesans and (former) Protestants. The last category had obvious reasons for feeling animosity towards Catholicism. The second, *libertines* in both senses of the word, had been coached by sceptical lovers.[192] For the first group, often similarly indoctrinated, mockery of commonly held beliefs was a facile means of creating a stir and of underlining superiority over the mob which carried little risk of retribution by burning at the stake on earth or in hell fire after death. The Almighty, as the Maréchale de la Meilleraye confidently averred, thought twice about damning any aristocrat.[193] Few persisted in their antagonism to the bitter end. When old age and decrepitude put a stop to debaucheries they remembered the God whom they had forsaken, attended to making their peace with Him, and died the most edifying deaths.

Religion was a phenomenon which affected the life of every seventeenth-century Frenchwoman. Her involvement in its mysteries was officially sealed at baptism and confirmed by participation in each of the sacraments that marked the salient events of the Christian[194] life. But a more active commitment was constantly and flatteringly invited from her. Ecclesiastics appealed to her reputed devoutness to help bring about mass spiritual regeneration. Priests solicited her charity for the infirm in body, mind or morals. Theologians wrote and disputed at her behest and with her tastes in mind. In an age when feelings, particularly on the emotive subject of religion, were easily aroused, the female response was predictably impassioned. Cloisters were crowded, invalids and outcasts succoured, spiritual directors cosseted and doctrines defended to the death. Of course there were numerous upsurges of the old Eve. Discontented nuns turned convents into hotbeds of intrigue and immorality. Pretty pharisees let their masks of devoutness slip too often for the public's liking. *Libertines* scandalised by their impudent sallies against Catholic bastions. But even the most obdurate sinners had a habit of wandering ultimately back to the spiritual fold, there to surround themselves with the ritual paraphernalia that had throughout the ages softened the blow of extinction.

14

Death

The omnipresence and inescapability of death was a reality vividly imprinted upon the seventeenth-century Frenchwoman's mind. Preachers brutally emphasised that her pampered flesh would one day rot and serve as worm-fodder.[1] Moralists urged her to prepare early for the last journey if she wished to lessen anxiety over departure and the risk of travelling to the wrong destination. Moribund parents had enacted before her eyes the sombre drama of which she herself was condemned one day to be the central figure, and infant offspring succumbing to disease and doctors reminded her that the final bow might well be taken prematurely. Criminals swinging from the gibbet along the highways; beggars withering in the gutters; dignitaries stonily recumbent on their tombs in churches; skeletons dancing and skulls grimacing in paintings, engravings and sculptures[2] – wherever she looked, gruesome images of humanity's ultimate fate seemed to stare her in the face.

She had a natural curiosity about death. The circumstances in which relatives, friends and celebrities had passed away were meticulously detailed in letters and memoirs. The ranks of contemporaries were watched for ominous signs of thinning with an uneasiness ill concealed by the nervous jest. 'Hélas! il n'y avait plus qu'elle entre la mort et moi', quipped octogenarian Mme Cornuel on learning that nonagenarian Mme de Villesavin had given up the ghost.[3] Opportunities for witnessing the death-throes of strangers were seized with alacrity. During a visit to the Val-de-Grâce convent in 1647 Anne d'Autriche watched intently the changing of dressings on a nun dying of breast cancer, the malady which was to end the queen's own life nearly twenty years later.[4] Her subjects flocked at regular intervals to the foot of the scaffold, drawn thither by a taste for the macabre or simply for a free show. Observation posts along the route to, and within, the public square where executions normally took place were booked in advance so that the countenance of the condemned could be studied at ease. Windows permitting a view of the parting between

Mme Tiquet's head and her body were hired for up to seven and eight *pistoles*, 'et elles étaient remplies de personnes de la cour et de la robe, jusque-là qu'on y voyait plusieurs hommes et femmes qui avaient été longtemps en commerce de société avec la dame'.[5] Vociferous female onlookers did not scruple to increase a wrongdoer's misery with their jeers and insults.[6] But if the accused showed resolution or the executioner discharged his functions clumsily, they were just as likely to be moved to sudden pity and to join in efforts to frustrate the law of its prey.[7]

Gazing upon the last agonies of indifferent parties and contemplating personal extinction were, however, two entirely different matters. It took an unusual fortitude, or insensitivity, to envisage loss of life without some quiver of fear. The idea of ceasing to exist was awful enough, but particularly repugnant to the fair sex was the thought of the physical and mental deterioration which in the ordinary course of events must precede the end. The flesh recoiled at the prospect of pains and infirmities, while the inevitability of faded beauty and dulled faculties revolted pride and vanity. 'Ah! ma bonne, que la lie de l'esprit et du corps sont humiliants à soutenir', lamented Mme de Sévigné to her daughter, 'et qu'à souhaiter il serait bien plus agréable de laisser de nous une mémoire digne d'être conservée, que de la gâter et la défigurer par toutes les misères que la vieillesse et les infirmités nous apportent!'[8] Better, she proposed, to submit to euthanasia at the hands of one's offspring than suffer such indignities. Less dramatically, the declining Mme de Maintenon requested her assistants at Saint-Cyr to warn her whenever they noticed her head beginning to shake or her speech becoming incoherent, in order to avoid mortifying comparisons being made between her age and her mental alertness.[9]

To help fight off dread and anguish women were almost unanimous in turning at some stage to the Christian religion,[10] which opened up pleasant vistas of definitive release from earthly tribulations and resurrection to eternal bliss, and comfortingly represented the process of dying as being in the natural and divinely established order of things. 'Un retour à la volonté de Dieu, et à cette loi universelle où nous sommes condamnés', Mme de Sévigné acknowledged, 'remet la raison à sa place, et fait prendre patience.'[11] Christian ministers and moralists applauded reflections along these lines, but urged that they should commence at an early age and be pursued thereafter without interruption.[12]

The slightest meditation on the actions that composed the daily
round – eating and wearing the remains of dead beasts, sinking
into unconsciousness during sleep, begetting heirs to take over
property – warned the attentive Christian that life was nothing but
a continual death.[13] Yet with typical human heedlessness the
worldlings of the seventeenth century tended to act as if they were
immortal and to think seriously about meeting their Maker only
when plagued by aches and wrinkles.

Je ne t'ai jamais bien connu,

the ageing Mme Deshoulières admitted in an appeal to God for
relief from suffering;

Hé, quel cœur sait le prix de ces douceurs charmantes
Que tu fais ici-bas goûter à tes Amantes,
S'il ne s'est avec toi souvent entretenu!
T'aimer semble un parti triste et bizarre à prendre,
Tant qu'à quelques plaisirs on peut encor prétendre.
On croit ne te devoir que la fin de ses jours,
Encore est-ce à regret qu'en ces instants funestes
     On te donne les affreux restes
D'une vie employée à t'offenser toujours.[14]

Previous neglect of, or indifference towards, God was not, however, a reason to despair, as some of the poetess's fellow-sinners
could have told her. Mme de la Sablière, crossed in love, gnawed
by cancer, haunted by the remembrance of a past 'qui a été long
dans un oubli et un abandon de Notre-Seigneur ... qui est
inconcevable', penned from her retreat at the Incurables' hospital a
moving testimony to the mysterious workings of the Divinity in
her tormented mind and body: 'au milieu de ce que tout le monde
jugerait un enfer ... je me trouve avec Dieu et dans un calme qui
surpasse tout entendement et toute expression'.[15] Mme de
Lafayette, herself wasted by years of painful maladies, felt something of it too, that peace which passes all understanding, as she
neared the end of her search for the God whose existence she had
doubted: 'Je me soumets sans peine à la volonté de Dieu – c'est le
tout-puissant et de tous côtés il faut enfin venir à lui.'[16] The Good
Shepherd manifestly honoured his obligation to take special care of
the stray sheep.

Spiritual preparation for death by means of the relevant contemplations and submission to the will of God was necessarily accompanied by a certain amount of material preparation. In the drafting of a testament the two considerations overlapped, since the testatrix was encouraged not only to content her descendants and dependents on earth but to boost her chances of salvation by posthumous donations to the poor and to charitable and religious institutions. Duties in the former respect were not always fulfilled with the exactitude desirable in persons about to render an account of their actions before the supreme tribunal. Great ladies were notorious for bequeathing to their relatives almost as many debts as solid effects,[17] and for making no provision whatsoever for the reward and upkeep of domestics.[18] In the matter of pious legacies the response was usually generous in proportion to available funds. Ladies who had placed their wealth at the disposal of charity workers in life found it natural to take steps to ensure the survival after their death of enterprises which they had helped to promote. The Duchesse de Montpensier, reputedly the wealthiest Frenchwoman of her day, donated in her will a phenomenal 57 000 *livres* to hospitals and religious communities which she had established and protected on her domains in Normandy.[19] Mme de Miramion, whose pecuniary resources were not quite equal to her bountiful impulses, expressly relied upon her daughter's financial assistance to help pay some of the 20 000 *livres* which she wanted distributed amongst all the major Parisian relief organisations with which she had been associated.[20] Those in whom charity had been one of the less outstanding virtues were persuaded by the imminence of the final reckoning to make tardy restitution for gains ill-gotten. Mme de Bresets, widow of a councillor in the Bordeaux Parlement, was successfully exhorted on her death-bed to leave for the construction of a poor-house 60 000 *écus* out of a fortune of 120 000 *écus* amassed through usury.[21] An ultimate gesture of philanthropy might also veil a licentious past and put a woman who had loved too much in a stronger position from which to implore divine forgiveness. Ninon de Lenclos eased her overburdened conscience by willing a token 200 *francs* to the poor.[22] Madeleine Béjart, the actress whose red hair had inflamed others besides Molière, backed her testamentary supplication to God to 'la vouloir admettre en son saint paradis' with a provision for the perpetual weekly donation of one *sou* each to five paupers, 'en l'honneur des cinq plaies de Notre-Seigneur'.[23]

Whatever the motive for the bequest, an ingrained piety or a guilt complex, the needy stood to profit, handsomely more often than not.

Dispositions for the actual interment were the subject of careful arrangement. Fastidious persons paid close attention to the containers and wrappings that would enfold their bones in the grave. Tallemant relates how one old Protestant maid inspected the joints of her coffin for fear of draughts and embroidered her own white satin shroud for subsequent use by all the spinsters of her diocese.[24] Amongst devout Catholic noblewomen it became fashionable to leave instructions for burial in the habit of a religious order. Marie-Thérèse was laid to rest in the habit of the Third Order of Saint Francis, of which she was a member.[25] The Duchesse de Vendôme ordered

> ... qu'on la mît en terre sans façon
> Son cadavre vêtu du seul caparaçon
> De capucine ...[26]

The theory behind the practice was that it honoured God and the particular founder of an order while testifying to a desire to have lived the kind of life implied by the robes.[27]

Any humility apparent in grave-clothes might be compensated by the choice of an appropriate burial-site. For the majority the obvious resting-place was the cemetery adjoining the parish church. The seventeenth-century French cemetery offered to uninitiated viewers the surprisingly lively spectacle of an inadequately demarcated precinct[28] over which roamed unimpeded humans and animals, the former pausing to chat, amuse themselves and ply their trade amidst the tombstones.[29] The very familiarity of its contours, surveyed thus in the course of the daily routine, tranquillised fears. 'Je vois ici tous les jours le lieu [cemetery of Saint-Sulpice] où je serai enterrée', wrote Mme de la Sablière, 'et je trouve cette vue-là si tranquille que je l'aime tout à fait.'[30] The fact that the family's forebears were often buried within its circumference added to the reassuringly homely atmosphere that pervaded the local graveyard. For relatives to be laid in the same tomb as their forefathers was a hallowed practice and one about which parishioners felt strongly. When a Languedoc priest attempted in 1688 to divert the burial of children from ancestral tombs to a special cemetery separate from that of the adults, on the grounds that this was done in all the best run churches, his distressed congregation appealed, successfully, to their bishop for the restoration of the old custom.[31]

Cemetery facilities were supplemented by the churches, parochial and conventual. Originally reserved for prelates, local magnates and benefactors, the honour of burial in church was gradually accorded to virtually anyone who expressed a desire for it, regardless of the damage caused to floors by ceaseless excavation and the unhealthy stench emanating from an accumulation of decaying corpses. Clauses decreeing that corpses, or parts thereof, should be deposited in some (illustrious) house of God were a regular feature of aristocratic wills.[32] But they were also encountered in testaments issuing from the lowest ranks of society. An illiterate servant, Edmée Lambert, specified in 1685 her wish to be buried in the church of Saint-Pierre-aux-Liens at Saint-Mesmin, 'proche l'eau bénitier et la petite porte de la dite église', in return for which privilege she bequeathed to the church one *écu* and a strip of land she owned on the parish boundary.[33] Plebeians, like patricians, had aspirations to moulder in state.

The physical and spiritual condition of individual women in the last days and hours of earthly life can often be reconstructed in fairly intimate detail. Members of royalty and of the aristocracy, who enjoyed no more privacy in death than at birth, had every last convulsion faithfully registered by variously concerned parties. The words and dispositions of bourgeois wives and mothers on the fatal threshold were reverently inscribed in memoranda and *Livres de Raison*. Even the death-throes of women of the people were considered worthy of preserving for posterity when interestingly directed by an executioner.

The degree of physical pain endured before final expiration emerges in harrowing terms from the different records of deaths. Criminals were obviously in a class apart. They were meant to suffer for their misdemeanours, even if on occasions the sight of inexpert axe-men hacking at half-severed heads, or of recourse to strangulation and scissors to finish off female delinquents, revolted hardened scaffold audiences.[34] But dying quietly at home in bed could become an equally prolonged and agonising ordeal for the woman abandoned to that other legalised order of tormentors, the surgeons and doctors. Medical men wielding their scalpels, lancets and cauteries gave many a defenceless patient a premature taste of purgatory. Anne d'Autriche, her body swelling, ulcerating and putrefying as cancer spread and gangrene set in, was obliged by her physician Alliot to undergo night and morning the operation of mortifying the suppurating flesh and slicing it off with a razor.[35] 'Cette princesse', exclaimed Mme de Motteville, indignant at the ignorance and prejudice of the royal doctors, 'fut contrainte de s'abandonner aux passions des hommes, qui la tourmentèrent plus que son propre mal.'[36] A kindred feeling seized Mme de Sévigné when she beheld the corpse of the Princesse de Conti (Anne-Marie Martinozzi), deceased from what was diagnosed as an apoplexy in 1672: 'Je vis hier sur son lit cette sainte princesse: elle était défigurée par les martyres qu'on lui avait fait souffrir pour tâcher de la faire revenir: on lui avait rompu les dents, et brûlé la tête; c'est-à-dire que si on ne mourait point de l'apoplexie, on serait à plaindre dans l'état où l'on met les pauvres patients.'[37] Ruffled by close-range observations of the antics of bungling operators, women understandably came to despise the medical fraternity for supplying more business for the grave-diggers than ever they took away.[38]

Despite intensity of suffering the moribund seem to have been remarkably attentive to bowing out of life on as edifying a note as possible. Stoic souls calmly discussed with their confessor the subject matter of their forthcoming funeral oration,[39] and with their surgeon the manner in which their entrails would be dissected at the autopsy.[40] Even those to whom the very mention of death had been intolerable were able to draw upon hitherto unsuspected reserves of bravery. The inordinate lengths to which Mme de Sablé went to avoid contact with illness and corpses were a well-worn joke amongst those who knew her,[41] but when escape was no longer possible, 'Cette crainte de la mort qu'elle avait fait tant de fois paraître ... après quelques derniers efforts, cessa enfin ... Elle s'abandonna aux décrets de la providence de Dieu avec des sentiments si religieux et si dévots, que pensant uniquement à son salut, elle compta le reste pour rien.'[42] Mme de Montespan's phobia of death reached such a pitch that she employed women solely to watch over her as she slept,[43] yet at the end 'elle a été aussi tranquille qu'elle a été agité sur la mort, dont on n'osait parler devant elle quand elle se portait bien'.[44] However unnerving in anticipation, the actual process of dying could still be borne with dignity and resolution.

On many occasions death struck too swiftly to allow for any grand finale: 'Madame se meurt! Madame est morte!'[45] But when the dying woman retained consciousness to the end a certain accepted ritual was followed. The Catholic, fortified by confession, viaticum and extreme unction, and the Protestant, taking courage from the belief that the faithful soul avoided the detour of Purgatory on its ascent to Heaven,[46] would have summoned to the bedside their family, intimates and domestics for the purpose of making the final farewells. This was the moment when taboos on overt demonstrations of affection could be swept aside without fear of blame or mockery. The wife of the Protestant controversialist Duplessis-Mornay took leave of him with the loving assurance 'qu'après la connaissance de son salut en Jésus Christ, elle n'avait de rien tant remercié Dieu que de l'avoir donnée à lui'.[47] The Duchesse de Liancourt looked to the moment when her husband would rejoin her – 'Je m'en vais: apparemment nous ne serons pas séparés longtemps; car à l'âge où nous sommes, le survivant suivra bientôt. Je pars donc dans l'espérance de vous revoir' – a pious hope fulfilled just seven weeks later.[48] Drawn momentarily closer perhaps than they had ever been before, partners would seek each other's forgiveness for mutual trespasses, a forgiveness which was subsequently asked of, and extended to, the whole assembled gathering. The children of the marriage would then kneel to receive their mother's benediction, and dutifully listen to her last instructions. Traditionally they would be exhorted not to appear to envy her, by their tears and laments, the bliss of imminent union with the Almighty, but to maintain family unity, and to serve God faithfully until their own personal call came.[49] Great store was set by death-bed counsels, particularly where impressionable youngsters were concerned.[50] But adults in attendance merely for decorum's sake blessed the potential sermoniser who slipped silently into eternity.[51]

The definitive cessation of respiration terminated the first act of the drama, but at the same time opened another, and in many ways a more colourful one: that of the funeral. Before an upper-class corpse was deposited in the waiting coffin two ceremonies were habitually performed. The first of these was the lying in state. The body would be placed on a bed known as the *lit de parade* which, in the case of princesses, was guarded by a number of their female peers and domestics proportionate to the closeness of the deceased's blood relationship to the king.[52] Finding suitable ladies to relay one another in the death-watch was no easy task. The fatigue alone repelled delicately nurtured constitutions, but more refusals still were caused by squabbles over precedence and etiquette. Disputes and protests over alleged failure to pay the respects and honours owing to individuals or companies were rife in the seventeenth century, not least amongst court ladies who had little else to fill their minds.[53] Scarcely any great ceremonial occasion passed without one or another prominent noblewoman sulking at home because a neighbour had been granted a longer train, extra fleurs-de-lys on her robe, a socially superior escort or a more elevated seat.[54] Burials were no exception. During Henriette d'Angleterre's lying in state in 1670 the services of the wives of the French marshals had to be dispensed with because they insisted on sharing with princesses and duchesses the right to remain seated by the coffin.[55] Twenty years later the corpse of the Dauphine de Bavière came near to being deprived of ceremonial dues altogether when women of the sovereign house of Savoy intimated that they would be demeaning themselves by guarding it and those of the Lorraine household promptly protested that the chore was beneath their dignity also.[56] In 1693 Louis XIV had to suspend the threat of exile over the Comtesse de Soissons to force her to do her duty by his defunct cousin the Duchesse de Montpensier.[57]

The second pre-burial procedure was the autopsy. Ignorance over the cause of maladies and perpetual apprehension of poisoning combined with considerations of piety to authorise the grisly operation of slitting open the carcass and scrutinising the viscera. Bodies which had been the object of reverence in life were suddenly exposed to the public gaze in all the repulsive deformity caused not only by the progress of old age and disease, but also by congenital malformations, dietary excesses and the like. Henriette d'Angleterre, for whom Louis XIV had known tenderer sentiments than those befitting a brother-in-law and whom the artistic world had idolised, was painstakingly dissected under a host of searching eyes to see whether there was any foundation in her death-bed allegations of having been poisoned: 'L'ambassadeur d'Angleterre y a assisté avec tous les Anglais qui étaient ici, des médecins et des chirurgiens de la même nation, et généralement tout ce qui se voulut trouver à Saint-Cloud, où les portes étaient ouvertes à toutes sortes de personnes. Le ventre était extraordinairement enflé à cette princesse depuis sa mort; dès le premier coup de bistouri qu'on donna dans son corps, il jeta une si grande puanteur que tous les assistants furent obligés de s'en éloigner et n'en purent approcher qu'après s'être bien munis contre une si mauvaise odeur'.[58] No formal traces of poison were found, but the presiding doctors readily informed the numerous enquirers who asked about the princess's body 'que rien au monde n'était si contrefait et si vilain'.[59] Rather than run the risk of similar indignities, or of posthumous mangling by unskilled hands,[60] ladies such as the Duchesse d'Aiguillon specified in their testament that they wished to be buried immediately after death, 'sans être ouverte'.[61] But the expectations of religious communities and charitable organisations, unwilling to forego the honour of preserving a tangible reminder of protectresses of note, were difficult to frustrate. The result was that a fair number of benefactresses went to the grave minus entrails or heart, which were embalmed in elaborate caskets and displayed where they might stimulate the charity of others.[62]

After one or more days' exposure to intermittent showers of tears and holy water from mourners and psalm-singing ecclesiastics,[63] the eviscerated corpse was finally prepared for consignment to the grave. Testamentary wishes for a simple burial ceremony were rarely respected to the letter by relatives who felt that they had a name and position to uphold in the sight of the community. The bigger and more resplendent the concourse following the coffin, it was reckoned, the more advantageous the idea that onlookers would conceive of a family's standing. Royalty and the aristocracy automatically had a head start in the prestige stakes. Their funeral trains, swollen by large retinues of officers and domestics, sombrely elegant in mourning liveries, files of bodyguards and luxuriously draped carriages filled with lordly occupants, rolled importantly along to churches draped, by special privilege, with black hangings.[64] Not to be outdone, the bourgeoisie summoned, by means of 'burial criers'[65] or written announcements,[66] kinsfolk and clients, fellow guildsmen and members of *confréries*[67] to honour their dead wives by carrying the rich pall[68] and the coffin in solemn procession behind the cross, priests, churchwardens, beadles and mace-bearers.[69] Both aristocrats and bourgeois liked to have amongst official mourners a contingent of persons recalling virtues that the deceased had possessed, or supposedly possessed: piety, charity, humility, purity. A group of the parish poor, specially dressed for the occasion, were favourite candidates for this function.[70] In certain districts of France, the Bourbonnais notably, girls called *pleureuses* were robed in symbolic white to accompany the dead to the grave.[71] White was the traditional colour of the lighted wax torches and tapers with which marchers in funeral processions were equipped. To add to the spectacular effect of these multiple *flambeaux*, and to make sure that they disappeared conspicuously from human view, persons of eminence arranged for their entombment to take place in the darkness of the night or early morning.[72]

Participants in the funerals of the great remembered the proceedings chiefly as a test of their endurance and stamina. The sheer number of riders and pedestrians escorting the coffin, in none too disciplined a fashion sometimes, lengthened interminably the march to the burial-place, even before the clergy commenced their protracted orations and the obligatory religious rites. In 1683 it took, in addition to preliminary delays while the procession assembled, a full twelve hours to convey Marie-Thérèse's remains from Versailles to the great mausoleum at Saint-Denis. The grumbles of the empty-bellied, the foot-weary and the saddle-sore were echoed in the *Mercure Galant*'s delicate allusion to the cavalcade's suffering from 'des fatigues, des besoins, et des incommodités, auxquelles il n'est pas aisé de remédier'.[73] In the relative privacy of her memoirs the Duchesse de Montpensier recalled with franker distaste the 'horrible coldness' of the January morning in 1666 when she was obliged to set out from the Louvre at seven in the wake of Anne d'Autriche's bier, spend four hours on the road to Saint-Denis, an hour waiting for the monks of the abbey there to return from a procession, and a further two hours listening to harangues, before bracing herself for the return march. 'J'étais si lasse et si accablée que j'appuyai ma tête contre la bière et que je l'y eus longtemps, sans m'en apercevoir', she confessed.[74]

Funerals were not all gloom, despondency and tedium. In marked contrast to their social superiors, common folk were speedily wound in the shroud that replaced a coffin[75] and bundled into the ground with the minimum of pomp. The Strasbourg traveller Brackenhoffer was taken aback to witness at Saumur the familiar church cross, *curé* and pall-bearers heading disorderly lines of male and female mourners, the latter attired in their colourful workaday clothes, and no marks of respect shown to the corpse beyond the sprinkling of the tomb with holy water.[76] The obsequies of the great had their lighter moments also. The pandemonium caused by the sudden explosion of the Duchesse de Montpensier's fermenting entrails from their casket subsided into irreverent mirth once the true cause of the phenomenon was ascertained.[77] Seventeenth-century mourners endeavoured not to let funerals interfere too much with their daily habits or weigh too heavily upon their spirits.

It was for totally different reasons that the Protestant section of the community made as little fuss as possible over the disposal of the deceased. Their religion commanded them to dispense with burial services and ceremonies, for fear of giving rise to the kind of superstitions that ran riot in the papist camp. The plainness and austerity which they affected in their mode of living ruled out the showy sepulchres in which Catholic plutocrats indulged. Thus one of their more notorious brethren, Tallemant des Réaux, could plausibly argue that dying cost them next to nothing.[78] But sobriety became as much a matter of necessity as of temperament and conviction. Once Louis XIV's ruthless drive towards mass conversion got under way, Protestant burial rights were held no more sacred than any others. Adherents of the Religion were peremptorily ordered to refrain from exposing corpses on the thresholds of houses, where they might mutely edify passers-by, and to avoid all exchanges of consolations and exhortations in the streets. Burial was restricted to cemeteries set apart from those assigned to Catholics, and to certain precise hours at daybreak and nightfall. In districts where public observance of the cult was conceded thirty persons only, including relatives, might accompany the funeral convoy, which was to proceed without stopping to the graveside. Everywhere else a mere ten mourners were to suffice.[79] One final crack of the royal whip – provision for the trial and punishment of corpses of relapsed converts[80] – and grieving Protestants were soon burying their dead with record speed, secrecy and economy.

Almost all necrological dramas, barring those in which Protestants were involved, had an epilogue consisting of steps taken to safeguard the eternal repose of the defunct and simultaneously to keep her memory fresh in the minds of the living.[81] Members of prominent families had the instructive interludes of their life-history embroidered in florid funeral orations and their departed souls formally recommended in church to the prayers of their fellow parishioners. If the latter were too indolent to pray personally they could always address themselves to one of the needy individuals accustomed to stand in the vicinity of graves and recite rapid orisons for the occupants at a *sou* a time.[82] But rather than compromise their eternal rest by relying on haphazard devotions, most women expressly set aside in their will a sum of money to pay for commemoration services – *annuels*,[83] *trentains*,[84] obits, masses – to be held in churches or monastic establishments on days which either had a personal significance for the testatrix or were important to Christian believers generally. Ninon de Lenclos deferred to pious custom to the extent of ordering fifty obituary masses at one *franc* apiece.[85] To be on the safe side the Duchesse d'Aiguillon commanded the celebration of ten thousand.[86] Testatrixes of bourgeois and peasant stock issued minute instructions regulating the form and periodicity of their memorial services. Catherine Dupré, widow of a wealthy bourgeois of Lyon, founded in the chapel of Notre-Dame de la Platière, which she and her husband had had built, 'pour le repos de son âme et de tous ces [sic] prédécesseurs, à perpétuité, une pension annuelle et perpétuelle de la somme de cent livres, pour et à icelle fin qu'il soit célébré tous les premiers vendredis des mois ... une messe basse "pro defunctis", et à la fin un Salve Regina'.[87] Guillemette Lamoignon thoughtfully provided for the distribution of ceremonial candles to those of her friends and relatives, municipal dignitaries of Bourges, who bestirred themselves to attend an annual Assumption Day service on her behalf: 'par son testament a fondé en l'église de Saint Bonnet de cette ville de Bourges, un salut solennel à chacun Jour de l'Assomption Notre Dame à sept heures du soir, où elle veut être distribué deux livres de bougie à ses parents et amis, qui y assisteront, et pour le dit salut a donné, à la dite fabrique de Saint Bonnet, neuf livres de rente foncière'.[88] Edmée Lambert, the stylish peasant of Saint-Mesmin, wanted a low mass to be said biennially the day after the feast of her patron saint, plus 'un libera sur sa fosse pour le repos de son âme tous les dimanches de l'année, un service complet au bout du mois et pareillement un service complet au bout de l'an'.[89] Low masses, ordinarily stipulated for these occasions, commended themselves to makers of wills because the fact that they were simply recited by a priest made them cheaper to repeat for maximum efficacy than high masses, sung with deacon and subdeacon present.

The founding of commemorative masses was looked upon as such an integral part of burial procedure that failure to conform caused eyebrows to be raised. Eléonore de Berg, Duchesse de Bouillon, sister-in-law of the famous general Turenne, was accused of concerning herself more with the temporal than with the spiritual advantages of her religion for having declared on her death-bed, 'pour ne point fonder de messes', that she 'était trop grande pécheresse pour sortir du purgatoire et qu'elle voulait y demeurer autant de temps qu'il plairait à Dieu; et ainsi mourut sans avoir contenté les prêtres à qui elle n'a rien laissé pour chanter à son honneur'.[90] Defiance of established rituals, albeit piously enveloped, was, however, an exceptional gesture for a moribund woman to make, one from which even the ultra-libertine Ninon had shrunk. Perhaps it would never have been recorded in this particular instance, in the journal of two itinerant Dutch Protestants, had the Duchesse not infuriated her Protestant husband's co-religionists by persuading him to abjure.

Prolonged periods of mourning over a dead female were not expected and, indeed, were criticised on occasions. The gap left in a commoner's household by a wife's premature demise was officially filled within the space of a few years, or sometimes months.[91] Possible replacements for the titled wife were reviewed before she was cold in her grave.[92] The rapidity with which the court forgot its illustrious dead was the subject of many a disillusioned commentary.[93] Memories of the charm and sparkle of Henriette d'Angleterre scarcely outlived her burial,[94] while the retiring Dauphine de Bavière, who had possessed neither, faded from recollection within a month.[95] Mme de Maintenon informed the Princesse des Ursins that a month-long demonstration of grief on the part of Mme de Montespan's bereaved daughters 'commence à paraître excessive; car on n'aime pas les longues afflictions à la cour'.[96] By a singular irony, those who had seemed best placed to cheat oblivion were some of the quickest to suffer its effects.

If the art of living well eluded them, seventeenth-century Frenchwomen made a determined effort to master the art of dying well. That they might better possess its secrets they studied avidly the comportment of the moribund, at first hand wherever possible. Material and spiritual preparations for departure they generally began in good time, at any event not later than the first prolonged illness of middle age, or the first irrefutable signs of charm and influence waning. The hope that their bequests and restitutions would make their peace with God and men, and the belief that their remains would rest in some favourite spot until the promised resurrection, helped to sustain them through the diverse torments inflicted upon their bodies by ignorant physicians and on their hearts by anguished relatives. Doubtless they experienced, and expressed, more sentiments of despair, terror and impatience than biographers anxious to moralise and to embellish their subject gave them credit for. But by no means all obituary notices were destined for perusal by the general public, and of those that were the constancy of the heroine is often vouchsafed by other, less suspect, sources.

The funeral was less the climax of the tragedy than its anti-climax, not a particularly edifying one at that. Coming after the dignified scene of the death-bed, the spectacle of corpses disgorging their putrescent organs under the surgeon's knife, or jolting along to their appointed repositories amidst straggling, dozing, laughing or sulking mourners, could not but strike a discordant note. As if anticipating posthumous affronts to their dignity, women repeatedly asked for burial-ceremonies to be abbreviated and simplified, choosing to reserve elaborate services for such time as their decomposing bodies were ornately hidden from profane eyes, beneath monuments and in mausoleums. When the sound of pulpit eulogies had died away, oblivion threatened to descend with a swiftness against which a grandiose tomb was but a fragile defence if the occupant's memory was not elsewhere enshrined, in human hearts.

Notes

CHAPTER 1

1. Pierre de l'Estoile, *Journal pour le règne de Henri IV*, Vol. II (ed. A. Martin) p. 86. The performance was repeated on the birth of Christine in 1606, ibid., p. 184.
2. *Valentin Conrart. Sa Vie et sa Correspondance* (eds R. Kerviler and E. de Barthélemy) p. 652.
3. Marquis de Sourches, *Mémoires* (eds Comte de Cosnac and A. Beltrand) Vol. I, p. 256 (June 1685: 'Mme de Richelieu accoucha d'une fille, au grand regret du duc, son époux, qui avait espéré un fils'); Vol. II, p. 232 (Sept. 1688: birth of Duchesse de Beauvillier's ninth daughter 'ne fut pas une médiocre épreuve pour la vertu de Monsieur son mari'); Vol. IV, p. 130 (Oct. 1692: 'On sut aussi que la duchesse de Choiseul était accouchée d'une fille ... Le 10, la duchesse d'Estrées accoucha aussi et ne fut pas plus heureuse que la duchesse de Choiseul').
4. *Lettres en Vers de la Gravette de Mayolas, Robinet, Boursault, Perdou de Subligny, Laurent et Autres* (ed. Baron James de Rothschild) Vol. I, p. 700. See also p. 150, and the *Mercure Galant* (ed. Jean Donneau de Visé) July 1685, pp. 76–81.
5. Mme de Sévigné, *Lettres* (Collection Grands Ecrivains de la France) Vol. II, p. 357.
6. Abbé de Choisy, *Mémoires* (Collection Michaud et Poujoulat) 3me Sér., Vol. VI, p. 594; Jean Loret, *La Muse Historique* (eds J. Ravenel and V. de la Pelouze) 5, 12, 19 Nov. 1661.
7. Théodore Godefroy, *Le Cérémonial Français*, Vol. II, p. 203.
8. Bussy-Rabutin, *Correspondance* (ed. L. Lalanne) Vol. V, p. 188. See also Antoine de Courtin, *Traité de la Jalousie*, 2me Partie, Ch. 2, p. 393.
9. Gui Patin, *Lettres* (ed. J.-H. Reveillé-Parise) Vol. III, p. 668.
10. Claude de Letouf, *Mémoires*, Vol. I, p. 8.
11. Lacroix, *Journal*, in *Mémoires de la Société d'Histoire et d'Archéologie de Chalon-sur-Saone*, Vol. VII, 1re Partie, p. 35.
12. Boyer, *Livre du Raison*, in *Revue du Lyonnais*, 5me Sér., Vol. VIII, p. 213.
13. Bourrut, *Papier de Raison*, in *Bulletin et Mémoires de la Société Archéologique et Mémoires de la Charente*, 7me Sér., Vol. III, p. 8.
14. Louise Bourgeoise, *Observations Diverses sur la stérilité, perte de fruit, fécondité, accouchements, et maladies des femmes, et enfants nouveaux-nés*, Liv. 1, Ch. 25, pp. 156–7; Philippe Peu, *Pratique des Accouchements*, Liv. 1, Ch. 12, pp. 199–201.
15. See Georges de La Tour's contemporary painting entitled *Le Nouveau-Né*.
16. Jacques Guillemeau, 'De la Nourriture et Gouvernement des Enfants', in *De la Grossesse et Accouchement des Femmes*, Ch. 5, pp. 776–7; Ch. 10, p. 799; François Mauriceau, *Traité des Maladies des Femmes*

Grosses, Liv. 3, Ch. 24, pp. 457–8; *Lettres Inédites de Mme de Mainte-non et de Mme la Princesse des Ursins* (ed. Bossange) Vol. I, p. 114.

17. Marguerite de Valois, *Mémoires et Lettres* (ed. M. F. Guessard) p. 96.
18. Pierre Charron, *De la Sagesse* (ed. A. Duval) Vol. III, Liv. 3, Ch. 14, p. 74; Antoine de Courtin, *Traité de la Paresse*, 5me Entretien, pp. 36–37; Esprit Fléchier, *Pensées sur l'Education des Enfants*, in *Œuvres Complètes* (ed. A.-V. Fabre de Narbonne) Vol. V, p. 434; Claude Joly, *Les Deux Livres de l'Etat du Mariage*, passim; Guillaume Le Roy, *Du Devoir des Mères avant et après la naissance de leurs enfants*, passim; Abel de Sainte-Marthe, *La Manière de Nourrir les Enfants à la Mamelle*, Liv. 1, pp. 8 et seq.
19. Marguerite Du Tertre, *Instruction familière et utile aux sages-femmes, pour bien pratiquer les accouchements*, 3me Partie, p. 98.
20. *Livre de Raison de la famille Froissard-Broissia (1532–1701)*, in *Mémoires de la Société d'Emulation du Jura*, 4me Sér., Vol. II, pp. 81, 83, 95; Jean Héroard, *Journal sur l'Enfance et la Jeunesse de Louis XIII* (eds E. Soulié and E. Barthélemy) Vol. I, pp. 8, 16, 18.
21. Medical men considered that *bouillie* could safely be administered after the first eight to ten days. See Charles de Saint-Germain, *L'Ecole méthodique et parfaite des sages-femmes, ou l'Art de l'Accouchement*, 4me Partie, Sect. 3, Ch. 1, p. 340. In Provence and Languedoc boiled bread was substituted for *bouillie*. See De Rostagny, *Traité de Primerose sur les erreurs vulgaires de la médecine*, Liv. 3, Ch. 13, p. 463.
22. Mauriceau, *Traité des Maladies*, Liv. 3, Ch. 25, p. 462; Patin, *Lettres*, Vol. I, pp. 317–18.
23. Bourgeoise, *Observations*, Liv. 1, Ch. 27; Guillemeau, *De la Nourriture des Enfants*, Ch. 1, pp. 753 et seq.; Mauriceau, *Traité des Maladies*, Liv. 3, Ch. 43.
24. Guillemeau, *De la Nourriture des Enfants*, Ch. 11, p. 800.
25. Locke, *Travels in France* (ed. J. Lough) p. 206.
26. Pierre de l'Estoile, *Journal*, Vol. II, p. 376.
27. Demaillasson, *Journal*, in *Archives Historiques du Poitou*, Vol. XXXVI p. 32; Mauriceau, *Traité des Maladies*, Liv. 3, Ch. 25, pp. 462–3. For other female infant victims of a nurse's negligence see Nicolas-Joseph Foucault, *Mémoires* (ed. F. Baudry) p. 3; Mme Guyon, *Vie de Mme Guyon écrite par elle-même*, 1re Partie, Ch. 15, p. 140. Records of male infants lost in this way tend to be more colourful, and in one instance led the bereft father to begin appending to the names of the numerous wet-nurses whom he engaged a heartfelt 'Dieu lui fasse la grâce de bien nourrir l'enfant que l'on lui commet' (see *Livre de Raison de la famille Froissard-Broissia*, pp. 82–3, 94).
28. Travellers through seventeenth-century French towns are unani-mous in remarking on the fact that houses rose to a height of as many as seven storeys and were badly over-populated. See Elie Brackenhoffer, *Voyage en France (1643–4)* (trans. H. Lehr) p. 58; Jean Dumont, *Voyages en France, en Italie, à Malthe, et en Turquie*, Vol. I, p. 82; Albert Jouvin, *Le Voyageur d'Europe*, Vol. I, p. 233; Martin Lister, *A Journey to Paris in the year 1698*, pp. 6–7; Sir John Reresby, *Travels and Memoirs*, p. 8. The one-room hovels of the peasantry,

described by Locke in *Travels in France,* pp. 229, 236, were scarcely less insalubrious.

29.   For example, a municipal ordinance of Nancy was issued in April 1607, and several times renewed subsequently, forbidding pig-keeping in houses. See *Archives de Nancy* (ed. H. Lepage) Vol. III, p. 215 et seq.

30.   Sébastien Locatelli, *Voyage de France (1664–5)* (trans. A. Vautier) p. 51; Patin, *Lettres,* Vol. II, p. 419, and Vol. III, p. 418.

31.   Père Anselme, *Histoire Généalogique et Chronologique de la Maison Royale de France,* Vol. IV, pp. 73, 217. This work will henceforth be referred to as *Maison Royale.*

32.   Le Marchand, *Journal* (ed. G. Vanel) pp. 9, 25, 27, 104, 110, 115, 125, 133, 139.

33.   Fleuriot, *Journal,* in *Le Cabinet Historique,* Vol. XXIV, p. 113.

34.   *Livre de Famille des Sieurs de la Brunye de Rochechouart* in *Livres de Raison, Registres de Famille et Journaux Individuels Limousins et Marchois* (ed. L. Guibert) p. 243.

35.   Boyer, *Livre de Raison,* pp. 459–60.

36.   Tour, *Livre Domestique,* in *Bulletin de la Société Archéologique, Historique, et Scientifique de Soissons,* 2me Sér., Vol. III, p. 57.

37.   Protestants opposed the idea that unbaptised infants were excluded from Paradise. See Jean Calvin, *Institution de la Religion Chrétienne* (ed. J.-D. Benoît) Liv. 4, Ch. 15, sect. 20, 22, and Ch. 16, sect. 26.

38.   P. J. J. G. Guyot, *Répertoire Universel et Raisonné de Jurisprudence,* Art. 'Baptême'; J.-B. Thiers, *Traité des Superstitions qui regardent tous les sacrements,* Vol. II, Liv. 1, Ch. 5, p. 39. Protestants showed a parallel concern for swift baptism. See E. Haag, *La France Protestante,* 'Pièces Justificatives', No. 33, Art. 10, p. 101; No. 46, Art. 23, p. 180; No. 87, Art. 12, p. 364. Like the Catholics they allowed a midwife to administer the *ondoiement* but only the form of baptism bestowed by the pastor in the temple was considered really valid. See Haag, ibid., No. 69, Art. 17, p. 277; also, preamble to Declaration of 20 Feb. 1680 forbidding Protestant midwives from exercising their profession, in *Recueil des Anciennes Lois Françaises* (eds F. A. Isambert et al.) Vol. XIX, p. 231.

39.   Du Tertre, *Instruction aux sages-femmes,* 3me Partie, pp. 101–2. Parents were advised to baptise their own children only in cases of extreme emergency when no one else was present, for by their action they would contract a spiritual alliance which removed their right to cohabit without special dispensation. See Du Tertre, ibid., p. 104; Guyot, *Répertoire,* Art. 'Baptême'.

40.   Du Tertre, *Instruction aux sages-femmes,* 3me Partie, p. 103; Peu, *Pratique des Accouchements,* Liv. 1, p. 179; Thiers, *Traité des Superstitions,* Vol. II, Liv. 1, Ch. 7, p. 76.

41.   Mairot, *Feuillets de Garde,* in *Mémoires de la Société d'Emulation du Jura,* 7me Sér., Vol. I, p. 203.

42.   *Livre de Raison de la famille Froissard-Broissia,* pp. 78–9, 82–3, 88–9.

43.   L'Estoile, *Journal,* Vol. II, p. 205. Louis's youngest sister Henriette, born on 26 Nov. 1609, was not baptised until 15 June 1614, together

with her brother Gaston d'Orléans, born on 25 Apr. 1608. See Héroard, *Journal*, Vol. II, p. 141.

44. Maréchal de Bassompierre, *Mémoires* (ed. Marquis de Chantérac) Vol. IV, p. 203.

45. Loret, *Muse Historique*, 16 June 1657.

46. Protestants seem to have been stricter than Catholics in this respect. The 5th National Synod of 1565 decreed that Protestant children be admitted as godparents only after their first communion, which was not to take place before twelve years as a rule. See Haag, *France Protestante*, 'Pièces Justificatives', No. 24, Art. 17, p. 75.

47. Tallemant des Réaux, 'Mme de Montausier', in *Historiettes* (ed. M. Monmerqué) Vol. III, p. 257.

48. Racine, 'Pièces Justificatives', in *Œuvres* (Collection Grands Ecrivains de la France) Vol. I, p. 192. See also Vol. VI, p. 553. It was not unknown for babies in arms to act as godparents (see Loret, *Muse Historique*, 8 July 1662).

49. Paul Scarron, *Le Roman Comique* (ed. E. Magne) 3me Partie, Ch. 10, p. 355.

50. In 1608 Louis XIII, who had already in 1606 been godfather to his *nourrice*'s daughter, acted in that same capacity again, with his two-year-old sister Christine as godmother, on the occasion of the baptism of a daughter of Christine's *nourrice*. In 1617 Louis and Christine were godparents to the daughter of Pluvinel, Louis's riding instructor. See Héroard, *Journal*, Vol. I, pp. 177, 371–2; Vol. II, p. 209.

51. Mairot, *Feuillets de Garde*, p. 204.

52. Foucault, *Mémoires*, pp. 41, 45, 78, 84, 108; *Livres de Raison . . . Limousins et Marchois* (ed. L. Guibert) p. 330; Marquis de Saint-Maurice, *Lettres sur la Cour de Louis XIV* (ed. J. Lemoine) Vol. I, p. 285. Thiers in *Traité des Superstitions*, Vol. II, Liv. 1, Ch. 9, pp. 99–101, roundly condemns the practice, which he attributes to parental laziness, avarice, or superstition, and demands to know how beggars can possibly fulfil their godparental duty of instructing children in the faith and in morals. Some parents also had misgivings. See *Livre de Raison de la famille Froissard-Broissia*, p. 94.

53. L'Estoile, *Journal*, Vol. II, p. 172.

54. Tallemant, *Historiette de M. de Guise, Fils du Balafré*, Vol. II, p. 22.

55. Jacqueline de Bouette de Blémur, *Eloges de Plusieurs Personnes Illustres en Piété de l'Ordre de St. Benoît*, Vol. I, p. 241.

56. Thiers, *Traité des Superstitions*, Vol. II, Liv. 1, Ch. 10, p. 118.

57. Ibid., p. 132.

58. Ibid., p. 126.

59. Anselme, *Maison Royale*, Vol. IV, pp. 722–3, 792–3. See also Vol. VII, pp. 573–4.

60. Tallemant, *Historiette de Mme de Montausier*, Vol. III, pp. 233–4.

61. See Edict of Feb. 1672 in Isambert, *Anciennes Lois Françaises*, Vol. XIX, p. 3.

62. The Protestant Church also had difficulty in stimulating the requisite reverence at baptisms. See Haag, *France Protestante*, 'Pièces Justificatives', No. 47, Art. 12, p. 182.

63. Anti-feminists pretended that it was more difficult to exorcise the devil in female infants than in males. See Jacques Olivier, *Alphabet de l'Imperfection et Malice des Femmes*, 'Letter H', p. 108.
64. The Church attempted in certain areas to prevent women from bell-ringing. See Thiers, *Traité des Superstitions*, Vol. I, Liv. 1, Ch. 12, pp. 162–3.
65. Ibid., Vol. II, Liv. 1, Ch. 9, pp. 104–5; Ch. 12, pp. 159–65.
66. The edicts are listed in Guyot, *Répertoire*, Art. 'Baptême'.
67. Guyon, *Vie*, 1re Partie, Ch. 2, p. 8.
68. *Souvenirs sur Mme de Maintenon* (eds Comte d'Haussonville and G. Hanotaux) p. 13.
69. See the burlesque marriage contract in G. M. de Brécourt, *La Noce de Village*, sc. 5; Bernard Le Bovier de Fontenelle, *Lettre à Mlle de C . . .* , *En lui envoyant un extrait de son baptême*, in *Œuvres*, Vol. I, p. 374; Charles de Marguetel de Saint-Evremond, *Lettres* (ed. R. Ternois) Vol. I, p. 234.
70. Blémur, *Eloges*, Vol. I, p. 499.
71. Loret, *Muse Historique*, 13 Dec. 1664.
72. Demaillasson, *Journal*, p. 106.
73. Maintenon, *Lettres* (ed. M. Langlois) Vol. IV, pp. 34–5. The Duchesse du Maine, Anne-Louise-Bénédicte de Bourbon, was newly married at the time and fifteen years old, but like all the grand-daughters of the great Condé, she possessed the diminutive stature of a much younger girl.
74. See below, Ch. 2, p. 22.
75. The early eighteenth century saw a revolt against the wearing of these *corps*, as they were called. See Maintenon, *Lettres Inédites de Mme de Maintenon et de Mme la Princesse des Ursins* (ed. Bossange) Vol. I, p. 257; Vol. II, pp. 105, 358, 368.
76. Bussy-Rabutin, *Histoire Amoureuse des Gaules* (ed. Garnier) Vol. II, p. 361.
77. Robert Dallington, *The View of France* (Shakespeare Association Facsimiles) No. 13, p. V.
78. Locatelli, *Voyage de France*, pp. 123, 160.
79. Maintenon, *Lettres et Entretiens sur l'Education des Filles* (ed. T. Lavallée) Vol. I, p. 261; Vol. II, pp. 254, 284.
80. Tallemant, *Historiette de Gombauld*, Vol. IV, p. 135; and *Historiette du Président Pascal*, Vol. V, pp. 134–5.
81. Marquis de Dangeau, *Journal* (eds E. Soulié, L. Dussieux et al.) Vol. VI, p. 443; Vol. VII, pp. 169, 205, 212 and others.
82. Maintenon, *Lettres et Entretiens*, Vol. I, p. 247; Elisabeth-Charlotte de Bavière, *Lettres Nouvelles Inédites* (ed. A.-A. Rolland) pp. 171–2. Elisabeth-Charlotte will henceforth be referred to in the notes as 'Bavière'.
83. Antoine Furetière, *Le Roman Bourgeois* (ed. P. Jannet) Vol. II, Liv. 2, p. 24; Garaby de la Luzerne, 'Le Citadin', in *Satires Inédites* (ed. E. de Beaurepaire) p. 40.
84. Bavière, *Lettres Inédites* (ed. Rolland) p. 272; *Choix de Mazarinades*, (ed. C. Moreau) Vol. I, p. 269.

85. D'Aumale, *Souvenirs*, p. 20; Ambroise Paccori, *Avis Salutaires à une Mère Chrétienne*, sect. 48.

86. Claude Perrault, *Voyage à Bordeaux (1669)* (ed. P. Bonnefon) p. 215.

87. *Mercure Galant*, Mar. 1699, pp. 97–8; Aug. 1699, p. 148; May 1700, p. 33.

88. Jean Louvet, *Journal: Récit véritable de tout ce qui est advenu digne de mémoire tant en la ville d'Angers, pays d'Anjou et autres lieux (depuis l'an 1560 jusqu'à l'an 1634)*, in *Revue de l'Anjou et de Maine et Loire*, Mar.–Apr. 1855, p. 135.

89. *Mercure Galant*, July 1685, pp. 170–1, 186–7.

90. Ibid., Mar. 1687, p. 163.

91. See below, Ch. 13, p. 209.

92. Lacroix, *Journal*, p. 55. Cf. *Journal de Deux Notaires Ciotadens au XVIIe siècle* (ed. A. Ritt) p. 36: 'Le mois de mai 1609 étant grand [sic] sécheresse, furent faites processions durant neuf jours par les capucins à la Ciotat et par les prêtres et pénitents, et icelles achevées, les enfants se sont mis à en faire autres [sic], et en après les filles, et après de jeunes hommes, le tout par troupes, de nuit'. The distinction made between 'enfants' and 'filles' suggests that the latter were more advanced in age than the former, but does not rule out the possibility of the presence of quite young girls.

93. *Mémoires d'un Bourgeois de Marseille* in *Publications spéciales de la Société pour l'Etude des Langues Romanes*, Vol. VIII, p. 41.

94. *Mercure Galant*, May 1681, pp. 48 et seq. The participation of children as a whole in celebrations of national, as opposed to local, import is rarely mentioned. But here again girls were not overlooked. Six little orphans, for example, 'nées de pauvres patrons pêcheurs', took part in festivities at Marseille in 1687 to give thanks for Louis XIV's recovery from a fistula operation. See *Mercure Galant*, Apr. 1687, p. 77.

95. Brackenhoffer, *Voyage en France*, p. 98.

96. Jouvin, *Le Voyageur d'Europe*, Vol. I, p. 123.

97. Richelieu, *Instruction du Chrétien*, Leçon 19.

98. *Etat de la Généralité d'Alençon sous Louis XIV* (ed. L. Duval) p. 126.

99. Locke, *Travels in France*, pp. 245–6.

100. See below, Ch. 2, n. 24.

101. Mortoft, *His Book, Being his Travels through France and Italy, 1658–59* (ed. M. Letts) p. 13. Sir John Lauder made the same observation about the beggar-women of Poitiers in the early 1660s in his *Journals* (ed. D. Crawford) pp. 54–5.

102. See below, Chs 3 and 4.

103. Bossuet, 'Méditation: De la Brièveté de la Vie', in *Sermons* (ed. Garnier) Vol. II, p. 467. See also his '2me Sermon pour le jour de la purification de la Sainte Vierge, 1666', in ibid., Vol. IV, pp. 327–8. The basic idea appears to stem from St Augustine, quoted by the Jansenist Pierre Nicole in his 'Traité des Quatre Dernières Fins de l'Homme', in *Essais de Morale*, Vol. IV, Liv. 3, Ch. 5, pp. 225 et seq. Cf. La Rochefoucauld's equation between childhood and folly in his *Maximes* (ed. J. Truchet) p. 403.

104. La Bruyère, 'De l'Homme', 50, in *Les Caractères* (ed. R. Garapon).
105. La Fontaine, *Fables* (ed. P. Clarac) Liv. 9. Nos 2, 5; Liv. 11, No. 2.
106. Nicolas Boileau-Despréaux, *l'Art Poétique*, in *Œuvres*, (ed. G. Mongrédien) Chant 3, vv. 696–702; Pierre Bayle, *Dictionnaire Historique et Critique*, Art. 'Andromaque H'.
107. A baby girl figures in Puget de la Serre's *Pandoste* (1631), 1re Journée, Acte IV, and a young boy in the Cinq Auteurs' *Aveugle de Smyrne* (1638), IV, iii, long before Molière's Louison (*Malade Imaginaire*) and Racine's Joas (*Athalie*), the two most frequently cited examples, appear on stage; but such parts remain rare in drama. The attitude of the novelists may be summed up in a quotation from Madeleine de Scudéry's *Artamène ou Le Grand Cyrus*, Vol. III, Liv. 2, p. 659, describing the upbringing of Princess Araminte, her sweetheart Prince Spitridate and their respective brothers and sisters: 'j'ose dire que par le soin que l'on prit à les élever, ils cessèrent d'être enfants, beaucoup plus tôt que leur âge ne semblait le devoir permettre. On voyait bien en leur conversation, la grâce, la naïveté et l'enjouement ordinaire de l'enfance: mais ils n'en avaient ni la sotte honte, ni la trop grande hardiesse, ni la simplicité, ni l'ignorance'.
108. Fortin de la Hoguette, *Testament ou Conseils Fidèles d'un Bon Père à ses Enfants*, 3me Partie, Ch. 3, pp. 272–3.
109. Cf. the more sympathetic analogy in La Bruyère, 'De l'homme', 128, in *Caractères*.
110. Coulanges, *Chansons Choisies*, pp. 71–6. Cf. Furetière, *Roman Bourgeois*, Vol. II, Liv. 2, p. 24.
111. Vigneul-Marville, *Mélanges d'Histoire et de Littérature*, Vol. II, p. 69. The moralist Jacques Esprit died in 1678.
112. Relations between *mother* and child will be considered in Ch. 5 below.
113. Henri IV, *Lettres Missives* (ed. J. Berger de Xivrey) Vol. VII, p. 18.
114. La Force, *Mémoires* (ed. Marquis de la Grange) Vol. I, pp. 310, 470.
115. Racine, *Œuvres*, Vol. VI, p. 546; Vol. VII, pp. 267, 274. Significantly, the dramatist feels obliged in a letter to his aunt, the mother superior of Port-Royal, to excuse himself for showing so much affection for his daughter Anne (see Vol. VII, p. 310).
116. Henri de Campion, *Mémoires* (ed. M. C. Moreau) pp. 243, 262–3.

CHAPTER 2

1. The number of panegyrists surpassed that of detractors in the seventeenth century, and the violent invective that had characterised contributions to the *Querelle* during the Middle Ages and the Renaissance virtually disappeared after a final explosion in Jacques Olivier's *Alphabet de l'Imperfection et Malice des Femmes* (1617). The debate was always conducted almost exclusively by men, who regarded it as a rhetorical exercise in which they changed sides at will to display their erudition and dialectical skills. The most powerful and rational advocate of women's rights in the century, Poulain de la Barre, thus followed his *De l'Egalité des Deux Sexes*

(1673) with a *De l'Excellence des Hommes contre l'Egalité des Sexes*
(1675). For a detailed exposition of the *Querelle* prior to, and during,
the period under review see G. Reynier, *La Femme au XVIIe Siècle*,
and P. Darmon, *Mythologie de la femme dans l'Ancienne France*.

2. Anon., *Les Caquets de l'Accouchée* (ed. E. Fournier) 6me Journée,
pp. 203–4.

3. Gournay, *L'Egalité des Hommes et des Femmes* (ed. M. Schiff) in *La Fille
d'Alliance de Montaigne-Marie de Gournay*, p. 65.

4. Louis Couvay, *L'Honnête Maîtresse*, Ch. 17, p. 98: 'Et premièrement,
qui est-ce qui m'osera nier que les dames ont une âme raisonnable
aussi bien que les hommes, et par conséquent un entendement
capable d'un parfait raisonnement? C'est-à-dire que quelques-unes
d'entre elles peuvent avoir de belles et hautes pensées, des concep-
tions fortes et relevées, des inventions aussi subtiles et aussi solides
que les meilleures têtes en peuvent avoir, puisqu'elles ne manquent
d'aucuns organes nécessaires, et que la nature leur peut donner le
tempérament propre pour élever leurs esprits à la dernière perfection.' See also Marguerite Buffet, *Nouvelles Observations sur la Langue
Française*, pp. 199 et seq.; Mme de Pringy, *Les Différents Caractères des
Femmes du Siècle*, Ch. 6, pp. 94–5; Samuel de Sorbière, *Lettres et
Discours*, p. 74.

5. Pierre Le Moyne, *La Galerie des Femmes Fortes*, pp. 251–2; C. M. D.
Noel, *Les Avantages du Sexe*, Ch. 14, pp. 90 et seq. '*Légèreté*' literally
means 'lightness', but with connotations of flightiness and moral
laxity.

6. Sappho, one of the dialogists in *Les Femmes Illustres*, published
under the name of Georges de Scudéry, goes so far as to say (Vol. I,
Harangue 20, p. 400) that for these reasons study should be permitted to women in preference to men who, when they indulge in
learned pursuits, 'steal' valuable time from the important business
of governing the world.

7. Nicolas Caussin, *La Cour Sainte*, 2me Partie, Vol. II, sect. 3, p. 468:
'Dieu nous ayant créés dans cette égalité des âmes, nous [femmes]
avons autant de droit aux connaissances qui nous sont nécessaires à
la grâce, à la vertu, et à la gloire, qu'en pourraient avoir les hommes.
Une chose avouerai-je, que la complexion d'un corps de femme
nous peut distiller en l'âme des inconstances, des infirmités, et des
passions, qui prendraient bien de l'essor si elles n'étaient réprimées
par la piété et par la raison.' Cf. François de Grenaille, *L'Honnête
Fille*, 3me Partie, Liv. 1, Ch. 1, p. 144: 'si l'esprit est nécessaire aux
hommes pour ne se pas laisser surprendre, il l'est beaucoup plus
aux filles qui sont sujettes à plus de surprises et ont moins de force
pour s'en garder'. See also Fléchier, *Œuvres Complètes*, Vol. IX,
Discours Académiques, No. 10, 'Les Passions des femmes sont plus
violentes que celles des hommes'; Mme de Pringy, *Différents Caractères des Femmes*, Ch. 6, p. 102; *Recueil Général des Questions Traitées
aux Conférences du Bureau d'Adresse, sur Toutes Sortes de Matières*,
Vol. IV, pp. 93–4; Saint-Gabriel, *Le Mérite des Dames*, 2me Partie,
pp. 159–60.

8. Urbain Chevreau, *Lettres Nouvelles*, No. 11, 'À M. Le Roy', pp. 50–1: 'les plus ignorantes ne sont pas toujours les plus chastes . . . En effet je m'imagine que les esprits sont aux femmes ce que les forteresses sont aux places, et qu'une niaise assiégée résisterait aussi peu qu'une ville qui n'aurait pas de quoi se défendre.' Cf. Jacques Du Bosc, *L'Honnête Femme*, 1re Partie, p. 114: 'celles qui n'ont pas assez de jugement pour connaître le vice, n'en ont pas davantage pour faire choix de la vertu . . . Le secours des lettres fortifie les meilleures inclinations, et ceux qui se persuadent que la lecture des livres est une école pour apprendre à faire le mal avec adresse, auraient meilleure grâce de croire que les dames y trouvent plus de moyens de se corriger que de se corrompre.' The original edition of Du Bosc's work having appeared in 1632, Molière in *L'Ecole des Femmes*, I. i.107 et seq., was merely repeating an old idea.

9. Caussin, *Cour Sainte*, 2me Partie, Vol. II, sect. 9, pp. 508–9; Du Bosc, *L'Honnête Femme*, 1re Partie, p. 115; De Grenaille, *L'Honnête Fille*, 3me Partie, Liv. 1, Ch. 1, p. 94.

10. De Grenaille, *L'Honnête Fille*, 3me Partie, Liv. 1, Ch. 1, p. 86: 'si les dames n'instruisent personne, elles s'instruisent elles-mêmes; si elles ne servent pas le public, elles se satisfont en particulier'. Cf. Du Bosc, *L'Honnête Femme*, 1re Partie, p. 113.

11. This anecdote, popularised by Montaigne in his *Essais* (ed. M. Rat) Vol. I, Liv. 1, Ch. 25, p. 150, is ridiculed by Du Bosc in *L'Honnête Femme*, 1re Partie, p. 112, and approved by Molière's Chrysale, with a slight variation, in *Femmes Savantes*, II, vii. See also Urbain Chevreau, *Chevraeana*, pp. 191–2.

12. La Bruyère, 'Des Femmes', 49, in *Caractères*.

13. Du Bosc, *L'Honnête Femme*, 1re Partie, p. 115; 3me Partie, sect. 1 passim.

14. Caussin, *Cour Sainte*, 2me Partie, Vol. II, sect. 9, p. 509.

15. Le Moyne, *Galerie des Femmes*, p. 253.

16. Saint-Gabriel in his *Mérite des Dames*, 3me Partie, p. 220, likewise preaches an empty revolution by taking refuge behind a barrage of rhetorical questions: 'Pourquoi exclure les dames des sciences? . . . Pourquoi leur interdire la prélature et la prêtrise? . . . Pourquoi leur ôter l'administration de la justice?'

17. Pierre Nicole, 'Combien les Entretiens des Hommes sont Dangereux', in *Essais de Morale*, Vol. II, 2me Partie, Ch. 6, p. 104.

18. Fénelon, *Traité de l'Education des Filles* (ed. P. Rousselot) Ch. 7, p. 80. For contemporary agreement with feminine concealment of knowledge, see D'Aumale, *Souvenirs*, p. 189; Guez de Balzac, letter to Mme Desloges, 20 Sept. 1628, in *Suite de la Seconde Partie des Lettres de M. de Balzac*, p. 266; Fontenelle, *Eloges des Académiciens de l'Académie Royale des Sciences, morts depuis l'an 1699*, in *Œuvres*, Vol. V, p. 306; Furetière, *Roman Bourgeois*, Vol. I, p. 111; La Fontaine, *Œuvres* (Collection Grands Ecrivains de la France) Vol. IX, p. 220; Chevalier de Méré, *Œuvres complètes* (ed. C. Boudhors) Vol. I, p. 9; Scarron, *Roman Comique*, 2me Partie, Ch. 8, p. 200; Scudéry, *Grand Cyrus*, Vol. X, Liv. 2, p. 678; Jean Regnauld de Segrais, *Segraisiana*, p. 102;

Mme de Villedieu, *Portrait des Faiblesses Humaines*, p. 254.

19. Mme de Maintenon, *Lettres et Entretiens*, Vol. II, pp. 296, 307, 308, 352.

20. Vincent de Paul, *Correspondance, Entretiens, Documents* (ed. P. Coste) Vol. III, p. 230.

21. Agrippa d'Aubigné, Mme de Maintenon's grandfather, pointed out to his daughters that knowledge was 'presque toujours inutile aux demoiselles de moyenne condition, comme vous', and likely to provide a rod for the back of a less well educated husband. See d'Aubigné, *Lettre à mes filles touchant les femmes doctes de notre siècle*, in *Œuvres* (Pléiade edn) p. 854.

22. De Grenaille, *L'Honnête Fille*, 3me Partie, Liv. 1, Ch. 1, p. 239.

23. Fortin de la Hoguette, *Testament*, 3me Partie, Ch. 3, p. 284. Cf. Montaigne, *Essais*, Vol. II, Liv. 3, Ch. 5, p. 281.

24. Mme de la Guette, *Mémoires* (ed. P. Moreau) p. 8. See also J.-J. Boileau, *La Vie de Mme la Duchesse de Liancourt, avec le Règlement qu'elle donna à sa petite-fille*, Art. 9, p. 50.

25. Bavière, *Correspondance* (trans. G. Brunet) Vol. I, p. 396.

26. Mme de Sévigné taught her daughter Mme de Grignan Italian (see her *Lettres*, Vol. II, p. 93). Mme d'Aubigné, mother of Mme de Maintenon, made the latter read and discuss Plutarch (see Maintenon, *Lettres et Entretiens*, Vol. II, p. 48; D'Aumale, *Souvenirs*, p. 17).

27. Montpensier, *Mémoires* (ed. A. Chéruel) Vol. III, p. 391.

28. Furetière, *Roman Bourgeois*, Vol. I, pp. 15, 21.

29. Mme de Maintenon, *Lettres et Entretiens*, Vol. I, pp. 360, 394; Vol. II, p. 114. Contemporary educationalists frequently stress that a girl should never be allowed out of her mother's sight. See Angélique Arnauld, *Lettres*, Vol. III, p. 430; Liancourt, *Règlement*, Art. 9, p. 52; Alexandre Varet, *De l'Education Chrétienne des Enfants*, Ch. 8, p. 148; De Vassetz, *De l'Obligation que les pères et mères ont d'instruire eux-mêmes leurs enfants*, Ch. 2, pp. 67–8.

30. Cardinal Richelieu, drawing up a list of servants to be engaged by the wife of his nephew, Du Pont de Courlay, in 1636, notes: 'Pour mesdemoiselles ses filles deux nourrices et une des femmes de chambre susdites, qui leur servira de gouvernante.' See Richelieu, *Lettres, Instructions Diplomatiques et Papiers d'Etat* (ed. Vicomte G. d'Avenel) Vol. V, p. 484. See also Marie de Gournay's preface to the *Essais* of Montaigne.

31. Audiger, *La Maison Réglée*, pp. 113–14; Claude Fleury, *Les Devoirs des Maîtres et des Domestiques*, p. 121; Maintenon, *Lettres* (ed. Langlois) Vol. III, pp. 128–9.

32. In the seventeenth century the moralising *Quatrains* of the Sieur de Pybrac or Pibrac, first published in 1574, became synonymous with a very narrow type of education. See Molière, *Sganarelle ou Le Cocu Imaginaire*, sc. 1.

33. Mme de Maintenon, *Lettres et Entretiens*, Vol. II, pp. 16–18. Cf. Fénelon, *Traité de l'Education des Filles*, Ch. 13.

34. Duc de Saint-Simon, *Mémoires* (ed. A. Chéruel) Vol. VI, p. 293.

35. Tallemant, *Historiette de Montauron*, Vol. VIII, p. 127.

36. Arnauld d'Andilly, *Journal Inédit* (ed. A. Halphen) p. 263; Tallemant, *Historiette de Menant et sa fille*, Vol. V, p. 167. François Hébert, *curé* of Versailles, learned from courtiers of Louis XIII's reign that it was quite customary then for girls to be given *gouvernantes* 'dont souvent la vertu était fort médiocre'. See Hébert, *Mémoires* (ed. G. Girard) p. 32.

37. Segrais, *Les Nouvelles Françaises ou Divertissements de la Princesse Aurélie*, Vol. I, p. 181; Tristan L'Hermite, 'La Gouvernante Importune', in *Les Amours et Autres Poésies Choisies* (ed. P. Camo) pp. 78–81; Mme de Villedieu, *Les Annales Galantes*, 6me Partie, p. 381. The theatre in the early part of the century is particularly fertile in portraits of the 'fragile' *gouvernante*. See Jean Auvray, *La Madonte* (1631); Pierre Du Ryer, *Argénis et Poliarque* (1630–1); Jean de Mairet, *La Virginie* (1635); Jean de Schelandre, *Tyr et Sidon* (ed. E. Viollet-le-Duc) (1628).

38. 'il n'y avait point de malice dont je ne m'avisasse pour me venger d'elle': Montpensier, *Mémoires*, Vol. I, p. 70.

39. Bavière, *Correspondance* (trans. Brunet) Vol. II, p. 35.

40. Liancourt, *Règlement*, Art. 9, p. 52; De Vassetz, *De l'Obligation*, Ch. 2, pp. 83, 141–3.

41. Abbé Genest, for example, tutor to Louis XIV's bastard Mlle de Blois (Françoise-Marie de Bourbon), was the son of a midwife who neglected his education completely until his early teens. See Paul Pellisson-Fontanier and Abbé d'Olivet, *Histoire de l'Académie Française* (ed. Ch. Livet) Vol. II, p. 370.

42. Méré, *Œuvres* (1692 edn) Vol. II, p. 28.

43. Tristan L'Hermite, *Amours et Autres Poésies Choisies*, p. 97.

44. Méré, *Œuvres* (1692 edn) Vol. II, p. 123.

45. Mme de Sévigné, *Lettres*, Vol. I, p. 370.

46. *Lettres de la Comtesse de La Fayette et de Gilles Ménage* (ed. H. Ashton) p. 99. The Comtesse's letters, with their repeated demands for attention, show that she gave all the platonic encouragement possible to a man who extolled her in prose and verse while acting in the capacity of general factotum.

47. The musician Michel Lambert married Mlle Dupuy, whom he taught to sing. See Tallemant, *Historiette de Niert, Lambert et Hilaire*, Vol. VIII, pp. 105–6. Louis de Lesclache, author of *Les avantages que les femmes peuvent recevoir de la philosophie et principalement de la morale* (1667), took to wife Mlle Giraut, a pupil of his who later gave philosophy lessons in her own right. See *Lettres en Vers* (ed. Rothschild) Vol. I, p. 389; Marguerite Buffet, *Traité sur les Eloges des Illustres Savantes Anciennes et Modernes*, appended to *Nouvelles Observations sur la Langue Française*, pp. 270–4.

48. Tallemant, *Historiette de Mme de Champré*, Vol. VI, p. 209.

49. This was the case of La Bruyère, ordered to extend his tutorship of the Duc de Bourbon to the latter's twelve-year-old bride after their marriage in 1685. La Bruyère's functions ceased the following year when the death of the Great Condé brought his pupils a step nearer to becoming the heads of the household. See La Bruyère's *Œuvres*

(Collection Grands Ecrivains de la France) Vol. II, pp. 500, 501–2, 507. See also Furetière, *Roman Bourgeois*, Vol. I, p. 110.

50. In Florent Dancourt's comedy *Les Bourgeoises à la Mode* (1692) II. vii, a young *bourgeoise* bitterly compares the interesting life of her coquettish and gambling stepmother with her own boring solitude: 'Je n'ai pour toute compagnie que des maîtres qui ne m'apprennent que des choses inutiles, la musique, la fable, l'histoire, la géographie: cela n'est-il pas bien divertissant?'

51. Conrart, *Mémoires*, Collection Michaud et Poujoulat, 3ᵐᵉ Sér., Vol. IV, p. 613.

52. J.-P. Nicéron, *Mémoires pour servir à l'histoire des hommes illustres*, Vol. III, pp. 126 et seq.

53. Ibid., Vol. XIV, pp. 168 et seq.; Fermel'huis, *Eloge Funèbre*, in *Archives de l'Art Français*, 2ᵐᵉ Sér., Vol. I, pp. 370 et seq. For examples other than the three quoted in the text see Jean-François de la Croix, *Dictionnaire Historique Portatif des Femmes Célèbres*, Art. 'Dupré'; Périer, *Lettres, Opuscules et Mémoires de Mme Périer et de Jacqueline, Sœurs de Pascal* (ed. P. Faugère) p. 436.

54. Charlotte de Bavière created a stir in 1718 by going to hear her son's bastard, the Abbé de Saint-Albin, defend his theses at the Sorbonne, 'où jamais femme n'était entrée'. See Dangeau, *Journal*, Vol. XVII, p. 248.

55. The *maître écrivain* or master scrivener who also privately tutored pupils in his home in elementary reading, writing and sometimes arithmetic, was *officially* banned from accepting girls. See Claude Joly, *Traité Historique des Ecoles Episcopales et Ecclésiastiques*, 3ᵐᵉ Partie, Ch. 23, p. 488.

56. For examples of the initiative of laywomen in this respect see below, Ch. 8, p. 121, and Ch. 13, p. 211.

57. Joly, *Traité*, 2ᵐᵉ Partie, Ch. 14, p. 270.

58. The *Etats Provinciaux* of Normandy called upon the king in their 1614 list of requests (Art. 36) to use revenues formerly employed to maintain leper hospitals for the upkeep of a schoolmaster. In the 1616 (Art. 18) and 1618 (Art. 28) lists they were still making the same supplication. See *Cahiers des Etats de Normandie sous les règnes de Louis XIII et de Louis XIV* (ed. Ch. de Robillard de Beaurepaire) Vol. I, pp. 115, 135, 189.

59. Joly, *Traité*, 2ᵐᵉ Partie, Ch. 17, pp. 294–5; 3ᵐᵉ Partie, Ch. 23, p. 491. See also Martin Sonnet, *Statuts et Règlements des Petites Ecoles de Paris* (1672), pp. 41 et seq.

60. Ursuline mistresses were advised not to 'mettre les filles de condition proche des plus pauvres et malpropres, pour ne leur point donner de dégoût'. See *Règlements des Religieuses Ursulines* (1751 edn) Liv. 1, 2ᵐᵉ Partie, Ch. 3, p. 166. The 'Approbation' of this work is dated 1652.

61. Angélique Arnauld, *Lettres*, Vol. III, p. 438. See also Thomas Du Fossé, *Mémoires* (ed. F. Bouquet) Vol. II, p. 64. Port-Royal took in only a very small number of boarders, daughters of élite Jansenist sympathisers.

62.   Mme de Maintenon, in *Lettres et Entretiens*, Vol. I, p. 17, describes
       teaching as 'une des plus grandes austérités que l'on puisse
       pratiquer, puisqu'il n'y en a guère qui n'aient quelque relâche, et
       que, dans l'instruction des enfants, il faut y employer toute la vie'.
       In her *Lettres* (ed. Langlois) Vol. IV, p. 458, she ends a letter to a
       'maîtresse des petites classes': 'il y a de grands dégoûts dans votre
       métier, mais ce sont là vos mortifications, et la récompense sera
       grande'. See also Angélique Arnauld, *Lettres*, Vol. I, p. 508.

63.   The remarks in this paragraph are based on the following works:
       Règlement des Religieuses Ursulines, Liv. 1, 1re Partie, Ch. 13, 'De
       l'ordre que les pensionnaires doivent garder'; *Coutumier ou Directoire
       des Religieuses Hospitalières de St Augustin* (1677), Ch. 21, 'Du Règle-
       ment des Pensionnaires'; *Usages des Religieuses de la Congrégation de
       Notre-Dame* (1690), 'Eclaircissements: Ordre de la journée pour les
       pensionnaires'; Maintenon, *Lettres et Entretiens*; Jacqueline Pascal,
       Règlement pour les Enfants [de Port-Royal] (1657) in *Jacqueline Pascal*
       (ed. V. Cousin).

64.   The only notable occasion on which regulations were relaxed was to
       allow pupils to act in edifying dramas. The performances of Racine's
       Esther (1689) and *Athalie* (1691) at Saint-Cyr are well known. See also
       Bossuet, *Correspondance* (eds C. Urbain and E. Levesque) Vol. VIII,
       Appendix 1, p. 478; Loret, *Muse Historique*, 15 Sept. 1652; *Journal
       d'un chanoine au diocèse de Cavaillon* in *Mémoires de l'Académie de Nîmes*,
       7me Sér., Vol. XXVI, p. 159; *Mercure Galant*, July 1685, pp. 186–7.

65.   This attitude, a cliché in instructional works generally (see, for
       example, Mme Guyon, *Instruction Chrétienne d'une mère à sa fille*, in
       Opuscules spirituels, Vol. II, sect. 5; Varet, *De l'Education Chrétienne
       des Enfants*, Ch. 8, pp. 144–5), is particularly pronounced in Mme de
       Maintenon's writings for Saint-Cyr. 'Tâchez de leur [aux élèves]
       donner de l'éloignement pour les hommes dont le commerce est
       toujours dangereux', she exhorts her class mistresses in1691, 'et de
       leur faire aimer la retraite, qui est la seule sûreté pour les femmes'
       (see Maintenon, *Lettres et Entretiens*, Vol. I, p. 82; also Vol. II, p. 330).
       She strongly disapproved, however, of the convent custom of never
       speaking to pupils about marriage (Ibid., Vol. II, pp. 270, 300).

66.   Both the Ursuline *Règlements* (Liv. 1, 1re Partie, Ch. 3, pp. 30–1) and
       those of the Congrégation de Notre-Dame (pp. 76–7) mention a
       morning and an evening hour of reading, the first session devoted
       to Latin books, the second to French.

67.   *Règlements des Ursulines*, Liv. 1, 1re Partie, Ch. 6, 'De la maîtresse de
       l'écriture'.

68.   Ibid., Ch. 8, 'De celle qui enseigne … l'orthographe', p. 87.

69.   *Congrégation de Notre-Dame*, Eclaircissements, pp. 77–8. This pre-
       scription is mentioned specifically in connection with day pupils,
       but it is permissible to suppose that it was also extended to the
       boarders.

70.   *Règlements des Ursulines*, Liv. 1, 1re Partie, Ch. 8, pp. 84–5.

71.   'Ouvrages manuels', mentioned in all the regulations, normally refer
       to some kind of sewing, though in addition pupils might be given

chores to do around the convent such as sweeping floors and laying tables.

72. *Règlements des Ursulines*, Liv. 1, 1re Partie, Ch. 3, p. 34: 'Elles [maîtresses] s'attacheront à les [élèves] rendre civiles et honnêtes, qu'elles parlent bien, se tiennent droites, et de bonne grâce, soient déférentes les unes aux autres, et portent du respect à toutes les religieuses.'

73. 'Il faut beaucoup exercer la mémoire des enfants; cela leur ouvre l'esprit, les occupe et les empêche de penser à mal' (Jacqueline Pascal, *Règlement*, p. 232).

74. Maintenon, *Lettres et Entretiens*, Vol. II, p. 228.

75. Ibid., Vol. I, pp. 226–7. Mme de Sablé, in a brief treatise significantly entitled 'Pour les enfants qu'on ne veut pas faire étudier à fond' in *La Marquise de Sablé et son Salon* (ed. N. Ivanoff) p. 150, stated that the study of history merely taught children a string of names, and facts irrelevant to modern life.

76. Maintenon, *Lettres et Entretiens*, Vol. I, p. 22. The study of modern foreign languages was not entirely unknown in the convents. See Blémur, *Eloges*, Vol. II, p. 189; Bossuet, *Correspondance*, Vol. VII, pp. 220–1; Claude Fleury, *Vie de la Vénérable Mère Marguerite d'Arbouze*, p. 5; Locatelli, *Voyage de France*, pp. 48, 49, 54–5.

77. De Vassetz, *De l'Obligation*, Ch. 2, p. 67. Arnauld d'Andilly sheds light on the level of female geographical knowledge with an anecdote about Mme Déageant, a government official's wife, who, hearing an ambassador from Venice mention 'la grandeur de la République', understood him to refer to a woman, for whom she proposed a match with the king's brother. See d'Andilly, *Mémoires*, Collection Michaud et Poujoulat, 2me Sér., Vol. IX, p. 427.

78. 'La peste des esprits, la ruine de la piété et la mère des hérésies' is Bossuet's definition of curiosity (see his 'Sermon pour le samedi après les cendres', 1660, in *Sermons*, Vol. I, p. 713). Cf. Fénelon ('La curiosité est une dangereuse maladie de l'esprit') in *Lettres spirituelles* (ed. Silvestre de Sacy) Vol. I, p. 52; and Mme de Maintenon ('On évite tout ce qui pourrait trop exciter leur [des élèves] esprit et leur curiosité') in *Lettres et Entretiens*, Vol. I, p. 10.

79. See below, Ch. 13.

80. Particularly true in comparison with the principal source of the play, Scarron's short story *La Précaution Inutile*, in *Œuvres* (1752 edn) Vol. III, p. 365, where Agnès's equivalent is described as 'sotte comme toutes les religieuses qui sont venues au monde sans esprit, et en ont été tirées dès l'enfance pour être enfermées dans un couvent'. Cf. *L'Ecole des Femmes*, I.i.135–6.

81. Fénelon, *Lettres spirituelles* (ed. Sacy) Vol. II, p. 432.

82. Mme de Staal, *Mémoires*, Collection Michaud et Poujoulat, 3me Sér., Vol. X, pp. 667–8. See also Comtesse de Murat, *Mémoires* (1740 edn) p. 7; Sévigné, *Lettres*, Vol. VIII, p. 427.

83. The ardour with which women involved themselves in legal matters may be judged from a letter of Mme de Lafayette to Ménage in 1657, concerning her husband's lawsuits: 'C'est une chose admirable que

ce que fait l'intérêt que [l'on] prend aux affaires. Si celles-ci n'étaient point les miennes je n'y comprendrais que le haut allemand et je les sais dans ma tête comme mon pater et dispute tous les jours contre nos gens d'affaires des choses dont je n'ai nulle connaissance et où mon intérêt seul me donne de la lumière.' See Mme de Lafayette, *Lettres* (ed. Ashton) p. 77.

84.   See Charles de Ribbe, *Une Grande Dame dans son Ménage au temps de Louis XIV*, pp. 351, 353–4, 361, 362, 371.

85.   Olivier de Serres, *Théâtre d'Agriculture et Ménage des Champs*, Liv. 8, Ch. 4, pp. 888 et seq.

86.   Scudéry, *Grand Cyrus*, Vol. X, Liv. 2, p. 727.

87.   See Méré's letters to the Duchesse de Lesdiguières, in *Œuvres* (1692 edn) Vol. II, expecially No. 144, p. 286: 'Vous me faites quelquefois l'honneur de m'écrire des lettres d'un air si délicat et si galant . . . Et vous m'en écrivez d'autres d'un tour grave et profond, comme celle où vous me questionnez sur l'immortalité de l'âme: et cette autre dans laquelle vous me demandez si nous devons croire qu'il y ait plusieurs mondes, et si ce grand nombre d'astres que nous appelons des étoiles ne sont point autant de soleils qui les éclairent.'

88.   Mme de Motteville, *Mémoires* (ed. F. Riaux) Vol. I, p. xxxii. The biographer hastens to add: 'Cela toutefois ne la délustre point, parce que le grand commerce que la Reine a eu avec les premiers de son siècle, la grande connaissance qu'elle a du monde, et la longue expérience des affaires et des intrigues de la cour . . . ont tout à fait réparé ce qui pouvait lui manquer du côté des livres.'

89.   Montpensier, *Mémoires*, Vol. II, p. 243; Murat, *Mémoires*, pp. 37–8; Princesse Palatine (Anne de Gonzague), *Mémoires*, pp. 70–1.

90.   *Caquets de l'Accouchée*, 3me Journée, p. 112.

91.   Huet, *Memoirs* (trans. from Latin by John Aikin) Bk 6, pp. 346–7.

92.   Where contemporaries prescribe books for female reading they are almost always of the devout kind. See Balzac, Letter to Mme de Campagnole, 15 April 1635, in *Suite de la Seconde Partie des Lettres*, pp. 282 et seq.; De Grenaille, *L'Honnête Fille*, 3me Partie, Liv. 1, Ch. 2, p. 241; Mme Guyon, *Instruction Chrétienne*, sect. 3, p. 429; Claude Joly, *Lettre à une jeune damoiselle de condition pour lui apprendre à se gouverner sagement*, in *Les Deux Livres de l'Etat du Mariage*, pp. 295–6. See also H.-J. Martin, *Livre, Pouvoirs et Société à Paris au XVIIe Siècle*, Vol. I, pp. 531–2; Vol. II, pp. 951–2. Mention is occasionally made of more original collections. Mme Lescot, wife of a Parisian municipal official, had a 'curieuse bibliothèque' containing 'un nombre prodigieux de bons livres, et de rares manuscrits' (Samuel Chappuzeau, in the dedication of *Le Colin-Maillard*, 1662). Mlle Chataignères, according to Bodeau de Somaize's *Dictionnaire des Précieuses* (ed. C. Livet) Vol. I, pp. 59–60, had a library of chemistry books to assist her in her experiments. The Protestant Mme de Lorme had a collection of all the novels published between 1642 and 1657, according to the *Journal du Voyage de Deux Jeunes Hollandais à Paris en 1656–8* (ed. A.-P. Faugère) p. 176.

93. Descartes, Letter to Père Vatier, 22 Feb. 1638, in *Correspondance* (eds Ch. Adam and G. Milhaud) Vol. II, p. 134.

94. A further stage of diffusion was reached when certain writers took to putting difficult subjects into verse. See Furetière, *Furetiriana*, p. 13; *Mercure Galant*, July 1684, pp. 5–15; Pierre Perrin, *Œuvres de Poésie*, pp. 3 et seq.; Saint-Martin, *Les Causes et les Admirables Effets des Météores* (British Library manuscript).

95. By René Bary and Abbé de Gérard respectively.

96. In Segrais's *Nouvelles Françaises*, Vol. I, p. 18, Princess Aurélie holds that 'Les beaux romans ne sont pas sans instruction ... principalement depuis qu'on y mêle l'histoire, et quand ceux qui les écrivent, savants dans les mœurs des nations, imaginent des aventures qui s'y rapportent, et qui nous en instruisent.' Madeleine de Scudéry cites the case of a friend 'qui n'eût jamais connu Xénophon ni Hérodote, si elle n'eût jamais lu le *Cyrus*, et qui en le lisant s'est accoutumée à aimer l'histoire et même la fable'. See *Mlle de Scudéry: Sa Vie et sa Correspondance* (eds E. Rathery and Boutron) p. 295. The theatre, which used much the same settings as the novels, and indeed often drew plots from them, also played an instructional role in this respect.

97. Somaize, *Dictionnaire*, Vol. I, p. 69.

98. Founded by Denis de Sallo in 1665, the *Journal*, which summarised the latest publications of scholars and men of letters, attracted the attention of 'des princesses curieuses'. See Jean Chapelain, *Lettres* (ed. P. Tamizey de Larroque) Vol. II, p. 397.

99. In the absence of fashion magazines, dolls dressed in the latest modes were circulated to fashion-conscious ladies in the provinces. See Furetière, *Roman Bourgeois*, Vol. I, pp. 53–4; *La Journée des Madrigaux* (ed. E. Colombey) p. 16.

100. See *Recueil Général des Questions Traitées aux Conférences du Bureau d'Adresse* (1660), No. 25, 'Quel est le plus noble de l'homme ou de la femme?'; No. 26, 'De la beauté'; No. 46, 'Du caprice des femmes'; No. 65, 'Si le mari et la femme doivent être de même humeur'; No. 106, 'S'il est expédient aux femmes d'être savantes'; No. 141, 'Lequel vaut mieux, se marier ou ne se marier point?'; and others.

101. Huygens, *Journal de Voyage à Paris et à Londres* (ed. H. L. Brugmans) in *Le Séjour de Christiaan Huygens à Paris*, pp. 138 (bis), 141, 145, 150, 154, 157. For Mmes de Guederville and de Bonneveau, see Marguerite Buffet, *Eloges des Illustres Savantes*, pp. 264–8; Jean de la Forge, *Le Cercle des Femmes Savantes* ('Barsine' and 'Galerite'); Somaize, *Dictionnaire*, Vol. I, p. 103 ('Galerice'). For the popularity of Rohault's 'conférences' with women generally, see Jean Clerselier's preface to Rohault's *Œuvres Posthumes* (1690), and below, p. 273, note 145.

102. Fontenelle, *Eloges*, p. 147.

103. Ibid., pp. 306–7.

104. In an anonymous critique of Cartesianism entitled *Voyage du Monde de Descartes* (1691), 2me Partie, p. 161, Aristotle is made to state that

'la mode d'être philosophe ne serait pas plus durable parmi les dames françaises que les autres modes'.

105. *Mercure Galant*, Nov. 1683, pp. 159–63.
106. Ibid., Apr. 1700, pp. 123–4.
107. Ladies were thus present when Colbert's son Seignelay defended his theses at the Collège de Clermont on 31 August 1668 (see Saint-Maurice, *Lettres*, Vol. I, p. 219) and when Abbé Le Boistel, whose father worked for Louvois, was put through his academic paces in the presence of the omnipotent War Minister (see *Mercure Galant*, Dec. 1677, p. 102). See also Loret, *Muse Historique*, 13 July 1658, 16 Aug. 1659, 11 Aug. 1663.
108. For a resumé of the question see E. Allain, *L'Instruction Primaire en France avant la Révolution*. P. Rousselot's monumental *Histoire de l'Education des Femmes en France* concentrates on the better known theorists of the period.
109. Towards the end of the nineteenth century Louis Maggiolo, rector of the Academy of Nancy, carried out research into the incidence of female signatures on marriage contracts in various French provinces at selected periods beginning with the late seventeenth century. His findings informed the articles of Ferdinand Buisson's *Dictionnaire de Pédagogie et d'Instruction Primaire en France* (1882–7), notably that entitled 'Illettrés', which alleged that for the period 1686–90 13.97 per cent of wives were able to sign as opposed to 29.06 per cent of husbands. Buisson himself, however, cast doubt on the validity of this method of research by noting that the signatures were often in the same writing as the text of a contract drafted by a priest (ibid., Art. 'Finistère'). More recently M. Fleury and P. Valmary in their article 'Les Progrès de l'Instruction Elémentaire de Louis XIV à Napoléon III' in *Population* (1957) pp. 71 et seq. and F. Furet and J. Ozouf in their book *Lire et Ecrire: L'Alphabétisation des Français de Calvin à Jules Ferry* (1977) have criticised other shortcomings in Maggiolo's methods, whilst accepting the global significance of the figures at which he arrived and adding little with respect to earlier decades of the century. The existence of 'popular' literature such as that composing the Bibliothèque Bleue of Troyes, analysed by R. Mandrou in *De la Culture Populaire aux XVIIe et XVIIIe Siècles*, offers no clue to the level of female literacy, since the author alleges (*Introduction*, p. 18) that these works were destined to be read aloud by literate male members of the community such as the priest or the beadle. See also R. Muchembled, *Culture Populaire et Culture des Elites dans la France Moderne (XV–XVIIIe Siècles)*, 2me Partie, Ch. 6.
110. The playing of a wind instrument like a flute is noted to be a great rarity amongst women. See *Noel sur les dames de la Cour* (1696) in *Recueil de Maurepas* (1865 edn), Vol. II, p. 273, n. 3. Perhaps disfigurement of the shape of the mouth was feared. Cf. Du Bellay, *La Deffence et Illustration de la Langue Francoyse* (ed. H. Chamard) Liv. 1, Ch. 9, p. 55.
111. Primi Visconti, *Mémoires sur la Cour de Louis XIV* (ed. J. Lemoine) p. 58.

112. *Mercure Galant*, June 1678, p. 225. See also Apr. 1685, p. 90.
113. Duchesse de Montpensier, *La Galerie des Portraits* (ed. E. de Barthélemy) p. 277. Mlle Petit was one of the female celebrities whom Huygens visited in Paris. See Huygens, *Journal de Voyage*, pp. 148, 155.
114. Duc de Sully, *Mémoires* (1767 edn) Vol. VIII, Supplément, p. 342.
115. Saint-Simon, *Mémoires*, Vol. VIII, p. 152.
116. Examples in Gautier de Costes de La Calprenède, *Cassandre*, Vol. IV, p. 476; Scudéry, *Grand Cyrus*, Vol. II, Liv. 2, p. 869.
117. J.-J. Boileau, *Vie de Mme la Duchesse de Liancourt*, p. vi.
118. Voiture, *Œuvres* (ed. A. Ubicini) Vol. I, p. 36. See also Tallemant, *Historiette de Mme de Rambouillet*, Vol. III, p. 213.
119. *Mémoires Inédits sur la Vie et les Ouvrages des Membres de l'Académie Royale de Peinture et de Sculpture* (ed. L. Dussieux) Vol. II, p. 87.
120. *Archives de l'Art Français*, 2me Sér., Vol. I, p. 304.
121. André Félibien, *Entretiens sur les Vies et sur les Ouvrages des Plus Excellents Peintres Anciens et Modernes* (1967 reprint), No. 7, pp. 400–1; Montpensier, *Galerie des Portraits*, p. 277.
122. Mlle Chéron, for example (see above, p. 24), and Catherine Perrot, who dedicated to one of her pupils, the Princesse de Guémené, *Les Leçons Royales contenant la pratique universelle de la peinture en miniature* (reprinted at the end of Félibien's *Entretiens* in the edn cited).
123. See below, Ch. 11.
124. Pellisson-Fontanier and d'Olivet, *Histoire de l'Académie*, Vol. II, p. 379; René Rapin, *Mémoires* (ed. L. Aubineau) Vol. I, pp. 109, 443. The same pious consideration dictated the occasional learning of Hebrew. See Bayle, *Dictionnaire*, Arts. 'Révérend-De-Bougy F' and 'Rohan, Anne de, B'; Huet, *Memoirs*, Bk 5, p. 234; La Croix, *Dictionnaire*, Art. 'Chéron'; Ménage, *Menagiana*, 1re Partie, p. 207. In all these instances, except the last, the women concerned were Protestants.
125. La Croix, *Dictionnaire*, Art. 'Dupré'; *Mercure Galant*, Feb. 1690, p. 233; Scudéry, *Correspondance*, p. 168; Sévigné, *Lettres*, Vol. V, pp. 249–50. See also references above to Mme Dacier and Mme de Castries, pp. 24 and 30.
126. Apart from the first two references given in n. 124 above, see Blémur, *Eloges*, Vol. II, pp. 189, 347; Bossuet, *Correspondance*, Vol. VI, p. 497; *Mercure Galant*, Nov. 1690, p. 9.
127. Examples in La Croix, *Dictionnaire*, Art. 'Patin'; *Mercure Galant*, Nov. 1681, p. 103; Titon du Tillet, *Le Parnasse Français*, p. 507.
128. Examples: Duchesse de Bouillon (Abbé de Chaulieu, *Œuvres*, Vol. I, p. 144); Mme de Brassac (Tallemant, *Historiette de M. et Mme de Brassac*, Vol. VI, p. 86); Maréchale de Clérembault (Bussy-Rabutin, *Correspondance*, Vol. V, pp. 34–5); Mme Deshoulières (*Epître à M. le Pelletier de Souzi*, in *Poésies de Mme et de Mlle Deshoulières*, Vol. II, p. 62); Mlle de Gournay (*Vie de la Demoiselle de Gournay*, appended to Liv. 2 of *Avis ou Présents*, 1641); Mme de Lafayette (Segrais, *Segraisiana*, p. 36); Mme de Maintenon

(D'Aumale, *Souvenirs*, p. 189); Comtesse de Marannes (La Croix, *Dictionnaire*, Art. 'Parthenai, Anne de'); Mme de Sévigné (*Lettres*, Vol. III, p. 150); Mlle des Vertus (Tallemant, *Historiette de la Comtesse des Vertus*, Vol. VI, p. 125); Mlle de Villenne (Montpensier, *Galerie des Portraits*, p. 233).

129. See Mme d'Aulnoy, *Mémoires de la Cour d'Espagne*, passim; D'Aumale, *Souvenirs*, p. 189; Bussy-Rabutin, *Correspondance*, Vol. I, pp. 221, 397; Ménage, *Menagiana*, 2me Partie, p. 7; *Mercure Galant*, July 1677, p. 76; Nov. 1679, p. 108; Jan. 1681, p. 293; Nov. 1690, p. 9; Aug. 1691, p. 259; Montpensier, *Galerie des Portraits*, pp. 133, 135, 139, 233, 254, 277, 426, 458, and *Mémoires*, Vol. III, p. 54; Motteville, *Mémoires*, Vol. I, p. 33; Mme de Sablé, 'Préface' to 1678 edn of *Maximes*; Sévigné, *Lettres*, Vol. I, pp. 375–6, Vol. II, pp. 93, 116 and others; Somaize, *Dictionnaire*, Vol. I, pp. 42, 68, 237; Tallemant, *Historiette de Mme de Rambouillet*, Vol. III, p. 212; Mme de Villars, *Lettres*, pp. 15, 32.

130. Dominique Bouhours, *Entretiens d'Ariste et d'Eugène* (ed. R. Radouant) *Sur la Langue Française*, p. 63: 'le français est infiniment éloigné de la rudesse de toutes les langues du nord, dont la plupart des mots écorchent le gosier de ceux qui parlent, et les oreilles de ceux qui écoutent'.

131. For a knowledge of German see Ezéchiel Spanheim, *Relation de la Cour de France en 1690* (ed. E. Bourgeois) p. 173; Tallemant, *Historiette du Chancelier de Bellièvre*, Vol. II, p. 97; Mme de Villedieu, *Mémoires de la Vie de Henriette Sylvie de Molière*, 1re Partie, p. 10.

132. Sévigné, *Lettres*, Vol. IX, p. 63.

133. Mme de Maintenon, *Lettres* (ed. Langlois) Vol. III, p. 170. See also Murat, *Mémoires*, p. 38; Scudéry, *Grand Cyrus*, Vol. X, Liv. 2, p. 680.

134. Saint-Evremond, *Lettres*, Vol. II, p. 207. The Duchesse's education had been extremely summary. See Mazarin, *Lettres du Cardinal Mazarin pendant son ministère* (eds A. Chéruel and Vicomte G. d'Avenel) Vol. IX, p. 436.

135. Segrais, *Segraisiana*, p. 34.

136. Montpensier, *Mémoires*, Vol. II, p. 17.

137. Montpensier, *Galerie des Portraits*, p. 167. See also Mme de Montespan's letters in *Mme de Montespan et Louis XIV* (ed. P. Clément) pp. 309, 310.

138. Sorbière begins thus a letter of 19 Oct. 1657 to one Mme ***: 'J'ai lu une partie de la lettre dont il vous a plu de m'honorer, et j'en ai deviné l'autre par la suite d'un très beau sens, qui répare le défaut de votre mauvaise écriture. Je vois bien en cette négligence de votre plume, ou en cette promptitude de votre main, que vous avez une habitude toute formée à penser subtilement et à vous exprimer de bonne grâce'. See Sorbière, *Lettres et Discours*, No. 48, pp. 354–5. See also Fénelon, *Correspondance: Commentaires de J. Orcibal*, Vol. II, pp. 262–3; Sévigné, *Lettres*, Vol. IX, pp. 76–7.

139. Charles Perrault, *L'Apologie des Femmes*, 'Préface', p. 35.

140. The *précieuses* were, however, credited with an attempt to simplify the spelling of French. See Somaize, *Dictionnaire*, Vol. I, Art. 'Orthographe'.

141. Saint-Evremond to Duchesse Mazarin: 'il n'est pas de la dignité d'une personne si considérable de bien orthographier. Il faut laisser cela aux auteurs'. See Saint-Evremond, *Lettres*, Vol. II, p. 227. Mme de Maintenon told the nuns at Saint-Cyr to avoid scrupulous exactitude in writing and spelling because 'cela sentait trop la pédanterie dans une personne de notre sexe, et l'envie de faire la savante'. See Dames de Saint-Cyr, *Mémoires sur Mme de Maintenon* (1846 edn) p. 257.

142. Malebranche, *De la Recherche de la Vérité* (ed. G. Rodis-Lewis) Liv. 2, 2me Partie, Ch. 1, sect. 1. Cf. La Bruyère, 'Des Femmes', 49, in *Caractères*.

143. Baillet, *Vie de Monsieur Descartes*, Vol. II, Liv. 8, Ch. 6, p. 500. Contemporary biographers credit other philosophers of the period with appreciating this particular disposition in women. See *Malebranche Vivant: Documents Biographiques et Bibliographiques* (ed. A. Robinet) in Malebranche, *Œuvres Complètes*, Vol. XX, pp. 26, 28. See also above, p. 33.

144. Sévigné, *Lettres*, Vol. III, p. 216. Mme de Sévigné herself was avowedly less well acquainted with the doctrine than her daughter (ibid., Vol. IV, p. 522).

145. Sablé, *Les Amis de la Marquise de Sablé: Recueil de Lettres des Principaux Habitués de son Salon* (ed. E. de Barthélemy) p. 306.

146. Staal, *Mémoires*, p. 669.

147. See De Bougainville's dedication to the Duchesse of *L'anti-Lucrèce, poème sur la Religion Naturelle, composé par M. le Cardinal de Polignac*. Other noted *cartésiennes* of the period included the philosopher's niece Mlle Descartes (Bouhours, *Recueil de Vers Choisis*, pp. 129 et seq.), Mlle Dupré, known as the *Cartésienne* (Sévigné, *Lettres*, Vol. III, p. 221; Titon du Tillet, *Parnasse Français*, p. 507), and Mlle de la Vigne (Bouhours, *Recueil*, pp. 27–32). Familiarity with Cartesian doctrines is also shown by women who opposed them, for example Mme de la Sablière (La Fontaine, *Fables*, Liv. 9, 'Discours à Mme de la Sablière) and the little known Geneviève Forest (*L'Histoire de la Philosophie des Héros*, 1681, Vol. I, Liv. 2, pp. 108–9, and *Le Fantôme du Sage*, 1681, 4me Partie, p. 27). The anti-Cartesian royal historiographer De Launay, who held conferences from 1656 onwards on, amongst other things, a modified form of Gassendism, had court ladies amongst his listeners (C. Le Maire, *Paris Ancien et Nouveau*, Vol. III, pp. 444–5).

148. See V. Cousin, *Fragments Philosophiques pour faire suite aux cours de l'histoire de la philosophie* (4me edn) Vol. III, Appendix, p. 515, also p. 480; *Le Père André, Jésuite: Documents pour servir à l'histoire philosophique, religieuse et littéraire du 18e siècle* (eds A. Charma and G. Mancel) Vol. I, p. 39. A list of the principal female *malebranchistes* is contained in Malebranche's *Œuvres Complètes*, Vol. XX, pp. 28, 189–201.

149. Bavière, *Lettres Inédites* (ed. Rolland) p. 231; Boileau, *Satire 10*, v. 426; Fontenelle, *Eloges*, pp. 470–1; Tallemant, *Historiette de M. et Mme de Brassac*, Vol. VI, p. 86.

150. *Mercure Galant*, Apr. 1685, p. 88; Apr. 1697, pp. 43 et seq.; Feb. 1698, p. 276. See also Loret, *Muse Historique*, 14 Apr. 1652, for the early interest shown by women in Pascal's calculating machine.

151. A poster affixed in Paris by the Italian herborist Paolo Boccone on his arrival there *circa* 1670 invites ladies of the capital to follow the example of two 'dames de condition' of Lyon whom he has taught, 'lesquelles en trois mois de temps connurent presque toutes les plantes qui naissent dans cette contrée'. See Boccone, *Avis aux Personnes d'Esprit et aux Curieux* (British Library).

152. For chemistry enthusiasts see Fontenelle, *Eloges*, p. 392, and above, n. 92.

153. Concern over women dabbling in alchemy was expressed more than once during the century. See Abbé de Gérard, *Philosophie des Gens de Cour*, 3me Entretien, pp. 63–4; Mlle de Gournay, *Peinture de Mœurs* (ed. Schiff) v. 94 et seq.; Lesclache, *Avantages que les femmes peuvent recevoir de la philosophie*, Ch. 1, p. 5.

154. Boileau, *Satire 10*, vv. 435–6; G. J. Duverney, *Œuvres Anatomiques*, prefatory 'Eloge', pp. x–xi.

155. Boileau, *Satire 10*, vv. 427–30; Abbé de Gérard, *Philosophie*, 3me Entretien, pp. 63–4; Lesclache, *Avantages*, Ch. 1, p. 5; Loret, *Muse Historique*, 10 Jan. 1665; Molière, *Femmes Savantes*, II.vii; Sourches, *Mémoires*, Vol. X, p. 79. Women even took to writing about astronomy: Jeanne Dumée published in 1680 some 'Entretiens sur l'Opinion de Copernic touchant la Mobilité de la Terre'; see *Journal des Savants*, Vol. VIII, 1682, pp. 304–5.

156. The heroine of Chappuzeau's *Académie des Femmes* (1661) is a pedantic *cartésienne* whose long-lost husband returns at the end of the play and orders her abruptly to get rid of all her books and attend to her household.

157. The ambiguous permission accorded to women in Molière's *Les Femmes Savantes* (1672), I.iii, to possess 'des clartés de tout' does not alter the fact that the sex's pursuit of higher forms of education is equated with mental derangement, and that Molière everywhere in his theatre prefers by implication the kind of untrained, unadorned common sense manifested here by Henriette, by the heroines of the *Critique de l'Ecole des Femmes*, and by Eliante in *Le Misanthrope*.

158. De la Roque, in *Journal des Savants*, 4 Mar. 1686: 'Depuis que les mathématiciens ont trouvé le secret de s'introduire jusque dans les ruelles et de faire passer dans le cabinet des dames les termes d'une science aussi solide et aussi sérieuse que la mathématique, par le moyen du *Mercure Galant*, on dit que l'empire de la galanterie va en déroute, qu'on n'y parle plus que problèmes, corollaires, théorèmes, angle droit, angle obtus, rhomboïdes, etc., et qu'il s'est trouvé depuis peu deux demoiselles dans Paris à qui ces sortes de connaissances ont tellement brouillé la cervelle, que l'une n'a point voulu entendre à une proposition de mariage, à moins que la personne qui la recherchait n'apprît l'art de faire des lunettes dont le *Mercure Galant* a si souvent parlé, et que l'autre a rejeté un parfaitement honnête homme, parce que dans un temps qu'elle lui

avait prescrit, il n'avait pu rien produire de nouveau sur la quadrature du cercle.'

159. Fatouville's *Fille Savante* (1690) portrays an insufferable *précieuse* who reads Aristotle and possesses mathematical instruments, but is finally converted and proclaims that 'la vraie science d'une femme, c'est d'être belle; l'étude et les livres ne servent qu'à la rendre insupportable'.

160. Boileau's educational ideal for women, as it emerges from his *Satire 10* (1694), is that of Port-Royal and Saint-Cyr, two establishments narrow in their outlook and practices.

CHAPTER 3

1. Maintenon, *Lettres et Entretiens*, Vol. II, p. 251.
2. Courtin, *Traité de la Jalousie*, 2me Partie, Ch. 2, p. 387.
3. Nicole, 'Pensées Diverses', in *Essais de Morale*, Vol. VI, p. 323.
4. Sales, *Lettres* (ed. Garnier) p. 501.
5. Le Moyne, *Galerie des Femmes Fortes*, p. 231. See also Antoine Arnauld, *Lettres*, Vol. I, pp. 69–70; Caussin, *Cour Sainte*, 1re Partie, Vol. I, Liv. 3, sect. 24, p. 604; Du Bosc, *L'Honnête Femme*, 2me Partie, p. 302; Du Fossé, *Mémoires*, Vol. I, p. 144.
6. La Rochefoucauld, *Maximes*, No. 113; La Bruyère, 'Des Biens de Fortune', 61, in *Caractères*; Maintenon, *Lettres et Entretiens*, Vol. II, p. 300.
7. D'Urfé, *l'Astrée* (ed. H. Vaganay) Vol. III, Liv. 10, p. 567. See also Mlle de la Roche-Guilhen, *Histoire des Favorites*, 1re Partie, p. 116; Scudéry, *Grand Cyrus*, Vol. IX, Liv. 3, pp. 1103–4.
8. Pierre Corneille, *Polyeucte*, I.iii and IV.iii. See also Molière, *Sganarelle*, I.v, and *L'Impromptu de Versailles*, sc. 1; Montfleury (Antoine Jacob), *Les Bêtes Raisonnables*, sc. 8; Jean Rotrou, *Les Ménechmes*, III.iii; Georges de Scudéry, *Orante*, II.i.
9. *Variétés Historiques et Littéraires* (ed. E. Fournier) Vol. IV, pp. 81–5.
10. Courval Sonnet, *Œuvres Poétiques* (ed. P. Blanchemain) Vol. III.
11. Molé, *Mémoires* (ed. A. Champollion-Figeac) Vol. II, p. 227. Montaigne had already said 'On ne se marie pas pour soi, quoi qu'on die; on se marie autant ou plus pour sa postérité, pour sa famille.' See his *Essais*, Vol. II, Liv. 3, Ch. 5, p. 273.
12. See German Vuillart's account of his negotiation of the marriage of Racine's daughter Marie-Catherine in the winter of 1698–9, in *Lettres à Louis de Préfontaine* (ed. R. Clark), p. 177.
13. Joachim Trotti de La Chétardie, *Instruction pour une jeune princesse*, p. 146.
14. Ménage, *Menagiana*, 2me Partie, p. 382: 'J'ai ouï dire à Mme la Maréchale d'Humières qu'une honnête fille peut bien dire, qu'elle ne veut pas d'un tel pour son mari, mais qu'elle ne peut pas dire aussi: Je veux un tel.' See also Motteville, *Mémoires*, Vol. II, p. 43.
15. Charron, *De la Sagesse*, Vol. I, Liv. 1, Ch. 48, p. 354.
16. The marriage of Henriette-Marie, youngest daughter of Henri IV,

to Charles I of England took place in 1625. Its unhappy sequel is well known.

17. Charles II of Spain is represented thus in the letters of Marie de Villars, wife of the French ambassador to Spain at the time of the king's marriage in 1679 to Marie-Louise d'Orléans, a niece of Louis XIV. The letters give a vivid picture of the boring, cloistered existence led by the new queen, who died ten years later. See Marie de Villars, *Lettres*, pp. 89, 99, 111, 227.

18. Marquis de Montglat, *Mémoires*, Collection Michaud et Poujoulat, 3me Sér., Vol. V, p. 25.

19. Comte de Montrésor, *Mémoires*, Collection Michaud et Poujoulat, 3me Sér., Vol. III, p. 209.

20. Richelieu was fully aware of this fact. See Richelieu, *Mémoires* (ed. Société de l'Histoire de France) Vol. VII, pp. 81–2. La Valette's ill-treatment of his devoted second wife was common knowledge. See Montpensier, *Mémoires*, Vol. III, pp. 239–43; Omer Talon, *Mémoires*, Collection Michaud et Poujoulat, 3me Sér., Vol. VI, p. 64.

21. The life of the Princesse de Condé can be traced in the following sources: Bussy-Rabutin, *Correspondance*, Vol. I, pp. 378–9, Vol. V, p. 305; Pierre Lenet, *Mémoires*, Collection Michaud et Poujoulat, 3me Sér., Vol. II, 1re Partie, passim; Montpensier, *Mémoires*, Vol. I, pp. 49 et seq., Vol. IV, pp. 254 et seq., 528; Motteville, *Mémoires*, Vol. III, pp. 178–9, 208, 230; Patin, *Lettres*, Vol. III, pp. 776, 777; Saint-Maurice, *Lettres*, Vol. II, pp. 10–11, 28–9; Saint-Simon, *Mémoires*, Vol. III, p. 178; Sévigné, *Lettres*, Vol. II, pp. 39–40, 49, Vol. VIII, p. 5; Spanheim, *Relation*, pp. 190–1.

22. Marquis de Fontenay-Mareuil, *Mémoires*, Collection Michaud et Poujoulat, 2me Sér., Vol. V, p. 153.

23. Richelieu, *Lettres*, Vol. II, p. 277; Vol. III, p. 489, n. 1; Vol. VII, p. 527; Tallemant, *Historiette de la Duchesse d'Aiguillon*, Vol. III, pp. 12–13.

24. Montglat, *Mémoires*, p. 48. The same author credits Richelieu with also contemplating a marriage between his niece and the unworthy Gaston d'Orléans (ibid., pp. 25, 49).

25. Examples: Caussin, *Cour Sainte*, 1re Partie, Vol. I, Liv. 3, sect. 35, p. 622; Dulorens, *Premières Satires* (ed. D. Jouast) No. 11, p. 84; L'Estoile, *Journal*, Vol. II, p. 449; Visconti, *Mémoires*, p. 251.

26. Louis Bourdaloue, *Sermon pour le 2me dimanche après l'épiphanie*, in *Sermons pour les Dimanches*, Vol. I, p. 68.

27. Furetière, *Roman Bourgeois*, Vol. I, p. 26.

28. The *franc*, like the *livre (tournois)* to which reference will be made later in the chapter, was worth 20 *sous*, and the two terms were used more or less interchangeably. The silver *écu* was worth three *livres*, the gold *écu* almost double. In Louis XIV's reign the Spanish *pistole* was equivalent to eleven *livres*. See Locke, *Travels in France*, p. 218.

29. Dangeau, *Journal*, Vol. III, p. 151; Sourches, *Mémoires*, Vol. III, p. 249.

30. Sully, *Mémoires*, Vol. IV, Liv. 12, pp. 15 et seq.; Richelieu, *Testament Politique* (ed. L. André) 1re Partie, Ch. 4, sect. 4, p. 251.

31. *Mémoires tirés des Archives de la Police de Paris* (ed. J. Peuchet) Vol. I,

p. 202; Sourches, *Mémoires*, Vol. XIII, p. 434, n. 1. The theatre of the late seventeenth century introduces rapacious aristocrats who sponge on wealthy women. See, for example, Dancourt's *Chevalier à la Mode* and *Folle Enchère*.

32. Saint-Simon, *Mémoires*, Vol. III, p. 121.
33. Tallemant, *Historiette du Maréchal de Gramont*, Vol. IV, pp. 97–8. For other examples see Daniel de Cosnac, *Mémoires* (ed. Comte Jules de Cosnac) Vol. I, p. 131; Saint-Simon, *Mémoires*, Vol. I, p. 75; Tallemant, *Historiette de l'Abbé Tallemant*, Vol. VIII, p. 182.
34. Montpensier, *Mémoires*, Vol. I, p. 62.
35. Bussy-Rabutin, *Correspondance*, Vol. V, p. 528.
36. Ibid., Vol. V, p. 182; Sévigné, *Lettres*, Vol. X, p. 456; Sourches, *Mémoires*, Vol. I, p. 135; Tallemant, *Historiette de Mlle et Mme de Marolles*, Vol. VIII.
37. A single entry in Héroard's *Journal*, Vol. II, pp. 243–4, contains the announcement of the betrothal in 1620 of the future Duchesse de Longueville (Anne-Geneviève de Bourbon), then aged six months, to the seven-year-old Prince de Joinville, and that of the Duc de Luynes's one-year-old daughter to a six-year-old prince of Lorraine. Neither marriage was ever celebrated.
38. Sully, *Mémoires*, Vol. V, Liv. 16, pp. 64–5, Liv. 20, pp. 440–3.
39. Ibid., Vol. VII, Liv. 25, pp. 7 et seq.
40. Bussy-Rabutin, *Correspondance*, Vol. III, pp. 442–3.
41. La Fontaine, *Œuvres*, Vol. IX, pp. 61–2.
42. See Le Grand Condé and Le Duc d'Enghien, *Lettres Inédites à Marie-Louise de Gonzague, Reine de Pologne, sur la Cour de Louis XIV* (ed. E. Magne) pp. 228–9, 336; Gatien Courtilz de Sandras, *Annales de la Cour et de Paris pour les années 1697 et 1698*, Vol. I, pp. 211–12; Maintenon, *Lettres* (ed. Langlois) Vol. II, p. 499; *Mercure Galant*, Dec. 1693, pp. 59–60; Comte de Souvigny, *Mémoires* (ed. Baron Ludovic de Cotenson) Vol. II, p. 72.
43. Varet, *De l'Education Chrétienne des Enfants*, Préface, pp. 2–3.
44. Mme de la Guette, *Mémoires*, p. 25.
45. Ferrand, *Histoire*, in *Lettres de la Présidente Ferrand au Baron de Breteuil* (ed. E. Asse) p. 192.
46. Mme Guyon, *Vie*, Ch. 6, pp. 50–1. For similar examples see Dangeau, *Journal*, Vol. IV, p. 275; Charles Perrault, *Mémoires* (Librairie des Bibliophiles edn) p. 120; Scudéry, *Grand Cyrus*, Vol. VI, Liv. 1, p. 169 (concerning Mme de Sablé); Tallemant, *Historiette de Mlle Garnier*, Vol. VIII, p. 31.
47. This attitude was often satirised in plays of the early seventeenth century. See Mairet, *Sylvie* (ed. J. Marsan) II.iv; Pichou, *Les Folies de Cardénio* (ed. E. Fournier) I.iv; Rotrou, *La Bague de l'Oubli*, II.ii; Veronneau, *L'Impuissance* (ed. E. Viollet-le-Duc) I.i. Dramatists perhaps remembered Andromache's words in Euripides' *Daughters of Troy* (Loeb Classical Library translation) v.665–6: 'And yet one night, they say, unknits the knot/Of woman's hate of any husband's couch.'
48. Abbé Arnauld professes complete incomprehension of those who

embark on loveless marriages: 'Je sais bien que c'est un sentiment assez particulier en ce temps-ci, et qui peut être traité de ridicule par ceux qui ne cherchent que de l'argent; mais je sais bien aussi que ceux-ci s'exposent souvent à quelque chose de pis que le ridicule.' See Arnauld, *Mémoires*, Collection Michaud et Poujoulat, 2ᵐᵉ Sér., Vol. IX, pp. 495–6. Furetière advises that young people of both sexes should be allowed to keep company under proper surveillance, and ridicules the custom of 'quantité de bons bourgeois' for contenting themselves with one mute glance at their future bride before marriage: Furetière, *Roman Bourgeois*, Vol. I, pp. 171, 184. Even the reactionary Caussin admits: 'C'est une chose ridicule de mettre des mariés au lit nuptial sans aucune connaissance, comme si on les avait portés là dans un sac.' See Caussin, *Cour Sainte*, 1ʳᵉ Partie, Vol. I, Liv. 3, sect. 36, p. 633.

49. Saint-Evremond, *Œuvres en Prose* (ed. R. Ternois) Vol. II, p. 28.
50. For the scarcity of novels dealing with married women prior to the 1660s see Furetière, *Roman Bourgeois*, Vol. I, p. 200.
51. Examples: Fléchier, *Pensées sur la nécessité de donner une éducation chrétienne aux enfants*, Nos 7 and 11, in *Œuvres*, Vol. V, pp. 451, 453; Liancourt, *Règlement*, Art. 9, p. 55; Mainville, *Du Bonheur et du Malheur du Mariage*, Lettre 11, p. 90; Louis Petit, *Satires Générales* (ed. O. de Gourcuff) No. 6, pp. 67–8.
52. Examples from the novel: Jean de Lannel, *Le Roman Satirique*, Liv. 1, pp. 109–12, Liv. 5, p. 978; Michel de Pure, *La Prétieuse* [sic] (ed. E. Magne) Vol. I, 2ᵐᵉ Partie, pp. 276 et seq., Vol. II, 3ᵐᵉ Partie, p. 66; Scudéry, *Grand Cyrus*, Vol. VI, Liv. 3, p. 1036, Vol. VII, Liv. 1, p. 115, and *Clélie*, 3ᵐᵉ Partie, Liv. 1, p. 593; D'Urfé, *L'Astrée*, Vol. III, Liv. 5, p. 245, Vol. IV, Liv. 3, p. 155. Examples from the theatre: Desmarets de Saint-Sorlin, *Mirame*, IV.iv; Du Ryer, *Alcimédon*, V.iii; Mairet, *Silvanire* (ed. R. Otto) III.iii and V.xi; Molière, *Tartuffe*, II.iii, and comedies passim; Rotrou, *L'Heureuse Constance*, I.iii, and *La Pèlerine Amoureuse*, I.i and III.vii.
53. *Déclaration sur les Formalités du Mariage*, 1639, Art. 2, in Isambert, *Anciennes Lois Françaises*, Vol. XVI, p. 522. Verbal *sommations* were customarily made to the parents by a minor legal official in the presence of other members of the family representing the petitioner (see Sourches, *Mémoires*, Vol. III, p. 249). The Paris Parlement took steps in 1692 to tighten regulations by decreeing that royal notaries should bear formal witness to acts of *sommation*. See *Recueil d'Edits et d'Ordonnances Royaux, augmenté sur l'édition de Messires Pierre Néron et Etienne Girard*, Vol. II, pp. 835–6 (this work will henceforth be referred to as *Recueil Néron*). Protestants had the right, by the disposition of the *Discipline Ecclésiastique* of May 1559, Art. 37, to appeal to the Consistory against obdurate parents.
54. By the terms of the *Ordonnance de Blois*, May 1579, Art. 42 (see Isambert, Vol. XIV, p. 392).
55. Nicolas Fabri de Peiresc, writing to Pierre Dupuy in 1627 about the frequent contraventions of the ordinances concerning clandestine marriages, tells how the efforts of the Provence Parlement to enforce

them are thwarted by the attitude of girls and their parents: 'je vous dirai que Messieurs de notre compagnie ont bien cru de pouvoir condamner à mort pour le rapt et l'ont fait souvent, n'y ayant pas de si fort mariage que la corde ne rompe, comme on dit. Mais cela n'a pas été capable de donner assez de terreur, et le consentement réciproque survenu à cela de s'entremarier du gré même des parents les plus indignés a vaincu la rigueur des juges et les a fait incliner à en laisser l'option aux querellés, de sorte que l'espérance que les filles ont eue de venir à ce point-là à l'extrémité les a fait plus librement abandonner à ces mariages clandestins.' See Peiresc, *Lettres* (ed. P. Tamizey de Larroque) Vol. I, p. 203.

56. Jules H. P. de La Mesnardière, 'Rondeau ou l'Enlèvement de Mlle de Bouteville', in *Poésies*, p. 32; François Sarasin, 'Ballade d'Enlever en Amour', in *Poésies* (ed. O. Uzanne) pp. 97–9; Voiture, *Œuvres*, Vol. II, pp. 380 et seq.

57. Bussy-Rabutin, *Mémoires* (ed. L. Lalanne) Vol. I, p. 163; Dubuisson-Aubenay, *Journal des Guerres Civiles* (ed. G. Saige) Vol. I, p. 6; Motteville, *Mémoires*, Vol. I, pp. 225–6; Olivier Lefèvre d'Ormesson, *Journal* (ed. A. Chéruel) Vol. I, p. 235; Tallemant, *Historiette de Mlle de Sallenauve*, Vol. VII, and *Mme d'Ableiges*, Vol. IX.

58. Dangeau, *Journal*, Vol. I, p. 62; Henri IV, *Lettres Missives*, Vol. VII, pp. 339–40; Richelieu, *Lettres*, Vol. VI, p. 39.

59. See below, Ch. 13, n. 7.

60. L'Estoile, *Journal*, Vol. II, p. 440.

61. Lorct, *Muse Historique*, 3 Dec. 1651; Patin, *Lettres*, Vol. II, pp. 601–2; Renaud de Sévigné, *Correspondance du Chevalier de Sévigné et de Christine de France* (eds J. Lemoine and F. Saulnier) p. 15; Tallemant, *Historiette de Varin*, Vol. IX.

62. Malebranche, *Traité de Morale* (1684) (ed. M. Adam) in *Œuvres Complètes*, Vol. XI, 2me Partie, Ch. 10, sect. 20: 'Que les enfants de leur côté obéissent à leurs parents comme à Dieu même, dont ils tiennent la place; qu'ils soient devant eux dans le respect, comme étant en la présence du Tout-puissant.' See also Charron, *De la Sagesse*, Vol. III, Liv. 3, Ch. 14, p. 120; De Vassetz, *De l'Obligation*, Ch. 6, p. 236; Paccori, *Avis Salutaires*, sect. 54, pp. 59–60. On the Protestant side Calvin, in *Institution de la Religion Chrétienne*, Liv. 2, Ch. 8, sect. 36, had quoted approvingly the scriptural precept that disobedience of parents should be punished by death.

63. Furetière, *Roman Bourgeois*, Vol. I, pp. 180–1; Nicolas Restif de la Bretonne, *Vie de mon père* (1931 edn) p. 12; Sully, *Mémoires, Supplément*, Vol. VIII, p. 334; Tallemant, *Historiette de Mme de Gondran*, Vol. VII, p. 198, n. 1.

64. Whence the use of corporal punishment, especially for the very young. See Liancourt, *Règlement*, Art. 9, p. 51; Maintenon, *Lettres* (ed. Langlois) Vol. IV, p. 457.

65. Spanheim, *Relation*, p. 391; Tallemant, *Historiette de la Comtesse de la Suze*, Vol. V, p. 212; Visconti, *Mémoires*, p. 227.

66. Louis XIV was apparently concerned to exercise sparingly his right to order daughters to be imprisoned on the instances of their family.

See *Correspondance Administrative sous Louis XIV* (ed. G. B. Depping) Vol. II, p. 267. Case histories in Frantz Funck-Brentano, *Les Lettres de Cachet*, Ch. 11, pp. 103 et seq., are taken mostly from the eighteenth century.

67. In those areas subject to the *droit coutumier* girls were emancipated by marriage, but in certain regions governed by the *droit écrit* offspring remained under paternal authority, whatever their age, until a formal emancipation had been granted by the father. See Guyot, *Répertoire Universel et Raisonné de Jurisprudence*, Art. 'Puissance Paternelle'. For the terms *droit coutumier* and *droit écrit* see Ch. 4 below.

68. Protestants were required by Art. 23 of the Edict of Nantes (1598) to abide by Catholic regulations concerning 'degrés de consanguinité et affinité' in marriage.

69. Guyot, *Répertoire*, Art. 'Empêchements'.

70. Antoine Arnauld, *Lettres*, Vol. VII, pp. 182 et seq; Nicolas Fontaine, *Mémoires pour servir à l'histoire de Port-Royal*, Vol. III, pp. 348 et seq.

71. Thiers, *Traité des Superstitions*, Vol. IV, Liv. 10, Ch. 2.

72. This is the usual pattern of the princely marriages reported, for example, in the *Mercure Galant*. The signing of the contract took place immediately before the betrothal ceremony, which in turn preceded the wedding by at the most twenty-four hours, and often considerably fewer.

73. Antoine Denesde, *Journal*, in *Archives Historiques du Poitou*, Vol. XV, p. 223 (betrothal on 14 Jan. 1635, marriage on 15 Jan.); Dusson, *Mémoires*, in *Mémoires de la Société Eduenne*, Nouvelle Sér., Vol. IV. p. 214 (betrothal on 27 Oct. 1670, marriage on 10 Nov.).

74. Pierre Boyer, *Livre de Raison*, p. 210 (betrothal on 8 Dec. 1620, marriage on 4 Feb. 1621); Robert Hodeau, *Mémoires Inédits*, in *Mémoires de la Société des Antiquaires du Centre*, Vol. VIII, p. 211 (betrothal on 28 Jan. 1626, marriage on 6 July); Simon Le Marchand, *Journal*, pp. 15, 19 (betrothal on 30 Jan. 1614, marriage on 31 July); Samuel Robert, *Livre de Raison*, in *Archives Historiques de la Saintonge et de l'Aunis*, Vol. XII, pp. 328–9 (betrothal on 17 July 1639, marriage on 15 Aug.).

75. The four witnesses, who were required to sign the marriage contract, were understood to be male. See Guyot, *Répertoire*, Art. 'Mariage'.

76. Isambert, *Anciennes Lois Françaises*, Vol. XVI, pp. 521–2.

77. *Code Matrimonial*, 1770, Vol. I, p. 187.

78. Isambert, *Anciennes Lois Françaises*, Vol. XX, pp. 293–4.

79. For the frequency with which advantage had been taken of these dispensations see Jean Plantavit de la Pause, Evêque de Lodève, *Journal des Actes (1626–1630)*, in *Annales du Midi*, 1913, passim.

80. Guyot, *Répertoire*, Art. 'Bans de Mariage'.

81. Paul de Vendée, *Journal* (ed. A. Drochon) pp. 40–1 (contract on 14 Mar. 1613, *fiançailles* on 15 Mar., marriage on 28 Apr.). See also above, n. 72.

82. Robert Hodeau, *Mémoires Inédits*, p. 233 (*fiançailles* on 31 Oct. 1660, contract on 16 Jan. 1661, marriage on 17 Jan.).

83. *Les Livres de Raison dans le Lyonnais* (ed. A. Vachez) p. 38. This latter procedure was associated with provinces governed by the *droit écrit*.

84. *Nouveau Coutumier Général* (ed. Charles A. Bourdot de Richebourg) Vol. III, 2me Partie, 1583 *Coutume* of Orléans, Ch. 10, Art. 202, p. 790: 'En traité de mariage, et avant la foi baillée et bénédiction nuptiale, homme et femme peuvent faire et apposer telles conditions, douaires, donations, et autres conventions que bon leur semblera.'

85. Guyot, *Répertoire*, Art. 'Articles de Mariage'.

86. Sourches, *Mémoires*, Vol. XII, p. 256, n. 1.

87. Furetière, *Roman Bourgeois*, Vol. I, pp. 31–2. See also *Caquets de l'Accouchée*, 1re Journée, pp. 13–16, 4me Journée, p. 129.

88. Colbert, *Lettres, Instructions et Mémoires* (ed. P. Clément) Vol. VI, pp. 13–14.

89. When Samuel Robert married Madeleine Merlat in 1639 he brought to the community a nominal 20 000 *livres* and his bride 6000, 'le tout en attendant la future succession des dits pères et mères (see Robert, *Livre de Raison*, p. 328).

90. Marie de Jassaud, marrying the *intendant* Foucault in 1675, brought him a dowry of 120 000 *livres* composed largely of sums owed by her parents' debtors (see Foucault, *Mémoires*, pp. 34–5), most of which were never paid.

91. Coulanges, *Mémoires* (ed. M. Monmerqué) p. 391; Dangeau, *Journal*, Vol. I, p. 368, Vol. II, pp. 24–5, 97, 353, Vol. IV, pp. 67, 456, Vol. V, pp. 174, 204, 349, Vol. VI, p. 281; D'Ormesson, *Journal*, Vol. I, p. 173.

92. Dangeau, *Journal*, Vol. I, p. 252, Vol. IV, p. 7, Vol. V, p. 314; Demaillasson, *Journal*, pp. 3, 137; *Livres de Raison Limousins et Marchois* (ed. Guibert) pp. 288, 302, 389, 390; and *Nouveau Recueil de Registres Domestiques Limousins et Marchois*, Vol. I, pp. 70–1.

93. On the death of the Princesse Palatine in 1684, 60 000 *écus* of her inheritance had to be earmarked for the unpaid dowry of her daughter the Princesse de Salms, married in 1671 (Dangeau, *Journal*, Vol. I, p. 34); see also Bavière, *Lettres Inédites* (ed. Rolland) p. 31.

94. Bussy-Rabutin, *Correspondance*, Vol. III, p. 205; Dangeau, *Journal*, Vol. I, p. 366, Vol. V, p. 367, Vol. VI, p. 29; Motteville, *Mémoires*, Vol. III, p. 29, Vol. IV, p. 238; Sourches, *Mémoires*, Vol. V, p. 217.

95. Sourches, *Mémoires*, Vol. III, p. 483.

96. *Caquets de l'Accouchée*, 1re Journée, p. 15.

97. Dangeau, *Journal*, Vol. III, p. 328.

98. A. Babeau, *La Vie Rurale dans l'Ancienne France*, Appendix 5, pp. 354–6; Brécourt, *La Noce de Village*, sc. 5.

99. Bussy-Rabutin, *Correspondance*, Vol. III, p. 39; Condé, *Lettres à la Reine de Pologne*, p. 167; Thiers, *Traité des Superstitions*, Vol. IV, Liv. 10, Ch. 3, p. 484; Nicolas Venette, *Tableau de l'amour considéré dans l'etat du mariage*, 2me Partie, Ch. 5, p. 167.

100.   Thiers, *Traité des Superstitions*, Vol. IV, Liv. 10, Ch. 3, pp. 492 et seq.
        Protestants similarly forbade marriages on holy communion days
        and at times of public fasting. See Haag, 'Pièces Justificatives', in
        France Protestante, pp. 101–2.
101.   Thiers, *Traité des Superstitions*, Vol. IV, Liv. 10, Ch. 4, pp. 508–10,
        Chs 7, 8, passim.
102.   Courtin, *Traité de la Jalousie*, 1re Partie, Ch. 5, p. 95, Ch. 6, p. 150.
103.   Brackenhoffer, *Voyage en France*, p. 114.
104.   *Journal du Voyage de Deux Hollandais à Paris*, p. 108.
105.   Michel de Marolles, *Mémoires*, 1re Partie, pp. 12–13.
106.   Letouf, *Mémoires*, Vol. I, p. 16; *Mercure Galant*, Oct. 1679, 2me
        Partie, p. 72.
107.   Loret, *Muse Historique*, 21 Feb. 1654; François de Malherbe, *Œuvres*
        (Collection Grands Ecrivains de la France) Vol. III, p. 92; *Mercure
        Galant*, Apr. 1684, p. 322, July 1688, p. 253, Feb. 1692, p. 318.
108.   Locatelli, *Voyage de France*, p. 67.
109.   For specimen Catholic condemnations of rowdy nuptials see Le
        Moyne, *Galerie des Femmes Fortes*, pp. 231–2; François de Sales,
        Introduction à la Vie Dévote (ed. C. Florisoone) Vol. II, p. 105.
        Protestant elders, after originally leaving it to the conscience of the
        faithful to decide if they were 'assez forts pour s'abstenir des
        dissolutions et autres péchés, que l'on commet ordinairement dans
        ces sortes d'assemblées, et aussi de les reprendre', finally banned
        attendance at Catholic weddings in 1596. Their attitude was a little
        self-righteous since the National Synod of 1617 called upon all their
        churches to 'réprimer soigneusement toutes les insolences' com-
        mitted at Protestant weddings. Sobriety was enforced by a decree
        of the royal council in 1670 which forbade more than twelve guests
        at Protestant baptisms and weddings. See Haag, 'Pièces Justifica-
        tives', in *France Protestante*, pp. 77, 215–16, 296, 372.
110.   *Mercure Galant*, Aug. 1687, 1re Partie, pp. 265–70; Thiers, *Traité des
        Superstitions*, Vol. IV, Liv. 10, Ch. 4, p. 524.
111.   The number of pieces of money varied, but was customarily fixed
        at thirteen. When, for example, Jacques de Fontainemarie, council-
        lor at the Customs and Excise Court (*Cour des Aides et Finances*) of
        Guyenne, married Jeanne de Saint-Angel at Bordeaux in 1661 he
        gave her 'treize louis d'or pour arrhes et quelques petites nippes
        avec un rond d'or'. See Fontainemarie, *Livre de Raison* (ed. P.
        Tamizey de Larroque) p. 13.
112.   Courtin, *Traité de la Jalousie*, 1re Partie, Ch. 5, pp. 95–6.
113.   Courtin, ibid., p. 96; Thiers, *Traité des Superstitions*, Vol. IV, Liv. 10,
        Ch. 4, p. 518.
114.   See an edict of Jan. 1629, Art. 134, regulating the number of
        courses at feasts, in Nicolas de La Mare, *Traité de la Police*, Vol. I,
        Liv. 3, Tit. 2, Ch. 3, p. 432.
115.   Venette, *Tableau de l'amour*, 3me Partie, Ch. 3, p. 266.
116.   Fléchier, *Mémoires sur les Grands Jours d'Auvergne en 1665* (ed. F.
        Dauphin) pp. 154–5.
117.   Pierre Davity, *Les Etats, Empires et Principautés du Monde*, 'Discours

de la France', p. 82; *Mercure Galant*, Dec. 1678, p. 22.

118. Furetière, *Roman Bourgeois*, Vol. I, p. 200: 'on a maintenant la sotte coutume de dépenser en meubles, présents et frais de noce la moitié de la dot d'une femme, et quelquefois le tout'. See also Montfleury, *La Femme Juge et Partie*, III.ii.

119. Davity, *Etats du Monde*, p. 82; Lauder, *Journals*, p. 124; Locatelli, *Voyage de France*, p. 69; Charles Sorel, *Histoire Comique de Francion* (ed. E. Roy) Vol. II, Liv. 6, p. 179.

120. Examples: Lenet, *Mémoires*, p. 452; *Lettres en Vers* (ed. Rothschild) Vol. I, pp. 390, 609–10, Vol. II, pp. 648, 713–16; Loret, *Muse Histori-que*, 21 Feb. 1654, 26 Feb. 1656, 1 July 1662; *Mercure Galant*, July 1677, p. 103, Sept. 1679, p. 110; Montpensier, *Mémoires*, Vol. IV, p. 74; Motteville, *Mémoires*, Vol. IV, p. 418; D'Ormesson, *Journal*, Vol. II, p. 285.

121. Bussy-Rabutin, *Correspondance*, Vol. V, p. 41.

122. D'Ormesson, *Journal*, Vol. II, p. 487: 'J'ai appris que le soir des fiançailles de sa fille [Colbert] avait dansé, dans son domestique, deux courantes, et fort bien.' See also Perdrix, *Chronique de J. G. Perdrix, Conseiller du Comte George de Montbéliard*, in *Compte-Rendu de la Situation et des Travaux de la Société d'Emulation de Montbéliard*, 1857, pp. 125–6.

123. *Mercure Galant*, June 1678, pp. 122–8; Dec. 1696, pp. 260–2.

124. One preacher, delivering a harangue to a titled bride, was heard to say: 'Madame, nous souhaitons qu'il puisse sortir autant de héros de votre ventre, qu'il en sortit jadis du cheval de Troie!' See Conrart, *Mémoires*, in Appendix Ch. 4 of *Valentin Conrart* (eds Kerviler and Barthélemy) p. 642.

125. Fléchier, *Grands Jours d'Auvergne*, p. 200.

126. Patin, *Lettres*, Vol. II, p. 186.

127. Sourches, *Mémoires*, Vol. I, p. 280, n. 1; Vol. V, p. 368, n. 1. The custom of separating young partners after a token bedding together was also practised amongst the aristocracy and upper bourgeoisie. See *Mercure Galant*, Feb. 1679, p. 171; Nov. 1680, pp. 268–9.

128. Dangeau, *Journal*, Vol. VI, p. 321; La Bruyère, 'De la Ville', 19, in *Caractères*; Sévigné, *Lettres*, Vol. VI, p. 120, Vol. VIII, p. 31, Vol. IX, p. 375; Sourches, *Mémoires*, Vol. II, p. 181.

129. Bayle, *Dictionnaire*, Art. 'Gonzague, Isabelle de, A'; *Lettres en Vers* (ed. Rothschild) Vol. II, pp. 677–8.

130. Tallemant, *Historiette de Mme de Gondran*, Vol. VII, p. 191.

131. Venette, *Tableau de l'Amour*, 2me Partie, Ch. 3, p. 99.

CHAPTER 4

1. Du Bosc, *L'Honnête Femme*, 2me Partie, p. 307: 'Pour ne point mentir, le malheur ou la félicité des mariages dépend bien souvent de leur [des femmes] conduite.'

2. Ibid., p. 313. See also Caussin, *Cour Sainte*, 1re Partie, Vol. I, Liv. 3,

sect. 36, p. 637; Fortin de La Hoguette, *Testament*, 3me Partie, Ch. 2, p. 261.

3. Courtin, *Traité de la Jalousie*, 2me Partie, Ch. 5, p. 453. Cf. *Ephesians* 5: 22–3.

4. Antoine Arnauld, *Lettres*, Vol. I, p. 69; Caussin, *Cour Sainte*, 2me Partie, Vol. II, sect. 10, p. 514; Charron, *De La Sagesse*, Vol. III, Liv. 3, Ch. 12, p. 62; Courtin, *Traité de la Jalousie*, 2me Partie, Ch. 2, p. 354; Liancourt, *Règlement*, Art. 4, p. 14; Malebranche, *Traité de Morale*, 2me Partie, Ch. 10, sect. 5; Motteville, *Mémoires*, Vol. I, p. 28; Vincent de Paul, *Correspondance*, Vol. II, p. 163.

5. Charron, *De la Sagesse*, Vol. III, Liv. 3, Ch. 12, p. 62. See also Hilarion de Coste, *Eloges et Vies des Reines, des Princesses, et des Dames illustres en Piété, en Courage, et en Doctrine*, 1re Partie, p. 62; Vigoureux, *La Défense des Femmes*, pp. 44–5. The mirror image is that of Plutarch in his 'Advice to Bride and Groom', in *Moralia* (Loeb Classical Library edn) Vol. II, sect. 4, pp. 309–10.

6. Guyot, *Répertoire*, Art. 'Paraphernal'.

7. See the *Digest*, Bk 23, Tit. 3, Art. 7.

8. See Justinian, *Institutes*, Bk 2, Tit. 8, and Guyot, *Répertoire*, Art. 'Dot'.

9. *Recueil Néron*, Vol. I, p. 722. The edict was renewed for Brittany in 1683 (ibid., Vol. II, pp. 188–9).

10. Ibid., Vol. II, p. 74. See also Guyot, *Répertoire*, Art. 'Senatus Consulte Velléien'.

11. According to the glossary of old French legal terms appended to the *Institutes Coutumières* of Antoine Loysel (ed. E. Laboulaye) *conquêts* was the general term for goods acquired during marriage while *acquêts* applied more specifically to *immeubles* acquired by means other than direct inheritance or donation (q.v., 'Acquest' and 'Conquest'). In legal documents of the seventeenth century the two terms are often coupled.

12. *Nouveau Coutumier Général*, Vol. III, 1re Partie, Tit. 10, Art. 225, p. 46.

13. Paris *Coutume*, Tit. 14, Art. 296, p. 51: 'Le mari par son testament . . . ne peut disposer des biens meubles et conquêts immeubles communs entre lui et sa femme, au préjudice de la dite femme, ni de la moitié qui lui peut appartenir en iceux par le trépas de son dit mari.'

14. Paris *Coutume*, Tit. 10, Art. 226, p. 46: 'Le mari ne peut vendre, échanger, faire partage ou licitation, charger, obliger, ni hypothéquer le propre héritage de sa femme, sans le consentement de sa dite femme, et icelle de par lui autorisée à cette fin.'

15. Ibid., Tit. 10, Art. 223, p. 45: 'La femme mariée ne peut vendre, aliéner ni hypothéquer ses héritages sans l'autorité et consentement exprès de son mari. Et si elle fait aucun contrat sans l'autorité et consentement de son dit mari, tel contrat est nul'.

16. Under certain *Coutumes* this right was extended to the fiancé. See *Coutumes* of Metz and Pays Messin, Tit. 1, Art. 9 (*Nouveau Coutumier Général*, Vol. II, 1re Partie, p. 396) and Auvergne, Ch. 14, Art. 1 (ibid., Vol. IV, 1re Partie, p. 1168).

17. See n. 15 above.

18. Paris *Coutume*, Tit. 10, Art. 224, p. 46: 'Femme ne peut ester en jugement sans le consentement de son mari, si elle n'est autorisée ou séparée par justice, et la dite séparation exécutée.'

19. Guyot, *Répertoire*, Art. 'Autorisation'.

20. Paris *Coutume*, Tit. 10, Art. 234, p. 46: 'Une femme mariée ne se peut obliger sans le consentement de son mari, si elle n'est séparée par effet, ou marchande publique'. For the rights of the separated wife see below, Ch. 6.

21. Examples are the *Coutume* of Nivernais, Ch. 23, Art. 1 (*Nouveau Coutumier Général*, Vol. III, 2me Partie, p. 1146) and that of Normandy, Art. 417 (ibid., Vol. IV, 1re Partie, p. 81).

22. Loysel, *Institutes Coutumières*, Vol. I, 2me Partie, Règle 22, pp. 159–60.

23. Charron, *De la Sagesse*, Vol. III, Liv. 3, Ch. 12, p. 62.

24. De Grenaille, *L'Honnête Mariage*, Liv. 3, Ch. 1, p. 225.

25. *Coutume* of Brittany, Tit. 20, Art. 451 (*Nouveau Coutumier Général*, Vol. IV, 1re Partie, p. 390): 'Femme qui laisse volontairement son mari et s'en va avec autre, et n'est avec son mari au temps de la mort, et aussi si elle le laisse et ne fait son devoir de le garder, et elle le peut faire, au cas que le mari ne la refuserait, jaçoit qu'elle ne s'en aille avec un autre, elle ne doit être endouairée'.

26. De Grenaille, *L'Honnête Mariage*, Liv. 3, Ch. 1, pp. 222–4.

27. Examples: Louise Bourgeoise, *Observations*, Liv. 2, pp. 40, 73; Conrart, *Mémoires*, p. 594; André Delort, *Mémoires de ce qui s'est passé de plus remarquable dans Montpellier depuis 1622 jusqu'en 1691* (ed. L. Gaudin) pp. 272–3; Mme Dunoyer, *Lettres Historiques et Galantes*, Vol. I, p. 207; Antoine Jacmon, *Mémoires* (ed. A. Chassaing) pp. 220–1; *Journal du Voyage de Deux Hollandais à Paris*, p. 169; Loret, *Muse Historique*, 23 July 1650, 14 May 1651; Samuel Robert, *Livre de Raison*, p. 368; Tallemant, *Historiettes*: 'Arnauld de Corbeville', Vol. IV, p. 58, 'Coustenan', Vol. VI, 'St Germain Beaupré', Vol. VII, p. 158, 'Turcan', Vol. VII, p. 224, 'Mlle et Mme de Marolles', Vol. VIII, p. 230; Saint-Simon, *Mémoires*, Vol. IV, pp. 293, 344.

28. Caussin, *Cour Sainte*, 2me Partie, Vol. II, sect. 4, p. 474: 'La femme qui a rencontré un mauvais mari n'est pas peu à plaindre, mais encore trouve-t-elle qu'étant dans la sujétion, elle n'est pas si éloignée du rang auquel nature l'a placée.'

29. Tallemant, *Historiette des Naïvetés*, Vol. X, p. 168: 'Il y a à Montmartre un tableau de Notre-Seigneur et de la Madeleine, de la bouche de laquelle sort un écriteau où il y a "Raboni". Les bonnes femmes en ont fait un Saint Rabonny qui "rabonnit" les maris, et on y fait des neuvaines pour cela.' See also Ménage, *Menagiana*, 2me Partie, p. 361; Henri Sauval, *Histoire des Antiquités de Paris* (1969 reprint) Vol. I, p. 357.

30. The remarks in this paragraph would not refer to girls of the lowest classes, who are generally regarded, on the authority of scattered examples unearthed by modern French social historians, as having married in their middle or late twenties. See, for example, P. Deyon, *Amiens, Capitale Provinciale*, p. 36; J.-L. Flandrin, *Familles, parenté,*

maison, *sexualité dans l'ancienne société*, p. 183; P. Goubert, *Beauvais et Le Beauvaisis de 1600 à 1730*, p. 32. Nor could it be claimed that such girls would be ignorant of the essentials of copulation, given the close physical proximity in which they lived with relatives and domestic animals.

31. Montpensier, *Mémoires*, Vol. I, p. 51; Sourches, *Mémoires*, Vol. V, p. 215.

32. Examples: Marquise de Courcelles, *Mémoires* (ed. P. Pougin) pp. 58–60; *Mercure Galant*, June 1680, p. 194, June 1682, pp. 41–2, Feb. 1694, p. 328, May 1694, pp. 306–7, Nov. 1694, p. 253, Mar. 1697, p. 248, June 1698, p. 264; Perrault, *Mémoires*, p. 120.

33. On Madeleine de Scudéry's love map, the Carte du Tendre, in Vol. I of her novel *Clélie*, it was possible for lovers to sail straight up the River Inclination to the ideal city of Tender-on-Inclination, but they might overshoot the mark and follow the river on into the Dangerous Sea, beyond which lay the Unknown Lands in question.

34. Bayle, *Dictionnaire*, Art. 'Gonzague, Isabelle de, A'.

35. Molière, *Précieuses Ridicules*, sc. 4.

36. The facts that the *Tableau* purports to be the manuscript of a Venetian doctor ('Au Lecteur') and has a 'Permission et Approbation' supposedly signed by the gods, seems to indicate a desire to elude the censorship of such works in France.

37. Dangeau, *Journal*, Vol. III, p. 127; Héroard, *Journal*, passim; L'Estoile, *Journal*, Vol. II, p. 488.

38. One of the results of this situation was the prevalence of venereal diseases in seventeenth-century society, from kings down to the humblest of their subjects. See, for example, Arnauld d'Andilly, *Journal Inédit*, p. 196; Bavière, *Correspondance* (trans. Brunet) Vol. I, p. 47; Cosnac, *Mémoires*, Vol. I, pp. 137–8; Fléchier, *Grands Jours d'Auvergne*, pp. 168, 218; L'Estoile, *Journal*, Vol. II, p. 42; Patin, *Lettres*, Vol. III, pp. 119, 742; Peiresc, *Lettres*, Vol. II, Appendix p. 694; Cardinal de Retz, *Mémoires* (ed. A. Feillet) Vol. II, p. 594; Saint-Simon, *Mémoires*, Vol. II, p. 10; Sévigné, *Lettres*, Vol. II, p. 168; Tallemant, *Historiettes*: 'Desportes', Vol. I, p. 130, 'Mme de St-Chaumont', Vol. IV, p. 102, 'Feu M. de Paris', Vol. V, p. 104, 'Maréchal de St-Luc', Vol. V, p. 223, 'Mme de Gondran', Vol. VII, pp. 194–5, 'Vandy', Vol. VIII, p. 214, 'Mlle et Mme de Marolles', Vol. VIII, p. 229, 'Maréchal de St-Géran', Vol. IX, p. 30, 'Président Tambonneau', Vol. IX, p. 152; Antoine Vallot, *Journal de la Santé du Roi Louis XIV* (ed. J.-A. Le Roi) pp. 26 et seq.

39. Charron, *De la Sagesse*, Vol. III, Liv. 3, Ch. 12, p. 64. Cf. Montaigne, *Essais*, Vol. I, Liv. 1, Ch. 30, p. 227.

40. This notion was already prominent in the works of medieval writers. The fourteenth-century poet Eustache Deschamps says in his *Miroir de Mariage* in *Œuvres Complètes* (ed. G. Raynaud) Vol. IX, vv. 5399–401:

> Saiges homs doit sa femme amer
> Pour avoir hoirs, non pour errer
> Es delis de la char mauvaise.

In the sixteenth and seventeenth centuries sexual excesses within marriage were strictly proscribed. See Calvin, *Institution de la Religion Chrétienne*, Liv. 2, Ch. 8, sect. 44; Courtin, *Traité de la Jalousie*, 1re Partie, Ch. 7, p. 198; François de Sales, *Introduction à la Vie Dévote*, 3me Partie, Ch. 39.

41. Montaigne, *Essais*, Vol. II, Liv. 3, Ch. 5, p. 273; also Vol. I, Liv. 1, Ch. 30, pp. 227, 228.

42. Motteville, *Mémoires*, Vol. IV, p. 322.

43. Woman's lust was a leit-motiv in every anti-feminist brochure, but serious writers also subscribed to the idea. See Venette, *Tableau de l'Amour*, 2me Partie, Ch. 4, p. 158.

44. Du Bosc, *La Femme Héroïque*, Vol. I, pp. 455–6; Paccori, *Avis Salutaires*, sect. 33.

45. Montaigne, *Essais*, Vol. II, Liv. 3, Ch. 5, p. 280.

46. Courtin, *Traité de la Jalousie*, 1re Partie, Ch. 9, pp. 270–3.

47. Courtin, ibid., p. 258; Du Bosc, *L'Honnête Femme*, 1re Partie, p. 85; François de Sales, *Introduction à la Vie Dévote*, Vol. II, p. 108.

48. Examples: Corneille, *L'Illusion*, V. ii; Montfleury, *Les Bêtes Raisonnables*, sc. 8; Rotrou, *Cléagénor et Doristée*, V. v.

49. Guyot, *Répertoire*, Art. 'Adultère'.

50. Richelieu, *Mémoires*, Vol. I, p. 8. Cf. La Chétardie, *Instruction pour une jeune princesse*, p. 149; 'Que si vous avez un mari qui n'ait pas pour vous toute la fidélité qu'il vous doit, n'y paraissez pas insensible; cela marquerait une indifférence, qui serait une mauvaise caution de votre tendresse. Plaignez-vous, mais gardez-vous bien qu'il entre de l'aigreur dans vos plaintes'; and Liancourt, *Règlement*, Art. 4, p. 16: 'Ce n'est pas une bonne méthode, à mon avis, de paraître ignorante ou indifférente sur ces choses-là; car cela semblerait venir de peu d'esprit, ou de peu d'amitié, ou de quelque attachement étranger; mais quand la tristesse que l'on en peut avoir est douce et sans murmure, ni chez soi, ni ailleurs, il n'est point mauvais qu'un mari voie qu'on est aussi sensible que patiente là-dessus: mais il ne faut pas que cela aille jusqu'à la froideur, et encore moins jusqu'à l'aigreur des reproches'. It will be seen that these writers come round in fact to advocating the alternative course.

51. Caussin, *Cour Sainte*, 2me Partie, Vol. II, sect. 10, p. 517. See also Du Bosc, *L'Honnête Femme*, 3me Partie, p. 487; J.D.D.C., *Les Agréments et les Chagrins du Mariage*, 2me Partie, pp. 101–3; Mainville, *Du Bonheur et du Malheur du Mariage*, Lettre 21, pp. 168 et seq.; Perrault, *L'Apologie des Femmes*, p. 45.

52. *Nouveau Coutumier Général*, Vol. IV, 2me Partie, *Coutumes* of Saint-Sever, Tit. 11, Art. 3, p. 941; Bayonne, Tit. 25, Arts 1 and 2, p. 962; Béarn, *Rubrica de penas et emendas* 16, p. 1089.

53. Lauder, *Journals*, pp. 69–70.

54. This penalty, known as the *Authentique Sed Hodie*, was derived from ancient Roman law. See *Code Matrimonial*, Vol. I, p. 237, note a; Guyot, *Répertoire*, Art. 'Authentique'.

55. Guyot, *Répertoire*, Art. 'Adultère'.

56.   Bayle, *Dictionnaire*, Art. 'Saint-Cyre B'; Villedieu, *Annales Galantes*, 2me Partie, p. 108.

57.   L'Estoile, *Journal*, Vol. II, p. 61.

58.   Joseph Guillaudeau, *Diaire*, in *Archives Historiques de la Saintonge et de l'Aunis*, Vol. XXXVIII, pp. 157–8; Parthenay, *Lettres de Catherine de Parthenay, Dame de Rohan-Soubise . . . à Charlotte-Brabantine de Nassau, Duchesse de la Trémoïlle* (ed. H. Imbert) p. 115.

59.   Peiresc, *Lettres*, Vol. I, p. 879.

60.   Fléchier, *Grands Jours d'Auvergne*, pp. 243–5. For further examples see Jean de Gaufreteau, *Chronique Bordeloise* [sic], Archives du Château de la Brède, Vol. II, p. 11; Tallemant, *Historiette de Mme de Reniez*, Vol. II, pp. 70–1.

61.   L'Estoile, *Journal*, Vol. II, p. 67.

62.   *Code Matrimonial*, Vol. I, p. 240.

63.   Guyot, *Répertoire*, Art. 'Adultère': 'quoiqu'il ne soit pas permis en France à un mari de tuer sa femme ni celui qu'il surprend en flagrant délit avec elle, cependant lorsque cela arrive il obtient facilement des lettres de rémission; ce qui ne serait pas s'il tuait les coupables autrement qu'en flagrant délit'.

64.   *Mémoire sur la Généralité de Limoges* (ed. A. Leroux) pp. 166–67; *Mémoire de la Généralité de Moulins* (ed. P. Flamant) pp. 12–13.

65.   Marolles, *Mémoires*, 1re Partie, pp. 2–3.

66.   Somaize, *Dictionnaire*, Vol. I, pp. 157, 173.

67.   Pure, *La Prétieuse*, Vol. II, 3me Partie, pp. 28 et seq.

68.   Sorel, *Discours pour et contre l'amitié tendre hors le mariage*, in *Œuvres Diverses* (1663), pp. 142–3.

69.   Donneau de Visé, *Nouvelles Nouvelles*, 3me Partie, p. 58.

70.   Hébert, *Mémoires*, pp. 34–5; Dancourt, *Foire de Besons*, I. 6.

71.   Charles Gobinet, *La Civilité qui se pratique en France parmi les honnêtes gens*, p. 22; Courtin, *Nouveau Traité de la Civilité qui se pratique en France parmi les honnêtes gens*, Ch. 5, p. 35.

72.   La Bruyère, 'De Quelques Usages', 35, in *Caractères*. See also Jean Pic, *Discours sur la Bienséance*, p. 220.

73.   La Rochefoucauld, *Maximes*, No. 364; Chevalier de Sévigné, *Correspondance*, p. 10.

74.   See, for example, the correspondence of La Rochefoucauld in *Œuvres* (Collection Grands Ecrivains de la France) Vol. III, 1re Partie, passim; and Président François de Maynard, *Lettres* (1652 edn) pp. 529–30, 549.

75.   Tallemant, *Historiettes*: 'l'Abbé Tallemant', Vol. VIII, p. 182, 'La Marquise de Brosses', Vol. X, p. 150, 'Naïvetés', Vol. X, p. 186.

76.   He ordered that the coffins of himself and his predeceased wife should be attached 'si étroitement ensemble et si bien rivés, qu'il soit impossible de les séparer l'un de l'autre sans les briser tous deux', and that a brass plaque riveted on each one should record 'la tendresse extrême et réciproque, la confiance sans réserve, l'union intime parfaite sans lacune, et si pleinement réciproque dont il a plu à Dieu bénir singulièrement tout le cours de notre mariage, qui a fait

de moi tant qu'il a duré, l'homme le plus heureux' (Saint-Simon, *Mémoires*, Vol. XIII, p. 103).

77. Demaillasson, *Journal*, Vol. XXXVII, p. 57.
78. Pierre Boyer, *Livre de Raison*, p. 459.
79. Claude du Tour, *Livre Domestique*, p. 57.
80. Etienne Borrelly, *Livre de Raison du Notaire* (ed. A. Puech) in *Les Nîmois dans la seconde moitié du XVIIe siècle*, pp. 217–18.
81. Sévigné, *Lettres*, Vol. VIII, pp. 88, 128.
82. Motteville, *Mémoires*, Vol. I, p. 35.
83. Maintenon, *Lettres* (ed. Langlois) Vol. II, pp. 23, 25.
84. Johann von Werth (*circa* 1600–52) was a German general captured while trying to relieve the siege of Rheinfelden in 1638 and subsequently taken to France, where he was imprisoned at Vincennes (see Molé, *Mémoires*, Vol. II, p. 394).
85. Deshoulières, 'Lettre en Chansons à M. Deshoulières', in *Poésies*, Vol. II, p. 75.

CHAPTER 5

1. Tallemant, *Historiette de Mme de Champré*, Vol. VI, p. 213.
2. Boyer, *Livre de Raison*, pp. 213, 216, 291, 298, 381, 385, 453, 457, 458.
3. Fontainemarie, *Livre de Raison*, pp. 14–17. For further examples see Mairot, *Feuillets de Garde*, p. 204; Froissard-Broissia, *Livre de Raison*, pp. 81 et seq.
4. Arnauld d'Andilly, *Mémoires*, p. 417; Comte de Brienne, *Mémoires* (ed. P. Bonnefon) Vol. III, p. 7; Anselme, *Maison Royale*, Vol. IV, pp. 128–9, 792–3.
5. Dubuisson-Aubenay, *Itinéraire de Bretagne en 1636* (Société des Bibliophiles Bretons) Vol. I, p. 21; Vol. II, p. 256.
6. Fléchier, *Grands Jours d'Auvergne*, p. 38.
7. Delort, *Mémoires*, pp. 56, 305.
8. Du Fossé, *Mémoires*, Vol. IV, p. 65.
9. *Anciennes Lois Françaises*, Vol. XVIII, pp. 90 et seq. For the exclusion of Protestants from the benefits of the edict see Colbert, *Lettres*, Vol. II, p. 72.
10. Colbert, *Lettres*, Vol. II, p. 119.
11. *Anciennes Lois Françaises*, Vol. XIX, p. 413.
12. *Correspondance des Contrôleurs Généraux des Finances* (ed. A. de Boislisle) Vol. I, p. 530, No. 1879.
13. *Code Matrimonial*, Vol. I, pp. 103–4.
14. Guyot, *Répertoire*, Art. 'Fornication'; *Variétés Historiques et Littéraires* (ed. Fournier) Vol. I, pp. 319–20.
15. Loysel, *Institutes Coutumières*, Vol. I, Liv. 1, Règle 40, pp. 87–8.
16. Ibid., Règle 42, pp. 91 et seq. Also Guyot, *Répertoire*, Art. 'Bâtard'.
17. Bavière, *Correspondance* (trans. Brunet) Vol. I, p. 297; Dangeau, *Journal*, Vol. XVII, p. 248; Montpensier, *Mémoires*, Vol. II, pp. 275–6, 384; Patin, *Lettres*, Vol. I, p. 336; Sévigné, *Lettres*, Vol. II, p. 547.
18. Saint-Simon, *Mémoires*, Vol. V, p. 300.

19. Sévigné, *Lettres*, Vol. II, pp. 222–3, 225, 383, 390, 424; Vol. IV, p. 373.
20. The *précieuse's* euphemism for pregnancy (see Somaize, *Dictionnaire*, Vol. I, p. xliv).
21. Pure, *Prétieuse*, Vol. I, 2me Partie, p. 285; Vol. II, 3me Partie, p. 39. Cf. Scudéry, *Grand Cyrus*, Vol. VII, Liv. 1, p. 349: '[Il faut] être exposée à toutes les fâcheuses suites du mariage: perdre peut-être la santé et la beauté tout ensemble, devant que de perdre la jeunesse: . . . et dans la fin de sa vie . . . se voir peut-être des enfants mal nés, mal faits, et ingrats.'
22. Desmarets de Saint-Sorlin, *Les Visionnaires* (ed. H. G. Hall) V. v; Donneau de Visé, *La Mère Coquette* (ed. P. Mélèse) III. i; Molière, *Femmes Savantes*, I. i, III. ii.
23. Saint-Germain, *L'Ecole Méthodique et Parfaite des Sages-Femmes*, 2me Partie, sect. 2, Ch. 8, pp. 117–18; Venette, *Tableau de l'Amour*, 3me Partie, Ch. 6, p. 399.
24. Marguerite Du Tertre, *Instruction aux Sages-Femmes*, 1re Partie, p. 44.
25. De Rostagny, *Traité de Primerose sur les erreurs vulgaires de la médecine*, Liv. 4, Ch. 31, p. 691.
26. See Mauriceau, *Traité des Maladies des Femmes Grosses*, Liv. 1, Ch. 11, 'De quelle façon se doit gouverner la femme pendant tout le cours de sa grossesse'.
27. Jolting was deliberately used to terminate unwanted pregnancies clandestinely. See Tallemant, *Historiette de Mme de Montbazon*, Vol. VI, p. 134.
28. Foucault, *Mémoires*, p. 45, describes how his daughter Marie was born 'fort contrefaite par la faute de sa mère qui, pour ne pas devenir trop épaisse, se faisait serrer le corps à force'. See also Maintenon, *Lettres à la Princesse des Ursins*, Vol. II, p. 368; Sainte-Marthe, *La Manière de Nourrir les Enfants à la Mamelle*, p. 15.
29. Bavière, *Correspondance* (trans. Brunet) Vol. I, p. 443.
30. Bernini, *Journal du Voyage en France du Cavalier Bernin* (ed. P. Freart de Chantelou) p. 233.
31. *Mercure Galant*, Sept. 1681, pp. 218–26. See also Bussy-Rabutin, *Correspondance*, Vol. I, p. 258; Malebranche, *Recherche de la Vérité*, Liv. 2, 1re Partie, Ch. 7, sect. 3; *Recueil des Questions traitées aux Conférences du Bureau d'Adresse*, Vol. I, pp. 197–8; Sourches, *Mémoires*, Vol. XII, p. 12, n. 1.
32. Guillemeau, *De la Grossesse et Accouchement des Femmes*, Liv. 1, Ch. 5, p. 40.
33. Mauriceau, *Traité des Maladies*, Liv. 1, Ch. 11, p. 120; Saint-Germain, *L'Ecole Méthodique*, 2me Partie, sect. 3, Ch. 3, pp. 143–4.
34. Patin, *Lettres*, Vol. III, p. 588.
35. Condé, *Lettres à la Reine de Pologne*, p. 219; *Mercure Galant*, Aug. 1682, pp. 30–1; Peu, *Pratique des Accouchements*, Liv. 1, Ch. 12, p. 169; Sourches, *Mémoires*, Vol. I, p. 26.
36. Mauriceau, *Observations sur la Grossesse et l'Accouchement des Femmes*, No. 20, p. 13, and *Traité des Maladies*, Liv. 1, Ch. 11, p. 121.
37. Mauriceau does, however, mention in his *Observations*, No. 66,

p. 40, the case of a woman, bled six times in one week, who gave premature birth to a still-born child.

38. Examples: Bassompierre, *Mémoires*, Vol. IV, pp. 256, 332; Condé, *Lettres à la Reine de Pologne*, pp. 213, 216, 217, 244; Dangeau, *Journal*, Vol. IV, p. 6; Patin, *Lettres*, Vol. I, p. 53; Richelieu, *Lettres*, Vol. III, p. 237; Sourches, *Mémoires*, Vol. I, p. 79.

39. Examples: La Fontaine, *Œuvres*, Vol. IX, p. 337; Jacqueline Pascal, 'Sonnet à la Reine sur le sujet de sa grossesse' and 'Epigramme sur le mouvement que la Reine a senti de son enfant', in *Lettres . . . de Mme Périer* (ed. Faugère) p. 121; Marc-Antoine Girard de Saint-Amant, *Œuvres* (eds J. Bailbé and J. Lagny) Vol. IV, pp. 197–203; Tristan L'Hermite, *Amours et Autres Poésies Choisies*, pp. 225–6.

40. Conrart, *Valentin Conrart, Sa Vie et Sa Correspondance* (eds Kerviler and Barthélemy) p. 647.

41. Bourgeoise, *Observations*, Liv. 2, pp. 159, 163.

42. Sourches, *Mémoires*, Vol. I, p. 133.

43. Godefroy, *Cérémonial Français*, Vol. II, p. 213.

44. Angot de l'Eperonnière, *Les Exercices de ce Temps* (ed. F. Lachèvre) Satire 7, vv. 61–2; Bourgeoise, *Observations*, Liv. 2, p. 155; Sévigné, *Lettres*, Vol. IV, p. 383, Vol. V, p. 335; Tallemant, *Historiettes*: 'Desportes', Vol. I, p. 130, 'L'Archevêque de Reims', Vol. III, p. 193, 'Mme de Montausier', Vol. III, p. 251.

45. Thiers, *Traité des Superstitions*, Vol. II, Liv. 1, Ch. 8, pp. 89–92.

46. G. Le Roy, *Du Devoir des Mères*, Ch. 1, pp. 23–4, Ch. 2, p. 65; H. Brémond, *Histoire Littéraire du Sentiment Religieux en France*, Vol. IX, pp. 302 et seq.

47. Bourgeoise, *Observations*, Liv. 1, Ch. 2, p. 37: 'Je me suis émerveillée autrefois de voir des femmes de village, jusqu'au jour qu'elles accouchent quelquefois de deux enfants, lever seules des faisceaux d'herbe sur leur tête, sans se blesser.'

48. See Ch. 8.

49. Bourgeoise, *Observations*, Liv. 2, p. 215. The preference which is here signalled in the early part of the century became still more widespread in Louis XIV's day, when *accoucheurs* such as Clément and Boucher regularly assisted royal and aristocratic mothers. See Dangeau, *Journal*, Vol. I, p. 377, Vol. II, p. 359, Vol. VI, p. 387, Vol. VII, p. 138, Vol. IX, p. 67, Vol. X, pp. 51, 163, Vol. XI, pp. 278, 367, Vol. XII, p. 336, Vol. XVI, p. 369; Fléchier, *Grands Jours d'Auvergne*, pp. 202–3; Locatelli, *Voyage de France*, p. 65; Patin, *Lettres*, Vol. II, p. 8; Visconti, *Mémoires*, p. 106.

50. Mauriceau, *Observations sur la Grossesse et l'Accouchement des Femmes*, pp. 53, 64, 382.

51. Bourgeoise, *Observations*, Liv. 1, Ch. 10; Du Tertre, *Instruction*, 2me Partie, p. 69; Guillemeau, *De la Grossesse et Accouchement des Femmes*, Liv. 2, Ch. 5, p. 165; Mauriceau, *Traité des Maladies*, Liv. 2, Ch. 7, p. 238; Peu, *Pratique des Accouchements*, Liv. 1, Ch. 12, p. 162; Saint-Germain, *L'Ecole Méthodique*, 3me Partie, sect. 2, Ch. 1, pp. 199–200.

52. Peu, *Pratique des Accouchements*, Liv. 1, Ch. 12, pp. 138–40.

53. De Rostagny, *Traité de Primerose*, Liv. 4, Ch. 31, p. 688.

54. Bourgeoise, *Observations*, Liv. 1, Ch. 18; Guillemeau, *De la Grossesse et Accouchement des Femmes*, Liv. 2, Ch. 9, pp. 184–6; Mauriceau, *Traité des Maladies*, Liv. 3, Ch. 2, pp. 365–7. The reference in Mauriceau shows that the wisdom of using the sheepskin was being questioned in the second half of the century, and it is not mentioned in the works of Marguerite Du Tertre and Charles de Saint-Germain.

55. Bourgeoise, *Observations*, Liv. 1, Ch. 22 et seq.

56. Anon, *Les Quinze Joies de Mariage* (ed. J. Rychner) No. 3; Angot de l'Eperonnière, *Exercices*, Satire 7, v. 165 et seq.; *Caquets de l'Accouchée*, passim; *Livres de Raison Limousins et Marchois* (ed. Guibert) pp. 178–80; Mauriceau, *Traité des Maladies*, Liv. 3, Ch. 3, p. 370; Sévigné, *Lettres*, Vol. X, p. 330.

57. Lauder, *Journals*, p. 74. See also Sévigné, *Lettres*, Vol. II, p. 451. Bayle, *Dictionnaire*, Art. 'Tibaréniens B', mentions an old custom of Béarn whereby a woman who had had a baby got up and her husband withdrew to bed!

58. Montpensier, *Mémoires*, Vol. IV, p. 48; D'Ormesson, *Journal*, Vol. II, pp. 69–70; Tallemant, *Historiette de Desportes*, Vol. I, p. 130.

59. Locatelli, *Voyage de France*, pp. 66–7; Thiers, *Traité des Superstitions*, Vol. II, Liv. 1, Ch. 12, pp. 167–73.

60. Baillet, *Vie de Descartes*, Vol. I, p. 14; Racine, *Œuvres*, Vol. VII, p. 369.

61. Saint-Simon, *Mémoires*, Vol. VIII, p. 182.

62. Dangeau, *Journal*, Vol. I, p. 151; Sourches, *Mémoires*, Vol. VI, p. 313; Villars, *Lettres*, p. 16.

63. Héroard, *Journal*, Vol. I, pp. 20, 81. Princes in Louis XIV's reign regularly called their *gouvernante* 'Mama(n)'. See Bavière, *Correspondance* (trans. Brunet) Vol. I, p. 318; Sourches, *Mémoires*, Vol. XIII, p. 308, n. 1; Spanheim, *Relation*, pp. 137, 138.

64. D'Aumale, *Souvenirs*, p. 18; Maintenon, *Lettres et Entretiens*, Vol. I, pp. 393, 396, Vol. II, p. 347.

65. See Ch. 2, p. 22, and Bavière, *Correspondance* (trans. Brunet) Vol. I, pp. 3, 7, 9, 64; Montpensier, *Mémoires*, Vol. I, p. 4.

66. See Donneau de Visé's *Mère Coquette*, and that of Quinault; in Mme de Lafayette's *Princesse de Clèves*, in *Romans et Nouvelles* (ed. E. Magne) p. 258, Mme de Chartres's pride and ambition lead her to marry the heroine to a man 'qu'elle ne pût aimer'.

67. Rou, *Mémoires Inédits et Opuscules* (ed. F. Waddington) Vol. I, p. 4.

68. Fontainemarie, *Livre de Raison*, pp. 63–4.

69. This was the age at which royal princes officially left the hands of their *gouvernante*, though in the case of lesser mortals it might be earlier. Fortin de la Hoguette, in *Testament*, 3me Partie, Ch. 3, p. 277, advises taking boys out of female care as soon as they can speak.

70. Bussy-Rabutin, *Correspondance*, Vol. IV, p. 276.

71. Courtin, *Traité de la Paresse*, 5me Entretien, pp. 42–3.

72. Murat, *Mémoires*, Liv. 1, pp. 6–7. See also Saint-Simon, *Mémoires*, Vol. I, p. 49, and below, Ch. 13, n. 12.

73. Quinault, *La Mère Coquette* (1666) II. i; Donneau de Visé, *La Mère Coquette*, (1666) III. i.

74. *Déclaration sur les Formalités du Mariage*, 1639, Art. 2, in *Anciennes Lois Françaises*, Vol. XVI, p. 522.
75. Souvigny, *Mémoires*, Vol. III, pp. 107, 112.
76. Hoguette, *Testament*, 3me Partie, Ch. 3, pp. 283–4.
77. Charron, *De la Sagesse*, Vol. I, Liv. 1, Ch. 49, p. 363.
78. *Règlement sur l'exercice de la Religion Prétendue Réformée*, 2 April 1666, Art. 45: 'Que les enfants dont les pères sont ou auront été catholiques seront baptisés et élevés en l'église catholique, quoique les mères soient de la religion prétendue réformée, comme aussi les enfants dont les pères sont décédés en la dite religion catholique seront élevés dans la dite religion, auquel effet ils seront mis entre les mains de leurs mères, tuteurs ou autres parents catholiques à leur réquisition, avec défenses très expresses de mener les dits enfants aux temples ni aux écoles des dits de la religion prétendue réformée, ni de les élever en icelle, encore que leurs mères soient de la dite religion prétendue réformée.' See *Anciennes Lois Françaises*, Vol. XVIII, p. 85. The clause was reiterated in Art. 39 of the royal declaration of Feb. 1669 'portant règlement des choses qui doivent être gardées et observées par ceux qui font profession de la R.P.R.' See *Edits, Déclarations et Arrêts concernant la Religion Prétendue Réformée, 1662–1751* (ed. L. Pilatte) p. 23.
79. Examples: *Coutumes* of Orléans (*Nouveau Coutumier Général*, Vol. III, 2me Partie, Ch. 9, Art. 180, p. 788), Nivernais (ibid., Ch. 30, Art. 7, p. 1153), Touraine (ibid., Vol. IV, 2me Partie, Tit. 32, Art. 350, p. 673).
80. Montaigne, in *Essais*, Vol. I, Liv. 2, Ch. 8, p. 438, had urged that mothers should not be left to distribute the paternal inheritance to children for fear of favouritism.
81. See Pierre-Jacques Brillon, *Dictionnaire des Arrêts ou Jurisprudence Universelle des Parlements de France*, Vol. II, Art. 'Mariage', No. 271, p. 700.

CHAPTER 6

1. See Ch. 3, p. 42, and Courval Sonnet, *Œuvres Poétiques*, Vol. III, p. 18.
2. Haag, 'Pièces Justificatives', in *France Protestante*, pp. 41, 59.
3. Paris *Coutume*, Tit. 10, Arts 224, 234 (*Nouveau Coutumier Général*, Vol. III, 1re Partie, p. 46); Guyot, *Répertoire*, Arts 'Autorisation', 'Séparation de Biens'; Loysel, *Institutes Coutumières*, Vol. I, Liv. 1, 2me Partie, Règle 24, pp. 160–1.
4. Loysel, *Institutes Coutumières*, Vol. I, Liv. 3, 3me Partie, Règle 18, p. 380. There were exceptions to this rule. The *Coutume* of Montargis (Ch. 8, Art. 6), notably, allowed the separated wife to 'contracter et disposer de ses biens meubles et immeubles, ainsi et en la manière qu'elle pourrait faire si elle n'était mariée'.
5. *Ordonnance du Commerce*, Tit. 8, Arts 1, 2, in *Anciennes Lois Françaises*, Vol. XIX, p. 102. See also Jacques Savary, *Le Parfait Négociant*, Liv. 2, Ch. 63.

6. Bussy-Rabutin, *Correspondance*, Vol. V, pp. 532–3.
7. Guyot, *Répertoire*, Art. 'Séparation de Corps et d'Habitation'.
8. Bussy-Rabutin, *Correspondance*, Vol. V, pp. 13–14.
9. Dangeau, *Journal*, Vol. IV, pp. 400–1.
10. Sévigné, *Lettres*, Vol. III, p. 358.
11. Tallemant, *Historiette de Mme de Liancourt*, Vol. VI, pp. 25–6.
12. Guillemeau, *Traité des abus*, p. 3 and passim. See also *Variétés Historiques et Littéraires* (ed. Fournier) Vol. VI, pp. 307–13, and for the second half of the century Raymond Poisson, *Les Faux Moscovites* (1668) sc. 5.
13. *Code Matrimonial*, Vol. I, p. 319. Cf. Vincent Tagereau, *Discours sur l'Impuissance de l'Homme et de la Femme*, Ch. 7, p. 184.
14. *Code Matrimonial*, Vol. I, p. 321.
15. Bayle, *Dictionnaire*, Art. 'Quellenec A'; Boileau, *Satire VIII*, vv. 143–6; Fléchier, *Grands Jours d'Auvergne*, p. 259; Tagereau, *Discours sur l'Impuissance*, Ch. 7, p. 146; Venette, *Tableau de l'Amour*, 4ᵐᵉ Partie, Ch. 1, pp. 463–4.
16. *Code Matrimonial*, Vol. I, p. 320; Dangeau, *Journal*, Vol. XIV, pp. 108, 159, 378, 456; Saint-Simon, *Mémoires*, Vol. VI, p. 302, Vol. VII, pp. 153–4.
17. The names of a number of rich widows who had made loans to the desperate superintendant of finances Particelli d'Hemery came to light in the troubled summer of 1648, when they were obliged to consent to a reduction of the huge interest rates initially promised. See Jean Vallier, *Journal (1648–1657)* (eds H. Courteault and P. de Vaissière) Vol. I, p. 56.
18. Clément Macheret, *Journal de ce qui s'est passé de mémorable à Lengres et aux environs depuis 1628 jusqu'en 1658* (ed. E. Bougard) Vol. II, p. 319.
19. Angélique Arnauld, *Lettres*, Vol. II, p. 590.
20. Examples: Comtesse de Montmorency-Bouteville (Richelieu, *Mémoires*, Vol. VII, pp. 63 et seq.); Duchesse de Nemours and Marquise de Sévigné (Conrart, *Mémoires*, pp. 587–8, 592). Louis de Pontis, in his *Mémoires*, Collection Michaud et Poujoulat, 2ᵐᵉ Sér., Vol. VI, p. 655, alleged that 930 *gentilshommes* had been killed in duels during Anne d'Autriche's regency alone, apart from those whose death was concealed or attributed to other causes.
21. Balzac, *Premières Lettres* (eds H. Bibas and K. Butler) Vol. I, No. 44; Tallemant, *Historiette de la Maréchale de Thémines*, Vol. V, pp. 187 et seq. See also above, Ch. 4, p. 68.
22. Loret, *Muse Historique*, 29 Mar. 1664; Montpensier, *Mémoires*, Vol. III, p. 432.
23. Caussin, *Cour Sainte*, 2ᵐᵉ Partie, Vol. II, sect. 4, p. 478; Charles Dufresny, *Amusements sérieux et comiques* (ed. J. Vic) No. 7, p. 112; La Bruyère, 'Des Femmes', 79, in *Caractères*; La Rochefoucauld, *Maximes*, No. 233; Le Moyne, *Galerie des Femmes Fortes*, p. 120. The prohibition spread even to literature. See Saint-Evremond, *Dissertation sur le Grand Alexandre*, in *Œuvres en Prose*, Vol. II, p. 97.
24. Thus Anne d'Autriche appeared in the Paris Parlement after Louis XIII's death in 1643 wearing the 'grand dueil' with a 'crêpe noir qui

lui descendait sur le visage et lui couvrait le front' (Marolles, *Mémoires*, 1re Partie, p. 138); see also Malherbe, *Œuvres*, Vol. III, p. 253.

25. Tallemant, *Historiette de Mme d'Aiguillon*, Vol. III, p. 12.
26. *Mercure Galant*, Vol. IV, p. 112.
27. Guyot, *Répertoire*, Art. 'Deuil'.
28. Saint-Simon, *Mémoires*, Vol. II, p. 68, Vol. XIII, p. 74.
29. See Ch. 5.
30. Charles Loyseau, *Cinq Livres du Droit des Offices* (1610 edn) Liv. 1, Ch. 9, sect. 69.
31. Guyot, *Traité des Droits, Fonctions, Franchises, Exemptions, Prérogatives et Privilèges*, Vol. IV, p. 31; Loyseau, *Cinq Livres*, Liv. 3, Ch. 9.
32. See Ch. 7.
33. Examples: *Coutumes* of Amiens, Tit. 6, Art. 124 (*Nouveau Coutumier Général*, Vol. I, 1re Partie, p. 180); Evêché de Metz, Tit. 1, Art. 7 (ibid., Vol. II, 1re Partie, p. 414); Bailliage de Vermandois, Art. 16 (ibid., Vol. II, 1re Partie, p. 456).
34. Paris *Coutume*, Tit. 10, Art. 221 (*Coutumier*, Vol. III, 1re Partie, p. 45): 'A cause de laquelle communauté, le mari est tenu personnellement payer les dettes mobiliaires deues à cause de sa femme, et en peut être valablement poursuivi durant leur mariage. Et aussi la femme est tenue après le trépas de son mari payer la moitié des dettes mobiliaires faites et accrues par le dit mari tant durant le dit mariage qu'auparavant icelui'. As the first part of the quotation shows, during his lifetime the husband was legally responsible for his wife's debts. 'Qui épouse la femme, il épouse les dettes', ran an old legal adage. See, for example, *Coutumes* of Bailliage de Meaux, Ch. 10, Art. 65 (*Coutumier*, Vol. III, 1re Partie, p. 387); Melun, Ch. 13, Art. 216 (ibid., p. 449); Blois, Ch. 13, Art. 180 (ibid., Vol. III, 2me Partie, p. 1060).
35. Guyot, *Répertoire*, Art. 'Renonciation'; Loysel, *Institutes Coutumières*, Vol. I, Liv. 1, 2me Partie, Règle 13. In past ages the widow publicised her decision to renounce by depositing on her husband's grave her keys, belt and purse, as a sign that she abandoned her part of the community and withheld nothing appertaining to it (ibid., Règle 30).
36. Examples: *Coutume* of Amiens, Tit. 5, Art. 101 (*Coutumier*, Vol. I, 1re Partie, p. 178): 'Aussi peut la dite veuve, nonobstant la dite renonciation, prendre et emporter une robe et l'un de tous ses habillements servant à son usage, non le meilleur ni le pire, mais le moyen quand il y en a plusieurs'; Comté d'Eu, Art. 89 (ibid., Vol. IV, 1re Partie, p. 186): 'une de ses robes moyenne, outre la sienne ordinaire, un lit fourni de couvertures, deux paires de draps, deux nappes, une demi-douzaine de serviettes, un escabeau, un pot de fer, un plat, deux écuelles, une jactelete [?], une chopine, un demyon, un chandelier, s'il s'en trouve'; Brittany, Tit. 20, Art. 436 (ibid., Vol. IV, 1re partie, p. 389): 'son lit garni, et son coffre, deux robes et accoutrements fournis à son usage, quels elle voudra choisir; et partie des joyaux et bagues selon l'état et qualité de la maison de son mari'; Touraine, Art. 293 (ibid., Vol. IV, 2me Partie,

p. 667): 'un lit garni, leurs heures et patenôtres, l'une de ses [sic] meilleures robes, et l'autre moyenne, tant d'hiver que d'été; mais n'aura bagues et joyaux'.

37. Normandy *Coutume*, Art. 367 (*Coutumier*, Vol. IV, 1re Partie, p. 78).
38. Brittany *Coutume*, Tit. 20, Art. 450 (*Coutumier*, Vol. IV, 1re Partie, p. 390).
39. Paris *Coutume*, Tit. 11, Art. 248 (*Coutumier*, Vol. III, 1re Partie, p. 47).
40. Paris *Coutume*, ibid.: 'Douaire coutumier est de la moitié des héritages que le mari tient et possède au jour des épousailles, et bénédiction nuptiale. Et de la moitié des héritages qui depuis la consommation du dit mariage, et pendant icelui, échoient et adviennent en ligne directe au dit mari.'
41. Examples: *Coutumes* of Perche, Tit. 6, Art. 111 (*Coutumier*, Vol. III, 2me Partie, p. 654), and Normandy, Art. 367 (ibid., Vol. IV, 1re Partie, p. 78).
42. Paris *Coutume*, Tit. 11, Art. 262 (*Coutumier*, Vol. III, 1re Partie, p. 48).
43. Examples: *Coutumes* of Paris, Tit. 11, Art. 261 (*Coutumier*, ibid.); Amiens, Tit. 5, Art. 100 (ibid., Vol. I, 1re Partie, p. 178); Bailliage de Vermandois, Art. 35 (ibid., Vol. II, 1re Partie, p. 458); Reims, Art. 244 (ibid., Vol. II, 1re Partie, p. 506); Bailliage de Meaux, Ch. 2, Art. 8 (ibid., Vol. III, 1re Partie, p. 382); Troyes, Tit. 5, Art. 87 (ibid., Vol. III, 2me Partie, p. 246); Perche, Tit. 6, Art. 112 (ibid., Vol. III, 2me Partie, p. 654).
44. As in the *Coutumes* of Boulenois, Tit. 23, Art. 101 (*Coutumier*, Vol. I, 1re Partie, p. 35): 'Le douaire est préféré au devant de toutes obligations personnelles précédentes [sic] le mariage, et de toutes hypothèques créées et engendrées depuis la consommation'; and Chaulny, Tit. 23, Art. 28 (ibid., Vol. II, 2me Partie, p. 689): 'Les dits douaires, tant préfix que coutumier, sont privilégiés en telle manière, qu'ils se prennent avant toutes autres dettes.'
45. See Ch. 4, n. 25. Also, *Coutumes* of Clermont, Ch. 13, Art. 14 (*Coutumier*, Vol. II, 2me Partie, p. 882); Normandy, Arts. 376, 377 (ibid., Vol. IV, 1re Partie, p. 79); Maine, 10me Partie, Art. 327 (ibid., Vol. IV, 1re Partie, p. 498); Anjou, 10me Partie, Art. 314 (ibid., Vol. IV, 1re Partie, p. 562); Touraine, Art. 336 (ibid., Vol. IV, 2me Partie, p. 672); and others.
46. Guyot, *Répertoire*, Arts 'Préciput' and 'Renonciation'. A *préciput légal*, one fixed by law, also existed, but mostly for the benefit of the nobility, and it was usually accorded on condition that the recipient paid the community debts.
47. Guyot, *Répertoire*, Art. 'Don Mutuel'. *Coutumes* varied greatly as to the amount of property that could be included in the *don* and whether that property might be fully owned or held only in usufruct.
48. Paris *Coutume*, Art. 280 (*Coutumier*, Vol. III, 1re Partie, pp. 49–50). In *Coutumes* where donations were permissible only in a partner's testament the same concern was shown for protecting the interests of children. The Amiens *Coutume*, for example, Tit. 5, Art. 106 (ibid., Vol. I, 1re Partie, p. 178), allowed couples to will to one another 'tous

leurs biens meubles, dettes, acquêts et conquêts immeubles, avec le
quint de leurs propres héritages à toujours ou à vie ... au cas
toutefois qu'il n'y ait enfants du dit mariage ou d'autre précédant, et
s'il y en a, ne peuvent donner l'un à l'autre que par usufruit'.

49. Examples: *Coutumes* of Anjou, 10me Partie, Art. 310 (*Coutumier*,
    Vol. IV, 1re Partie, p. 562); Poitou, Tit. 4, Art. 266 (ibid., Vol. IV, 2me
    Partie, pp. 800–1); Touraine, Tit. 30, Art. 337 (ibid., Vol. IV, 2me
    Partie, p. 672).

50. Guyot, *Répertoire*, Art. 'Augment'.

51. Ibid., Art. 'Bagues et Joyaux'. In Provence, Bresse and Mâconnais
    the *augment de dot* and *bagues et joyaux* were replaced by the *donation
    de survie* (ibid., Art. 'Gains Nuptiaux et Gains de Survie').

52. Ibid., Arts 'Dot' and 'Année de Viduité'.

53. Ibid., Art. 'Gains Nuptiaux et Gains de Survie'.

54. De Grenaille, *L'Honnête Veuve*, Liv. 1, Ch. 1, p. 18.

55. François de Sales, *Introduction à la Vie Dévote*, Vol. II, 3me Partie,
    Ch. 40.

56. Arnauld d'Andilly, *Mémoires*, p. 417.

57. For Mme de Chantal see biography by Françoise-Madeleine de
    Chaugy in *Sainte Jeanne de Chantal, Sa Vie et ses Œuvres* (ed. Plon)
    Vol. I; for Mmes de Belle-Isle and de Lestonnac see La Croix,
    Dictionnaire, Arts 'Belle-Isle' and 'Lestonac' [sic].

58. Mme de Montmorency was the wife of the rebel governor of
    Languedoc, executed in 1632 for active participation in one of the
    conspiracies hatched by Louis XIII's brother and his henchmen
    against Richelieu. After her husband's death she withdrew to the
    Visitandine convent of Moulins where she built a superb mauso-
    leum in his memory and eventually took the veil. See Deshoulières,
    *Poésies, Epître à Mlle ***, Vol. II, p. 242; Loret, *Muse Historique*, 13 Oct.
    1657; Mairet, Dedication of *Le Grand et Dernier Soliman*; Montpensier,
    Mémoires, Vol. III, pp. 349–52; Saint-Evremond, *Lettres*, Vol. II, p. 37;
    Sévigné, *Lettres*, Vol. IV, p. 449.

59. Rapin, *Mémoires*, Vol. I, p. 173.

60. Mme de Caylus, *Souvenirs*, Collection Michaud et Poujoulat, 3me
    Sér., Vol. VIII, p. 476; Maintenon, *Lettres* (ed. Langlois) Vol. II, p. 25;
    Tallemant, *Historiette du Petit Scarron*, Vol. IX, pp. 126, 129.

61. Sévigné, *Lettres*, Vol. X, p. 189.

62. Campion, *Mémoires*, p. 4.

63. Gaufreteau, *Chronique Bordeloise*, Vol. II, p. 174.

64. Souvigny, *Mémoires*, Vol. I, p. 154.

65. Sourches, *Mémoires*, Vol. IV, p. 328, n. 5. See also p. 454, concerning
    the Comtesse de Matignon.

66. For recollections and re-tellings of the story, see Bussy-Rabutin,
    Correspondance, Vol. III, p. 331; La Fontaine, *Fables*, Liv. 12, No. 26;
    Méré, *Œuvres* (1692 edn) Vol. II, pp. 100–3; Patin, *Lettres*, Vol. III,
    p. 129; Pure, *La Prétieuse*, Vol. II, 3me Partie, pp. 95–7; Saint-
    Evremond, *Œuvres en Prose*, Vol. I, pp. 189–95.

67. Donneau de Visé, *La Veuve à la Mode* (1667) passim. For other
    skittish widows in drama see Discret, *Alizon*; Du Ryer, *Alcimédon*;

Mairet, *Les Galanteries du Duc d'Ossonne*; Molière, *Le Misanthrope*;
Antoine Le Metel D'Ouville, *L'Esprit Folet*. For novels see D'Urfé,
L'Astrée, Vol. I, Liv. 5.

68. Maintenon, *Lettres* (ed. Langlois) Vol. II, p. 52. Cf. Saint-Maurice,
     Lettres, Vol. II, p. 159.

69. Montpensier, *Mémoires*, Vol. IV, pp. 327–8, 385. Cf. Bussy-Rabutin,
     Histoire Amoureuse des Gaules (ed. Garnier) Vol. II, p. 41.

70. Bassompierre, *Mémoires*, Vol. I, p. 143.

71. Bussy-Rabutin, *Mémoires*, Vol. I, p. 31.

72. Tallemant, *Historiette de Mme d'Aiguillon*, Vol. III, pp. 14 et seq.,
     Mmes de Rohan, Vol. V, p. 22, *Les Amours de l'Auteur*, Vol. X, pp. 88 et
     seq.

73. Bossuet, *Correspondance*, Vol. VI, pp. 419–20.

74. Caussin, *Cour Sainte*, 1re Partie, Vol. I, Liv. 3, sect. 37, pp. 651–2; De
     Grenaille, *L'Honnête Veuve*, Liv. I, Ch. 3.

75. Guyot, *Répertoire*, Art. 'Noces'.

76. As in the *Coutume* of the Bailliage de Vermandois, Art. 15 (*Coutu-
     mier*, Vol. II, 1re Partie, p. 456).

77. The nobility of other provinces pressed for the enforcement of this
     provision on a national scale. See *Deux Cahiers de la Noblesse pour les
     Etats Généraux de 1649–1651* (eds R. Mousnier et al.) p. 151.

78. Examples: *Coutumes* of Calais, Ch. 5, Art. 71 (*Coutumier*, Vol. I, 1re
     Partie, p. 6); Amiens, Tit. 5, Art. 107 (ibid., Vol. I, 1re Partie, p. 179);
     Laon, Art. 29 (ibid., Vol. II, 1re Partie, p. 457); Châlons, Art. 35
     (ibid., Vol. II, 1re Partie, p. 477); Sedan, Art. 100 (ibid., Vol. II, 2me
     Partie, p. 825). See also Guyot, *Répertoire*, Art. 'Noces'.

79. *Coutumes* of Châteauneuf, Ch. 15, Art. 106 (*Coutumier*, Vol. III, 2me
     Partie, p. 688); Maine, 11me Partie, Art. 334 (ibid., Vol. IV, 1re Partie,
     p. 499).

80. See above, Ch. 5, p. 82, and note.

81. Durand, *Journal* (ed. B. Prost) p. 92.

82. Delort, *Mémoires*, pp. 124–5; Gaufreteau, *Chronique Bordeloise*,
     Vol. II, pp. 251–2.

83. *Archives de Nancy* (ed. H. Lepage) Vol. II, pp. 27–8; Gaufreteau,
     Chronique Bordeloise, Vol. II, p. 252; Thiers, *Traité des Superstitions*,
     Vol. IV, Liv. 10, Ch. 5, pp. 536 et seq.

CHAPTER 7

1. Charron, *De la Sagesse*, Vol. III, Liv. 3, Ch. 12, p. 63.

2. See Ch. 2, p. 19.

3. Caussin, *Cour Sainte*, 1re Partie, Vol. I, Liv. 2, sect. 6, pp. 272–3;
    Courcelles, *Mémoires*, p. 167; Gabriel Gilbert, *Les Intrigues
    Amoureuses*, IV. ii; Lannel, *Roman Satirique*, Liv. 1, pp. 69–70; and
    others.

4. Saint-Simon, *Mémoires*, Vol. III, p. 74; Vol. VIII, p. 120.

5. A post created in 1664. See Condé, *Lettres à la Reine de Pologne*, pp.
    2–4.

6. Contemporaries disagree as to when this post was created and the person for whom it was originally destined. Dubuisson-Aubenay, in *Journal*, Vol. I, p. 198, names Mme de Brégy, wife of the French ambassador to Sweden, at the date of 1650. Bussy-Rabutin, *Correspondance*, Vol. II, pp. 237–8, 240, Marquis de La Fare, *Mémoires*, Collection Michaud et Poujoulat, 3me Sér., Vol. VIII, p. 283, and Saint-Maurice, *Lettres*, Vol. II, p. 524, specify that the post was designed for Mme Dufresnoy, mistress of Louvois, in 1673.

7. For details of the functions attached to these posts, see Guyot, *Traité des Droits*, Vol. II, 1re Partie, Ch. 68.

8. Bassompierre, *Mémoires*, Vol. III, p. 181; Condé, *Lettres à la Reine de Pologne*, p. 2; Sévigné, *Lettres*, Vol. VII, p. 381.

9. Héroard, *Journal*, Vol. I, p. 373.

10. Dangeau, *Journal*, Vol. VI, pp. 269–70. Gratifications on the occasion of marriage, such as the one thousand *écus* which Louis XIV gave to *femmes de chambre* of the royal household, were common. See Dangeau, ibid., Vol. II, p. 433; Sully, *Mémoires*, Vol. V, Liv. 20, p. 443.

11. Her chief *femme de chambre* slept in the same room as the queen (see Motteville, *Mémoires*, Vol. II, p. 285). After the birth of a royal baby the queen's *surintendante* slept for the first three nights in her mistress's chamber (see Guyot, *Traité des Droits*, Vol. II, 1re Partie, Ch. 68, p. 245).

12. Guyot, *Traité des Droits*, ibid., pp. 244 et seq.

13. Fontenay-Mareuil, *Mémoires*, p. 175; Motteville, *Mémoires*, Vol. IV, pp. 262 et seq.; Pellisson-Fontanier, *Lettres Historiques*, Vol. II, p. 3.

14. Fontenay-Mareuil, *Mémoires*, p. 35.

15. Montpensier, *Mémoires*, Vol. IV, p. 411.

16. Spanheim, *Relation*, p. 131.

17. Saint-Simon, *Mémoires*, Vol. I, p. 219.

18. Pierre de La Porte, *Mémoires*, Collection Michaud et Poujoulat, 3me Sér., Vol. VIII, pp. 30–1; Motteville, *Mémoires*, Vol. I, pp. 67, 103, 129, 131–4, 162–6.

19. Motteville, *Mémoires*, Vol. IV, pp. 314 et seq.; D'Ormesson, *Journal*, Vol. II, pp. 166, 176.

20. Patin, *Lettres*, Vol. I, p. 405.

21. Montpensier, *Mémoires*, Vol. I, p. 170; Vol. II, p. 266.

22. This state of affairs persisted in the early eighteenth century. Mme de Staal, who as Mlle de Launay had entered the service of the Duchesse du Maine at Sceaux, was given an apartment consisting of 'un entresol si bas et si sombre, que j'y marchais pliée, et à tâtons: on ne pouvait y respirer, faute d'air, ni s'y chauffer, faute de cheminée'. See Staal, *Mémoires*, pp. 691–2.

23. Motteville, *Mémoires*, Vol. I, p. 174.

24. Maintenon, *Lettres et Entretiens*, Vol. I, p. 381.

25. Sourches, *Mémoires*, Vol. IX, p. 181, n. 2.

26. For kneeling see Héroard, *Journal*, Vol. I, p. 145; Mme de Lafayette, *Histoire de Madame Henriette d'Angleterre*, Collection Michaud et

Poujoulat, 3me Sér., Vol. VIII, p. 188; Motteville, *Mémoires*, Vol. II, pp. 353, 420; Sévigné, *Lettres*, Vol. II, pp. 34, 55–6.

27.   Dangeau, *Journal*, Vol. I, p. 154; Vol. II, p. 61.
28.   Montpensier, *Mémoires*, Vol. IV, pp. 108 et seq., 339, 341. See also D'Ormesson, *Journal*, Vol. II, p. 585; Pellisson-Fontanier, *Lettres Historiques*, Vol. III, p. 372; *Recueil de Pièces Galantes en Prose et en Vers* (eds Comtesse de la Suze and Pellisson-Fontanier) Vol. I, pp. 118 et seq.; Saint-Maurice, *Lettres*, Vol. I, p. 95; Saint-Simon, *Mémoires*, Vol. VIII, pp. 156–8; Sourches, *Mémoires*, Vol. I, pp. 28, 44–5; E. de Barthélemy, *La Marquise d'Huxelles et ses amis*, p. 320.
29.   Guyot, *Traité des Droits*, Vol. II, 1re Partie, Ch. 68, p. 245.
30.   Dangeau, *Journal*, Vol. I, pp. 245, 422; Motteville, *Mémoires*, Vol. IV, pp. 419, 429; Sourches, *Mémoires*, Vol. IV, p. 231. The references in Dangeau and Sourches indicate that ladies-in-waiting devoted enough to nurse mistresses with smallpox more than once caught the disease.
31.   Dangeau, *Journal*, Vol. XIV, pp. 87–8.
32.   Saint-Simon, *Mémoires*, Vol. I, p. 27.
33.   Molière, *Tartuffe*, II. iii. In the same vein see La Rochefoucauld, *Œuvres*, Vol. III, 1re Partie, pp. 177–8; Marquis de Racan, *Œuvres* (ed. Tenant de Latour) Vol. I, pp. 315–6; Sévigné, *Lettres*, Vol. I, pp. 348–50.
34.   The salient passages of the *Journal* were published by Charles de Ribbe in *Une Grande Dame dans son Ménage au temps de Louis XIV*.
35.   Ibid., pp. 369, 375.
36.   Ibid., p. 348.
37.   Ibid., pp. 349, 351.
38.   Ibid., p. 353.
39.   Ibid., p. 349.
40.   Ibid., p. 356.
41.   See Ch. 2, n. 84.
42.   Rochefort, ibid., pp. 355, 362, 370.
43.   Examples from Rochefort, *Journal*: 'J'arrêtai mon compte avec M. Michel, marchand d'Arles, et j'ai vu que je lui devais 1053 livres. M. Michel m'a promis de se contenter des intérêts pour cette année' (p. 358); 'j'avais le dessein d'aller aujourd'hui à la Bégude. La pluie m'en ayant empêchée, j'ai arrête le compte du rentier du Grès, et j'ai vu qu'il me devra encore de l'argent à la foire. J'ai arrêté aussi le compte du meunier, qui me devra encore' (p. 352); 'Le 26 juillet, j'ai arrêté les comptes de plusieurs de mes domestiques' (p. 379).
44.   Example, ibid.: 'Sur une lettre des religieuses de Sainte-Claire d'Avignon, j'ai répondu qu'il m'était impossible de payer avant la récolte, et que, si l'on me presse davantage, je me servirai des lettres d'état pour arrêter les poursuites' (p. 351). She was subsequently informed that the *lettres* were valueless (p. 386).
45.   Ibid., pp. 355, 369.
46.   Ibid., p. 382.
47.   Ibid., p. 379.
48.   Ibid., pp. 351, 354, 375, 376.

49. Ibid., p. 363.
50. Ibid., pp. 362, 369.
51. Ibid., p. 367.
52. Ibid., p. 363.
53. Ibid., p. 352.
54. Ibid., pp. 390, 391.
55. Colbert, *Lettres*, Vol. II, p. 643; *Correspondance des Contrôleurs Généraux*, Vol. I, p. 61, No. 235; La Mare, *Traité de la Police*, Vol. IV, Liv. 6, Tit. 12, Ch. 2, pp. 438–9, Tit. 14, Ch. 10, p. 624; Abraham du Pradel, *Le Livre Commode des Adresses de Paris pour 1692* (ed. E. Fournier) Vol. I, pp. 266, 269, Vol. II, pp. 161, 166; Sauval, *Antiquités de Paris*, Vol. I, p. 192; Sourches, *Mémoires*, Vol. V, p. 322, note; Tallemant, *Historiette de Mme de Cavoye*, Vol. VII, p. 17.
56. *Correspondance des Contrôleurs Généraux*, Vol. I, p. 325, No. 1197.
57. *Mémoires des Intendants sur l'Etat des Généralités*, Vol. I (ed. A. Boislisle) Appendix 10, p. 612.
58. Chappuzeau, *L'Académie des Femmes*, III. iii, and *Le Colin-Maillard*, sc. 3; Dancourt, *Les Bourgeoises à la Mode*, passim; La Bruyère, 'De la Ville', 16, in *Caractères; Variétés Historiques et Littéraires* (ed. Fournier) Vol. I, p. 62.
59. Peiresc, *Lettres*, Vol. VI, p. 4 ('Mademoiselle ma mère'). Towards the end of the century the title of 'Madame' had been usurped by the humblest classes of society. See Edme Boursault, *Les Mots à la Mode* (1694) sc. 6.
60. *An Historical View of the Negotiations between the Courts of England, France, and Brussels from the year 1592 to 1617* (ed. Thomas Birch) p. 435.
61. *Correspondance des Contrôleurs Généraux*, Vol. I, p. 477, No. 1703.
62. Locatelli, *Voyage de France*, p. 45.
63. Ibid., p. 122.
64. Sévigné, *Lettres*, Vol. IX, pp. 277, 448, 474.
65. Examples: *Coutumes* of Trois Bailliages de Lorraine, Nancy, Vosges et Allemagne, Tit. 1, Art. 21 (*Nouveau Coutumier Général*, Vol. II, 2me Partie, p. 1100); Paris, Tit. 10, Arts 234–6 (ibid., Vol. III, 1re Partie, p. 46); Blois, Ch. 1, Art. 3 (ibid., Vol. III, 2me Partie, pp. 1047–8); Bourbonnais, Ch. 15, Art. 168 (ibid., Vol. III, 2me Partie, pp. 1243–4); Britanny, Tit. 20, Art. 448 (ibid., Vol. IV, 1re Partie, p. 390); Poitou, Tit. 3, Art. 227 (ibid., Vol. IV, 2me Partie, p. 797). See also Guyot, *Répertoire*, Art. 'Autorisation'.
66. Examples: 1608 Statutes of Paris fruit merchants (*marchands fruitiers-orangers*), Art. 8: 'Item, les veuves des maîtres jouiront des privilèges des maîtres pendant qu'elles sont en viduité, pourront continuer leurs apprentis et apprenties qui étaient accueillis à [sic] leur défunt mari, et néanmoins n'en pourront prendre ni accueillir de nouveaux, et perdront leurs privilèges en se remariant avec un homme d'un autre métier.' See *Métiers et Corporations de la Ville de Paris* (ed. R. de Lespinasse) Vol. I, p. 486.

1637 Statutes of Clermont-Ferrand apothecaries, Art. 18: 'advenant le décès de quelqu'un des dits maîtres apothicaires, donnons pouvoir et permission à la veuve délaissée de faire valoir et tenir la boutique ouverte pendant sa viduité, et y faire exercer l'art de pharmacie par un serviteur capable qu'elle présentera au maître garde, pour recevoir d'icelui le serment en tel cas requis.' See *Histoire des Communautés des Arts et Métiers de l'Auvergne* (ed. J.-B. Bouillet) p. 9.

1640 Statutes of Le Mans chandlers: 'Les veuves des dits maîtres ciergers jouiront des mêmes droits, honneurs et privilèges que les autres maîtres de la dite vocation demeurant en la dite ville et faubourgs du Mans, au moyen qu'elles seront contribuables aux frais qu'il conviendra faire en leur communauté et qu'elles répondront de la fidélité de toutes les marchandises et ouvrages qui seront vendus et débités en leurs boutiques.' See *Documents relatifs à l'Histoire des Corporations d'Arts et Métiers du Diocèse du Mans* (ed. T. Cauvin) p. 386.

1661 Statutes of Amiens haberdashers, wax-chandlers, grocers, druggists (*merciers-ciriers-épiciers-droguistes*), Art. 24: 'Item, que toutes les femmes veuves des maîtres du dit état pourront entretenir et continuer leur métier pendant leur viduité comme elles faisaient pendant que leurs maris vivaient, et au cas qu'elles se remarient à d'autres personnes qui ne soient maîtres du dit état, elles ne pourront tenir ni continuer le dit métier, ains elles seront privées du dit état et maîtrise.' See *Recueil des Monuments Inédits de l'Histoire du Tiers Etat* (ed. A. Thierry) 1re Sér., Vol. III, p. 123.

A fifth condition, found especially in old statutes and sometimes preserved in seventeenth-century revisions was the obligation for the widow to be of 'bonne vie et honnête conversation'.

67. The widows of Paris smiths (*orfèvres*) were forbidden by a *Règlement* of 1679 (Art. 5) from using their husband's hallmark even if they refrained from remarriage. If they wished to continue the business they had to do so under the aegis of a master smith whose seal they adopted and who was held responsible for any contraventions of regulations. See *Métiers de Paris* (ed. Lespinasse) Vol. II, p. 45.

68. Example: 1676 Statutes of Paris nailers, Art. 14: 'et si les dites veuves de maîtres ou filles épousent un compagnon soit de la ville ou forain, elles l'exempteront du service qu'il est obligé de rendre aux maîtres de la dite communauté et de la moitié des droits, et ne feront que légère expérience qui leur sera donnée'. See Lespinasse, ibid., Vol. II, p. 583. This relaxation of guild rules in favour of journeymen marrying the widows or daughters of master craftsmen was by no means universal. Dijon, in particular, seems to have been hostile to the idea. See A.-V. Chapuis, *Les Anciennes Corporations Dijonnaises*, passim.

69. 1660 Statutes, Arts 4, 14, 19; Lespinasse, *Métiers de Paris*, Vol. III, p. 195 note, 197, 198.

70. Statutes of *couturières*, Arts 1, 2, 3, and final preamble; Lespinasse, ibid., Vol. III, pp. 233, 235.

71. See *Les Métiers de Blois* (ed. A. Bourgeois) Vol. II, p. 60; *Correspondance des Contrôleurs Généraux*, Vol. I, pp. 49–50, No. 185. Also

P. Boissonnade, *Essai sur l'Organisation du Travail en Poitou* in *Mémoires de la Société des Antiquaires de l'Ouest*, 2me Sér., Vol. XXI, p. 297; E. Cornaaert, *Les Corporations en France avant 1789*, pp. 198–9.

72. This was the case elsewhere in France. The *lingères-toilières* of Rouen counted 'plus de mille maîtresses et de deux cents marchandes en boutique'. See *Correspondance des Contrôleurs Généraux*, Vol. I, p. 253, No. 966.

73. Lespinasse, ibid., Vol. III, pp. 62 et seq. Likewise at Nantes. See *Les Anciens Corps d'Arts et Métiers de Nantes* (ed. E. Pied) Vol. III, p. 275.

74. 1595 Statutes of *grainiers*, confirmed 1612 and 1656, Art. 6, Lespinasse, ibid., Vol. I, p. 230; 1616 Statutes of *perruquiers*, Art. 1, ibid., Vol. III, p. 655.

75. 1608 Statutes, Art. 23, Lespinasse, ibid., Vol. I, p. 488.

76. The 1551 Statutes of the embroiderers and clerical outfitters (*brodeurs-chasubliers*), for example, dilate on the reception of women into the *maîtrise*. See Art. 25, Lespinasse, ibid., Vol. II, p. 177. But the 1648 version follows a reference to 'maîtres et maîtresses' with clauses describing the election of '*jurés*' and the necessity for 30 '*maîtres*' to be present for the discussion of guild affairs. See ibid., Art. 26, p. 179, note. See also Jacques Savary des Bruslons and Philemon Louis Savary, *Dictionnaire Universel de Commerce*, Art. 'Sayetteur'.

77. *Métiers de Blois* (ed. Bourgeois) Vol. II, p. 213.

78. 1653 Statutes of *passementiers-boutonniers*, Art. 12 (Lespinasse, ibid., Vol. II, pp. 154–5); 1599 Statutes of *plumassiers*, Art. 22 (ibid., Vol. III, p. 299); 1595 Statutes of *ceinturiers*, Art. 14 (ibid., Vol. III, p. 395); 1664 Statutes of *fripiers*, Art. 14 (ibid., Vol. III, p. 432, note); *monnayeurs* (*Mercure Galant*, April 1690, pp. 30–1; Savary, *Dictionnaire de Commerce*, Art. 'Ouvriers').

79. *Recueil des Monuments Inédits* (ed. Thierry) Vol. IV, p. 506.

80. *Histoire des Anciennes Corporations de la Capitale de la Normandie* (ed. Ch. Ouin-Lacroix) p. 685.

81. Lespinasse, ibid., Vol. I, p. 233.

82. A sample contract of apprenticeship to a 'maîtresse couturière' (1663) can be found in M. Jurgens and E. Maxfield-Miller, *Cent Ans de Recherches sur Molière, sur sa famille et sur les comédiens de sa troupe*, pp. 383–4.

83. Savary, *Dictionnaire de Commerce*, Arts 'Esnoueuses' and 'Esplucheuses'. Both types of women were employed in the wool trade.

84. Lespinasse, ibid., Vol. II, p. 303. These women participated in the manufacture of cloth of gold and silver.

85. Savary, *Dictionnaire de Commerce*, Art. 'Meneuse'. The *meneuse* sorted playing-cards into packs.

86. Lespinasse, ibid., Vol. III, p. 660, note; *Métiers de Nantes* (ed. Pied) Vol. I, p. 53. *Tresseuses* assisted barbers and wig-makers.

87. Funerals of guild members were elaborate affairs in which the whole of the professional community marched in procession bearing lighted torches and candles. Wives of *maîtres*, as well as widows and

maîtresses, normally had the right to full ceremonial honours. See
Lespinasse, ibid., Vol. II, pp. 90, 298; *Recueil* (ed. Thierry) Vol. III,
p. 127, Vol. IV, pp. 504, 509; *Les Anciennes Corporations Ouvrières à
Bourges* (ed. E. Toubeau de Maisonneuve) pp. 36–7, 50, 144–5, 196,
255, 262, 282.

88. Example: 1677 Statutes of Paris *bouquetières*, Art. 20 (Lespinasse,
ibid., Vol. III, p. 620).

89. E. Cornaaert, *Les Compagnonnages en France du Moyen Age à Nos
Jours*, pp. 178–9, 228.

90. Lespinasse, ibid., Vol. II, pp. 449, note 2, 450.

91. *Recueil* (ed. Thierry) Vol. III, p. 125.

92. Lespinasse, ibid., Vol. I, p. 487.

93. *Corporations de la Capitale de la Normandie* (ed. Ouin-Lacroix) p. 686.

94. Lespinasse, ibid., Vol. I, p. 434 (for 1681 *Ordonnance sur le Commerce
du Poisson*, Art. 6); Patin, *Lettres*, Vol. III, p. 619.

95. In the words of D'Argenson, Lieutenant-General of Police, in
Correspondance des Contrôleurs Généraux, Vol. II, p. 89, No. 326.

96. *Le Journal de [François] Colletet, Premier Petit Journal Parisien* (1676)
(ed. A. Heulhard) p. 60.

97. Savary, *Dictionnaire de Commerce*, Art. 'Revendeur'.

98. See the portrait of Ragonde in Claude de L'Estoile's comedy
L'Intrigue des Filous (1648) and Molière, *L'Ecole des Femmes*, IV. v.

99. *Archives de Nancy* (ed. Lepage), Vol. III, pp. 222–3.

100. Boissonnade, *Travail en Poitou*, Vol. XXI, p. 238.

101. *Journal de Colletet*, p. 218.

102. Lespinasse, ibid., Vol. III, p. 198; *Corporations à Bourges* (ed.
Toubeau de Maisonneuve) pp. 71–2.

103. Savary, *Dictionnaire de Commerce*, Art. 'Crieur'.

104. H. Hauser, *Les Débuts du Capitalisme*, Chs 4 and 6. See also
A. Rébillon, 'Recherches sur les Anciennes Corporations de
Rennes', in *Annales de Bretagne*, Vol. XX, p. 220.

105. Boissonnade, *Travail en Poitou*, Vol. XXII, p. 4. The same was true
in the Nivernais area. See L. Gueneau, *L'Organisation du Travail à
Nevers*, 1re Partie, Ch. 1.

106. The section in this chapter concerning the role of women in the
guilds first appeared in the form of an article in the 1981 issue of
the *Newsletter* (subsequently renamed *Seventeenth-Century French
Studies*) of the Society for Seventeenth-Century French Studies,
and is reprinted here by kind permission of the editor.

CHAPTER 8

1. *Métiers de Paris* (ed. Lespinasse) Vol. III, p. 635, n. 1; Pradel, *Adresses de Paris*, Vol. II, p. 49.

2. Babeau, *La Vie Rurale dans l'Ancienne France*, Appendix 5, pp. 354–6;
Sorel, *Francion*, Vol. I, Liv. 2, p. 62.

3. *Caquets de l'Accouchée*, 1re Journée, p. 15; Maintenon, *Lettres* (ed.
Langlois) Vol. II, p. 97.

4.   Charron, *De la Sagesse*, Vol. III, Liv. 3, Ch. 15, p. 125; Claude Fleury, *Devoirs des Maîtres et des Domestiques*, passim; Mme Guyon, *Instruction d'une mère à sa fille*, sect. 5, p. 437; Fortin de la Hoguette, *Testament*, 3me Partie, Ch. 5; Liancourt, *Règlement*, Art. 11; Jacqueline Pascal, Letter to Gilberte Périer, in V. Cousin, *Jacqueline Pascal*, pp. 240–5; Pic, *Discours sur la Bienséance*, p. 235; François de Sales, *Lettres*, p. 392.
5.   Fénelon, *Traité de l'Education des Filles*, Ch. 12, p. 126.
6.   Chappuzeau, *L'Académie des Femmes*, I. iii; Molière, *Le Misanthrope*, III. iv, *Tartuffe*, I. i, *Femmes Savantes*, II. v; Pierre Troterel, *Gillette*, IV. ii. In François Le Metel de Boisrobert's *Trois Orontes* V. i, a servant girl is tortured by her employer.
7.   Peu, *Pratique des Accouchements*, Liv. 1, Ch. 8, pp. 71–2, 74–5, 83.
8.   Dubuisson-Aubenay, *Journal*, Vol. II, pp. 99–100; Loret, *Muse Historique*, 30 July and 13 Aug. 1651; Tallemant, *Historiette de Mme de Vervins*, Vol. VIII, p. 79.
9.   Tallemant, *Historiette de Mme d'Aymet*, Vol. VI, p. 238.
10. Bavière, *Correspondance* (trans. Brunet), Vol. II, p. 337.
11. Bavière, ibid., p. 338; Saint-Simon, *Mémoires*, Vol. II, p. 417. For further testimonies to servant-beating see Boileau, *Satire X*, vv. 289–90; Courtin, *Nouveau Traité de la Civilité*, Ch. 11, pp. 143–4; Patin, *Lettres*, Vol. II, p. 346.
12. See Ch. 2, p. 21. In Charles Sorel's novel *Polyandre* (1648) Vol. I, Liv. 3, p. 400, a vexed servant-girl protests at the consideration accorded to a *suivante* in preference to herself: 'Pensez-vous que les servantes de chambre ou de charge ne valent pas bien les demoiselles suivantes, ou plutôt demoiselles servantes, car elles servent aussi bien que moi, et il n'y a que l'escoiffion qui mette différence entre nous deux.'
13. Courtin, *Nouveau Traité de la Civilité*, Ch. 5, p. 50; Molière, *Comtesse d'Escarbagnas*, sc. 2 et seq.
14. Boursault, *Les Mots à la Mode*, sc. 3.
15. Comtesse de Murat, *Voyage de Campagne*, Vol. I, 1re Partie, p. 348.
16. Audiger, *La Maison Réglée*, pp. 162 et seq.
17. Examples: Marguerite Laurens, engaged in 1601 by Martial de Gay de Nexon, Lieutenant-General at Limoges, for three *écus* and a pair of shoes per annum (see *Nouveau Recueil de Registres Domestiques Limousins et Marchois*, Vol. I, p. 479); Marie, serving Paul de Vendée, a Huguenot captain, for eleven *livres*, a chemise and a pair of shoes a year in 1622 (see Paul de Vendée, *Journal*, p. 161); Jeanne Grase, hired for fourteen *livres* and a pair of shoes by the notary Etienne Borrelly in 1658 (see Borrelly, *Livre de Raison*, p. 144); 'la fille de la Perse', employed by Pierre Bourrut, Parlement advocate, in 1697 for nine *livres* per annum and two ells of coarse cloth (see Bourrut, *Papier de Raison*, p. 24).
18. Quinault, *La Mère Coquette*, II. i.
19. Mercier, *Livre de Raison* (ed. J. Pannier) in *Bulletin de la Société de l'Histoire du Protestantisme Français*, 5me Sér., Vol. III, p. 521, note.
20. Ibid., pp. 501, 505, 509.

21.   See *La Maltôte des Cuisinières ou la manière de bien ferrer la mule: Dialogue entre une vieille cuisinière et une jeune servante*, in *Variétés Historiques et Littéraires*, Vol. V, pp. 243–57.

22.   Maidservants were credited with a passion for the type of lottery known as *la blanque*, in which cards were drawn, the losing ones being white or unmarked. See La Mare, *Traité de la Police*, Vol. I, Liv. 3, Tit. 4, p. 507; L'Estoile, *Journal*, Vol. II, pp. 440–1; *Variétés Historiques et Littéraires*, Vol. I, pp. 313 et seq., Vol. III, p. 102.

23.   See, for example, the *Cahiers de Doléances des Paroisses du Bailliage de Troyes pour les Etats Généraux de 1614* (ed. Y. Durand) p. 144: 'Que défenses seront faites aux dits serviteurs et servantes de porter soie, argenterie ni habits non convenables à leurs état et condition.'

24.   *Coutume* of Bouillon, Ch. 19, Art. 18, in *Nouveau Coutumier Général*, Vol. II, 2me Partie, p. 858. See also Guyot, *Répertoire*, Art. 'Vol'.

25.   Louvet, *Journal*, in *Revue de l'Anjou*, Mar.–Apr. 1855, pp. 183–4.

26.   Patin, *Lettres*, Vol. I, p. 392.

27.   Claude Fleury, *Devoirs des Maîtres et des Domestiques*, pp. 69–70: 'La plupart des domestiques n'osent penser à se marier, parce que la plupart des maîtres n'en voudraient plus. De là vient qu'il y en a tant, qui se précipitent dans la débauche'.

28.   Liancourt, *Règlement*, Art. 11, pp. 63–4.

29.   Bayle, *Dictionnaire*, Art. 'Aurélien B'.

30.   References in both factual and fictional literature to the sexual licence of masters and maids are legion. See, for example, Charles d'Assoucy, *Aventures Burlesques* (ed. E. Colombey) p. 119; Jean-Jacques Bouchard, *Confessions* (ed. Gallimard) passim; *Le Cabinet Satirique* (1618), pp. 613–16; Hauteroche, *Crispin Médecin*, II. i; Patin, *Lettres*, Vol. I, p. 45; Tabarin, *Œuvres* (ed. G. d'Harmonville) pp. 399 et seq.; Tallemant, *Historiettes*: 'Faure Père et Fils', Vol. II, p. 104, 'Maris cocus par leur faute', Vol. II, pp. 139–40, 'Mme d'Atis', Vol. V, p. 146, 'Mme de Saint-Ange', Vol. IX, p. 150; Troterel, *Gillette*, passim; *Variétés Historiques et Littéraires*, Vol. I, pp. 313 et seq., Vol. II, pp. 237 et seq., Vol. III, pp. 344–5, Vol. V, pp. 299 et seq., Vol. IX, p. 172. The servants of ecclesiastics were always, according to Bayle's *Dictionnaire*, Art. 'Launoi, Matthieu de, E', reputed to be their concubines, and not without foundation. See *Cahiers de Doléance du Bailliage de Troyes*, pp. 80, 87–8.

31.   Misalliances of this kind were by no means rare in the different sections of society. The painter Du Moustier, the poet Colletet, the controller-general of finances Cornuel and the Duc de Saint-Aignan were among those who contracted them. For Du Moustier see Tallemant's *Historiette*, Vol. V, p. 58; for Colletet see Tallemant, Vol. IX, p. 179, and Chapelain, *Lettres*, Vol. II, p. 23; for Cornuel see Tallemant, *Historiette de Mme Coulon*, Vol. VI, p. 171; for Saint-Aignan see Bussy-Rabutin, *Correspondance*, Vol. V, p. 60, and Saint-Simon, *Mémoires*, Vol. II, p. 428.

32.   Lannel, *Roman Satirique*, Liv. 3, pp. 370–1; Mauriceau, *Observations sur la Grossesse et l'Accouchement des Femmes*, p. 104.

33.   Anon, *Les Amours, Intrigues et Cabales des Domestiques des grandes*

maisons de ce temps (1632), p. 127; Bayle, *Dictionnaire*, Art. 'Patin F'.

34. Audiger, *La Maison Réglée*, pp. 162–3. See also L'Estoile, *Journal*, Vol. II, p. 468; Saint-Maurice, *Lettres*, Vol. I, p. 406.

35. Bayle, *Dictionnaire*, Art. 'Judith D'.

36. Murat, *Mémoires*, Liv. 6, p. 189. Cf. Maintenon, *Lettres et Entretiens*, Vol. I, pp. 384–5.

37. Abbé d'Aubignac, *Conseils d'Ariste à Célimène sur les moyens de conserver sa réputation*, sect. 13, p. 60. Same note in Jean-Pierre Camus, *Flaminio et Colman*, 'Avant-Propos' ('les adversaires étrangers ne peuvent jamais tant nuire que ceux qui vivent, mangent et dorment parmi nous, et auxquels nous nous fions de nos biens et de nos vies'), and in Olivier de Serres, *Théâtre d'Agriculture*, Liv. 1, Ch. 6, p. 39.

38. As was Louise Bourgeoise, midwife to Marie de Médicis (see Bourgeoise, *Observations*, Liv. 2, pp. 104 et seq.).

39. Guillemeau's *Traité des Abus qui se commettent sur les procédures de l'impuissance*, p. 10, recalls that the midwives' report was the decisive factor in judgements of impotence cases.

40. Bourgeoise, *Observations*, Liv. 2, p. 220; Guyot, *Répertoire*, Art. 'Accouchement'; Patin, *Lettres*, Vol. III, p. 236. See also below, Ch. 9, n. 53.

41. Peu, *Pratique des Accouchements*, Liv. 2, Ch. 1, pp. 261–2.

42. Guillemeau, *Traité des Abus*, p. 11: 'quelle anatomie, quelle dissection de corps ont-elles jamais fait entre elles, ou avec autres plus entendues qu'elles ne sont?'

43. Bourgeoise, *Observations*, Liv. 1, Ch. 36, p. 183.

44. Venette, *Tableau de l'Amour*, 2me Partie, Ch. 1, p. 87. Tardy letters patent of 1664 rectified the situation in Paris at least. See *Métiers de Paris* (ed. Lespinasse) Vol. III, p. 635.

45. Lespinasse, ibid.

46. *Corporations de la Capitale de la Normandie* (ed. Ouin-Lacroix) pp. 313–14.

47. The standard formula for such oaths is given in the *Dictionnaire de Droit Canonique et de Pratique Bénéficiale* (ed. Durand de Maillane) Art. 'Sage-Femme'.

48. L. Nardin and J. Mauveaux, 'Histoire des Corporations d'Arts et Métiers des Ville et Comté de Montbéliard', in *Mémoires de la Société d'Emulation de Montbéliard*, Vol. XXXIX, pp. 131–2.

49. Boissonnade, *Travail en Poitou*, Vol. XXI, p. 490; François Lebrun, *Les Hommes et la Mort en Anjou au 17e et 18e Siècles*, p. 213.

50. Bayle, *Dictionnaire*, Art. 'Sapho E': 'Les accoucheuses étaient surnommées sages, non pas à cause de leur vertu, mais à cause qu'elles savaient beaucoup de choses inconnues aux autres femmes. On les nomme encore les femmes sages en Guyenne et en Languedoc, mais dans les provinces où la langue française est plus exacte on use de transposition afin d'ôter l'équivoque, et on les nomme sages-femmes.'

51. Michel Lalande, *Notes* (ed. J. Sahuc) pp. 36–7.

52. Protestant midwives were forbidden in 1680 to exercise their profession. See *Anciennes Lois Françaises*, Vol. XIX, p. 231–2.

53. See Ch. 5, n. 49.
54. Lepage, *Archives de Nancy*, Vol. I, p. 312.
55. Pradel, *Adresses de Paris*, Vol. II, p. 75.
56. Patin, *Lettres*, Vol. III, p. 373. For a reflection of the same prejudices in seventeenth-century England see De Rostagny, *Traité de Primerose sur les Erreurs Vulgaires de la Médecine*, Liv. 1, Ch. 5.
57. Fléchier, *Grands Jours d'Auvergne*, p. 91; Racine, *Abrégé de l'Histoire de Port-Royal*, in *Œuvres Complètes* (Éditions du Seuil) p. 324. Convent regulations invariably contain a section devoted to the duties of the *infirmière* and her assistants.
58. See Ch. 2, n. 85. J. Devaux, in *Le Médecin de Soi-même* (2me edn, Leyden, 1687) 3me Partie, p. 157, declared: 'Il n'y a pas à présent jusqu'à la moindre femme, qui n'ait dans son faible cerveau une pharmacie entière'. The first edition was in 1682.
59. James Howell, *Familiar Letters* (ed. J. Jacobs) p. 136.
60. Audiger, *La Maison Réglée*, p. 108; Patin, *Lettres*, Vol. I, p. 23.
61. Donneau de Visé, *La Veuve à la Mode*, scenes 1–4, 22; Peu, *Pratique des Accouchements*, Liv. 2, Ch. 1, p. 263; Saint-Germain, *L'Ecole Méthodique*, 4me Partie, sect. 1.
62. *Cahiers de Doléance du Bailliage de Troyes*, Appendix 14, p. 332. See also L'Estoile, *Journal*, Vol. II, p. 237.
63. D'Ormesson, *Journal*, Vol. II, pp. 251–2; Patin, *Lettres*, Vol. III, p. 494; Saint-Simon, *Mémoires*, Vol. VIII, p. 248; Sévigné, *Lettres*, Vol. I, pp. 443, 447–8. In 1755 Mme Fouquet's *emplâtres* were still being used by the Dauphine: see Marquis d'Argenson, *Journal et Mémoires* (ed. E. J. B. Rathery) Vol. IX, p. 137.
64. 'Comme ce n'est pas le fait d'une femme de faire des livres, je n'aurais jamais pris le dessein de donner ces leçons au public, si Messieurs les Administrateurs de l'Hôtel-Dieu, pour qui j'ai toute sorte de déférence, ne m'y eussent engagée' (Du Tertre, *Instruction Familière*, Prefatory 'Avis').
65. Bussy-Rabutin, *Correspondance*, Vol. V, p. 517; Dangeau, *Journal*, Vol. I, p. 296; Sourches, *Mémoires*, Vol. V, p. 181 and n. 1.
66. Lister, *A Journey to Paris in the year 1698*, p. 239.
67. As happened with the Filles de la Croix. See Sauval, *Antiquités de Paris*, Vol. I, p. 678.
68. Such as the Benedictines of Notre-Dame de Liesse. See Jaillot, *Recherches Critiques, Historiques et Topographiques sur la Ville de Paris*, Vol. V, 19me Quartier, Le Luxembourg, pp. 94–6.
69. Claude Joly, *Traité Historique des Ecoles Épiscopales et Ecclésiastiques*, pp. 283–4; Martin Sonnet, *Statuts et Règlements des Petites Ecoles de Paris*, p. 25.
70. Sonnet, ibid., p. 14.
71. Joly, *Traité*, p. 491.
72. See above, Ch. 2, p. 25.
73. Sonnet, *Statuts*, pp. 20, 27.
74. Ibid., pp. 23, 28.
75. Joly, *Traité*, p. 283.
76. Du Fossé, *Mémoires*, Vol. IV, pp. 9–10.

77. *Déclaration du Roi qui pourvoit à l'instruction de ceux qui sont rentrés dans le sein de l'Eglise Catholique, et de leurs enfants*, Art. 9, in *Recueil Néron*, Vol. II, p. 978.

78. Foucault, *Mémoires*, pp. 209, 216–17.

79. *Correspondance des Contrôleurs Généraux*, Vol. I, p. 523, No. 1857; Vol. II, p. 14, No. 49.

80. Ibid., Vol. I, p. 387, No. 1420, note.

81. Ibid., Vol. II, p. 59, No. 207.

82. Women were banned by a decree of the Paris Parlement dated 24 July 1600 from becoming churchwardens. See Brillon, *Dictionnaire des Arrêts*, Art. 'Marguilliers', No. 39, Vol. II, p. 679.

83. Vauban, *Dîme Royale*, (ed. E. Cornaaert) p. 73.

84. Ibid., p. 81.

85. Often done over the side of boats on the river. See Brackenhoffer, *Voyage en France*, p. 114; *Journal de Colletet*, p. 89; La Mare, *Traité de la Police*, Vol. I, Liv. 4, Tit. 3, Ch. 5; Louvet, *Journal*, in *Revue de l'Anjou*, Mar.–Apr. 1856, p. 133.

86. For water carriers see La Mare reference in previous note and Lauder, *Journals*, p. 68. For souvenir vendors see Fénelon, *Correspondance* (ed. Orcibal) Vol. II, p. 69; Locke, *Travels in France*, p. 81.

87. Jouvin de Rochefort, *Voyageur d'Europe*, Vol. I, p. 39.

88. Colbert, *Lettres*, Vol. IV, p. 339, Vol. V, pp. 151, 186; Guyot, *Répertoire*, Art. 'Femme'.

89. *Journal de Deux Notaires Ciotadens au XVII Siècle*, p. 30; Locke, *Travels in France*, p. 18.

90. Lister, *Journey to Paris*, p. 13.

91. Dunoyer, *Lettres*, Vol. III, pp. 311–12.

92. Borrelly, *Livre de Raison*, p. 243; Guyot, *Répertoire*, Art. 'Fouet'; *Variétés Historiques et Littéraires*, Vol. I, p. 43. The wives of jailers commonly assisted their husband in the exercise of his functions. See, for example, *Mémoires des Intendants sur l'Etat des Généralités*, Vol. I, Appendix 15, p. 733.

93. Locke, *Travels in France*, p. 18.

94. Colbert, *Lettres*, Vol. V, p. 151.

95. Locke, *Travels in France*, p. 217.

96. Ibid., pp. 236–7.

97. Vauban, *Dîme Royale*, p. 7.

98. Saint-Simon, *Mémoires*, Vol. III, pp. 391 et seq.

99. Brienne, *Mémoires*, Vol. III, pp. 67–8; Choisy, *Mémoires*, p. 588; Héroard, *Journal*, Vol. I, pp. 77, 117, 187, 241, 243, 246, 251, 291, 354, 359, 361; Sévigné, *Lettres*, Vol. II, p. 301.

100. The Duchesse de Bourgogne, who had arrived in France in 1696, went to Paris for the first time on 18 Aug. 1698, to the fair of Saint-Laurent. See Sourches, *Mémoires*, Vol. VI, p. 56.

101. La Bruyère, 'De la Ville', 21, in *Caractères*.

102. In 1709 the Dauphin's carriage was several times stopped by women demanding bread. See Dangeau, *Journal*, Vol. XII, pp. 399, 403–4.

CHAPTER 9

1. Nicole, *Essais de Morale*, Vol. III, pp. 272–3. See also Desmarets de Saint-Sorlin, *Les Visionnaires*, V. v.

2. Chappuzeau, *Le Théâtre Français*, Liv. 3, pp. 140–1; Dorimon, *La Comédie de la Comédie*, scenes 1 and 2.

3. This apologetic literature also reveals the presence of other women besides the stars working in the theatre, for example, usherettes (*ouvreuses de loge*) and refreshment sellers. See David de Brueys, *Le Grondeur*, Prologue, sc. 2, in *Œuvres de Théâtre de Mssrs de Brueys et de Palaprat*, Vol. II; Chappuzeau, *Théâtre Français*, Liv. 3, pp. 232, 250; Dancourt, *Les Trois Cousines*, Prologue. The famous *Registre* kept by his fellow actor La Grange suggests that Molière readily attached women to his troupe in the capacity of receivers of takings, as well as usherettes and caretakers. See La Grange, *Registre* (eds B. E. Young and G. P. Young) Vol. I, pp. 18, 29, 47, 126, 232, 259, 314, 344, 348.

4. See S. W. Deierkauf-Holsboer, *La Vie d'Alexandre Hardy, Poète du Roi (1572–1632)*, Appendices 22, p. 192; 28, p. 196; 30, p. 198. Arrangements might be less formal for actors' and dramatists' children introduced onto the stage at an early age. See Tralage, *Notes et Documents sur l'Histoire des Théâtres de Paris au XVIIe Siècle: Extraits du Manuscrit de J. N. Du Tralage* (ed. P. L. Jacob) p. 84.

5. Chappuzeau, *Théâtre Français*, Liv. 3, p. 147. See also Gougenot, *La Comédie des Comédiens*, I. ii, III. ii; Holsboer, *Alexandre Hardy*, Appendices 21, p. 191, and 38, p. 209.

6. Chappuzeau, *Théâtre Français*, Liv. 2, p. 83.

7. Chappuzeau, ibid., Liv. 3, pp. 148–9, 174–5; Corneille, *L'Illusion*, V. v.

8. Pierre Juvernay, *Discours Particulier contre les femmes débraillées de ce temps*, Ch. 8, p. 44; Timothée Philalèthe, *De la Modestie des femmes et des filles chrétiennes*, Motif 4, p. 90; Motif 8, p. 183.

9. Chappuzeau, *L'Académie des Femmes*, II. vi.

10. Dorimon, *La Comédie de la Comédie*, sc. 4; Rotrou, *Le Martyre de Saint Genest*, II. ii; Scarron, *Roman Comique*, 1re Partie, Ch. 8, p. 24, Ch. 10, pp. 42–3; Georges de Scudéry, *La Comédie des Comédiens*, I. iii.

11. Pellisson-Fontanier, *Histoire de l'Académie*, Vol. II, p. 238; Sévigné, *Lettres*, Vol. II, p. 536; A. Gasté, *La Querelle du Cid*, p. 86.

12. Gougenot, *Comédie des Comédiens*, II. ii. See also La Calprenède's *Mort de Mithridate* (1636), 'Au Lecteur'.

13. Tallemant, *Historiette de Mondory*, Vol. X, p. 43.

14. Abbé d'Aubignac, *Projet pour le Rétablissement du Théâtre Français*, in *La Pratique du Théâtre* (ed. P. Martino) pp. 390–1.

15. Three apprenticeship contracts published by Holsboer in *Alexandre Hardy*, pp. 194–6, may be taken as representative. In 1609 Jeanne Crevé, daughter of a Paris shoemaker, and Judith Messier, daughter of a process-server (*huissier*) in the bailliwick of Beauvais, contracted to serve with a troupe directed by Mathieu Le Febvre, known as Laporte. Early in 1610 they were joined by Elisabeth Duje, daughter

of a certain captain La Vallée of Brittany, who signed on for seven years' apprenticeship.

16. Holsboer, ibid., Appendix 45, p. 221. Marriages into the nobility were not unknown. See H. Chardon, *Nouveaux Documents sur la Vie de Molière: M. de Modène, ses deux femmes et Madeleine Béjart*, Vol. I passim. In contemporary fiction members of the profession are often represented as being drawn from the respectable bourgeoisie and even the gentry. See Corneille, *L'Illusion*; Gougenot, *Comédie des Comédiens*; Scarron, *Roman Comique*.

17. Gougenot, *Comédie des Comédiens*, III.i,ii; Scarron, *Roman Comique*, 1re Partie, Ch. 21, p. 129.

18. Tallemant, *Historiette de Mondory*, Vol. X, p. 42.

19. See Ch. 3, p. 57.

20. Richelieu, *Lettres*, Vol. IV, pp. 644–5.

21. Chappuzeau, *Théâtre Français*, Liv. 3, p. 152.

22. Holsboer, *Alexandre Hardy*, pp. 192, 196, 199.

23. Locatelli, *Voyage de France*, p. 181.

24. Tallemant, *Historiette de Mondory*, Vol. X, p. 39.

25. For theatrical wardrobes see Chappuzeau, *Théâtre Français*, Liv. 3, pp. 170–1; Dorimon, *Comédie de la Comédie*, sc. 4; Gougenot, *Comédie des Comédiens*, III.ii; Holsboer, *Alexandre Hardy*, pp. 174, 188, 203; Jurgens and Maxfield-Miller, *Cent Ans de Recherches sur Molière*, pp. 506–8, 570–2; *Lettres en Vers* (ed. Rothschild) Vol. II, p. 886; *Mascarade: La réception faite par un gentilhomme de campagne à une compagnie*, Entrée 8, in *Les Contemporains de Molière* (ed. V. Fournel) Vol. II; Raymond Poisson, *Le Baron de la Crasse*, in ibid., Vol. I, p. 428, note. The costumes of provincial troupes remained makeshift, according to Scarron's *Roman Comique*, 1re Partie, Ch. 2, p. 7, though they too profited from seigneurial liberalities (see 2me Partie, Ch. 3, p. 172).

26. For supporting testimonies about actresses see Tallemant, *Historiettes*: 'Boisrobert', Vol. III, p. 155, and 'Mondory', Vol. X, p. 40.

27. Scarron, *Roman Comique*, 2me Partie, Ch. 1, p. 160. See also O. S. de Claireville, *Le Gascon Extravagant: Histoire Comique* (ed. F. Robello) pp. 296–305.

28. Scudéry, *Comédie des Comédiens*, I.iii.

29. 'En cas que les dits comédiens règlent tellement les actions du théâtre, qu'elles soient du tout exemptes d'impureté, Nous voulons que leur exercice, qui peut innocemment divertir nos peuples de diverses occupations mauvaises, ne puisse leur être imputé à blâme, ni préjudicier à leur réputation dans le commerce public'. See François and Claude Parfaict, *Histoire du Théâtre Français*, Vol. VI, pp. 132–3.

30. Bavière, *Correspondance* (trans. Brunet) Vol. I, pp. 259, 264; Dunoyer, *Lettres*, Vol. I, pp. 23–4; Saint-Simon, *Mémoires*, Vol. IV, p. 78, Vol. V, p. 445. For the situation in England see John Evelyn, *Diary* (ed. E. S. de Beer) Vol. III, p. 466. One mortified royal wife, the Dauphine de Bavière, hit on a novel way to tackle the problem. By prevailing upon her father-in-law Louis XIV to set her up as an

official superintendant of drama she was able, in the 1680s, to dismiss actresses who displeased her and to regulate the professional life of the acting community generally. See Dangeau, *Journal*, Vol. I, p. 28; La Grange, *Registre* (eds B. E. and G. P. Young) Vol. I, pp. 335, 351–2.

31.   Hébert, *Mémoires*, pp. 36–7.

32.   Bossuet, *Maximes et Réflexions sur la Comédie*, sect. 8.

33.   Voltaire, *La Mort de Mlle Lecouvreur*, in *Œuvres Complètes* (ed. Garnier) Vol. IX, pp. 369–71.

34.   La Bruyère, 'De Quelques Usages', 21, in *Caractères*.

35.   *Journal du Voyage de Deux Hollandais à Paris*, p. 34; Locatelli, *Voyage de France*, p. 35; Scarron, *Roman Comique*, 2me Partie, Ch. 6, p. 184; Tallemant, *Historiette de La Du Ryer*, Vol. IX, p. 223.

36.   Huet, *Memoirs*, Vol. II, Bk 4, p. 42.

37.   Scarron, *Roman Comique*, 1re Partie, Ch. 1, p. 5; 2me Partie, Ch. 6, p. 184; Ch. 8, p. 196.

38.   Locatelli, *Voyage de France*, pp. 35–6.

39.   L'Estoile, *Journal*, Vol. I (ed. L.-R. Lefèvre) pp. 613, 614; Mme de Mornay, *Mémoires* (ed. Mme de Witt) Vol. I, p. 392.

40.   See Samuel Pepys's experience at a Dutch inn in 1660, in *Diary* (eds. R. Latham and W. Matthews) Vol. I, p. 150.

41.   Locatelli, *Voyage de France*, pp. 31–2, 84, 252.

42.   Francis Mortoft, *His Book, Being his Travels through France and Italy, 1658–59*, p. 22; Tallemant, *Historiette de La Du Ryer*, p. 223.

43.   O. S. de Claireville, *Le Gascon Extravagant*, pp. 127–30; Gillet de La Tessonerie, *Comédie de Francion*, I.vii; Quinault, *Les Rivales*, passim; Rotrou, *Les Deux Pucelles*, passim.

44.   Tallemant, *Historiette de La Du Ryer*, p. 224.

45.   'En ce même temps [1644] a paru un certain jeune homme qui se disait connaître les sorciers et l'on l'appelait le prophète d'Arcée, et les peuples du duché de Bourgogne et particulièrement aux environs de Flavigny y ajoutaient une telle foi que le menant par les villages et faisant passer les communautés par devant lui, ceux qu'il regardait en passant et disait celui-là ou celle-là est sorcier ou sorcière, on les prenait incontinent et on les noyait et leur donnait-on tant de coups de perche qu'enfin ils mouraient en l'eau; d'autres faisaient chauffer des fours et jettaient dedans tous ceux qu'il disait être sorciers'. See Macheret, *Journal*, Vol. II, pp. 317–18. See also *Lettres et Mémoires adressés au Chancelier Séguier* (ed. R. Mousnier) Vol. I, pp. 636–7.

46.   Denesde, *Journal*, p. 108; Gaufreteau, *Chronique Bordeloise*, Vol. II, p. 121; L'Estoile, *Journal*, Vol. I, p. 619, Vol. II, pp. 154, 470.

47.   Richelieu, *Lettres*, Vol. I, p. 99.

48.   Périer, *Mémoire sur la Vie de M. Pascal, écrit par Mlle Marguerite Périer, sa nièce*, in *Lettres* (ed. Faugère) pp. 447–52.

49.   Vigneul-Marville, *Mélanges d'Histoire et de Littérature*, Vol. I, p. 231.

50.   Saint-Simon, *Mémoires*, Vol. II, p. 18.

51.   Visconti, *Mémoires*, p. 55.

52.   Ibid., pp. 61–3, 70–3.

53. A number of midwives worked in collusion with the *devineresses*: la Callet, la Bouffet, la Desponts, la Leclerc and in particular the last-named's mother, la Lepère. See *Archives de la Bastille* (ed. F. Ravaisson) Vol. VI, pp. 180, 198, 273, 445, 461; Vol. VII, pp. 72, 114. Leclerc and Lepère were said to have procured more than 10 000 abortions (ibid., Vol. VI, p. 164). La Voisin burned the foetuses in an oven (ibid., Vol. VI, p. 37).

54. *Archives* (ed. Ravaisson) Vol. VI, pp. 232, 252, 259, 294–5, 334, 335, 444–5, and so on.

55. For la Brinvilliers see La Fare, *Mémoires*, p. 291; Sévigné, *Lettres*, Vol. IV, pp. 411, 423, 425–6, 428–9, 435, 504, 507, 513–14, 523, 526, 528–30, 533–4, 551; Visconti, *Mémoires*, pp. 278–9.

56. Bussy-Rabutin, *Correspondance*, Vol. V, p. 46; Visconti, *Mémoires*, pp. 285–6.

57. *Archives* (ed. Ravaisson) Vol. VI, pp. 289, 295, 334.

58. Ibid., Vol. VI, pp. 4, 5, 7.

59. Ibid., Vol. VI, pp. 259, 312.

60. Bussy-Rabutin, *Correspondance*, Vol. IV, pp. 347–8; Sévigné, *Lettres*, Vol. VI, pp. 230, 277; Visconti, *Mémoires*, pp. 296–7.

61. Sévigné, *Lettres*, Vol. VI, p. 231.

62. Visconti, *Mémoires*, pp. 277–8.

63. Sévigné, *Lettres*, Vol. VI, p. 225.

64. Ibid., 31 Jan. 1680, p. 230.

65. Bussy-Rabutin, *Correspondance*, Vol. V, pp. 44–5; Sévigné, *Lettres*, Vol. VI, pp. 213–14. The Vicomtesse de Polignac also fled before she could be arrested; see *Archives* (ed. Ravaisson) Vol. VI, pp. 129–30.

66. La Fare, *Mémoires*, p. 291; Sévigné, *Lettres*, Vol. VI, p. 229.

67. Sévigné, *Lettres*, Vol. VI, pp. 229 et seq. The actual text of the interrogation is given in *Archives* (ed. Ravaisson) Vol. VI, pp. 117 et seq.

68. Sévigné, *Lettres*, Vol. VI, p. 266. Uninfluential clients of the *devineresses* paid the full penalty. Mme Brunet, for example, who had poisoned her husband in order to marry the royal flautist Philibert, had her hand cut off before being hanged in June 1679. See *Archives* (ed. Ravaisson) Vol. V, p. 399.

69. Louvois to *intendant* Chauvelin regarding the imprisonment of eleven men in the citadel of Besançon and thirteen women in the Fort-Saint-André at Salins. See *Archives* (ed. Ravaisson) Vol. VII, p. 119.

70. Sévigné, *Lettres*, Vol. VI, p. 280; *Archives*, ibid., Vol. V, p. 360.

71. *Archives*, ibid., Vol. VI, pp. 174 et seq.

72. Sévigné, *Lettres*, Vol. VI, p. 278.

73. Ibid., pp. 279–80.

74. Visconti, *Mémoires*, pp. 292–3.

75. *Anciennes Lois Françaises*, Vol. XIX, pp. 396–401.

76. Bayle, *Dictionnaire*, Art. 'Métella A'; Donneau de Visé, *Les Dames Vengées*, I.vii; Dufresny, *Amusements*, p. 94; La Chétardie, *Instruction pour une jeune princesse*, pp. 157–8; La Fontaine, *Fables*, Liv. 7, No. 15.

77. *Correspondance des Contrôleurs Généraux*, Vol. II, pp. 76–7, No. 281.

In asserting that such rumours were not new, the attorney was quite correct. See d'Assoucy, *Aventures Burlesques*, p. 132; *Archives* (ed. Ravaisson) Vol. VI, pp. 288, 433.

78. Witch-hunts by the police continued well into the eighteenth century. See Argenson, *Notes de René d'Argenson, Lieutenant-Général de Police* (Collection des Petits Mémoires Inédits) pp. 26, 66–8, 88–90, 103.

79. *Notes*, ibid., p. 71; Mathurin Régnier, *Œuvres Complètes* (ed. G. Raibaud) Satire 12, v. 181 et seq.

80. La Mare, *Traité de la Police*, Vol. I, Liv. 3, Tit. 5, Ch. 4; *Lettres en Vers* (ed. Rothschild) Vol. II, pp. 417–18, 430–1.

81. Sauval, *Antiquités de Paris*, Vol. I, pp. 700–1.

82. *Anciennes Lois Françaises*, Vol. XIX, pp. 443–5. Similarly, at Lyon, unmarried prostitutes were imprisoned in La Charité, 'et on les contraint aux travaux forcés ou on leur inflige une pénitence corporelle, voire même par le fouet'. See Brackenhoffer, *Voyage de France*, pp. 108–9.

83. *Correspondance des Contrôleurs Généraux*, Vol. I, p. 381, No. 1389; La Mare, *Traité de la Police*, Vol. I, Liv. 3, Tit. 5, Ch. 4; Lepage, *Archives de Nancy*, Vol. III, p. 221; L'Estoile, *Journal*, Vol. II, p. 341; Antoine Mareschal, *Le Railleur*, II.ii; *Variétés Historiques et Littéraires*, Vol. V, pp. 321 et seq.

84. *Anciennes Lois Françaises*, Vol. XIX, p. 464; Vol. XX, p. 47.

85. *Journal du Voyage de Deux Hollandais*, p. 225; La Fontaine, *Œuvres Complètes*, Vol. IX, p. 410; Tallemant, *Historiette de Gens Guéris ou Sauvés par Moyens Extraordinaires*, Vol. II, p. 126.

86. In the *Caquets de l'Accouchée* (1ʳᵉ Journée, p. 37) police commissioners are accused of accepting pensions from prostitutes and procuresses. See also L'Estoile, *Journal*, Vol. II, p. 470.

87. Jacmon, *Mémoires*, pp. 149–50.

88. Tallemant, *Historiette de Ninon*, Vol. VII, p. 236.

89. Tallemant, *Historiette de Marion*, Vol. V, p. 99, and *Historiette de Ninon*, Vol. VII, pp. 225, 230; Douxménil, *Mémoires et Lettres pour servir à l'histoire de la vie de Ninon*, pp. 18, 19.

90. Tallemant, *Historiette de Richelieu*, Vol. II, pp. 194–5, and *Historiette de Marion*, passim.

91. Tallemant, *Historiette de Boisrobert*, Vol. III, p. 164.

92. Ninon, *Correspondance Authentique* (ed. E. Colombey) passim; Saint-Evremond, *Lettres*, Vol. I, pp. 232 et seq., Vol. II, pp. 255 et seq.

93. Ninon, *Correspondance*, p. 219.

94. Ninon, *Correspondance*, p. 79; Saint-Simon, *Mémoires*, Vol. III, pp. 207–8.

95. *Journal du Voyage de Deux Hollandais*, p. 193.

96. Saint-Simon, *Mémoires*, Vol. III, p. 207.

97. Tallemant, *Historiette de Ninon*, passim.

98. Saint-Evremond, who defined his relationship with Ninon as 'ni de simple ami, ni de véritable amant', praised her probity where her friends were concerned. See his *Lettres*, Vol. I, p. 237; Vol. II, p. 258.

99. Saint-Simon, *Mémoires*, Vol. III, p. 207.
100. Saint-Simon, ibid.; Ninon, *Correspondance*, pp. 112, 224.
101. Saint-Simon, *Mémoires*, Vol. III, p. 208.
102. Dubuisson-Aubenay, *Journal*, Vol. I, p. 283; Tallemant, *Historiette de Marion*, Vol. V, p. 101. The piety of courtesans was a favourite subject with satirists, who naturally represented it as false. See Mareschal, *Le Railleur*, II.ii; Régnier, *Satire 13*; Sorel, *Francion*, Vol. I, Liv. 2, p. 103.
103. Tallemant, *Historiette de Marion*, Vol. V, p. 101.

CHAPTER 10

1. Examples: Marie de Médicis, governor of Normandy, then of Anjou (Fontenay-Mareuil, *Mémoires*, p. 138; Malherbe, *Œuvres*, Vol. III, p. 261); Anne d'Autriche, Grand-Maître, Chef et Surintendant Général de la Navigation et du Commerce (Guyot, *Traité des Droits*, Vol. II, 1ʳᵉ Partie, Ch. 67, p. 215; Vallier, *Journal*, Vol. II, p. 129); Duchesse d'Aiguillon, governor of Le Havre (Motteville, *Mémoires*, Vol. I, p. 108; Patin, *Lettres*, Vol. II, p. 59).
2. D'Aubignac, *Zénobie*, IV.iii; Bayle, *Dictionnaire*, Art. 'Junon M'.
3. Poulain de la Barre, *De l'Egalité des Deux Sexes*, p. 162. See also Du Bosc, *L'Honnête Femme*, 1ʳᵉ Partie, pp. 106, 108; Le Moyne, *Galerie des Femmes Fortes*, pp. 10–12.
4. Saint-Evremond, *Sur l'Amitié*, in *Œuvres en Prose*, Vol. III, p. 317.
5. The *sacre* of queens differed from that of kings in that they made no formal promises to the nation. For details of this and the queen's other prerogatives see Guyot, *Traité des Droits*, Vol. II, 1ʳᵉ Partie, Ch. 67.
6. For a potted history of the female regency in France see an anonymous pamphlet of 1652, *Le Sceptre de France en Quenouille*, attributed to Claude Dubosc de Montandré.
7. Louis XIV several times gave (nominal) regency powers to Marie-Thérèse when he went campaigning. See Colbert, *Lettres*, Vol. II, p. 81; Saint-Maurice, *Lettres*, Vol. I, p. 52. Louis XIII preferred to leave his mother in command (Colbert, *Lettres*, Vol. VI, p. 289; Peiresc, *Lettres*, Vol. VII, p. 424), but after her exile he vested authority in Anne d'Autriche, for example in 1636 when he went to repel a Spanish invasion of Picardy (Molé, *Mémoires*, Vol. II, p. 356).
8. Guyot, *Traité des Droits*, Vol. II, 1ʳᵉ Partie, Ch. 67, pp. 226–7, 228–30.
9. For Marie de Médicis see Richelieu, *Mémoires*, Vol. I, pp. 20, 395; Duc de Rohan, *Mémoires*, Collection Michaud et Poujoulat, 2ᵐᵉ Sér., Vol. V, p.493. For Anne d'Autriche see Bavière, *Correspondance* (trans. Brunet) Vol. I, p. 440; Montglat, *Mémoires*, p. 194; Duchesse de Nemours, *Mémoires*, Collection Michaud et Poujoulat, 2ᵐᵉ Sér., Vol. IX, p. 638; Talon, *Mémoires*, p. 432.
10. Richelieu, in his *Mémoires*, Vol. I, pp. 395–6, represents her as also confiding in various ministers alternatively.

11. Anne's reliance on Mazarin did not prevent her from occasionally thinking and acting independently, as he himself complained. See Mazarin, *Lettres*, Vol. IV, p. 429. See also Motteville, *Mémoires*, Vol. III, pp. 30–3.
12. Bavière, *Correspondance* (trans. Brunet) Vol. I, p. 456; *Recueil de Maurepas*, Vol. I, p. 32.
13. Lord Herbert of Cherbury, *Autobiography* (1886 edn) pp. 192–3; Pontchartrain, *Mémoires*, Collection Michaud et Poujoulat, 2me Sér., Vol. V, p. 379. But Héroard notes that Louis attended a council meeting in his mother's presence as early as 26 June 1610 (Héroard, *Journal*, Vol. II, p. 11) and that after his majority in 1614 such attendances were fairly regular (ibid., pp. 159 et seq.).
14. No first-hand evidence has so far come to light to prove or disprove Anne's marriage to Mazarin. All that can be said is that Mazarin wrote letters to Anne in tones more passionate than would be expected from a prime minister addressing his sovereign; for example on 11 May 1651: 'jamais il n'y a eu une amitié approchante à celle que j'ai pour vous ... [je] donnerais ma vie pour vous revoir et vous pouvoir dire des choses, devant de mourir, qui assurément n'ont jamais été imaginées'. See Mazarin, *Lettres du Cardinal Mazarin à la Reine, à la Princesse Palatine, etc.* (ed. J. Ravenel) pp. 31, 36.
15. Over against the testimony of Choisy (*Mémoires*, p. 577) to Anne's resentment at having to hand over government completely to Louis, and that of the Duchesse de Montpensier (*Mémoires*, Vol. I, p. 316) to Louis's impatience of maternal domination, must be placed that of Mme de Motteville, which stresses the respect that Anne always showed to her son in public, the obedience towards him which she inculcated into his brother and Louis's confidence in her in later years. See Motteville, *Mémoires*, Vol. I, p. 397, Vol. IV, pp. 54, 284. Louis's lack of political education is contradicted notably by the assertions of Brienne (*Mémoires*, Vol. II, p. 22, Vol. III, pp. 96–7), Choisy (*Mémoires*, p. 569), D'Ormesson (*Journal*, Vol. I, p. 768), Maréchal du Plessis (*Mémoires*, Collection Michaud et Poujoulat, 3me Sér., Vol. VII, p. 441) and Rapin (*Mémoires*, Vol. III, p. 103).
16. Sully, *Mémoires*, Vol. III, Liv. 10, pp. 243 et seq., 378 et seq.; Vol. V, Liv. 17, pp. 168 et seq.
17. For Mlle de Lafayette see Motteville, *Mémoires*, Vol. I, pp. 58 et seq. For Mme de Hautefort see above, Ch. 7, p. 99.
18. Perrault, *Mémoires*, pp. 25–6. See also Louis's own memoirs (ed. J. Longnon) pp. 258–60.
19. Saint-Maurice, *Lettres*, Vol. I, p. 350. Also La Fare, *Mémoires*, p. 264.
20. Bavière, *Correspondance* (trans. Brunet) Vol. I, p. 307; Bussy-Rabutin, *Histoire Amoureuse des Gaules*, Vol. I, p. 261; Choisy, *Mémoires*, p. 582; Saint-Simon, *Mémoires*, Vol. VIII, p. 77; Visconti, *Mémoires*, p. 39.
21. Bussy-Rabutin, *Correspondance*, Vol. V, pp. 30–1, and *Histoire Amoureuse des Gaules*, Vol. I, p. 269; *Mercure Galant*, Sept. 1680, 1re Partie, pp. 242–3; D'Ormesson, *Journal*, Vol. II, p. 506; Sévigné, *Lettres*, Vol. VI, pp. 195 et seq.
22. Sourches, *Mémoires*, Vol. I, p. 18, no. 2.

23. Bussy-Rabutin, *Correspondance*, Vol. I, p. 343; Saint-Maurice, *Lettres*, Vol. I, p. 514.
24. Clément, *Mme de Montespan et Louis XIV*, pp. 256, 338.
25. For example, Louis had a casket of jewels prepared from which to give her periodic presents (Clément, ibid., pp. 221–2), paid her gambling debts (Bussy-Rabutin, *Correspondance*, Vol. IV, p. 320) and had the estate of Clagny laid out for her (Sévigné, *Lettres*, Vol. III, pp. 477, 480, Vol. IV, p. 21).
26. Saint-Simon, *Mémoires*, Vol. VIII, p. 137; Sévigné, *Lettres*, Vol. VI, pp. 533–4.
27. Examples: separate carriage and royal groom and guards to escort her on a trip to Luxembourg in 1687 (Sourches, *Mémoires*, Vol. II, p. 55); expulsion of Italian actors in 1697 for performing *La Fausse Prude*, thought to satirise her (Saint-Simon, *Mémoires*, Vol. I, p. 274); marked attentions paid to her by Louis at the magnificent military review at Compiègne in 1698 (Saint-Simon, Vol. I, pp. 390–1).
28. Dangeau mentions such an event for the first time in 1689 in his *Journal*, Vol. II, p. 405.
29. Dangeau, *Journal*, Vol. III, pp. 21, 27; Vol. IV, pp. 16, 439; Vol. V, pp. 281, 288, 309, 311, 319, 322, 373, 388, 389; Vol. VI, pp. 185, 215, 278, 452; Vol. VII, p. 321 and elsewhere.
30. Ibid., Vol. IV, p. 210; Vol. VI, p. 41, and elsewhere.
31. Sourches, *Mémoires*, Vol. XII, p. 179, n. 2.
32. Saint-Simon, *Mémoires*, Vol. VIII, p. 152.
33. Ibid., Vol. II, p. 131.
34. Ibid., Vol. VIII, p. 153.
35. Louis's brother, Monsieur, disliked her – see Saint-Simon, *Mémoires*, Vol. II, p. 214; Visconti, *Mémoires*, p. 269 – and she was execrated by Monsieur's second wife – see Bavière, *Correspondance* (trans. Brunet) Vol. I, p. 114, Vol. II, p. 289 and passim. Relations with their son, the future Regent, were strained – see Saint-Simon, Vol. IV, pp. 168–9; likewise with the Dauphin – see Pierre Narbonne, *Journal des Règnes de Louis XIV et Louis XV de l'année 1701 à l'année 1744* (ed. J.-A. Le Roi) pp. 10–11; Saint-Simon, Vol. V, p. 442.
36. D'Aumale, *Souvenirs*, p. 110.
37. Choisy, *Mémoires*, p. 623; Saint-Simon, *Mémoires*, Vol. VIII, pp. 93 et seq.
38. Maintenon, *Lettres* (ed. Langlois) Vol. V, pp. 18, 48–9, 81, 251; Saint-Simon, Vol. IV, p. 286. Mme de Maintenon was alleged to resent the Jesuits in general because of the influence which their order had acquired over the king.
39. On 5 Dec. 1706 Mme de Maintenon wrote to the Princesse des Ursins: 'je reçois très souvent des lettres anonymes, où l'on me dit des injures sur tous les maux que je fais à l'état; on me demande ce que je veux faire, à la veille de ma mort, de tout l'argent que j'amasse. Il n'y a sur tout cela, madame, qu'à prendre patience.' See Maintenon, *Lettres Inédites* (ed. Bossange) Vol. I, p. 66.
40. Saint-Simon, *Mémoires*, Vol. V, p. 137, Vol. VIII, pp. 152–3.
41. Spanheim, *Relation*, p. 91; Sourches, *Mémoires*, Vol. I, p. 379.

Saint-Simon represents her as scheming always to have one
minister completely dependent upon her. See his *Mémoires*, Vol. II,
p. 31; Vol. IV, pp. 142, 400 et seq.

42. Saint-Simon, Vol. II, pp. 354–5; Vol. IV, p. 262.

43. Maintenon, *Lettres* (ed. Langlois) Vol. V, p. 6.

44. Bavière, *Lettres Inédites* (ed. Rolland) pp. 194–5; Saint-Simon,
Mémoires, Vol. VIII, pp. 155–6; Sourches, *Mémoires*, Vol. III, pp. 363–
4. Mme de Maintenon herself testified to the difficulty that she had
in persuading Louis to comply with her wishes. See her *Lettres* (ed.
Langlois) Vol. III, p. 325, and *Lettres Inédites* (ed. Bossange) Vol. II,
p. 64.

45. Maintenon, *Lettres* (ed. Langlois) Vol. II, pp. 367, 376, 383–4, 404,
466–7; Vol. III, p. 12.

46. Spanheim, *Relation*, p. 92. Cf. Dames de Saint-Cyr, *Mémoires sur
Mme de Maintenon*, p. 31; Saint-Simon, *Mémoires*, Vol. VIII, p. 143.
Initially Mme de Maintenon was a partisan of persuasion rather
than violence to achieve conversions – see her *Lettres* (ed. Langlois)
Vol. II, p. 65 – but her attitude seems to have hardened – ibid.,
Vol. V, p. 369.

47. The memory of her association with Fénelon continued to trouble
her many years after his disgrace in 1699. See a letter of 16 July 1714
to the Princesse des Ursins in Maintenon, *Lettres Inédites* (ed.
Bossange) Vol. III, p. 87; also Saint-Simon, Vol. I, pp. 192–3, 347 et
seq.

48. Mme de Maintenon had been instrumental in the appointment of
Noailles, through whom (always according to Saint-Simon) she
proposed to gain that control over the distribution of ecclesiastical
benefices which La Chaise had resisted. See Saint-Simon, *Mémoires*,
Vol. I, p. 182; Vol. IV, p. 286; Vol. VIII, pp. 162 et seq. Her own
letters (ed. Langlois) Vol. V, p. 13, and the *Souvenirs* of Mlle
d'Aumale (p. 181) attest that she did influence the choice of
beneficiaries but only after checking their worthiness with men of
the Church.

49. Bavière, *Correspondance* (trans. Brunet) Vol. I, p. 295; Saint-Simon,
Mémoires, Vol. VI, pp. 410–11.

50. Saint-Simon, a personal friend of the Princesse des Ursins, alleges in
his *Mémoires*, Vol. III, p. 4, that she flattered Mme de Maintenon into
swallowing the bait of being able to govern Spain, through the
agency of the Princesse, along with France. The published correspondence of the two women between 1705 and 1715 leaves no doubt
about the Princesse's initial use of hyperbolical flattery. See, for
example, Maintenon, *Lettres Inédites*, Vol. III, p. 203. But relations
quickly became strained when Mme de Maintenon was obliged to
represent the necessity for an exhausted France to sue for peace
with the Allies at the cost of abandoning Philip V, while Mme des
Ursins pressed for the war to continue and for French troops to be
sent to Spain. For the Princesse's break with Mme de Maintenon
and fall from power, see Charles Duclos, *Mémoires Secrets*,
Collection Michaud et Poujoulat, 3me Sér., Vol. X, pp. 461

et seq.; Saint-Simon, *Mémoires*, Vol. VII, pp. 39 et seq., 284 et seq.

51.   One noblewoman, Mme de Villiers, was decapitated in 1674 for being implicated in the Chevalier de Rohan's treasonable plot to introduce the Dutch enemy into France, but she was not the prime mover of the conspiracy and had joined only for love of the ringleader's nephew. See La Fare, *Mémoires*, pp. 279–80; *Lettres et Rapports de Police* in P. Clément, *La Police sous Louis XIV*, pp. 424–5.

52.   Rapin, *Mémoires*, Vol. III, p. 430.

53.   Bavière, *Correspondance* (trans. Brunet) Vol. II, p. 9.

54.   Lafayette, *La Princesse de Clèves*, p. 252.

55.   Amongst examples of battling females in the late sixteenth century may be noted those of Claude de la Tour, Comtesse de Roussillon – see François de Belleforest, *Histoire Universelle du Monde*, dedicatory 'Epître'; Hilarion de Coste, *Eloges*, 2me Partie, pp. 475–86; Mme de Neuvy – see Jacques de Thou, *Histoire Universelle* (1734 edn) Vol. V, pp. 659–60; and Maréchale de Balagny – see Le Moyne, *Galerie des Femmes Fortes*, p. 156; Louis Moréri, *Grand Dictionnaire Historique*, Art. 'Montluc, Jean de'.

56.   Balzac to Mme des Loges, 20 Sept. 1628, in *Suite de la Seconde Partie des Lettres de M. de Balzac*, p. 259; La Guette, *Mémoires*, pp. 8–9; *Mercure Galant*, Feb. 1679, pp. 55–8, Nov. 1681, p. 56 et seq., Apr. 1687, p. 95; Scarron, *Poésies Diverses* (ed. M. Cauchie) Vol. II, p. 335; Tallemant, *Historiette de Villarceaux*, Vol. VII, p. 239.

57.   Abbé Arnauld, *Mémoires*, pp. 494–5; D'Assoucy, *Aventures Burlesques*, p. 119; Dunoyer, *Lettres*, Vol. II, pp. 329 et seq.; Fléchier, *Grands Jours d'Auvergne*, p. 179; *Lettres en Vers* (ed. Rothschild) Vol. I, pp. 4–5, 22–3, 94, 198, Vol. II, pp. 81–2; *Mercure Galant*, Jan. 1681, pp. 334–8; Patin, *Lettres*, Vol. III, pp. 536–7; Tallemant, *Historiette de Mlle du Tillet*, Vol. I, p. 187, *Femmes Vaillantes*, Vol. VIII, *Mondory*, Vol. X, p. 49; *Variétés Historiques et Littéraires*, Vol. II, pp. 357–63.

58.   Dubuisson-Aubenay, *Journal*, Vol. II, p. 154; *Lettres en Vers*, Vol. II, p. 1004; *Mercure Galant*, Sept. 1692, pp. 328–31, May 1695, pp. 211–12.

59.   Protestant women distinguished themselves in this respect. See Ch. 13, p. 232.

60.   Examples of amazons in novels: Talestris in La Calprenède's *Cassandre*, Vol. II, pp. 334 et seq., and Hermione in Vol. III, pp. 547 et seq.; Menalippe in the same author's *Cléopâtre*, 8me Partie, Liv. 2–4, pp. 222 et seq.; Melandre in D'Urfé, *l'Astrée*, Vol. I, Liv. 12. For amazons on stage see especially the plays of Antoine Mareschal (*La Généreuse Allemande; La Sœur Valeureuse*) and those of Jean Rotrou (passim).

61.   Attached to *La Pucelle* is an interesting feminist preface in which the indefatigability of aristocratic huntresses and the robustness of peasant women doing the same jobs as their husbands is used as an argument for forming armies composed of females. See Chapelain, *Opuscules Critiques* (ed. A. Hunter) p. 264.

62.   Fontenay-Mareuil, *Mémoires*, p. 104. For other examples of women

peacemakers see Rohan, *Mémoires*, pp. 552–3; Sully, *Mémoires*, Vol. III, Liv. 11, pp. 498 et seq.

63. Hilarion de Coste, *Eloges*, 2me Partie, pp. 286–7; Souvigny, *Mémoires*, Vol. I, pp. 45–6.
64. Arnauld d'Andilly, *Journal*, pp. 203–4; Fontenay-Mareuil, *Mémoires*, p. 110.
65. Fontenay-Mareuil, *Mémoires*, pp. 176 et seq.; Richelieu, *Mémoires*, Vol. VI, pp. 101 et seq.
66. Fontenay-Mareuil, *Mémoires*, pp. 200 et seq.; Richelieu, *Lettres*, Vol. IV, p. 95.
67. Montpensier, *Mémoires*, Vol. III, pp. 351–2.
68. Motteville, *Mémoires*, Vol. I, pp. 51–2; Richelieu, *Lettres*, Vol. IV, pp. 432–3, 436, and *Mémoires*, Vol. VII, p. 90, Vol. VIII, pp. 93 et seq.
69. La Porte, *Mémoires*, pp. 19 et seq.; La Rochefoucauld, *Mémoires*, Collection Michaud et Poujoulat, 3me Sér., Vol. V, pp. 386 et seq.; Richelieu, *Lettres*, Vol. V, pp. 836–7.
70. Richelieu, *Mémoires*, Vol. I, p. 184.
71. Richelieu, *Lettres*, Vol. VI, p. 122. See also Vol. V, p. 689, and *Testament Politique*, 1re Partie, Ch. 8, sect. 5, p. 301, 2me Partie, Ch. 7, p. 362, and Ch. 8, p. 370.
72. He was credited with a passion for both the Duchesse de Chevreuse and Anne d'Autriche. See Motteville, *Mémoires*, Vol. I, pp. 29, 51.
73. Montglat, *Mémoires*, p. 73; Richelieu, *Lettres*, Vol. VI, pp. 73 et seq. As soon as she became regent Anne dismissed Mmes de Brassac and de Lansac and replaced them by Mme de Senecé, whom Richelieu had ousted for intriguing against him. See Motteville, *Mémoires*, Vol. I, p. 125; Richelieu, *Lettres*, Vol. VI, pp. 93, 235–6.
74. Lenet, *Mémoires*, p. 463.
75. La Porte, *Mémoires*, pp. 38–9; Tallemant, *Historiette de Bazinière*, Vol. VI, p. 112.
76. Tallemant, *Historiette de Mme de Rambouillet*, Vol. III, p. 214.
77. La Rochefoucauld, *Mémoires*, p. 383; Tallemant, *Historiette de Richelieu*, Vol. II, p. 230.
78. Through Mlles de Roussereau and de Chamarante Mazarin kept an eye on one of Louis XIV's ephemeral mistresses, Mlle de la Mothe-Argencourt (La Fare, *Mémoires*, p. 262). Mme de Navailles, *gouvernante* of the royal *filles d'honneur*, remained a devoted agent throughout the Fronde (Motteville, *Mémoires*, Vol. III, pp. 260, 343–4), as did the Marquise d'Ampus (Retz, *Mémoires*, Vol. II, p. 558).
79. Retz, *Mémoires*, Vol. I, p. 210.
80. Scudéry, *Grand Cyrus*, Vol. IX, Liv. 3, p. 1049.
81. Lenet, *Mémoires*, p. 254; Benjamin Priolo, *Ab Excessu Ludovici XIII De Rebus Gallicis, Historiarum Libri XII*, Lib. II, p. 58.
82. Tallemant, *Historiette de Mme de Montausier*, Vol. III, p. 256.
83. Nemours, *Mémoires*, p. 635.
84. Montpensier, *Mémoires*, Vol. I, pp. 313 et seq.
85. *Choix de Mazarinades* (ed. C. Moreau) Vol. I, pp. 431, 435; Talon, *Mémoires*, p. 348. The distribution of *tabourets* escalated into a major political issue. See Motteville, *Mémoires*, Vol. II, pp. 262 et seq.,

Vol. III, pp. 56–7, 70 et seq.; Retz, *Mémoires*, Vol. II, pp. 540–3.

86. Princesse Palatine, *Mémoires*, pp. 115–16.
87. Nemours, *Mémoires*, p. 635.
88. Lenet, *Mémoires*, passim.
89. Montpensier, *Mémoires*, Vol. I, p. 335, Vol. II, p. 111.
90. La Rochefoucauld, *Mémoires*, p. 451; Motteville, *Mémoires*, Vol. III, p. 391.
91. Nemours, *Mémoires*, p. 619; Palatine, *Mémoires*, p. 121.
92. La Rochefoucauld, *Mémoires*, p. 478; Lenet, *Mémoires*, pp. 218–19; Motteville, *Mémoires*, Vol. IV, pp. 9–11.
93. Palatine, *Mémoires*, pp. 196–7.
94. Ibid., p. 111.
95. Lenet, *Mémoires*, p. 376; Montpensier, *Mémoires*, Vol. I, p. 203.
96. Montglat, *Mémoires*, pp. 207–8, 275.
97. Retz, *Mémoires*, Vol. II, pp. 190–1.
98. Lenet, *Mémoires*, p. 254.
99. *De Rebus Gallicis*, Lib. II, pp. 58–9.
100. Bayle, *Dictionnaire*, Art. 'Denys A'; Colbert, *Lettres*, Vol. I, p. 345; Davity, *Les Etats, Empires et Principautés du Monde*, p. 82; Saint-Evremond, *Sur les Historiens Français*, in *Œuvres en Prose*, Vol. III, p. 92; Saint-Simon, *Mémoires*, Vol. V, p. 254. For the first half of the century see Nicolas Faret, *L'Honnête Homme ou l'Art de Plaire à la Cour* (ed. M. Magendie) pp. 40, 90.
101. Saint-Maurice, *Lettres*, Vol. I, pp. 294, 296; Visconti, *Mémoires*, p. 174. In Giovanni Marana's *L'Esploratore turco* (1684) spies insinuate themselves among the women of Paris as the persons most likely to have information at their command (an English translation of 1741, *Letters writ by a Turkish spy*, has been used: Vol. I, Bk 1, Letter 8).
102. Condé's nickname for Mazarin (Retz, *Mémoires*, Vol. II, p. 85).
103. Saint-Maurice, *Lettres*, Vol. I, p. 512. Cf. Patin, *Lettres*, Vol. III, p. 784.
104. In 1662 the Comtesse de Soissons had played a leading part in a conspiracy to dislodge Mlle de La Vallière from favour. See Lafayette, *Histoire d'Henriette d'Angleterre*, p. 190; Montpensier, *Mémoires*, Vol. III, pp. 551–2; Motteville, *Mémoires*, Vol. IV, pp. 325–6.
105. Hébert, *Mémoires*, pp. 22 et seq.
106. D'Ormesson, *Journal*, Vol. I, pp. 267, 332–3. In 1648 these incidents multiplied. See Guy Joly, *Mémoires*, Collection Michaud et Poujoulat, 3ᵐᵉ Sér., Vol. II, p. 7; Molé, *Mémoires*, Vol. IV, pp. 306–7; Motteville, *Mémoires*, Vol. II, p. 8; D'Ormesson, *Journal*, Vol. I, p. 414; Talon, *Mémoires*, p. 273.
107. Dubuisson-Aubenay, *Journal*, Vol. II, pp. 125, 169, 248, 260, 277, 279.
108. Dubuisson-Aubenay, *Journal*, Vol. II, pp. 102, 104; Guy Joly, *Mémoires*, p. 19; Montglat, *Mémoires*, p. 286; Rapin, *Mémoires*, Vol. I, pp. 268–9.
109. Vallier, *Journal*, Vol. I, p. 336.

110.   Patin, *Lettres*, Vol. I, p. 440.

111.   Talon, *Mémoires*, p. 483. See also ibid., pp. 139–41, 254; Dubuisson-Aubenay, *Journal*, Vol. I, p. 181; D'Ormesson, *Journal*, Vol. I, pp. 267, 270, 334.

112.   Joseph Ancillon, an advocate in the Parlement of Metz, relates a typical instance of how one Le Verrier brought to the town a royal decree stipulating that trades not in guilds should become incorporated, and authorisation for a census of the number of taxable persons in each trade; 'mais comme cela faisait grand bruit dans la ville et que quelques femmes eurent donné l'épouvante, il s'en retourna sans rien faire'. See Ancillon, *Recueil Journalier de ce qui s'est passé de plus mémorable dans la cité de Metz* (ed. F. Chabert) Vol. I, p. 107.

113.   *Documents de l'Histoire de la Provence* (ed. E. Baratier) p. 198; Louvet, *Journal*, in *Revue de l'Anjou*, Sept.–Oct. 1856, p. 137; B. Porchnev, *Les Soulèvements Populaires en France de 1623 à 1648*, p. 634.

114.   *Lettres et Mémoires adressés au Chancelier Séguier*, Vol. II, p. 767.

115.   *Correspondance des Contrôleurs Généraux*, Vol. I, p. 249, No. 955.

116.   Ibid., pp. 514–15, No. 1829, note.

117.   Women were suspected at times of being 'used' by masculine rebels who wanted to hide their hand. A *Relation de la Révolte de la Basse-Normandie*, published by A.-P. Floquet in his edition of the *Diaire ou Journal du Voyage du Chancelier Séguier en Normandie après la sédition des Nu-Pieds (1639–1640)*, ends with the observation: 'Toutefois, on peut encore ajouter que ceux qui n'osaient pas se déclarer pour rebelles, par la crainte de la perte de leurs biens, fomentaient secrètement la rébellion, et faisaient agir les femmes de basse et mauvaise condition dans toutes les actions susdites, lesquelles s'y portaient avec autant [sic] plus d'ardeur et de furie que ce sexe indiscret et imprudent en considérait moins l'importance' (p. 420).

118.   Delort, *Mémoires*, pp. 82 et seq. See also *Correspondance des Contrôleurs Généraux*, Vol. I, p. 404, No. 1471.

119.   M. Foisil, *La Révolte des Nu-Pieds et les Révoltes Normandes*, p. 174.

120.   *Une Emeute à Agen en 1635, Publiée d'après le manuscrit de Malebaysse* (ed. A. Magen) in *Recueil des Travaux de la Société d'Agriculture, Science et Arts d'Agen*, Vol. VII, pp. 210, 217. The word *gabelle* was often used in a broad sense, as in this instance, to denote any new tax. Similarly *gabeleur* was a global term of abuse levelled against fiscal agents, but also used of anyone considered guilty of profiteering and oppression.

121.   Michel Béziers, *Mémoires pour servir à l'état historique et géographique du Diocèse de Bayeux* (ed. G. Le Hardy) Vol. I, p. 176; *Correspondance des Contrôleurs Généraux*, Vol. I, pp. 428–9, No. 1546; *Correspondance Administrative sous Louis XIV* (ed. Depping) Vol. III, p. 168; Delort, *Mémoires*, p. 88; *Une Emeute à Agen* (ed. Magen) p. 224.

122.   See *Chacun fait le métier d'autrui*, *Ballet* (ed. V. Fournel) in *Les Contemporains de Molière*, Vol. II, p. 496; *Choix de Mazarinades*, Vol. I, p. 16, Vol. II, p. 276; Montpensier, *Mémoires*, Vol. I, pp. 92–3.

123. For Beaufort's familiarity with the women of the Halles see *Choix de Mazarinades*, Vol. II, p. 85; Loret, *Muse Historique*, 18 June 1651; Patin, *Lettres*, Vol. II, pp. 513–14. For his stupidity see Retz, *Mémoires*, Vol. II, pp. 177–8 and passim; and for his tresses, Retz, ibid., Vol. II, p. 194.

124. The word *pair* was used for female peers in their own right, *pairesse* denoting the wife of a peer. See Fléchier, *Oraison Funèbre pour la Duchesse d'Aiguillon*, in *Œuvres Complètes*, Vol. I, p. 47; Guyot, *Répertoire*, Art. 'Pair'; Malherbe, *Œuvres*, Vol. III, p. 454.

125. Fiefs were commonly made into duchies at the same time as peerages, though this was not always automatic. See next note.

126. The *seigneurie* of Piney, for example, which became a duchy in 1576 and a peerage in 1581, was passed on through females and possessed in the early seventeenth century by Marguerite-Charlotte de Luxembourg. Her daughter Madeleine-Charlotte, the sole heiress, on marrying the future Maréchal de Luxembourg in 1661, transmitted the dukeship to him. Luxembourg obtained the peerage, in the face of strong opposition, in 1662. See Anselme, *Maison Royale*, Vol. III, pp. 589, 733, Vol. IV, pp. 327–8; Saint-Simon, *Mémoires*, Vol. I, p. 86.

127. Anselme, *Maison Royale*, Vol. IV, p. 736.

128. Ibid., Vol. V, pp. 26–7.

129. The estate of D'Aubigny in Berry was elevated into a *duché-pairie* in favour of herself and Charles's bastard the Duke of Richmond, but the *lettres d'érection* were never formally registered. See Anselme, ibid., Vol. V, pp. 919 et seq.; Dangeau, *Journal*, Vol. I, p. 126.

130. The Duchesse d'Aiguillon passed hers to her niece and the Marquise de Senecé transmitted hers to her daughter. See Anselme, ibid., Vol. IV, pp. 483–4, 735.

131. Male heirs to the *duché-pairie* of Hallwin having become extinct in 1598, the sister of the original beneficiary of the honour, Anne d'Hallwin, was allowed to retain it in favour of her marriage to the Comte de Candale in 1611. When the marriage was nullified the *duché-pairie* was recreated (1620) in favour of Anne's second marriage to Charles de Schomberg, to whom she passed on the peerage. See Anselme, ibid., Vol. III, p. 900, Vol. IV, p. 330.

132. Sourches, *Mémoires*, Vol. I, p. 19, n. 2.

133. According to Guyot, *Répertoire*, Art. 'Pair', women in the Middle Ages had possessed this right.

134. Guyot, *Répertoire*, Art. 'Femme'; Loysel, *Institutes Coutumières*, Vol. I, Liv. 1, Règle 35.

135. Examples: Molé, *Mémoires*, Vol. I, pp. 126–7, Vol. II, p. 152, Vol. III, p. 57; D'Ormesson, *Journal*, Vol. I, p. 310.

136. Delort, *Mémoires*, p. 287; D'Ormesson, *Journal*, Vol. II, p. 427.

137. Dubuisson-Aubenay, *Journal*, Vol. I, p. 181, Vol. II, p. 87; D'Ormesson, *Journal*, Vol. I, p. 588, Vol. II, pp. 131–2, 353; Retz, *Mémoires*, Vol. III, pp. 445–7.

138. Women did not participate in either of the two *Assemblées des Notables* held in 1617–18 and 1626–7.

139. In exceptional cases, such as that of Marie de Médicis, election-rigging seems to be proven. See J. M. Hayden, *France and the Estates General of 1614*, pp. 77, 78.

140. For the procedure of these rural assemblies, which had their equivalent in the towns, see A. Babeau, *Le Village sous l'Ancien Régime*, Liv. I, Ch. 2, and *La Ville sous l'Ancien Régime*, Vol. I, Liv. 1, Ch. 3.

141. La Poix de Freminville, *Traité Général*, Ch. 10, pp. 189–91.

142. Babeau's citation of a ban on female participation in mayoral elections at Dijon in Louis XIII's reign (see *La Ville sous l'Ancien Régime*, Vol. I, Liv. 1, Ch. 4, p. 71) is evidence of an official desire to preclude the ordinary townswoman from voting at least for the municipal authorities who elected deputies. Openings always existed, however, for women of substance to put their protégés into office. See *Correspondance des Contrôleurs Généraux*, Vol. I, p. 306, No. 1150; *Mémoire de la Généralité de Moulins* (ed. P. Flamant) p. 114.

143. J. Russell Major in *The Deputies to the Estates General in Renaissance France*, a work which covers the 1614 Estates and the projected Estates of 1649 and 1651, occasionally mentions the summoning of heads of female religious communities to participate in sixteenth-century elections of deputies for the clergy (pp. 101, 105). But only a single such instance, in connection with the 1651 Estates, is cited for the seventeenth century (p. 107).

144. *Cahiers* (ed. Durand) pp. 85, 95, 168, 242.

145. Ibid., p. 85. However, when representatives of the nobility assembled at Troyes during the Fronde to draft a *Cahier* in preparation for a meeting of the Estates General which never materialised, no woman sat in their midst. See *Deux Cahiers de la Noblesse pour les Etats Généraux de 1649–1651* (ed. Mousnier) p. 155.

146. *Des Etats Généraux et Autres Assemblées Nationales* (ed. Charles Mayer) Vol. XVI, 1789, p. 99.

147. Bouche, *La Chorographie ou Description de Provence*, Vol. II, pp. 418, 833, 837, 857, 858, 862, 888, 918. In his addenda to Vol. I, p. 22, Bouche notes that those who assisted at the Provençal Estates, which ceased after 1639, included 'tous les gentilshommes possédant fiefs'.

148. *Cahiers des Etats de Normandie* (ed. Beaurepaire) passim; H. Beaune and J. d'Arbaumont, *La Noblesse aux Etats de Bourgogne de 1350 à 1789*, pp. 20–56.

149. A. Rébillon, *Les Etats de Bretagne de 1661 à 1789*, p. 86. The Estates of Foix similarly allowed women to pass on entry rights to husbands, sons and sons-in-law. See G. Arnaud, *Mémoire sur les Etats de Foix (1608–1789)*, p. 14.

150. Dom J. Vaissète and Dom C. Devic, *Histoire Générale de Languedoc*, Vol. XI, pp. 896, 898.

151. Ibid., Vol. XIV, pp. 555–6. A *Règlement* of 1685 repeated the same provisions and clearly stated that only men were to sit on the Estates (pp. 1319 et seq.).

152. *Cahiers des Etats de Normandie*, Vol. III, pp. xviii–xix; Vaissète, *Histoire*, Vol. XI, pp. 887, 913 and passim.
153. Sévigné, *Lettres*, Vol. II, pp. 309–10, and Letter 191 passim. Cf. Coulanges, 'L'Adieu des Etats de Bretagne', in *Chansons Choisies*, pp. 58–60.
154. Bayle, *Dictionnaire*, Art. 'Junon M'.
155. These harangues were a standing joke. See Chaulieu, *Œuvres*, Vol. I, p. 3 (*A Mme la Duchesse du Maine*); Dunoyer, *Lettres*, Vol. II, pp. 46–7; Sarasin, 'Vers Irréguliers à Mme la Princesse de Condé la douairière', in *Œuvres* (ed. Gilles Ménage) pp. 80 et seq.
156. For typical examples of ceremonial entries see Loret, *Muse Historique*, 20 Sept. 1653; *Mercure Galant*, Oct. 1685, pp. 167 et seq.; May 1686, pp. 165 et seq. Exceptionally, a high-born lady making her official entry might be offered a richly embroidered canopy (the *poêle* or *dais*) beneath which to process, but this honour, along with the presentation of the town's keys, was normally reserved for those of royal blood. See René de Brilhac, *Extraits des Mémoires* in *Archives Historiques du Poitou*, Vol. XV, pp. 38–9; Joseph Guillaudeau, *Diaire*, p. 391; Jousselin, *Journal de M. Jousselin, curé de Sainte-Croix d'Angers (1621–52)* (ed. C. Port) in *Inventaire Analytique des Archives Anciennes de la Mairie d'Angers*, p. 431; Loret, *Muse Historique*, 18 Aug. 1652; Louvet, *Journal*, in *Revue de l'Anjou*, Mar.–Apr. 1855, p. 135, and May–June 1855, p. 312; *Journal Historique de Vitré* (ed. Abbé P. Paris-Jallobert) p. 88; C.-A. Parmentier, *Archives de Nevers*, Vol. II, pp. 186, 211.
157. Vaissète, *Histoire*, Vol. XI, p. 920. See also *Correspondance des Contrôleurs Généraux*, Vol. I, p. 304, No. 1147. Gratifications were given not only for specific attendance at the Estates but also for general services rendered to the province. In 1628 the Prince de Condé was awarded 48 000 *livres* by the Languedoc Estates 'pour lui témoigner l'honneur qu'ils recevaient de ce qu'il avait le commandement des armes dans la Province', and his wife (Charlotte de Montmorency) received 12 000 *livres*. In 1641 she obtained a further 12 000 *livres* and her husband 50 000 (Vaissète, ibid., Vol. XI, pp. 1023, 1126).
158. Lepage, *Archives de Nancy*, Vol. II, pp. 16–17.
159. Nicolas Chorier, *Mémoires*, (trans. F. Crozet) Liv. 3, p. 173.
160. Locke, *Travels in France*, p. 124.
161. *Grands Jours d'Auvergne*, pp. 85 et seq.
162. Sourches, *Mémoires*, Vol. III, pp. 39–40.
163. French writers mocked and criticised the Italian Marie de Médicis, the Spanish Anne d'Autriche and the German Dauphine, Marie-Anne-Victoire de Bavière, for preserving overt loyalties to their native land or for failing to acquire fluency in French. See Caylus, *Souvenirs*, p. 496; Dangeau, *Journal*, Vol. III, p. 102; Tallemant, *Historiette de Richelieu*, Vol. II, p. 164, and *Historiette de M. de Bullion*, Vol. III, p. 6.
164. Bavière, *Lettres Inédites* (ed. Rolland) pp. 93, 95.

165. For the tragic life of Henriette see Lafayette, *Histoire de Madame Henriette d'Angleterre*, passim.
166. Montpensier, *Mémoires*, Vol. IV, p. 306; Sévigné, *Lettres*, Vol. II, p. 324.
167. Jean Le Laboureur, *Relation du Voyage de la Reine de Pologne et du Retour de Mme la Maréchale de Guébriant*, 3me Partie, pp. 3 et seq.
168. Anselme, *Maison Royale*, Vol. II, p. 87.
169. Dangeau, *Journal*, Vol. I, p. 3.
170. On the sudden death of the ambassador to Turkey in 1685 his wife, Mme de Guilleragues, was able to take his place until a successor could be sent out. See Dangeau, *Journal*, Vol. I, p. 165; Sourches, *Mémoires*, Vol. I, p. 378.
171. Villars, *Lettres* (1759 edn) pp. 8–9.
172. Ibid., p. 15.
173. Ibid., pp. 38–9.
174. Ibid., pp. 85, 161.
175. Ibid., pp. 110–11.
176. Ibid., pp. 51, 109, 121, 127. The accusations probably contained more than a grain of truth in view of the 'salée, plaisante, méchante' personality that Saint-Simon attributed to Mme de Villars. See his *Mémoires*, Vol. III, p. 288.
177. See *Recueil des Instructions données aux Ambassadeurs et Ministres de France*, Vol. XI, Tome 1 (ed. A. Morel-Fatio) pp. 275 et seq.
178. Richelieu, *Lettres*, Vol. VI, p. 539.

CHAPTER 11

1. A popular means of rewarding artists, all the more so since it cost little, was for great ladies to act as godmothers to their infants. See *Lettres en Vers* (ed. Rothschild) Vol. III, p. 587.
2. Details in L. Batiffol, *La Vie Intime d'une Reine de France au XVIIe Siècle*, Ch. 7. Two other outstanding builders of *châteaux* were the Duchesse de Longueville (Catherine de Gonzague), who had one erected at Coulommiers in Brie (see Marolles, *Mémoires*, 1re Partie, p. 67), and the Duchesse de Montpensier, responsible for the construction of Choisy on the Seine (see *Mercure Galant*, July 1686, 1re Partie, pp. 154 et seq.).
3. Sauval, *Antiquités de Paris*, Vol. II, pp. 200–1. Several Paris town houses were rebuilt on the initiative of women. See, for example, Sauval, Vol. II, p. 122 (Duchesse de Mercœur), and Germain Brice, *Description Nouvelle de la Ville de Paris* (1700 edn) Vol. II, pp. 261–2, 265 (Duchesses de Chevreuse and de la Meilleraye).
4. Sévigné, *Lettres*, Vol. III, p. 504; Vol. IV, p. 21.
5. Maintenon, *Lettres* (ed. Langlois) Vol. II, pp. 152–3, 180, 183–4, 381, 446–7.
6. *Mémoires Inédits sur la Vie et les Ouvrages des Membres de l'Académie Royale de Peinture et de Sculpture* (ed. Dussieux) Vol. I, pp. 155, 167,

168, 169. This work contains examples of the same kind on every other page.

7. The *Livre de Raison* of the painter Hyacinthe Rigaud (ed. J. Roman) shows the extent to which this fashion had spread from women of the aristocracy to the Parisian and provincial bourgeoisie by the 1680s. Wives of magistrates, tax officials and municipal notabilities are listed repeatedly as sitters. This, despite the sharp rise in the painter's fees from the 11 *livres* paid in 1681 by Mme Dupin, wife of a salt-tax collector of Montluçon (see ibid., p. 1), to the 140 *livres* paid in 1699 by Mme Delaborde of Pau, wife of a tax-farmer (see ibid., p. 72).

8. Félibien, *Entretiens sur les Vies et sur les Ouvrages des plus excellents peintres anciens et modernes*, No. 7, pp. 410–25.

9. Dussieux, *Mémoires Inédits*, Vol. I, pp. 143–4; Félibien, *Entretiens*, No. 10, p. 334; *Lettres en Vers* (ed. Rothschild) Vol. III, pp. 543–4.

10. Félibien, *Entretiens*, No. 9, p. 269. Mme de Montespan was painted, twice, as Mary Magdalen (see Clément, *Mme de Montespan et Louis XIV*, p. 430), and Mme de Maintenon as Ste Françoise (see Dussieux, *Mémoires Inédits*, Vol. II, p. 96). See also *Lettres en Vers*, Vol. III, pp. 1093–4; Rapin, *Mémoires*, Vol. II, p. 493.

11. Originally painted for Monsieur's [Louis XIV's brother] *château* at Saint-Cloud in 1670, the portrait contained eighteen life-size figures in all. See Dussieux, *Mémoires Inédits*, Vol. I, p. 313; E. Soulié, *Notice du Musée Impérial de Versailles* (2me edn) 2me Partie, p. 198.

12. The portrait of Mme de Chevreuse is reproduced in L. Batiffol, *La Duchesse de Chevreuse*. For Mme de Montbazon see Loret, *Muse Historique*, 29 Oct. 1650.

13. Félibien, *Entretiens*, No. 8, pp. 18, 24; Marolles, *Suite des Mémoires*, p. 267.

14. *Nouvelles Archives de l'Art Français* (1878) p. 266.

15. *Journal du Voyage de Deux Hollandais*, p. 317; *Mercure Galant*, Nov. 1697, p. 225.

16. Bavière, *Lettres Inédites* (ed. Rolland) p. 210; Brice, *Description de Paris*, Vol. II, pp. 299–300, 302; Loret, *Muse Historique*, 10 Nov. 1663; Marolles, *Suite des Mémoires*, p. 267.

17. Patriotic women periodically took their silver plate to the Mint to be melted down to help Louis XIV's war effort. See Sévigné, *Lettres*, Vol. IX, pp. 359, 366, 377, 406; Sourches, *Mémoires*, Vol. XI, p. 350; Jacques Vergier, 'A Mme la Comtesse d'Ars, qui avait prié l'auteur de faire recevoir sa vaisselle d'argent à la Monnaie', in *Œuvres*, Vol. II, pp. 163–5.

18. Bavière, *Correspondance* (trans. Brunet) Vol. I, pp. 141, 169, Vol. II, p. 259; Sauval, *Antiquités*, Vol. I, p. 20, Vol. II, p. 346.

19. Boisrobert, *Epîtres en Vers* (ed. M. Cauchie) Vol. II, pp. 46 et seq.

20. Pradel, *Adresses de Paris pour 1692*, Vol. I, pp. 231–6; and above, note 15.

21. Piganiol de La Force, *Nouveau Voyage de France*, Vol. I, p. 343.

22. Dussieux, *Mémoires Inédits*, Vol. I, p. 288.

23. Charles Perrault, *Les Hommes Illustres*, Art. 'Sarrasin'.

24. Molière, *La Gloire du Val de Grâce*, in *Œuvres Complètes* (ed. Garnier) Vol. II, pp. 858 et seq.; Sauval, *Antiquités*, Vol. I, p. 439.
25. Dussieux, *Mémoires Inédits*, passim; Félibien, *Entretiens*, No. 7, pp. 390 (Jacques Blanchart), 398 (Simon Vouet), No. 10, pp. 316, 317, 323 (Philippe de Champaigne), 411 (Jacques Stella), 424 (Charles du Fresnoy) and others.
26. See Ch. 2, p. 35.
27. Molière, *La Princesse d'Elide*, 3me Intermède, sc. 1. Cf. De Grenaille, *Les Plaisirs ou les Honnêtes Divertissements des Dames* (1647), where the concert figures as the penultimate example of the honest diversions in question. See also Bavière, *Lettres Inédites* (ed. Rolland) p. 140; Loret, *Muse Historique*, 7 Dec. 1652, 25 Jan. 1653, 15 Aug. 1654.
28. Scipion Dupleix, *Histoire de Louis Le Juste*, p. 72.
29. Montpensier, *Mémoires*, Vol. III, pp. 255 et seq.
30. Benserade, 'Epître à Mme la Duchesse d'Epernon', in *Œuvres*, Vol. I, p. 100; *Journal du Voyage de Deux Hollandais*, p. 317; La Fontaine, *Le Songe de Vaux*, in *Œuvres*, Vol. VIII, pp. 271 et seq.; Perrin, *Œuvres de Poésie*, p. 194; Mme de Saintot, *Correspondance* (ed. P. d'Estrée) in *Revue d'Histoire Littéraire* (1894) p. 366.
31. Loret, *Muse Historique*, 1 Jan. 1651.
32. Ibid. Loret misleadingly calls Hilaire the 'sœur' of Lambert.
33. Montpensier, *Mémoires*, Vol. III, p. 348.
34. Tralage, *Extraits du Manuscrit de Tralage* (ed. P. L. Jacob) p. 81.
35. *Lettres en Vers* (ed. Rothschild) Vol. I, pp. 357–8, 484–5, 509; Vol. II, pp. 407–10, 1123; Vol. III, p. 20.
36. D'Aumale, *Souvenirs*, p. 170; Bavière, *Lettres Inédites* (ed. Rolland) p. 260; Dangeau, *Journal*, Vol. X, pp. 161, 428; Maintenon, *Lettres Inédites* (ed. Bossange) Vol. II, pp. 339, 350.
37. The reputation of opera-singers was, if possible, even more execrable than that of ordinary actresses. See Bavière, *Correspondance* (trans. Brunet) Vol. I, p. 44; Dufresny, *Amusements Sérieux et Comiques*, No. 5; Dunoyer, *Lettres*, Vol. IV, pp. 408–9; La Bruyère, 'Des Jugements', 16, in *Caractères*; Courtilz de Sandras, *Annales de la Cour et de Paris pour les années 1697 et 1698*, Vol. I, pp. 33 et seq; Spanheim, *Relation*, p. 214; Tralage, *Extraits du Manuscrit*, pp. 92–3.
38. Occasionally a woman ventured to compose an opera, for example, Mme de Saintonge, wife of an advocate in the Paris Parlement. See *Mercure Galant*, Feb. 1696, p. 320; Titon du Tillet, *Parnasse Français*, p. 563. Outstanding operatic patrons were notoriously masculine.
39. Thus Bassompierre could dance with other lords the *Ballet des Lavandières* and the *Ballet des Nymphes* in 1600 (see his *Mémoires*, Vol. I, p. 79).
40. See Mlle de Gournay, *Œuvres* (1626 edn) Liv. 2, pp. 1138 et seq. Later on Mme de Maintenon deigned to supply the outlines for ballets that Mme de Montespan commissioned the Abbé Genest to write. See Pellisson-Fontanier, *Histoire de l'Académie Française*, Vol. II, p. 384.
41. Bassompierre, *Mémoires*, Vol. I, p. 300.
42. See *Ballets et Mascarades de Cour sous Henri IV et Louis XIII (1581–1652)*

(ed. P. Lacroix) Vol. II, pp. 63 et seq.; Bassompierre, *Mémoires*, Vol. II, pp. 1–2; Malherbe, *Œuvres*, Vol. III, pp. 488–9.

43. According to Bassompierre, *Mémoires*, Vol. I, p. 223, she last danced in a ballet on 8 Mar. 1609.
44. Malherbe, *Œuvres*, Vol. III, pp. 61, 131, 479.
45. Bassompierre, *Mémoires*, Vol. II, p. 111; P.-F. Godard de Beauchamps, *Recherches sur les Théâtres de France*, Vol. III, pp. 78, 84, 85, 92, 101.
46. Loret, *Muse Historique*, 11 Feb. 1662, 16 Feb. 1664.
47. The dancing skill of the Princesse de Conti (Marie-Anne de Bourbon), Louis XIV's daughter by La Vallière, is often lauded by contemporaries. See La Fontaine, *Œuvres*, Vol. VIII, p. 451; Sourches, *Mémoires*, Vol. I, pp. 56, 289; Spanheim, *Relation*, p. 201.
48. Benserade, *Œuvres*, Vol. II, passim; Loret, *Muse Historique*, 18 Apr. 1654, 22 Jan. 1656, 22 Feb. 1659, 19 Feb. 1661, 31 July 1661, 11 Feb. 1662, 20 Jan. 1663, 16 Feb. 1664, 31 Jan. 1665; *Lettres en Vers*, Vol. I, pp. 302–3, Vol. II, pp. 549–52, Vol. III, pp. 498, 505–6.
49. The exception is Angélique Paulet, who sang in the *Ballet de la Reine* of 1609. See Tallemant, *Historiette de Mlle Paulet*, Vol. IV, p. 8.
50. The names of Mlles Hilaire (Dupuy), de la Barre, Cercamanan, Bergerotti and Saint-Christophle recur frequently in contemporary accounts of ballets. See above, note 48.
51. For example, at Marguerite de Valois's Hôtel in the Rue de Seine. See Lord Herbert of Cherbury, *Autobiography*, p. 105; Tallemant, *Historiette de Marguerite de Valois*, Vol. I, p. 165.
52. Chapelle, *Voyage de Chapelle et de Bachaumont*, in *Œuvres de Chapelle* (ed. Tenant de Latour) p. 56.
53. Tallemant, *Historiette de Richelieu*, Vol. II, p. 191.
54. Benserade, *Œuvres*, Vol. II, p. 332.
55. For the Maréchale relations with men of letters see *Mercure Galant*, Aug. 1691, pp. 258–9.
56. While rarely acknowledging the receipt of material benefits from them, Loret speaks of many other women (for example, the Maréchale de l'Hôpital, wife of the governor of Paris) in terms which suggest that they paid more than their gazette money.
57. See *Lettres en Vers*, Vol. I, passim, Vol. II, pp. 767 et seq.
58. 'Elles [les précieuses] ont un homme d'esprit, pauvre et malheureux, auquel elles donnent un dîner par semaine, et un habit par an, et le font travailler tout leur saoul sur toutes les pensées qui leur tombent dans l'esprit' (De Pure, *La Prétieuse*, Vol. I, 1ʳᵉ Partie, p. 90). This tyranny was exercised over the greatest writers, as was evident in the case of Racine and Boileau, forced to apply themselves to the composition of opera and history at the whim of Mme de Montespan – see Boileau, *Prologue d'un Opéra*, in *Œuvres*, p. 262; Caylus, *Souvenirs*, p. 490 – and that of La Fontaine writing the *Poème du Quinquina* for the Duchesse de Bouillon – see his *Œuvres*, Vol. VI, p. 316, vv. 10–11.
59. Examples: Boisrobert, *Epîtres en Vers*, Vol. II, pp. 119 et seq.; La Fontaine, *Œuvres*, Vol. VIII, pp. 447–8; René Le Pays, *Amitiés*,

Amours et Amourettes, Liv. 1, p. 16; Voiture, *Œuvres*, Vol. II, pp. 367, 375, 399.

60. Examples: Chorier, *Mémoires*, p. 28; Maintenon, *Lettres* (ed. Langlois) Vol. III, p. 177; Montpensier, *Mémoires*, Vol. II, p. 248.

61. Tallemant, *Historiette de Voiture*, Vol. IV, pp. 34 et seq.

62. Segrais, *Les Nouvelles Françaises ou Les Divertissements de la Princesse Aurelie* [Duchesse de Montpensier], passim.

63. Two stalwarts of contemporary salons, the academicians Conrart and Chapelain, were notorious for their dirty habits (see their respective *Historiettes* by Tallemant, Vol. IV, pp. 153, 177). But these were always an extra diversion.

64. The *ruelle* was technically the space between the wall and the side of the bed on which ladies liked to recline to receive visitors (*Dictionnaire de l'Académie*, 'Ruelle'). Recesses designed for conversation with intimates were also known as *réduits* and *alcôves*, and those who frequented them as *alcôvistes* (Somaize, *Dictionnaire des Précieuses*, passim).

65. See Ch. 10, p. 150.

66. Tallemant, *Historiette de Mme des Loges*, Vol. IV.

67. Rapin, *Mémoires*, Vol. I, p. 218; Vol. III, pp. 72–3.

68. Members of the Hôtel de Rambouillet included the Duchesse d'Aiguillon, of lesbian tendencies; the Princesse de Condé, mistress of the Cardinal de La Valette; Angélique Paulet, who numbered Henri IV among a long succession of lovers; Malherbe, who boasted of his VD attacks; and so on. See their *Historiettes* by Tallemant, a fellow frequenter of the salon.

69. Mme Tambonneau, wife of a president in the Chambre des Comptes, once launched in society by her lover the Duc de Mortemart, 'avait trouvé le secret par son seul esprit d'attirer chez elle tout ce qu'il y avait de plus considérable à la cour, de l'un et de l'autre sexe'. See *Recueil de Maurepas*, Vol. II, p. 83, n. 4. See also Tallemant, *Historiette du Président et de la Présidente Tambonneau*, Vol. IX.

70. The Rambouillet salon set the tone. See Abbé Arnauld, *Mémoires*, pp. 482–3; Tallemant, *Historiette de Mme de Rambouillet*, Vol. III, pp. 216, 230, and *Historiette de Mlle Paulet*, Vol. IV, p. 14; Voiture, *Œuvres*, Vol. I, pp. 46–7.

71. Abbé Arnauld, *Mémoires*, p. 485; Voiture, *Œuvres*, Vol. I, p. 258.

72. Staal, *Mémoires*, p. 693.

73. For Mme Deshoulières's circle see her daughter's 'Epître à Benscrade', in *Poésies de Mme et de Mlle Deshoulières*, Vol. II, pp. 209 et seq., and Louis Le Gendre, *Mémoires*, (ed. M. Roux) Liv. 4, pp. 173–4. For her philosophical ideas see her 'Idylles' and 'Ode à M.L.D.D.L.R.', in *Poésies*, Vol. I, pp. 151 et seq.

74. For Mme de la Sablière's erudition and acquaintances see above, Ch. 2, n. 147, and Boileau, *Satire 10*, vv. 425–6; for her love-life see Sévigné, *Lettres*, Vol. VI, pp. 79–80, 527–8, and S. Menjot-d'Elbenne, *Mme de La Sablière*, passim.

75. Tallemant, *Historiette de Ninon*, Vol. VII, pp. 229, 230.

76. Scudéry, *Clélie*, 4me Partie, Liv. 2, pp. 959 et seq.; Liv. 3, pp. 1211 et seq.
77. Ibid., 2me Partie, Liv. 1, pp. 307 et seq. (kindness); 4me Partie, Liv. 1, pp. 82 et seq. (idleness); 105 et seq. (ingratitude); 5me Partie, Liv. 1, pp. 77 et seq. (exactitude and mendacity); 1re Partie, Liv. 3, pp. 1252 et seq., 3me Partie, Liv. 2, pp. 674 et seq., 4me Partie, Liv. 1, pp. 59 et seq. (death). Her previous ten-volume novel *Le Grand Cyrus* contains conversations on patriotism (Vol. VIII, Liv. 2, pp. 746 et seq.), old age (ibid., pp. 844 et seq.), suicide (ibid., pp. 1006 et seq.), mockery (ibid., Vol. IX, Liv. 3, pp. 967 et seq.).
78. Examples in: Coulanges, *Mémoires*, pp. 396–401; *La Journée des Madrigaux* (ed. E. Colombey) passim.
79. *Questions d'Amour proposées par Mme de Brégy* in La Suze-Pellisson, *Recueil de Pièces Galantes*, Vol. IV, p. 137. For the origins of love-questions, with which contemporary literature bristles, see T. F. Crane, *Italian Social Customs of the Sixteenth Century*, passim.
80. Scudéry, *Clélie*, 3me Partie, Liv. 1, pp. 60 et seq., Liv. 2, pp. 732–3; Somaize, *Dictionnaire des Précieuses*, Vol. I, pp. 121, 131.
81. Mlle de Scudéry's 'Carte du Tendre' was only one of many. See E. Magne, *Mme de la Suze et la Société Précieuse*, pp. 206 et seq.
82. Examples: Anon, *Les Lois de la Galanterie* (1855 reprint); Bussy-Rabutin, *Mémoires*, Vol. II, pp. 160 et seq.; Scudéry, *Clélie*, 3me Partie, Liv. 3, pp. 1362 et seq.; D'Urfé, *L'Astrée*, Vol. II, Liv. 5, pp. 181–3, 195–7.
83. Sorel, *La Maison des Jeux*, Vol. I, pp. 283–4.
84. Salons enjoyed putting on their own plays. See Abbé Arnauld, *Mémoires*, p. 490; Maintenon, *Lettres Inédites* (ed. Bossange) Vol. I, pp. 78, 81, Vol. III, p. 148; Segrais, *Les Nouvelles Françaises*, Vol. II, pp. 173 et seq.
85. Scudéry, *Grand Cyrus*, Vol. X, Liv. 2, p. 727.
86. Scudéry, *Clélie*, 3me Partie, Liv. 2, pp. 1075 et seq. (poetry composition by the *honnête homme*); 4me Partie, Liv. 1, pp. 56–7 (epitaphs); Liv. 2, pp. 794 et seq., 1124 et seq. (novels); Liv. 2, pp. 866 et seq. (burlesque); 5me Partie, Liv. 1, pp. 284 et seq. (portraits); Segrais, *Les Nouvelles Françaises*, passim (novels).
87. Mlle de La Force, *Les Jeux d'Esprit* (ed. Marquis de la Grange) pp. 75 et seq.; Sorel, *Maison des Jeux*, Vol. II, pp. 393 et seq.
88. *La Guirlande de Julie* (ed. O. Ozanne) 1875. Some thirty other poems were written for the *Guirlande* but not included in the original presentation. See E. Magne, *Voiture et les Années de Gloire de l'Hôtel de Rambouillet*, p. 220, note.
89. A present given by Conrart to Mme Aragonais, friend of Mlle de Scudéry, was the origin of the most famous poetic tournament in salon history, the *Journée des Madrigaux*. See Colombey edition, passim.
90. Pets occupy considerable space in the poetry of the day. See Benserade, *Œuvres*, Vol. I, pp. 137, 179–81, 182, 278; Charles Cotin, *Œuvres Mêlées*, pp. 51–2; Deshoulières, *Poésies*, Vol. II, pp. 158 et seq.; La Suze-Pellisson, *Recueil*, Vol. I, pp. 168 et seq., Vol. II,

pp. 126 et seq., Vol. III, pp. 14–15, Vol. IV, pp. 252–3; Le Pays, *Nouvelles Œuvres* (ed. A. de Bersaucourt) pp. 60–1; Loret, *Muse Historique*, 29 Nov. 1653, 19 June 1655; Etienne Pavillon, *Œuvres* pp. 25–6, 220; and others.

91. See Ch. 12, p. 195.
92. See Ch. 12, p. 193.
93. Somaize, *Dictionnaire des Précieuses*, Art. 'Toxaris', Vol. I, p. 232.
94. Boursault, *Lettres de Respect, d'Obligation et d'Amour*, p. 93.
95. Scudéry, Dedication of *Le Vassal Généreux*.
96. Claude-Nicolas Le Cat, *Eloge de Fontenelle*, pp. 3–4; Pellisson-Fontanier, *Histoire de l'Académie Française*, Vol. II, p. 194; Sévigné, *Lettres*, Vol. II, pp. 470, 524; Tallemant, *Historiette de Tallemant, Le Maître des Requêtes*, Vol. VIII, p. 141; Vigneul-Marville, *Mélanges d'Histoire et de Littérature*, Vol. I, p. 160.
97. The salon of Mme du Plessis-Guénégaud played a leading role in diffusing his *Provinciales*. See Rapin, *Mémoires*, Vol. II, pp. 367, 375.
98. Racine, dedicatory epistle of *Andromaque*, and letter of 1688 to Mme de Maintenon, in *Œuvres*, Vol. VII, pp. 5–6; Coulanges, *Mémoires*, p. 384.
99. Antoine Arnauld, *Lettres*, Vol. VII, pp. 330–1; Boileau-Despréaux, *Bolaeana*, pp. 124–5; Coulanges, *Mémoires*, p. 384; Pellisson-Fontanier, *Histoire de l'Académie*, Vol. II, pp. 159–60; Charles Perrault, preface to *L'Apologie des Femmes*; Louis Racine, *Mémoires sur la Vie de Jean Racine*, in the latter's *Œuvres* (Editions du Seuil) pp. 24, 43; Sévigné, *Lettres*, Vol. III, pp. 315–6, 369; E. de Barthélemy, *La Marquise d'Huxelles et ses Amis*, p. 96.
100. The principal feminine influences on the career of La Fontaine were Mme de la Sablière (see La Fontaine, 'Discours à Mme de la Sablière', in *Fables*, Liv. 9); the Duchesse de Bouillon, to whom authors declaimed in the midst of her snapping dogs (see Chaulieu, *Œuvres*, Vol. I, pp. 64, 87, 95; La Fontaine, *Œuvres*, Vol. IX, pp. 394–5); Mme d'Hervart, a financier's wife (see La Fontaine, *Œuvres*, Vol. IX, pp. 74–6, 378 et seq., 461–4; Vergier, *Œuvres*, Vol. II, pp. 133, 162); and Mme Ulrich, who published his *Œuvres Posthumes* in 1696 (see the 'Préface').
101. François Le Dieu, *Mémoires et Journal sur la Vie et les Ouvrages de Bossuet* (ed. Abbé Guettée) Vol. I, pp. 18–19; Tallemant, *Historiette de Voiture*, Vol. IV, p. 52.
102. La Rochefoucauld, *Œuvres*, Vol. III, 1re Partie, pp. 147, 156. Mme de Lafayette was also credited with having had 'bonne part' in the *Maximes* (see Huet, *Huetiana*, p. 248).
103. This was the attitude constantly adopted by Mme de Lafayette – see Lafayette, *Correspondance éditée d'après les travaux d'A. Beaunier*, Vol. I, p. 211; Lafayette, *Lettres* (ed. Ashton) pp. 43, 92–3, 95 – and by Mlle de Scudéry – see Scudéry, *Correspondance*, pp. 145–6, 302; 'Documents Inédits sur la Société et la Littérature Précieuses' (ed. L. Belmont) in *Revue d'Histoire Littéraire* (1902) p. 661.
104. Chapelain, *Lettres*, Vol. I, pp. 221–2. See also pp. 215–16, and Tallemant, *Historiette de la Vicomtesse d'Auchy*, Vol. II, p. 4.

105. Donneau de Visé, *Nouvelles Nouvelles*, 3ᵐᵉ Partie, p. 162.
106. De Pure, *La Prétieuse*, Vol. I, 1ʳᵉ Partie, pp. 16, 20.
107. Furetière, *Roman Bourgeois*, Vol. I, p. 114.
108. Molière, *Femmes Savantes*, III.ii.
109. Boileau, '1ʳᵉ Réflexion sur Longin', in *Dialogues, Réflexions Critiques, Œuvres Diverses* (ed. C. Boudhors) p. 56. For other authors who favoured this procedure see Bouhours, *Entretiens d'Ariste et d'Eugène*, 'Le Bel Esprit', p. 161; Pellisson-Fontanier, *Histoire de l'Académie*, Vol. I, pp. 246–7.
110. Ninon, *Correspondance*, p. 219. Ninon shared the honour with another gallant lady, Honorée de Bussy (see Tallemant, *Historiette du Maréchal de Brézé*, Vol. III, p. 35, n. 2). When Molière read his plays to ladies of the court he ignored their opinions. See the anecdote about Madame and *Le Misanthrope* in Le Gallois de Grimarest's *Vie de Molière* (Renaissance du Livre edn) pp. 59–60.
111. Marolles, *Mémoires*, 1ʳᵉ Partie, p. 105.
112. Gournay, *Les Idées Littéraires de Mlle de Gournay* (ed. A. Uildriks) pp. 106, 117, 182. The *Défense de la Poésie* and *De la Façon d'Ecrire de Messieurs Du Perron et Bertaut* from which these expressions are taken were both published in the *Œuvres* of 1626.
113. Malherbe, *Œuvres*, Vol. IV, p. 90; Tallemant, *Historiette de Vaugelas*, Vol. IV, p. 124.
114. Molière, *Femme Savantes*, II.vi–vii.
115. Bouhours, *Entretiens*, 'Sur la Langue Française', p. 100; Margucrite Buffet, *Nouvelles Observations sur la Langue Française*, 4ᵐᵉ Partie, pp. 183, 185, 188; Gournay, *Défense de la Poésie* (ed. Uildriks) pp. 129–30; François de Maucroix, *Lettres* (ed. R. Kohn) pp. 91–2; Molière, *Femmes Savantes*, III.ii; Chevalier de Sévigné, *Correspondance*, p. 246; La Suze-Pellisson, *Recueil*, Vol. V, p. 39.
116. Somaize, *Dictionnaire des Précieuses*, Vol. I, pp. lvii, liii, xliv, lxiii.
117. De Pure, *La Prétieuse*, Vol. I, 1ʳᵉ Partie, p. 5.
118. Boursault, *Les Mots à la Mode*; Delosme de Montchenay, *La Cause des Femmes*; Fatouville, *La Fille Savante*; Molière, *Femmes Savantes*; and so on.
119. *Variétés Historiques et Littéraires*, Vol. IX, pp. 79–89.
120. Tallemant, *Historiette de la Marquise de Rambouillet*, Vol. III, p. 232, and *Historiette de Mme de Montausier*, Vol. III, p. 253.
121. Cf. Mlle de Scudéry's publication of all her early works under her brother Georges's name. See *Journal des Savants*, 11 July 1701 (Bosquillon's 'Eloge'); Tallemant, *Historiette de Scudéry*, Vol. IX, p. 140.
122. Lafayette, *Lettres* (ed. Ashton) p. 108.
123. Lafayette, *Correspondance* (ed. Beaunier) Vol. I, p. 175.
124. Ibid., Vol. II, p. 63.
125. Ménage, *Menagiana*, 2ᵐᵉ Partie, p. 137.
126. Puget de La Serre's *Secrétaire de la Cour*, for example, contains specimen feminine replies to an offer of service, a projected absence, a lover's inconstancy, departure, farewell and so on. See 1624 edn, pp. 143–6, 172–4, 192–3, 270–6, 405–7, 438–41.

127. La Bruyère, 'Des Ouvrages de l'Esprit', 37, in *Caractères*. Cf. Maintenon, *Lettres* (ed. Langlois) Vol. III, p. 170; Segrais, *Segraisiana*, p. 34.

128. Brégy, *Lettres et Poésies*, addressed to Anne d'Autriche, Christina of Sweden, the exiled queen of England and her daughter, the Duchesse de Longueville, and others.

129. Balzac, *Lettres Choisies* (1647 edn) 1re Partie, No. 13, to Ménage.

130. Malherbe, *Œuvres*, Vol. IV, p. 22.

131. Tallemant, *Historiette de Mme des Loges*, Vol. IV, pp. 212, 213.

132. Chapelain, *Lettres*, Vol. I, p. 504 (Oct. 1639).

133. Sévigné, *Lettres*, Vol. IV, p. 246. Mme de Sévigné insists with suspect regularity on the negligence of her style. See Vol. II, pp. 374, 487, 519; Vol. V, pp. 241, 425, 551–2, and so on.

134. Her term, in Sévigné, *Lettres*, Vol. VI, p. 551.

135. Sévigné, *Lettres*, Vol. II, p. 101; Vol. III, p. 198; Vol. VIII, pp. 378–9.

136. Motteville, *Mémoires*, Vol. IV, p. 312.

137. Lafayette, *Histoire de Madame Henriette d'Angleterre*, p. 181.

138. See Ch. 2, n. 88.

139. Lafayette, *Histoire*, p. 182.

140. Guyon, *Vie de Mme Guyon, écrite par elle-même*, passim.

141. Montpensier, *Mémoires*, Vol. I, p. 2; Vol. IV, p. 18. The *Mémoires*, were interrupted between 1660 and 1677 (Vol. III, p. 370). When the Duchesse resumed them she had her amorous advances towards an ugly and arrogant social inferior, Lauzun, to justify to posterity (Vol. IV, pp. 386 et seq.).

142. Comtesse de Murat, *Mémoires* (1740 edn) Liv. 1, p. 5. These *Mémoires* were originally published in 1697.

143. By Mme de Villedieu and Présidente Ferrand respectively.

144. For other examples see the *Mémoires* of the Marquise de Courcelles and those attributed to the Duchesse Mazarin.

145. Bayle, *Dictionnaire*, Art. 'Virgile A'.

146. The output of novels in the seventeenth century is so vast and diverse that it is impossible to resume in a few neat formulas. Apart from the representative romance described in the text, women also dabbled in ghost stories – see, for example, the Comtesse de Murat's *Lutins du Château de Kernosy* and *Voyage de Campagne* – and in fairy-tales – see *Mercure Galant*, April 1698, p. 208; M. E. Storer, *La Mode des Contes de Fée, 1685–1700*.

147. Examples of bibliographies in Marie-Jeanne l'Héritier de Villandon, preface to *La Tour Ténébreuse*, and Mme de Villedieu, *Annales Galantes*.

148. Scudéry, *Grand Cyrus*, Vol. I, Liv. 1, p. 34; Vol. VI, Liv. 3, p. 1298; Vol. VIII, Liv. 3, p. 1343. *Enlèvements* were such a persistent feature of novels as to excite the hilarity of sceptics and satirists. See Bayle, *Dictionnaire*, Art. 'Hélène E'; Boileau, *Dialogue sur les Héros de Roman*, in *Œuvres*, p. 291; Furetière, *Roman Bourgeois*, Vol. I, p. 190; Gabriel Guéret, *Le Parnasse Réformé* (1671 edn) pp. 136–7; Sorel, *Le Berger Extravagant*, Vol. III, pp. 381–2, and *De la Connoissance des Bons Livres* (ed. H. Béchade) p. 114.

149. Lafayette, *Romans et Nouvelles*, p. 337: 'La singularité d'un pareil aveu, dont elle ne trouvait point d'exemple ... un remède si extraordinaire ...'
150. Scudéry, *Correspondance*, pp. 294–5.
151. Mme de Villedieu, for example, has one of the heroes of her *Annales Galantes* tossed into a mud-patch (4me Partie, pp. 239–40) and describes thus an ageing *gouvernante* surprised in her bed: 'C'était une vieille qui pliait sous le faix des années, et cependant quand elle vit un homme, elle fit un cri, et cacha son visage sous la couverture, comme si sa vertu eut encore été dans la saison des périls' (6me Partie, p. 381). The tone is prolonged in the frequent interruptions of the narrative to mock traditional modes of novel-writing (2me Partie, pp. 131–2; 4me Partie, pp. 217–18; 8me Partie, p. 490; and so on).
152. Pointing out in her *Désordres de L'Amour*, 2me Partie, pp. 137–8, that love leads to despair, Villedieu adds: 'Je ne doute point qu'en cet endroit plus d'un lecteur ne dise d'un ton ironique que je n'en ai pas toujours parlé de cette sorte, mais c'est sur cela même que je me fonde pour en dire tant de mal, et c'est pour en avoir fait une parfaite expérience que je me trouve autorisée à le peindre avec de si noires couleurs.' See E. Magne, *Mme de Villedieu*, passim.
153. Villedieu, *Annales Galantes*, 'Avant-Propos'.
154. See above, Ch. 2, p. 31.
155. Mme de Sablé's 81 *Maximes* were published in 1678. For those of Mme de Maintenon see *Lettres et Entretiens*, Vol. II, pp. 401–7, 410–12.
156. They are published with the Comtesse de Murat's *Voyage de Campagne*, Vol. I, pp. 351 et seq., Vol. II, pp. 132 et seq.; but see Catherine Durand's own *Œuvres* (1737 edn) Vol. II. Mme de Maintenon also tried her hand at proverb composition for Saint-Cyr (see Dames de Saint-Cyr, *Mémoires sur Mme de Maintenon*, p. 421).
157. Pringy, *Les Différents Caractères des Femmes du Siècle*, passim.
158. Scudéry, *Correspondance*, pp. 479–80; Sévigné, *Lettres*, Vol. VIII, p. 372. For a complete bibliography of the *Conversations* see *Revue d'Histoire Littéraire* (1933) pp. 555–9.
159. The work by Mlle de Gournay (1641).
160. The work by Mme de Pringy.
161. See above, Ch. 2, pp. 30–1, 32.
162. L'Héritier de Villandon, *La Tour Ténébreuse*, pp. 154–5, 184; *Les Bigarrures Ingénieuses*, pp. 69 et seq. See also Murat, 'Le Bonheur des Moineaux', in *Nouveaux Contes des Fées*, pp. 157–9.
163. Deshoulières, *Poésies*, Vol. I, pp. 94 et seq.; Vol. II, pp. 119 et seq., 150 et seq. For the idylls, ibid., passim.
164. See Ch. 14, p. 241.
165. Deshoulières, 'Imitation de la 1re Ode d'Horace', in *Poésies*, Vol. I, p. 13.
166. Villedieu, *Jouissance*, in La Suze-Pellisson, *Recueil*, Vol. I, pp. 13–14.
167. Examples of poems by Mlles Catherine Bernard, d'Alerac de La

Charce, l'Héritier de Villandon, Itier, Marie de Razilly, de Scudéry and others will readily be found in the *Mercure Galant* and in De Vertron, *La Nouvelle Pandore ou Les Femmes Illustres du Siècle de Louis le Grand*.

168. The Revocation of the Edict of Nantes, for example. See Deshoulières, *Poésies*, Vol. I, pp. 82–3; De Vertron, *Nouvelle Pandore*, Vol. I, pp. 387–8 (Mlle Roland); *Mercure Galant*, Jan. 1686, p. 28 (Mlle de Scudéry).

169. Deshoulières, *Poésies*, Vol. I, pp. 101–3; De Vertron, *Nouvelle Pandore*, Vol. II, pp. 388–9.

170. De Vertron, *Nouvelle Pandore*, Vol. I, p. 230; Vol. II, pp. 328–9, 337–42, 362.

171. Deshoulières, 'Epître à M. le Duc de Montausier', 'Epître à Mgr sur son départ pour l'Allemagne', 'Epître à Mgr le Duc de Bourgogne sur la Prise de Mons', in *Poésies*, Vol. II, pp. 16–20, 103–7, 152–7.

172. Deshoulières, *Poésies*, Vol. I, p. 115.

173. Deshoulières, 'Placet au Roi', 'Epître à M. de Pontchartrain', 'Au Roi Madrigal', in *Poésies*, Vol. II, pp. 135–7, 155–7, 162–3. Mlle Bernard addressed a straightforward *Requête* to the king for payment of her pension of 200 *écus* (see De Vertron, *Nouvelle Pandore*, Vol. II, pp. 366–7).

174. See, for example, *Mercure Galant*, Sept. 1693, p. 224; May 1697, p. 245; Sept. 1697, p. 14; Sept. 1698, pp. 12, 50; June 1700, p. 226.

175. The exception was Marie de Pech de Calages of Toulouse, authoress of *Judith* (1660). The poem is analysed in detail by R. A. Sayce, *The French Biblical Epic in the Seventeenth Century*, Ch. 9, Part 2.

176. For Mme de Villedieu see D'Aubignac, *Remarques sur la Tragédie de M. Corneille intitulée Sertorius*, pp. 96–7; Tallemant, *Historiette de Mlle Desjardins*, Vol. X, pp. 221 et seq.; Titon du Tillet, *Parnasse Français*, p. 542. For Mlle Bernard see La Croix, *Dictionnaire des Femmes Célèbres*, Art. 'Bernard'; *Mercure Galant*, Dec. 1690, pp. 288–9.

177. Apart from *Genséric*, Mme Deshoulières partly composed a play called *Jules Antoine*. See the 'Eloge Historique' by her friend Chambors at the head of the 1754 edition of her *Poésies*, pp. xxx–xxxii. Chambors formally attributes to her the sonnet parodying *Phèdre* (p. xxvii) and it is printed amongst her poems. See also Louis Racine, *Mémoires*, p. 33.

178. These three provincials, together with Mmes Deshoulières and de Villedieu, are mentioned in Jean de la Forge's *Cercle des Femmes Savantes* (1663). For analyses of their plays see H. Carrington Lancaster, *A History of French Dramatic Literature in the Seventeenth Century*, Part 2, Vol. II, pp. 671–4, Part 3, Vol. I, p. 158, n. 2.

179. Mme Deshoulières, for example, produced an 'Imitation de la 1re Ode d'Horace', an 'Imitation de Lucrèce, en galimatias fait exprès', and several paraphrases of Latin psalms.

180. Though not unique. Mlle de Gournay in her *Avis ou Présents* had included translations of extracts from several Latin authors,

notably Virgil. But she left a rather different memory from that of her illustrious successor.

181. For Mme Dacier's biography see Nicéron, *Mémoires pour servir à l'histoire des hommes illustres*, Vol. III, pp. 126 et seq., and above, Ch. 2, p. 24.

182. Bayle, *Dictionnaire*, Arts 'Anacréon K.' and 'Sappho A'; Boileau-Despréaux, *Bolaeana*, p. 43.

183. Dacier, *Des Causes de la Corruption du Goût* (1714) p. 4. For the circumstances of the quarrel with La Motte see the opening pages of this work, and for the sequel see Montesquieu, *Lettres Persanes*, No. 36; Staal, *Mémoires*, p. 752.

184. Ferrand, 'Lettre de la Présidente Ferrand sur Mme Dacier' (ed. P. B.) in *Revue d'Histoire Littéraire* (1906) pp. 326 et seq.; Lister, *Journey to Paris*, p. 77; Nicéron, *Mémoires*, Vol. III, p. 137; Saint-Simon, *Mémoires*, Vol. XI, p. 331.

185. Agrippa d'Aubigné, *Histoire Universelle* (ed. Baron A. de Ruble) Liv. 7, Ch. 20, 1576, Vol. V, p. 3, and *Lettre à mes filles*, in Pléiade edition of *Œuvres*, pp. 852–3; Brantôme, *Œuvres* (ed. L. Lalanne) Vol. 9, p. 709 ('Discours sur les femmes mariées, les veuves, et les filles').

186. De Vertron, *Nouvelle Pandore*, Vol. I, pp. 425 et seq.; *Mercure Galant*, Sept. 1699, pp. 135–6.

187. *Mercure Galant*, May 1691, p. 118.

188. Ibid., May 1698, p. 200; June 1698, p. 84.

189. It is true that three learned French associates of the academy, Mme Hommetz Patin and her daughters Gabrielle and Charlotte, were resident in Padua, but they passed for Italian. See La Croix, *Dictionnaire*, Art. 'Patin'.

190. After admitting only a handful of women as Academicians at well-spaced intervals from the 1660s onwards, the Academy of Painting decided in 1706 to admit no more, and did not lift its ban until 1770. See *Procès verbaux de l'Académie Royale de Peinture et de Sculpture, 1648–1792* (ed. A. de Montaiglon) Vol. IV, pp. 33–4; Vol. VIII, p. 53. For the Academy of Music see Claude-François Ménestrier, *Des Représentations en Musique Anciennes et Modernes* (1972 reprint) p. 236.

191. Private academies were sometimes disposed to be less rigid. The Abbé d'Aubignac founded an Académie des Belles-Lettres to examine works of eloquence and poetry, and planned to introduce therein women such as Mmes Deshoulières and de Villedieu. But the academy was disbanded before the candidates proposed were able to take their places. See *Mercure Galant*, 1673, Vol. I, pp. 80–2.

192. *Mercure Galant*, May 1691, pp. 117–18.

193. See, however, Bussy-Rabutin, *Correspondance*, Vol. I, p. 369, Vol. II, p. 132, Vol. VI, p. 116; Ménage, *Anti-Baillet*, Vol. I, p. 304; Pellisson-Fontanier, *Histoire de l'Académie*, Vol. II, pp. 295, n. 1, 408, 462.

194. Article 1 of the Statutes of the Académie Française declared that no one should be received therein who was not agreeable to the Protector. See Pellisson-Fontanier, *Histoire de l'Académie*, Vol. I, p. 489.

195. D'Argenson, *Journal et Mémoires*, Vol. I, p. 164.

CHAPTER 12

1. Saint-Gabriel, *Le Mérite des Dames*, p. 42.
2. Malebranche, *Recherche de la Vérité*, Liv. 2, 2me Partie, Ch. 1, sect. 1.
3. Fléchier, *Réflexions sur les Caractères des Hommes*, in *Œuvres*, Vol. IX, Ch. 17, p. 397; Fontenelle, *Fontenelliana*, p. 82; Furetière, *Roman Bourgeois*, Vol. I, p. 18; De Grenaille, *L'Honnête Fille*, 3me Partie, Liv. 1, Ch. 1, pp. 78–9, and *L'Honnête Mariage*, Liv. 3, Ch. 1, p. 235; Méré, *Œuvres Complètes* (ed. C. Boudhors) Vol. I, pp. 17–18, Vol. II, p. 80; Perrault, *L'Apologie des Femmes*, p. 42; Poulain de la Barre, *De l'Education des Dames*, p. 24, and *De l'Egalité des Deux Sexes*, p. 37; Scudéry, *Grand Cyrus*, Vol. X, Liv. 2, pp. 888–9; François du Soucy, *Le Triomphe des Dames*, Ch. 7, pp. 108, 132–3.
4. Jean Hérault de Gourville, *Mémoires*, Collection Michaud et Poujoulat, 3me Série, Vol. V, p. 568. For Mme de Sablé's gallant youth see Tallemant's *Historiette*, Vol. IV, pp. 74 et seq.
5. Gaspard de Chavagnac, *Mémoires*, pp. 58–9. Cf. *Journal du Voyage de Deux Hollandais*, pp. 193–4. For other examples of female mentors see Choisy, *Mémoires*, p. 567; Marquis de Franclieu, *Mémoires* (ed. L. de Germon) pp. 13–14; Lenet, *Mémoires*, p. 447; Motteville, *Mémoires*, Vol. III, p. 111.
6. Charles Perrault, *Iris*, in Montpensier, *Galerie des Portraits*, pp. 174–5. See also Lignières's portrait of Mlle Petit, ibid., p. 276, and Le Pays, *Amitiés, Amours et Amourettes*, Liv. 2, p. 88.
7. Particularly explicit descriptions and actions are to be found in Balthasar Baro, *La Clorise*, IV.i; Auvray, *La Dorinde*, I.i and *La Madonte*, II.iii; Jean Durval, *Agarite*, III.ii.
8. Guillaume Colletet, 'La Chute Risible', in *La Muse Coquette*, p. 14; Le Pays, *Amitiés*, Liv. 1, p. 22; Loret, *Muse Historique*, 3 Sept. 1651; Voiture, 'Sur une dame dont la jupe fut retroussée', in *Œuvres*, Vol. II, pp. 303–6.
9. Dubuisson-Aubenay, *Journal*, Vol. II, p. 212; Sarasin, 'A Alcidiane prenant médecine', in *Poésies* (ed. Uzanne) pp. 248–9; Scarron, 'Epitaphe sur une dame qui mourut constipée', in *Poésies Diverses*, Vol. I, p. 401; Voiture, 'Rondeau' No. 35, in *Œuvres*, Vol. II, p. 321. Women were, in return, minutely informed of the inner workings of the men of their acquaintance. (St) Vincent de Paul candidly wrote to Louise de Marillac: 'Votre médecine, Mademoiselle, m'a fait faire neuf opérations' (see his *Correspondance, Entretiens, Documents*, Vol. I, p. 581).
10. Boursault, *Lettres de Respect, d'Obligation et d'Amour*, p. 250; Tallemant, *Historiette de Mme de Saint-Ange*, Vol. IX, p. 151.
11. Arnauld d'Andilly, *Journal Inédit*, p. 92; Dubuisson-Aubenay, *Journal*, Vol. I, p. 343; Henri IV, *Lettres Missives*, Vol. VII, pp. 538–9; Malherbe, *Œuvres*, Vol. III, pp. 50, 525; Mazarin, *Lettres*, Vol. III, p. 906; Saint-Maurice, *Lettres*, Vol. II, p. 579.
12. Scarron, *Poésies Diverses*, Vol. I, pp. 55–9.
13. Malherbe, *Œuvres*, Vol. III, p. 324.

14. Courtin, *Nouveau Traité de la Civilité*, Ch. 5, pp. 43, 44, Ch. 6, p. 58.
15. Ibid., Ch. 6, pp. 66–7, 69.
16. Furetière, *Furetiriana*, p. 56.
17. Saint-Simon, *Mémoires*, Vol. II, p. 77. See also Conrart, *Mémoires*, p. 557.
18. Scudéry, *Grand Cyrus*, Vol. X, Liv. 2, pp. 888–9.
19. Examples: Bussy-Rabutin, *Mémoires*, Vol. I, pp. 50, 55; Caylus, *Souvenirs*, p. 489; Lenet, *Mémoires*, p. 218; Nemours, *Mémoires*, pp. 630–1; Tallemant, *Historiettes*: 'Malherbe', Vol. I, pp. 257–8, 'Guise, Fils du Balafré', Vol. II, p. 26, 'La Tour-Roquelaure', Vol. VII, p. 139, 'Président Tambonneau', Vol. IX, pp. 157–8.
20. Tallemant, *Historiette de Mme de Gondran*, Vol. VII, p. 198.
21. Malherbe, *Œuvres*, Vol. III, p. 245.
22. Retz, *Mémoires*, Vol. II, pp. 538–9.
23. Tallemant, *Historiette de Malherbe*, Vol. I, pp. 269–70. For other incidents of the same kind see Bussy-Rabutin, *Correspondance*, Vol. IV, p. 26; Conrart, *Mémoires*, pp. 596–7; Saint-Maurice, *Lettres*, Vol. II, p. 196; Tallemant, *Historiette de La Présidente Lescalopier*, Vol. VI, p. 175, and *Historiette du Président Tambonneau*, Vol. IX, p. 153.
24. Motteville, *Mémoires*, Vol. II, p. 38. Cf. Donneau de Visé, *Les Dames Vangées*, I.vi.
25. Saint-Maurice, *Lettres*, Vol. I, pp. 8–9; Tallemant, *Historiettes*: 'Mme d'Aiguillon', Vol. III, p. 17, 'Roquelaure', Vol. VII, pp. 130–1, 'Villarceaux', Vol. VII, p. 239.
26. For the insolence of lackeys towards women see Courtilz de Sandras, *Annales de la Cour*, Vol. II, pp. 501–2; L'Héritier de Villandon, *Bigarrures Ingénieuses*, p. 122; Maucroix, *Lettres*, pp. 154–5.
27. Patin, *Lettres*, Vol. II, pp. 320–1. On several previous occasions Monsieur was seen to strike ladies-in-waiting (see Loret, *Muse Historique*, 17 Sept. and 3 Dec. 1651; Chevalier de Sévigné, *Correspondance*, p. 14).
28. D'Aumale, *Souvenirs*, p. 77.
29. Deshoulières, 'Epître au Duc de Montausier', in *Poésies*, Vol. I, p. 46.
30. Fontenay-Mareuil, *Mémoires*, pp. 6, 61. See also Abbé Arnauld, *Mémoires*, pp. 514, 520; Mme d'Aulnoy, *Mémoires de la Cour d'Espagne*, passim; Bavière, *Correspondance* (trans. Brunet) Vol. II, p. 124; Gournay, *L'Egalité des Hommes et des Femmes* (ed. Schiff) p. 65; Huet, 'Traité de l'Origine des Romans', prefacing *Zaïde*, attributed to Segrais, pp. 62–3; Le Pays, *Amitiés*, Liv. 2, p. 172; Duchesse Mazarin, *Mémoires*, p. 21; Montpensier, *Mémoires*, Vol. III, p. 562; Gaston d'Orléans, *Mémoires*, Collection Michaud et Poujoulat, 2me Sér., Vol. IX, p. 592; Charles Robinet, *Panégyrique de l'Ecole des Femmes*, sc. 6; Saint-Evremond, *Sur les Comédies*, in *Œuvres en Prose*, Vol. III, p. 43; Scarron, *Roman Comique*, 2me Partie, Ch. 19, pp. 274, 278; Sorel, *Francion*, Vol. IV, Liv. 12, pp. 83, 90–1; Tallemant, *Historiette de Catalogne*, Vol. VI, pp. 153 et seq.; Villars, *Lettres*, pp. 11–12, 187.
31. Philip Skippon, *An Account of a Journey made thro' part of the Low*

Countries, Germany, Italy, and France (1732 edn) Vol. VI, p. 733.
32. Brackenhoffer, *Voyage en France*, pp. 101, 180; Locatelli, *Voyage de France*, p. 39.
33. *Aventures d'un grand seigneur italien à travers l'Europe (1606)* (ed. E. Rodocanachi) p. 286; Locatelli, *Voyage de France*, pp. 29–32.
34. Tallemant, *Historiette du Connétable de Montmorency*, Vol. I, p. 174.
35. La Fare, *Mémoires*, p. 264. Cf. Visconti, *Mémoires*, pp. 219–20.
36. Scudéry, *Grand Cyrus*, Liv. 2, pp. 898–9. See also Bourdaloue, 'Sermon sur l'Impureté', in *Sermons pour le Carême*, Vol. II, p. 120. Du Bosc had already said in *L'Honnête Femme*, 3me Partie, p. 497: 'véritablement si elles [femmes] témoignent plus d'inclination à la vertu, les hommes y seraient plus portés'.
37. Jacques Boileau, *De l'Abus des Nudités de Gorge*, passim; Louis de Bouvignes, *Le Miroir de la Vanité des Femmes Mondaines*, Ch. 2, p. 48; Juvernay, *Discours contre les Femmes Débraillées*, Ch. 8; Timothée Philalèthe, *De la Modestie des Femmes et des Filles Chrétiennes*, Motif 12. Racine noted that the fashion had spread to the provinces (see Racine, *Œuvres*, Vol. VI, p. 469), but its popularity underwent fluctuations (see Rapin, *Mémoires*, Vol. I, p. 333; Saint-Maurice, *Lettres*, Vol. I, p. 383).
38. D'Aumale, *Souvenirs*, p. 50; Voiture, *Œuvres*, Vol. I, p. 58.
39. Courtin, *Nouveau Traité de la Civilité*, Ch. 6, p. 61; *Recueil de Maurepas*, Vol. II, p. 255; Tallemant, *Historiette de la Duchesse d'Aiguillon*, Vol. III, p. 20, n. 1.
40. Skippon, *Account of a Journey*, Vol. VI, p. 733.
41. *Recueil de Maurepas*, Vol. I, p. 99.
42. Saint-Maurice, *Lettres*, Vol. I, p. 169.
43. Bavière, *Correspondance* (trans. Brunet) Vol. I, p. 409.
44. Spanheim, *Relation*, pp. 291–2; Visconti, *Mémoires*, p. 301.
45. See Ch. 8, n. 22.
46. Gaufreteau, *Chronique Bordeloise*, Vol. II, pp. 111–12.
47. Boileau, *Satire X*, v. 216 et seq.; Bourdaloue, 'Sermon sur les Divertissements du Monde', in *Sermons pour les Dimanches*, Vol. II, pp. 89 et seq.; Coulanges, 'Chanson sur les Modes', in *Chansons Choisies*, p. 158; Dufresny, *Amusements*, No. 11, pp. 151–2; Jacques Goussault, *Le Portrait d'une Femme Honnête*, Ch. 7, pp. 97 et seq.; La Bruyère, 'Des Femmes', 43, in *Caractères*; Pavillon, *Conseils à une Jeune Demoiselle*, in *Œuvres*, p. 36; and so on.
48. Visconti, *Mémoires*, p. 46.
49. Ibid.
50. Saint-Simon, *Mémoires*, Vol. V, p. 125; Visconti, *Mémoires*, p. 208.
51. Bussy-Rabutin, *Correspondance*, Vol. IV, p. 320. As a result of this incident basset playing was banned by Louis.
52. Dangeau, *Journal*, Vol. VII, p. 311.
53. Marie-Thérèse, hampered by lack of intelligence and doubtless by honesty, lost often and heavily. See Bavière, *Correspondance* (trans. Brunet) Vol. I, p. 281; Dangeau, *Journal*, Vol. I, p. 6; Sévigné, *Lettres*, Vol. IV, p. 247; Visconti, *Mémoires*, pp. 45–6.
54. Dancourt, *Les Bourgeoises à la Mode*, I.xii.

55. See above, Ch. 10, p. 154.
56. Dancourt, *Les Bourgeoises à la Mode*, I.xii, and *La Désolation des Joueuses*, scenes 6 and 8.
57. Jean de la Forge, *La Joueuse Dupée*, scenes 4 and 6; Saint-Simon, *Mémoires*, Vol. II, p. 414; Staal, *Mémoires*, p. 689; Tallemant, *Historiette du Président Tambonneau*, Vol. IX, pp. 156–7.
58. Chevreau, *Chevraeana*, p. 105; Hébert, *Mémoires*, p. 21; Visconti, *Mémoires*, p. 133.
59. Dancourt, *Désolation des Joueuses*, sc. 10.
60. La Forge, *Joueuse Dupée*, sc. 7.
61. Maintenon, *Lettres et Entretiens*, Vol. II, p. 114; Visconti, *Mémoires*, p. 128.
62. De la Mare, *Traité de la Police*, Vol. I, Liv. 3, Tit. 4, Ch. 6.
63. Particularly apparent in the late 1650s and early 1660s. See Loret, *Muse Historique*, 2 Feb. 1658, 6 Apr. 1658, 18 May 1658, 20 Mar. 1661.
64. De la Mare, *Traité de la Police*, Vol. I, Liv. 3, Tit. 4, Ch. 7.
65. *Correspondance Administrative* (ed. Depping) Vol. II, pp. 563, 572, 719, 742, 748–9, 766, 782, 813–14, 820, 825; Delosme de Montchenay, *La Cause des Femmes*, I.i; Dunoyer, *Lettres*, Vol. I, pp. 325 et seq.; Furetière, *Roman Bourgeois*, Vol. I, p. 29.
66. Sourches, *Mémoires*, Vol. III, p. 334. The reference is to 1690. In 1698 Dangeau noted that gambling stakes at the court were higher than ever before (see his *Journal*, Vol. VI, p. 275).
67. Racine, *Les Plaideurs*, I.vii. The fictional Comtesse was said by Pierre Le Verrier to have a real-life counterpart in the Comtesse de Crissey. See Le Verrier, *Les Satires de Boileau commentées par lui-même* (ed. F. Lachèvre) p. 35. See also Boileau, *Satire X*, v. 724 et seq.
68. Pringy, *Différents Caractères*, 1re Partie, Ch. 11, p. 171.
69. Furetière, *Roman Bourgeois*, Vol. II, pp. 84–5.
70. *Lettres et Mémoires addressés au Chancelier Séguier*, Vol. II, p. 728.
71. Reprinted in Shakespeare Association Facsimiles, No. 13, p. T2.
72. D'Ormesson, *Journal*, Vol. II, pp. 494, 495. Cf. Maintenon, *Lettres* (ed. Langlois) Vol. V, pp. 60–1, 392.
73. Bavière, *Correspondance* (trans. Brunet) Vol. I, p. 393, Vol. II, p. 146; Conrart, *Valentin Conrart, Sa Vie et sa Correspondance* (eds Kerviler and Barthélemy) Appendix Ch. 4, p. 646; Patin, *Lettres*, Vol. III, p. 224.
74. Saint-Simon, *Mémoires*, Vol. VIII, p. 157. At Louis's autopsy in 1715, 'Son estomac surtout étonna, et ses boyaux par leur volume et leur étendue au double de l'ordinaire, d'où lui vint d'être si grand mangeur et si égal' (ibid., pp. 32–3).
75. D'Argenson, *Journal et Mémoires*, Vol. I, pp. 147–8; Bavière, *Correspondance* (trans. Brunet) Vol. I, p. 357; Bayle, *Dictionnaire*, Art. 'Lycurge G'; Bayle, *Lettres Choisies* (1714 edn) Vol. II, pp. 512–3 (to Abbé du Bos, 29 Oct. 1696); Courtilz de Sandras, *Annales de la Cour*, Vol. I, p. 27; L'Héritier de Villandon, *Les Bigarrures Ingénieuses*, p. 39.
76. For alcoholic excesses amongst women in Louis XIV's reign see Bavière, *Correspondance* (trans. Brunet) Vol. I, pp. 40, 75, 238–9, 361,

and *Lettres Inédites* (ed. Rolland) p. 157; Bayle, *Dictionnaire*, Art. 'Wert B'; Caylus, *Souvenirs*, p. 477; Coulanges, *Chanson sur les Modes*, p. 158; Hébert, *Mémoires*, pp. 33–4; L'Héritier de Villandon, *L'Erudition Enjouée*, Lettre 1, p. 39; *Recueil de Maurepas*, Vol. II, pp. 24, n. 1, 208, n. 1; Saint-Evremond, *Lettres*, Vol. II, p. 307; Chevalier de Sévigné, *Correspondance*, p. 71; Mme de Sévigné, *Lettres*, Vol. X, pp. 442–3; Tallemant, *Historiette de Mme de Gondran*, Vol. VII, p. 206. The problem was by no means confined to France. See Dunoyer, *Mémoires*, (1760 edn) 1re Partie, p. 201; Furetière, *Furetiriana*, pp. 176–9; Le Pays, *Amitiés*, Liv. 2, p. 146; Saint-Amant, *Œuvres*, Vol. III, pp. 264, 329–30.

77. Saint-Simon, *Mémoires*, Vol. II, p. 414.
78. Bussy-Rabutin, *Correspondance*, Vol. III, p. 456.
79. Bayle, *Lettres Choisies*, Vol. II, pp. 512–13; Coulanges, *Chanson sur les Modes*, p. 159.
80. Isaac Dumont de Bostaquet, *Mémoires Inédits* (eds C. Read and F. Waddington) pp. 217–18.
81. Saint-Simon, *Mémoires*, Vol. I, p. 185.
82. Bavière, *Correspondance* (trans. Brunet) Vol. I, pp. 138–9, 174, 179; Boileau, *Satire X*, vv. 669–72; Maintenon, *Lettres Inédites* (ed. Bossange) Vol. I, p. 138, Vol. II, p. 360.
83. Saint-Evremond, *Lettres*, Vol. II, p. 307.
84. *Correspondance Administrative* (ed. Depping) Vol. II, p. 645; Sévigné, *Lettres*, Vol. X, p. 163.
85. Variations on the 'straight' form of sex referred to in the text persisted, earning the distasteful publicity that was characteristic of the last decades of Louis XIV's reign. The star performer in the field was the Comtesse de Murat, exiled in 1702 for lesbianism. See D'Argenson, *Rapports Inédits* (ed. P. Cottin) pp. 11, 97–8; Dunoyer, *Lettres*, Vol. II, p. 430.
86. On ne leur [aux hommes] donne pas le temps de souhaiter
Ce qu'au moins par des pleurs, des soins, des complaisances
On devrait leur faire acheter.
On les gâte. On leur fait de honteuses avances,
Qui ne font que les dégoûter.
(Deshoulières, 'Epître Chagrine à Mlle de la Charce', in *Poésies*, Vol. I, p. 89.) See also *Lettres en Vers* (ed. Rothschild) Vol. II, pp. 354–6.
87. Visconti, *Mémoires*, p. 57. See also Lafayette, *Histoire d'Henriette d'Angleterre*, p. 176; Molière, *Amphitryon*, III.x.
88. Saint-Maurice, *Lettres*, Vol. I, pp. 235–6.
89. Examples: Henriette d'Angleterre choosing her ladies-in-waiting 'parmi les plus belles pour attirer le roi chez elle' (Visconti, *Mémoires*, p. 205) and scheming to replace Mlle de La Vallière by Mme de Monaco (Cosnac, *Mémoires*, Vol. II, p. 213); the Comtesse de Soissons promoting Mlle de la Mothe-Houdancourt (Lafayette, *Histoire d'Henriette d'Angleterre*, p. 192; Montpensier, *Mémoires*, Vol. III, p. 540); Mme de Montespan trying to interest Louis in her niece, Diane Gabrielle Damas de Thianges, Duchesse de Nevers

(Caylus, *Souvenirs*, p. 488; Sévigné, *Lettres*, Vol. VI, p. 455; Visconti, *Mémoires*, p. 240).

90. A *mazarinade* of 1649 entitled *Les Logements de la Cour à St Germain-en-Laye* significantly lodged the *filles d'honneur* at the hostelry of Petite Vertu (see *Choix de Mazarinades*, Vol. I, p. 173). The joke was more than substantiated. See, for example, Sourches, *Mémoires*, Vol. II, pp. 97–8, and n. 92 below.

91. La Fare, *Mémoires*, p. 262; Saint-Simon, *Mémoires*, Vol. I, p. 69; Visconti, *Mémoires*, p. 161.

92. The expression is that of Visconti (*Mémoires*, p. 46). La Vallière, la Fontanges, La Mothe-Houdancourt and La Mothe-Argencourt were selected as mistresses from the ranks of the ladies-in-waiting. Established favourites like Mmes de Montespan and de Maintenon were rewarded for their services by the posts of *surintendante* to the queen and second *dame d'atours* to the Dauphine de Bavière respectively.

93. Bavière, *Correspondance* (trans. Brunet) Vol. I, p. 286; Saint-Simon, *Mémoires*, Vol. III, p. 72.

94. Bourdaloue, 'Sermon sur l'Impureté', in *Sermons pour le Carême*, Vol. II, p. 119.

95. 'Il y a à Paris plus de vingt mille gentilshommes qui n'ont pas un sou et qui subsistent pourtant par le jeu et les femmes' (Visconti, *Mémoires*, p. 252). See also Maréchal de Gramont, *Mémoires*, Collection Michaud et Poujoulat, 3me Sér., Vol. VII, p. 237.

96. Bussy-Rabutin, *Correspondance*, Vol. I, pp. 426–7; Saint-Maurice, *Lettres*, Vol. II, pp. 106–8; Sévigné, *Lettres*, Vol. II, pp. 305, 331; Visconti, *Mémoires*, p. 93.

97. Bussy-Rabutin, *Correspondance*, Vol. V, pp. 60–1; Visconti, *Mémoires*, p. 147.

98. La Bruyère, 'Des Femmes', 33 and 'Des Jugements', 16, 17, in *Caractères*. The same sources indicate the dubious popularity of musicians and dancers.

99. Bussy-Rabutin, *Histoire Amoureuse des Gaules*, Vol. II, p. 7; Locatelli, *Voyage de France*, p. 187; Maintenon, *Lettres* (ed. Langlois) Vol. IV, p. 442; Motteville, *Mémoires*, Vol. IV, p. 68.

100. Bayle, *Dictionnaire*, Art. 'Anchise A'; Guyot, *Répertoire*, Art. 'Fornication'; Lauder, *Journals*, p. 111.

101. Visconti, *Mémoires*, p. 160.

102. For examples of misalliances between mistresses and domestics see *Mémoires tirés des Archives de la Police de Paris* (ed. Peuchet) Vol. I, p. 203; *Recueil de Maurepas*, Vol. V, p. 55; Saint-Simon, *Mémoires*, Vol. V, p. 194; Visconti, *Mémoires*, p. 67.

103. Bavière, *Correspondance* (trans. Brunet) Vol. I, p. 39.

104. For the Tiquet affair see Bavière, *Correspondance* (trans. Brunet) Vol. I, p. 37; Dangeau, *Journal*, Vol. VII, pp. 70, 93, 94, 100; Dunoyer, *Lettres*, Vol. II, pp. 49 et seq.; Saint-Simon, *Mémoires*, Vol. II, p. 62; Sourches, *Mémoires*, Vol. VI, pp. 144, 145, 162, 165–6; Vuillart, *Lettres*, pp. 214, 238, 243.

105. Fléchier, *Grands Jours d'Auvergne*, pp. 14–15.

106.   Racine, *Œuvres*, Vol. VI, pp. 449, 484–5; Sévigné, *Lettres*, Vol. VI, p. 305.
107.   Examples: *Correspondance Administrative* (ed. Depping) Vol. II, p. 190; Demaillasson, *Journal*, Vol. XXXVI, p. 294; Fléchier, *Grands Jours d'Auvergne*, pp. 118, 121–2; Guillaudeau, *Diaire*, pp. 410–12; *Journal de J. Baudouin sur les Grands-Jours de Languedoc (1666–1667)* (ed. P. Le Blanc) pp. 53, 64; Sévigné, *Lettres*, Vol. II, p. 260.
108.   Examples: Delort, *Mémoires*, p. 246; *Journal de Toisonnier* (ed. M. Saché) p. 47; *Lettres en Vers* (ed. Rothschild) Vol. II, pp. 755–6, 995–8; Loret, *Muse Historique*, 16 Dec. 1662; Patin, *Lettres*, Vol. III, p. 569; Tallemant, *Historiette de Mme de Taloet*, Vol. IX, p. 171.
109.   Examples: Denesde, *Journal*, p. 108; Foucault, *Mémoires*, p. 310; Gaufreteau, *Chronique Bordeloise*, Vol. II, p. 121; Huet, *Memoirs*, Bk 6, p. 359; Marana, *Turkish Spy*, Vol. IV, Bk 3, Letter 9; Perdrix, *Chronique*, p. 120.
110.   The most resounding trial of the early seventeenth century had been that of the priest Urbain Grandier, burned alive at Loudun in 1634 for allegedly causing the demoniacal possession of local Ursuline nuns and laywomen who had been schooled by his enemies in faking wounds and convulsions that continued to provide a tourist attraction for several years after the execution. See Denesde, *Journal*, pp. 66 et seq.; *Histoire des Diables de Loudun* (1693) passim; Tallemant, *Historiette du Père Joseph*, Vol. II, p. 245; Voiture, *Œuvres*, Vol. I, pp. 304, 305.
111.   See preceding note and following chapter.

CHAPTER 13

1.   Bayle, *Pensées sur la Comète* (ed. A. Prat) Vol. II, No. 142, p. 25; Caussin, *Cour Sainte*, 1re Partie, Vol. I, Liv. 3, sect. 34, p. 610; Louis Machon, *Discours ou Sermon Apologétique en faveur des Femmes*, p. 102; Noel, *Les Avantages du Sexe*, Ch. 13, p. 72; Patin, *Lettres*, Vol. I, p. 305; and others.
2.   Blémur, *Eloges*, Vol. I, pp. 230, 361; Vol. II, pp. 413, 432.
3.   L'Estoile, *Journal*, Vol. II, p. 207; Peiresc, *Lettres*, Vol. I, p. 520.
4.   The memorable example was the Duchesse de Ventadour, Marie-Liesse de Luxembourg, who took her vows in 1641 at the Carmelite convent of Chambéry, which she had founded, and remained there till her death in 1660. Her husband, Henri de Lévis, renounced his duchy and became a canon of Notre-Dame. See Anselme, *Maison Royale*, Vol. III, p. 732. See also Peiresc, *Lettres*, Vol. I, p. 93.
5.   Jeanne de Chantal stepped dramatically over the body of her distraught son as he tried to bar her way to the cloister. See Chaugy, *Sainte Jeanne de Chantal, Sa Vie et ses Œuvres*, Vol. I, Ch. 28, p. 129. The Marquise de Belle-Isle, Antoinette d'Orléans, similarly left two young sons in the care of their grandparents when she embarked upon her conventual career with the Feuillantines of Toulouse in

1599. See *Vie de la Mère Antoinette d'Orléans* (ed. Abbé Petit) pp. 96–7.

6. Examples: Loret, *Muse Historique*, 17 Sept. 1650, 17 Mar. 1652; Perrault, *Les Hommes Illustres*, Art.'Bérulle'; Rapin, *Mémoires*, Vol. I, p. 118; Saint-Simon, *Mémoires*, Vol. I, p. 294; Sourches, *Mémoires*, Vol. III, p. 270, n. 2, Vol. IV, p. 139; Barthélemy, *La Marquise d'Huxelles et ses Amis*, p. 55.

7. Examples: Abbé Arnauld, *Mémoires*, p. 491; Gaufreteau, *Chronique Bordeloise*, Vol. II, p. 159; Lenet, *Mémoires*, p. 207; Motteville, *Mémoires*, Vol. I, p. 280; D'Ormesson, *Journal*, Vol. II, p. 386.

8. Louise de La Vallière, the best known example (Saint-Simon, *Mémoires*, Vol. VIII, p. 77), had been shown the way by Louison Roger, ex-mistress of Gaston d'Orléans (Dangeau, *Journal*, Vol. IV, pp. 156–7), and by Mlle de la Mothe-Argencourt, one of Louis XIV's passing fancies, who entered a convent without taking vows (La Fare, *Mémoires*, p. 262).

9. Bourdaloue, 'Sermon sur le Devoir des Pères', in *Sermons pour le Dimanche*, Vol. I, p. 19.

10. Blémur, *Eloges*, Vol. I, pp. 144–5, 292, 324–5, 429, 499, Vol. II, pp. 144, 187, 290, 347–8, 481, 554. See also *Caquets de l'Accouchée*, 2ᵐᵉ Journée, p. 90; Letouf, *Mémoires*, Vol. I, p. 9; Malherbe, *Œuvres*, Vol. III, pp. 144–5; *Mercure Galant*, Oct. 1688, 1ʳᵉ Partie, p. 79, Apr. 1696, p. 13; Peiresc, *Lettres*, Vol. VII, p. 590, n. 1.

11. Oudard Coquault, *Mémoires*, (ed. C. Loriquet) Vol. II, pp. 379–80; Donneau de Visé, *Mère Coquette*, III.i.

12. See Mme de Sévigné on the veiling of her elder grand-daughter and the projected veiling of the younger one in her *Lettres*, Vol. V, pp. 212, 228, 346, Vol. VI, pp. 442–3.

13. Bourdaloue, 'Sermon sur l'Ambition', in *Sermons pour le Carême*, Vol. I, p. 520; Foucault, *Mémoires*, p. 45; Spanheim, *Relation*, p. 193.

14. The Duc de la Rochefoucauld (François V), the Duc de Saint-Aignan and President Molé of the Paris Parlement each set up several sons and married off one privileged daughter by dint of veiling five remaining sisters. Saint-Aignan's son, the Duc de Beauvillier, put seven daughters into the convent for the benefit of an eighth. See Anselme, *Maison Royale*, Vol. IV, pp. 429, 720–1, 722–3; Vol. VI, p. 575.

15. Anselme, *Maison Royale*, Vol. I, pp. 151, 223, Vol. III, p. 857; Tallemant, *Historiette de Voiture*, Vol. IV, p. 52.

16. Anselme, *Maison Royale*, Vol. III, p. 386; Blémur, *Eloges*, Vol. II, p. 115; Gaufreteau, *Chronique Bordeloise*, Vol. II, pp. 98–9.

17. Bourdaloue, *Sermon sur le Devoir des Pères*, p. 21.

18. Ordinance of Blois, Art. 28. See Isambert, *Anciennes Lois Françaises*, Vol. XIV, pp. 388–9.

19. Bossuet, *Correspondance*, Vol. VI, p. 154; Vol. VII, p. 127.

20. The *Constitutions* of Port-Royal (1665) declare in Ch. 14, p. 94: 'L'on emploiera les sœurs converses au plus grand travail, comme la cuisine, la boulangerie, la lessive, le soin des vaches et des poules, la cordonnerie, et choses semblables.'

21. See above, Ch. 8, p. 121, and Jaillot, *Recherches sur la Ville de Paris*,

Vol. V, 19e Quartier, Le Luxembourg, pp. 30–3 (Religieuses de N-D de Miséricorde).

22. Gaufreteau, *Chronique Bordeloise*, Vol. II, pp. 21–2.
23. A notable exception appears to have been Port-Royal, much vaunted by its supporters for its disinterestedness. See Angélique Arnauld, *Lettres*, Vol. II, p. 355; Antoine Arnauld, *Lettres*, Vol. I, p. 77; Du Fossé, *Mémoires*, Vol. I, pp. 78, 154; Fontaine, *Mémoires*, Vol. II, p. 207; Racine, *Abrégé de l'Histoire de Port-Royal*, pp. 323, 332. Hostile witnesses concur. See Hébert, *Mémoires*, p. 101; Rapin, *Mémoires*, Vol. III, pp. 308–9.
24. Coquault, *Mémoires*, Vol. II, pp. 516–17.
25. Hodeau, *Mémoires*, pp. 221, 232.
26. Renaudot, *Journal*, in *Mémoires de la Société de l'Histoire de Paris et de l'Ile-de-France*, Vol. IV, pp. 257, 258.
27. Locatelli, *Voyage de France*, p. 63.
28. Louis-Isaac Le Maistre de Sacy, *Choix de Lettres Inédites* (ed. G. Delassault) p. 86.
29. Boyer, *Livre de Raison*, p. 297.
30. Amelot de la Houssaye, *Mémoires Historiques, Critiques, Politiques et Littéraires*, Vol. II, Art. 'Camus'; Le Gendre, *Mémoires*, p. 170; Ménage, *Menagiana*, 1re Partie, p. 75.
31. Clamours for the suppression or diminution of conventual dowries were a regular item in aristocratic *Cahiers de Doléances*. See *Deux Cahiers de la Noblesse pour les Etats Généraux de 1649–1651* (ed. Mousnier) p. 138; *Cahiers des Etats de Normandie* (ed. Beaurepaire) Vol. II, pp. 95, 171–2; Y.-M. Bercé, *Histoire des Croquants, Etude des Soulèvements Populaires au XVIIe Siecle dans le Sud-Ouest de la France*, Vol. II, 'Pièces Justificatives', p. 818.
32. *Caquets de l'Accouchée*, 5me Journée, p. 188; Coquault, *Mémoires*, Vol. I, p. 129.
33. In towns without Parlements these sums were reduced by 150 *livres* and 2000 *livres* respectively. The communities in question were also allowed to accept up to 2000 *livres* for the nun's clothes, furniture and so on. See Brillon, *Dictionnaire des Arrêts*, Art. 'Dot', Vol. I, p. 872, No. 436; Guyot, *Répertoire*, Art. 'Dotation'; *Recueil Néron*, Vol. II, pp. 247–8, *Déclaration concernant la réception et dots des personnes qui entrent dans les monastères pour y embrasser la profession religieuse*, 28 April 1693.
34. Le Gendre, *Mémoires*, p. 170.
35. Anselme, *Maison Royale*, Vol. VII, p. 572; Du Fossé, *Mémoires*, Vol. I, p. 68. See also Bossuet, *Oraisons Funèbres* (ed. A. Rébelliau) Anne de Gonzague, pp. 309–10.
36. For a striking instance of these conventual dynasties see Anselme, *Maison Royale*, Vol. VII, pp. 573–4.
37. Graphic examples in Foucault, *Mémoires*, p. 44; Olivier Patru, *Œuvres Diverses*, Vol. I, Plaidoyer No. 16, pp. 429 et seq. Two groups of nuns in particular, those of Poissy and the Urbanistes, achieved a certain celebrity by the length and tenacity of their resistance to the royal will. For Poissy see Anselme, *Maison Royale*, Vol. IV, p. 324;

Saint-Simon, *Mémoires*, Vol. III, pp. 379–81; Sourches, *Mémoires*, Vol. X, p. 392. For the Urbanistes see Hébert, *Mémoires*, pp. 74 et seq.; Patru, *Œuvres Diverses*, Vol. II, Plaidoyer No. 17, pp. 3 et seq.

38. Relatively more democratic because votes were often swayed by intimidation from an abbess or from factions that arose amongst the sisters at election times. See Bossuet, *Correspondance*, Vol. VI, p. 226; Richelieu, *Testament Politique*, 1re Partie, Ch. 2, sect. 8, p. 201; P. Clément, *Une Abbesse de Fontevrault au XVIIe Siècle*, pp. 112, 145.

39. Thomas Corneille, *Dictionnaire Universelle, Géographique et Historique*, Art. 'Fontevrault'; Clément, *Une Abbesse de Fontevrault*, pp. 63–4; Religieuses de Ste Marie de Fontevrault, *Histoire de l'Ordre de Fontevrault*, passim.

40. Pierre Hélyot, *Dictionnaire des Ordres Religieux*, Art. 'Fontevrault'.

41. Moréri, *Grand Dictionnaire Historique*, Art. 'Roncerai, N-D de'.

42. Thiers, *Traité des Superstitions*, Vol. IV, Liv. 9, p. 429. The question of admitting women to the priesthood was raised from time to time during the seventeenth century. See Noel, *Les Avantages du Sexe*, Ch. 13, pp. 83–7; Poulain de la Barre, *De l'Education des Dames*, p. 30, and *De l'Egalité des Deux Sexes*, pp. 163–5; Saint-Gabriel, *Le Mérite des Dames*, 3me Partie, p. 219; Thiers, ibid., pp. 435 et seq.

43. Bossuet, *Correspondance*, Vol. IV, pp. 57 et seq., 480 et seq.; Vol. V, pp. 497 et seq.

44. Bussy-Rabutin, *Correspondance*, Vol. IV, pp. 232–3, 288, 293. For other examples of resistance see Peiresc, *Lettres*, Vol. I, pp. 290–1; Clément, *Une Abbesse de Fontevrault*, pp. 155 et seq., 200 et seq., 221 et seq.

45. Information concerning the officers of convents has been derived from the convent regulations listed above in Ch. 2, n. 63, plus the following: *Constitutions de Port-Royal* (1665); *La Règle du Bienheureux Père St Benoît, avec les constitutions qui y ont été accommodées pour la réforme de l'abbaye royale de Notre-Dame du Val de Grâce* (1676); *La Règle et Statuts des Religieuses de Ste Claire, pour l'usage des Dames Religieuses de Patience de Laval* (1651).

46. Examples: *Arrêts du Conseil du Roi* (ed. M. Le Pesant) Vol. I, p. 22, No. 219; Blémur, *Eloges*, Vol. II, p. 151; La Mare, *Traité de la Police*, Vol. I, Liv. 2, Tit. 13, p. 408; Loret, *Muse Historique*, 29 Mar. 1664; Rapin, *Mémoires*, Vol. I, p. 445; *Les Papiers de Richelieu* (ed. P. Grillon) Vol. I, pp. 123, 125.

47. Huet, *Memoirs*, Bk 6, p. 348; Saint-Simon, *Mémoires*, Vol. III, p. 84; Sévigné, *Lettres*, Vol. V, pp. 249–50; Clément, *Une Abbesse de Fontevrault*, p. 173.

48. Fléchier, *Grands Jours d'Auvergne*, p. 54.

49. The ruling made at the 25th session of the Council of Trent, allowing five years after the pronouncement of the final vows for a religious to declare them null and void if any coercion had been involved, was observed in France. See Guyot, *Répertoire*, Art. 'Profession Monastique'.

50. Dubuisson-Aubenay, *Journal*, Vol. II, p. 65; Sourches, *Mémoires*, Vol. I, p. 206.

51. Bossuet, *Correspondance*, Vol. II, p. 352; *Choix de Mazarinades*, Vol. II,
     p. 528; Dubuisson-Aubenay, *Journal*, Vol. I, p. 13; Loret, *Muse
     Historique*, 22 May 1660; Louvet, *Journal*, in *Revue de l'Anjou*, July–
     Aug. 1855, pp. 1–2; Montpensier, *Mémoires*, Vol. I, p. 29.
52. Dangeau, *Journal*, Vol. II, p. 162; Fléchier, *Grands Jours d'Auvergne*,
     p. 25; Loret, *Muse Historique*, 29 Oct. 1651; D'Ormesson, *Journal*,
     Vol. I, pp. 470–1; Peiresc, *Lettres*, Vol. I, p. 901; Sourches, *Mémoires*,
     Vol. III, p. 59; Vuillart, *Lettres*, p. 202.
53. Furetière, *Roman Bourgeois*, Vol. I, p. 187. Cf. Bussy-Rabutin, *Corres-
     pondance*, Vol. III, p. 290; L'Estoile, *Journal*, Vol. II, p. 328.
54. D'Argenson, *Rapports Inédits*, pp. 29–30; *Correspondance Administra-
     tive* (ed. Depping) Vol. II, p. 795, Vol. IV, p. 197.
55. See below, p. 219 and n. 71.
56. J.-B. Thiers, in the preface of his *Traité de la Clôture des Religieuses*
     (1681), notes that 'il n'y a guère aujourd'hui de point de discipline
     ecclésiastique qui soit ou plus négligé, ou plus ignoré que celui de la
     clôture des religieuses'.
57. Blémur, *Eloges*, Vol. I, pp. 298, 429, Vol. II, p. 256; Fleury, *Vie de
     Marguerite d'Arbouze*, pp. 34–5.
58. Coquault, *Mémoires*, Vol. II, p. 357.
59. Bossuet, *Correspondance*, Vol. VI, pp. 240–1, Vol. X, p. 185.
60. Ibid., Vol. V, pp. 498–500.
61. Ibid., Vol. V, pp. 501–2; Fléchier, *Grands Jours d'Auvergne*, p. 44;
     Ménage, *Menagiana*, 2me Partie, p. 60; Clément, *Une Abbesse de
     Fontevrault*, p. 168.
62. Blémur, *Eloges*, Vol. I, p. 562; Locke, *Travels*, p. 79; Tallemant,
     Historiette de Richelieu, Vol. II, p. 191; Vuillart, *Lettres*, p. 203.
63. See for example A. Dutilleux and J. Depoin, *L'Abbaye de Maubuisson,
     Histoire et Cartulaire*, 1re Partie, 'Chartes concernant la fondation de
     l'abbaye', pp. 21–2.
64. At the consecration of the Abbess of Chelles in August 1680,
     'l'Eglise était tout ornée de riches tapisseries de soie, relevées d'or et
     d'argent, et le Grand-Autel rempli de vases d'argent, de six beaux
     chandeliers, et d'une fort grande croix ... des lustres, des girand-
     oles et des flambeaux disposés partout en très bon ordre. Depuis
     l'Autel jusqu'au fond du Chœur il y avait des tapis de pied. Tout le
     Chœur était couvert d'un seul tapis de Perse de soie. Mme l'Abbesse
     de Chelles avait Mmes les Abbesses de Montmartre et de Farmous-
     tier pour Assistantes. Les trois Prie-Dieu destinés pour elles, et le
     trône de la nouvelle abbesse, étaient couverts de tapis de Perse à
     fond d'or, avec des carreaux de velours bleu tous brodés d'or'
     (*Mercure Galant*, Sept. 1680, 1re Partie, pp. 242–3).
65. Borrelly, *Livre de Raison*, p. 279; Coquault, *Mémoires*, Vol. II, p. 516;
     Loret, *Muse Historique*, 19 June 1653, 14 Feb. 1654, 26 May 1657;
     Mercure Galant, July 1683, pp. 151–2. Sumptuous repasts at normal
     times are attested by witnesses who include Coquault, *Mémoires*,
     Vol. II, pp. 380–1; Locatelli, *Voyage de France*, p. 61; Vuillart, *Lettres*,
     p. 203.
66. Blémur, *Eloges*, Vol. I, p. 569.

67. Benserade, 'Stances à Mlle de Brionne' and 'Stances pour une abbesse', in *Œuvres*, Vol. I, pp. 67, 334; Mlle de La Roche-Guilhen, *Histoire des Favorites*, 2ᵐᵉ Partie, pp. 57 et seq.; Villedieu, *Annales Galantes*, 2ᵐᵉ Partie, p. 113.

68. *Journal du Voyage de Deux Hollandais*, p. 271; D'Ormesson, *Journal*, Vol. I, p. 60; Patin, *Lettres*, Vol. II, p. 340; Peiresc, *Lettres*, Vol. I, p. 290, Vol. VI, p. 580; Spanheim, *Relation*, p. 413.

69. As did Anne de Beauvillier, daughter of the Duc de Saint-Aignan. See Le Gendre, *Mémoires*, p. 137; Saint-Simon, *Mémoires*, Vol. II, pp. 227–8. See also Peiresc, *Lettres*, Vol. I, pp. 652–3.

70. Bavière, *Correspondance* (trans. Brunet) Vol. I, p. 218. The dissoluteness of nuns authorised the saucy poems and letters addressed to them. See Benserade, 'Stances pour une abbesse', in *Œuvres*, Vol. I, pp. 330 et seq.; La Fontaine, 'Épître à Mme de Coucy', in *Œuvres*, Vol. IX, pp. 102–6; Le Pays, 'Sonnet pour une belle personne à qui les tetons étaient venus depuis qu'elle était religieuse', in *Amitiés*, p. 260; Voiture, 'Lettre à Mme l'Abbesse d'Yeres', in *Œuvres*, Vol. I, p. 424.

71. Blémur, *Eloges*, Vol. II, p. 120. See also Vol. I, p. 325; and Clément, *Une Abbesse de Fontevrault*, pp. 136, 144.

72. Blémur, *Eloges*, Vol. I, p. 166.

73. Ibid., Vol. II, pp. 154–5.

74. La Fontaine, *Contes* ('Conte de *'; 'Mazet de Lamporechio'; 'L'Abbesse'; 'Le Psautier'; 'Les Lunettes'; 'Le Tableau'); Saint-Evremond, *Lettres*, Vol. I, pp. 245–6, 332–3, 388 et seq., Vol. II, p. 46.

75. Coquault, *Mémoires*, passim; L'Estoile, *Journal*, Vol. II, p. 207.

76. Colbert, *Lettres*, Vol. VI, p. 3.

77. Ibid., p. 10. See also Bayle, *Dictionnaire*, Art. 'Bucer E'.

78. Foucault, *Mémoires*, p. 38; La Mare, *Traité de la Police*, Vol. I, Liv. 2, Tit. 13, p. 408.

79. 1664 was the year of the first performance of Molière's *Tartuffe* at a court *fête*, and of the disgrace of Mme de Navailles for barring the king's way to the ladies-in-waiting. See Louis's *Mémoires*, pp. 220–1.

80. La Mare, *Traité de la Police*, Vol. I, Liv. 2, Tit. 13, pp. 408–10. The wish expressed by Richelieu in his *Testament Politique*, 1ʳᵉ Partie, Ch. 2, sect. 8, p. 201, that the monarch would arrest 'le trop grand nombre des nouveaux monastères, qui s'établissent tous les jours', thereby seemed close to realisation.

81. Isambert, *Anciennes Lois Françaises*, Vol. XVIII, pp. 90–1, and above, Ch. 5, p. 71.

82. In some *Tiers Ordres* – the Franciscan Ordre de la Pénitence, for example, and the Dominican Milice de Jésus-Christ – vows were taken and observed as in a regular religious order. See Hélyot, *Dictionnaire des Ordres Religieux*, Arts 'Milice de Jésus-Christ', and 'Pénitence, Ordre de la'.

83. *La Règle, le Cérémonial et le Directoire des Sœurs du Tiers-Ordre de Notre-Dame du Mont-Carmel et de Sainte Thérèse*, p. x. The 'Approbation' of the work is dated 1708.

84. Ibid., Chs 1–3.

85.   Ibid., Ch. 13.
86.   Ibid., Ch. 4 et seq.
87.   Ibid., Chs 12, 16–19.
88.   Guyot, *Répertoire*, Art. 'Chanoinesses Régulières'.
89.   Ibid., Art. 'Chanoinesses Séculières'.
90.   In 1686, for example, the memorialist Dangeau married Sophie de Levenstein (variously spelt 'Lowestein' and 'Lovestein' by the French), a canoness belonging to a branch of the Bavarian royal family degraded by a misalliance. See Saint-Simon, *Mémoires*, Vol. I, p. 222; Spanheim, *Relation*, pp. 271–2.
91.   Her senior officers, the *Doyenne* and the *Sacristine*, each had similar powers in her own right. See Hélyot, *Dictionnaire des Ordres Religieux*, Art. 'Remiremont'; La Houssaye, *Mémoires*, Vol. I, Art. 'Abbayes'.
92.   Du Fossé, *Mémoires*, Vol. III, p. 192; Huygens, *Journal du Voyage à Paris*, p. 123; *Mercure Galant*, May 1692, pp. 286–7.
93.   Villedieu, *Mémoires de Henriette Sylvie de Molière*, 6ᵐᵉ Partie, p. 6.
94.   Bassompierre, *Mémoires*, Vol. I, p. 373; Le Gendre, *Mémoires*, p. 139.
95.   See François de Sales, *Introduction*, passim, and his *Lettres* (ed. Garnier) p. 102; also Du Bosc, *L'Honnête Femme*, 1ʳᵉ Partie, p. 73, 3ᵐᵉ Partie, p. 377.
96.   Maintenon, *Lettres et Entretiens*, Vol. I, p. 37.
97.   François de Sales, *Lettres*, pp. 121–2, 135, 214–15, 218, 290, and passim.
98.   See Louis Abelli, *Vie de Vincent de Paul*, Liv. 1, Ch. 10.
99.   See *Règlement Général des Charités de Femmes* in Vincent de Paul's *Correspondance* (ed. Coste) Vol. XIII, pp. 419 et seq.
100.   Vincent de Paul, *Correspondance*, Vol. IV, p. 71.
101.   The Dames de l'Hôtel-Dieu, created by Vincent in 1634 at the request of Présidente Goussault, assisted the nursing nuns there by taking round food and dispensing spiritual comfort. See Abelli, *Vie de Vincent de Paul*, Liv. 1, Ch. 29.
102.   For the origins of the foundling hospital, see Abelli, ibid., Liv. 1, Ch. 30.
103.   For the history and functions of the Filles de la Charité see Vincent de Paul, *Correspondance*, Vol. II, pp. 548–53; Vol. XIII, pp. 551 et seq.
104.   For her emaciation see Vincent de Paul, *Correspondance*, Vol. III, pp. 256–7, and passim for her relations with the saint.
105.   Vincent de Paul, *Correspondance*, is full of references to her. See, for example, Vol. II, pp. 6, 42–3, 284–5, 535–6. See also A. Bonneau-Avenant, *La Duchesse d'Aiguillon*, passim.
106.   Vincent de Paul, *Correspondance*, Vol. I, p. 448.
107.   The leading names are listed amongst the Dames de Charité, ibid., Vol. XIV, pp. 108–9.
108.   Report from a priest at Saint-Quentin in 1652: 'La famine est telle que nous voyons les hommes mangeant la terre, broutant l'herbe,

arrachant l'écorce des arbres, déchirant les méchants haillons dont ils sont couverts, pour les avaler. Mais ce que nous n'oserions dire si nous ne l'avions vu, et qui fait horreur, ils se mangent les bras et les mains et meurent dans ce désespoir.' See Vincent de Paul, *Correspondance*, Vol. IV, p. 300.

109. The incident was represented in bas-relief on her tomb. See Le Maire, *Paris Ancien et Nouveau*, Vol. II, p. 61. The memory of Mme Fouquet, charitable mother of the disgraced superintendant of finances, was similarly hallowed. See Saint-Simon, *Mémoires*, Vol. VIII, p. 248.

110. Vincent de Paul, *Correspondance*, Vol. V, p. 591.

111. Examples: The Filles de la Providence, a community instituted by Mme de Polaillon (or Pollalion) to safeguard the chastity of indigent girls, were authorised by letters patent of 1643 to move from Charonne to Paris where they came under the direction of Vincent and the protection of Anne d'Autriche (see Jaillot, *Recherches sur la Ville de Paris*, Vol. IV, 17ᵐᵉ Quartier St-Benoît, pp. 8–12; Sauval, *Antiquités de Paris*, Vol. I, p. 709). The association of Filles de Ste Geneviève, begun in 1636 by Mlle du Blosset for the relief and education of the poor, amalgamated in 1665 with the more famous Miramionnes, separately founded by Mme de Miramion for a similar purpose *circa* 1660. The Miramionnes extended their sphere of influence as provincial charity groups requested affiliation (see Bossuet, *Correspondance*, Vol. VII, pp. 31 et seq.; Sauval, *Antiquités*, Vol. I, pp. 691–6; A. Bonneau-Avenant, *Mme de Miramion*, Ch. 8 et seq.). The Filles de St Joseph, originally from Bordeaux, were established in Paris in the early 1640s by Marie Delpech to succour poor orphaned girls. Mme de Montespan interested herself in the community and withdrew after her disgrace to a house which she had had built there for retreats (see Jaillot, *Recherches*, Vol. V, 20ᵐᵉ Quartier St Germain-des-Prés, pp. 41–2; Sauval, *Antiquités*, Vol. I, p. 699; Sourches, *Mémoires*, Vol. III, p. 365).

112. The benefactress in question, the Princesse de Conti (Anne-Marie Martinozzi), had the incident commemorated on a funeral monument (Le Maire, *Paris Ancien et Nouveau*, Vol. I, pp. 280–2; Loret, *Muse Historique*, 20 May 1662). Anne d'Autriche had made a similar gesture during the Fronde (Motteville, *Mémoires*, Vol. II, pp. 339–40).

113. *Lettres en Vers* (ed. Rothschild) Vol. I, pp. 837–8. The action was part of an Easter ritual which French queens performed in imitation of the king. Cf. Loret, *Muse Historique*, 11 Apr. 1654.

114. D'Aumale, *Souvenirs*, p. 157. The numerous charitable works performed by Mme de Maintenon are detailed on pp. 152–67.

115. Goussault, *Portrait d'une Femme Honnête*, Ch. 10, p. 156; Perrault, *L'Apologie des Femmes*, pp. 41–2.

116. The Religieuses (Bénédictines) du Saint-Sacrement, for example, founded in Paris in 1654 for the perpetual adoration of the holy sacrament (Jaillot, *Recherches*, Vol. V, 19ᵉ Quartier, Le

Luxembourg, pp. 18–22), and the nursing congregation of Augustine nuns known as the Filles St Thomas de Villeneuve, founded in Brittany by Père Ange Proust, prior of Lamballe, and granted letters patent in 1661 (Jaillot, ibid., pp. 88–90).

117. Brienne, *Mémoires*, Vol. III, pp. 159–60; Rapin, *Mémoires*, Vol. II, pp. 146 et seq., 420.

118. Mazarin, *Lettres*, Vol. III, pp. 760–1; Rapin, *Mémoires*, Vol. I, pp. 173 et seq., Vol. III, pp. 430–1; Tallemant, *Historiette de Mme de Sablé*, Vol. IV, pp. 78, 84; V. Cousin, *Mme de Sablé*, Appendix 2, pp. 370–1.

119. Which included also the Princesse de Guémené (see Rapin, *Mémoires*, Vol. I, pp. 29–30, 46; Retz, *Mémoires*, Vol. I, pp. 104–6, 130–2), the Comtesse de Maure (see Rapin, ibid., p. 208; Tallemant, *Historiette de Mme de Sablé*, Vol. IV, p. 84, and *Historiette du Comte et de la Comtesse de Maure*, Vol. IV, pp. 89 et seq.; E. de Barthélemy, *Mme la Comtesse de Maure, Sa Vie et sa Correspondance*, passim) and Mme du Plessis-Guénégaud (see above, Ch. 11, p. 175).

120. Ninon de Lenclos, an old acquaintance of Mme de Maintenon, categorically affirmed that she had often made available one of her rooms for use by the then Mme Scarron and the Marquis de Villarceaux, the man popularly credited with having been the favourite's lover; see Lenclos, *Correspondance* (ed. Colombey) p. 79. See also Huygens, *Journal de Voyage à Paris*, p. 153.

121. Maintenon, *Lettres* (ed. Langlois) Vol. II, pp. 523–4.

122. Saint-Simon, *Mémoires*, Vol. IV, p. 110.

123. Boileau, *Satire X*, v. 523 et seq.; Deshoulières, 'Epître Chagrine au T.-R. Père de la Chaise', in *Poésies*, Vol. II, pp. 92–3; Dulorens, *Satires* (1646), No. 1, pp. 5–6; Fléchier, *Réflexions sur les caractères des hommes*, in *Œuvres*, Vol. IX, pp. 344–5; De Grenaille, *L'Honnête Fille*, 2ᵐᵉ Partie, Liv. 1, Ch. 3, pp. 63 et seq.; La Bruyère, 'Des Femmes', 43 and 44, in *Caractères*; Molière, *Le Misanthrope*, III.iv; Pringy, *Caractères des Femmes*, Ch. 3; Régnier, *Satire XIII*; Saint-Evremond, *Lettre à une dame galante qui voulait devenir dévote*, and *Que la dévotion est le dernier de nos amours*, in *Œuvres en Prose*, Vol. IV, pp. 212–17, 359–61; Visconti, *Mémoires*, p. 273.

124. Boileau, *Satire X*, v. 556 et seq.; La Bruyère, 'Des Femmes', 45, in *Caractères*; Molière, *Tartuffe*; Petit, *Satires*, No. 12, pp. 108–9; Saint-Evremond, *Œuvres en Prose*, Vol. IV, p. 216; Sévigné, *Lettres*, Vol. X, p. 127.

125. 'M. Arnauld, son directeur, étant devenu son amant spirituel, elle [Duchesse de Longueville] en était folle comme elle l'avait été, en d'autres temps, du duc de la Rochefoucauld' (Brienne, *Mémoires*, Vol. III, pp. 159–60).

126. D'Aumale, *Souvenirs*, pp. 186–7; Le Verrier, *Les Satires de Boileau commentées par lui-même* (ed. Lachèvre) p. 121.

127. For the Fréquente Communion affair, triggered off by Mmes de Guémené and de Sablé, see Antoine Arnauld's preface to *De la Fréquente Communion* (1643); Rapin, *Mémoires*, Vol. I, pp. 29–30; Tallemant, *Historiette d'Antoine Arnauld*, Vol. IV, p. 71.

128. See above, Ch. 12, p. 199.
129. This seventeenth-century equivalent of a hassock was a prerogative of the nobility. See Boileau, *Satire X*, vv. 502–4; Courval Sonnet, *Œuvres Poétiques*, Vol. I, *Satire V*, p. 140.
130. Provincial noblewomen were particularly sensitive on this point. See Bossuet, *Correspondance*, Vol. III, pp. 2–4, and above, Ch. 7, p. 102. At the Protestant temple of Charenton, just outside Paris, disputes over seats were so frequent that women took to paying individuals to reserve their places. See *Une Femme de Qualité au milieu du XVIIᵉ siècle* [Marguerite Mercier] (ed. J. Pannier) p. 485; Tallemant, *Historiette de Mme de Beringhen et son fils*, Vol. IV, p. 216.
131. For gallantry and so on in church see D'Aubignac, *Histoire du Temps ou Relation du Royaume de Coquetterie*, p. 63; Balzac, Letter to Mme de Campagnole, 3 May 1635, in *Suite de la Seconde Partie des Lettres*, pp. 294 et seq.; Bouvignes, *Miroir de la Vanité des Femmes Mondaines*, Ch. 3; La Houssaye, *Mémoires*, Art. 'Camus'; Furetière, *Roman Bourgeois*, Vol. I, p. 9; Scarron, *Roman Comique*, 1ʳᵉ Partie, Ch. 9, p. 26; Sorel, *Francion*, Vol. II, Liv. 5, p. 107.
132. La Mare, *Traité de la Police*, Vol. I, Liv. 2, Tit. 11.
133. See the map entitled 'La France Religieuse au Temps de Louis XIV', in *La France au Temps de Louis XIV* (Collection Ages d'Or et Réalités) p. 279.
134. For pilgrimages see Angot de L'Eperonnière, *Exercices de ce Temps*, No. 3; *Caquets de l'Accouchée*, 4ᵐᵉ Journée, pp. 126–7, 7ᵐᵉ Journée, p. 217; Lauder, *Journals*, p. 23; François de Sales, *Lettres*, p. 135; Tallemant, *Historiette de Tallemant, Le Maitre des Requêtes*, Vol. VIII, p. 146.
135. Bossuet, *Correspondance*, Vol. IV, p. 118. The dangers of Bible reading for the laywoman are stressed in the *Caquets de l'Accouchée*, 2ᵐᵉ Journée, p. 53.
136. Brégy, *Lettres et Poésies*, pp. 50–1; Maintenon, *Lettres* (ed. Langlois) Vol. IV, p. 376; Maure, *Correspondance* (ed. Barthélemy) pp. 189, 190–1; Montpensier, *Mémoires*, Vol. III, p. 69; Motteville, *Mémoires*, Vol. I, pp. 321 et seq. See also *Caquets de l'Accouchée*, 2ᵐᵉ Journée, p. 88.
137. For female involvement in Jansenism see Hébert, *Mémoires*, pp. 98–100, 111–12; Rapin, *Mémoires*, passim. Some important ladies who had no direct association with the Jansenists were avid readers of their works and admirers of their virtue. See Montpensier, *Mémoires*, Vol. III, pp. 67 et seq.; Motteville, *Mémoires*, Vol. IV, p. 105; Scudéry, *Clélie*, 3ᵐᵉ Partie, Liv. 2, pp. 1138 et seq.; Sévigné, *Lettres*, Vol. III, p. 390, and passim for references to reading of Nicole, Pascal and others; Clément, *Une Abbesse de Fontevrault*, p. 107.
138. Le Dieu, *Mémoires*, Vol. I, p. 37; Motteville, *Mémoires*, Vol. I, p. 323; Rapin, *Mémoires*, Vol. , p. 37.
139. Dames de Saint-Cyr, *Mémoires*, pp. 72, 237–9; Saint-Simon, *Mémoires*, Vol. III, pp. 155–6, Vol. V, p. 72.
140. Sourches, *Mémoires*, Vol. VI, pp. 168–9.

141. Sévigné, *Lettres*, Vol. VI, p. 196.
142. Du Fossé, *Mémoires*, p. 96; Foucault, *Mémoires*, p. 350; Hébert, *Mémoires*, pp. 314–16; Rapin, *Mémoires*, Vol. III, pp. 166 et seq., 378–9.
143. For the salient events of the persecution of the nuns see Jérôme Besoigne, *Histoire de l'Abbaye de Port-Royal* (1752 edn) Vol. I, Liv. 5, pp. 426 et seq., Vol. II, Liv. 10, pp. 422–9, Liv. 11, pp. 506 et seq., Vol. III, Liv. 14, pp. 144–223; Hébert, *Mémoires*, pp. 197–200; Racine, *Abrégé de l'Histoire de Port-Royal*, passim; Saint-Simon, *Mémoires*, Vol. V, pp. 75–6; Sourches, *Mémoires*, Vol. XII, p. 108, n. 1.
144. The career of Mme Guyon has been reconstructed from the following sources, in addition to her own *Vie*: Bossuet, *Correspondance*, Vols VI, VII, VIII; Dangeau, *Journal*, Vol. VI, p. 361, Vol. IX, p. 153, Vol. XVII, p. 106; Fénelon, *Correspondance* (ed. Orcibal) Vol. II, pp. 102 et seq., Vol. IV, pp. 57–8, 60–4, 89–94; Hébert, *Mémoires*, pp. 212 et seq.; Dames de Saint-Cyr, *Mémoires sur Mme de Maintenon*, pp. 298 et seq.; Saint-Simon, *Mémoires*, Vol. I, pp. 177–8, 191–3, 261 et seq.
145. Catherine de Parthenay, *Lettres à la Duchesse de la Trémoille*, p. 139.
146. Rohan, *Mémoires*, pp. 547, 589; Saint-Simon, *Mémoires*, Vol. I, p. 362; Sourches, *Mémoires*, Vol. I, p. 177.
147. Bassompierre, *Mémoires*, Vol. II, p. 322; Héroard, *Journal*, Vol. II, p. 276; Puységur, *Mémoires*, Vol. I, pp. 13–14; Richelieu, *Mémoires*, Vol. III, p. 237, Vol. IX, p. 367; Souvigny, *Mémoires*, Vol. I, p. 113; Tallemant, *Historiette des Femmes Vaillantes*, Vol. VIII, p. 217; Tristan l'Hermite, *Le Page Disgracié* (ed. A. Dietrich) pp. 408–9; Vaissète, *Histoire Générale de Languedoc*, Vol. XI, pp. 976, 1021.
148. *Edits, Déclarations et Arrêts concernant la Religion Prétendue Réformée* (ed. L. Pilatte) pp. 61–2.
149. Rather than attend mass and confession, formalities without which couples were refused the marriage sacrament, Protestants had recourse to vagabond priests and to the passing of simple contracts between parties. See *Correspondance des Contrôleurs Généraux*, Vol. I, p. 373, No. 1359, Vol. II, p. 47, No. 167.
150. Declaration of 16 June 1685 in *Edits* (ed. Pilatte) pp. 194–6.
151. Declaration of 20 Feb. 1680, ibid., pp. 49–51.
152. Ibid., p. 261.
153. Declaration of 6 Aug. 1686, ibid., p. 297. See also Brillon, *Dictionnaire des Arrêts*, Art. 'Exhérédation', Vol. II, p. 153, No. 66.
154. Revocation of the Edict of Nantes, Art. 7, in *Edits* (ed. Pilatte) p. 243.
155. Edict of Jan. 1686, ibid., pp. 259–60.
156. Declaration of 9 July 1685, plus Ordinance of 11 Jan. 1686, ibid., pp. 203–4, 268–9.
157. As did Mme Dacier (see Nicéron, *Mémoires*, Vol. III, pp. 132–4). Her reward was a royal pension of 500 *livres* and 1500 for her husband.
158. Bayle, *Dictionnaire*, Art. 'Claude D'; Le Dieu, *Mémoires*, Vol. I, pp. 171–2; Haag, *France Protestante*, Vol. III, Art. 'Claude'.

159. Dangeau, *Journal*, Vol. I, pp. 216, 218, 226, 227, 228, 230, 231–2, and so on.
160. *Correspondance Administrative* (ed. Depping) Vol. IV, pp. 338, 351; *Correspondance des Contrôleurs Généraux*, Vol. I, p. 316, No. 1175; Argenson, *Notes*, p. 12.
161. Bossuet, *Correspondance*, Vol. III, p. 224, Vol. IX, p. 322; Jean Cavalier, *Mémoires sur la Guerre des Camisards* (ed. F. Puaux) pp. 33 et seq., *Correspondance des Contrôleurs Généraux*, Vol. I, p. 316, No. 1175; Fléchier, *Œuvres*, Vol. X, pp. 59, 69–72; Argenson, *Notes*, p. 49; Savois, 'Abrégé de l'Histoire de l'origine, de la sortie de France et de la vie d'Alexandre Savois', in *Bulletin de la Société de l'Histoire du Protestantisme Français*, 5me Sér., Vol. III, p. 42.
162. A graphic description of the indignities perpetrated on a female corpse is to be found in *Recueil de Journaux Caennais (1661–1707)* (ed. G. Vanel) pp. 11–12. In 1699 Louis XIV had second thoughts about subjecting relapsed Catholics to this punishment. See *Correspondance Administrative* (ed. Depping) Vol. IV, p. 432.
163. *Correspondance Administrative*, Vol. IV, p. 375.
164. Louis granted formal permission to some of his Huguenot courtiers to retire abroad, but penalised them cruelly by forbidding them to be accompanied by their younger, convertible, children. The Comtesse de Roye was thus authorised to rejoin her husband in Denmark with their two eldest daughters, but had to leave five children behind in France. See Dangeau, *Journal*, Vol. I, pp. 280–1.
165. *Correspondance des Contrôleurs Généraux*, Vol. I, p. 538, No. 1908.
166. The central government was frequently notified of cases of converted husbands with unconverted wives. See Colbert, *Lettres*, Vol. V, p. 136; *Correspondance Administrative* (ed. Depping) Vol. IV, pp. 367–8; *Correspondance des Contrôleurs Généraux*, Vol. I, pp. 57, No. 215, 520–1, No. 1847.
167. The classic example is that of the Duc and Duchesse de La Force, arrested in 1689 after the dispersal of their children to Catholic establishments. When the Duc, a great-grandson of the famous marshal who served under Henri IV and Louis XIII, lay dying in 1698 his wife was first refused access to him except in the hearing of a police official, for fear of her swaying him back to Protestantism, then finally prevented from seeing him altogether. See *Correspondance Administrative*, Vol. IV, pp. 349, 391–2, 410, 422–3, 464, 480, 482, 486.
168. *Correspondance Administrative*, Vol. IV, pp. 373, 394, 408, 414, 419, 451, 511, 512; *Correspondance des Contrôleurs Généraux*, Vol. I, p. 90, No. 351.
169. *Correspondance des Contrôleurs Généraux*, Vol. I, p. 148, No. 564.
170. For the attachment of Protestants to their psalms see Bavière, *Correspondance* (trans. Brunet) Vol. II, p. 259.
171. For Protestant prophetesses see Fléchier, *Récit fidèle de ce qui s'est passé dans les assemblées des Fanatiques [Protestants] du Vivarais*, *Mémoire touchant la bergère de Crest*, *Mémoire sur les visions de la fille du diocèse de Castres*, in *Œuvres*, Vol. IX, pp. 441 et seq.

172. Cavalier, *Mémoires*, p. 143. For the Camisard uprising in general see Antoine Court, *Histoire des Troubles des Cévennes ou de la Guerre des Camisards* (1760) passim.
173. *Correspondance des Contrôleurs Généraux*, Vol. II, p. 44, No. 152.
174. Saint-Simon, *Mémoires*, Vol. I, p. 263.
175. Bossuet, *Correspondance*, Vol. VI, p. 27.
176. Dec. 1655. Quoted by V. Cousin, *Mme de Sablé*, pp. 94–5.
177. The convents had already become infected by doubt, owing to the infiltration into the cloister of propagandist works from Dutch presses. See Clément, *Une Abbesse de Fontevrault*, p. 193.
178. Bayle, *Dictionnaire*, Art. 'Barbe A'; Bayle, *Pensées sur la Comète*, Vol. II, No. 142, pp. 25 et seq.
179. The brochure is reproduced in A. Devyver, *Le Sang Epuré: Les Préjugés de Race chez les Gentilshommes Français de l'Ancien Régime 1560–1720*, pp. 485–97. The passage quoted is on p. 487.
180. Claveret, *L'Esprit Fort*, III.iii. The 'Achevé d'imprimer' is dated 30 Aug. 1637, but the 'Avertissement au Lecteur' describes the play as having been written nearly seven years previously.
181. Already in 1646, when the Chevalier de Roquelaure was imprisoned in the Bastille on a charge of committing blasphemies such as baptising and marrying dogs, the Duchesse de Longueville and the ladies of the court had complained loudly 'qu'on n'avait jamais vu arrêter un homme de condition pour des bagatelles comme cela'. See Tallemant, *Historiette du Chevalier de Roquelaure*, Vol. III, pp. 143–4.
182. Montpensier, *Mémoires*, Vol. III, pp. 213–4.
183. Tallemant, *Historiette de Ninon*, Vol. VII, p. 231.
184. Bavière, *Lettres Inédites* (ed. Rolland) p. 288; Dangeau, *Journal*, Vol. I, p. 34.
185. The Temple was a vast enclosure containing a fortress that had once been the Paris headquarters of the Knights Templars, of which the younger Vendôme brother was Grand Prior. For the Vendômes see Saint-Simon, *Mémoires*, Vol. III, pp. 249 et seq.; for Temple society and pastimes see La Fontaine's *Epître à Mgr le Duc de Vendôme* (1689), in *Œuvres*, Vol. IX, pp. 446 et seq., and G. Desnoiresterres, *Les Cours Galantes*, passim.
186. Mazarin's nieces, of whom this Duchesse (Marie-Anne Mancini) was one, had very little piety according to the *Mémoires* of her sister, the Duchesse Mazarin (pp. 14–15; below, Ch. 14, n. 10). The Duchesse Mazarin herself, who died in exile in England (1699), had set up there a private little court, the leading light of which was the sceptic Saint-Evremond.
187. Bayle, *Lettres Choisies*, Vol. II, pp. 555–6 (on the impious *noëls* of Mlle de La Force); Deshoulières, 'Ode à M.L.D.D.L.R.', in *Poésies*, Vol. I, pp. 151 et seq. (exposé of materialist doctrines); Dunoyer, *Lettres*, Vol. III, pp. 293, 294 ('Croyez-moi, ma chère Madame, les miracles sont rares, et je crois, entre nous, que la plupart de ceux que notre Sainte Mère Eglise nous oblige de croire, sont un peu sujets à caution ... On n'a jamais moins cru, et on n'a jamais fait

semblant de tant croire!'); La Roche-Guilhen, *Histoire des Favorites*, 1re Partie, p. 193, 2me Partie, pp. 73, 225 (attacks on pope and Vatican mores).

188. The reaction of their peers to the perpetration of such acts is significant. In 1659 a young tailor and his girlfriend were caught fornicating in the church of St Etienne at Bourges, while a second girl kept watch. All three were whipped, branded, pilloried, fined and banished, but the unplacated 'peuple' clamoured for them to be hanged and burned. See *Chroniques Berrichonnes du XVIIe siècle* (ed. H. Jongleux) pp. 178–9.

189. See, for example, *Journal d'un chanoine au diocèse de Cavaillon*, p. 134; Louvet, *Journal*, in *Revue de l'Anjou*, July–Aug. 1855, p. 13.

190. Angélique Arnauld, *Lettres*, Vol. I, pp. 61–2; Sévigné, *Lettres*, Vol. III, p. 172, Vol. VII, p. 209.

191. Geneviève Forest, for example, wrote a string of poems denouncing atheists and materialists. See her *Le Fantôme du Sage*, 1re Partie, pp. 80 et seq.

192. Le Verrier, *Les Satires de Boileau*, p. 124; Tallemant, *Historiette de Des Barreaux*, Vol. V, p. 93, and *Ninon*, Vol. VII, p. 230.

193. Dangeau, *Journal*, Vol. IV, p. 371.

194. Judaism was tolerated in seventeenth-century France, but Jews were confined to ghettos in large towns and obliged to wear distinctive clothing (see, for example, Jouvin, *Voyageur d'Europe*, Vol. I, p. 97). They were perpetual objects of dislike and suspicion to the Christian population, who accused them amongst other things of sacrificing infants (see Ancillon, *Recueil Journalier*, Vol. I, p. 64). But the government hesitated to expel them because of their usefulness in trade and business. See *Correspondance Administrative* (ed. Depping) Vol. III, pp. 286–7, 294–5; *Correspondance des Contrôleurs Généraux*, Vol. I, p. 148, No. 567.

CHAPTER 14

1. Bussy-Rabutin, *Correspondance*, Vol. V, p. 262; Sévigné, *Lettres*, Vol. IX, p. 463.

2. See A. Chastel, 'L'Art et Le Sentiment de la Mort au XVIIe Siècle', in *Dix-Septième Siècle*, July–Oct. 1957; E. Mâle, *L'Art Religieux du XVIIe Siècle*, Ch. 5; C. Nisard, *Histoire des Livres Populaires ou de la Littérature de Colportage* (2me edn) Vol. I, Ch. 2, pp. 90–8, Vol. II, Ch. 10, pp. 275–331.

3. Ménage, *Menagiana*, 1re Partie, pp. 66–7.

4. Motteville, *Mémoires*, Vol. I, p. 333.

5. Sourches, *Mémoires*, Vol. VI, p. 165.

6. Gaufreteau, *Chronique Bordeloise*, Vol. II, pp. 112–13.

7. The execution of Hélène Gillet was a case in point. See *Deux Livres de Raison Bourguignons* (ed. C. Oursel) pp. 362–3; *Variétés Historiques et Littéraires* (ed. Fournier) Vol. I, pp. 35–47.

8. Sévigné, *Lettres*, Vol. VII, p. 458. Cf. Bavière, *Correspondance* (trans.

Brunet) Vol. II, p. 311: 'Je ne trouve pas qu'une bien grande vieillesse soit quelque chose d'agréable; on a trop à souffrir, et, sous le rapport de la souffrance je suis un grand poltron.'

9. D'Aumale, *Souvenirs*, p. 228.

10. When little enthusiasm could be generated for religion, purely philosophical consolations might be substituted. Chaulieu thus addressed to Mazarin's niece the Duchesse de Bouillon a rhymed *Epître* expounding the epicurean view of death:

> Aux pensées de la mort accoutume ton âme:
> Hors son nom seulement, elle n'a rien d'affreux.
> Détaches-en l'horreur d'un séjour ténébreux,
> De démons, d'enfer, et de flamme;
> Qu'aura-t-elle de douloureux?
> La mort est simplement le terme de la vie.
> De peines, ni de biens, elle n'est point suivie...
>   (Chaulieu, *Œuvres*, Vol. II, pp. 317 et seq.)

11. Sévigné, *Lettres*, Vol. IX, p. 334. See also Vol. X, p. 344.

12. Du Bosc, *L'Honnête Femme*, 2me Partie, p. 334; Goussault, *Portrait d'une Femme Honnête*, Ch. 20; La Chétardie, *Instruction pour une jeune princesse*, p. 167.

13. For a lengthy development on this theme see the Protestant pastor Charles Drelincourt's *Consolations de l'Ame Fidèle contre les Frayeurs de la Mort* (1651), Ch. 7, '1er remède contre les frayeurs de la mort. Y penser souvent.'

14. Deshoulières, 'Ode', in *Poésies*, Vol. I, p. 106.

15. Sablière, *Lettres*, in Menjot d'Elbenne, *Mme de la Sablière*, pp. 295, 324.

16. Lafayette, *Lettres* (ed. Ashton) pp. 152–3. For Mme de Lafayette's religious doubts see her *Correspondance* (ed. Beaunier) pp. 143–5.

17. Examples: *Archives Curieuses de l'Histoire de France* (eds L. Cimber and F. Danjou) 2me Sér., Vol. V, pp. 175–7 (Marie de Médicis's will); Bussy-Rabutin, *Correspondance*, Vol. IV, p. 124; Dangeau, *Journal*, Vol. I, p. 34; Maintenon, *Lettres* (ed. Langlois) Vol. II, p. 389; Malherbe, *Œuvres*, Vol. III, p. 493.

18. The Duchesse de Montpensier made a special point of leaving legacies to all her domestics 'pour les empêcher, dit-elle, de mourir de faim, comme ceux de plus grandes princesses qu'elle a vus en ce triste état-là' (see Dangeau, *Journal*, Vol. IV, p. 260).

19. Plus 10 000 *livres* to the Carmelites of Saint-Denis (see *Mercure Galant*, Apr. 1693, pp. 153–5).

20. Bonneau-Avenant, *Mme de Miramion*, pp. 412 et seq. For other outstanding examples of charitable bequests see Loret, *Muse Historique*, 14 Dec. 1658; *Mercure Galant*, Mar. 1700, p. 210; Sévigné, *Lettres*, Vol. II, p. 491; Vincent de Paul, *Correspondance*, Vol. II, p. 127; Bonneau-Avenant, *La Duchesse d'Aiguillon*, pp. 461 et seq.

21. Gaufreteau, *Chronique Bordeloise*, Vol. II, pp. 77–8. For the difficulties encountered in executing the testatrix's last wishes see *Mémoires et Documents pour servir à l'Histoire du Commerce et de l'Industrie en France* (ed. J. Hayem) 4me Sér., pp. 85 et seq.

22. The will is quoted in E. Magne, *Ninon de Lanclos*, p. 196.
23. The will is cited in E. Soulié, *Recherches sur Molière et sur sa Famille*, pp. 243–4.
24. Tallemant, *Historiette de Jeanne Arnauld*, Vol. IV, p. 66.
25. *Mercure Galant*, Aug. 1683, p. 63.
26. *Lettres en Vers* (ed. Rothschild) Vol. III, pp. 909–10. See also Anselme, *Maison Royale*, Vol. III, p. 488.
27. Bouvignes, *Miroir de la Vanité des Femmes Mondaines*, Ch. 5, p. 171.
28. Louvet, *Journal*, in *Revue de l'Anjou*, Nov.–Dec. 1856, p. 348.
29. R. Sauzet, *Les Visites Pastorales dans le diocèse de Chartres pendant la première moitié du XVIIᵉ siècle*, pp. 260–1, 325. The famous 'Secretaries' of the Holy Innocents cemetery in Paris, clerks who earned a living by writing letters for the illiterate, used the gravestones there as tables (see Evelyn, *Diary*, Vol. I, p. 85).
30. Sablière, *Lettres* (ed. Menjot d'Elbenne) p. 334.
31. Lalande, *Notes* (ed. Sahuc) p. 13.
32. The church of the great Carmelite convent in the Faubourg Saint-Jacques in Paris was a favourite rendezvous for the remains of noblewomen. See, for example, J. F. Bourgoin de Villefore, *Vie de Mme la Duchesse de Longueville*, p. 179; *Lettres en Vers* (ed. Rothschild) Vol. I, p. 594; Saint-Simon, *Mémoires*, Vol. I, p. 197.
33. Babeau, *La Vie Rurale dans l'Ancienne France*, Appendix 9.
34. See above, n. 7, and Ch. 12, p. 207.
35. Motteville, *Mémoires*, Vol. IV, p. 405.
36. Ibid., p. 364.
37. Sévigné, *Lettres*, Vol. II, p. 491. For further testimonies to her own scorn, and that of the public, for doctors see ibid., Vol. VI, p. 94; Vol. VII, p. 189; Vol. IX, pp. 254–5.
38. See Bavière, *Correspondance* (trans. Brunet) Vol. I, pp. 2–3, 5, 266, 353, Vol. II, pp. 188, 201; Lafayette, *Histoire d'Henriette d'Angleterre*, p. 204; Sablé, *Discours contre les Médecins*, in N. Ivanoff, *La Marquise de Sablé et son Salon*, pp. 109–20; Barthélemy, *Les Amis de la Marquise de Sablé*, p. 208.
39. Bussy-Rabutin, *Correspondance*, Vol. VI, p. 322.
40. Malherbe, *Œuvres*, Vol. III, p. 362.
41. In addition to the Rapin and Tallemant references given above in Ch. 13, n. 118, see Voiture, *Œuvres*, Vol. I, pp. 224, 329; Barthélemy, *Les Amis de la Marquise de Sablé*, pp. 108 et seq.
42. Abbé d'Ailly's preface to the 1678 edition of Sablé, *Maximes*.
43. Saint-Simon, *Mémoires*, Vol. IV, p. 10.
44. Maintenon, *Lettres Inédites* (ed. Bossange) 19 June 1707, Vol. I, p. 140.
45. Bossuet, *Oraisons Funèbres* (ed. A. Rébelliau) p. 160 (on the death of Henriette d'Angleterre).
46. Purgatory was qualified by Calvin as 'une fiction pernicieuse de Satan'. See his *Institution de la Religion Chrétienne*, Liv. 3, Ch. 5, sect. 6. See also the Protestant pastor Moyse Amyraut's *Discours de l'Etat des Fidèles après la Mort*, sect. 2, 'Quelle est la félicité des âmes fidèles séparées du corps, et quel le lieu où elles sont recueillies'.

47. Mornay, *Mémoires*, Vol. II, p. 116.
48. J.-J. Boileau, *Vie de Madame la Duchesse de Liancourt*, pp. xi–xii.
49. For 'classic' deaths see *Livre de Raison de la Famille de Froissard-Broissia*, p. 99; *Livres de Raison Limousins et Marchois* (ed. Guibert) pp. 228–9; Marolles, *Mémoires*, 1ʳᵉ Partie, p. 80; Nicolas Pasquier, *Lettres*, Liv. 5, No. 8, in Etienne Pasquier, *Œuvres* (1723 edn) Vol. II.
50. De Vassetz, *De l'obligation que les pères et mères ont d'instruire eux-mêmes leurs enfants*, Ch. 2, p. 86.
51. Montpensier, *Mémoires*, Vol. II, p. 289.
52. Saint-Simon, *Mémoires*, Vol. I, p. 27.
53. A few examples amongst many: Bussy-Rabutin, *Correspondance*, Vol. V, pp. 415–16, 506; Condé, *Lettres à la Reine de Pologne*, pp. 24 n. 1, 89–90, 122–3, 292; Fontenay-Mareuil, *Mémoires*, p. 16; Lafayette, *Mémoires de la Cour de France*, Collection Michaud et Poujoulat, 3ᵐᵉ Sér., Vol. VIII, p. 228; Molé, *Mémoires*, Vol. I, p. 451; Montpensier, *Mémoires*, Vol. I, p. 132, Vol. III, pp. 476–7; Motteville, *Mémoires*, Vol. I, pp. 220–1, 344; Richelieu, *Lettres*, Vol. II, p. 481; Saint-Maurice, *Lettres*, Vol. I, pp. 8, 374–5; Saint-Simon, *Mémoires*, Vol. I, pp. 324, 363, 419 et seq., Vol. II, p. 224.
54. Saint-Simon, *Mémoires*, Vol. I, pp. 417–18.
55. Saint-Maurice, *Lettres*, Vol. I, p. 452.
56. Sourches, *Mémoires*, Vol. III, p. 230.
57. Saint-Simon, *Mémoires*, Vol. I, p. 27.
58. Saint-Maurice, *Lettres*, Vol. I, p. 453.
59. Montpensier, *Mémoires*, Vol. IV, p. 151; D'Ormesson, *Journal*, Vol. II, p. 594. For other examples of the detailed divulgence of autopsy findings see Saint-Simon, *Mémoires*, Vol. I, pp. 381, 382; Sévigné, *Lettres*, Vol. X, p. 108; Sourches, *Mémoires*, Vol. III, p. 229.
60. The fate of Mme de Montespan (see Saint-Simon, *Mémoires*, Vol. IV, p. 13). Bodies of female criminals could be taken for use in public demonstrations of dissection. See Patin, *Lettres*, Vol. I, p. 216, Vol. II, p. 93, Vol. III, pp. 635, 722.
61. Bonneau-Avenant, *La Duchesse d'Aiguillon*, p. 462.
62. Examples: Marguerite de Valois's heart, deposited in the monastery of the Petits Augustins in the Faubourg St Jacques which she had founded; Anne d'Autriche's heart, bequeathed to the Val-de-Grâce convent, completely renovated at her instigation; Duchesse de Longueville's entrails put in the Eglise St Jacques du Haut Pas, rebuilt at her expense. See Le Maire, *Paris Ancien et Nouveau*, Vol. I, pp. 345, 582; Vol. II, pp. 349 et seq.
63. *Mercure Galant*, Apr. 1693, pp. 160–2 (lying-in-state of Duchesse de Montpensier).
64. In the course of the funeral at Angers of the Comtesse de Carvaz in 1626, for example, the corpse was taken to the church of St-Aulbin, 'la nef de laquelle était toute tendue à noir, jusqu'à la grande porte de la rue, et le chœur tendu à velours tout autour'. See Louvet, *Journal*, in *Revue de l'Anjou*, Mar.–Apr. 1856, p. 180.
65. An edict creating 'jurés crieurs héréditaires d'enterrements' throughout the realm was promulgated in Jan. 1690. Another,

creating two sworn criers in every town, followed in Dec. 1694. See Isambert, *Anciennes Lois Françaises*, Vol. XX, pp. 102, 233.

66. For *billets d'enterrement* see Boursault, *Le Mercure Galant ou La Comédie Sans Titre*, II.vii; Patin, *Lettres*, Vol. III, pp. 510, 740. An illustration of one such document has been published in P. Goubert and D. Roche, *Les Français et l'Ancien Régime* (Paris, 1984) Vol. II, p. 166.

67. Apart from the *confréries* associated with the guilds there existed in some parts of France specialist *Confréries des Agonisants*, members of which bound themselves to say prayers for the dying. See Bessot, *Livre-Journal de Pierre de Bessot (1609–1652)*, in *Bulletin de la Société Historique et Archéologique du Périgord*, Vol. XX, p. 180.

68. The quality of the cloth from which the pall was made indicated the rank of the deceased. The rich had a black velvet pall, overlaid with a white satin cross. See *Livre de Raison de la Famille de Froissard-Broissia*, p. 85; Locatelli, *Voyage de France*, pp. 70–1.

69. Borrelly, *Livre de Raison*, p. 218; Simon Le Marchand, *Journal*, p. 35. See also Ch. 7, n. 87.

70. 'Je désire ... une bière de bois, et portée par des pauvres de la paroisse, vraiment pauvres, à qui l'on donnera de quoi s'habiller, comme aussi aux enfants pauvres qui porteront les chandeliers et flambeaux; ils seront de la paroisse' – Mme de Miramion's will in Bonneau-Avenant, *Mme de Miramion*, p. 411.

71. *Mercure Galant*, Sept. 1681, p. 360.

72. Bouvignes, *Miroir de la Vanité des Femmes Mondaines*, Ch. 5, pp. 164–5; Brackenhoffer, *Voyage en France*, p. 213.

73. *Mercure Galant*, Aug. 1683, p. 97.

74. Montpensier, *Mémoires*, Vol. IV, p. 30. Cf. Condé, *Lettres à la Reine de Pologne*, p. 257.

75. Ménage, *Menagiana*, 1re Partie, p. 145.

76. Brackenhoffer, *Voyage en France*, p. 213.

77. Saint-Simon, *Mémoires*, Vol. I, p. 28.

78. Tallemant, *Historiette de Gombauld*, Vol. IV, p. 150.

79. *Arrêt du Conseil* of 7 Aug. 1662 (Isambert, *Anciennes Lois Françaises*, Vol. XVIII, p. 20); *Règlement* of 2 Apr. 1666 (Isambert, Vol. XVIII, p. 80); *Déclaration du Roi* of Feb. 1669 (*Recueil Néron*, Vol. II, p. 963).

80. See Ch. 13, n. 162.

81. According to Calvin in *Institution de la Religion Chrétienne*, Liv. 3, Ch. 5, sect. 10, there was no scriptural authority for the practice of praying for the dead, which was therefore tantamount to profaning the name of God.

82. Brackenhoffer, *Voyage en France*, p. 165; Fléchier, *Grands Jours d'Auvergne*, pp. 96–7.

83. A service in honour of the dead performed once a week throughout a year.

84. A series of thirty masses.

85. Magne, *Ninon de Lanclos*, p. 196.

86. Bonneau-Avenant, *La Duchesse d'Aiguillon*, p. 462.

87. *Récits de Messire P. Millet, Curé de Notre-Dame de la Platière* (ed. F. Frécon) p. 18.

88. Hodeau, *Mémoires*, pp. 221–2.
89. Babeau, *La Vie Rurale dans l'Ancienne France*, Appendix 9. See also the testament of an illiterate widow reproduced in full in P. Chaunu, *La Mort à Paris*, Annexe IV.
90. *Journal du Voyage de Deux Hollandais*, p. 214.
91. Examples: Dudrot de Capdebosc, *Livre de Raison de la Famille* (ed. P. Tamizey de Larroque) p. 25 (bereavement on 27 Oct. 1621, remarriage on 23 Oct. 1622); Demaillasson, *Journal*, Vol. XXXVI, pp. 1, 3 (bereavement on 3 July 1644, remarriage on 3 June 1647); *Mémoires d'un Bourgeois de Marseille*, pp. 44, 47 (bereavement on 31 Oct. 1689, remarriage on 13 July 1691); Dusson, *Mémoires*, pp. 271, 272 (bereavement in Feb. 1685, remarriage on 13 Nov. 1685); Noé Lacroix, *Journal*, pp. 32, 34 (bereavement on 12 Jan. 1611, remarriage on 18 June 1611).
92. Examples: Bussy-Rabutin, *Correspondance*, Vol. IV, p. 69, Vol. V, p. 60; Loret, *Muse Historique*, 8 Jan. and 16 July 1651; Maintenon, *Lettres* (ed. Langlois) Vol. III, p. 467; Sévigné, *Lettres*, Vol. X, p. 456.
93. Bavière, *Lettres Inédites* (ed. Rolland) p. 120; Sévigné, *Lettres*, Vol. X, p. 229.
94. She died on 30 June 1670. By 5 Aug. Bussy-Rabutin had heard from one of his correspondents that the princess was 'déjà presque oubliée'. See Bussy-Rabutin, *Correspondance*, Vol. I, p. 303.
95. Sévigné, *Lettres*, Vol. IX, p. 512.
96. Maintenon, *Lettres Inédites* (ed. Bossange) Vol. I, p. 142.

Appendix:
Translations of French
Passages

Page references for each passage are given on the left.

TO THE READER

vii   An author on his knees, in a humble preface/Begs mercy in vain
       from the reader whom he bores;/He will get nowhere with this
       irritated judge,/Who is fully authorised to put him on trial.

CHAPTER 1

1   It's a girl!
1   wept loud and long
1   could not reconcile herself to the fact
1   said that it would have to be thrown in the river, and showed her
     extreme disappointment to everyone
1   But since it is only a female cherub,/Husband and wife, redoub-
     ling their efforts,/Will work all over again/To produce a male
     cherub afterwards.
1   become a girl
1   signs of rejoicing in the customary manner
1   that it was not the custom to hold any ceremonies for girls, except
     for the first-born one, and that no such ceremony was registered in
     the Rolls, in the Church of Paris, or in the Town Hall
2   The males are the props and supports of a big family's lastingness.
2   God give her the grace to be mindful to fear and love Him, and fill
     her with His gifts.
2   God give her the grace to be pure white [blanche] in fact as in
     name, before God and men.
2   God give this child the grace to live and die with a holy fear and
     love of Him!
5   many little children ... stifled by their wet-nurses
5   God grant her peace.
5   May God through His grace deign to have had mercy upon her,
     not charging her with the sins of her father and mother, albeit that
     these sully her profoundly.
5   God has given, God has taken away, blessed be the name of the
     Lord. Her soul is in heaven and her body in our tomb, near that of
     her good mother. May it please the divine majesty that their souls
     be together in heaven.

363

6   She was well taught and full of promise ... Had considerable intelligence, knew how to read at five years and had all the good inclinations and sentiments of her late mother.

9   I was born, according to what some people say, the day before Easter, 13 April (although my baptism was not until 24 May) of the year 1648.

9   in order that it would please her [the Virgin] to be her Protectress, and to agree to let her wear the white habit in her honour, till the age of seven

10   She staggers under gold and jewels ... and her coiffure weighs more than her whole person. She will be prevented from growing and being healthy.

12   the smallest children are trained to work

12   You see there ... even very little children ... working

13   Childhood is the life of an animal

13   Children ... are already men

13   a very obscure feeling of affection on the part of father towards son, son towards father ... which subsists only as long as it is necessary for them to work together

14   Know, furthermore, good people, / That nothing is more intolerable / Than to see your little children / Strung like onions round the big table, / With runny noses and greasy chins, / Poking their fingers in all the dishes.

14   Learned men have their ridiculous side as well. Who would not have laughed at seeing Melancthon, the most serious and erudite of the Lutheran theologians, reading from a book held in one hand, and with the other rocking his child to sleep? I saw on one occasion the late Monsieur Esprit in a very similar posture. He was reading Plato, and from time to time he would stop reading, shake his infant's rattle, and play with this kid.

14   our daughter conversed with my wife and myself and the whole company for three hours this evening, and nearly made us die laughing

15   so beautiful and so pleasing that from the moment of her birth I loved her with a tenderness that I cannot put into words

15   When I reflected that I was separated for the whole of my life from what was most dear to me, I could find no pleasure in the world, outside of which lay my happiness. I know that many will tax me with weakness and with a lack of fortitude over an accident that they will not consider one of the worst; but to that I would reply that things only affect us according to the feelings that we have for them, and that therefore one should not make blanket judgements as if we all had the same way of thinking. It is necessary to know how highly we rate things before praising the patience we show on losing them ... I confess that I would be acting like a woman if I pestered people with my laments; but always to cherish what I loved most of all, to think about her continually and to want to rejoin her, I consider that the sentiment of a man who knows what love is, and who, believing firmly in the immortality of the soul,

feels that the departure of his dear daughter is a temporary absence, and not an eternal separation.

CHAPTER 2

17 you would see miracles

17 And why should their training or upbringing in business affairs and cultural pursuits on an equal footing with men not fill this gap ordinarily apparent between men's intelligence and their own?

18 a cabinet piece, displayed to the curious, but of no use

18 Sibyls and Muses

18 an honest knowledge of things useful for moral guidance

18–19 Nevertheless, despite what I have said, it is not my intention to summon women to college. I do not want to make graduates of them, nor exchange their needles and wools for astrolabes and globes. I have too much respect for the dividing line between us; and I pose the question only of what they are able to do, not what they must do, given the way in which things have been arranged, either by a decree of nature, or by a time-honoured custom as old as nature.

19 There are high-born ladies very knowledgeable in the humanities who hide that fact as if it were somewhat shameful, and they are right to do so ... because it is always somewhat shameful to have loaded oneself with useless knowledge.

19 Keep their mind as much as you can within average limits and teach them that their sex should show in matters of learning a modesty almost as fierce as that inspired by horror of vice.

20 that the girls learn to write

20 for queens before working for ladies' maids

21 good mother

21 and made me always give an account of what she had ordered me to do

21 I was asked how I went about bringing her up so well: I replied that it was by always talking reason to her, by showing her why such and such a thing was bad or good, by not indulging any of her whims, by ensuring as far as possible that she saw no bad example, by not repelling her with fits of bad temper, by praising virtue and by inspiring in her a horror of vice in general.

21 Stand up straight; raise your head

21 your mother would have at most two chambermaids, one of whom would be your *gouvernante*. What education do you think such a woman would give you? they are ordinarily peasants, or at best petty *bourgeoises* who only know how to teach their charges to stand up straight, adjust a bodice-stiffener properly, and curtsey well ... The cleverest is the one who knows four silly little verses, one or two stanzas of Pibrac that she has you say on every occasion, and that you recite like a little parrot.

22 so many blows to her old belly that she fell headlong ... and nearly died

23	they are vagabonds who go hither and thither only to bring scandal and to seduce some unsuspecting female, and when you think you have laid hold of them they never fail to skedaddle.
23	To his Pupil: You who are truly more than mortal, / Ever-present Love / Makes me guide your hand / To form fine letters: / But seeing your eyes inflame me with passion / The traitor quietly tells me / That I profit from instructing you / And that I learn how to love well / While I am showing you how to write well. /
23	your truest friend for life
23	sweetest Laverna
25	It is not necessary that a girl should know how to form her letters perfectly: but it is necessary that she should be in a place that is safe and above suspicion.
26	We are very happy to serve these little souls in order to try to help them preserve their innocence. But after all, if God allows them to be taken away from us, we shall be more at peace and less distracted, since serving them gives us a lot to do.
27	gracefully, with three fingers
28	All that should be permitted to them is to say simply what they do not understand and to ask for explanations . . . beware of making of them chatterboxes who ask questions for the pleasure of speaking.
28	the simplicity appropriate to our sex
28	take up time that could be employed more usefully
28	a son can embark upon a voyage, cross seas, go to the ends of the earth; but a daughter must not even go out of her house without permission
28	avoid, if you can, a convent. The best one will constrain her, bore her, repel her, make her insincere and eager for a worldly existence.
29	more often of ordinary and gallant things than of elevated ones
30	had not read
30	even women could understand something of it
31	worldly wit
32	the variety of subject matter in my letters . . . being such that there is no one, whatever their taste, who cannot find therein something to suit them
33	a very clever adept of Descartes
33	Many women
34	at the back behind the circles of chairs for the guests, so that without being seen much they can see and hear the respondent.
35	played the harpsichord, the bass viol and various other instruments
35	played admirably well the lute, theorbo, clavichord and guitar
35	relaxed during her leisure hours by doing tapestry and embroidery work, with her daughters and her ladies-in-waiting
36	a thousand grammar mistakes
36	you could not handle syntax any more than spelling
37	spelling was non-existent in her letters

37	I write so badly that it is an awful job to read my handwriting
37	More often than not my pen gets swept along by the vivacity of my thoughts, causing me to scribble and spell badly
37	They have considerable difficulty in forming proper [true] letters; how would they be clever enough to produce false ones?
38	For the most part they are incapable of probing those truths that are somewhat difficult to discover. Everything abstract is incomprehensible to them
38	more gentle, more patient, more docile, in short, more free from prejudices and false doctrines than many men
39	live and die
39	even amongst the ladies of the court and the capital
39	What an age this is! What morals have come to! [Ciceronian interjection]

CHAPTER 3

41	the lot that falls to our sex
41	Whoever speaks of woman, speaks of a dependent thing
41	they cannot hold themselves upright or subsist by themselves; they need a prop, even more for their mind than for their body
41	Better to marry than to burn [I Corinthians 7:9]
41	The estate of matrimony is one which requires more virtue and constancy than any other; it is a perpetual exercise in self-mortification
42	It is a word which signifies servitude and suffering, a community of woes and troubles, a relationship of cares and duties
42	no such thing as a pleasurable marriage; heavy burden beneath which man succumbs; the estate in which one experiences the most tribulations
42	There is a great difference between love and marriage . . . because love lasts only as long as it is pleasing, but marriage becomes all the more lengthy in that it is more boring: love is the symbol of freedom because it constrains no one against their will; marriage, on the other hand, is the symbol of servitude, because only death can break its bonds.
42	As long as they are only lovers, we [women] reign supreme, / And they treat us like queens until they have us in their power; / But after marriage they are kings in turn
42	My surrender has made me odious to you!
43	marriages take place, not out of consideration for the contracting party, but for the honour and advantage of families; . . . the contract is made not as a private agreement, but one which is common to all the relatives, since they are being given heirs and allies, something which they cannot accept against their wishes.
43	few marriages turn out well when they start and progress on the basis of physical charms and amorous desires
44	ungainly and blotchy

44   that she could not stand

45   crowned slaves

45   linchpin of nearly all alliances

45   the exact amount of his assets, whether he was not financially
        embarrassed, and whether he had not contracted . . . debts

45   in solid effects

46   that it was His Eminence whom he was marrying, not his female
        relatives, and that he would take the one given to him

46   Do you love him? No, Sire, she replied, but he is a man of very
        high rank that I would rather marry than any other.

47   a fifteen-minute affair: while Sanguin's son was being praised to
        his father, the latter praised Mlle de Saint-Aignan as well. The
        duke said to him: 'Should we unite the two of them in marriage?'
        Sanguin replied: 'You would do me too much honour, sir, even if
        you only gave her a pair of gloves' [that is, as a dowry]. 'Let us go
        and speak to the king' said the duke. They did so, and that is how
        the marriage came about.

47   I recommend you to receive him graciously, since I intend to make
        him your husband

47   intolerable hatred

47   As soon as he [her father] had found a prospective partner who
        was as suitable to my family as he was unsuitable to my taste, he
        committed me to marriage, as is the custom, without mentioning
        the matter to me, and informed me that, in order to consummate
        this terrible business, it only required my consent, which he did
        not think that he would have to ask me for.

47   It [the marriage] was arranged without my being notified . . . and I
        was even made to sign the marriage articles without being told
        what they were . . . I did not see my betrothed until two or three
        days before the marriage.

48   In France, where marriage almost always takes place out of self-
        interest, the persons [of prospective partners] are rarely con-
        sidered, and the settling of the formalities often precedes simple
        curiosity to see one another. The reason is that one seeks less to
        possess the other person's heart than to procure material advan-
        tages; that one concentrates more on the well-being of a household
        and on ways of spending money than on compatibility of tempera-
        ments and on the qualities of one's future wife. However beautiful
        she may be, we are all prepared not to love for long that which
        cannot be loved forever, and forestalling the sentiment of pleasure
        by imagining future aversion, we enter upon matrimony with
        indifference, fully intent on consoling ourselves elsewhere for a
        tedious home life and wearisome company. In Holland, where
        people surrender their freedom in good faith and where the
        finesse of these reservations is scarcely understood, they think
        that you can never know enough about that which you want to
        love forever.

49   and what follows

50   as a result of which she died three-quarters of an hour later

without making any other sound, except to say: 'I must die, because my father's avarice has willed it so.'

53 married publicly

53 we order that the proclamation of the banns shall be made by the parish priest of each of the contracting parties, with the consent of fathers, mothers, guardians or trustees, if they are minors, or in the power of others. And that at the celebration of the marriage four credible witnesses shall be present, apart from the priest who will receive the parties' consent, and join them in matrimony according to the form practised in the church.

53 very frequent in the dioceses

54 their word to marry

58 incessantly of presents to Church and State

CHAPTER 4

59 convinced that, when she speaks to her husband, she speaks to her master, her lord, her King, and, what is infinitely more important, that she speaks to Jesus Christ Himself, whose person and authority he represents where she is concerned

59 the good mirror which faithfully reflects the face, having no objective, love, thought different from his

61 The husband is lord of the movables and immovable *conquêts* made by him during the marriage of himself and his wife. So that he can sell, alienate or mortgage them, and do with and dispose of them by donation or other agreement made between living parties, according to his will and pleasure, without the consent of his said wife, for the benefit of a competent person and without fraud being involved.

61 master and gracious lord

61 honour, reverence and respect

62 sleep alongside a stark naked man

63 religious and devout relationship

63 efforts and extravagances associated with uninhibited love

63 little refreshment

63–4 M. Oh! it's not the same thing. A man's glory consists in cajoling more than one woman, but a wife's virtue consists in listening only to her husband.
D. I don't believe that men are more privileged in this matter than women, and that they should be permitted to do what women would not dare to do.
M. The law has willed it so.
D. The situation should be quite the opposite.

64 When a sin has been committed, let us weep over it, let us try to remedy the matter through prayers, discretion, patience ... we shall gain fortitude from silence and hope, and not from constant moaning, which only scratches wounds and brings fresh disasters.

65   after making her pray to God
65   It is not permitted to the husband to kill his wife, even though he
      takes her in adultery, wherever it may be; it is only permitted to
      the father to do so, in his own home, or that of his son-in-law. It is
      repugnant to the principles of justice and humanity to give an
      individual freedom to avenge himself. The husband is not there-
      fore exempt from punishment when it happens that he kills his
      wife surprised in adultery, but the laws have mercy on him. He is
      punished for transgressing the law; but the punishment is light.
66   the ruin of freedom
66   It seems that marriage partners are each condemned to keep aloof
      from the other. To behave in any other way is to live like simple
      folk of yore, at least, as far as those who put on fashionable society
      airs are concerned. It is enough to turn the stomach of gallant
      persons, just seeing husband and wife in the same carriage. Fashion
      dictates that the two should keep at a distance from one another.
66   utterly ridiculous
66   She was a very worthy and very virtuous person with whom I had
      lived amicably during our marriage
67   dear wife
67   God grant me the grace to see her in heaven
67   great affliction
67   all her life virtuous and obliging
67   Lived well and died well . . . She was the best woman in the world
67   Saturday 20 November [1683], at half past five in the morning
      precisely, according to my watch and the town clock with which it
      tallied exactly, my wife gave up her soul to God . . . She was a good
      soul; she made confession and took communion every Saturday;
      consequently she saw with joy her last hour approach . . . She was
      aged 45 years, 10 months, 5 days.
68   unhappily married women
68   [his death] has caused me quite a lot of pain and trouble
68   I am honest enough to own that I love my husband, though in
      Paris this weakness is regarded as one of the vices of Johann von
      Werth's time, which the mores of the century have corrected.
68   If one dared write to husbands / On a tender note, / I would give
      vent to some 'Alas's; / But where the dear *précieuses* are concerned /
      Fashion decrees against it.

CHAPTER 5

70   the biggest booby
71   was in fairly good health
71   a whole register
73   the repercussions of permitted love
73   every year to a fresh burden, to a visible danger, to an importunate
      responsibility, to indescribable pains, and to a thousand and one
      unpleasant consequences

73 After this first production and this sign of a blessing on the honourable love which mutually consumed them, they would share the booty; to the father would be awarded the child and to the woman her freedom which the father would acknowledge by a considerable sum proportionate to the merit of what she had produced.

75 the Princes were beneath the great pavilion, opposite to her

75 I believe that there were two hundred persons, so that it was impossible to make shift to carry the Queen to her bed.

75 the Dauphine's pains began to increase after she had been bled; and the King, with all the royal family, having returned to her room, the whole court remained in her apartment

76 Concerning a woman who had had two disagreeable deliveries, in which her infants had had arms and legs broken, through the fault of the midwife and surgeon who had delivered her;

76 Concerning a woman who died through the ignorance of a surgeon who violently pulled her womb, believing it to be a foreign body;

77 Concerning a woman who died on the day of her delivery, her midwife having proceeded too violently to free her of the afterbirth remaining in the womb.

77 beds of misery

79–80 that my mother, whose indulgence towards me I still admire whenever I think about it, took the trouble, in order to bolster my courage, of learning all my lessons along with me, promising me umpteen 'sweeties', as they say, if I was the first to accomplish our innocent task

80 As soon as I was capable of profiting from the initial instructions given to children, my mother took personal care to teach me how to pray to God; then she taught me the catechism, after which she showed me how to read, and finally it was she who started me off in Latin. Never did a mother show more attention than she to the education of her family and there are few who have shown as much; she neglected nor spared nothing to make us all upright citizens, and she worked at all times with singular application and unwavering tenderness to inspire in us sentiments of piety, honour and probity.

81 covered all over with pink ribbons, neckline plunging, saying that she was only thirty-two, and that when one had grown-up children at that age, one still wore colours

81 too young to watch growing up beside her a daughter who would have so clearly indicated her age

82 She is so good and prudent that I doubt not that when I am gone you will find in her alone the affection of a mother and of a father. If that happens, since her kindly offices towards you will redouble, if you wish God's blessing to accompany you, you will then also unite all the forces of your soul to render to her alone all the honour and respect that you owe to the two of us jointly.

CHAPTER 6

85   There are a lot of women who want separations: mme de Fonten-
      illes, mme de Saint-Géran, mme de Foix; mme de Poussé has
      already taken the plunge; the marquise de Coislin and a dozen
      others; the majority because they overspend. Husbands used not
      to object because lovers made their wives presents of skirts; now
      that lovers want to make love on equal terms, the husbands
      grumble, and moreover they do not possess the talents proper to
      end the dispute; so the wives prefer to obtain a separation.

86   Monsieur de Ventadour told the king that he was very upset that his
      wife found him uglier than when she married him, but that it was not
      his fault; that one could not be handsome at will, and that if one could
      choose one's looks, he would be made exactly like His Majesty.

87   so frequent and common nowadays that it seems our courtrooms
      and lawyers' speeches resound with no other complaints

88   many poor widows ... lumbered with children

88   in order not to wear a *bandeau*

89   of the commonest people

90   good and honest

90   the wife earns her dower on getting into bed

90   having put her foot in the bed

92   very lovable

92   several persons of rank and wealth

93   in order to be able, she told those who urged her to remarry, to
      rear her children and see them comfortably settled in life through
      her care and attention

93   widowed at twenty-two, with an only son, she did not wish to
      remarry for love of him, had him reared with great care, restored
      her ruined household through her economy, and then enriched it
      with her brother's inheritance ... She crowned a life so praise-
      worthy in the eyes of the world by much alms-giving and piety
      during her last years.

CHAPTER 7

97   the most useful and honourable science and occupation of woman

97   their needles and wools

98   fille d'honneur = maid of honour or lady-in-waiting
      dame d'atours = wardrobe mistress
      femme de chambre = chambermaid
      dame du palais = lady of the palace
      dame du lit = lady of the bed
      dame d'honneur = (senior) lady-in-waiting
      surintendante = superintendant or chief lady-in-waiting

99   sole depositary of her thoughts, reflections and conduct

99   adapt to his wishes while preserving some semblance of honour

99   with a sudden and intolerable stench

101   For a start you will be introduced into elegant society; / You will visit, by way of a reception committee, / The bailiff's lady wife, and the tax-adjudicator's, / Who will honour you with a folding chair. / At carnival time you can look forward to / The ball and the big band, in other words, a couple of bagpipes / And, occasionally, Fagotin [a performing monkey] and the puppets.

102   to several places to get money

102   [her] son the chevalier

103   From 10 November to 1 February I was so overwhelmed by melancholy, owing to the bad state in which I saw my affairs to be, that I could neither eat nor sleep; I had lost a lot of weight, and I was certainly in a position to fear anything . . . In the end the good Lord has been graciously pleased to remedy the state of our affairs, at the time when I least expected it. I hope, with His grace, to get them settled a few years hence. But in order to do that the household must be well organised; it will even be necessary to economise as much as possible; because otherwise we shall not be able to make ends meet in bad years.

104–5 Wives, out of ambition and vanity, urge their husbands to buy offices which have some distinction or which give them some status.

105   The women have the most important jobs there; they keep double-entry accounts, they sell, they invite customers to buy, politely show them the merchandise, count the money, put it away and look after it . . . In short, the husbands and fathers act as assistants and errand-boys.

105   the comeliest and prettiest

106   Let no man nor woman . . .

108   workwomen

110   to plot and intrigue amongst themselves

110   Item, in order to regulate in future the unrestrained number of those involved in selling and reselling the said commodities, all persons, whether men or women, are henceforth forbidden, on pain of confiscation and arbitrary fine, to resell in public squares or other parts of the said town any kind of fruits, eggs, butters and cheeses.

110   All *revenderesses*, of old clothes are forbidden to display or carry round the streets or to houses any cloths, in pieces or lengths, hand-worked or not.

111   A forward and tumultuous nation

111   to revile or insult any townsman in the process of buying

111   If any charitable persons want lace-making done on the needlework pattern, we know of a poor widow who will do the job conscientiously and to the satisfaction of those who honour her with employment; provided that she is given a small, reasonable sum to cover the cost of her thread and to procure her the wherewithal to live.

CHAPTER 8

114   almost like horses

114   beat her lady-in-waiting outrageously

114 Hey, one of you!
115 I have paid Esther for the whole of 1651. When we come to the end of the year 1654 I shall owe her three years' wages
115 shoe the mule
116 when they are sent to buy something most people ask them, 'Aha, my girl, so you are now with Monsieur or Madame so-and-so?' 'Yes, Madame', the servant girl replies. 'Have you been with them long?', replies the questioner. 'No, Madame', replies the girl again. 'They certainly change servants often', the questioner continues. 'What sort of folk are they then, what do they get up to? How do they live? They must be very choosy since they make so many changes.' At that point the servant girl really gets going and tells everything she knows, and does not know, about her master and mistress.
117 the most dangerous of our enemies
117 in the light of their own base nature and infamous debaucheries
117 Some, timid or disconcerted, do not dare to make known the true state of affairs and to seek help. Others, devoted to their own interests, try to do without help. The majority, infatuated with their own supposed skill, want no help whatsoever ... Necessity compels me to reveal what it has grieved me to see: cords broken; infants contused, bruised, dislocated or dead; placentas in pieces; wombs sagging, prolapsed and displaced; women inopportunely forced to lose blood, a source of the worst possible labour symptoms.
118 sworn midwives
118–19 On 21 March 1697, the midwife who formerly assisted in delivering women and rearing children having become incapable of continuing due to illness and old age ... it was necessary to find a replacement. I, the rector, did so by examining the votes of approval given by the women to Marianne Sonière, wife of Jean Cros of this parish, in the form of the confidence with which they would send for her and their testimony to her eminent fitness for the job. I was all the more favourably inclined in that I see that she is the mother of a considerable number of children, and she seems to me to set a good example in the parish by her conduct. That is why, being additionally assured of her faith in the Church and her adequate knowledge of [Catholic] doctrine, and having particularly instructed her in the way to administer baptism in case of necessity, I received her oath, which she made by placing her hand on the holy scriptures, that she would do her job carefully, diligently and conscientiously, for the salvation of children and mothers. I thus received her as midwife in the presence of several other women who formed a procession in church for the rising from childbed of Thérèse Falquière, wife of Jean Cathala.
119–20 A woman who meddles in our profession is a stupid animal; that prerogative belongs only to those who wear trunk-hose and are of sound mind.
120 an experienced woman, long versed in such matters ... in order to give [them] treatment and medicaments in accordance with the

instructions issued to her by the doctor and surgeon in charge of public health

122   If some of them do not possess this talent he permits them to summon to their schools, at their own expense, other women with the necessary expertise, or schoolmasters, and even sworn scriveners, to teach their girls in their presence.

122   We were very edified to see at Pluviers two very sensible ladies who ran the girls' school and acquitted themselves of the task with all possible care and skill. It was curious to hear these young girls all reciting collectively, and individually, the different articles of the catechism or whatever else was required of them. For, at the same time as the mistress finished her question, the first girl on the bench began her reply; the second continued; the third took up where the previous one left off; and so on, each in turn . . .

123   to provide for the upkeep of three or four schoolmasters and two or three schoolmistresses

124   the common people . . . the dregs of the people

124   all the heavy jobs in the towns and countryside, without which neither they, nor others, could exist

CHAPTER 9

127–8   . . . women, chiefly, taking pleasure in the adoration onstage of the members of their sex . . . have this sort of life so firmly imprinted on their imagination that household trivia become intolerable to them. And when they return home in this giddy frame of mind they find everything disagreeable, especially their husbands who, going about their own business, are not always in the mood to pay them the ridiculous attentions that women get in plays . . .

128   The authority of the [theatrical] state is shared between the two sexes, the women being as useful as the men or more so, and they have a vote in all affairs that concern the common interest.

129   whatever trouble the best actor in the world takes, the women are always thought to do better . . . It's true. The other day I was at the Hôtel de Bourgogne [the leading Paris theatre] where I heard umpteen voices, some of which were saying: Ha! there's a woman who performs well! and others: That woman's doing even better.

130   libertinism, a permit for vice, impurity, idleness and dissoluteness

130   That is not to say that there are not some women of the profession who do not lack virtue, but according to public opinion, which is perhaps mistaken, they are less burdened with it than with old embroidery and make-up.

131   People were horrified to see them dressed like princesses, possessing magnificent furniture, superb equipages, fine town and country houses bought by their gallants, accumulating wealth, creating incomes for themselves, in short, profiting as much as possible from their crimes and piling up in their homes spoils from the greatest households in the realm.

he woman to whom ancient Greece would have raised altars. The whole of Europe is horrified, and those who read about us a century hence will pity those who were witnesses to these accusations.

4   these sorceresses . . . horrify the whole of Europe over a mere trifle
134 entered like a little queen
135 prevent anyone from hearing the absurdities they might shout out loud, having often said some about Mme de Montespan which are entirely without foundation; threaten to administer such cruel correction at the slightest sound they make that there is not one of them who dares to breath a word
135 She was given the ordinary degree of torture, then the extraordinary one, and so extraordinarily extraordinary that she almost died in the process.
135 in passing . . . another woman who expired, with the doctor taking her pulse
136 certain little leniencies
137 These visions and upsurges of popular fury are not new; I have seen some . . . taken to such an extreme that in various quarters of Paris women have been nearly felled with blows and on the point of being thrown into the river and into drains because they were accused of abducting children.
137 for the longest period and at the hardest tasks that their strength and the places where [they] are permit
138 good ladies
139 You are given red-carpet treatment even at the theatre, / Your box is reserved, and the valiant porter / By keeping it for you shows he is doing his job; / Your carriage is followed by lackeys and pages; / They are so feared by your [professional] sisters that you have the latter in your employ; / The number of lords who pass through your arms / Raises the income from your bedsheets to two thousand *écus*.
139 Any other woman, doing what she did, would have dishonoured her family; yet with what respect she was treated!
139 The consideration, paradoxically, in which she had come to be held, the number and distinguished nature of her friends and acquaintances [continued] when her charms ceased to attract company
140 gave to God
140 after a most Christian fashion
140 She was laid out in state in her finery and seen by everyone the next day, as if she had been a princess. She had a circlet of orange blossom on her head.

CHAPTER 10

141 If women are as capable as we men of conducting themselves properly they are capable of directing others also and of having a share in the jobs and dignities of civic society.

141   for I found some of them more enlightened and more capable than
        men

142   weak, uncertain, too much in subjection to the fragility of their
        nature. The woman who would govern a realm wisely today,
        would tomorrow become a master whom one would not allow to
        govern a dozen hens, in the words of Cardinal Mazarin.

145   boundless ambition

146   much less habitual

146   this adroit woman did almost all she wanted but not everything,
        nor when and how she wanted

147   hide many things

148   after the king took over his own affairs, the ladies no longer
        meddled in anything and were rarely listened to

148   In his day ladies had been taught not to speak about state affairs;
        that had not been the custom.

148–9   Many people disapproved of women being seated and having a
        say in an assembly like that, but the situation had to be tolerated in
        order to oblige them to desire peace and to contribute to bring it
        about as much as they had the war.

150   One often finds, in palace intrigues, stumbling-blocks much more
        dangerous than in the most difficult state affairs; and indeed it is
        more perilous to meddle with those in which women participate
        . . . than with the most grandiose plans that kings can make in
        other spheres.

150   there is nothing so capable of ruining a state as disruptive persons,
        screened by the weakness of their sex

150   so good!

151   let us talk of affairs of state, now that I am five years old

151   negotiations, nocturnal rendezvous and disguises had . . . infinite
        charm

151   had developed such a taste for intrigues that she threw her-
        self headlong into them, without bothering about the issues at
        stake

152   Plans had nothing fixed about them; brilliant qualities, courage,
        wit, shone forth in some persons. But self-interest alone directed
        all those who stoked the fire of faction; no system ruled them.

153   capable of overthrowing ten states

153   b(eggar) of a Sicilian

153–4   thus, old and decrepit as she is, without budging from her cabinet,
        she governs the court

155   since their bread was being taken away

156   that they [the members of Parlement] were amusing themselves
        working and earning money while they [the women] were dying
        of hunger

156   begun by the women and pursued with great fervour by their
        husbands

156   a kind of riot . . . incited by some women, who have beaten up one
        of the agents of the person arranging the sale of public criers'
        offices

roup of about five or six hundred women gathered in the Place
s Terreaux, at the foot of the town hall steps, and the number
,rew every minute; some men joined in
over the *gabelle* [meaning salt-tax; but see note 120]
extraordinary services

᠔8   Considering that it behoves the prudence and justice of kings, as
well as their grandeur and munificence, not only to uphold the
principal households in their realm, through titles and prerogatives of honour, but also to promote them, and to elevate those
who are sprung from them, and who by their virtues and outstanding services have won esteem, and distinguished themselves
from others, honouring them with the supreme dignities, which
enable them to preserve a rank proportionate to their merits, and
inform posterity of the consideration in which their persons were
held; a practice that in our opinion should apply to women as well
as men when the former have attained a high degree of virtue, and
possess all the rare qualities and have rendered all the services of
which their sex is capable.

160   it is necessary for all the inhabitants to be assembled without
exception

160   the greatest and best [or most sane] part of the inhabitants

160   in person and not by proxy

160   everywhere was full of married and unmarried ladies, gentlemen
and other persons, as if they had gone there to be entertained by
some play

161   The Magnificent Lady of Baux, Phanete de Baux, wife of Berenguier de Pontivez, Chevalier Lord of Lambesc, Lady of la Barben

161   lords and gentlemen

161   gentlemen, of ancient lineage, in name, and arms

162   It was a great joy to see myself at the Estates, where I had never
been in my life; I didn't want to see the opening, it was too early.
The Estates aren't likely to take long; it's only a question of
demanding what the King wants; nobody says a word: there's
business over and done with. As for the governor, he finds, I don't
know how, more than forty thousand *écus* coming his way. A
multitude of other presents, pensions, repairs to roads and towns,
fifteen or twenty high tables, continual gambling, non-stop balls,
plays three times a week, tremendous expenditure on fine clothes,
that's the Estates.

163   a woman very greedy for money, and as prodigal as she was
greedy

163   a sure prey

163   which upset her terribly

166   I haven't wanted to receive visitors yet. I'm waiting for the return
of Monsieur de Villars. There are so many customs and so many
ceremonies to observe that he'll have to instruct me in everything
. . . Nothing here resembles what is done in France.

166   How I dread dressing up and starting to appear in public! I'm not
at all cut out to be a representative.

166   I won't tell you about the steps that are counted in going to receive ladies, some at the first dais, others at the second, or at the third: because, by the way, I have a very large apartment. Imagine from that what it costs to furnish it, and pity me. On entering and leaving it's necessary to pass in front of all these ladies. The one who was acting as my guide had quite a job putting me right. Because I often forgot the ceremonial. These visits last the whole day.

166   When such disorders arise, complaints are unfailingly made to France, and a poor ambassador is condemned without a hearing.

167   Government by women is ordinarily the downfall of states.

CHAPTER 11

171   Most women nowadays can be captured by the ear; they are the reason why everyone dabbles in music, and the only way to succeed with them is to provide little songs and verses for them to hear.

171   a sizeable number of excellent musicians and players of instruments that she employed at religious services and for her customary recreation

172   many beauties

173–4   It is true that I emerge from my deep cave / To pay faithful homage to the Goddess; / And what all the other nereids do for pleasure, / I do for the honour of dancing with her: / But I shall dance better, and much more appropriately, / On the return of a Husband so famous at sea; / With what transports of joy my soul will be filled! / At every moment I think he is coming back, / And everything reminds me of him, / Right down to the smallest Whale.

176   Order of Gypsies

176   Order of the Bee

177   Whether the presence of the beloved causes more joy than the marks of his / her indifference cause pain; whether it is pleasanter to love someone whose heart is elsewhere engaged than another whose heart is unfeeling; whether worthiness to be loved should compensate for the chagrin of being unloved

177   love [or friendship]

177   esteem

177   obligingness

177   persons of good birth, nurtured on civility and gallantry

177   kissing (games)

178   usually on ordinary and gallant matters

178   Novel Game

178–9   I shall not have the benefit of submitting my play to you tomorrow for correction, from which I derive more profit than from anything I could learn in books. You are so used to talking common sense that your approval alone controls the destiny of all works shown to you.

179   to regard as indubitable maxims all [her] opinions, and as sover-
        eign decrees all the sentiments of those excellent persons who
        performed a miracle in producing [her]
179   you know ... that maxims are not maxims until you have
        approved them ... I send you what I have in part taken from you.
        I beg you very humbly to tell me if I have not spoilt it, and whether
        you find the rest to your liking.
179   ridiculous novelty
179   hags
179   women only receive and men ... keep on giving
180   dolly-pedagogues
180   precious *Ruelles*
180   snap up good dinners
180   cushions of love; virginal urinal; bottom saucer; antipodes hole
180   of a roughness fit to skin the poor throat uttering them
181   Would you have believed it?
181   arse
181   a bit too fussy
181   fainted whenever she heard an improper word
182   if you hear it talked about, to act as if you had never seen it and to
        deny that it is my work if by chance people should say so
182   but I did not hand it to you to give to her as one of my works. She
        will think that I am a real professional author, to distribute my
        books like that.
182   It was the most agreeable present that gallants could give to their
        lady-loves.
183   They choose their words felicitously, and place them so appositely
        that, although well-known, they have the charm of novelty; ...
        only women can evoke in a single word a whole range of feeling,
        and render delicately a delicate thought ... If women were always
        grammatically accurate, I would venture to say that the letters of
        some of them would perhaps be amongst the best written produc-
        tions in our language.
183   the first person of her sex to write reasonable letters
184   not all that wonderful
184   it was a great consolation to see that my sentiments agree with
        yours concerning the Marquise de Sablé's way of writing. Certain-
        ly it is not possible to express one's thoughts more delicately or
        flatteringly than she has in that letter of hers which I sent you, and
        if all those that she writes are in the same style, which I believe to
        be the case, I have no doubt that I must prefer her to your friend
        [Mme des Loges], to whom one cannot deny considerable wit and
        eloquence, but who writes so pretentiously and prides herself so
        on roundabout a dozen [?] polished letters, that it is as much as I
        can do to put up with her.
185   the grace and charm ... spread over the whole of her person
185   the miracle of inflaming the heart of this prince was not reserved
        for any woman in the world
185   some persons of whom I am fond

185 damsel who disliked self-restraint

185 avoid the misfortunes which pass for crimes, and steer clear of the occasions that can harm the reputation of women

186 Our best French novels have for a long time been composed by spinsters or married women.

187 a little extra morality, in order to set them apart from those novels inimical to good morals, which can only be time-wasting

187 In addition I have tried to enclose a moral message in the things that seem most immoral ... if I push the debauchery of some female characters to the point of effrontery, it is in order to paint immodesty in stronger colours. It is sometimes dangerous to make only a faint sketch of vice: such and such a person yields to temptation who might, perhaps, have overcome it if she had known all the consequences: and so as to encapsulate useful precepts in the examples I put forward, I observe strictly the maxim that vice should be punished and virtue rewarded.

188 treatise on the passions

189 I celebrate on my lyre / Either the God of Warriors, or the God of Lovers.

189 Today I lay prostrate with passion in your arms, / Today, dear Tircis, your amorous ardour / Triumphs with impunity over all my modesty, / And I yield to the transports that spellbind my soul.

189 No, since I have spoken the language of the Gods, / I have never been known to lavish flattery

190 how can one see what one loves in such a pitiful state and not run to help!

CHAPTER 12

193 Women are of a more delicate substance than men.

193 It is for women to pronounce on fashions, to judge language, to discern the well-bred air and good manners. They have more knowledge, skill, and finesse than men in these matters. Everything dependent upon taste is their province.

194 all the young men used to be very assiduous in paying [her] their respects, because having been schooled for a while by her qualified them for entry into [high] society

194 When someone at court had a son who was still 'green', he was sent to her for tuition. The education that she dispensed was so excellent that it was easy to tell the difference between a young man who had been trained at [Ninon's] hands, and one who had not. She taught them love-making, delicacy of expression, winning ways; however little trouble she took, provided that she was dealing with a docile soul, she made him an *honnête homme* in no time.

194-5 Her breast, where desire wanders, / Is separated into two little mountains, / Far enough from one another; / Hidden by an importunate veil / They repel it with great indignation, / And seem to be angered by it.

195   Laugh, jump, dance, lucky Countess. / From the belly whence comes the hot water that you piss / May a fortunate lineage soon emerge.

195   It is not the mark of a man of quality, if he is in the company of Ladies . . . to kiss them unawares, to remove their coiffe, neckerchief, or bracelet, to appropriate a ribbon, make it out to be a favour, and wear it in order to act the gallant, the passionate lover; to take a Lady's letters, or some of her books; to look through her memoranda, etc.

196   something half open which must be closed for decency's sake

196   horribly filthy talk

196   thought to perform a fine act of gallantry

196   all sorts of advantages over her

197   strange and lascivious terms

197   If submissive, faithful, discreet lovers / Still exist, their number is small. / A month-old love is a decrepit love. / Brutal lovers get most approval. / Sighs and tears would betoken stupidity. / Favour is no sooner obtained than broadcast. / Men no longer love as they used to.

197   without making them frequent society, as happens in France

197   Women are not visited as freely as they are in France, and they hardly go out except to church, and other places whither duty impels them.

198   almost everywhere else they are virtually imprisoned, and cannot indulge in gallantry, because they see no men

198   Simultaneously proud and polite, she knew better than anyone what is meant by holding court, and although virtuous she tolerated and even took pleasure in that air of gallantry necessary to render a court agreeable and to maintain there that courtesy which everyone at the time considered important, but which has since become useless, and perhaps even ridiculous. It could be said that the mores of men and women have entirely changed . . . for example, it is certain that, since women seemed to have more self-respect than nowadays, they were also more respected.

199   Women must be blamed for the decline of masculine gallantry: because if they knew how to use properly all the privileges of their sex, they would teach men to be truly gallant, and would never permit them to lose in their presence the respect which they owe women.

199   highly immodest action

199   that, although his potency was great . . . his sceptre was very small.

200   there is no decency, no politeness, and no gallantry, which are the three sources of fine and elevated conversations

200   but it must be owned that women have for some time now rendered conversation a little too licentious and unruly on the pretext of greater freedom and gaiety . . . Women have become used to crude and ambiguous words, and the licence they have granted to their cavaliers to proffer them means that nowadays they are in no position to take offence.

200   I dislike innocent pleasures

202   which took no account of the misery to which the best part of the realm was reduced at the time

202   life without litigation, is that happiness?

202   They nurture, they kindle, they satisfy all their passions by this means.

203   I've already ruined seven well-to-do peasants and four bourgeois families, and there are three nobles that I'm holding by the backside and breeches. If God grants me the grace to go on living, I intend to send them to the workhouse.

203   which, having eaten away the immediately surrounding flesh, starts on that which is further off

203   although she only has one opposing party in the criminal proceedings brought against her in Parlement, she there entangles lawsuits in which she is involved against her brothers, others contested against individuals, and others against those whom she alleges to be legal opponents but who are not, and thus wears out the opposition financially, forcing them to abandon litigation. There are more than eighty witnesses against her to be examined, and without assisting the *procureur général* [official representing the interests of the king and the public within the jurisdiction of a tribunal like Parlement] in his investigations, she plans to evoke cases, and as her opponents are not in a position to sustain these heavy expenses, she will get off, and be a pest that will ruin the country.

204   the ladies of the court smelt of nothing but soup and stew and had drunk at nine in the morning five or six kinds of wine

205   There is no lady of quality whose ambition is not to become the king's mistress. A number of women, married or not, have assured me that it constituted no offence to husband, father or even God to succeed in being loved by one's king.

206   as a lover would do with his mistresses

CHAPTER 13

210   a kind of law

212   the familiar converse that several women and girls of the people had had with her in her initial position

212   the said nuns alleging ... that her father had not wished to give her the sums of money that they wanted, an attitude that was considered very strange on the part of religious persons who have left aside worldly things

214   a great number of benefices, [*curés'*] livings, prebends and chapels

218   did a novitiate in coquetry while it was believed that they were doing one in religion

220   useless people in this world

221   people in society, so that they can share in the spiritual benefits accruing from so many good works being performed by religious

orders, simply by wearing an adapted version of the habit of the order, and observing at home the points of the rule which are compatible with their station

222–3 female lover of God

224 the lowest and basest jobs

224 good country girls

225 remembering the large amount of alms which she had liberally bestowed on them during her lifetime

226 I believe that the queen has asked God to convert the whole court: the king's conversion is admirable, and the ladies who seemed furthest removed from the idea no longer budge from the churches. Mme de Montchevreuil, Mmes de Chevreuse and de Beauvilliers, the Princesse d'Harcourt, and, in short, all our devout ladies, do not go there more often than Mmes de Montespan, de Thianges, the Comtesse de Grammont, the Duchesse du Lude and Mme de Soubise; ordinary Sundays are, as in the past, like Easter days [every French Catholic was expected to take communion at Easter, if at no other time].

230 The Most Christian King

235 The remedy for so many evils is to leave the Protestants in peace, and not one will leave [the realm]; but forcibly seizing their children, like we do, imprisoning fathers and maltreating mothers, as is happening to a lady ... reputed to be the most virtuous woman in France, gives rise to a lot of murmuring on the part of Catholics and makes them doubt religion, a cause of great scandal amongst us. I have been assured that there is a parish here where several persons did not wish to take Easter communion.

235 Make my religion a bit more solid; it's getting so subtle that it's all evaporating

235 create freethinkers and ungodly persons. I speak from experience, seeing the extent to which the courtiers and worldlings have gone astray since the advent of these propositions on grace, saying all the time: 'Well, what does it matter how one behaves, since if we possess grace, we'll be saved, and if we don't, we'll be damned.' And then they conclude: 'It's all twaddle.'

236 several married and unmarried ladies

236 barely or not at all pious

236 impious and ridiculous grimace

236 never follow the common belief

CHAPTER 14

239 Alas! only she stood between death and me

240 and they were full of persons belonging to the court and the magistracy, to the extent that one saw there several men and women who had long been socially intimate with the lady

240 Ah, my good child, how humiliating it is to sustain a decrepit mind and body, and, if we had the choice, how much more

pleasant it would be to leave a memory worth preserving, rather than spoil and disfigure it by all the miseries that old age and infirmities bring!

240 Reconsideration of the will of god, and of this universal law by which we are condemned, restores reason and gives patience.

241 I have never been well acquainted with you; / Alas, what heart knows the value of those sweet charms / Savoured by your Beloveds here below, / If it has not been in frequent converse with you! / Loving you seems a sorry and strange move to make / As long as one can still aspire to a few pleasures. / One believes that only the end of one's days is your due; / Even then it is only grudgingly that in these funereal moments / You are given the awful remnants / Of a life employed in constantly offending you.

241 long spent in an inconceivable forgetfulness and abandonment of Our Lord

241 amidst what the world would deem hell . . . I find myself with God and in a state of calm which surpasses all understanding and all expression

241 I submit myself without difficulty to the will of God – He is the Almighty and from all sides one must come to Him in the end.

242 deign to admit her into His holy paradise

242 in honour of the five wounds of Our Lord

243 . . . that she should be put unceremoniously into the earth, / Her corpse clothed only in the garb / Of a Capuchin nun . . .

243 I see here every day the place where I shall be buried, and I find the view so calm that I really love it.

244 near the holy water stoup and the little door of the said church

245 This princess . . . was constrained to abandon herself to the passions of men, who tormented her more than her own malady.

245 I saw yesterday this pious princess laid on her bed: she was disfigured by the torture that she had been made to suffer in an attempt to bring her round: her teeth had been broken, and her head burned; that is to say that if one did not die of apoplexy, one would deserve pity, given the state to which poor patients are reduced.

245 This fear of death that she had so many times shown . . . after some final efforts, ceased at last . . . She abandoned herself to the decrees of divine providence with such pious and devout sentiments that, concentrating solely on her salvation, she counted all else as nought.

245 she was as calm as she had previously been agitated over death, about which one did not venture to speak to her when she was in good health

245 Madame is dying! Madame is dead!

246 that after the knowledge of her salvation in Jesus Christ, she had thanked God for nothing as much as for having given her to him

246 I am going: to all appearances we shall not be separated long; for at our age the survivor will soon follow. I leave, then, in the hope of seeing you again

247–8 The ambassador of England was present with all the English who were here, doctors and surgeons of the same nation, and everyone generally who wished to be at Saint-Cloud, where the doors were open to all kinds of persons. The princess's belly had swollen extraordinarily since her death; at the first incision made in her body, it gave off such a great stench that all those present were obliged to retreat, and could only approach after well protecting themselves against such a bad odour.

248 that nothing in the world was so mis-shapen and so ugly

248 without being opened

249 fatigues, needs and incommodities difficult to remedy

249 I was so weary and so overcome that I leaned my head against the bier and kept it there for a long time, without noticing

251 for the repose of her soul and that of all her predecessors, in perpetuity, an annual and perpetual pension of the sum of one hundred *livres*, for and to the end that there should be celebrated every first Friday of the month . . . a low mass 'for the dead', and at the end a Salve Regina

251 in her will she founded in the church of Saint Bonnet in this town of Bourges a solemn service to be held every Assumption Day at seven in the evening, at which she wanted two pounds of candles to be distributed to relatives and friends there present, and in return for the said service she gave to the said church funds of Saint Bonnet nine *livres* of ground rent

251 a *libera* [a prayer for the dead] on her grave, for the repose of her soul, every Sunday in the year, a complete service at the end of the month and one likewise at the end of the year

252 in order not to found masses . . . was too great a sinner to leave purgatory and that she wanted to stay there for as long as it pleased God; and thus she died without having satisfied the priests, to whom she left no wherewithal to chant in her honour.

252 is beginning to seem excessive, for prolonged grief is not liked at court.

NOTES

Chapter 1

254 *n. 3* Mme de Richelieu gave birth to a daughter, to the great regret of the duke, her husband, who had hoped for a son
was no mean test of the virtue of her husband
It was known also that the Duchesse de Choiseul had given birth to a daughter . . . On the 10th the Duchesse d'Estrées was delivered also and was no more fortunate than the Duchesse de Choiseul.

255 *n. 27* God give her the grace to feed [rear] well the infant committed to her care

259　　*n. 92*　There being a great drought in May 1609, processions were made for nine days by the Capuchins at La Ciotat and by the priests and penitents, and when these were over the children began to make others, then the girls, and afterwards young men, all in groups, at night

259　　*n. 94*　daughters of impoverished skippers

260　　*n. 107*　I venture to say that, owing to the care with which they were raised, they ceased to be children much earlier than their age seemed to permit. The grace, naivety and normal gaiety of childhood were clearly visible in their conversation; but they had none of childhood's bashfulness, nor effrontery, nor simpleness, nor ignorance.

Chapter 2

261　　*n. 4*　For a start, who will deny me that ladies have a rational soul as well as men, and consequently an understanding capable of perfect reasoning? That is to say that some of them can have fine and lofty thoughts, powerful and elevated notions, ideas as subtle and as solid as those of the best brains, since they lack none of the necessary organs, and nature can give them the temperament proper to raise their minds to the highest perfection.

261　　*n. 7*　God having created us equal in soul, we women have as much right to the knowledge necessary for the possession of grace, virtue and glory as men could have. One thing I will confess, that woman's body is so constituted as to be capable of secreting into our soul inconstancies, infirmities and passions which would develop rapidly if not suppressed by piety and reason.

　　　if intelligence is necessary to men in order not to be taken by surprise, it is much more necessary to girls, who are more prone to such surprises, from which they have less strength to preserve themselves.

262　　*n. 8*　the most ignorant are not always the most chaste . . . In fact I imagine that wits are to women what fortresses are to fortified places, and that a besieged simpleton would offer as little resistance as a town lacking the wherewithal to defend itself.

　　　those women without enough judgement to know what vice is, have not enough to choose virtue either . . . Education helps to fortify the best inclinations and those convinced that the reading of books is a school for learning to do evil adroitly would do better to believe that ladies find in this occupation more means to reform than to corrupt themselves.

262　　*n. 10*　if the ladies instruct no one else, they instruct themselves; if they do not serve the public, they satisfy themselves in private

263　　*n. 16*　Why exclude women from learning? . . . Why forbid them the prelacy and the priesthood? . . . Why take from them the administration of justice?

263　　*n. 21*　almost always useless to young women of middling nobility, like you

263   *n. 30* For his daughters two wet-nurses and one of the aforementioned chambermaids, who will serve them as *gouvernante*.

264   *n. 36* whose virtue was often very mediocre

264   *n. 38* there was no piece of malice that I did not think up to get my revenge on her

265   *n. 50* The only company I have is masters who teach me nothing but useless things, music, mythology, history, geography: how's that for real amusement?

265   *n. 54* where no woman had ever entered

265   *n. 60* put girls of high rank next to the poorest and dirtiest, in order not to disgust them

266   *n. 62* one of the greatest austerities that one can practise, since there are scarcely any that offer no respite, and in the instruction of children one must employ a whole lifetime
mistress of one of the lower forms
there are some very off-putting things in your job, but those are your mortifications, and the reward will be great

266   *n. 65* Try to steer your pupils clear of men, dealings with whom are always dangerous . . . and to make them like a withdrawn life, which is the only security for women

266   *n. 71* manual labours

267   *n. 72* Mistresses will study to render pupils civil and honest, see that they speak well, walk tall and gracefully, behave deferentially towards one another, and show respect to all the nuns.

267   *n. 73* It is necessary to exercise the memory of children a great deal; that opens up their minds, occupies them and stops them from thinking of evil

267   *n. 75* 'For children that one does not wish to make study in depth'

267   *n. 78* The plague of minds, the ruin of piety and the mother of heresies
Curiosity is a dangerous malady of the mind
Everything that could over-stimulate the pupils' minds and curiosity is avoided.

267   *n. 80* stupid like all the nuns who have come into the world without intelligence, and have been removed from it in infancy in order to be shut up in a convent

267–8   *n. 83* It is remarkable what [one's] interest in affairs can do. If the affairs were not mine they would be like double Dutch to me, and yet I know them in my head like I do the Lord's Prayer and argue every day with professionals in the field over things of which I have no knowledge and about which self-interest alone enlightens me.

268   *n. 87* Sometimes you do me the honour of writing me letters with such a delicate and such a gallant air . . . And you write me others in a serious and profound style, such as the one where you question me on the immortality of the soul: and that other one where you ask me if we should believe that there are several worlds, and whether this great number of celestial bodies that we call stars are not so many suns that give light to them.

268   *n. 88*   However, that does not take the shine off her, because the many exchanges that the Queen has had with the leading persons of her century, the great knowledge that she has of the world, and her long experience of affairs and court intrigues ... have totally compensated for what she might lack on the side of books.

268   *n. 92*   curious library ... a prodigious number of good books and rare manuscripts

269   *n. 96*   Good novels are not without providing instruction ... especially since history has been brought into them, and when the authors, knowledgeable about the mores of nations, imagine adventures which appertain thereto and which instruct us on the subject.

who would never have known Xenophon or Herodotus if she had never read *Cyrus*, and who in reading it came to love history and even mythology

269   *n. 98*   enquiring princesses

269   *n. 100*   'Which is the more noble, man or woman?'; 'On beauty'; 'On feminine caprice'; 'If husband and wife should be of the same temperament'; 'If it is expedient for women to be learned'; 'Which is better, to marry or not to marry?'

270   *n. 104*   the fashion for being a philosopher would not last longer among French ladies than the other fashions

272   *n. 130*   French is infinitely far from possessing the roughness of all the northern languages, most of the words of which skin the throat of those who speak, and the ears of those who listen

272   *n. 138*   I have read part of the letter with which you were pleased to honour me, and I have guessed the other from the continuation of a splendid line of argument which makes up for the imperfection of your bad handwriting. I see clearly from this negligence of your pen, or this speed of your hand, that you have a long-standing habit of thinking subtly and expressing yourself gracefully.

273   *n. 141*   it is not consistent with the dignity of such a notable person to spell well. That must be left to authors

that would smack too much of pedantry in a person of our sex, and of the desire to play the bluestocking

274   *n. 151*   ladies of quality ... who in three months knew almost all the plants that grow in this region

274   *n. 157*   glimmers of knowledge about everything

274–5   *n. 158*   Ever since the mathematicians found the secret of infiltrating the salons and introducing into ladies' studyrooms the vocabulary of a science as solid and serious as mathematics, via the *Mercure Galant*, people say that the empire of gallantry is going to pieces, that the only talk therein is of problems, corollaries, theorems, right angle, obtuse angle, rhomboids, etc, and that recently two damsels were discovered in Paris with their brains so confused by this kind of knowledge that the one refused to listen to a marriage proposal unless her suitor learned the art of making telescopes, so often discussed in the *Mercure Galant*, and the other rejected a perfectly honourable man because he failed within her prescribed time-limit to produce anything new on the squaring of the circle.

275   *n. 159*   the true science of a woman is to be beautiful; study and books only serve to make her intolerable

Chapter 3

275   *n. 11*   One does not marry for oneself, whatever people may say; one marries as much or more for one's posterity, for one's family.

275   *n. 14*   I have heard the Maréchale d'Humières declare that an honest girl may well say that she does not want so-and-so for a husband but that she cannot say as well: I want so-and-so.

278   *n. 48*   I know full well that this is a rather peculiar opinion nowadays, and open to ridicule from those who seek only money; but I know also that such persons often expose themselves to something worse than ridicule.
a fair number of worthy bourgeois
It is ridiculous to put a married couple in the nuptial bed without their knowing one another, as if they had been carried there in a sack.

279   *n. 55*   I shall tell you that the gentlemen of our Company really thought that they could pronounce the death penalty for *rapt* [the strong term, with its significant overtones of possession by abduction and violence, used in Article 42 of the Ordinance of Blois to denote the subornation of a minor for the purpose of marriage], and have often done so, there being no marriage bond so strong that the rope cannot break it, as the saying goes. But that has not proved capable of causing enough terror, and subsequent reciprocal consent to marry with the approval of even the most indignant parents has softened the rigour of the judges and inclined them to leave matters up to the aggrieved parties, so that hope of coming to that point in the end has made girls abandon themselves more freely to these clandestine marriages.

279   *n. 62*   Let children for their part obey their parents as they would God, whose place they take; let children stand before parents with respect, as if they were in the presence of the Almighty.

280   *n. 68*   degrees of consanguinity and affinity

281   *n. 84*   In the marriage contract, before the plighting of troths and nuptial benediction, the man and the woman can make and insert such conditions, dowers, donations and other conventions as they see fit.

281   *n. 89*   the whole lot in expectation of the future inheritance from the said fathers and mothers

282   *n. 109*   strong enough to abstain from the debaucheries and other sins ordinarily committed at these kinds of assemblies, and also to censure them
carefully repress all the impertinences

282   *n. 111*   thirteen gold *louis* [a coin, named after Louis XIII, bearing the king's effigy] as a deposit, and a few little items of adornment, together with a gold ring

283   *n. 118* there is a foolish custom nowadays for spending in furniture, presents and wedding expenses half a woman's dowry, and sometimes the lot

283   *n. 122* I learned that on the evening of his daughter's betrothal Colbert had, in the privacy of his home, twice danced the coranto, expertly at that.

283   *n. 124* Madame, we wish that there may issue as many heroes from your belly as there once did from that of the Trojan horse!

Chapter 4

283   *n. 1* To tell the truth, the unhappiness or happiness of marriages very often depends upon the behaviour of wives.

284   *n. 13* The husband in his testament ... cannot dispose of the movable goods and immovable *conquêts* held in common with his wife, in a way prejudicial to the said wife, nor of half of what may belong to her out of these possessions as a result of her said husband's death.

284   *n. 14* The husband cannot sell, exchange, divide up, auction, encumber, place under obligation, or mortgage the wife's own inheritance, without the consent of the said wife, she being authorised by him for that purpose.

284   *n. 15* The married woman cannot sell, alienate or mortgage her inheritances without the authority and express consent of her husband. And if she makes any contract without the authority and consent of her said husband, such a contract is null

285   *n. 18* A wife cannot appear in court without the consent of her husband, unless she is authorised to do so or is judicially separated from him, and the said separation has been carried out.

285   *n. 20* A married woman cannot enter into a legal obligation without the consent of her husband, unless she is effectively separated from him, or she is a public merchant

285   *n. 25* A wife who voluntarily leaves her husband and goes off with another man, and is not with her husband at the time of death, and also if she leaves him and shirks her duty to look after him, whilst being capable of doing so, in the case of the husband not refusing her, although she does not go off with another, she must not have her dower.

285   *n. 28* The woman who has come up against a bad husband is deserving of no small amount of pity, but even so she finds that, being in subjection, she is not so far removed from the station assigned to her by nature

285   *n. 29* There is at Montmartre a painting of Our Lord and of Mary Magdalen, out of whose mouth the word 'Raboni' is depicted as emerging. The good wives have made of this a Saint Rabonny who 'improves' husbands, and they offer up novenas there to that end.

286   *n. 40* A wise man should love his wife / In order to have heirs, not to err / In the pleasures of evil flesh.

287   *n. 50* If you have a husband who does not show you all the

fidelity that he owes you, do not appear insensitive to the situation; that would signify an indifference which would be a poor guarantee of your affection. Complain, but be careful to let no sharpness enter into your complaints

It is not a good method, in my opinion, to appear ignorant or indifferent about such things; because that would seem to stem from scant intelligence or affection, or from some outside attachment; but when one's sadness is mild and uncomplaining, whether at home or elsewhere, it is not a bad thing to let a husband see that one is as sensitive as patient over the matter; but this must not be taken to the point of coldness, still less to that of sharp reproaches.

288   *n. 63* although in France a husband is not permitted to kill his wife nor the man whom he catches in the act of adultery with her, however when that happens he easily obtains letters of remission, something that would not be possible if he killed the guilty parties other than in the act of adultery

288–9   *n. 76* so closely together and so well fastened that it is impossible to separate the one from the other without breaking both . . .

the extreme and reciprocal affection; the unreserved trust; the perfect, uninterrupted, intimate and so fully reciprocal union with which it has pleased God to particularly bless the whole duration of our marriage, making of me, while it lasted, the happiest of men

Chapter 5

290   *n. 21* [One has] to be exposed to all the unpleasant consequences of marriage: perhaps to lose health and beauty simultaneously, before losing youth: . . . and at the end of life . . . perhaps to see oneself the mother of ill-born, ill-formed and ungrateful children.

290   *n. 26* 'How a woman should look after herself throughout her pregnancy.'

290   *n. 28* very deformed through the fault of her mother who, in order not to become too bulky, had her body tightly constricted

291   *n. 47* I marvelled in the past to see village women, right up to the day that they gave birth sometimes to two children, lift, unaided, bundles of grass onto their head, without suffering a miscarriage.

292   *n. 66* whom she could not love

293   *n. 78* Children whose fathers are or have been Catholics will be baptised and raised in the Catholic church, although the mothers are of the R.P.R. ['supposedly reformed religion', the name given by Catholics to the Protestant faith], as also the children whose fathers have died in the said Catholic religion shall be raised in the said religion, for which purpose they will be placed in the hands of their mothers, guardians or other Catholic relatives, at the request of the latter, with very strict prohibitions against taking the said children to temples or schools belonging to those of the R.P.R., and against raising them in that religion, even though their mothers are of the said R.P.R.

containing regulations for the things that must be heeded and observed by those professing the R.P.R.

Chapter 6

293   *n. 4*   make contracts and dispose of her movable and immovable property in the way that she could if she were not married

294–5   *n. 24*   deep mourning . . . black crape coming down over her face and covering her forehead

295   *n. 34*   On account of which community, the husband is personally obliged to pay debts on movable property due because of his wife, and he can be legitimately pursued for these debts during their marriage. And also the wife, after the death of her husband, is held responsible for paying half the debts on movable property incurred and increased by the said husband during as well as prior to the said marriage

He who marries the woman, marries the debts

295–6   *n. 36*   Also the said widow, notwithstanding the said renunciation, can take and remove a robe and one of all the items of clothing she uses, not the best nor the worst, but one in between when there are several

one of her middle-quality robes, apart from her habitual one, a bed provided with coverlets, two pairs of sheets, two table-cloths, half a dozen napkins, a stool, an iron pot, a dish, two bowls, [*jactelete* does not figure in any dictionary that I have been able to consult; perhaps a diminutive form of *jatte*, meaning bowl or basin], a half-litre measure, a quarter-litre measure, a chandelier, if there is

one her bed with bed-linen, and her coffer, two robes and accoutrements provided for her use, whichever she wishes to choose; and part of the jewels and rings according to the situation and social standing of her husband's household

a bed with bed-linen, their books of hours and paternosters, one of her best robes, and another middle-quality one, both for winter and summer use; but she shall not have rings and jewels

296   *n. 40*   Under customary law the dower consists of half the property that the husband has and possesses on the day of the wedding and nuptial benediction. And of half the property which since the consummation of the said marriage and during the latter, has come and fallen into the possession of the said husband by direct succession.

296   *n. 44*   The dower has preference over all personal obligations preceding the marriage, and over all mortgages that have been created and come into being since the consummation of the marriage

The said dowers, *préfix* as well as *coutumier*, are privileged in such a way that they are paid prior to all other debts.

296–7   *n. 48*   all their movable goods, debts, immovable *acquêts* and *conquêts*, with a fifth of their personal inheritances in perpetuity or for life . . . in the case, however, where there are no children of the said marriage or a preceding one; and if there are children, they [the testators] can only give to each other in usufruct

Chapter 7

299   *n. 22*   an entresol so low and so dark that I used to bend and grope to walk round it: you could not breath in there, for lack of air, nor keep warm, for lack of a chimney

300   *n. 43*   I made up my account with Monsieur Michel, a merchant of Arles, and I saw that I owed him 1053 *livres*. Monsieur Michel has promised to be satisfied with payment of interest only this year I had planned to go to La Bégude today. Rain stopped me, so I made up the account of the tenant of Le Grès, and I saw that he will owe me more money at the time of the fair. I also made up the account of the miller, who will owe me more
On 26 July I made up the accounts of several of my domestics

300   *n. 44*   To a letter from the nuns of Sainte-Claire at Avignon, I replied that it was impossible for me to pay before the harvest, and that if I am pressed any more, I shall use *lettres d'état* [permitting persons occupied with important state matters, especially army and navy officers, to defer legal proceedings of a non-criminal nature] to stop prosecution

301–2   *n. 66*   Item, the widows of masters will enjoy the privileges of masters while they remain widows, will be able to continue with the male and female apprentices taken in by their late husband, and nevertheless will not be able to accept or take on new ones, and will lose their privileges on remarriage with a man of another profession. in the event of one of the said master apothecaries dying, we give power and permission to the forsaken widow to exploit and keep open the shop during her widowhood, and to have the art of pharmacy practised therein by a competent journeyman that she will present to the master guard [of the guild] so that the latter can receive the oath required in such a case.
The widows of the said master chandlers will enjoy the same rights, honours and privileges as the other masters of the said profession living in the said town and suburbs of Le Mans, and will consequently be liable for contribution to appropriate expenses paid by their community and responsible for the good quality of all the merchandise and goods sold in and issuing from their shops. Item, that all the widows of masters of the said estate will be able to keep up and continue their trade during their widowhood as they did during their husband's lifetime, and if they remarry with other persons who are not masters of the said estate, they will not be able to carry on or continue with the said trade, but will be deprived of the said estate and mastership.
good morals and honourable to frequent

302   *n. 68*   and if the said widows or daughters of masters marry a journeyman who either belongs to the town or is an outsider, they will exempt him from doing the service that he is obliged to render to the masters of the said community and from half of the fees, and [such journeymen] will only be given a simple test of their expertise

303   *n. 72* more than a thousand mistresses and two hundred merchant-women in shops

Chapter 8

305   *n. 12* Do you think that maidservants or those keeping house are not more than equal to lady companions, or rather lady servants, since they serve like me, and there's only the head-dress that marks a difference between the two of us.

306   *n. 23* The said male and female servants shall be prohibited from wearing silk, silver, and garments unsuitable to their estate and condition.

306   *n. 27* The majority of domestics dare not contemplate marriage, because the majority of masters would no longer want them. Whence the fact that so many throw themselves into debauchery.

307   *n. 37* foreign enemies can never do as much harm as those who live, eat, and sleep amongst us, and to whom we confide our goods and our lives

307   *n. 42* what close examination, what dissection of bodies have they ever carried out amongst themselves, or with others more competent than they are?

307   *n. 50* Midwives were nicknamed *sages* [good or wise], not because of their virtue but because they knew many things unknown to other women. They are still called *femmes sages* in Guyenne and Languedoc, but in the provinces where the French language is more precise the words are transposed to remove ambiguity, and they are called *sages-femmes*.

308   *n. 58* At the moment there is not the most insignificant female who does not carry an entire pharmacy in her feeble head.

308   *n. 64* Since it is not suitable for a woman to produce books, I would never have planned to give these lessons to the public, if the Administrators of the Hôtel-Dieu, for whom I have every kind of respect, had not urged me to do so

Chapter 9

311   *n. 29* Supposing that the said actors so regulate actions on stage as to render them completely free from impurity, it is our wish that the exercise of their profession, which can harmlessly divert our subjects from various undesirable occupations, should not be considered blameworthy, nor prejudicial to their reputation in public life

312   *n. 45* At this same time there appeared a certain young man who said he could detect sorcerers, and he was known as the prophet of Arcée, and the people of the duchy of Burgundy, and especially from around Flavigny, put such faith in him that, leading him through the villages and getting the inhabitants to pass before him, those whom he looked at as they went by and said 'he or she is a sorcerer or witch' were immediately seized and drowned, and

were given so many blows with poles that they finally died in the water; others heated ovens and threw inside all whom he said were sorcerers

314   *n. 82*   and they are forced to do hard labour and have inflicted upon them corporal penitence, indeed even via the whip

314   *n. 98*   neither that of simple friend, nor of real lover

Chapter 10

316   *n. 14*   there has never been an affection ['*amitié*' is an ambiguous term, often used in the seventeenth century to mean 'love' as well as 'friendship'] like that which I have for you . . . [I] would give my life to see you again and be able to tell you things, before I die, which most certainly have never been imagined

317   *n. 39*   I often receive anonymous letters in which I am insulted for all the evils that I do in the state; I am asked what I intend to do, on the eve of my death, with all the money that I am piling up. There is nothing for it, madame, but to be patient about all that.

322   *n. 112*   but since that made a great stir in the town and several women had given the alarm, he went away without doing anything

322   *n. 117*   However, one could add that those who did not dare to declare themselves as rebels, for fear of losing their property, secretly fomented the rebellion, and directed women of low and disreputable condition in all the aforementioned events; these women complied with all the more ardour and fury in that this indiscreet and imprudent sex was less able to judge the importance of its actions.

324   *n. 147*   all gentlemen possessing fiefs

325   *n. 157*   as a token of the honour they received from his command of arms in the Province

326   *n. 176*   piquant, facetious, malicious

Chapter 11

329   *n. 58*   The *précieuses* have a man of wit, poor and wretched, to whom they give a dinner once a week, and an outfit once a year, and make him work to their heart's content on all the ideas that come into their mind

330   *n. 69*   had found the secret, through her wit alone, of attracting to her home all that was most reputed at court, of both sexes

332   *n. 102*   a good share

335   *n. 149*   The singularity of such an avowal, of which she could find no example . . . such an extraordinary remedy . . .

335   *n. 151*   She was an old woman bent beneath the burden of the years, and yet when she saw a man, she gave a cry, and hid her face beneath the coverlet, as if her virtue had still been ripe for exposure to risks

335   *n. 152*   I do not doubt that at this juncture more than one reader

will say in an ironic tone that I have not always spoken of it [love] in this way, but that is exactly why I denigrate it so, and it is because I have complete experience of it that I find myself authorised to portray it in such black colours.

Chapter 12

338 *n. 9* Your medicine, Mademoiselle, has worked me nine times
340 *n. 36* truly, if women show more inclination towards virtue, men would be more inclined thereto
341 *n. 74* His stomach above all caused astonishment, and his bowels by their size and length which were twice that of the ordinary man's, whence the fact that he ate such large amounts and so consistently
342 *n. 86* Men are not given time to desire / What – at the least with tears, assiduity, attention to pleasing –/ They ought to be made to purchase. / They are spoilt. Shameful advances are made to them, / Which only disgust them.
342 *n. 89* from amongst the most beautiful, in order to attract the king to her
343 *n. 95* There are in Paris more than twenty thousand penniless gentlemen who yet subsist through gambling and women

Chapter 13

345 *n. 20* The *sœurs converses* will be employed on the heaviest work, such as cooking, bread-making, laundry, caring for cows and hens, shoemending and similar things.
348 *n. 56* there is scarcely any point of ecclesiastical discipline nowadays which is either more neglected, or more ignored, than that of the enclosure of nuns
348 *n. 64* the church was all adorned with rich silken tapestries, embellished with gold and silver, and the high altar filled with silver vessels, with six fine chandeliers, and with a huge cross . . . candelabras, girandoles [branched candlesticks] and torches placed everywhere in very good order. From the altar right up to the back of the chancel there were foot carpets. The whole of the chancel was covered with one single Persian silk carpet. The Abbess of Chelles had the Abbesses of Montmartre and Farmoustier as assistants. The three kneeling-desks destined for them, and the throne of the new abbess, were covered by Persian carpets worked with gold, and had blue velvet cushions all embroidered with gold
349 *n. 80* the excessive number of religious communities being established every day
350–1 *n. 108* The famine is such that we see men eating earth, cropping grass, stripping bark from trees, tearing at the miserable rags with which they are covered, in order to swallow them. But what we would not dare to speak of if we had not actually seen it, and what

is horrifying, they eat their arms and hands and die in this state of desperation.

352   *n. 125*   Monsieur Arnauld, her director, having become her spiritual lover, she was crazy over him, as she had been in former times over the Duc de la Rochefoucauld

356   *n. 181*   that people had never seen a man of quality arrested for trifles like that

356–7   *n. 187*   Believe me, my dear Madame, miracles are rare, and I believe, just between the two of us, that the majority of those which our Holy Mother Church obliges us to believe are a little subject to caution ... People have never believed less, and never pretended to believe so much!

Chapter 14

358   *n. 8*   I do not think that a very great age is something pleasant; there is too much to suffer, and where suffering is concerned I am a great coward.

358   *n. 10*   Accustom your soul to thoughts of death: / Apart from its name alone, death holds no terrors. / Take away from it the horror of a dark sojourn, / Of demons, hell, and fire; / What will be left that is painful? / Death is simply the end of life. / It is not followed by either penalties or benefits ...

358   *n. 13*   'First remedy against fear of death. Think of it often.'

358   *n. 18*   to prevent them, she says, from dying of hunger, like those of greater princesses that she has seen in that sorry state

359   *n. 46*   a pernicious invention of Satan 'What is the felicity of faithful souls separated from the body, and in what place they are received.'

360   *n. 64*   the nave of which was completely hung with black, right up to the great street door, and the chancel draped all around with velvet

360   *n. 65*   sworn hereditary criers of burials

361   *n. 70*   I desire ... a wooden bier, carried by poor people of the parish, truly poor, to whom shall be given the wherewithal to clothe themselves, as also to the poor children who will carry the candlesticks and torches; they shall be from the parish

362   *n. 94*   almost forgotten already

Bibliography

The bibliography is divided into the following sections:
I   Primary sources
   A   Law
   B   Government and political history
   C   Guilds
   D   Religious history (Sects, Convent regulations)
   E   Local history
   F   Travel literature and topography
   G   Anas, compilations and dictionaries
   H   Memoirs
   I   Livres de raison
   J   Correspondence
   K   Biographies and panegyrics
   L   Gazettes and periodicals
   M   Philosophy and science
   N   Medicine, obstetrics and child welfare
   O   Moral, educational, feminist and anti-feminist works
   P   Literary and linguistic treatises; criticism
   Q   Novels, short stories, romanticised memoirs
   R   Poetry, satire, chansons
   S   Theatre and ballet
   T   Miscellaneous
II Secondary sources

The following abbreviations have been used:
GEF   Collection Grands Ecrivains de la France
MP   Nouvelle Collection des Mémoires pour servir à l'histoire de France depuis le XIIIe siècle jusqu'à la fin du XVIIIe (eds J. F. Michaud and J. J. Poujoulat) 1836–9, 32 vols
PUF   Presses Universitaires Françaises
RHL   Revue d'Histoire Littéraire
SHF   Société de l'Histoire de France
STFM   Société des Textes Français Modernes
UP   University Press

Unless otherwise stated the place of publication is Paris.

I   PRIMARY SOURCES

A   Law

Archives de la Bastille, ed. F. Ravaisson, Vols V, VI, VII (Durand et Pedone-Lauriel, 1872–4).

Argenson, René-Louis, Marquis d', *Notes* (Collection des Petits Mémoires Inédits, Voitelain, 1866).

Argenson, René-Louis, Marquis d', *Rapports Inédits (1697–1715)*, ed. P. Cottin (Plon, 1891).

Arrêts du Conseil du Roi, ed. M. Le Pesant, Vol. I (Archives Nationales, 1976).

Bourdot de Richebourg, Charles A., *Nouveau Coutumier Général* (Robustel, 1724, 8 vols).

Brillon, Pierre-Jacques, *Dictionnaire des Arrêts ou Jurisprudence Universelle des Parlements de France* (Osmont, 1711, 3 vols).

Code Criminel (1670) (Le Boucher, 1786).

Code Matrimonial (Hérissant le Fils, 1770, 2 vols).

Edits, Déclarations et Arrêts concernant la Religion Prétendue Réformée, ed. L. Pilatte (Fischbacher, 1885).

Guyot, Pierre J. J. G., *Répertoire Universel et Raisonné de Jurisprudence*, 2me edn (Panckoucke, 1776–83, 64 vols).

Guyot, Pierre J. J. G., *Traité des Droits, Fonctions, Franchises, Exemptions, Prérogatives et Privilèges* (Visse, 1786–8, 4 vols).

Isambert, François A. et al., *Recueil Général des Anciennes Lois Françaises*, Vols XIV–XX (Belin-Leprieur, 1829–30).

La Mare, Nicolas de, *Traité de la Police*, 2me edn augmentée (Brunet, 1719–38, 4 vols).

La Poix de Freminville, Edme de, *Traité Général des biens et affaires des communautés d'habitants des villes, bourgs, villages et paroisses du royaume* (Gissey, 1760).

Lettres et Rapports de Police, ed. P. Clément, in *La Police sous Louis XIV*, 2me edn (Didier, 1866).

Loyseau, Charles, *Cinq Livres du Droit des Offices* (Châteaudun: L'Angelier, 1610).

Loysel, Antoine, *Institutes Coutumières*, ed. E. Laboulaye (Videcoq, 1846, 2 vols).

Mémoires tirés des Archives de la Police de Paris, ed. J. Peuchet, Vol. I (Levavasseur, 1838).

Recueil d'Edits et d'Ordonnances Royaux, augmenté sur l'édition de Pierre Néron et Etienne Girard (Montalant, 1720, 2 vols).

B   Government and political history

Archives Curieuses de l'Histoire de France, eds L. Cimber and F. Danjou, 2me Sér., Vol. V (1838).

Aubigné, Agrippa d', *Histoire Universelle*, ed. Baron A. de Ruble (SHF, 1886–1925, 10 vols and Supplément).

Baudouin, J., *Journal sur les Grands-Jours de Languedoc (1666–67)*, ed. P. Le Blanc (Dumoulin, 1869).

Belleforest, François de, *Histoire Universelle du Monde*, (Mallot, 1570).

Cahiers de Doléance des Paroisses du Bailliage de Troyes pour les Etats Généraux de 1614, ed. Y. Durand (PUF, 1966).

Cahiers des Etats de Normandie sous les règnes de Louis XIII et de Louis XIV, ed. C. de Robillard de Beaurepaire (Rouen: Société de l'Histoire de Normandie, 1876–8, 3 vols).

Carew, Sir George, 'A Relation of the State of France', in *An Historical View of the Negotiations between the Courts of England, France, and Brussels from the year 1592 to 1617*, ed. Thomas Birch (London: Millar, 1749).

Choix de Mazarinades, ed. C. Moreau (Renouard, 1853, 2 vols).

Des Etats Généraux et Autres Assemblées Nationales, ed. Charles J. Mayer, Vol. XVI (Buisson, 1789).

Deux Cahiers de la Noblesse pour les Etats Généraux de 1649–1651, eds R. Mousnier, J.-P. Labatut, Y. Durand (PUF, 1965).

Dubosc de Montandré, *Le Sceptre de France en Quenouille* (no place of publication, 1652).

Dupleix, Scipion, *Histoire de Louis Le Juste* (Sonnius, 1635).

Etat de la Généralité d'Alençon sous Louis XIV, ed. L. Duval (1890).

Fléchier, Esprit, *Mémoires sur les Grands Jours d'Auvergne en 1665*, ed. F. Dauphin (Jonquières, 1930).

Mémoires et Documents pour servir à l'histoire du commerce et de l'industrie en France, ed. J. Hayem (Hachette, 4me Sér., 1916).

Mémoire de la Généralité de Moulins, ed. P. Flamant (Moulins: Librairie Historique du Bourbonnais, 1906).

Mémoire sur la Généralité de Limoges, ed. A. Leroux, in *Documents Historiques Bas-Latins, Provençaux et Français concernant principalement La Marche et Le Limousin*, Vol. II (Limoges, 1885).

Mémoires des Intendants sur L'Etat des Généralités, Vol. I, Paris, ed. A. de Boislisle (Imprimerie Nationale, 1881).

Priolo, Benjamin, *Ab Excessu Ludovici XIII De Rebus Gallicis, Historiarum Libri XII* (Charleville, 1665).

Recueil des Instructions données aux Ambassadeurs et Ministres de France, Vol. XI, Tome I, ed. A. Morel-Fatio (Alcan, 1894).

Richelieu, Armand-Jean du Plessis de, Cardinal, *Testament Politique*, ed. L. André (Laffont, 1947).

Richelieu, Armand-Jean du Plessis de, Cardinal, *Papiers*, ed. P. Grillon, Vol. I (Pedone, 1975).

Thou, Jacques-Auguste de, *Histoire Universelle 1543–1610*, traduite sur l'édition latine de Londres (London, 1734).

Vauban, Sébastien Le Prestre, Maréchal de, *Projet d'une dîme royale*, ed. E. Coornaert (Alcan, 1933).

C   Guilds

The works listed in this section reproduce original guild statutes. They are arranged according to editors' names.

Bouillet, J.-B., *Histoire des Communautés des Arts et Métiers de l'Auvergne* (Clermont Ferrand, 1857).

Bourgeois, A., *Les Métiers de Blois* (Blois: Société des Sciences et Lettres de Loir-et-Cher, Vol. XIII, 1892).

Cauvin, T., *Documents relatifs à l'histoire des corporations d'arts et métiers du diocèse du Mans* (Le Mans, 1860).

Chapuis, A. V., *Les Anciennes Corporations Dijonnaises* (Dijon, 1906).

Lespinasse, R. de, *Les Métiers et Corporations de la Ville de Paris* (Imprimerie Nationale, 1886–97, 3 vols).

Maisonneuve, E. Toubeau de, *Les Anciennes Corporations Ouvrières à Bourges* (Bourges, 1881).

Nardin, L., and Mauveaux, J., 'Histoire des Corporations d'Arts et Métiers des Ville et Comté de Montbéliard', in *Mémoires de la Société d'Emulation de Montbéliard*, Vol. XXXIX (1910).

Ouin-Lacroix, C., *Histoire des Anciennes Corporations d'Arts et Métiers et des Confréries Religieuses de la Capitale de la Normandie* (Rouen, 1850).

Pied, E., *Les Anciens Corps d'Arts et Métiers de Nantes* (Nantes, 1903, 3 vols).

Thierry, A., *Recueil des Monuments Inédits de l'Histoire du Tiers Etat, 1ere Sér.*, *Région du Nord* (Imprimerie Impériale, 1853–70, 4 vols).

D   Religious history

(i) Sects

Arnauld, Antoine, *De la Fréquente Communion* (Vitré, 1643).

Besoigne, Jérôme, *Histoire de l'Abbaye de Port-Royal* (Cologne, 1756, 6 vols).

Court, Antoine, *Histoire des troubles des Cévennes ou de la Guerre des Camisards* (Villefranche, 1760, 3 vols).

Fontaine, Nicolas, *Mémoires pour servir à l'histoire de Port-Royal* (Cologne, 1753, 4 vols).

Racine, Jean, *Abrégé de l'Histoire de Port-Royal*, in *Œuvres Complètes* (Editions du Seuil, 1962).

(ii) Convent regulations

Augustin, *Coutumier ou Directoire des Religieuses Hospitalières de Saint Augustin* (Arles: Mesnier, 1677).

Benoît, *La Règle du Bienheureux Père Saint Benoît, avec les constitutions qui y ont été accommodées pour la réforme de l'Abbaye Royale de Notre-Dame du Val de Grâce* (Billaine, 1676).

Claire, *La Règle et Statuts des Religieuses de Sainte Claire, Pour l'usage des Dames Religieuses de Patience de Laval* (Laval: Cormier, 1651).

Notre-Dame, *Usages des Religieuses de la Congrégation de Notre-Dame* (Châlons: Seneuze, 1690).

Notre-Dame du Mont-Carmel et de Sainte-Thérèse, *La Règle, Le Cérémonial et Le Directoire des Sœurs du Tiers Ordre de Notre-Dame du Mont-Carmel et de Sainte-Thérèse* (Brussels: Foppens, 1733).

Port-Royal du Saint Sacrement, *Constitutions* (Mons: Migeot, 1665).

Thiers, Jean-Baptiste, *Traité de la Clôture des Religieuses* (Dezallier, 1681).

Ursulines, *Règlements des Religieuses Ursulines* (Josse, 1751, 3 vols).

E   Local history

Archives de Nancy, ed. H. Lepage, Vols I–IV (Nancy: Wiener, 1865).

Archives de Nevers, ed. C.-A. Parmentier (1842, 2 vols).

Béziers, Michel, *Mémoires pour servir à l'état historique et géographique du*

Diocèse de Bayeux, ed. G. Le Hardy (Société de l'Histoire de Normandie, 1896, 1895, 2 vols).

Bouche, Honoré, *La Chorographie, ou Description de Provence* (Aix: David, 1664).

Delort, André, *Mémoires de ce qui s'est passé de plus remarquable dans Montpellier depuis 1622 jusqu'en 1691*, ed. L. Gaudin (Montpellier, 1876).

Diaire ou Journal du Voyage du Chancelier Séguier en Normandie après la sédition des Nu-Pieds (1639–1640), ed. A.-P. Floquet (Geneva: Slatkine Reprints, 1975).

Documents de l'Histoire de la Provence, ed. E. Baratier (Privat, 1971).

Dubuisson-Aubenay, Nicolas-François Baudot, Seigneur de, *Itinéraire de Bretagne en 1636* (Nantes: Sociéte des Bibliophiles Bretons, 1898, 2 vols).

Gaufreteau, Jean de, *Chronique Bordeloise* (Bordeaux: Archives du Château de la Brède, 1877–8, 2 vols).

Journal Historique de Vitré, ed. Abbé P. Paris-Jallobert (Vitré, 1880).

Louvet, Jean, *Journal: Récit véritable de tout ce qui est advenu digne de mémoire tant en la ville d'Angers, pays d'Anjou et autres lieux (depuis l'an 1560 jusqu'à l'an 1634)*, in *Revue de l'Anjou et de Maine et Loire*, May–June 1854 to Sept.–Oct. 1856.

Macheret, Clément, *Journal de ce qui s'est passé de mémorable à Lengres et aux environs depuis 1628 jusqu'en 1658*, ed. E. Bougard (Langres, 1880, 2 vols).

Malebaysse, *Une Emeute à Agen, Publiée d'après le manuscrit de Malebaysse*, ed. A. Magen, in *Recueil des Travaux de la Société d'Agriculture, Science et Arts d'Agen*, Vol. VII (1854–5).

Vaissète, Dom. J., and Devic, Dom. C., *Histoire Générale de Languedoc* (Osnabrück: Zeller, 1973, 16 vols).

F Travel literature and topography

Aventures d'un grand seigneur italien à travers l'Europe (1606), ed. E. Rodocanachi (Flammarion, no date).

Bernini, Gian Lorenzo, called Le Cavalier Bernin, *Journal du Voyage en France du Cavalier Bernin*, ed. P. Freart de Chantelou (Stock, 1930).

Brackenhoffer, Elie, *Voyage en France 1643–44*, trans. H. Lehr (Berger-Levrault, 1925).

Brice, Germain, *Description Nouvelle de la Ville de Paris*, 4me edn (Le Gras, 1700, 2 vols).

Dallington, Robert, *The View of France* (Shakespeare Association Facsimiles, No. 13; Oxford UP, 1936).

Davity, Pierre, *Les Etats, Empires, et Principautés du Monde* (Rouen: Ouin et Cailloue, 1640).

Dumont, Jean, *Voyages en France, en Italie, à Malthe, et en Turquie* (Hague, 1699, 4 vols).

Howell, James, *Familiar Letters*, ed. J. Jacobs (London, 1890).

Huygens, Christiaan, *Le Séjour de C. Huygens à Paris, suivi de son Journal de Voyage à Paris et à Londres*, ed. and trans. H. L. Brugmans (Droz, 1935).

Jaillot, J.-B. Michel Renou de Chevigné, *Recherches Critiques, Historiques, et Topographiques sur la Ville de Paris* (Le Boucher, 1782, 5 vols).

Journal du Voyage de Deux Jeunes Hollandais à Paris en 1656–58, ed. A.-P. Faugère (Champion, 1899).

Jouvin, Albert, *Le Voyageur d'Europe* (Thierry, 1672–6, 7 vols).

Lauder, Sir John, *Journals*, ed. D. Crawford (Scottish History Society, No. 36; Edinburgh UP, 1900).

Le Laboureur, Jean, *Relation du Voyage de la Reine de Pologne et du retour de Mme la Maréchale de Guébriant* (Veuve Jean Camusat, 1647).

Le Maire, C., *Paris Ancien et Nouveau* (Vaugon, 1685, 3 vols).

Lister, Martin, *A Journey to Paris in the year 1698* (London, 1699).

Locatelli, Sébastien, *Voyage de France (1664–65)* trans. A. Vautier (Picard, 1905).

Locke, John, *Travels in France*, ed. J. Lough (Cambridge UP, 1953).

Marana, Giovanni Paolo, *L'esploratore Turco* [originally published 1684] translated as *Letters writ by a Turkish Spy*, 11th edn (London, 1741, 8 vols).

Montesquieu, Charles-Louis de Secondat, Baron de, *Lettres Persanes*, ed. P. Vernière (Garnier, 1960).

Mortoft, Francis, *His Book, Being his Travels through France and Italy, 1658–59*, ed. M. Letts (London: Hakluyt Society, 1925).

Perrault, Claude, *Voyage à Bordeaux (1669)*, ed. P. Bonnefon (Renouard, 1909).

Piganiol de La Force, Jean Aimar, *Nouveau Voyage de France* (Desprez, 1755, 2 vols).

Pradel, Abraham du, [pseudonym of Nicolas de Blégny], *Le Livre Commode des Adresses de Paris pour 1692*, ed. E. Fournier (1878, 2 vols).

Reresby, Sir John, *Travels and Memoirs*, 2nd edn (London, 1821).

Sauval, Henri, *Histoire des Antiquités de Paris* ([no place of publication] Gregg International Publishers, 1969, 3 vols).

Skippon, Philip, *An Account of a Journey made thro' part of the Low Countries, Germany, Italy, and France*, in *A Collection of Voyages and Travels* (London, 1732, 6 vols).

G Anas, compilations and dictionaries

Académie Française, *Dictionnaire de l'*, 5me edn (Bossange et al., 1814, 2 vols).

Anselme, Pierre de Guibours, Père, *Histoire Généalogique et Chronologique de la Maison Royale de France* (New York and London: Johnson Reprint Corporation, 1967, 9 vols).

Bayle, Pierre, *Dictionnaire Historique et Critique* (Desoer, 1820, 16 vols).

Boileau-Despréaux, Nicolas, *Bolaeana* (Amsterdam: Chez LHonoré, 1742).

Chevreau, Urbain, *Chevraeana* (Delaulne, 1697).

Corneille, Thomas, *Dictionnaire Universel, Géographique et Historique* (Coignard, 1708, 3 vols).

Durand de Maillane, Pierre Toussaint, *Dictionnaire de Droit Canonique et de Pratique Bénéficiale* (Lyon: Duplain, 1776, 5 vols).

Fontenelle, Bernard Le Bovier de, *Fontenelliana* (Marchand, 1801).

Furetière, Antoine, *Furetiriana* (Brussels: Foppens, 1696).

Huet, Pierre Daniel, *Huetiana* (Estienne, 1722).

La Croix, Jean-François de, *Dictionnaire Historique Portatif des Femmes Célèbres* (Cellot, 1769, 2 vols).

La Houssaye, Nicolas Amelot de, *Mémoires Historiques, Politiques, Critiques, et Littéraires* (Amsterdam: Chatelain, 1737, 3 vols).

Ménage, Gilles, *Menagiana*, 3me edn (Amsterdam: De Coup, 1713, 4 vols).

Montpensier, Anne-Marie-Louise d'Orléans, Duchesse de, *La Galerie des Portraits*, ed. E. de Barthélemy (Didier, 1860).

Moréri, Louis, *Le Grand Dictionnaire Historique* (Libraires Associés, 1759, 10 vols).

Recueil Général des questions traitées aux Conférences du Bureau d'Adresse, sur toutes sortes de matières (Lyon: Valançol, 1666, 6 vols).

Savary des Bruslons, Jacques, and Savary, Philemon Louis, *Dictionnaire Universel de Commerce* (Estienne, 1723–30, 3 vols).

Segrais, Jean Regnauld de, *Segraisiana* (Hague: Gosse, 1722).

Somaize, Antoine Bodeau de, *Le Dictionnaire des Précieuses*, ed. C. Livet (Jannet, 1856, 2 vols).

Vigneul-Marville, [Pseudonym of Noël Bonaventure d'Argonne], *Mélanges d'Histoire et de Littérature* (Besoigne, 1699–1701, 3 vols).

H Memoirs

Argenson, René-Louis, Marquis d', *Journal et Mémoires*, ed. E. Rathery (SHF, 1859–67, 9 vols).

Arnauld, Antoine, Abbé, *Mémoires* (MP, 2me Sér., Vol. IX).

Arnauld d'Andilly, Robert, *Journal Inédit*, ed. A. Halphen (Techener, 1857).

Arnauld d'Andilly, Robert, *Mémoires* (MP, 2me Sér., Vol. IX).

Aumale, Marie-Jeanne d', *Souvenirs sur Mme de Maintenon*, eds Comte d'Haussonville and G. Hanotaux (Calmann-Lévy, no date).

Bassompierre, François, Maréchal de, *Mémoires*, ed. Marquis de Chantérac (SHF, 1870–7, 4 vols).

Bouchard, Jean-Jacques, *Confessions* (Gallimard, 1930).

Brantôme, Pierre de Bourdeille, Seigneur de, *Œuvres Complètes*, ed. L. Lalanne (SHF, 1864–82, 11 vols).

Brienne, Louis Henri de Loménie, Comte de, *Mémoires*, ed. P. Bonnefon (SHF, 1916–19, 3 vols).

Bussy, Roger de Rabutin Chantal, Comte de, *Mémoires*, ed. L. Lalanne (Flammarion, 1882, 2 vols).

Campion, Henri de, *Mémoires*, ed. M. C. Moreau (Jannet, 1857).

Cavalier, Jean, *Mémoires sur la Guerre des Camisards*, ed. F. Puaux (Payot, 1973).

Caylus, Marguerite de Villette de Murçay, Comtesse de, *Souvenirs* (MP, 3me Sér., Vol. VIII).

Chavagnac, Gaspard, Comte de, *Mémoires* (Besançon: Rigoine, 1699, 2 vols).

Cherbury, Edward, Lord Herbert of, *Autobiography* (London: Nimmo, 1886).

Choisy, François-Timoléon, Abbé de, *Mémoires* (MP, 3me Sér., Vol. VI).

Chorier, Nicolas, *Mémoires*, trans. F. Crozet (Grenoble, 1868).

Conrart, Valentin, *Mémoires*, (MP, 3me Sér., Vol. IV).

Cosnac, Daniel de, *Mémoires*, ed. Comte J. de Cosnac (SHF, 1852, 2 vols).

Coulanges, Philippe Emmanuel de, *Mémoires* [See Correspondence section under Pomponne].

Dames de Saint-Cyr, *Mémoires sur Mme de Maintenon* (Olivier-Fulgence, 1846).

Dangeau, Philippe de Courcillon, Marquis de, *Journal*, eds E. Soulié, L. Dussieux et al. (Firmin-Didot, 1854–60, 18 vols and Table).

Dubuisson-Aubenay, Nicolas-François Baudot, Seigneur de, *Journal des Guerres Civiles (1648–1652)*, ed. G. Saige (Champion, 1883–5, 2 vols).

Duclos, Charles Pinot, *Mémoires Secrets sur les Règnes de Louis XIV et de Louis XV* (MP, 3me Sér., Vol. X).

Du Fossé, Pierre Thomas, *Mémoires*, ed. F. Bouquet (Rouen: Société de l'Histoire de Normandie, 1876–9, 4 vols).

Dunoyer, Anne Marguerite Petit, *Mémoires* (Amsterdam, 1760).

Evelyn, John, *The Diary*, ed. E. S. de Beer (Oxford: Clarendon Press, 1955, 6 vols).

Fontenay-Mareuil, François Duval, Marquis de), *Mémoires* (MP, 2me Sér., Vol. V).

Foucault, Nicolas-Joseph, *Mémoires*, ed. F. Baudry (Imprimerie Impériale, 1862).

Franclieu, Jacques-Laurent-Pierre-Charles Pasquier de, Marquis, *Mémoires (1680–1745)*, ed. L. de Germon (1896).

Gourville, Jean Hérault de, *Mémoires* (MP, 3me Sér., Vol. V).

Gramont, Antoine III, Maréchal de, *Mémoires* (MP, 3me Sér., Vol. VII).

Guyon, Jeanne-Marie Bouvier de la Motte, known as Mme Guyon, *Vie de Mme Guyon écrite par elle-même* (Cologne: La Pierre, 1720, 3 vols).

Hébert, François, Curé de Versailles, *Mémoires (1686–1704)*, ed. G. Girard (Editions de France, 1927).

Héroard, Jean, *Journal sur l'enfance et la jeunesse de Louis XIII, 1601–1628*, eds E. Soulié and E. Barthélemy (Firmin-Didot, 1868, 2 vols).

Huet, Pierre Daniel, *Memoirs*, trans. J. Aikin (London, 1810, 2 vols).

Joly, Guy, *Mémoires* (MP, 3me Sér., Vol. II).

La Fare, Charles Auguste, Marquis de, *Mémoires* (MP, 3me Sér., Vol. VIII).

Lafayette, Marie-Madeleine de la Vergne, Comtesse de, *Histoire de Madame Henriette d'Angleterre* (MP, 3me Sér., Vol. VIII).

Lafayette, Marie-Madeleine de la Vergne, Comtesse de, *Mémoires de la Cour de France*, ibid.

La Force, Jacques Nompar de Caumont, Duc de, *Mémoires Authentiques*, ed. Marquis de la Grange (Charpentier, 1843, 4 vols).

La Guette, Catherine Meudrac, Mme de, *Mémoires*, ed. P. Moreau, (Jannet, 1856).

La Porte, Pierre de, *Mémoires* (MP, 3me Sér., Vol. VIII).

La Rochefoucauld, François VI, Duc de, *Mémoires* (MP, 3me Sér., Vol. V).

Le Gendre, Louis, Abbé, *Mémoires*, ed. M. Roux (Charpentier, 1865).

Letouf, Claude de, Baron de Sirot, *Mémoires* (Barbin, 1683, 2 vols).

Lenet, Pierre, *Mémoires* (MP, 3me Sér., Vol. II).

L'Estoile, Pierre de, *Journal pour le règne de Henri IV*, Vol. I, 1589–1600, ed.

L.-R. Lefèvre (Gallimard, 1948); Vol. II, 1601–9, ed. A. Martin (Gallimard, 1958).

Louis XIV, *Mémoires*, ed. J. Longnon (Tallandier, 1927).

Marguerite de Valois, *Mémoires et Lettres*, ed. M. F. Guessard (SHF, 1842).

Marolles, Michel de, *Mémoires* and *Suite des Mémoires* (Sommaville, 1656–7).

Molé, Mathieu, *Mémoires*, ed. A. Champollion-Figeac (SHF, 1855–7, 4 vols).

Montglat, François de Paule de Clermont, Marquis de, *Mémoires* (MP, 3me Sér., Vol. V).

Montpensier, Anne-Marie-Louise d'Orléans, Duchesse de, *Mémoires*, ed. A. Chéruel (Charpentier, 1857–9, 4 vols).

Montrésor, Claude de Bourdeille, Comte de, *Mémoires* (MP, 3me Sér., Vol. III).

Mornay, Charlotte Arbaleste de la Borde, Mme de, *Mémoires*, ed. Mme de Witt (SHF, 1868–9, 2 vols).

Motteville, Françoise Bertaut de, *Mémoires*, ed. F. Riaux (Charpentier, 1911, 4 vols).

Narbonne, Pierre, *Journal des Règnes de Louis XIV et Louis XV de l'année 1701 à l'année 1744*, ed. J.-A. Le Roi (Versailles: Bernard, 1866).

Nemours, Marie de Longueville, Duchesse de, *Mémoires* (MP, 2me Sér., Vol. IX).

Orléans, Gaston, Duc d', *Mémoires* (MP, 2me Sér., Vol. IX).

Ormesson, Olivier Lefèvre d', *Journal*, ed. A. Chéruel (Imprimerie Impériale, 1860–1, 2 vols).

Palatine, Anne de Gonzague, Princesse, *Mémoires*, 2me edn (Prault, 1789).

Pepys, Samuel, *The Diary*, eds R. Latham and W. Matthews (London: Bell and Sons, 1970–6, 9 vols).

Périer, Gilberte, *Lettres, Opuscules et Mémoires de Mme Périer et de Jacqueline, Sœurs de Pascal*, ed. P. Faugère (Vaton, 1845).

Perrault, Charles, *Mémoires* (Librairie des Bibliophiles, 1878).

Plessis Praslin, César, Duc de Choiseul, Comte du, *Mémoires* (MP, 3me Sér., Vol. VII).

Pontchartrain, Paul Phélypeaux, Seigneur de, *Mémoires* (MP, 2me Sér., Vol. V).

Pontis, Louis de, *Mémoires* (MP, 2me Sér., Vol. VI).

Puységur, Jacques de Chastenet, Seigneur de, *Mémoires* (Jombert, 1747, 2 vols).

Rapin, René, *Mémoires*, ed. L. Aubineau ([no place of publication] Gregg International Publishers, 1972, 3 vols).

Retz, Paul de Gondi, Cardinal de, *Mémoires*, ed. A. Feillet (GEF, Hachette, 1870–80, 5 vols).

Richelieu, Armand-Jean du Plessis de, Cardinal, *Mémoires* (SHF, 1907–31, 10 vols).

Rohan, Henri, Duc de, *Mémoires* (MP, 2me Sér., Vol. V).

Saint-Simon, Louis de Rouvroy, Duc de, *Mémoires*, ed. A. Chéruel (Hachette, 1904–6, 13 vols).

Sourches, Louis-François Du Bouchet, Marquis de, *Mémoires*, eds Comte G.-J. de Cosnac and A. Bertrand (Hachette, 1882–93, 13 vols).

Souvigny, Jean Gangnières, Comte de, *Mémoires*, ed. Baron L. de Cotenson (SHF, 1906–9, 3 vols).

Spanheim, Ezéchiel, *Relation de la Cour de France en 1690*, ed. E. Bourgeois (Picard, 1900).

Staal de Launay, Marguerite Jeanne Cordier, Baronne de, *Mémoires* (MP 3me Sér., Vol. X).

Sully, Maximilien de Béthune, Duc de, *Mémoires* (London, 1767, 8 vols).

Tallemant des Réaux, Gédéon, *Les Historiettes*, 3me edn, ed. M. Monmerqué (Garnier, 1840, 10 vols).

Talon, Omer, *Mémoires* (MP, 3me Sér., Vol. VI).

Vallier, Jean, *Journal*, eds H. Courteault and P. de Vaissière (SHF, 1902–18, 4 vols).

Visconti, Primi, *Mémoires sur la Cour de Louis XIV*, ed. J. Lemoine (Calmann-Lévy, 1908).

I Livres de raison

Generally included under this heading are all memoirs by those members of the bourgeoisie and minor provincial nobility who write chiefly about family affairs and events taking place in the immediate locality.

Ancillon, Joseph, *Recueil Journalier de ce qui s'est passé de plus mémorable dans la cité de Metz, pays messin et aux environs, de 1656 à 1674*, ed. F. M. Chabert (Metz and Paris, 1860–6, 2 vols).

Bessot, Pierre de, 'Livre-Journal', ed. P. Tamizey de Larroque, in *Bulletin de la Société Historique et Archéologique du Périgord*, Vol. XX (1893).

Borrelly, Etienne, Notaire, 'Livre de Raison (1654–1717)', in A. Puech, *Les Nîmois dans la seconde moitié du XVIIe siécle* (Nîmes, 1888).

Bourrut, Pierre, Sieur des Pascauds, 'Papier de Raison (1692–1725)', ed. A. Mazière, in *Bulletin et Mémoires de la Société Archéologique et Historique de la Charente*, 7me Sér., Vol. III (1902–3).

Boyer, Pierre, Dr en Médecine à St-Bonnet-Le Château, 'Livre de Raison (1620–34)', ed. A. Vachez, in *Revue du Lyonnais*, 5me Sér., Vol. VIII (1889).

Brilhac, René de, Sieur du Parc, Conseiller, 'Extraits des Mémoires (1573–1622)', ed. B. Ledain, in *Archives Historiques du Poitou*, Vol. XV (1885).

Chroniques Berrichonnes du XVIIe Siècle, ed. H. Jongleux (Bourges, 1881).

Coquault, Oudard, Bourgeois de Reims, *Mémoires*, ed. C. Loriquet (Reims, 1875, 2 vols).

Demaillasson, Avocat du Roi à Montmorillon, 'Journal', ed. V. Bardet, in *Archives Historiques du Poitou*, Vol. XXXVI (1907) and Vol. XXXVII (1908).

Denesde, Antoine, Marchand Ferron à Poitiers, 'Journal (1628–1687)', ed. E. Bricauld de Verneuil, in *Archives Historiques du Poitou*, Vol. XV (1885).

'Deux Livres de Raison Bourguignons', ed. C. Oursel, in *Mémoires de la Société Bourguignonne de Géographie et d'Histoire*, Vol. XXIV (1908).

Dudrot de Capdebosc, *Livre de Raison de la Famille (1522–1675)*, ed. P. Tamizey de Larroque (Picard, 1891).

Dumont de Bostaquet, Isaac, *Mémoires Inédits*, eds C. Read and F. Waddington (Lévy, 1864).

Durand, Guillaume, Chirurgien à Poligny, *Journal (1610–1623)*, ed. B. Prost (Champion, 1883).

Dusson, Claude, Jacques and N., 'Memoires', ed. H. de Fontenay, in *Mémoires de la Société Eduenne* (Autun, Nouvelle Sér., Vol. IV, 1875).

Fleuriot, René, Gentilhomme Breton, 'Journal (1593–1624)', ed. A. de Barthélemy, in *Le Cabinet Historique*, Vol. XXIV (1878).

Fontainemarie, Famille de, *Livre de Raison (1640–1774)*, ed. P. Tamizey de Larroque (Agen: Lamy, 1889).

Froissard-Broissia, 'Livre de Raison de la Famille (1532–1701)', in *Mémoires de la Société d'Emulation du Jura* (Lons-Le-Saunier, 4ᵐᵉ Sér., Vol. II, 1886).

Guillaudeau, Joseph, Sieur de Beaupréau, 'Diaire (1584–1643)', in *Archives Historiques de la Saintonge et de l'Aunis*, Vol. XXXVIII (1908).

Hodeau, Robert, Ancien Maire de Bourges, 'Mémoires Inédits', ed. P. Riffé, in *Mémoires de la Société des Antiquaires du Centre* (Bourges, Vol. VIII, 1879).

Jacmon, Antoine, Bourgeois du Puy, *Mémoires*, ed. A. Chassaing (Le-Puy-en-Velay, 1885).

Journal de Deux Notaires Ciotadens au XVIIᵉ Siècle, ed. A. Ritt (Marseille, 1919).

'Journal d'un Chanoine du Diocèse de Cavaillon', ed. M. Jouve, in *Mémoires de l'Académie de Nîmes*, 7ᵐᵉ Sér., Vol. XXVI (1903).

Jousselin, Curé de Ste-Croix d'Angers, 'Journal (1621–52)', ed. C. Port, in *Inventaire Analytique des Archives Anciennes de la Mairie d'Angers* (1861).

Lacroix, Noé, Chalonnais, 'Journal (1610–1631)', ed. A. de Charmasse, in *Mémoires de la Société d'Histoire et d'Archéologie de Chalon-sur-Saone*, Vol. VII, 1ʳᵉ Partie (1883).

Lalande, Michel, Recteur de Siran, *Notes (1685–1712)*, ed. J. Sahuc (Narbonne, 1898).

Le Marchand, Simon, Bourgeois de Caen, *Journal (1610–1693)*, ed. G. Vanel (Caen: Jouan, 1903).

Les Livres de Raison dans le Lyonnais, ed. A. Vachez (Lyon, no date).

Livres de Raison, Registres de Famille et Journaux Individuels Limousins et Marchois, ed. L. Guibert (Paris: Picard and Limoges: Veuve Ducourtieux, 1888).

Mairot, 'Feuillets de Garde', ed. J. Feuvrier, in *Mémoires de la Société d'Emulation du Jura*, 7ᵐᵉ Sér., Vol. I (1901).

'Mémoires d'un Bourgeois de Marseille (1674–1726)', ed. J.-F. Thénard, in *Publications Spéciales de la Société pour l'étude des Langues Romanes* (Montpellier, Vol. VIII, 1881).

Mercier, Marguerite, 'Une Femme de Qualité au Milieu du XVIIᵉ Siècle (1650–61)', ed. J. Pannier, in *Bulletin de la Société de l'Histoire du Protestantisme Français*, 5ᵐᵉ Sér., Vol. III (1905).

Millet, P., Curé de Notre-Dame de la Platière, *Récits*, ed. F. Frécon (Lyon, 1888).

Nouveau Recueil de Registres Domestiques Limousins et Marchois, ed. L. Guibert (Limoges, 1895, 1903, 2 vols).

Perdrix, J. G., Conseiller du Comte George de Montbéliard, 'Chronique', ed. L. Wetzel, in *Compte-Rendu de la Situation et des Travaux de la Société d'Emulation de Montbéliard* (1857).

Plantavit de la Pause, Jean, Evêque de Lodève, 'Journal des Actes (1626–30)', ed. M. Luthard, in *Annales du Midi* (1913).

Recueil de Journaux Caennais, ed. G. Vanel (Rouen: Société de l'Histoire de Normandie, 1904).

Renaudot, Eusèbe, Régent en Médecine à Paris, 'Journal (1646–79)', ed. C. Tronchin, in *Mémoires de la Société de l'Histoire de Paris et de l'Ile de France*, Vol. IV (1877).

Rigaud, Hyacinthe, Peintre, *Livre de Raison*, ed. J. Roman (Laurens, 1919).

Robert, Samuel, Lieutenant Particulier en l'Election de Saintes, 'Livre de Raison', ed. G. Tortat, in *Archives Historiques de la Saintonge et de l'Aunis*, Vol. XII (1884).

Rochefort, Ursule des Porcellets, Comtesse de, 'Journal', in *Une Grande Dame dans son ménage au temps de Louis XIV*, ed. C. de Ribbe (Palmé, 1890).

Rou, Jean, *Mémoires Inédits et Opuscules (1638–1711)*, ed. F. Waddington, Société de l'Histoire du Protestantisme Français (1857, 2 vols).

Savois, Alexandre, 'Abrégé de l'Histoire de l'origine, de la sortie de France et de la vie d'Alexandre Savois', ed. Ch. G., in *Bulletin de la Société de l'Histoire du Protestantisme Français*, 5me Sér., Vol. VIII (1905).

Toisonnier, Etienne, *Journal (1683–1713)*, ed. M. Saché (Angers, 1930).

Tour, Claude du, 'Livre Domestique', ed. La Prairie, in *Bulletin de la Société Archéologique, Historique, et Scientifique de Soissons*, 2me Sér., Vol. III (1862).

Vendée, Paul de, Capitaine Huguenot, *Journal (1611–1623)*, ed. A. Drochon (Niort: Clouzot, 1880).

J Correspondence

Arnauld, Angélique, *Lettres* (Utrecht, 1742–4, 3 vols).

Arnauld, Antoine, Dr de la Sorbonne, *Lettres* (Nancy, 1727–43, 9 vols).

Balzac, Guez de, *Premières Lettres (1618–1627)*, eds H. Bibas and K. Butler (STFM, 1933–4, 2 vols).

Balzac, Guez de, *Lettres Choisies*, 1re Partie (Courbé, 1647).

Balzac, Guez de, *Suite de la Seconde Partie des Lettres*, 2me edn (Rocolet, 1637).

Bavière, Elisabeth Charlotte de, Princesse Palatine, Duchesse d'Orléans, *Correspondance*, trans. G. Brunet (Charpentier, 1857, 2 vols).

Bavière, Elisabeth Charlotte de, Princesse Palatine, Duchesse d'Orléans, *Lettres Nouvelles Inédites de la Princesse Palatine*, ed. A.-A. Rolland (Firmin-Didot, no date).

Bayle, Pierre, *Lettres Choisies* (Rotterdam: Fritsch and Böhm, 1714, 3 vols).

Bossuet, Jacques-Bénigne, *Correspondance*, eds C. Urbain and E. Levesque (Hachette, 1909–25, 15 vols).

Boursault, Edme, *Lettres de Respect, d'Obligation et d'Amour* (Guignard, 1669).

Brégy, Charlotte Saumaise de Chazan, Comtesse de), *Lettres et Poésies* (Leyden: Du Val, 1666).

Bussy, Roger de Rabutin Chantal, Comte de, *Correspondance*, ed. L. Lalanne (Charpentier, 1858–9, 6 vols).

Chapelain, Jean, *Lettres*, ed. P. Tamizey de Larroque (Collection de

Documents Inédits sur l'Histoire de France, 2me Sér., Imprimerie Nationale, 1880–3, 2 vols).

Chevreau, Urbain, *Lettres Nouvelles* (Besongne, 1642).

Colbert, Jean-Baptiste, *Lettres, Instructions et Mémoires*, ed. P. Clément (Imprimerie Impériale, 1861–82, 8 vols).

Condé, Le Grand, and Le Duc d'Enghien, *Lettres Inédites à Marie-Louise de Gonzague, Reine de Pologne, sur la Cour de Louis XIV (1660–67)*, ed. E. Magne (Emile-Paul, 1920).

Conrart, Valentin, letters, eds R. Kerviler and E. de Barthélemy, in *Valentin Conrart, Sa Vie et sa Correspondance*, Appendix Ch. 3 (Librairie Académique, 1881).

Correspondance Administrative sous Louis XIV, ed. G. B. Depping (Imprimerie Nationale, 1850–5, 4 vols).

Correspondance des Contrôleurs Généraux des Finances, ed. A. de Boislisle (Imprimerie Nationale, 1874–97, 3 vols).

Descartes, René, *Correspondance*, eds C. Adam and G. Milhaud (Alcan and PUF, 1936–63, 8 vols).

Dunoyer, Anne Marguerite Petit, *Lettres Historiques et Galantes* (Cologne: Marteau, 1707–18, 7 vols).

Fénelon, François de Salignac de la Mothe-, *Correspondance de Fénelon: Commentaires*, ed. J. Orcibal (Editions Klincksieck, 1972–6, 5 vols).

Fénelon, François de Salignac de la Mothe-, *Lettres Spirituelles*, ed. Silvestre de Sacy (Techener, 1856, 3 vols).

Ferrand, Anne de Bellinzani, Présidente, *Une Lettre de la Présidente Ferrand sur Mme Dacier*, ed. P.B., in *RHL* (1906).

Fontenelle, Bernard Le Bovier de, 'Lettres Galantes', in *Œuvres* (Saillant et al., 1767, Vol. I).

Henri IV, *Lettres Missives*, ed. J. Berger de Xivrey (Imprimerie Impériale, 1843–58, 7 vols).

Huxelles, Marie Le Bailleul, Marquise d', letters, ed. E. de Barthélemy, in *La Marquise d'Huxelles et ses amis* (Firmin-Didot, 1881).

La Bruyère, Jean de, letters, in *Œuvres*, ed. G. Servois (GEF, Hachette, 1865, Vol. II).

Lafayette, Marie-Madeleine de la Vergne, Comtesse de, *Lettres de la Comtesse de La Fayette et de Gilles Ménage*, ed. H. Ashton (Liverpool UP, 1924).

Lafayette, Marie-Madeleine de la Vergne, Comtesse de, *Correspondance éditée d'après les travaux d'A. Beaunier* (Gallimard, 1942, 2 vols).

La Fontaine, Jean de, letters, in *Œuvres*, ed. H. Régnier (GEF, Hachette, 1883–92, Vol. IX).

La Rochefoucauld, François VI, Duc de, letters, in *Œuvres*, eds J. Gourdaut and D. L. Gilbert (GEF, Hachette, 1868–83, Vol. III, 1re Partie).

La Serre, Puget de, *Le Secrétaire de la Cour* (Billaine, 1624).

Le Maistre de Sacy, Louis-Isaac, *Choix de Lettres Inédites (1650–83)*, ed. G. Delassault (Nizet, 1959).

Maintenon, Françoise d'Aubigné, Marquise de, *Lettres*, ed. M. Langlois (Letouzey and Ané, 1935–9, 4 vols).

Maintenon, Françoise d'Aubigné, Marquise de, *Lettres et Entretiens sur l'Education des Filles*, ed. T. Lavallée (Charpentier, 1861, 2 vols).

Maintenon, Françoise d'Aubigné, Marquise de, *Lettres Inédites de Mme de Maintenon et de Mme la Princesse des Ursins* (Bossange, 1826, 3 vols).

Malherbe, François de, letters in *Œuvres*, ed. L. Lalanne (GEF, Hachette, 1862–9, Vols III and IV).

Maucroix, François de, *Lettres*, ed. R. Kohn (PUF, 1962).

Maure, Anne Doni d'Attichy, Comtesse de, letters, in *Mme la Comtesse de Maure, sa vie et sa correspondance*, ed. E. de Barthélemy (Gay, 1863).

Maynard, François de, Président, *Lettres* (Quinet, 1652).

Mazarin, (Giulio Mazarini), *Lettres du Cardinal Mazarin pendant son ministère*, eds A. Chéruel and Vicomte G. d'Avenel (Imprimerie Nationale, 1872–1906, 9 vols).

Mazarin, (Giulio Mazarini), *Lettres du Cardinal Mazarin à la Reine, à la Princesse Palatine, etc.*, ed. J. Ravenel (SHF, 1836).

Méré, Antoine Gombaud, Chevalier de, letters, in *Œuvres*, Vol. II (Amsterdam: Mortier, 1692, 2 vols).

Montespan, Françoise-Athénaïs de Rochechouart de Mortemart, Marquise de, letters, in P. Clément, *Mme de Montespan et Louis XIV*, 2me edn Appendix A (Didier, 1868).

Ninon de Lenclos, *Correspondance Authentique*, ed. E. Colombey (Dentu, 1886).

Parthenay, Catherine de, Dame de Rohan-Soubise, 'Lettres de Catherine de Parthenay . . . et de ses deux filles Henriette et Anne à Charlotte-Brabantine de Nassau, Duchesse de la Trémoïlle', ed. H. Imbert, in *Mémoires de la Société de Statistique des Deux-Sèvres*, Vol. XII (Niort, 1874).

Pasquier, Nicolas, 'Lettres', in *Œuvres d'Etienne Pasquier*, Vol. II (Amsterdam, 1723).

Patin, Gui, *Lettres*, ed. J.-H. Reveillé-Parise (Baillière, 1846, 3 vols).

Peiresc, Nicolas-Claude Fabri de, *Lettres*, ed. P. Tamizey de Larroque (Imprimerie Nationale, 1888–98, 7 vols).

Pellisson-Fontanier, Paul, *Lettres Historiques* (Nyon, 1729, 3 vols).

Pomponne, Simon Arnauld, Marquis de, letters, in *Mémoires de M. de Coulanges*, ed. M. Monmerqué (1820).

Racan, Honorat de Bueil, Marquis de, letters, in *Œuvres*, ed. Tenant de Latour, Vol. I, (Jannet, 1857, 2 vols).

Racine, Jean, letters, in *Œuvres*, ed. P. Mesnard, Vols VI and VII (GEF, Hachette, 1888–1912, 8 vols).

Richelieu, Armand-Jean du Plessis de, Cardinal, *Lettres, Instructions Diplomatiques et Papiers d'Etat*, ed. Vicomte G. d'Avenel (Imprimerie Impériale, 1853–74, 7 vols).

Rochechouart de Mortemart, Gabrielle de, Abbesse, letters, in P. Clément, *Une Abbesse de Fontevrault au XVIIe Siècle* (Didier, 1869).

Sablé, Madeleine de Souvré, Marquise de, *Les Amis de la Marquise de Sablé: Recueil de Lettres des principaux habitués de son salon*, ed. E. de Barthélemy (Dentu, 1865).

Sablière, Marguerite Hessein, Mme de la, letters, in Vicomte S. Menjot-d'Elbenne, *Mme de la Sablière* (Plon, 1923).

Saint-Evremond, Charles de Marguetel de Saint-Denis de, *Lettres*, ed. R. Ternois (SFTM, 1967–8, 2 vols).

Saint-Maurice, Thomas François Chabod, Marquis de, *Lettres sur la Cour de Louis XIV, 1667–70, 1671–3,* ed. J. Lemoine (Calmann-Lévy, 1910, 1912, 2 vols).

Saintot, Marguerite Vion, Mme de, *Correspondance,* ed. P. d'Estrée (RHL, 1894).

Sales, François de, Saint, *Lettres* (Garnier, no date).

Scudéry, Madeleine de, letters, in *Mlle de Scudéry, Sa Vie et sa Correspondance,* eds E. Rathery and Boutron (Techener, 1873).

Scudéry, Madeleine de, letters, in *Documents Inédits sur la Société et la Littérature Précieuses,* ed. L. Belmont (RHL, 1902).

Séguier, Pierre, *Lettres et Mémoires adressés au Chancelier Séguier,* ed. R. Mousnier (PUF, 1964, 2 vols).

Sévigné, Marie de Rabutin Chantal, Marquise de, *Lettres,* ed. M. Monmerqué (GEF, Hachette, 1862–1925, 14 vols).

Sévigné, Renaud de, Chevalier, *Correspondance du Chevalier de Sévigné et de Christine de France,* eds J. Lemoine and F. Saulnier (SHF, 1911).

Sorbière, Samuel de, *Lettres et Discours* (Clousier, 1660).

Villars, Marie de, *Lettres* (Lambert, 1759).

Vincent de Paul, Saint, *Correspondance, Entretiens, Documents,* ed. P. Coste (Lecoffre, 1920–5, 14 vols).

Vuillart, Germain, *Lettres de G. Vuillart, Ami de Port-Royal, à Louis de Préfontaine (1694–1700),* ed. R. Clark (Geneva: Droz, and Lille: Giard, 1951).

K Biographies and panegyrics

Abelli, Louis, *La Vie du Vénérable Serviteur de Dieu, Vincent de Paul* (Lambert, 1664, 3 vols).

Baillet, Adrien, *Vie de Monsieur Descartes* (Horthemels, 1691, 2 vols).

Blémur, Jacqueline de Bouette de, *Eloges de plusieurs personnes illustres en piété de l'Ordre de St Benoît* (Billaine, 1679, 2 vols).

Boileau, Jean-Jacques, Abbé, *Vie de Mme la Duchesse de Liancourt, avec le règlement qu'elle donna à sa petite-fille* (Cretté, 1814).

Bossuet, Jacques-Bénigne, *Oraisons Funèbres,* ed. A. Rébelliau, 16me edn (Hachette, 1931).

Bourgoin de Villefore, J., *Vie de Madame la Duchesse de Longueville* (1738).

Chaugy, Françoise-Madeleine de, *Ste Jeanne Françoise Frémyot de Chantal, Sa Vie et ses Œuvres* (Plon, 1874–8, 8 vols). (*Vie* in Vol. I.)

Coste, Hilarion de, *Les Eloges et les Vies des Reines, des Princesses, et des Dames illustres en piété, en courage, et en doctrine* (Cramoisy, 1647).

Douxménil, *Mémoires et Lettres pour servir à l'histoire de la vie de Ninon* (Rotterdam, 1752).

Félibien, André, *Entretiens sur les vies et sur les ouvrages des plus excellents peintres anciens et modernes* (Hants: Gregg Press Ltd reprint, 1967).

Fleury, Claude, *La Vie de la Vénérable Mère Marguerite d'Arbouze* (Veuve Gervais Clouzier, 1684).

Fontenelle, Bernard Le Bovier de, *Eloges des Académiciens morts depuis l'an 1699,* in *Œuvres,* Vol. V (Saillant et al., 1767).

Grimarest, Jean Léonor Le Gallois de, *Vie de Molière* (Renaissance du Livre, 1930).

Le Cat, Claude-Nicolas, *Eloge de Fontenelle* (Rouen, 1759).

Le Dieu, François, Abbé, *Mémoires et Journal sur la vie et les ouvrages de Bossuet*, ed. Abbé Guettée (Didier, 1856–7, 4 vols).

Mémoires Inédits sur la vie et les ouvrages des membres de l'Académie Royale de Peinture et de Sculpture, eds L. Dussieux et al. (Dumoulin, 1854, 2 vols).

Nicéron, Jean-Pierre, *Mémoires pour servir à l'histoire des hommes illustres* (Briasson, 1729–45, 43 vols).

Orléans, Antoinette d', Marquise de Belle-Isle, *Vie de la Mère Antoinette d'Orléans*, ed. Abbé Petit (Haton, 1880).

Pellisson-Fontanier, Paul, and D'Olivet, P.-J., Abbé, *Histoire de l'Académie Française*, ed. C. Livet (Didier, 1858, 2 vols).

Perrault, Charles, *Les Hommes Illustres qui ont paru en France pendant ce siècle* (Dezallier, 1696, 2 vols).

Racine, Louis, *Mémoires sur la Vie de Jean Racine*, in the latter's *Œuvres* (Editions du Seuil, 1962).

Restif de la Bretonne, Nicolas, *La Vie de Mon Père* (Editions du Trianon, 1931).

Titon du Tillet, Evrard, *Le Parnasse Français* (Coignard, 1732).

Vallot, Antoine, *Journal de la Santé du Roi Louis XIV*, ed. J.-A. Le Roi (Durand, 1862).

L Gazettes and periodicals

Donneau de Visé, Jean, *Le Mercure Galant*, 1672 et seq.

Le Journal de [François] Colletet, Premier Petit Journal Parisien, ed. A. Heulhard (Le Moniteur du Bibliophile, 1878).

Loret, Jean, *La Muse Historique*, eds J. Ravenel and V. de la Pelouze (Jannet, 1857–78, 4 vols).

Lettres en Vers de la Gravette de Mayolas, Robinet, Boursault, Perdou de Subligny, Laurent et autres, ed. Baron J. de Rothschild (Morgand et Fatout, 1881–99, 3 vols).

Sallo, Denis de et al., *Le Journal des Savants*, 1665 et seq.

M Philosophy and science

Anon, *Voyage du Monde de Descartes* (Veuve Simon Bénard, 1691).

Bayle, Pierre, *Pensées sur la Comète*, ed. A. Prat (STFM, 1911–12, 2 vols).

Boccone, Paulo, *Avis aux Personnes d'Esprit et aux Curieux* (c. 1670; British Library, shelf-mark 444.i.12.[4]).

De Bougainville, *L'Anti-Lucrèce, poème sur la religion naturelle, composé par M. le Cardinal de Polignac, traduit par M. de Bougainville, de l'Académie Royale des Belles-Lettres* (Guérin, 1749).

Fontenelle, Bernard Le Bovier de, *Entretiens sur la Pluralité des Mondes*, ed. A. Calame (STFM, 1966).

L'Isle André, Yves M., *Le Père André, Jésuite: Documents pour servir à l'histoire philosophique, religieuse, et littéraire du 18e siècle*, eds A. Charma and G. Mancel (Hachette, 1856, 1857, 2 vols).

Malebranche, Nicolas de, *Œuvres Complètes* (Bibliothèque des Textes Philosophiques, Vrin, 1962–70, 20 vols and Index). [Vols I–III contain *De la Recherche de la Vérité*, ed. G. Rodis-Lewis; Vol. XI contains the *Traité de Morale*, ed. M. Adam; Vol. XX, *Documents Biographiques et Bibliographiques*, ed. A. Robinet.]

Meurdrac, Marie, *La Chimie charitable et facile en faveur des dames*, 3me edn (Houry, 1687).

Rohault, Jacques, *Œuvres Posthumes* (Hague: Van Bulderen, 1690, 2 vols).

Saint-Martin, *Les Causes et les Admirables Effets des Météores, ou Diverses Impressions de l'Air* (British Library, Additional Manuscript 15, 912).

N   Medicine, obstetrics and child welfare

Bourgeoise, Louise, *Observations Diverses, sur la stérilité, perte de fruit, fécondité, accouchements, et maladies des femmes, et enfants nouveaux-nés* (Saugrain, 1617).

De Rostagny, *Traité de Primerose sur les erreurs vulgaires de la Médecine* (Lyon: Certe, 1689).

Devaux, J., *Le Médecin de Soi-Même*, 2me edn (Leyden, 1687).

Du Tertre, Marguerite, *Instruction Familière et Utile aux Sages-Femmes pour bien pratiquer les accouchements* (d'Houry, 1710).

Duverney, Guichard Joseph, *Œuvres Anatomiques* (Jombert, 1761, 2 vols).

Guillemeau, Jacques, *De la Grossesse et Accouchement des Femmes* (Pacard, 1620).

Le Roy, Guillaume, *Du Devoir des Mères avant et après la naissance de leurs enfants* (Desprez, 1675).

Mauriceau, François, *Observations sur la grossesse et l'accouchement des femmes* (Chez l'Auteur, 1695).

Mauriceau, François, *Traité des maladies des femmes grosses*, 3me edn (Chez l'Auteur, 1681).

Peu, Philippe, *Pratique des Accouchements* (Boudot, 1694).

Saint-Germain, Charles de, *L'Ecole Méthodique et Parfaite des Sages-Femmes, ou l'Art de l'Accouchement* (Clousier, 1650).

Sainte-Marthe, Abel de, *La Manière de Nourrir les Enfants à la Mamelle* (De Luyne et al., 1698).

O   Moral, educational, feminist and anti-feminist works

Anon., *Les Caquets de l'Accouchée*, ed. E. Fournier (Jannet, 1855).

Anon., *Les Quinze Joies de Mariage*, ed. J. Rychner (Textes Littéraires Français, 1963).

Amyraut, Moyse, *Discours de l'Etat des Fidèles après la Mort* (Saumur: Lesnier, 1646).

Aubignac, François Hédelin, Abbé d', *Les Conseils d'Ariste à Célimène sur les moyens de conserver sa réputation* (Hague: Arondeus, 1687).

Aubignac, François Hédelin, Abbé d', *Histoire du Temps ou Relation du Royaume de Coquetterie* (De Sercy, 1654).

Aubigné, Agrippa d', *Œuvres* (Bibliothèque de la Pléiade, Gallimard, 1969).

Audiger, *La Maison Réglée* (Amsterdam: Marret, 1700).

Bary, René, *La Fine Philosophie accommodée à l'intelligence des dames* (Piget et Chez l'Auteur, 1660).

Boileau, Jacques, *De l'Abus des Nudités de Gorge* (Brussels: Foppens, 1675).

Bouvignes, Louis de, *Le Miroir de la Vanité des Femmes Mondaines*, 2me edn (Namur: La Fabrique, 1684).

Calvin, Jean, *Institution de la Religion Chrétienne*, ed. J.-D. Benoît (Vrin, 1957–63, 5 vols).

Caussin, Nicolas, *La Cour Sainte* (Sonnius et Bechet, 1645, 6 vols).

Charron,Pierre, *De la Sagesse*, ed. A. Duval (Rapilly, 1827, 3 vols).

Courtin, Antoine de, *Nouveau Traité de la Civilité qui se pratique en France parmi les honnêtes gens* (Amsterdam: Le Jeune, 1672).

Courtin, Antoine de, *Traité de la Jalousie ou moyens d'entretenir la paix dans le mariage* (Josset, 1685).

Courtin, Antoine de, *Traité de la Paresse ou l'art de bien employer le temps en toute sorte de conditions* (Josset, 1677).

Couvay, Louis, *L'Honnête Maîtresse* (De Luyne, 1654).

Drelincourt, Charles, *Les Consolations de l'Ame Fidèle contre les frayeurs de la mort* (Dernière edn de celles qui ont été revues et corrigées par l'auteur, Geneva: Chouet, 1686).

Du Bosc, Jacques, *La Femme Héroïque* (Sommaville et Courbé, 1645, 2 vols).

Du Bosc, Jacques, *L'Honnête Femme* (Lyon: Grégoire, 1665).

Faret, Nicolas, *L'Honnête Homme ou l'Art de Plaire à la Cour*, ed. M. Magendie (Geneva: Slatkine Reprints, 1970).

Fénelon, François de Salignac de la Mothe-, *Traité de l'Education des Filles*, ed. P. Rousselot, 3me edn (Delagrave, 1864).

Fléchier, Esprit, *Œuvres Complètes*, ed. A.-V. Fabre de Narbonne (Boiste et al., 1828, 10 vols).

Fleury, Claude, *Les Devoirs des Maîtres et des Domestiques* (Amsterdam: Mortier, 1688).

Forest, Geneviève, *Le Fantôme du Sage* (L'Espicier, 1682).

Gérard, Abbé de, *La Philosophie des Gens de Cour*, 3me edn (Loyson, 1685).

Gobinet, Charles, *La Civilité qui se pratique en France parmi les honnêtes gens, pour l'éducation de la jeunesse* (Orléans: Le Gall, 1772).

Gournay, Marie Le Jars de, *Avis ou Présents*, 3me edn (Du Bray, 1641).

Gournay, Marie Le Jars de, 'L'Egalité des Hommes et des Femmes', ed. M. Schiff, in *La Fille d'Alliance de Montaigne – Marie de Gournay* (Champion, 1910).

Gournay, Marie Le Jars de, *Œuvres* (Libert, 1626).

Goussault, Jacques, *Le Portrait d'une Femme Honnête, Raisonnable, et Véritablement Chrétienne* (Brunet, 1694).

Grenaille, François de, *L'Honnête Fille* (Sommaville et Quinet, 1640).

Grenaille, François de, *L'Honnête Mariage* (Sommaville et Quinet, 1640).

Grenaille, François de, *L'Honnête Veuve* (Sommaville, 1640).

Grenaille, François de, *Les Plaisirs ou les Honnêtes Divertissements des Dames* (Clousier, 1647).

Guyon, Jeanne-Marie Bouvier de la Motte, Mme, 'Instruction Chrétienne d'une mère à sa fille', in *Opuscules Spirituels*, Vol. II (1790).

J.D.D.C., *Les Agréments et les Chagrins du mariage* (Hague: Van Ellinkhuysen, 1692).

Joly, Claude, *Les Deux Livres de l'Etat du Mariage par François Barbaro, Traduction Nouvelle* (De Luyne, 1667).

Joly, Claude, *Traité Historique des Ecoles Episcopales et Ecclésiastiques* (Muguet, 1678).

Juvernay, Pierre, *Discours Particulier contre les Femmes Débraillées de ce temps* (Geneva: Gay reprint of 1637 edn, 1867).

La Bruyère, Jean de, *Les Caractères*, ed. R. Garapon (Garnier, 1962).

La Chétardie, Joachim Trotti de, Chevalier, *Instruction pour une Jeune Princesse* (Amsterdam, 1754).

La Hoguette, Fortin de, *Testament ou Conseils Fidèles d'un Bon Père à ses Enfants* (Vitré, 1653).

La Rochefoucauld, François VI, Duc de, *Maximes*, ed. J. Truchet (Garnier, 1967).

Le Moyne, Pierre, *La Galerie des Femmes Fortes* (Sommaville, 1647).

Lesclache, Louis de, *Les avantages que les femmes peuvent recevoir de la philosophie et principalement de la morale, ou l'Abrégé de cette science* (Chez l'Auteur et Rondet, 1667).

Machon, Louis, *Discours ou Sermon Apologétique en faveur des Femmes* (Blaise, 1641).

Mainville, *Du Bonheur et du Malheur du Mariage* (Veuve Sébastien Hure, 1683).

Méré, Antoine Gombaud, Chevalier de, *Œuvres Complètes*, ed. C. Boudhors (Les Belles Lettres, 1930, 3 vols).

Montaigne, Michel de, *Essais*, ed. M. Rat. (Garnier, 1962, 3 vols).

Nicole, Pierre, *Essais de Morale* (Desprez, 1755, 6 vols).

Noel, C. M. D., *Les Avantages du Sexe ou Le Triomphe des Femmes* (Antwerp: Sleghers, 1698).

Olivier, Jacques, *Alphabet de l'Imperfection et Malice des Femmes* (Petit-Pas, 1617).

Paccori, Ambroise, *Avis Salutaires à une mère chrétienne pour se sanctifier dans l'éducation de ses enfants*, 4ᵐᵉ edn (Orléans: Rouzeau, 1691).

Perrault, Charles, *L'Apologie des Femmes* (Amsterdam: Braakman, 1694).

Philalèthe, Timothée, *De la Modestie des Femmes et des Filles Chrétiennes dans leurs habits et dans tout leur extérieur* (Lyon: Plaignard, 1686).

Pic, Jean, *Discours sur la Bienséance* (Veuve de Sébastien Mabre-Cramoisy, 1688).

Poulain de la Barre, *De l'Education des Dames pour la conduite de l'esprit dans les sciences et dans les moeurs* (Dezallier, 1679).

Poulain de la Barre, *De l'Egalité des Deux Sexes* (Du Puis, 1673).

Poulain de la Barre, *De l'Excellence des Hommes contre l'Egalité des Sexes* (Du Puis, 1690).

Pringy, Mme de, *Les Différents Caractères des Femmes du Siècle*, 2ᵐᵉ edn (Brunet, 1699).

Richelieu, Armand-Jean du Plessis de, Cardinal, *Instruction du Chrétien* (Imprimerie Nationale, 1944).

Sablé, Madeleine de Souvré, Marquise de, *Maximes et Pensées Diverses* (Mabre-Cramoisy, 1678).

Saint-Evremond, Charles de Marguetel de Saint-Denis de, *Œuvres en Prose*, ed. R. Ternois (STFM, 1962, 4 vols).

Saint-Gabriel, *Le Mérite des Dames* (Le Gras, 1660).

Sales, François de, Saint, *Introduction à la Vie Dévote*, ed. C. Florisoone (Les Belles Lettres, 1961, 2 vols).

Scudéry, Georges de, *Les Femmes Illustres* (Courbé, 1654–55, 2 vols).

Sonnet, Martin, *Statuts et Règlements des Petites Ecoles de Grammaire de la Ville, Cité, Université, Faubourgs et Banlieue de Paris* (1672).

Soucy, François du, *Le Triomphe des Dames* (Chez l'Auteur, 1646).

Thiers, Jean-Baptiste, *Traité des Superstitions qui regardent tous les sacrements* (Nully, 1704, 4 vols).

Varet, Alexandre, *De l'Education Chrétienne des Enfants* (Brussels: Foppens, 1669).

Vassetz, De, *De l'Obligation que les pères et mères ont d'instruire eux-mêmes leurs enfants* (Coignard, 1695).

Venette, Nicolas, *Tableau de l'Amour considéré dans l'état du mariage*, 'Parme; Chez Franc d'Amour' (1688).

Vertron, Guyonnet de, *La Nouvelle Pandore ou Les Femmes Illustres du Siècle de Louis le Grand* (Veuve C. Mazuel, 1698, 2 vols).

Vigoureux, *La Défense des Femmes contre l'Alphabet* (Chevalier, 1617).

P Literary and linguistic treatises; criticism

Aubignac, François Hédelin, Abbé d', *Seconde Dissertation concernant le Poème Dramatique en forme de remarques sur la tragédie de M. Corneille intitulée Sertorius* (Du Breuil, 1663).

Boileau-Despréaux, Nicolas, *Dialogues, Réflexions Critiques, Oeuvres Diverses*, ed. C. Boudhors (Les Belles Lettres, 1960).

Bouhours, Dominique, Père, *Entretiens d'Ariste et d'Eugène*, ed. R. Radouant (Bossard, 1920).

Buffet, Marguerite, *Nouvelles Observations sur la Langue Française* (Cusson, 1668).

Chapelain, Jean, *Opuscules Critiques*, ed. A. Hunter (Droz, 1936).

Dacier, Anne Le Fèvre, Mme, *Des Causes de la Corruption du Goût* (Rigaud, 1714).

Gournay, Marie le Jars de, *Les Idées Littéraires*, ed. A. Uildriks (Groningen, 1962).

Huet, Pierre Daniel, *Traité de l'Origine des Romans*, published with 'Segrais's' *Zaïde* (1671).

Le Verrier, Pierre, *Les Satires de Boileau commentées par lui-même*, ed. F. Lachèvre (Le Vésinet, 1906).

Ménage, Gilles, *Anti-Baillet ou Critique du livre de M' Baillet intitulé Jugements des Savants* (The Hague: Foulque and L. Van Dole, 1688 (Vol. I) and L. and H. Van Dole, 1690 (Vol. II)).

Sorel, Charles, *De la Connoissance des Bons Livres*, ed. H. Béchade (Geneva: Slatkine, 1981).

Vaugelas, Claude Favre de, *Remarques sur la Langue Française*, ed. J. Streicher (STFM, 1934).

Q Novels, short stories, romanticised memoirs

Assoucy, Charles d', *Aventures Burlesques*, ed. E. Colombey (1858).

Aubignac, François Hédelin, Abbé d', *Macarise ou La Reine des Iles Fortunées, Histoire Allégorique* (Dubreuil, 1664).

Aulnoy, Marie-Catherine Le Jumel de Berneville, Comtesse d', *Mémoires de la Cour d'Espagne*, 2me edn (The Hague: Moetjens, 1692).

Camus, Jean-Pierre, *Flaminio et Colman* (Lyon: Chard, 1626).

Claireville, O. S. de, *Le Gascon Extravagant: Histoire Comique*, ed. F. Robello, (Abano Terme: Piovan, 1984).

Courcelles, Marie-Sidonia de Lenoncourt, Marquise de, *Mémoires*, ed. P. Pougin (Jannet, 1855).

Courtilz de Sandras, Gatien, *Annales de la Cour et de Paris pour les années 1697 et 1698* (Cologne: Marteau, 1701).

Donneau de Visé, Jean, *Nouvelles nouvelles* (Ribou, 1663).

Durand, Catherine, *Œuvres* (Prault, 1737, 6 vols).

Ferrand, Anne de Bellinzani, Présidente, 'Histoire des Amours de Cléante et de Bélise', in *Lettres de la Présidente Ferrand au Baron de Breteuil*, ed. E. Asse (Charpentier, 1880).

Forest, Geneviève, *L'Histoire de la Philosophie des Héros, Nouveau Roman ou Philosophie Nouvelle* (L'Espicier, 1681).

Furetière, Antoine, *Le Roman Bourgeois*, ed. P. Jannet (Picard, 1868, 2 vols).

La Calprenède, Gautier de Costes de, *Cassandre* (Courbé, 1653–4, 5 vols).

La Calprenède, Gautier de Costes de, *Cléopâtre* (Sommaville et De Luyne, 1647–63, 12 parts).

Lafayette, Marie-Madeleine de la Vergne, Comtesse de, *Romans et Nouvelles*, ed. E. Magne (Garnier, 1961).

La Fontaine, Jean de, *Contes*, in *Œuvres*, ed. H. Régnier, Vols IV, V, VI (GEF, Hachette, 1883–92).

La Force, Charlotte Rose de Caumont, Demoiselle de, *Les Jeux d'Esprit*, ed. Marquis de la Grange (1862).

Lannel, Jean de, *Le Roman Satirique* (Du Bray, 1624).

La Roche-Guilhen, Mlle de, *Histoire des Favorites* ('Imprimé à Constantinople cette année présente', no date).

L'Héritier de Villandon, Marie-Jeanne, *Les Bigarrures Ingénieuses* (Guignard, 1696).

L'Héritier de Villandon, Marie-Jeanne, *L'Erudition Enjouée* (Ribou, 1703).

L'Héritier de Villandon, Marie-Jeanne, *La Tour Ténébreuse* (Amsterdam: Des Bordes, 1706).

Mazarin, Hortense Mancini, Duchesse, *Mémoires* (Cologne: Du Marteau, 1675).

Murat, Henriette-Julie de Castelnau, Comtesse de, *La Défense des Dames, ou Les Mémoires de Mme la Comtesse de **** (no place, no publisher, 1740).

Murat, Henriette-Julie de Castelnau, Comtesse de, 'Les Lutins du Château de Kernosy', in *Voyages Imaginaires, Songes, Visions et Romans Cabalistiques*, Vol. XXXV (Amsterdam, 1789).

Murat, Henriette-Julie de Castelnau, Comtesse de, *Nouveaux Contes des Fées* (Barbin, 1698).

Murat, Henriette-Julie de Castelnau, Comtesse de, *Le Voyage de Campagne* (Veuve Claude Barbin, 1699, 2 vols).

Pure, Michel de, *La Prétieuse*, ed. E. Magne (Droz, 1938, 2 vols).

Scarron, Paul, 'La Précaution Inutile', in *Œuvres*, Vol. III (Amsterdam: Wetstein, 1752, 7 vols).

Scarron, Paul, *Le Roman Comique*, ed. M. Simon (Garnier, 1973).

Scudéry, Madeleine de, *Artamène ou Le Grand Cyrus*, 2me edn (Courbé, 1650–5 [sic], 10 vols).

Scudéry, Madeleine de, *Clélie, Histoire Romaine* (Courbé, 1658–62 [sic], 10 parts).

Segrais, Jean Regnauld de, *Les Nouvelles Françaises ou Divertissements de la Princesse Aurélie* (Huart, 1722, 2 vols).

Sorel, Charles, *Le Berger Extravagant* (Rouen, 1640, 3 vols).

Sorel, Charles, *Histoire Comique de Francion*, ed. E. Roy (STFM, Hachette, 1924–31, 4 vols).

Sorel, Charles, *Polyandre, Histoire Comique* (Courbé, 1648, 2 vols).

Tristan l'Hermite, François, *Le Page Disgracié*, ed. A. Dietrich (Bibliothèque Elzévirienne, 1898).

Urfé, Honoré d', *L'Astrée*, ed. H. Vaganay (Lyon: Masson, 1925, 5 vols).

Villedieu, Hortense Desjardins, Mme de, *Les Annales Galantes* (The Hague: Van Dole, 1700).

Villedieu, Hortense Desjardins, Mme de, *Les Aventures ou Mémoires de la Vie de Henriette Sylvie de Molière* (Barbin, 1674, 6 parts).

Villedieu, Hortense Desjardins, Mme de, *Les Désordres de l'Amour* (Lyon: Guerrier, 1697).

Villedieu, Hortense Desjardins, Mme de, *Portrait des Faiblesses Humaines* (Barbin, 1685).

R   Poetry, satire, chansons

Angot de l'Eperonnière, *Les Exercices de ce Temps*, ed. F. Lachèvre (STFM, 1924).

Benserade, Isaac de, *Œuvres* (De Sercy, 1697, 2 vols).

Boileau-Despréaux, Nicolas, *Œuvres*, ed. G. Mongrédien (Garnier, 1961).

Boisrobert, François Le Metel de, Abbé, *Epîtres en Vers*, ed. M. Cauchie (STFM, 1921–7, 2 vols).

Bouhours, Dominique, Père, *Recueil de Vers Choisis* (Josse, 1693).

Bussy, Roger de Rabutin Chantal, Comte de, *Histoire Amoureuse des Gaules* (Garnier, [1868], 2 vols).

Cabinet Satirique, Le (Billaine, 1618).

Chapelle, Claude Emmanuel Luillier, and Bachaumont, François Le Coigneux, Sieur de, *Œuvres*, ed. Tenant de Latour (Jannet, 1854).

Chaulieu, Guillaume Amfrye, Abbé de, *Œuvres*, ed. Saint Marc (David et al., 1757, 2 vols).

Colletet, Guillaume, *La Muse Coquette* (Loyson, 1665).

Cotin, Charles, Abbé, *Œuvres Mêlées* (Sommaville, 1659).

Coulanges, Philippe Emmanuel de, *Chansons Choisies* (Valleyre et Cailleau, 1754).

Courval Sonnet, *Œuvres Poétiques*, ed. P. Blanchemain (Librairie des Bibliophiles, 1876, 3 vols).

Deschamps, Eustache, *Le Miroir de Mariage*, in *Œuvres Complètes*, ed. G. Raynaud, Vol. IX (Société des Anciens Textes Français, Firmin Didot, 1894).

Deshoulières, Antoinette du Ligier de la Garde, Mme, *Poésies* (Brussels: Foppens, 1708, 2 vols).

Dufresny, Charles, *Amusements Sérieux et Comiques*, ed. J. Vic (Collection des Chefs-d'œuvre Méconnus, Bossard, 1921).

Dulorens, Jacques, *Premières Satires*, ed. D. Jouast (Librairie des Bibliophiles, 1876).

Dulorens, Jacques, *Satires* (Sommaville, 1646).

Garaby de la Luzerne, *Satires Inédites*, ed. E. de Beaurepaire (Rouen: Société Rouennaise de Bibliophiles, 1888).

Guéret, Gabriel, *Le Parnasse Réformé*, Nouvelle édn, reveue, corrigée et augmentée (Jolly, 1671).

La Journée des Madrigaux, ed. E. Colombey (Aubry, 1856).

La Fontaine, Jean de, *Fables*, ed. P. Clarac (Livre de Poche, 1972).

La Fontaine, Jean de, *Œuvres Posthumes*, ed. Mme Ulrich (De Luyne, 1696).

La Guirlande de Julie, ed. O. Uzanne (Librairie des Bibliophiles, 1875).

La Mesnardière, J. H. Pilet de, *Poésies* (Sommaville, 1656).

La Suze, Henriette de Coligny, Comtesse de, and Pellisson-Fontanier, Paul, *Recueil de Pièces Galantes en Prose et en Vers* (Trévoux, 1748, 5 vols).

Le Pays, René, *Amitiés, Amours et Amourettes* (Amsterdam: Zetter, 1665).

Le Pays, René, *Nouvelles Œuvres*, ed. A. de Bersaucourt (Collection des Chefs-d'Œuvre Méconnus, 1925).

Pavillon, Etienne, *Œuvres*, (The Hague: Du Sauzet, 1715).

Perrin, Pierre, *Œuvres de Poésie* (Loyson, 1661).

Petit, Louis, *Satires Générales*, ed. O. de Gourcuff (Librairie des Bibliophiles, 1883).

Recueil de Maurepas (Leyden, 1865, 6 vols).

Régnier, Mathurin, *Œuvres Complètes*, ed. G. Raibaud (STFM, 1958).

Saint-Amant, Marc-Antoine Girard de, *Œuvres*, eds J. Bailbé and J. Lagny (STFM, 1971, 4 vols).

Sarasin, François, *Œuvres*, ed. Gilles Ménage (Billaine, 1663).

Sarasin, François, *Poésies*, ed. O. Uzanne (Librairie des Bibliophiles, 1877).

Scarron, Paul, *Poésies Diverses*, ed. M. Cauchie (STFM, 1947–61, 2 vols).

Tristan l'Hermite, François, *Les Amours et Autres Poésies Choisies*, ed. P. Camo (Garnier, 1925).

Vergier, Jacques, *Œuvres* (Lausanne: Briaconnet, 1752, 2 vols).

Voiture, Vincent, *Œuvres*, ed. A. Ubicini (Charpentier, 1855, 2 vols).

Voltaire, (François Marie Arouet), *La Mort de Mlle Lecouvreur*, in *Œuvres Complètes*, Vol. IX (Garnier, 1877).

S Theatre and ballet

Aubignac, François Hédelin, Abbé d', *La Pratique du Théâtre*, ed. P. Martino (Algiers: Carbonel, 1927).

Aubignac, François Hédelin, Abbé d', *Zénobie* (Sommaville, 1647).

Auvray, Jean, *La Dorinde* (Sommaville et Soubron, 1631).

Auvray, Jean, *La Madonte* (Sommaville, 1631).

Baro, Balthasar, *La Clorise* (Sommaville, 1634).

Beauchamps, Pierre-François Godard de, *Recherches sur les Théâtres de France* (Prault, 1735, 3 vols).

Boisrobert, François Le Metel de, *Les Trois Orontes* (Courbé, 1653).

Bossuet, Jacques-Bénigne, *Maximes et Réflexions sur la Comédie*, in *Œuvres Complètes*, Vol. XI (Lefèvre, 1836, 12 vols).

Boursault, Edme, *Le Mercure Galant ou La Comédie sans Titre* (Brussels: Guillain, no date).

Boursault, Edme, *Les Mots à la Mode*, in Vol. I of Fournel, *Petites Comédies Rares* (see below).

Brécourt, Guillaume Marcoureau de, *La Noce de Village* (Girard, 1666).

Brueys, David Augustin de, *Œuvres de Théâtre de Mssrs de Brueys et de Palaprat* (Briasson, 1755–6, 5 vols).

Chappuzeau, Samuel, *L'Académie des Femmes*, in Vol. III of Fournel, *Contemporains* (see below).

Chappuzeau, Samuel, *Le Colin-Maillard* (Loyson, 1662).

Chappuzeau, Samuel, *Le Théâtre Français* (Guignard, 1674).

Cinq Auteurs [Boisrobert, P. Corneille, Rotrou, Colletet, L'Estoile], *L'Aveugle de Smyrne* (Courbé, 1638).

Claveret, Jean, *L'Esprit Fort* (Targa, 1637).

Corneille, Pierre, *Théâtre Choisi*, ed. M. Rat (Garnier, no date).

Corneille, Thomas, and Donneau de Visé, Jean, *La Devineresse* (Exeter UP, 1971).

Dancourt, Florent, *Théâtre* (Brussels: Foppens, 1696–8, 3 vols).

Dancourt, Florent, *Théâtre Choisi*, ed. F. Sarcey (Garnier, no date).

Delosme de Montchenay, Jacques, *La Cause des Femmes*, in Vol. II of Gherardi, *Théâtre* (see below).

Desmarets de Saint-Sorlin, Jean, *Mirame* (Le Gras, 1642).

Desmarets de Saint-Sorlin, Jean, *Les Visionnaires*, ed. H. G. Hall (STFM, 1963).

Discret, *Alizon*, in Fournier, *Théâtre Français* (see below).

Donneau de Visé, Jean, *Trois Comédies* [*La Mère Coquette; La Veuve à la Mode; Les Dames Vangées*], ed. P. Mélèse (Droz, 1940).

Dorimon, *La Comédie de la Comédie*, in Vol. I of Fournel, *Petites Comédies Rares* (see below).

Durval, Jean Gilbert, *Agarite* (Targa, 1636).

Du Ryer, Pierre, *Alcimédon* (Sommaville, 1634).

Du Ryer, Pierre, *Argénis et Poliarque* (Bessin, 1630, 1631).

Fatouville, Nolant de, *La Fille Savante*, in Vol. III of Gherardi, *Théâtre* (see below).

Fournel, V., ed., *Les Contemporains de Molière* (Firmin Didot, 1863–75, 3 vols).

Fournel, V., ed., *Petites Comédies Rares et Curieuses du XVIIᵉ Siècle* (Geneva: Slatkine Reprints, 1968, 2 vols).

Fournier, E., ed., *Le Théâtre Français au XVIᵉ et au XVIIᵉ Siècle* (Laplace et al., [1871]).

Gherardi, Evaristo, *Théâtre Italien, ou Le Recueil Général de toutes les comédies et scènes françaises jouées par les Comédiens Italiens du Roi pendant tout le temps qu'ils ont été au service de sa Majesté* (Amsterdam: Braakman, 1701, 6 vols).

Gilbert, Gabriel, *Les Intrigues Amoureuses*, in Vol. II of Fournel, *Contemporains* (see above).

Gougenot, *La Comédie des Comédiens*, in Fournier, *Théâtre* (see above).

Hauteroche, Noel Le Breton, Sieur de, *Crispin Médecin*, in Vol. II of Fournel, *Contemporains* (see above).

La Calprenède, Gautier de Costes de, *La Mort de Mithridate* (Sommaville, 1636).

Lacroix, P., ed., *Ballets et Mascarades de Cour sous Henri IV et Louis XIII (1581–1652)* (Geneva: Gay, 1868–70, 6 vols).

La Forge, Jean de, *Le Cercle des Femmes Savantes* (Loyson, 1663).

La Forge, Jean de, *La Joueuse Dupée*, in Vol. III of Fournel, *Contemporains* (see above).

La Grange, Charles Varlet, *Le Registre*, eds B. E. and G. P. Young (Droz, 1947, 2 vols).

La Tessonerie, Gillet de, *La Comédie de Francion* (Quinet, 1642).

La Serre, Puget de, *Pandoste* (Billaine, 1631).

L'Estoile, Claude de, *L'Intrigue des Filous*, in Fournier, *Théâtre* (see above).

Mairet, Jean de, *Les Galanteries du Duc d'Ossonne*, in Fournier, *Théâtre* (see above).

Mairet, Jean de, *Le Grand et Dernier Soliman* (Courbé, 1639).

Mairet, Jean de, *Silvanire*, ed. R. Otto (Bamberg, 1890).

Mairet, Jean de, *Sylvie*, ed. J. Marsan (STFM, 1932).

Mairet, Jean de, *La Virginie* (Rocolet, 1635).

Mareschal, Antoine, *La Généreuse Allemande* (Rocolet, 1630).

Mareschal, Antoine, *La Soeur Valeureuse* (Sommaville, 1634).

Mareschal, Antoine, *Le Railleur*, in Fournier, *Théâtre* (see above).

Menestrier, Claude-François, *Des Représentations en Musique Anciennes et Modernes* (Geneva: Minkoff Reprint, 1972).

Molière, [Jean-Baptiste Poquelin], *Œuvres Complètes*, ed. R. Jouanny, (Garnier, 1962, 2 vols).

Montfleury, [Antoine Jacob], *Les Bêtes Raisonnables* (De Luyne, 1661).

Montfleury, [Antoine Jacob], *La Femme Juge et Partie*, in *Répertoire du Théâtre Français*, ed. M. Petitot (Didot, 1804, Vol. VIII).

Ouville, Antoine Le Metel d', *L'Esprit Folet* (Quinet, 1642).

Parfaict, Claude and François, *Histoire du Théâtre Français*, Vol. VI (Le Mercier et Saillant, 1746).

Pichou, *Les Folies de Cardénio*, in Fournier, *Théâtre* (see above).

Poisson, Raymond, *Le Baron de la Crasse*, in Vol. I of Fournel, *Contemporains* (see above).

Poisson, Raymond, *Les Faux Moscovites*, in Vol. I of Fournel, *Contemporains* (see above).

Quinault, Philippe, *Théâtre Choisi*, ed. V. Fournel (Laplace et al., 1882).

Robinet, Charles, *Le Panégyrique de l'Ecole des Femmes*, in *La Querelle de l'Ecole des Femmes*, ed. G. Mongrédien, Vol. I (STFM, 1971, 2 vols).

Rotrou, Jean, *Œuvres* (Desoer, 1820, 5 vols).

Schelandre, Jean de, *Tyr et Sidon*, ed. E. Viollet-le-Duc, in *Ancien Théâtre Français*, Vol. VIII (Plon, 1854, 10 vols).

Scudéry, Georges de, *La Comédie des Comédiens* (Courbé, 1635).

Scudéry, Georges de, *Orante* (Courbé, 1635).

Scudéry, Georges de, *Le Vassal Généreux* (Courbé, 1636).

Tabarin, [Antoine Girard], *Œuvres*, ed. G. d'Harmonville (Delahays, 1858).

Tralage, J. N. Du, *Notes et Documents sur l'Histoire des Théâtres de Paris au XVIIe Siècle: Extraits du Manuscrit de J. N. Du Tralage*, ed. P. L. Jacob (Librairie des Bibliophiles, 1880).

Troterel, Pierre, *Gillette* (Rouen: Petit Val, 1620).

Veronneau, *L'Impuissance*, in *Ancien Théâtre Français*, ed. E. Viollet-le-Duc, in *Ancien Théâtre Français*, Vol. VIII (Plon, 1854, 10 vols).

T   Miscellaneous

Anon., *Les Amours, Intrigues et Cabales des Domestiques des grandes maisons de ce temps* (De Villac, 1632).

Anon., *Histoire des Diables de Loudun* (Amsterdam: Wolfgang, 1693).

Anon., *Les Lois de la Galanterie* (Collection Trésor des Pièces Rares ou Inédites, Aubry, 1855).

Bossuet, Jacques-Bénigne, *Sermons* (Garnier, 1872–3, 4 vols).

Bourdaloue, Louis, *Sermons pour le Carême* (Imprimerie Royale, 1716, 3 vols).

Bourdaloue, Louis, *Sermons pour les Dimanches* (Rigaud, 1716, 3 vols).

Godefroy, Théodore, *Le Cérémonial Français* (Cramoisy, 1649, 2 vols).

Guillemeau, Charles, *Traité des Abus qui se commettent sur les procédures de l'impuissance des hommes et des femmes* (Pacard, 1620).

Patru, Olivier, *Œuvres Diverses* (Mabre-Cramoisy, 1692, 2 vols).

Procès Verbaux de l'Académie Royale de Peinture et de Sculpture, 1648–1792, ed. A. de Montaiglon (Société de l'Histoire de l'Art Français, 1875–1909, 10 vols and Table).

Savary, Jacques, *Le Parfait Négociant*, (Billaine, 1675).

Serres, Olivier de, *Théâtre d'Agriculture et Ménage des Champs* (Métayer, 1600).

Sorel, Charles, *La Maison des Jeux* (Sommaville, 1657, 2 vols).

Sorel, Charles, *Œuvres Diverses* (1663).

Tagereau, Vincent, *Discours sur l'Impuissance de l'Homme et de la Femme* (Veuve Du Brayet et Rousset, 1612).

Variétés Historiques et Littéraires, ed. E. Fournier (Jannet, 1855–63, 10 vols).

II   SECONDARY SOURCES

Reference is made here only to works cited in the text.

Allain, E., *L'Instruction Primaire en France avant la Révolution* (Geneva: Slatkine Reprints, 1970).

Archives de l'Art Français, 2me Sér., Vol. I, ed. A. de Montaiglon, (1861); *Nouvelles Archives de l'Art Français* (1878).

Arnaud, G., *Mémoire sur les Etats de Foix* (Toulouse, 1904).

Babeau, A., *La Vie Rurale dans l'Ancienne France*, 2me edn (Perrin, 1885).

Babeau, A., *Le Village sous l'Ancien Régime* (Didier, 1882).

Babeau, A., *La Ville sous l'Ancien Régime* (Didier, 1884, 2 vols).

Batiffol, L., *La Duchesse de Chevreuse* (Hachette, 1927).

Batiffol, L., *La Vie Intime d'une Reine de France au XVIIᵉ Siècle* (Calmann-Lévy, 1906).

Beaune, H. and D'Arbaumont, J., *La Noblesse aux Etats de Bourgogne de 1350 à 1789* (Dijon: Lamarche, 1864).

Bercé, Y.-M., *Histoire des Croquants, Etude des Soulèvements Populaires au XVIIᵉ Siècle dans le Sud-Ouest de la France* (Geneva: Droz, 1974, 2 vols).

Boissonnade, P., 'Essai sur l'Organisation du Travail en Poitou', in *Mémoires de la Société des Antiquaires de l'Ouest*, 2me Sér., Vol. XXI (1898), and Vol. XXII (1899).

Bonneau-Avenant, A., *La Duchesse d'Aiguillon* (Didier, 1879).

Bonneau-Avenant, A., *Mme de Miramion* (Didier, 1873).

Brémond, H., *Histoire Littéraire du Sentiment Religieux en France* (Bloud et Gay, 1924–36, 11 vols and Index).

Buisson, F., *Dictionnaire de Pédagogie et d'Instruction Primaire* (Hachette, 1882–7, 2 parts, 4 vols).

Chardon, H., *Nouveaux Documents sur la Vie de Molière, M. de Modène, ses deux femmes, et Madeleine Béjart* (New York: Lenox Hill reprint, 1972, 2 vols).

Chastel, A., 'L'Art et le Sentiment de la Mort au XVIIᵉ Siècle', in *Dix-Septième Siècle*, July–Oct. 1957.

Chaunu, P., *La Mort à Paris* (Fayard, 1978).

Coornaert, E., *Les Compagnonnages en France du Moyen Age à nos jours* (Editions Ouvrières, 1966).

Coornaert, E., *Les Corporations en France avant 1789*, 2me edn (Editions Ouvrières, 1968).

Cousin, V., *Fragments Philosophiques pour faire suite aux cours de l'histoire de la philosophie*, 4me edn (1847, 4 vols).

Cousin, V., *Jacqueline Pascal* (Didier, 1845).

Cousin, V., *Mme de Sablé* (Didier, 1859).

Crane, T. F., *Italian Social Customs of the Sixteenth Century* (New Haven: Yale UP, 1920).

Darmon, P., *Mythologie de la femme dans l'Ancienne France* (Seuil, 1983).

Desnoiresterres, G., *Les Cours Galantes* (Dentu, 1860–3, 3 vols).

Devyver, A., *Le Sang Epuré: Les Préjugés de Race chez les Gentilshommes Français de l'Ancien Régime (1560–1720)* (Editions de l'Université de Bruxelles, 1973).

Deyon, P., *Amiens, Capitale Provinciale* (Mouton, 1967).

Dutilleux, A., and Depoin, J., *L'Abbaye de Maubuisson, Histoire et Cartulaire* (Pontoise: Amédée Paris, 1882).

Flandrin, J.-L., *Familles, parenté, maison, sexualité dans l'ancienne société* (Hachette, 1976).

Fleury, M., and Valmary, P., 'Les Progrès de l'Instruction Elémentaire de Louis XIV à Napoléon III', in *Population* (1957).

Foisil, M., *La Révolte des Nu-Pieds et les Révoltes Normandes* (PUF, 1970).

Fontevrault, Religieuses de Sainte-Marie de, *Histoire de l'Ordre de Fontevrault* (Auch: Cocharaux, 1911–15, 3 vols).

France au temps de Louis XIV, La (Collection Ages d'Or et Réalités, Hachette, 1965).

Funck-Brentano, F., *Les Lettres de Cachet* (Hachette, 1926).

Furet, F., and Ozouf, J., *Lire et Ecrire: L'alphabétisation des Français de Calvin à Jules Ferry* (Editions de Minuit, 1977, 2 vols).

Gasté, A., *La Querelle du Cid* (Wetter, 1898).

Goubert, P., *Beauvais et le Beauvaisis de 1600 à 1730* (Imprimerie Nationale, 1960).

Gueneau, L., *L'Organisation du Travail à Nevers (1660–1790)* (Hachette, 1919).

Haag, E., *La France Protestante* (Geneva: Slatkine Reprints, 1966, 9 vols and Pièces Justificatives).

Hauser, H., *Les Débuts du Capitalisme* (Alcan, 1931).

Hayden, J. M., *France and the Estates General of 1614* (Cambridge UP, 1974).

Helyot, P., 'Dictionnaire des Ordres Religieux', in *Encyclopédie Théologique*, ed. J.-P. Migne, Vols XX–XXIII (1847–59).

Holsboer, S. W. D., *La Vie d'Alexandre Hardy, Poète du Roi, 1572–1632* (Nizet, 1972).

Ivanoff, N., *La Marquise de Sablé et son Salon* (Presses Modernes, 1927).

Jurgens, M., and Maxfield-Miller, E., *Cent Ans de Recherches sur Molière, sur sa famille et sur les comédiens de sa troupe* (Imprimerie Nationale, 1963).

Lancaster, H. C., *A History of French Dramatic Literature in the Seventeenth Century* (Baltimore: John Hopkins Press, 1929–42, 9 vols).

Lebrun, F., *Les Hommes et la Mort en Anjou au 17ᵉ et 18ᵉ Siècles* (Mouton, 1971).

Magne, E., *Ninon de Lanclos*, 7ᵐᵉ edn (Emile-Paul, 1925).

Magne, E., *Mme de la Suze et la Société Précieuse* (Mercure de France, 1908).

Magne, E., *Mme de Villedieu* (Mercure de France, 1907).

Magne, E., *Voiture et les Années de Gloire de l'Hôtel de Rambouillet (1635–1648)* (Emile-Paul, 1930).

Major, J. Russell, *The Deputies to the Estates General in Renaissance France* (Madison: University of Wisconsin Press, 1960).

Mâle, E., *L'Art Religieux du XVIIᵉ Siècle* (Colin, 1951).

Mandrou, R., *De la Culture Populaire au XVIIᵉ et XVIIIᵉ Siècles* (Editions Stock, 1964).

Martin, H.-J., *Livre, Pouvoirs et Société à Paris au XVIIᵉ Siècle* (Geneva: Droz, 1969, 2 vols).

Mongrédien, G., 'Bibliographie des Œuvres de Georges et de Madeleine de Scudéry', in *RHL* (1933).

Muchembled, R., *Culture Populaire et Culture des Elites dans la France Moderne (XV–XVIIIᵉ Siècles)* (Flammarion, 1978).

Nisard, C., *Histoire des Livres Populaires ou de la Littérature de Colportage*, 2ᵐᵉ edn (Dentu, 1864, 2 vols).

Porchnev, B., *Les Soulèvements Populaires en France de 1623 à 1648* (SEVPEN, 1963).

Rébillon, A., *Les Etats de Bretagne de 1661 à 1789* (Picard, 1932).

Rébillon, A., 'Recherches sur les Anciennes Corporations Ouvrières et

Marchandes de la Ville de Rennes' in *Annales de Bretagne*, Vol. XVIII (1902–3) and Vol. XX (1904–5).

Reynier, G., *La Femme au XVIIe Siècle: ses ennemis et ses défenseurs* (Tallandier, 1929).

Rousselot, P., *Histoire de l'Education des Femmes en France* (Didier, 1883, 2 vols).

Sauzet, R., *Les Visites Pastorales dans le diocèse de Chartres pendant la première moitié du XVIIe siècle* (Rome, 1975).

Sayce, R. A., *The French Biblical Epic in the Seventeenth Century* (Oxford: Clarendon Press, 1955).

Soulié, E., *Notice du Musée Impérial de Versailles*, 2me edn (De Mourgues, 1859–80, 3 parts).

Soulié, E., *Recherches sur Molière et sur sa famille* (Hachette, 1863).

Storer, M. E., *La Mode des Contes de Fées (1685–1700)* (Champion, 1928).

Index